Lecture Notes in Computer Science   3132

Commenced Publication in 1973
Founding and Former Series Editors:
Gerhard Goos, Juris Hartmanis, and Jan van Leeuwen

T0223585

Bart Demoen   Vladimir Lifschitz (Eds.)

Logic Programming

20th International Conference, ICLP 2004
Saint-Malo, France, September 6-10, 2004
Proceedings

 Springer

Volume Editors

Bart Demoen
Catholic University of Leuven
Department of Computer Science
Celestijnenlaan 200A, 3001 Leuven, Belgium
E-mail: Bart.Demoen@cs.kuleuven.ac.be

Vladimir Lifschitz
University of Texas at Austin
Department of Computer Sciences
Austin, TX 78712-1188, USA
E-mail: vl@cs.utexas.edu

Library of Congress Control Number: 2004110708

CR Subject Classification (1998): D.1.6, I.2.3, D.3, F.3, F.4

ISSN 0302-9743
ISBN 3-540-22671-0 Springer Berlin Heidelberg New York

Springer is a part of Springer Science+Business Media

springeronline.com

© Springer-Verlag Berlin Heidelberg 2004
Printed in Germany

Typesetting: Camera-ready by author, data conversion by Olgun Computergrafik
Printed on acid-free paper   SPIN: 11307471   06/3142   5 4 3 2 1 0

Preface

This volume contains the papers presented at the 20th International Conference on Logic Programming, held in Saint-Malo, France, September 6–10, 2004. Since the first meeting in this series, held in Marseilles in 1982, ICLP has been the premier international conference for presenting research in logic programming. This year, we received 70 technical papers from countries all over the world, and the Program Committee accepted 28 of them for presentation; they are included in this volume.

A stand-by-your-poster session took place during the conference. It served as a forum for presenting work in a more informal and interactive setting. Abstracts of the 16 posters selected by the Program Committee are included in this volume as well.

The conference program also included invited talks and invited tutorials. We were privileged to have talks by three outstanding researchers and excellent speakers: Nachum Dershowitz (Tel Aviv University, Israel) talked on *Termination by Abstraction*, Michael Gelfond (Texas Tech University, USA) on *Answer Set Programming and the Design of Deliberative Agents*, and Gérard Huet (INRIA, France) on *Non-determinism Lessons*. Two of the invited talks appear in these proceedings. The tutorials covered topics of high interest to the logic programming community: Ilkka Niemelä gave a tutorial on *The Implementation of Answer Set Solvers*, Andreas Podelski on *Tree Automata in Program Analysis and Verification*, and Guillermo R. Simari on *Defeasible Logic Programming and Belief Revision*.

Satellite workshops made the conference even more interesting. Six workshops collocated with ICLP 2004:

- CICLOPS 2004, Colloquium on Implementation of Constraint and Logic Programming Systems, organized by Manuel Carro.
- COLOPS 2004, 2nd International Workshop on Constraint & Logic Programming in Security, organized by Frank Valencia.
- MultiCPL 2004, 3rd International Workshop on Multiparadigm Constraint, organized by Petra Hofstedt.
- TeachLP 2004, 1st International Workshop on Teaching Logic Programming, organized by Dietmar Seipel.
- WLPE 2004, 14th Workshop on Logic Programming Environments, organized by Susana Muñoz-Hernández and José Manuel Gómez-Perez.
- PPSWR 2004, Workshop on Principles and Practice of Semantic Web Reasoning, organized by Hans Jürgen Ohlbach and Sebastian Schaffert.

The traditional Prolog Programming Contest was organized by Tom Schrijvers and Remko Tronçon.

We take this opportunity to thank the many people who helped in the processing of the submissions and in the local organization of the conference. In particular we are grateful to Tristan Denmat, Ludovic Langevine, Elisabeth Lebret, Joohyung Lee, Lydie Mabil, Matthieu Petit, Olivier Ridoux and Benjamin Sigonneau. We also thank the organizers of the workshops and the Prolog Programming Contest.

Finally, we thank all the authors of the submitted papers, the Program Committee members, and the referees for their time and effort spent in the reviewing process, Pål Halvorsen and Ketil Lund for their conference management software, ConfMan, and the conference chair Mireille Ducassé and her équipe in Rennes for the excellent organization.

June 2004   Bart Demoen, Vladimir Lifschitz

Organization

Conference Organization

Program Chairs	Bart Demoen (K.U.Leuven, Belgium)
	and Vladimir Lifschitz (University of Texas, USA)
General Chair	Mireille Ducassé (INSA/IRISA, Rennes, France)
Workshop Chair	Fausto Spoto (University of Verona, Italy)
Publicity Chair	Arnaud Gotlieb (INRIA/IRISA Rennes, France)
Programming Contest	Tom Schrijvers (K.U.Leuven, Belgium)
	and Remko Tronçon (K.U.Leuven, Belgium)

Program Committee Members

Chitta Baral	Arizona State University, USA
Piero Bonatti	Università di Napoli Federico II, Italy
Gerhard Brewka	Leipzig University, Germany
Michael Codish	Ben-Gurion University, Israel
Veronica Dahl	Simon Fraser University, Canada
Bart Demoen	Katholieke Universiteit Leuven, Belgium
Juergen Dix	University of Manchester, UK
Mireille Ducassé	INSA/IRISA, Rennes, France
Francois Fages	INRIA Rocquencourt, France
John Gallagher	Roskilde University, Denmark
Gopal Gupta	University of Texas, USA
Manuel Hermenegildo	Universidad Politécnica de Madrid, Spain
Antonis Kakas	University of Cyprus, Cyprus
Andy King	University of Kent, UK
Evelina Lamma	University of Ferrara, Italy
Vladimir Lifschitz	University of Texas, USA
Fangzhen Lin	University of Science and Technology, Hong Kong
Naomi Lindenstrauss	Hebrew University, Israel
Michael Maher	Loyola University, Chicago, USA
Dale Miller	INRIA Futurs, France
Stephen Muggleton	Imperial College London, UK
Ilkka Niemelä	Helsinki University of Technology, Finland
Andreas Podelski	Max Planck Institute, Germany
Kostis Sagonas	Uppsala University, Sweden
Chiaki Sakama	Wakayama University, Japan
Vitor Santos Costa	Universidade Federal do Rio de Janeiro, Brasil
Zoltan Somogyi	University of Melbourne, Australia
Peter Stuckey	University of Melbourne, Australia
Paul Tarau	University of North Texas, USA

Referees

Dulce Aguilar Solis
Marco Alberti
Matteo Baldoni
Marcello Balduccini
Peter Baumgartner
Torben Braüner
Antonio Brogi
Maurice Bruynooghe
Henning Christiansen
Anna Ciampolini
Anna Corazza
Saumya K. Debray
Marc Denecker
Pierre Deransart
Daniel de Rauglaudre
Michael Elhadad
Gérard Ferrand
Michel Ferreira
Maurizio Gabbrielli
Marco Gavanelli
Michael Gelfond
Hai-Feng Guo
Rémy Haemmerlé

Andreas Herzig
Glendon Holst
Katsumi Inoue
Tomi Janhunen
Gerda Janssens
Kathrin Konczak
Hristo Koshutanski
Ludovic Langevine
Nicola Leone
Michael Leuschel
Thomas Linke
Jorge Lobo
Yann Loyer
Lunjin Lu
Kim Marriott
Alberto Martelli
Paola Mello
Michela Milano
Alberto Momigliano
Emilia Oikarinen
Nicola Olivetti
Catuscia Palamidessi
David Pearce

Nikolay Pelov
Frank Pfenning
Enrico Pontelli
C.R. Ramakrishnan
Claus Reinke
Fabrizio Riguzzi
Ricardo Rocha
Francesca Rossi
Ken Satoh
Tom Schrijvers
Alexander Serebrenik
Kish Shen
Axel Simon
Luke Simon
Kostas Stathis
Alwen Tiu
Ana Paula Tomás
Paolo Torroni
Cao Son Tran
Jørgen Villadsen
Kewen Wang
Qian Wang

Best Paper Award

Constraint Handling Rules and Tabled Execution
Tom Schrijvers and David S. Warren

Sponsoring Institutions

ICLP 2004 was organized by INRIA.
ICLP 2004 was sponsored by the Association for Logic Programming, INRIA,
INSA, the Université de Rennes 1, Région Bretagne, CologNet, REWERSE, the
Universidad Politécnica de Madrid, CNRS, and the Association Française pour
la Programmation en Logique et la programmation par Contraintes.

Table of Contents

Alternative Paradigms II

Poster Presentations

Termination by Abstraction

Nachum Dershowitz*

School of Computer Science, Tel-Aviv University,
Ramat Aviv, Tel-Aviv 69978, Israel
nachum.dershowitz@cs.tau.ac.il

Abstract. Abstraction can be used very effectively to decompose and simplify termination arguments. If a symbolic computation is nonterminating, then there is an infinite computation with a top redex, such that all redexes are immortal, but all children of redexes are mortal. This suggests applying weakly-monotonic well-founded relations in abstraction-based termination methods, expressed here within an abstract framework for term-based proofs. Lexicographic combinations of orderings may be used to match up with multiple levels of abstraction.

> *A small number of firms*
> *have decided to terminate*
> *their independent abstraction schemes.*
>
> – Netherlands Ministry of Spatial Planning,
> Housing and the Environment (2003)

1 Introduction

For as long as there have been algorithms, the question of their termination – though undecidable, in general – has had to be addressed. Not surprisingly, one of the earliest proofs of termination of a computer program was by Turing himself [43], mapping the program state to the ordinal numbers.

Floyd [22] suggested using arbitrary well-founded (partial) orderings; this direction was developed further by Manna [34]. Such a termination proof typically involves several steps:

1. Choose an appropriate well-founded set.
2. Choose a set of points in each potentially infinite computation at which to measure progress towards termination.
3. Establish invariant properties that always hold at those points.
4. Choose a mapping from states to the well-founded set by which to measure progress.
5. Show a necessary decrease in this measure with each transition from point to point.

---

* Research supported in part by the Israel Science Foundation (grant no. 254/01).

B. Demoen and V. Lifschitz (Eds.): ICLP 2004, LNCS 3132, pp. 1–18, 2004.

For a survey of termination methods for ordinary programs, see [30][1].

Showing termination of symbolic computations often requires special tools, since state transitions involve symbolic expressions that may grow bigger and bigger, while progress is being made towards a final result. Therefore, one often resorts to powerful term-based orderings, such as have been developed for rewrite systems [13]. We are mainly interested here in relatively simple symbolic termination functions, mapping symbolic states to terms, and in sophisticated methods of showing that they decrease. More complicated symbolic transformations have been considered, for example in [3, 4].

We use rewriting [15, 20, 42] as a prototypical symbolic computation paradigm (and employ terminology and notation from [20]). A rewrite system is *(uniformly) terminating* if there is no term to which rules in can be applied over-and-over-again forever; see [13]. Narrowing (a unification-based version of rewriting) has been proposed as a basis for functional-logic programming; see [19, 27]. Termination of narrowing has been considered in several works [28, 21, 6]. Much effort has also been devoted to devising methods for establishing termination of logic programs. For a survey, see [10]; a recent dissertation on the subject is [39]; interfaces to several automated tools (cTI, Hasta-La-Vista, TALP, TermiLog, and TerminWeb) are available over the web. Methods have been suggested for converting well-moded logic programs into rewrite systems with identical termination behavior [2, 36].

In the next section, we sketch how abstraction is used to decompose termination proofs. Section 3 introduces notation and monotonicity properties, and is followed by a section containing some termination methods for rewriting based on those properties. In Section 5, we look at constricting derivations, which are used in the following section to design dependency-based approaches, in which the symbolic state is a "critical" immortal subterm. Correctness of the various methods and their interrelatedness are the subjects of Section 7. We conclude with an example.

2   Abstraction

A *transition system* is a graph in which vertices are states (S) of a computation and edges ($\leadsto$) are state-transitions, as defined by some program. A *computation*

---

[1] It is misleading to suggest (cf. [26]) that – for deterministic (or bounded-nondeterministic) programs – it suffices to use the natural numbers as the well-founded set (Step 1), claiming that – after all – the (maximum) number of iterations of any terminating loop is fixed and depends only on the values of the inputs. This fixation on the naturals begs the real issue, since the proof (Step 5) may require transfinite induction over ordinals much larger than ω. For example, one can easily program the deterministic Battle of Hercules and Hydra (or Goodstein sequences) [31]. Though there exists an integer-valued function that counts how many steps it takes Hercules to eliminate any Hydra, *proving* that it is well-defined, and that it decreases with each round of the battle, provably *requires* a stronger principle of induction (viz. ε_0) than that provided by the Peano Axioms of arithmetic.

is a sequence $s_0 \rightsquigarrow s_1 \rightsquigarrow \cdots$ of states, where the arrows represent transitions. We say that a binary relation $\gg$ (over some S) is *terminating* if there are no infinite descending sequences $s_1 \gg s_2 \gg \cdots$ (of elements $s_i \in S$). This property will be denoted $\mathrm{SN}(\gg)$ for "strongly normalizing". Thus, we aim to show $\mathrm{SN}(\rightsquigarrow)$, that is, that the transition relation $\rightsquigarrow$ is terminating, for given transition systems $\rightsquigarrow$. To show that no infinite computation is possible, one can make use of any other terminating relation $\gg$, and show that transitions $\rightsquigarrow$ are decreasing in $\gg$. That is, we need $s \rightsquigarrow s'$ to imply $s \gg s'$, or $\rightsquigarrow \subseteq \gg$, for short.

Abstraction and dataflow analysis can be used to restrict the cases for which a reduction needs to be confirmed. The underlying idea is that of abstract interpretation, as introduced by Sintzoff [40], Wegbreit [45], and others, and formalized by Cousot and Cousot [9]. The property we are concerned with here is termination. For use of abstraction in termination of logic programs, see [44].

A partial ordering $>$ is *well-founded* if it is terminating. If $\geq$ is a quasi-ordering (i.e. a reflexive-transitive binary relation) and $\leq$ its inverse, then we can use $\simeq$ to denote the associated equivalence ($\geq \cap \leq$, viewing orderings as sets of ordered pairs) and $>$ to denote the associated partial ordering ($\geq \setminus \leq$). We will say that a quasi-ordering $\geq$ is well-founded whenever its strict part $>$ is. We often use well-founded partial and quasi-orderings in proofs, since they are transitive. Specifically, we know that $s \geq t > u$ and $s > t \geq u$ each imply $s > u$.

As is customary, for any binary relation $\rightarrowtail$, we use $\rightarrowtail^+$ for its transitive closure, $\rightarrowtail^*$ for its reflexive-transitive closure, and $\rightarrowtail^-$ (or $\leftarrowtail$, typography permitting) for its inverse. If a relation $\twoheadrightarrow$ is terminating, then both its transitive closure $\twoheadrightarrow^+$ and reflexive-transitive closure $\twoheadrightarrow^*$ are well-founded. *In what follows, we will dedicate the symbol $\twoheadrightarrow$ for terminating relations, $\succ$ for well-founded partial orderings, and $\succsim$ for well-founded quasi-orderings.* The intersection of a terminating relation with any other binary relation is terminating:

$$\mathrm{SN}(\twoheadrightarrow) \quad \Rightarrow \quad \mathrm{SN}(\twoheadrightarrow \cap \gg). \tag{1}$$

It is often convenient to introduce an intermediate notion in proofs of termination, namely, a "termination function" τ, mapping states to some set W, and show that state transition $s \rightsquigarrow s'$ implies $\tau(s) \twoheadrightarrow \tau(s')$, for some terminating relation $\twoheadrightarrow$. Accordingly, one can view $\tau(s)$ as an "abstraction" of state s for the purposes of a termination proof. Instead of proving that $\rightsquigarrow$ is terminating, one considers the abstracted states $\tau(S) = \{\tau(s) \mid s \in S\} \subseteq W$ and supplies a proof of termination for the abstract transition relation $\tau(\rightsquigarrow)$, defined as $\{\tau(s) \rightsquigarrow \tau(s') \mid s \rightsquigarrow s'\}$.

Suppose the only loops in the abstracted transition graph $\tau(S)$ are self-loops. That is, $\tau(s) \rightsquigarrow^* \tau(s') \rightsquigarrow^* \tau(s)$ implies $\tau(s) = \tau(s')$. Then termination can be decomposed into subproofs for each of the loops and for the remainder of the graph, *sans* loops. For the latter, one needs to check that $\tau(\rightsquigarrow)$ has no infinite chains, which is trivially true when the abstract graph is finite. For each of the self-loops, one needs to reason on the concrete level, but under the assumption that τ remains invariant (its value is some constant).

Oftentimes [34], one maps states to a lexicographically-ordered tuple of elements, a pair $\langle \tau_1(s), \tau_2(s) \rangle$, say. Then one needs to show, separately (if one wishes), that every transition $s \rightsquigarrow s'$ implies $\tau_1(s) \succsim \tau_1(s')$, for some well-founded quasi-ordering $\succsim$, and that $s \rightsquigarrow s'$ and $\tau_1(s) \simeq \tau_1(s')$ imply $\tau_2(s) \succ\!\!\!\succ \tau_2(s')$, for some terminating relation $\succ\!\!\!\succ$.

In the symbolic case, the set of ground terms in a computation can be divided according to some set of patterns of which they are instances. If there are only a finite number of different patterns, and computations do not cycle among the patterns, then one only needs to show termination of computations involving a single pattern. In logic programming, these can be predicate names and argument modes. For rewriting, syntactic path orderings [12, 13], based on a precedence of function symbols, are used, but one must consider subterms, as well as the top-level term. Abstraction is also the essence of the "operator derivability" method of [21] for pruning unsatisfiable narrowing goals (as used for functional-logic programming), where terms $f(\cdots)$ are represented by their outermost symbol f. A more sophisticated use of patterns to prune narrowing-based goal solving was developed in [6].

Example 1. The rewrite system

$$
\begin{array}{rclcrclcrcl}
\varepsilon @ z & \rightarrow & z & \quad & \varepsilon = \varepsilon & \rightarrow & T & \quad & \varepsilon = x\!:\!y & \rightarrow & F \\
(x\!:\!y) @ z & \rightarrow & x\!:\!(y @ z) & \quad & x\!:\!y = x\!:\!z & \rightarrow & y = z & \quad & x\!:\!y = \varepsilon & \rightarrow & F,
\end{array}
$$

for appending and comparing lists, can be used to compute directly by rewriting (using pattern matching), or can be used to solve goals by narrowing (using unification), or by their pleasant combination [19]: eager simplification interspersed between outermost narrowing steps. The goal $z @ (b\!:\!\varepsilon) = a\!:\!b\!:\!\varepsilon$, for example, where z is the existential "logic" variable being solved for, narrows to the subgoal $b\!:\!\varepsilon = a\!:\!b\!:\!\varepsilon$ (applying the first rule and assigning $z \mapsto \varepsilon$), which dies (for lack of applicable rule). The original goal also narrows to $x\!:\!(z' @ (b\!:\!\varepsilon)) = a\!:\!b\!:\!\varepsilon$ via the bottom-left rule (with $z \mapsto x\!:\!z'$), which narrows to $z' @ (b\!:\!\varepsilon) = b\!:\!\varepsilon$ ($x \mapsto a$), which narrows to $b\!:\!\varepsilon = b\!:\!\varepsilon$ ($z' \mapsto \varepsilon$), which simplifies to T.

Suppose we are interested in solving goals of that form, $z @ A = B$, where A and B are (fully instantiated) lists. As abstract states, we can take the goal patterns $\{z @ A = B, \; x\!:\!(z @ A) = a\!:\!B\}$, $\{A = B\}$, and $\{T, F\}$, where a can be any atom. As we just saw, a goal of the form $z @ A = B$ can narrow to one of the forms $A = B$ and $x\!:\!(z' @ A) = B$. In the second event, if $B = \varepsilon$, then the goal simplifies to F; otherwise, it is of the form $x\!:\!(z @ A) = a\!:\!B$. For the latter goal, we have $x\!:\!(z @ A) = a\!:\!B \rightsquigarrow z @ A = B$. All told, the possible abstract transitions are

$$
\{z @ A = B, \; x\!:\!(z @ A) = a\!:\!B\} \quad \rightsquigarrow \quad \{A = B\}
$$
$$
\{T, F\}
$$

Since there are self-loops for the top two pattern sets, a proof of termination only requires showing that with each trip around these loops some measure decreases. For the right loop, we measure a goal $A = B$ by the list B under the sublist (or list length) ordering. For the left loop, we first look at its pattern [with $z@A = B \ll x : (z@A) = a : B$], and, for like patterns, take B.   □

In general, consider an infinite computation $s_0 \rightsquigarrow s_1 \rightsquigarrow \cdots$, and let τ assign one of finitely many colors to each state. By the Pigeonhole Principle, infinitely many states must share the same color. Hence, there must be a subcomputation $s_i \rightsquigarrow^+ s_j$ $(i < j)$ for which $\tau(s_i) = \tau(s_j)$. So if we show the impossibility of this happening infinitely often for any color, then we have precluded having infinite computations altogether.

Rather than just coloring vertices (states) of the transition graph, it is even better to also color its edges and paths: each subcomputation $s_i \rightsquigarrow^+ s_j$ $(i < j)$ is assigned one of a finite palette A of colors. Then, by (a simple case of) the infinite version of Ramsey's Theorem, there is an infinite (noncontiguous) subsequence of states $s_{i_1} \rightsquigarrow^+ s_{i_2} \rightsquigarrow^+ \cdots$, such that every one of its subcomputations $s_{i_j} \rightsquigarrow^+ s_{i_k}$ has the identical color $a \in A$ [and also $\tau(s_{i_j}) = \tau(s_{i_k})$]. So, to preclude nontermination, we need only show every such cyclical subcomputation decreases in some well-founded sense.

As shown in [16, Lemma 3.1], this fact can be applied to the call tree of a logic program. (See also the discussion in [7].) This leads to the *query-mapping method* of Sagiv [38, 16] and to similar techniques [8, 33].

3   Formalism

Let F be some vocabulary of (ranked) function symbols, and T the set of (ground) terms built from them. A *flat context* ℓ is a term of the form $f(t_1, \ldots, t_{i-1}, \Box, t_{i+1}, \ldots, t_n)$, where $f \in F$ is a function symbol of arity $n > 0$, the t_i are any terms, and $\Box$ is a special symbol denoting a "hole". If ℓ is such a flat context and t a term (or context), then by $\ell[t]$ we denote the term (or context) $f(t_1, \ldots, t_{i-1}, t, t_{i+1}, \ldots, t_n)$. We will view ℓ also as the binary relation $\{\langle t, \ell[t] \rangle \mid t \in T\}$, mapping a term t to the term $\ell[t]$, containing t as its immediate subterm. The inverse of flat ℓ, with its hole at position i, is the projection π_i. Let L be the set of all flat contexts (for some vocabulary), and $\Pi = L^-$, the set of all projections.

A *context* c is just an element of L^*, that is, the relation between any term t and some particular superterm $c[t]$ containing t where c's hole was. It has the shape of a "teepee", a term minus a subterm, so may be represented by a term $c[\Box]$ with one hole. Let $C = L^* \subseteq T \times T$ denote all contexts; put another way, C is just the subterm relation $\unlhd$. Its inverse $\unrhd$ is the superterm relation and its strict part $\rhd$ is proper superterm.

A *rewrite system* is a set of rewrite rules, each of the form $l \rightarrow r$, where l and r are (first-order) terms. Rules are used to compute by replacing a subterm of a term t that matches the left-side pattern l with the corresponding instance of the right side r. For a rewrite system R, viewed as a binary relation (set of pairs of terms), we will use the notation $\propto_R$ to signify all its ground instances (a set of pairs of ground terms), and $\to_R$ for the associated rewrite relation (also on ground terms). The latter is the relevant transition relation.

Composition of relations will be indicated by juxtaposition. If S and R are binary relations on terms, then by $S[R]$ we denote the composite relation:

$$S[R] = \bigcup_{x \in S} x^- Rx,$$

which takes a backwards S-step before R, and then undoes that S-step. Let Γ be the set of all ground instantiations, where a ground instantiation γ is the relation $\langle t, t\gamma \rangle$, where $t\gamma$ is the term t with its variables instantiated as per γ. The inverse operation γ^{-1} is "generalization", which replaces subterms by variables. With this machinery in place, the *top-rewrite relation* (rule application) and *rewrite steps* (applying a rule at a subterm) are definable as follows:

$$\propto_R = \Gamma[R]$$
$$\to_R = C[\propto_R].$$

Thus,

$$\propto_R = \{l\gamma \propto r\gamma \mid l \to r \in R,\ \gamma \in \Gamma\}$$
$$\to_R = \{c[l\gamma] \to c[r\gamma] \mid l \to r \in R,\ \gamma \in \Gamma,\ c \in C\}.$$

Of course,

$$\propto_R \ \subseteq \ \to_R . \tag{2}$$

Since we will rarely talk about more than one system at a time, we will often forget subscripts.

Two properties of relations are central to the termination tools we describe:

$$\boxed{\begin{array}{l} \text{Mono}(\sqsupset): \quad \sqsupset \ell \subseteq \ell \sqsupset \\ \text{Harmony}(\sqsupset, \gg): \quad \sqsupset \ell \subseteq \ell \gg \end{array}}$$

where $\sqsupset$ and $\gg$ are arbitrary binary relations over terms and ℓ is an arbitrary flat context. See the diagrams in Fig. 1. Mono is "monotonicity", a.k.a. the "replacement property" (relations are inherited by superterms). Rewriting is monotonic:

$$\text{Mono}(\to). \tag{3}$$

Harmony means that

$$s \sqsupset t \quad \Rightarrow \quad \ell[s] \gg \ell[t]$$

for all $\ell \in L$ and $s, t \in T$ [2]. So, monotonicity of a relation is self-harmony:

$$\text{Harmony}(\gg, \gg) \Leftrightarrow \text{Mono}(\gg). \tag{4}$$

---

[2] Harmony is called "quasi-monotonicity of $\gg$ with respect to $\sqsupset$" in [5].

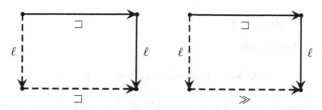

Fig. 1. Monotonicity and harmony.

Clearly:

$$\text{Mono}(\gg) \wedge \text{Mono}(\sqsupset) \Rightarrow \text{Mono}(\gg \cap \sqsupset) \qquad (5)$$

$$\text{Mono}(\gg) \Rightarrow \text{Mono}(\rightarrow \cap \gg) \qquad (6)$$

$$\text{Mono}(\gg \cap \sqsupset) \Rightarrow \text{Harmony}(\gg \cap \sqsupset, \gg) \qquad (7)$$

$$\text{Harmony}(\looparrowright, \gg) \wedge \text{Harmony}(\looparrowright, \sqsupset) \Leftrightarrow \text{Harmony}(\looparrowright, \gg \cap \sqsupset), \qquad (8)$$

for any relations $\gg, \sqsupset, \looparrowright$.

All such relations refer to ground terms. They may be lifted to free terms in the standard manner: Demanding that $u \gg v$, for terms u and v with free variables, means that $u\gamma \gg v\gamma$ for all substitutions γ of ground terms for those variables.

Let $\rightarrow$ be a rewrite relation, the termination of which is in question and $\propto$, its rule application relation. To prove $\text{SN}(\rightarrow)$, we make use of various combinations of conditions involving two basic properties:

$$
\begin{array}{lll}
\text{Rule}(\sqsupset): & \propto & \subseteq \ \sqsupset \\
\text{Reduce}(\sqsupset): & \rightarrow & \subseteq \ \sqsupset
\end{array}
$$

The following relations are all easy:

$\text{Rule}(\propto)$	(9)	$\text{Rule}(\gg) \wedge \text{Rule}(\sqsupset) \Leftrightarrow \text{Rule}(\gg \cap \sqsupset)$	(12)
$\text{Rule}(\rightarrow)$	(10)	$\text{Reduce}(\gg) \wedge \text{Reduce}(\sqsupset) \Leftrightarrow \text{Reduce}(\gg \cap \sqsupset)$	(13)
$\text{Reduce}(\rightarrow)$	(11)	$\text{Rule}(\gg) \wedge \text{Mono}(\rightarrow \cap \gg) \Leftrightarrow \text{Reduce}(\gg)$	(14)

$$\text{Rule}(\gg) \wedge \text{Harmony}(\rightarrow \cap \gg, \gg) \Leftrightarrow \text{Reduce}(\gg) \qquad (15)$$

$$\text{Reduce}(\gg) \wedge \text{Harmony}(\gg, \sqsupset) \Rightarrow \text{Mono}(\rightarrow \cap \sqsupset) \qquad (16)$$

Statements (14,15) are by induction on term structure.

As described in Section 2, one can (always) prove termination by showing that $\rightarrow$ is contained in some terminating relation $\succ$. Accordingly, the first, and most general, method employed in termination arguments is[3]:

---

[3] These two methods are usually phrased in terms of well-founded orderings, rather than terminating binary relations.

Obvious ($\nrightarrow$): Reduce($\nrightarrow$).

More precisely, this means

$$\mathrm{SN}(\nrightarrow) \wedge \mathrm{Reduce}(\nrightarrow) \quad \Rightarrow \quad \mathrm{SN}(\rightarrow)\,,$$

where $\mathrm{SN}(\nrightarrow)$ makes explicit the assumption that $\nrightarrow$ is terminating.

Since Reduce refers to the "global" rewriting of any term at any redex, it is easier to deal with Rule, which is a "local" condition on rules only, and impose monotonicity on the relation:[3]

Standard ($\nrightarrow$) [32]: Rule($\nrightarrow$), Mono($\nrightarrow$).

4   Harmonious Methods

The following properties can be used to show that the union of two relations is terminating:

$$\begin{array}{ll} \mathrm{Commute}(\sqsupset,\gg)\colon & \sqsupset\gg \ \subseteq \ \gg^{+}\sqsupset^{*} \\ \mathrm{Compat}(\sqsupset,\gg)\colon & \sqsupset\gg \ \subseteq \ \sqsupset \end{array}$$

For example [3]:

$$\mathrm{Commute}(\nrightarrow,\nrightarrow') \wedge \mathrm{SN}(\nrightarrow) \wedge \mathrm{SN}(\nrightarrow') \quad \Rightarrow \quad \mathrm{SN}(\nrightarrow \cup \nrightarrow')\,.$$

Obviously, if $>$ is the strict part of a quasi-order $\geq$, then:

$$\mathrm{Compat}(>,\geq)\,. \tag{17}$$

Requiring that the relation $\nrightarrow$ be monotonic, as in the **Standard** method of the previous section, may be too restrictive; all that is actually needed is that it be harmonious with rewriting:

Kamin & Lévy ($\nrightarrow$) [29]: Rule($\nrightarrow$), Harmony($\rightarrow \cap \nrightarrow, \nrightarrow$).

When terms are larger than their subterms, monotonicity can be weakened to refer instead to a non-strict quasi-ordering $\succsim$ ($\succ$ is its strict part)[4]:

Quasi-Simplification Ordering ($\succsim$) [12]: Rule($\succ$), Sub($\succsim$), Mono($\succsim$).

where a binary relation has the *subterm property* (Sub) if it contains the superterm relation ($\trianglerighteq$):

$$\mathrm{Sub}(\sqsupset)\colon \quad \trianglerighteq \ \subseteq \ \sqsupset$$

---

[4] We are ignoring the fact that the subterm and monotonicity conditions for quasi-simplification orderings obviate the separate need to show that the ordering is well-founded [12].

By definition:

$$\mathrm{Sub}(\unrhd)\,. \tag{18}$$

As illustrated in [1], the fact that the **Quasi-Simplification Ordering** method, as well as the ones developed in Section 6 below, do not require $\mathrm{Mono}(\succ)$ means that selected function symbols and argument positions can be ignored completely (cf. the use of weak monotonicity in [14]). See the example in Section 8.

As before, what is actually needed is that the relation $\succsim$ be monotonic when restricted to pairs that are related by rewriting:

Subterm $(\succsim)$ [13]: $\mathrm{Rule}(\succ)$, $\mathrm{Sub}(\succsim)$, $\mathrm{Harmony}(\to\,\cap\,\succsim,\succsim)$.

Furthermore, the proof of this method in [13] is based on the requirements:

Right $(\succsim)$: $\mathrm{Right}(\succ)$, $\mathrm{Harmony}(\to\,\cap\,\succsim,\succsim)$.

Here, we are using the property

$$\boxed{\quad \mathrm{Right}(\sqsupset)\!: \quad \propto\,\unrhd\,\subseteq\,\sqsupset \quad}$$

meaning that left-hand sides are bigger than all right-side subterms. The composite relation $\propto\,\unrhd$ comprises the "dependency pairs" of [1]. Trivially:

$$\mathrm{Right}(\gg) \Rightarrow \mathrm{Rule}(\gg)\,, \tag{19}$$

In the following formulations, $\succ\!\!\!\succ$ is terminating, but $\gg$ need not be. If one relation is monotonic, then the other should live harmoniously with it:

Harmony $(\succ\!\!\!\succ,\gg)$: $\mathrm{Rule}(\succ\!\!\!\succ\,\cap\,\gg)$, $\mathrm{Mono}(\gg)$, $\mathrm{Harmony}(\succ\!\!\!\succ\,\cap\,\gg,\succ\!\!\!\succ)$.

The *semantic path ordering* of [29] (see [13]) is a special case, using $\to$ for $\gg$, for which only the conditions of the **Kamin & Lévy** method need be shown (see Lemma 5 below).

Monotonicity $(\succ\!\!\!\succ,\gg)$: $\mathrm{Rule}(\succ\!\!\!\succ\,\cap\,\gg)$, $\mathrm{Mono}(\gg)$, $\mathrm{Harmony}(\gg,\succ\!\!\!\succ)$.

The *monotonic semantic path ordering* of [5] uses a semantic path ordering for $\succ\!\!\!\succ$, demanding $\mathrm{Rule}(\gg^*\cap\succ)$ and $\mathrm{Harmony}(\gg,\gg^*\cap\succsim)$, in the final analysis.

The correctness of these methods is proved in Section 7 below. A more complicated alternative is

Weak $(\succ\!\!\!\succ,\gg)$: $\mathrm{Right}(\succ\!\!\!\succ)$, $\mathrm{Harmony}(\propto\,\cap\,\succ\!\!\!\succ,\gg)$, $\mathrm{Harmony}(\to\,\cap\,\gg,\gg)$,
$\mathrm{Commute}(\gg,\succ\!\!\!\succ)$.

5 Constrictions

The goal we haven been pursuing is to establish finiteness of sequences of transitions, beginning in any valid state. It will be convenient to define the set (monadic predicate) $\leadsto^\infty$ of elements that can initiate infinite chains in a relation $\leadsto$, as follows:

$$\leadsto^\infty \quad = \quad \{s_0 \,|\, \exists\, s_1, s_2, \dots . \,\forall j.\, s_j \leadsto s_{j+1}\}\,.$$

Thus, $\leadsto^\infty$ is the set of "immortal" initial states. With this notation in mind, termination of a transition system, $SN(\leadsto)$, is emptiness of $\leadsto^\infty$ (that is, denial of immortality):

$$SN(\gg) \quad \Leftrightarrow \quad \gg^\infty = \emptyset\,.$$

For rewriting, since contexts and rewrites commute ($\rhd \to \,\subseteq\, \to\, \rhd$), meaning that if a subterm can be rewritten, so can the whole term, we have [15]:

$$\to^\infty \quad = \quad (\to \cup \rhd)^\infty\,. \tag{20}$$

Two important observations on nontermination of rewriting can be made:

- If a system is nonterminating, then there is an infinite derivation with at least one redex at the top of a term. In fact, any immortal term has a subterm initiating such a derivation:

$$\to^\infty \quad \subseteq \quad \rhd \to^* \propto \to^\infty\,. \tag{21}$$

See, for example, [11],[12, p. 287].
- If a system is nonterminating, then there is an infinite derivation in which all proper subterms of every redex are mortal. By *mortal*, we mean that it initiates finite derivations only. Let's call such redexes *critical*. Rewriting at critical redexes yields a "constricting" derivation in the sense of Plaisted [37].

For given rewrite relation $\to$, let T_∞ be its immortal terms ($T_\infty = \to^\infty$), $T_{<\infty}$ the mortal ones ($T \setminus T_\infty$), and $T_\circ = T_\infty \cap L[T_{<\infty}]$ the critical terms (immortal terms all of whose subterms are mortal). To facilitate composition, it will be convenient to associate a binary relation $P?$ with monadic predicates P:

$$P? \quad = \quad \{\langle x, x \rangle \,|\, x \in P\},$$

the identity relation restricted to the domain of P. Let $\propto_\circ = T_\circ? \propto$ be a constricting rewrite step (at a critical redex) and $\to_\circ = C[\propto_\circ]$ be the corresponding rewrite relation. The following facts hold:

$$\to T_\infty? \,\subseteq\, T_\infty? \tag{22}$$
$$\rhd\, T_\infty? \,\subseteq\, T_\infty? \tag{23}$$
$$\to_\circ T_{<\infty}? \,\subseteq\, T_{<\infty}?\,. \tag{24}$$

In words: mortals remain mortal after rewriting; mortals beget mortal subterms; immortals remain immortal after constriction.

Let a non-top constriction be denoted $\to_B = \Pi[\to_\circ]$. Let $\to_D$ be a top constriction, followed by a sequence of projections, followed by a sequence of non-top constrictions: $\to_D = \propto_\circ \trianglerighteq \to_B^*$. Considering constrictions suffices for termination [37][5]:

$$\to^\infty \quad = \quad \to_\circ^\infty \quad = \quad \trianglerighteq \to_B^* \to_D^\infty \ . \tag{25}$$

Thus, we aim to show only that $\to_D$ is terminating. To prove this one can use compatible well-founded orderings $\succ$ and $\succsim'$ such that $\propto_\circ \trianglerighteq \subseteq \succ$ and $\to_B \subseteq \succsim'$. This is the basis for the various dependency-pair methods[6]. Since constricting redexes don't have immortal children, termination follows even if the condition $\propto_\circ \trianglerighteq \subseteq \succ$ is weakened to $\propto_\circ \trianglerighteq \subseteq (\succ \cup \triangleright)$ [7].

Therefore, we can restrict the following two properties of rewrite sequences to refer only to constrictions:

$$\boxed{\begin{array}{ll} \mathrm{Subrule}(\sqsupseteq): & \propto_\circ \subseteq \sqsupseteq \cup \triangleright \\ \mathrm{Depend}(\sqsupseteq): & \propto_\circ \trianglerighteq \subseteq \sqsupseteq \cup \triangleright \end{array}}$$

where:

$$\mathrm{Depend}(\gg) \quad \Rightarrow \quad \mathrm{Subrule}(\gg) \tag{26}$$

$$\mathrm{Rule}(\sqsupseteq) \quad \Rightarrow \quad \mathrm{Subrule}(\sqsupseteq) \tag{27}$$

$$\mathrm{Subrule}(\gg) \wedge \mathrm{Sub}(\sqsupseteq) \wedge \mathrm{Compat}(\gg, \sqsupseteq) \quad \Rightarrow \quad \mathrm{Depend}(\gg) \tag{28}$$

$$\mathrm{Subrule}(\succ) \wedge \mathrm{Sub}(\succsim) \quad \Rightarrow \quad \mathrm{Depend}(\succ) . \tag{29}$$

Statement (29) follows from (17,28).

All this establishes the correctness of the following method:

Basic $(\succsim)$: Depend$(\succ)$, Reduce$(\succsim)$.

6 Dependency Methods

In what follows, let $\succsim$ and $\succsim'$ be arbitrary well-founded quasi-orderings, and $\succ$ and $\succ'$ their associated strict well-founded partial orderings.

The dependency-pair method [1] of proving termination of rewriting takes into account the possible transitions from one critical term to the next $(\to_D)$ in an infinite rewriting derivation. Using the notations of the previous sections, we have two additional variations on this theme:

---

[5] The idea is reminiscent of Tait's reducibility predicate [41]. Constricting derivations were also used by [24] to argue about the sufficiency of "forward closures" for proving termination of "overlaying" systems (see [13]).

[6] Another way to understand the dependency method is to transform ordinary rewrite rules into equational Horn clauses (i.e. conditional rewrite rules; see [42, Sect. 3.5]). A rule $l \to f(r_1, \ldots, r_n)$ has the same operational behavior as the flat, conditional rule $r_1 \to^* y_1, \ldots, r_n \to^* y_n : l \to f(y_1, \ldots, y_n)$. Using the *decreasing method* [18] for operational termination requires that $l \succ r_1, \ldots, r_n, f(y_1, \ldots, y_n)$ for all y_i such that $r_i \to^* y_i$.

[7] For proving "call-by-value" termination, or for (locally-confluent overlay) rewrite systems for which innermost derivations are the least likely to terminate, the conditions can be simplified, since $\to_B$ steps cannot preceded a $\to_D$ step. See [1].

Main ($\succsim$) [1]: Depend($\succ$), Mono($\rightarrow \cap \succsim$).

Intermediate ($\succsim, \succ'$): Depend($\succ'$), Reduce($\succsim$), Compat($\succ', \succsim$).

More specific techniques may be derived from these. For example, the dependency method of [20] may be expressed as follows[8]:

Harmonious Dependency ($\succsim, \succsim'$) [20]: Depend($\succ'$), Rule($\succsim$), Mono($\succsim$), Harmony($\succsim, \succsim'$).

Let $\widehat{F}$ be a mirror image of F: $\widehat{F} = \{\widehat{g} \mid g \in F\}$. Denote by $\widehat{s}$ the term $s = f(u_1, \ldots, u_n)$ with root symbol $f \in F$ replaced by its mirror image $\widehat{f} \in \widehat{F}$, that is, $\widehat{s} = \widehat{f}(u_1, \ldots, u_n)$. Let $\widehat{T}$ be T's image under $\widehat{\cdot}$. If $\succ$ is a partial ordering of $\widehat{T}$, define another partial ordering $\widehat{\succ}$ as $u \mathrel{\widehat{\succ}} v$, for terms $u, v \in T$, when $\widehat{u} \succ \widehat{v}$. The original dependency-pair method is approximately[8]:

Dependency Pairs ($\succsim$) [1]: Depend($\widehat{\succ}$), Rule($\succsim$), Mono($\succsim$).

Here, Mono applies to both hatted ($f \in \widehat{F}$) and bareheaded ($f \in F$) terms, hence implies Harmony.

A more recent version of the dependency-pair method is essentially:

Variant ($\succsim, \succ'$) [25]: Depend($\succ'$), Rule($\succsim$), Mono($\succsim$), Compat($\succ', \succsim$).

7   Method Dependencies

Entailments between the methods are depicted in Fig. 2. The following series of lemmata justify the figure, by establishing dependencies between the different methods and their correctness. As a starter, take:

Lemma 1 ([32]). Obvious ($\nrightarrow$) $\Rightarrow$ Standard ($\nrightarrow$) .

In general, such an implication $\mathbf{M} \Rightarrow \mathbf{M'}$ means that method $\mathbf{M'}$ is a special case of method $\mathbf{M}$. To prove the implication, viz. that correctness of the antecedent method $\mathbf{M}$ implies correctness of the consequent $\mathbf{M'}$, one shows that the *requirements* for $\mathbf{M'}$ imply the requirements for $\mathbf{M}$. This includes the requirement that any terminating relation(s) or well-founded ordering(s) used by $\mathbf{M}$ should be a derivative of those used by $\mathbf{M'}$.

Suppose method $\mathbf{M}(\nrightarrow)$ has requirements C and $\mathbf{M'}(\nrightarrow')$ requires C'. Then, to claim $\mathbf{M} \Rightarrow \mathbf{M'}$ one needs to establish

$$C' \wedge \mathrm{SN}(\nrightarrow') \wedge \neg\mathrm{SN}(\rightarrow) \quad \Rightarrow \quad C \wedge \mathrm{SN}(\nrightarrow).$$

In particular, to prove Lemma 1, we show that the conditions for the latter imply the conditions for the former:

---

[8] The dependency-pair methods of [1, 20, 25] exclude only variables u in r, rather than all left-side proper subterms, from the requirement that $l \succ' u$ of Depend($\succ'$) or $l \mathrel{\widehat{\succ}} u$ of Depend($\widehat{\succ}$). This can make a practical difference [35].

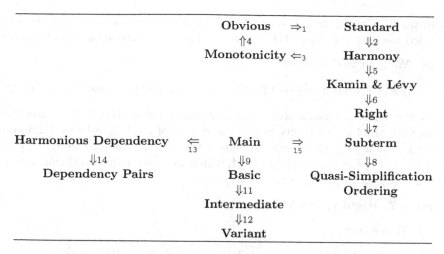

Fig. 2. Dependencies of methods. (Numbers refer to lemmata.)

Proof. By (6,14),

$$\mathrm{SN}(\succ) \wedge \mathrm{Rule}(\succ) \wedge \mathrm{Mono}(\succ) \;\Rightarrow\; \mathrm{SN}(\succ) \wedge \mathrm{Reduce}(\succ). \qquad \square$$

Lemma 2. Standard ($\succ \cap \gg$) $\Rightarrow$ Harmony ($\succ, \gg$).

Here, the implication means that correctness of **Harmony**, using the terminating relation $\succ$, follows from the **Standard** method, using the restricted relation $\rightarrow \cap \succ$ (which is also terminating, by Eq. 1).

Lemma 3. Harmony ($\succ, \gg$) $\Rightarrow$ Monotonicity ($\succ, \gg$).

This circle of dependencies can be closed:

Lemma 4. Monotonicity ($\succ, \rightarrow$) $\Rightarrow$ Obvious ($\succ$).

The correctness of **Obvious** – using the ordering $\succ$, follows from the **Monotonicity** method – using the monotonic rewrite relation $\rightarrow$ for $\gg$.

Lemma 5. Harmony ($\succ, \rightarrow$) $\Rightarrow$ Kamin & Lévy ($\succ$).

Proof. We need

$$\mathrm{Rule}(\succ) \wedge \mathrm{Harmony}(\rightarrow \cap \succ, \succ)$$
$$\Rightarrow \quad \mathrm{Rule}(\rightarrow \cap \succ) \wedge \mathrm{Harmony}(\rightarrow \cap \succ, \succ) \wedge \mathrm{Mono}(\rightarrow),$$

which follows from (10,3,12). $\qquad \square$

We have split the argument of [12] for the **Quasi-Simplification Ordering** method into three parts, with the **Right** and **Subterm** methods as intermediate stages:

Lemma 6. Kamin & Lévy $(\succ^\omega) \Rightarrow$ **Right** $(\succsim)$, where $s \succ^\omega t$ is the well-founded multiset extension [17] of $\succ$ to the bags of all the subterms of s and t.

Proof. We need to show that

$$\text{Right}(\succ) \wedge \text{Harmony}(\rightarrow \cap \succsim, \succsim) \quad \Rightarrow \quad \text{Rule}(\succ^\omega) \wedge \text{Mono}(\rightarrow \cap \succ^\omega).$$

For $u \propto v$, Right$(\succ)$ means that a bag containing u alone is strictly greater than a bag with all of v's subterms. So, by the nature of the bag ordering (adding to a bag makes it bigger), Rule$(\succ^\omega)$ follows. If $u \succ^\omega w$, one only needs to know that $\ell[u] \succsim \ell[v]$ for $\ell[u] \succ^\omega \ell[v]$ to hold, which we have thanks to Harmony (and Eqs. 15, 19), as long as $u \rightarrow v$. □

Lemma 7. Right $(\succsim) \Rightarrow$ **Subterm** $(\succsim)$.

Proof. To see that

$$\text{Rule}(\succ) \wedge \text{Sub}(\succsim) \wedge \text{Harmony}(\rightarrow \cap \succsim, \succsim) \Rightarrow \text{Right}(\succ) \wedge \text{Harmony}(\rightarrow \cap \succsim, \succsim),$$

note that Right$(\succ)$ follows from Rule$(\succ)$, Sub$(\succsim)$, and the compatibility of a quasi-ordering with its strict part (17). □

Lemma 8. Subterm $(\succsim) \Rightarrow$ **Quasi-Simplification Ordering** $(\succsim)$.

Proof. Harmony$(\rightarrow \cap \succsim, \succsim)$ follows from Mono$(\succsim)$ and (3,5,7). □

Turning to the dependency methods:

Lemma 9 ([1]). Main $(\succsim) \Rightarrow$ **Basic** $(\succsim)$.

Proof. Follows from (14). □

Lemma 10. Basic $(\succsim) \Rightarrow$ **Main** $(\succsim)$, for constrictions $\rightarrow_\circ$.

Proof. From Subrule$(\succsim)$ and Mono$(\rightarrow_\circ \cap \succsim)$, one can show Reduce$(\succsim)$ for constrictions. □

Lemma 11. Basic $(\succsim^*) \Rightarrow$ **Intermediate** $(\succsim, \succ')$, where $\succsim^*$ symbolizes the transitive closure of $\succsim \cup \succ'$.

Proof. We need

$$\text{Depend}(\succ') \wedge \text{Reduce}(\succsim) \wedge \text{Compat}(\succ', \succsim) \quad \Rightarrow \quad \text{Depend}(\succ^*) \wedge \text{Reduce}(\succsim^*).$$

Note that $\succsim^*$ is well-founded on account of Compat$(\succ', \succsim)$. The rest is straightforward. □

Lemma 12. Intermediate $(\succsim, \succ') \Rightarrow$ **Variant** $(\succsim, \succ')$.

Proof. By (6,14). □

Lemma 13. Main $(\succsim') \Rightarrow$ **Harmonious Dependency** $(\succsim, \succsim')$.

Proof. By (14,16). □

Lemma 14. Harmonious Dependency $(\gtrsim,\widehat{\gtrsim}) \Rightarrow$ Dependency Pairs $(\gtrsim)$.

Proof. Harmony$(\gtrsim,\widehat{\gtrsim})$ holds trivially.   □

The linchpin step is:

Lemma 15. Main $(\gtrsim) \Rightarrow$ Subterm $(\gtrsim)$.

Proof. This follows from (27,29).   □

8   Illustrations

We conclude with an example.

Example 2. Consider the seven rules:

$$
\begin{array}{rclcrcl}
0 + x & \to & x & \quad & s(x) + y & \to & s(x + y) \\
0 - x & \to & 0 & & s(x) - s(y) & \to & x - y \\
0 \times x & \to & 0 & & s(x) \times y & \to & y + (x \times y) \\
& & & & s(x) \times (y + z) & \to & x \times (y + z) + (y + z)
\end{array}
$$

To prove termination by the **Harmonious Dependency** method, we can use the style of the general path ordering [14, 23], which allows one to compare terms by comparing a mix of precedences, interpretations, and *selected* arguments. Take a "natural" interpretation $[\![\cdot]\!]$ to show that $s \to t$ preserves the value of the interpretation (this natural equivalence of value will be $\gtrsim$), and for $\succ'$ use a termination function based on an interpretation $\{\!\!\{\cdot\}\!\!\}$, where:

$$
\begin{array}{rcl}
[\![0]\!] & = & 0 \\
[\![s(x)]\!] & = & [\![x]\!] + 1 \\
[\![x + y]\!] & = & [\![x]\!] + [\![y]\!] \\
[\![x - y]\!] & = & [\![x]\!] - \min([\![x]\!], [\![y]\!]) \\
[\![x \times y]\!] & = & [\![x]\!] \cdot [\![y]\!]
\end{array}
\qquad
\begin{array}{rcl}
\{\!\!\{s(x)\}\!\!\} & = & \langle s, 0, 0 \rangle \\
\{\!\!\{x + y\}\!\!\} & = & \langle +, [\![y]\!], [\![x]\!] \rangle \\
\{\!\!\{x - y\}\!\!\} & = & \langle -, [\![x]\!], 0 \rangle \\
\{\!\!\{x \times y\}\!\!\} & = & \langle \times, [\![x]\!], 0 \rangle,
\end{array}
$$

with triples ordered lexicographically. The precedence $\times > + > - > s$ is the abstraction[9]. Terms in the same abstract class are compared by the remaining components, which express the recursion scheme. Harmony follows from the use of $[\![\cdot]\!]$ in $\{\!\!\{\cdot\}\!\!\}$. Now, one shows the following inequalities for constricting transitions:

$$
\begin{aligned}
\{\!\!\{s(x) + y\}\!\!\} &> \{\!\!\{s(x + y)\}\!\!\}, \ \{\!\!\{x + y\}\!\!\} \\
\{\!\!\{s(x) - s(y)\}\!\!\} &> \{\!\!\{x - y\}\!\!\} \\
\{\!\!\{s(x) \times y\}\!\!\} &> \{\!\!\{y + (x \times y)\}\!\!\}, \ \{\!\!\{x \times y\}\!\!\} \\
\{\!\!\{s(x) \times (y + z)\}\!\!\} &> \{\!\!\{x \times (y + z) + (y + z)\}\!\!\}, \ \{\!\!\{x \times (y + z)\}\!\!\}. \qquad \square
\end{aligned}
$$

---

[9] There is no need to explicitly exclude the case that u is headed by a constructor (as done in [1]). One simply makes terms headed by constructors smaller than terms headed by defined symbols, which is why s is minimal. The constructor 0 need not be interpreted, since it appears on the left of every rule in which it appears at all.

Rather than a simple precedence, one can devise a "pattern-based" ordering. Patterns that can never have a top redex are made minimal in the surface ordering, and safely ignored. Symbolic inductive techniques may be used to discover patterns that generalize terms in computations.

References

1. Thomas Arts and Jürgen Giesl. Termination of term rewriting using dependency pairs. *Theoretical Computer Science*, 236:133–178, 2000.
2. Thomas Arts and Hans Zantema. Termination of logic programs using semantic unification. In M. Proietti, editor, *Proceedings of the Fifth International Workshop on Logic Program Synthesis and Transformation*, volume 1048 of *Lecture Notes in Computer Science*, pages 219–233, Berlin, 1996. Springer-Verlag.
3. Leo Bachmair and Nachum Dershowitz. Commutation, transformation, and termination. In J. H. Siekmann, editor, *Proceedings of the Eighth International Conference on Automated Deduction (Oxford, England)*, volume 230 of *Lecture Notes in Computer Science*, pages 5–20, Berlin, July 1986. Springer-Verlag.
4. Françoise Bellegarde and Pierre Lescanne. Termination by completion. *Applied Algebra on Engineering, Communication and Computer Science*, 1(2):79–96, 1990.
5. Cristina Borralleras, Maria Ferreira, and Albert Rubio. Complete monotonic semantic path orderings. In *Proceedings of the Seventeenth International Conference on Automated Deduction (Pittsburgh, PA)*, volume 1831 of *Lecture Notes in Artificial Intelligence*, pages 346–364. Springer-Verlag, June 2000.
6. Jacques Chabin and Pierre Réty. Narrowing directed by a graph of terms. In R. V. Book, editor, *Rewriting Techniques and Applications: Proceedings of the Fourth International Conference (RTA-91)*, pages 112–123. Springer, Berlin, 1991.
7. Michael Codish, Samir Genaim, Maurice Bruynooghe, John Gallagher, and Wim Vanhoof. One loop at a time. In *6th International Workshop on Termination (WST 2003)*, June 2003.
8. Michael Codish and Cohavit Taboch. A semantic basis for the termination analysis of logic programs. *J. Logic Programming*, 41(1):103–123, 1999.
9. Patrick M. Cousot and Radhia Cousot. Abstract interpretation: A unified lattice model for static analysis of programs by construction or approximation of fixpoints. In *Conference Record of the Fourth Annual ACM SIGPLAN-SIGACT Symposium on Principles of Programming Languages*, pages 238–252, Los Angeles, California, 1977. ACM Press, New York, NY.
10. Danny De Schreye and Stefaan Decorte. Termination of logic programs: The never-ending story. *J. Logic Programming*, 19/20:199–260, 1993.
11. Nachum Dershowitz. Termination of linear rewriting systems. In *Proceedings of the Eighth International Colloquium on Automata, Languages and Programming (Acre, Israel)*, volume 115 of *Lecture Notes in Computer Science*, pages 448–458, Berlin, July 1981. European Association of Theoretical Computer Science, Springer-Verlag.
12. Nachum Dershowitz. Orderings for term-rewriting systems. *Theoretical Computer Science*, 17(3):279–301, March 1982.
13. Nachum Dershowitz. Termination of rewriting. *J. Symbolic Computation*, 3(1&2):69–115, February/April 1987.
14. Nachum Dershowitz and Charles Hoot. Natural termination. *Theoretical Computer Science*, 142(2):179–207, May 1995.

15. Nachum Dershowitz and Jean-Pierre Jouannaud. Rewrite systems. In J. van Leeuwen, editor, *Handbook of Theoretical Computer Science*, volume B: Formal Methods and Semantics, chapter 6, pages 243–320. North-Holland, Amsterdam, 1990.

16. Nachum Dershowitz, Naomi Lindenstrauss, Yehoshua Sagiv, and Alexander Serebrenik. A general framework for automatic termination analysis of logic programs. *Applicable Algebra in Engineering, Communication and Computing*, 12(1/2):117–156, 2001.

17. Nachum Dershowitz and Zohar Manna. Proving termination with multiset orderings. *Communications of the ACM*, 22(8):465–476, August 1979.

18. Nachum Dershowitz, Mitsuhiro Okada, and G. Sivakumar. Confluence of conditional rewrite systems. In S. Kaplan and J.-P. Jouannaud, editors, *Proceedings of the First International Workshop on Conditional Term Rewriting Systems (Orsay, France)*, volume 308 of *Lecture Notes in Computer Science*, pages 31–44, Berlin, July 1987. Springer-Verlag.

19. Nachum Dershowitz and David A. Plaisted. Equational programming. In J. E. Hayes, D. Michie, and J. Richards, editors, *Machine Intelligence 11: The logic and acquisition of knowledge*, chapter 2, pages 21–56. Oxford Press, Oxford, 1988.

20. Nachum Dershowitz and David A. Plaisted. Rewriting. In A. Robinson and A. Voronkov, editors, *Handbook of Automated Reasoning*, volume I, chapter 9, pages 535–610. Elsevier Science, 2001.

21. Nachum Dershowitz and G. Sivakumar. Goal-directed equation solving. In *Proceedings of the Seventh National Conference on Artificial Intelligence*, pages 166–170, St. Paul, MN, August 1988. AAAI.

22. Robert W. Floyd. Assigning meanings to programs. In *Proceedings of Symposia in Applied Mathematics, XIX: Mathematical Aspects of Computer Science*, pages 19–32, Providence, RI, 1967. American Mathematical Society.

23. Alfons Geser. An improved general path order. *Applicable Algebra in Engineering, Communication, and Computing*, 7(6):469–511, 1996.

24. Oliver Geupel. Overlap closures and termination of term rewriting systems. Report MIP-8922, Universität Passau, Passau, West Germany, July 1989.

25. Jürgen Giesl and Deepak Kapur. Dependency pairs for equational rewriting. In *Proceedings of the Twelfth International Conference on Rewriting Techniques and Applications (Utrecht, The Netherlands)*, volume 2051 of *Lecture Notes in Computer Science*, pages 93–107. Springer-Verlag, 2001.

26. David Gries. Is sometime ever better than alway? *ACM Transactions on Programming Languages and Systems*, 1(2):258–265, October 1979.

27. Michael Hanus. The integration of functions into logic programming: From theory to practice. *J. Logic Programming*, 19&20:583–628, 1994.

28. Jean-Marie Hullot. Canonical forms and unification. In R. Kowalski, editor, *Proceedings of the Fifth International Conference on Automated Deduction (Les Arcs, France)*, volume 87 of *Lecture Notes in Computer Science*, pages 318–334, Berlin, July 1980. Springer-Verlag.

29. Sam Kamin and Jean-Jacques Lévy. Two generalizations of the recursive path ordering, February 1980. Unpublished note, Department of Computer Science, University of Illinois, Urbana, IL.
    Available at http://www.ens-lyon.fr / LIP / REWRITING / OLD_PUBLICATIONS_ON_ TERMINATION / KAMIN_LEVY (viewed June 2004).

30. Shmuel M. Katz and Zohar Manna. A closer look at termination. *Acta Informatica*, 5(4):333–352, December 1975.

31. Laurie Kirby and Jeff Paris. Accessible independence results for Peano arithmetic. *Bulletin London Mathematical Society*, 14:285–293, 1982.
32. Dallas S. Lankford. On proving term rewriting systems are Noetherian. Memo MTP-3, Mathematics Department, Louisiana Tech. University, Ruston, LA, May 1979. Revised October 1979.
33. Chin Soon Lee, Neil D. Jones, and Amir M. Ben-Amram. The size-change principle for program termination. In *Conference Record of the Twenty-Eighth Symposium on Principles of Programming Languages*, volume 36 (3), pages 81–92, London, UK, January 2001. ACM SIGPLAN Notices.
34. Zohar Manna. *Mathematical Theory of Computation*. McGraw-Hill, New York, 1974.
35. Aart Middeldorp, June 2003. Personal communication.
36. Enno Ohlebusch, Claus Claves, and Claude Marché. TALP: A tool for the termination analysis of logic programs. In P. Narendran and M. Rusinowitch, editors, *Proceedings of the Tenth International Conference on Rewriting Techniques and Applications (Trento, Italy)*, volume 1631 of *Lecture Notes in Computer Science*, pages 270–273, Berlin, July 1999. Springer-Verlag.
37. David A. Plaisted. Semantic confluence tests and completion methods. *Information and Control*, 65(2/3):182–215, 1985.
38. Yehoshua Sagiv. A termination test for logic programs. In *Logic Programming: Proceedings of the 1991 International Symposium*, pages 518–532, San Diego, CA, October 1991. MIT Press.
39. Alexander Serebrenik. *Termination Analysis of Logic Programs*. PhD thesis, Katholieke Universiteit Leuven, Leuven, Belgium, July 2003.
40. Michele Sintzoff. Calculating properties of programs by valuations on specific models. *Proceedings of the ACM Conference on Proving Assertions About Programs*, 7(1):203–207, January 1972.
41. William W. Tait. Intensional interpretations of functionals of finite type I. *Journal of Symbolic Logic*, 32(2):198–212, 1967.
42. "Terese" (M. Bezem, J. W. Klop and R. de Vrijer, eds.). *Term Rewriting Systems*. Cambridge University Press, 2002.
43. Alan M. Turing. Checking a large routine. In *Report of a Conference on High Speed Automatic Calculating Machines*, pages 67–69, Cambridge, England, 1949. University Mathematics Laboratory.
44. Kristof Vershaetse and Danny De Schreye. Deriving termination proofs for logic programs, using abstract procedures. In K. Furukawa, editor, *Proceeedings of the Eighth International Conference on Logic Programming*, pages 301–315, Cambridge, MA, 1991. The MIT Press.
45. Ben Wegbreit. Property extraction in well-founded property sets. *IEEE Transactions on Software Engineering*, SE-1(3):270–285, September 1975.

Answer Set Programming
and the Design of Deliberative Agents

Michael Gelfond

Department of Computer Science
Texas Tech University
Lubbock, TX 79409, USA
mgelfond@cs.ttu.edu

1   Introduction

Answer set programming (ASP) (see, for instance, [22]) is a new declarative programming paradigm suitable for solving a large range of problems related to knowledge representation and search. The paradigm is rooted in recent developments in several areas of artificial intelligence. ASP starts by encoding relevant domain knowledge as a (possibly disjunctive) logic program, Π. The connectives of this program are normally understood in accordance with the answer set (stable model) semantics [12, 13]. The corresponding language is frequently referred to as A-Prolog (or ANS-Prolog). The language's ability to express defaults, i.e. statements of the form "normally, objects of class C have property P", coupled with its natural treatment of recursion, and other useful features, often leads to a comparatively concise and clear representation of knowledge. Insights on the nature of causality and its relationship with the answer sets of logic programs [14, 21, 25] allows for the description of the effects of actions which solves the frame, ramification, and qualification problems, which for a long time have caused difficulties in modeling knowledge about dynamic domains.

In the second stage of the ASP programming process, a programming task is reduced to finding the answer sets of a logic program $\Pi \cup R$ where R is normally a simple and short program corresponding to this task. The answer sets are found with the help of programming systems [23, 9, 10, 16, 20] implementing various answer set finding algorithms.

During the last few years the answer set programming paradigm seems to have crossed the boundaries of artificial intelligence and has started to attract people in various areas of computer science. The recent book [6] contains the first comprehensive introduction to the subject.

In this talk I will discuss the use of ASP for the design and implementation of software components of deliberative agents capable of reasoning, planning and acting in a changing environment. We assume that such an agent has knowledge about its domain and about its own capabilities and goals. It constantly

B. Demoen and V. Lifschitz (Eds.): ICLP 2004, LNCS 3132, pp. 19–26, 2004.
© Springer-Verlag Berlin Heidelberg 2004

1. observes the world, explains the observations, and updates its knowledge base;
2. selects an appropriate goal, G;
3. looks for a plan (sequence of actions $a_1, \ldots, a_n$) to achieve G;
4. executes some initial part of the plan, updates the knowledge base, and goes back to step (1).

Initially we will assume [8] that

- The agent's environment can be viewed as a transition diagram whose states are sets of fluents[1] and whose arcs are labeled by actions.
- The agent is capable of making correct observations, performing actions, and remembering the domain history.
- Normally the agent is capable of observing all relevant exogenous events occurring in its environment.

The ASP methodology of design and implementation of such agents consists in

- Using A-Prolog for the description of a transition diagram representing possible trajectories of the domain, history of the agent's observations, actions, occurrences of exogenous events, agent's goals and information about preferred or most promising actions needed to achieve these goals, etc.
- Reducing the reasoning tasks of an agent (including planning and diagnostics) to finding answer sets of programs containing this knowledge.

In this talk I illustrate the basic idea of this approach by discussing its use for the development of the USA-Advisor decision support system for the Space Shuttle. The largest part of this work was done by my former and current students Dr. Monica Nogueira, Marcello Balduccini, and Dr. Richard Watson, in close cooperation with Dr. Matt Barry from the USA Advanced Technology Development Group [1, 2, 5, 24]. From the standpoint of engineering, the goal of our project was to design a system to help flight controllers plan for correct operations of the shuttle in situations where multiple failures have occurred. While the methods used in this work are general enough to model any of the subsystems of the shuttle, for our initial prototypes we modeled the Reaction Control System (RCS). The project consisted of two largely independent parts: modeling of the RCS, and the development of a planner for the RCS domain.

2   Modeling the RCS

The RCS is a system for maneuvering the spacecraft which consists of fuel and oxidizer tanks, valves, and other plumbing needed to deliver propellant to the maneuvering jets, electrical circuitry to control the valves, and to prepare the jets to receive firing commands. The RCS is controlled by flipping switches and issuing computer commands to open and close the corresponding valves. We

---

[1] Fluent is a propositions whose truth values may change as a result of actions.

are interested in a situation when a shuttle controller has the description of the RCS, and a collection of faults reported to him by the observers, e.g. switch 5 and valve 8 are stuck in the open position, circuit 7 is malfunctioning, valve 3 is leaking, etc. The controller's goal is to find a sequence of actions (a plan), to perform a desired maneuver. Controller may use the USA-Advisor to test if the plan he came up with manually, actually satisfies the goal, and/or find a plan to achieve this goal. The USA-Advisor consists of a collection of largely independent modules, represented by A-Prolog programs. A Java interface asks the user about the history of the RCS, its faults, and the task to be performed. Based on this information, the interface selects an appropriate combination of modules and assembles them into an A-Prolog program. The program is passed as an input to a reasoning system for computing stable models (SMODELS). The desired plans are extracted from these models by the Java interface.

In its simplest form, the RCS can be viewed as a directed graph, with nodes corresponding to tanks, pipe junctions, and jets, and links labeled by valves, together with a collection of switches controlling the positions of valves.

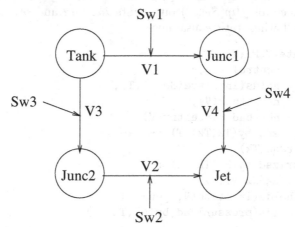

This information can be encoded by facts describing objects of the domain and their connections:

```
tank_of(tank,fwd_rcs).
jet_of(jet,fwd_rcs).
link(tank,junc2,v3).
controls(sw3,v3).
```

A state of the RCS is given by fluents, including:
$pressurized\_by(N, Tk)$ - node N is pressurized by a tank Tk
$in\_state(V, P)$ - valve V is in valve position P
$in\_state(Sw, P)$ - switch Sw is in switch position P
A typical action is:
$flip(Sw, P)$ - flip switch Sw to position P

Our description of the corresponding transition diagram is based on McCain-Turner style theories of action and change [21, 18] and a number of results establishing the relationship between these theories and logic programs [14, 25]. In this approach the direct effects of actions are specified by dynamic causal laws:

$$holds(f, T + 1) \text{ :- } holds(p, T), occurs(a, T)$$

static causal laws:

$$holds(f, T) \text{ :- } holds(p, T)$$

and impossibility conditions:

$$\text{:- } occurs(a, T), holds(p, T).$$

Below are several examples of such laws in the context of the RCS:

Direct effect of $flip(Sw, P)$ on in_state:

```
holds(in_state(Sw,P),T+1) :-
            occurs(flip(Sw,P),T),
            not stuck(Sw).
```

Indirect effects of $flip(Sw, P)$ on fluents in_state and $pressurized\_by$ are given by the following static causal laws

```
holds(in_state(V,P),T) :-
            controls(Sw,V),
            holds(in_state(Sw,P),T),
            not stuck(V),
            not bad_circuitry(V).
holds(pressurized_by(Tk,Tk),T) :-
            tank(Tk).
holds(pressurized_by(N1,Tk),T) :-
            link(N2,N1,V),
            holds(in_state(V,open),T),
            holds(pressurized_by(N2,Tk),T).
```

Note that the last law is recursive and that the effect of a single action propagates and affects several fluents.

Similar simple laws (including a simple theory of electrical circuits) constitutes a commonsense theory, EMD, of simple electro-mechanical devices. Program T consisting of EMD together with a collection, S, of atoms describing the RCS (which can be automatically generated from the RCS schematics) incorporates the controller's knowledge about the RCS.

3   The USA Planning Module

The structure of the USA Planning Module described in this section follows the generate and test approach from [11, 17]. The following rules, PM, form the heart of the planner. The first rule states that, for each moment of time from $[0, n)$ if the goal has not been reached for one of the RCS subsystems, then an action should occur at that time.

```
1{occurs(A,T):action_of(A,R)}1 :- T < n,
                                   system(R),
                                   not goal(T,R).
```

The second rule states that the overall goal has been reached if the goal has been reached on each subsystem at some time.

```
goal :- goal(T1,left_rcs),
        goal(T2,right_rcs),
        goal(T3,fwd_rcs).
:- not goal.
```

Finally, the last rule states that failure to achieve a goal is not an option. Based on results from [25] one can show that, given a collection of faults, I, and a goal G, finding a plan for G of max length n can be reduced to finding an answer set of the program

$$T \cup I \cup PM$$

Since the RCS contains more than 200 actions, with rather complex effects, this standard approach needs to be substantially improved to provide the necessary efficiency.

To improve the efficiency of the planner, and the quality of plans, we will expand our planning module with control knowledge from the operating manual for system controllers. For instance, we include a statement "Normal valve, connecting node $N1$ with node $N2$, shall not be open if $N1$ is not pressurized" which can be expressed in A-Prolog as follows:

```
holds(pressurized(N),T) :-
              node(N), tank(Tk),
              holds(pressurized_by(N,Tk),T).
:- link(N1,N2,V),
   not stuck(V),
   holds(in_state(V,open),T),
   not holds(pressurized(N1),T).
```

After the basic planning module is expanded by about twenty such rules, planning becomes efficient, and the quality of the returned plans improves dramatically. We ran thousands of experiments in which faults were generated at random, and the planner was run in a loop with n ranging from 0 to the maximal possible length (easily available for the RCS system). In most cases the answers were found in seconds. We always were able to find plans or discover that the goal cannot be achieved in less than 20 minutes - the time limit given to us by the USA controllers.

It may be instructive to do some comparison of ASP planning with more traditional approaches.

– The ability to specify causal relations between fluents is crucial for the success of our project. 'Classical' planning languages cannot express such relations.

– We do not use any specialized planning algorithm. Finding a plan is reduced to finding an answer set of a program. This is of course similar to satisfiability planning [15]. In fact recent results [20] show that in many cases finding a stable model of a program can be reduced to finding classical models of its "propositional translation". However in [19] the authors show that any equivalent transformation from logic programs to propositional formula involves a significant increase in size. This confirms our experience that the ability of A-Prolog to represent the domain's transition diagram, its control knowledge, the complex initial situations, allows to naturally formalize domains for which propositional formalizations are far from obvious.

– The program is fully declarative. This means that if the causal laws correctly describe the system's behavior then the plans returned by our system are provenly correct. This also simplifies informal validation of our model and allows for simple modification and reuse.

– One can move from sequential to parallel planning by simply changing a constant.

– Finally, recent work on extensions of A-Prolog allowed us to declaratively specify preferences between plans. E.g. the system returns plans which use computer commands only if it is unavoidable, etc. (See [5]).

4   Future Work

The discussion above shows that ASP planning works well in domains where actions have complex effects depending on a large body of knowledge, and where plans are comparatively short. If we are interested in long plans, or in plans which require non-trivial computation, current answer set solvers do not work well. This is due to the fact that all the solvers start their work by grounding the corresponding program. Even though the grounding algorithms are smart and economical and the current solvers can deal with hundreds of thousands of ground rules this is still a very serious limitation. Finding new algorithms with some kind of "grounding on demand" mechanism is a very interesting and important research problem.

Now a few words about other reasoning steps in the agent observe-think-act loop. In [3] we showed how the process of diagnostics (finding an explanation for an unexpected observation) can be reduced to finding answer sets of a logic program. In the context of the RCS, this program consists of the controller's knowledge T, observations on the values of fluents, and a diagnostics module DM similar to PM. The program efficiently finds collections of faults (a stuck valve, a malfunctioning electrical circuit, etc) which explain the unexpected observation. It is important to notice that the same knowledge, T, is used for diagnostics and for planning. In other knowledge representation languages this is usually not the case - each task requires its own representation. It is important to make sure that the system has enough information to first return diagnoses which are most plausible or most suitable for testing, etc. To achieve this goal we need to better understand how such information can be expressed in A-Prolog and its extensions. Some of the ideas related to this task are discussed in [4, 7] but much more work is needed to make these ideas practical.

References

1. M. Balduccini, M. Barry, M. Gelfond, M. Nogueira, and R. Watson An A-Prolog decision support system for the Space Shuttle. *Lecture Notes in Computer Science – Proceedings of Practical Aspects of Declarative Languages'01*, (2001), 1990:169–183
2. M. Balduccini, M. Gelfond, M. Nogueira, and R. Watson Planning with the USA-Advisor. In 3rd International NASA Workshop on Planning and Scheduling for Space, Sep 2002.
3. M. Balduccini and M. Gelfond Diagnostic reasoning with A-Prolog. Theory and Practice of Logic Programming, 3(4-5):425-461, Jul 2003.
4. M. Balduccini and V. Mellarkod A-Prolog with CR-Rules and Ordered Disjunction. In ICISIP'04, pages 1-6, Jan 2004.
5. M. Balduccini USA-Smart: Improving the Quality of Plans in Answer Set Planning. In PADL'04, Lecture Notes in Artificial Intelligence (LNCS), Jun 2004.
6. C. Baral. Knowledge representation, reasoning and declarative problem solving. Cambridge University Press, 2003.
7. C. Baral, M. Gelfond and N. Rushton. Probabilistic reasoning with answer sets. The Proceedings of the 7th International Conference on Logic Programming and Nonmonotonic Reasoning, pp 21-33, 2004.
8. C. Baral and M. Gelfond. Reasoning agents in dynamic domains. In J Minker, editor, *Logic Based AI*. pp. 257–279, Kluwer, 2000.
9. S. Citrigno, T. Eiter, W. Faber, G. Gottlob, C. Koch, N. Leone, C. Mateis, G. Pfeifer and F. Scarcello. The dlv system: Model generator and application frontends. In *Proceedings of the 12th Workshop on Logic Programming*, 128–137, 1997.
10. P. Cholewinski, W. Marek and M. Truszczyński. Default Reasoning System DeReS. In *International Conference on Principles of Knowledge Representation and Reasoning*, 518-528. Morgan Kauffman, 1996.
11. Dimopoulos, Y., Nebel, B., and Koehler, J.: Encoding planning problems in nonmonotonic logic programs. *Lecture Notes in Artificial Intelligence – Recent Advances in AI Planning, Proceedings of the 4th European Conference on Planning, ECP'97*, (1997), 1348:169–18
12. M. Gelfond and V. Lifschitz. The Stable Model Semantics for Logic Programs. In *Proceedings of the 5th International Conference on Logic Programming*, 1070-1080, 1988.
13. M. Gelfond and V. Lifschitz. Classical Negation in Logic Programs and Disjunctive Databases. *New Generation Computing*, 9(3/4):365-386, 1991.
14. M. Gelfond and V. Lifschitz. Representing Actions and Change by Logic Programs. *Journal of Logic Programming*, 17:301–323, 1993.
15. H. Kautz and B. Selman. Planning as Satisfiability. In Proc. of ECAI-92, pp. 359-363, 1992
16. Yu. Lierler and M. Maratea Cmodels-2: SAT-based Answer Sets Solver Enhanced to Non-tight Programs, In Proc. of LPNMR-7, 2004.
17. V. Lifschitz Answer set programming and plan generation Artificial Intelligence, Vol. 138, 2002, pp. 39-54.

18. V. Lifschitz and H. Turner, Representing transition systems by logic programs. In Proc. of the Fifth Int'l Conf. on Logic Programming and Nonmonotonic Reasoning (LPNMR'99), pp. 92-106, 1999.
19. V. Lifschitz and A. Razborov Why are there so many loop formulas? ACM Transactions on Computational Logic, to appear.
20. F. Lin and Yu. Zhao ASSAT: Computing Answer Sets of A Logic Program By SAT Solvers In Proc. of AAAI-02, pp. 112-117, 2002.
21. N. McCain and H. Turner. Causal theories of action and change. In *14th National Conference of Artificial Intelligence (AAAI'97)*, 460–465, 1997.
22. W. Marek, and M. Truszczyński. Stable models and an alternative logic programming paradigm. In *The Logic Programming Paradigm: a 25-Year Perspective*, 375–398, Spring-Verlag. 1999.
23. I. Niemelä, and P. Simons. Smodels – an implementation of the stable model and well-founded semantics for normal logic programs. In *Proceedings of the 4th International Conference on Logic Programming and Non-Monotonic Reasoning*, 420–429, 1997.
24. M. Nogueira. Building Knowledge Systems in A-Prolog. PhD thesis, University of Texas at El Paso, May 2003.
25. H. Turner. Representing actions in logic programs and default theories: A situation calculus approach. *Journal of Logic Programming*, Vol. 31, No. 1-3, 245-298, 1997.

Abstract Domains Based on Regular Types*

John P. Gallagher and Kim S. Henriksen

Computer Science, Building 42.1, P.O. Box 260, Roskilde University,
DK-4000 Denmark
{jpg,kimsh}@ruc.dk

Abstract. We show how to transform a set of regular type definitions into a finite pre-interpretation for a logic program. The derived pre-interpretation forms the basis for an abstract interpretation. The core of the transformation is a determinization procedure for non-deterministic finite tree automata. This approach provides a flexible and practical way of building program-specific analysis domains. We argue that the constructed domains are condensing: thus goal-independent analysis over the constructed domains loses no precision compared to goal-dependent analysis. We also show how instantiation modes such as *ground, variable* and *non-variable* can be expressed as regular types and hence integrated with other regular types. We highlight applications in binding time analysis for offline partial evaluation and infinite-state model checking. Experimental results and a discussion of complexity are included.

1 Background

There is a well-established connection between regular types and finite tree automata (FTAs) [1], although typical regular type definition notations [2, 3] usually correspond to top-down deterministic FTAs, which are less expressive than FTAs in general. We show how to build an analysis domain from any FTA on a given program's signature, by transforming it to a *pre-interpretation* for the signature. The main contribution of this paper is thus to link the rich descriptive framework of arbitrary FTAs, which includes modes and regular types, to the analysis framework based on pre-interpretations, and demonstrate the practicality of the link and the precision of the resulting analyses.

In Section 2, we introduce the essential concepts from types and FTAs [4] and a review of the approach to logic program analysis based on pre-interpretations [5–7]. In Section 3 it is shown how to determinize a given FTA on order to construct a pre-interpretation. Section 4 contains some examples. Implementation and complexity issues are discussed in Section 5.

An informal example is given first, to give some intuition into the procedure.

Example 1. Given a program containing functions [], [_|_] and unary function f, let the type *list* be defined by $list = []; [any|list]$ and the type *any* as $any =$

---

* Work supported in part by European Framework 5 Project ASAP (IST-2001-38059), and the IT-University of Copenhagen.

B. Demoen and V. Lifschitz (Eds.): ICLP 2004, LNCS 3132, pp. 27–42, 2004.
© Springer-Verlag Berlin Heidelberg 2004

$f(any)$; $[\,]$; $[any|any]$. Clearly *list* and *any* are not disjoint: *any* includes *list*. We can *determinize* the types, yielding two types *list* and *nonlist* (l and nl) with type rules $l = [\,]$; $[nl|l]$; $[l|l]$ and $nl = [nl|nl]$; $[l|nl]$; $f(l)$; $f(nl)$. Every ground term in the language of the program is in exactly one of the two types.

Computing a model of the usual *append* program over the elements l and nl (using a procedure to be described) we will obtain the following "abstract model" of the relation *append*/3: $\{append(l, l, l), append(l, nl, nl)\}$. This can be interpreted as showing that for any correct answer to $append(X, Y, Z)$, X is a *list*, and Y and Z are of the same type (*list* or *nonlist*). Note that it is not possible to express the same information using only *list* and *any*, since whenever *any* is associated with an argument position, its subtype *list* is automatically associated with that argument too. Hence a description of the model of the program using the original types could be no more precise than $\{append(list, any, any)\}$.

2   Preliminaries

Let Σ be a set of function symbols. Each function symbol in Σ has a rank (arity) which is a natural number. Whenever we write an expression such as $f(t_1, \ldots, t_n)$, we assume that $f \in \Sigma$ and has arity n. We write f^n to indicate that function symbol f has arity n. If the arity of f is 0 we write the term $f()$ as f and call f a *constant*. The set of *ground terms* (or *trees*) Term_Σ associated with Σ is the least set containing the constants and all terms $f(t_1, \ldots, t_n)$ such that $t_1, \ldots, t_n$ are elements of Term_Σ and $f \in \Sigma$ has arity n.

A *finite tree automaton (FTA)* is a means of finitely specifying a possibly infinite set of terms. An FTA is defined as a quadruple $\langle Q, Q_f, \Sigma, \Delta \rangle$, where Q is a finite set of *states*, $Q_f \subseteq Q$ is the set of accepting (or final) states, Σ is a set of ranked function symbols and Δ is a set of *transitions*. Each element of Δ is of the form $f(q_1, \ldots, q_n) \rightarrow q$, where $f \in \Sigma$ and $q, q_1, \ldots, q_n \in Q$.

FTAs can be "run" on terms in Term_Σ; a successful run of a term and an FTA is one in which the term is *accepted* by the FTA. When a term is accepted, it is accepted by one or more of the final states of the FTA. Different runs may result in acceptance by different states. At each step of a successful bottom-up run, some subterm identical to the left-hand-side of some transition is replaced by the right-hand-side, until eventually the whole term is reduced to some accepting state. The details can be found elsewhere [4]. Implicitly, a tree automaton R defines a set of terms (or tree language), denoted $L(R)$, which is the set of all terms that it accepts.

Tree Automata and Types. An accepting state of an FTA can be regarded as a type. Given an automaton $R = \langle Q, Q_f, \Sigma, \Delta \rangle$, and $q \in Q_f$, define the automaton R_q to be $\langle Q, \{q\}, \Sigma, \Delta \rangle$. The language $L(R_q)$ is the set of terms corresponding to type q. A term t *is of type* q if and only if $t \in L(R_q)$.

A transition $f(q_1, \ldots, q_n) \rightarrow q$, when regarded as a type rule, is usually written the other way around, as $q \rightarrow f(q_1, \ldots, q_n)$. Furthermore, all the rules defining the same type, $q \rightarrow R_1, \ldots, q \rightarrow R_n$ are collected into a single equation of the form $q = R_1; \ldots; R_n$. When speaking about types we will usually follow the type notation, but when discussing FTAs we will use the notation for transitions, in order to make it easier to relate to the literature.

Example 2. Let $Q = \{listnat, nat\}$, $Q_f = \{listnat\}$, $\Sigma = \{[], [-|-], s^1, 0^0\}$, $\Delta = \{[] \rightarrow listnat, [nat|listnat] \rightarrow listnat, 0 \rightarrow nat, s(nat) \rightarrow nat\}$. The type $listnat$ is the set of lists of natural numbers in successor notation; the type rule notation is $listnat = []; [nat|listnat]$, and $nat = 0; s(nat)$.

Let $\Sigma = \{[], [-|-], s^1, 0^0\}$, $Q = \{zero, one, list_0, list_1\}$, $Q_f = \{list_1\}$, and $\Delta = \{[] \rightarrow list_1, [one|list_1] \rightarrow list_1, [zero|list_0] \rightarrow list_1, [] \rightarrow list_0, [zero|list_0] \rightarrow list_0, 0 \rightarrow zero, s(zero) \rightarrow one\}$, or $list_1 = []; [one|list_1]; [zero|list_0]$ and $list_0 = []; [zero|list_0]$. The type $list_1$ is the set of lists consisting of zero or more elements $s(0)$ followed by zero or more elements 0 (such as $[s(0), 0]$, $[s(0), s(0), 0, 0, 0]$, $[0, 0], [s(0)], \ldots$). This kind of set is not normally thought of as a type.

Deterministic and Non-deterministic Tree Automata. It can be shown that (so far as expressiveness is concerned) we can limit our attention to FTAs in which the set of transitions Δ contains no two transitions with the same left-hand-side. These are called *bottom-up deterministic* finite tree automata. For every FTA R there exists a bottom-up deterministic FTA R' such that $L(R) = L(R')$. The sets of terms accepted by states of bottom-up deterministic FTAs are disjoint. Each term in $L(R')$ is accepted by exactly one state.

An automaton $R = \langle Q, Q_f, \Sigma, \Delta \rangle$ is called *complete* if for all n-ary functions $f \in \Sigma$ and states $q_1, \ldots, q_n \in Q$, it contains a transition $f(q_1, \ldots, q_n) \rightarrow q$. We may always extend an FTA $\langle Q, Q_f, \Sigma, \Delta \rangle$ to make it complete, by adding a new state $q^\flat$ to Q. Then add transitions of the form $f(q_1, \ldots, q_n) \rightarrow q^\flat$ for every combination of f and states $q_1, \ldots, q_n$ (including $q^\flat$) that does not appear in Δ. A complete bottom-up deterministic finite tree automaton in which every state is an accepting state partitions the set of terms into disjoint subsets (types), one for each state. In such an automaton $q^\flat$ can be thought of as the error type, that is, the set of terms not accepted by any other type.

Example 3. Let $\Sigma = \{[], [-|-], 0^0\}$, and let $Q = \{list, listlist, any\}$. We define the set Δ_{any}, for a given Σ, to be the set of transitions $\{f(\overbrace{any, \ldots, any}^{n \text{ times}}) \rightarrow any \mid f^n \in \Sigma\}$. Let $Q_f = \{list, listlist\}$, $\Delta = \{[] \rightarrow list, [any|list] \rightarrow list, [] \rightarrow listlist, [list|listlist] \rightarrow listlist\} \cup \Delta_{any}$. The type $list$ is the set of lists of any terms, while the type $listlist$ is the set of lists whose elements are of type $list$; note that $list$ includes $listlist$.

The automaton is not bottom-up deterministic; for example, three transitions have the same left-hand-side, namely, $[] \rightarrow list$, $[] \rightarrow listlist$ and $[] \rightarrow any$. So for example the term $[[0]]$ is accepted by $list, listlist$ and any. A determinization algorithm can be applied, yielding the following. q_1 corresponds to the type $any \cap list \cap listlist$, $q2$ to the type $(list \cap any) - listlist$, and q_3 to $any - (list \cup listlist)$. Thus q_1, q_2 and q_3 are disjoint. The automaton is given by $Q = \{q_1, q_2, q_3\}$, Σ as before, $Q_f = \{q_1, q_2\}$ and $\Delta = \{[] \rightarrow q_1, [q_1|q_1] \rightarrow q_1, [q_2|q_1] \rightarrow q_1, [q_1|q_2] \rightarrow$

$q_2, [q_2|q_2] \rightarrow q_2, [q_3|q_2] \rightarrow q_2, [q_3|q_1] \rightarrow q_2, [q_2|q_3] \rightarrow q_3, [q_1|q_3] \rightarrow q_3, [q_3|q_3] \rightarrow q_3, 0 \rightarrow q_3\}$. This automaton is also complete; the determinization of this example will be discussed in more detail in Section 3.

An FTA is *top-down deterministic* if it has no two transitions with both the same right-hand-side and the same function symbol on the left-hand-side. Top-down determinism introduces a loss in expressiveness. It is *not* the case that for each FTA R there is a top-down deterministic FTA R' such that $L(R) = L(R')$. Note that a top-down deterministic automaton can be transformed to an equivalent bottom-up deterministic automaton, as usual, but the result might not be top-down deterministic.

Example 4. Take the second automaton from Example 2. This is not top-down deterministic, due to the presence of transitions $[one|list_1] \rightarrow list_1, [zero|list_0] \rightarrow list_1$. No top-down deterministic automaton can be defined that has the same language. Thus the set accepted by $list_1$ could not be defined as a type, using type notations that require top-down deterministic rules (e.g. [2, 3]).

Example 5. We define the set Δ_{any} as before. Consider the automaton with transitions $\Delta_{any} \cup \{[] \rightarrow list, [any|list] \rightarrow list\}$. This is top-down deterministic, but not bottom-up deterministic (since $[] \rightarrow list$ and $[] \rightarrow any$ both occur). Determinizing this automaton would result in one that is not top-down deterministic.

2.1   Analysis Based on Pre-interpretations

We now define the analysis framework for logic programs. Bottom-up declarative semantics captures the set of logical consequences (or a model) of a program. The standard, or concrete semantics is based on the Herbrand pre-interpretation. The theoretical basis of this approach to static analysis of definite logic programs was set out in [5, 6] and [7]. We follow standard notation for logic programs [8].

Let P be a definite program and Σ the signature of its underlying language L. A *pre-interpretation* of L consists of

1. a non-empty domain of interpretation D;
2. an assignment of an n-ary function $D^n \rightarrow D$ to each n-ary function symbol in Σ ($n \geq 0$).

Correspondence of FTAs and Pre-interpretations. A pre-interpretation with a finite domain D over a signature Σ is equivalent to a complete bottom-up deterministic FTA over the same signature, as follows.

1. The domain D is the set of states of the FTA.
2. Let $\hat{f}$ be the function $D^n \rightarrow D$ assigned to $f \in \Sigma$ by the pre-interpretation. In the corresponding FTA there is a set of transitions $f(d_1, \ldots, d_n) \rightarrow d$, for each $d_1, \ldots, d_n, d$ such that $\hat{f}(d_1, \ldots, d_n) = d$. Conversely the transitions of a complete bottom-up deterministic FTA define a function [4].

Semantics Parameterized by a Pre-interpretation. We quote some definitions from Chapter 1 of [8]. Let J be a pre-interpretation of L with domain D. Let V be a mapping assigning each variable in L to an element of D. A *term assignment* $T_J^V(t)$ is defined for each term t as follows:

1. $T_J^V(x) = V(x)$ for each variable x.
2. $T_J^V(f(t_1, \ldots, t_n)) = f'(T_J^V(t_1), \ldots, T_J^V(t_n))$, $(n \geq 0)$ for each non-variable term
   $f(t_1, \ldots, t_n)$, where f' is the function assigned by J to f.

Let J be a pre-interpretation of a language L, with domain D, and let p be an n-ary function symbol from L. Then a *domain atom* for J is any atom $p(d_1, \ldots, d_n)$ where $d_i \in D$, $1 \leq i \leq n$. Let $p(t_1, \ldots, t_n)$ be an atom. Then a *domain instance* of $p(t_1, \ldots, t_n)$ with respect to J and V is a domain atom $p(T_J^V(t_1), \ldots, T_J^V(t_n))$. Denote by $[A]_J$ the set of all domain instances of A with respect to J and some V.

The definition of domain instance extends naturally to formulas. In particular, let C be a clause. Denote by $[C]_J$ the set of all domain instances of the clause with respect to J.

Core Bottom-Up Semantics Function T_P^J. The core bottom-up declarative semantics is parameterised by a pre-interpretation of the language of the program. Let P be a definite program, and J a pre-interpretation of the language of P. Let $Atom_J$ be the set of domain atoms with respect to J. The function $T_P^J : 2^{Atom_J} \to 2^{Atom_J}$ is defined as follows.

$$T_P^J(I) = \left\{ A' \left| \begin{array}{l} A \leftarrow B_1, \ldots, B_n \in P \\ A' \leftarrow B_1', \ldots, B_n' \in [A \leftarrow B_1, \ldots, B_n]_J \\ \{B_1', \ldots, B_n'\} \subseteq I \end{array} \right. \right\}$$

$\mathsf{M}^J[\![P]\!] = \mathsf{lfp}(T_P^J)$: $\mathsf{M}^J[\![P]\!]$ is the minimal model of P with pre-interpretation J.

Concrete Semantics. The usual semantics is obtained by taking J to be the Herbrand pre-interpretation, which we call H. Thus $Atom_H$ is the Herbrand base of (the language of) P and $\mathsf{M}^H[\![P]\!]$ is the minimal Herbrand model of P.

The minimal Herbrand model consists of ground atoms. In order to capture information about the occurrence of variables, we extend the signature with an infinite set of extra constants $\mathcal{V} = \{v_0, v_1, v_2, \ldots\}$. The Herbrand pre-interpretation over the extended language is called HV. The model $\mathsf{M}^{HV}[\![P]\!]$ is our concrete semantics.

The elements of $\mathcal{V}$ do not occur in the program or goals, but can appear in atoms in the minimal model $\mathsf{M}^{HV}[\![P]\!]$. Let $\mathcal{C}(P)$ be the set of all atomic logical consequences of the program P, known as the Clark semantics [9]; that is, $\mathcal{C} = \{A \mid P \models \forall A\}$, where A is an atom. Then $\mathsf{M}^{HV}[\![P]\!]$ is isomorphic to $\mathcal{C}(P)$. More precisely, let Ω be some fixed bijective mapping from $\mathcal{V}$ to the variables in L. Let A be an atom; denote by $\Omega(A)$ the result of replacing any constant

v_j in A by $\Omega(v_j)$. Then $A \in \mathsf{M}^{HV}[\![P]\!]$ iff $P \models \forall(\Omega(A))$. By taking the Clark semantics as our concrete semantics, we can construct abstractions capturing the occurrence of variables. This version of the concrete semantics is essentially the same as the one discussed in [7].

In our applications, we will always use pre-interpretations that map all elements of $\mathcal{V}$ onto the same domain element, say d_v. In effect, we do not distinguish between different variables. Thus, a pre-interpretation includes an infinite mapping $\{v_0 \mapsto d_v, v_1 \mapsto d_v, \ldots\}$. For such interpretations, we can take a simpler concrete semantics, in which the set of extra constants $\mathcal{V}$ contains just one constant v instead of an infinite set of constants. Then pre-interpretations are defined which include a single mapping $\{v \mapsto d_v\}$ to interpret the extra constant. Examples are shown in Section 4.

Abstract Interpretations. Let P be a program and J be a pre-interpretation. Let $Atom_J$ be the set of domain atoms with respect to J. The *concretisation function* $\gamma : 2^{Atom_J} \to 2^{Atom_{HV}}$ is defined as $\gamma(S) = \{ A \,|\, [A]_J \subseteq S \}$

$\mathsf{M}^J[\![P]\!]$ is an abstraction of the atomic logical consequences of P, in the following sense.

Proposition 1. *Let P be a program with signature Σ, and $\mathcal{V}$ be a set of constants not in Σ (where $\mathcal{V}$ can be either infinite or finite). Let HV be the Herbrand interpretation over $\Sigma \cup \mathcal{V}$ and J be any pre-interpretation of $\Sigma \cup \mathcal{V}$. Then $\mathsf{M}^{HV}[\![P]\!] \subseteq \gamma(\mathsf{M}^J[\![P]\!])$.*

Thus, by defining pre-interpretations and computing the corresponding least model, we obtain safe approximations of the concrete semantics.

Condensing Domains. The property of being a *condensing* domain [10] has to do with precision of goal-dependent and goal-independent analyses (top-down and bottom-up) over that domain. Goal-independent analysis over a condensing domain loses no precision compared with goal-dependent analysis; this has advantages since a single goal-independent analysis can be reused to analyse different goals (relatively efficiently) with the same precision as if the individual goals were analysed.

The abstract domain is 2^{Atom_J}, namely, sets of abstract atoms with respect to the domain of the pre-interpretation J, with set union as the upper bound operator. The conditions satisfied by a condensing domain are usually stated in terms of the abstract unification operation (namely that it should be idempotent and commutative) and the upper bound $\sqcup$ on the domain (which should satisfy the property $\gamma(X \sqcup Y) = \gamma(X) \cup \gamma(Y)$). The latter condition is clearly satisfied ($\sqcup = \cup$) in our domain). Abstract unification is not explicitly present in our framework. However, we argue informally that the declarative equivalent is the abstraction of the equality predicate $X = Y$. This is the set $\{d = d \mid d \in D_J\}$ where D_J is the domain of the pre-interpretation. This satisfies an idempotency property, since for example the clause $p(X, Y) \leftarrow X = Y, X = Y$ gives the same result as $p(X, Y) \leftarrow X = Y$. It also satisfies a relevant commutativity property, namely that the solution to the goal $q(X, Y), X = Y$ is the same as the solution to $q(X, Y)$, where each clause $q(X, Y) \leftarrow B$ is replaced by $q(X, Y) \leftarrow X = Y, B$. These are informal arguments, but we also note that the goal-independent analysis yields the *least*, that is, the most precise, model for the given pre-interpretation, which provides support for our claim that domains based on pre-interpretations are condensing.

3   Deriving a Pre-interpretation from Regular Types

As mentioned above, a pre-interpretation of a language signature Σ is equivalent to a complete bottom-up deterministic FTA over Σ. An arbitrary FTA can be transformed to an equivalent complete, bottom-up deterministic FTA. Hence, we can construct a pre-interpretation starting from an arbitrary FTA.

An algorithm for transforming a non-deterministic FTA (NFTA) to a deterministic FTA (DFTA) is presented in [4]. The algorithm is shown in a slightly modified version.

> **input:** NFTA $R = \langle Q, Q_f, \Sigma, \Delta \rangle$,
>   Set Q_d to $\emptyset$; set Δ_d to $\emptyset$
> **repeat**
>   Set Q_d to $Q_d \cup \{s\}$, Δ_d to $\Delta_d \cup \{f(s_1, \ldots, s_n) \rightarrow s\}$
>   **where**
> $\forall f^n \in \Sigma, \forall s_1, \ldots, s_n \in Q_d, \mathcal{C} = s_1 \times \ldots \times s_n$
> $s = \{q \in Q | \exists (q_1, \ldots, q_n) \in \mathcal{C}, f(q_1, \ldots, q_n) \rightarrow q \in \Delta\}$
> **until** no rule can be added to Δ_d
> Set Q_{d_f} to $\{s \in Q_d \mid s \cap Q_{d_f} \neq \emptyset\}$
> **output:** DFTA $R_d = \langle Q_d, Q_{d_f}, \Sigma, \Delta_d \rangle$

Description: The algorithm transform the NFTA from one that operates on states, to one that operates on sets of states from the NFTA. In the DFTA, the output of the algorithm, all reachable states in the NFTA are contained in sets that make up the new states - these are contained in the set Q_d. A state in the NFTA *can* occur in more than state in the DFTA. Potentially every non-empty subset of the set of states of the NFTA can be a state of the DFTA.

The sets in Q_d and the new set of transitions, Δ_d, are generated in an iterative process. In an iteration of the process, a function f is chosen from Σ. Then a number of sets, $s_1, \ldots, s_n$ corresponding to the arity of f, is selected from Q_d - the same set can be chosen more than once. The cartesian product is then formed, $(s_1 \times \cdots \times s_n)$, and for each element in the cartesian product, $q_1, \ldots, q_n$, such that a transition $f(q_1, \ldots, q_n) \rightarrow q$ exists, q is added to a set s. When all elements in the cartesian product have been selected, the set s is added to Q_d if s is non-empty and not already in Q_d. A transition $f(s_1, \ldots, s_n) \rightarrow s$ is added to Δ_d if s is non-empty.

The algorithm terminates when Q_d is such that no new transitions are added. Initially Q_d is the empty set, so no set containing a state can be chosen from Q_d and therefore only the constants (0-ary functions) can be selected on the first iteration.

Example 6. In Example 3 a non-deterministic FTA is shown; $\Sigma = \{[]^0, [\_ \mid \_]^2, 0^0\}$, $Q = \{list, listlist, any\}$, $\Delta = \Delta_{any} \cup \{[] \rightarrow list, [any \mid list] \rightarrow list, [] \rightarrow listlist, [list \mid listlist] \rightarrow listlist\}$.

A step by step application of the algorithm follows:

Step 1: $Q_d = \emptyset, \Delta_d = \emptyset$. Choose f as a constant, $f = []$. Now $s = \{q \in Q \mid [] \rightarrow q \in \Delta\} = \{any, list, listlist\}$. Add s to Q_d and the transition $[] \rightarrow \{any, list, listlist\}$ to Δ_d.

Step 2: Choose $f = 0$. Now $s = \{q \in Q \mid 0 \rightarrow q \in \Delta\} = \{any\}$. Add s to Q_d and the transition $0 \rightarrow \{any\}$ to Δ_d.

Step 3: Choose $f = [\_ \mid \_]$, $s_1 = s_2 = \{any, list, listlist\}$. Now $s = \{q \in Q \mid \exists q_1 \in s_1, \exists q_2 \in s_2, [q_1 \mid q_2] \rightarrow q \in \Delta\} = \{any, list, listlist\}$. Add s to Q_d and the transition $[\{any, list, listlist\} \mid \{any, list, listlist\}] \rightarrow \{any, list, listlist\}$ to Δ_d.

Step 4: Choose $f = [\_ \mid \_]$, $s_1 = s_2 = \{any\}$. Now $s = \{q \in Q \mid \exists q_1 \in s_1, \exists q_2 \in s_2, [q_1 \mid q_2] \rightarrow q \in \Delta\} = \{any\}$. Add s to Q_d and the transition $[\{any\} \mid \{any\}] \rightarrow \{any\}$ to Δ_d.

Step 5: Choose $f = [\_ \mid \_]$, $s_1 = \{any\}, s_2 = \{any, list, listlist\}$. Now $s = \{q \in Q \mid \exists q_1 \in s_1, \exists q_2 \in s_2, [q_1 \mid q_2] \rightarrow q \in \Delta\} = \{any, list\}$. Add s to Q_d and the transition $[\{any\} \mid \{any, list, listlist\}] \rightarrow \{any, list\}$ to Δ_d.

Step 6: Choose $f = [\_ \mid \_]$, $s_1 = \{any, list, listlist\}, s_2 = \{any\}$. Now $s = \{q \in Q \mid \exists q_1 \in s_1, \exists q_2 \in s_2, [q_1 \mid q_2] \rightarrow q \in \Delta\} = \{any\}$. Add s to Q_d and the transition $[\{any, list, listlist\} \mid \{any\}] \rightarrow \{any\}$ to Δ_d.

Step 7 to 11: No new sets added to Q_d. New transitions added to Δ_d: $[\{any, list\} \mid \{any, list\}] \rightarrow \{any, list\}$, $[\{any, list\} \mid \{any, list, listlist\}] \rightarrow \{any, list, listlist\}$, $[\{any, list, listlist\} \mid \{any, list\}] \rightarrow \{any, list\}$, $[\{any\} \mid \{any, list\}] \rightarrow \{any, list\}$, $[\{any, list\} \mid \{any\}] \rightarrow \{any\}$.

The states of states Q_d and the transitions Δ_d in the resulting DFTA are equivalent to the states and transitions in Example 3. $q_1 = \{any, list, listlist\}$, $q_2 = \{any, list\}$ and finally $q_3 = \{any\}$.

In a naive implementation of the algorithm where every combination of arguments to the chosen f would have to be tested in each iteration, the complexity lies in forming and testing each element in the cartesian product, for every combination of states in Q_d. It is possible to estimate of the number of operations required in a single iteration of the process, where an operation is the steps necessary to determine whether $f(q_1, \ldots, q_n) \rightarrow q \in \Delta$. Since Δ is static, an operation on Σ can be considered to be of constant time. The number of operations can be estimated by the formula $\#op = (s * e)^a$, where s is the number of states in Q_d, e is the average number of elements in a single state in Q_d and a is the arity of the chosen f. Every time a state is added to Q_d, an iteration in the algorithm will require additional operations. The worst case is if the algorithm causes an exponential blow-up in the number of states[4].

Obtaining a Complete FTA: The determinization procedure does not return a complete FTA in general. We can complete it as outlined in Section 2, by adding an extra state and corresponding transitions. Another way is to ensure that the input NFTA accepts every term. We can easily do this by adding the standard transitions Δ_{any} to the input NFTA. The output DFTA is then guaranteed to be complete.

The algorithm's efficiency can be improved by generating the new states, Q_d, before the new transitions, Δ_d, are generated. Each iteration in the naive algorithm will redo work from previous iterations, though only combinations containing a newly added state can result in new states. The transitions can be generated in one iteration if all states in Q_d are known.

The new states are formed based on the transitions in the NFTA. The NFTA does not change during the algorithm and a preprocessing of the NFTA can be used to determine, for a given f^n, which states from Q_d can possibly occur as arguments in transitions: those states in Q_d not containing a state from the NFTA that occurring as and argument of f cannot result in any new state being added to Q_d.

Experimental results using an optimised version of the above algorithm (to be described in detail in a forthcoming paper) show that the algorithm can handle automata with hundreds of transitions. Table 3 in Section 5 gives some experimental results.

4   Examples

In this section we look at examples involving both types and modes. The usefulness of this approach in a binding time analysis (BTA) for offline partial evaluation will be shown. We also illustrate the applicability of the domains to model-checking.

We assume that Σ includes one special constant v (see Section 2.1). The standard type any is assumed where necessary (see Example 3), and it includes the rule $v \rightarrow any$.

Definition of Modes as Regular Types. Instantiation modes can be coded as regular types. In other words, we claim that *modes are regular types*, and that this gives some new insight into the relation between modes and types. The set of ground terms over a given signature, for example, can be described using regular types, as can the set of non-ground terms, the set of variables, and the set of non-variable terms. The definition of the types *ground* (g) and *variable* (var) are $g = 0; []; [g|g]; s(g)$ and $var = v$ respectively. Using the determinization algorithm, we can derive other modes automatically. For these examples we assume the signature $\Sigma = \{[], [\_|\_], s, 0\}$ with the usual arities, though clearly

Input states	Output states	Corresponding modes
g, var, any	{any,g}, {any,var}, {any}	ground, variable, non-ground-non-variable
g, any	{any,g}, {any}	ground, non-ground
var, any	{any,var}, {any}	variable, non-variable

Fig. 1. Mode pre-interpretations obtained from g, var and any

the definitions can be constructed for any signature. Different pre-interpretations are obtained by taking one or both of the modes g and var along with the type any, and then determinizing. The choices are summarised in Figure 1. We do not show the transitions, due to lack of space. To give one example, the mode $non\text{-}variable$ in the determinized FTA computed from var and any is given by the transitions for $\{any\}$.

$$\{any\} = 0; []; [\{any\}|\{any\}]; [\{any, var\}|\{any\}]; [\{any\}|\{any, var\}];$$
$$[\{any, var\}|\{any, var\}]; s(\{any\}); s(\{any, var\})$$

Let P be the naive reverse program shown below.

$$rev([],[]). \qquad rev([X|U], W) \leftarrow rev(U, V), app(V, [X], W).$$
$$app([], Y, Y). \qquad app([X|U], V, [X|W]) \leftarrow app(U, V, W).$$

Input types	Model
g, v, any	$\{rev(g, g), rev(ngnv, ngnv), app(g, var, ngnv), app(g, var, var),$
	$app(g, g, g), app(g, ngnv, ngnv), app(ngnv, X, ngnv)\}$
g, any	$\{rev(g, g), rev(ng, ng), app(g, X, X), app(ng, X, ng)\}$
var, any	$\{rev(nv, nv), app(nv, X, X), app(nv, X, nv)\}$

Fig. 2. Abstract Models of Naive Reverse program

The result of computing the least model of P is summarised in Figure 2, with the abbreviations ground=g, variable=v, non-ground=ng, non-variable=nv and non-ground-non-variable=$ngnv$. An atom containing a variable X in the abstract model is an abbreviation for the collection of atoms obtained by replacing X by any element of the abstract domain. The analysis based on g and any is equivalent to the well-known Pos abstract domain [10], while that based on g, var and any is the **fgi** domain discussed in [7]. The presence of var in an argument indicates possible freeness, or alternatively, the absence of var indicates definite non-freeness. For example, the answers for rev are definitely not free, the first argument of app is not free, and if the second argument of app is not free then neither is the third.

Combining Modes with Other Types. Consider the usual definition of lists, namely $list = []; [any|list]$. Now compute the pre-interpretation derived from the types $list$, any and g. Note that $list$, any and g intersect. The set of disjoint types is $\{\{any, ground\}, \{any, list\}, \{any, ground, list\}, \{any\}\}$ (abbreviated as $\{g, ngl, gl, ngnl\}$ corresponding to ground non-lists, non-ground lists, ground lists, and non-ground-non-lists respectively). The abstract model with respect to the pre-interpretation is

$$\{rev(gl, gl), rev(ngl, ngl),$$
$$app(gl, X, X), app(ngl, ngnl, ngnl), app(ngl, gl, ngl), app(ngl, ngl, ngl)\}$$

Types for Binding Time Analysis. Binding time analysis (BTA) for offline partial evaluation in LOGEN [11] distinguishes between various kinds of term instantiations. *Static* corresponds to *ground*, and *dynamic* to *any*. In addition LOGEN has the binding type *nonvar* and user-defined types.

A given set of user types can be determinized together with types representing *static*, *dynamic* (that is, g and *any*) and *var*. *Call types* can be computed from the abstract model over the resulting pre-interpretation, for example using a query-answer transformation (magic sets). This is a standard approach to deriving call patterns; [12] gives a clear account and implementation strategy.

Let P be the following program for transposing a matrix.

$$transpose(Xs, []) \leftarrow$$
$$\quad nullrows(Xs).$$
$$transpose(Xs, [Y|Ys]) \leftarrow$$
$$\quad makerow(Xs, Y, Zs),$$
$$\quad transpose(Zs, Ys).$$

$$makerow([], [], []).$$
$$makerow([[X|Xs]|Ys], [X|Xs1], [Xs|Zs]) \leftarrow$$
$$\quad makerow(Ys, Xs1, Zs).$$
$$nullrows([]).$$
$$nullrows([[]|Ns]) \leftarrow nullrows(Ns).$$

Let *row* and *matrix* be defined as $row = []; [any|row]$ and $matrix = []; [row|matrix]$ respectively. These are combined with the standard types g, *var* and *any*. Given an initial call of the form $transpose(matrix, any)$, BTA with respect to the disjoint types results in the information that every call to the predicates *makerow* and *transpose* has a matrix as first argument. More specifically, it is derived to have a type $\{any, matrix, row, g\}$ or $\{any, matrix, row\}$, meaning that it is either a ground or non-ground matrix. Note that any term of type *matrix* is also of type *row*. This BTA is optimal for this set of types.

Infinite-State Model Checking. The following example is from [13].

$$gen([0, 1]).$$
$$gen([0|X]) \leftarrow gen(X).$$
$$reachable(X) \leftarrow$$
$$\quad gen(X).$$
$$reachable(X) \leftarrow$$
$$\quad reachable(Y), trans(Y, X).$$

$$trans1([0, 1|T], [1, 0|T]).$$
$$trans1([H|T], [H|T1]) \leftarrow$$
$$\quad trans1(T, T1).$$
$$trans2([0], [1]).$$
$$trans2([H|T], [H|T1]) \leftarrow$$
$$\quad trans2(X, Y).$$

$$trans(X, Y) \leftarrow$$
$$\quad trans1(X, Y).$$
$$trans([1|X], [0|Y]) \leftarrow$$
$$\quad trans2(T, T1).$$

It is a simple model of a token ring transition system. A state of the system is a list of processes indicated by 0 and 1 where a 0 indicates a waiting process and a 1 indicates an active process. The initial state is defined by the predicate *gen* and the the predicate *reachable* defines the reachable states with respect to the transition predicate *trans*. The required property is that exactly one process is active in any state. The state space is infinite, since the number of processes (the length of the lists) is unbounded. Hence finite model checking techniques do not suffice. The example was used in [14] to illustrate directional type inference for infinite-state model checking.

We define simple regular types defining the states. The set of "good" states in which there is exactly one 1 is *goodlist*. The type *zerolist* is the set of list of zeros. (Note that it is not necessary to give an explicit definition of a "bad" state).

$$one = 1 \qquad goodlist = [zero|goodlist]; \ [one|zerolist]$$
$$zero = 0 \qquad zerolist = []; \ [zero|zerolist]$$

Determinization of the given types along with *any* results in five states representing disjoint types: $\{any, one\}$, $\{any, zero\}$, the good lists $\{any, goodlist\}$, the lists of zeros $\{any, zerolist\}$ and all other terms $\{any\}$. We abbreviate these as *one*, *zero*, *goodlist*, *zerolist* and *other* respectively. The least model of the above program over this domain is as follows.

$gen(goodlist)$ $trans1(goodlist, goodlist), trans1(other, other)$
$trans2(other, other)$ $trans(goodlist, goodlist), trans(other, other)$
$trans2(goodlist, other)$ $reachable(goodlist)$
$trans2(goodlist, goodlist)$

The key property of the model is the presence of $reachable(goodlist)$ (and the absence of other atoms for *reachable*), indicating that if a state is reachable then it is a *goodlist*. Note that the transitions will handle *other* states, but in the context in which they are invoked, only *goodlist* states are propagated. In contrast to the use of set constraints or directional type inference to solve this problem, no goal-directed analysis is necessary. Thus there is no need to define an "unsafe" state and show that it is unreachable.

In summary, the examples show that accurate mode analysis can be performed, and that modes can be combined with arbitrary user defined types. Types can be used to prove properties expressible by regular types. Note that no assumption needs to be made that programs are well-typed; the programmer does not have to associate types with particular argument positions.

5   Implementation and Complexity Issues

The implementation is based on two components; the FTA *determinization* algorithm described in Section 3, which yields a pre-interpretation, and the computation of the least model of the program with respect to that pre-interpretation.

We have designed a much faster version of the determinization algorithm presented in Section 3. Clearly the worst-case number of states in the determinized FTA is exponential, but our algorithm exploits the structure of the given FTA to reduce the computation. Nevertheless the scalability of the determinization algorithm is a critical topic for future study and experiment. A forthcoming publication will describe our algorithm and its performance for typical FTAs. We note that, although the states in the determinized FTA are formed from subsets of the powerset of the set of states in the input FTA, most of the subsets are empty in the examples we have examined. This is because there are many cases of subtypes and disjoint types among the given types.

The number of transitions in the determinized FTA can increase rapidly, even when the number of states does not, due to the fact that the output is a complete FTA. Hence, for each n-ary function, there are m^n transitions, if there are m states in the determinized automaton. We can alleviate the complexity greatly by making use of "don't care" arguments of functions in the transitions, of which there are usually several, especially in the transitions for the $\{any\}$ state, which represents terms that are not of any other type. If there exists an n-ary function f and states $q_1, \ldots, q_{j-1}, q_{j+1}, \ldots, q_n, q$ such that for all states q_j, there is a transition $f(q_1, \ldots, q_j, \ldots, q_n) \to q$, then we can represent all such transitions by the single transition $f(q_1, \ldots, q_{j-1}, X, q_{j+1}, , \ldots, q_n) \to q$. The jth argument is called a *don't care* argument. Our algorithm generates the transitions of the determinized FTA with some "don't care" arguments (though not all the possible don't cares are generated in the current version), which is critical for the scalability of the model computation.

Abstract Compilation of a Pre-interpretation. The idea of abstract compilation was introduced first by Debray and Warren [15]. Operations on the abstract domain are coded as logic programs and added directly to the target program, which is then executed according to standard concrete semantics. The reason for this technique is to avoid some of the overhead of interpreting the abstract operations.

A pre-interpretation can be defined by a predicate $\to$ /2 defining the FTA transitions. We introduce the predicate $\to$ /2 directly into the program to be analysed, as follows. Each clause of the program of the form is transformed

Prog	Pre-int	NFTA		DFTA		Det.Time	Model time
P / $|P|$ / $|\Sigma|$	J	Q	Δ	Q_d	Δ_d	Secs	Secs
trans / 6 / 2	g,any	2	5	2	6	0.0	0.02
	var,any	2	4	2	7	0.0	0.02
	list,any	2	5	2	5	0.0	0.01
	matrix,row,any	3	7	3	8	0.0	0.03
	g,var,any	3	6	3	8	0.0	0.03
peep / 227 / 110	g,any	2	221	2	279	0.07	2.25
	var,any	2	112	2	349	0.05	1.29
	list,any	2	113	2	347	0.05	1.28
	matrix,row,any	3	115	3	515	0.05	1.98
	g,var,any	3	222	3	446	0.08	3.03
plan / 29 / 13	g,any	2	25	2	24	0.01	0.21
	var,any	2	14	2	30	0.01	0.11
	list,any	2	15	2	33	0.01	0.03
	matrix,row,any	3	17	3	34	0.0	0.13
	g,var,any	3	26	3	81	0.04	0.07
press / 155 / 32	g,any	2	66	2	58	0.03	0.92
	var,any	2	33	2	67	0.03	0.67
	list,any	2	34	2	65	0.02	0.66
	matrix,row,any	3	36	3	91	0.03	0.85
	g,var,any	3	64	3	83	0.03	1.01

Fig. 3. Experimental results

by repeatedly replacing non-variable terms occurring in the clause, of form $f(x_1, \ldots, x_m)$ where $x_1, \ldots, x_m$ ($m \geq 0$) are variables, by a fresh variable u and adding the atom $f(x_1, \ldots, x_m) \to u$ to the clause body, until the only non-variables in the clause occur in the first argument of $\to$. If P is the original program, the transformed program is called $\bar{P}$.

When a specific pre-interpretation J is added to $\bar{P}$, the result is a *domain program* for J, called $\bar{P}^J$. Clearly $\bar{P}^J$ has a different language than P, since the definition of $\to /2$ contains elements of the domain of interpretation. It can easily be shown that least model $\mathsf{M}^J[\![P]\!] = \mathsf{lfp}(T_P^J)$ is obtained by computing $\mathsf{lfp}(T_{\bar{P}^J})$, and then restricting to the predicates in P (that is, omitting the predicate $\to /2$ which was introduced in the abstract compilation). An example of the domain program for *append* and the pre-interpretation for variable/non-variable is shown below. (Note that don't care arguments are used in the definition of $\to /2$).

$$app(U, Y, Y) \leftarrow \quad [\,] \to U. \qquad app(U, Y, V) \leftarrow app(X, Y, Z), [X|X] \to U, [X|Z] \to V.$$
$$v \to var. \quad [\,] \to nonvar. \qquad [\_|\_] \to nonvar.$$

Computation of the Least Domain Model. The computation of the least model is an iterative fixpoint algorithm. The iterations of the basic fixpoint algorithm, which terminates when a fixed point is found, can be decomposed into a sequence of smaller fixpoint computations, one for each *strongly connected component (SCC)* of the program's predicate dependency graph. These can be computed in linear time [16]. In addition to the SCC optimisation, our implementation incorporates a variant of the *semi-naive* optimisation [17], which makes use of the information about new results on each iteration. A clause body containing predicates whose models have not changed on some iteration need not be processed on the next iteration.

Experimental Results. Figure 3 shows a few experimental results (space does not permit more). For each program, the table shows the number of clauses and the number of function symbols. The time to perform the determinization and compute the least model is shown. Timings were obtained using Ciao Prolog running on a machine with 4 Intel Xeon 2 GHz processors and 1 GByte of memory. The determinization algorithm currently does not find all the "don't care" arguments. Insertion of don't care values by hand indicates that the method scales better when this is done. More generally, finding efficient representations of sets of domain atoms is a critical factor in scalability. For two-element pre-interpretations such as Pos, BDDs [18] or multi-headed clauses [19] can be used.

6   Related Work and Conclusions

Prior work on propagating type information in logic programs goes back to [20] and [21]. Our work can be seen partly as extending and generalising the approach of Codish and Demoen [22]. Analysis of logic programs based on types was performed by Codish and Lagoon [23]. Their approach was similar in that given types were used to construct an abstract domain. However their types were quite restricted; each function symbol had to be of exactly one type (which is even more restrictive than top-down deterministic FTAs). Hence several of the application discussed in this paper are not possible, such as modes, or types such as the *goodlist* type of Example 4. On the other hand, their approach used a more complex abstract domain, using ACI unification to implement the domain operations, which allowed polymorphic dependencies to be derived. Like our approach, their domain was condensing.

Work on regular type inference is complementary to our method. The types used as input in this paper could be derived by a regular type inference, or set constraints. One possible use for the method of this paper would be to enhance the precision given by regular type inference. For example, (bottom-up) regular type inference derives the information that the first argument of $rev/2$ in the naive reverse program is a list; using a pre-interpretation derived from the inferred type, it can then be shown that the second argument is also a list. This approach could be used to add precision to regular type inference and set constraint analysis, which are already promising techniques in infinite state model-checking [14].

Applications in binding time analysis for offline partial evaluation have been investigated, with promising results. As noted in Section 4 various mode analyses can be reproduced with this approach, including Pos analysis [24].

References

1. Frühwirth, T., Shapiro, E., Vardi, M., Yardeni, E.: Logic programs as types for logic programs. In: Proceedings of the IEEE Symposium on Logic in Computer Science, Amsterdam. (1991)
2. Mishra, P.: Towards a theory of types in Prolog. In: Proceedings of the IEEE International Symposium on Logic Programming. (1984)
3. Yardeni, E., Shapiro, E.: A type system for logic programs. Journal of Logic Programming **10(2)** (1990) 125–154
4. Comon, H., Dauchet, M., Gilleron, R., Jacquemard, F., Lugiez, D., Tison, S., Tommasi, M.: Tree Automata Techniques and Applications. http://www.grappa.univ-lille3.fr/tata (1999)
5. Boulanger, D., Bruynooghe, M., Denecker, M.: Abstracting s-semantics using a model-theoretic approach. In Hermenegildo, M., Penjam, J., eds.: Proc. 6th International Symposium on Programming Language Implementation and Logic Programming, PLILP'94. Volume 844 of Springer-Verlag Lecture Notes in Computer Science. (1994) 432–446
6. Boulanger, D., Bruynooghe, M.: A systematic construction of abstract domains. In Le Charlier, B., ed.: Proc. First International Static Analysis Symposium, SAS'94. Volume 864 of Springer-Verlag Lecture Notes in Computer Science. (1994) 61–77
7. Gallagher, J., Boulanger, D., Sağlam, H.: Practical model-based static analysis for definite logic programs. In Lloyd, J.W., ed.: Proc. of International Logic Programming Symposium, MIT Press (1995) 351–365
8. Lloyd, J.: Foundations of Logic Programming: 2nd Edition. Springer-Verlag (1987)
9. Clark, K.: Predicate logic as a computational formalism. Technical Report DOC 79/59, Imperial College, London, Department of Computing (1979)

42   John P. Gallagher and Kim S. Henriksen

10. Marriott, K., Søndergaard, H.: Bottom-up abstract interpretation of logic programs. In: Proceedings of the Fifth International Conference and Symposium on Logic Programming, Washington. (1988)
11. Leuschel, M., Jørgensen, J.: Efficient specialisation in Prolog using the handwritten compiler generator LOGEN. Elec. Notes Theor. Comp. Sci. **30(2)** (1999)
12. Codish, M., Demoen, B.: Analysing logic programs using "Prop"-ositional logic programs and a magic wand. In Miller, D., ed.: Proceedings of the 1993 International Symposium on Logic Programming, Vancouver, MIT Press (1993)
13. Roychoudhury, A., Kumar, K.N., Ramakrishnan, C.R., Ramakrishnan, I.V., Smolka, S.A.: Verification of parameterized systems using logic program transformations. In Graf, S., Schwartzbach, M.I., eds.: Tools and Algorithms for Construction and Analysis of Systems, 6th Int. Conf., TACAS 2000. Volume 1785 of Springer-Verlag Lecture Notes in Computer Science. (2000) 172–187
14. Charatonik, W.: Directional type checking for logic programs: Beyond discriminative types. In Smolka, G., ed.: Programming Languages and Systems, 9th European Symposium on Programming, ESOP 2000. Volume 1782 of Springer-Verlag Lecture Notes in Computer Science. (2000) 72–87
15. Debray, S., Warren, D.: Automatic mode inference for logic programs. Journal of Logic Programming **5(3)** (1988) 207–229
16. Tarjan, R.: Depth-first search and linear graph algorithms. SIAM Journal of Computing **1(2)** (1972) 146–160
17. Ullman, J.: Implementation of Logical Query Languages for Databases. ACM Transactions on Database Systems **10(3)** (1985)
18. Schachte, P.: Precise and Efficient Static Analysis of Logic Programs. PhD thesis, Dept. of Computer Science, The University of Melbourne, Australia (1999)
19. Howe, J.M., King, A.: Positive Boolean Functions as Multiheaded Clauses. In Codognet, P., ed.: International Conference on Logic Programming. Volume 2237 of LNCS. (2001) 120–134
20. Bruynooghe, M., Janssens, G.: An instance of abstract interpretation integrating type and mode inferencing. In Kowalski, R., Bowen, K., eds.: Proceedings of ICLP/SLP, MIT Press (1988) 669–683
21. Horiuchi, K., Kanamori, T.: Polymorphic type inference in prolog by abstract interpretation. In: Proc. 6th Conference on Logic Programming. Volume 315 of Springer-Verlag Lecture Notes in Computer Science. (1987) 195–214
22. Codish, M., Demoen, B.: Deriving type dependencies for logic programs using multiple incarnations of Prop. In Le Charlier, B., ed.: Proceedings of SAS'94, Namur, Belgium. Volume 864 of Springer-Verlag Lecture Notes in Computer Science. (1994) 281–296
23. Codish, M., Lagoon, V.: Type dependencies for logic programs using ACI-unification. Theoretical Computer Science **238(1-2)** (2000) 131–159
24. Marriott, K., Søndergaard, H.: Precise and efficient groundness analysis for logic programs. LOPLAS **2(1-4)** (1993) 181–196

Termination of Logic Programs
Using Various Dynamic Selection Rules

Jan-Georg Smaus

Institut für Informatik, Universität Freiburg,
Georges-Köhler-Allee 52, 79110 Freiburg im Breisgau, Germany
smaus@informatik.uni-freiburg.de

Abstract. We study termination of logic programs with dynamic scheduling, as it can be realised using delay declarations. Following previous work, our minimum assumption is that derivations are *input-consuming*, a notion introduced to define dynamic scheduling in an abstract way. Since this minimum assumption is sometimes insufficient to ensure termination, we consider here various *additional* assumptions on the permissible derivations. In one dimension, we consider derivations parametrised by any property that the selected atoms must have, e.g. being ground in the input positions. In another dimension, we consider both *local* and non-local derivations. In all cases, we give sufficient criteria for termination. The dimensions can be combined, yielding the most comprehensive approach so far to termination of logic programs with dynamic scheduling. For non-local derivations, the termination criterion is even necessary.

1 Introduction

Termination of logic programs has been widely studied for the LD selection rule, i.e., derivations where the leftmost atom in a query is selected [1, 4, 8–11, 16]. This rule is adequate for many applications, but there are situations, e.g., in the context of parallel executions or the test-and-generate paradigm, that require *dynamic scheduling*, i.e., some mechanism to determine at runtime which atom is selected. Dynamic scheduling can be realised by *delay declarations* [12, 23], specifying that an atom must be instantiated to a certain degree to be selected.

Termination of logic programs with dynamic scheduling has been studied for about a decade [3, 6, 7, 13–15, 17, 19, 22], starting with observations of surprisingly complex (non-)termination behaviour of simple programs such as APPEND or PERMUTE with delay declarations [17]. In our own research [7, 19, 22], we found that *modes* (input and output), while arguably compromising the "pure logical" view of logic programming, are the key to understanding this behaviour and achieving or verifying termination. We have proposed *input-consuming derivations* (where in each resolution step, the input arguments of the selected atom do not become instantiated) as a reasonable minimum assumption about the selection rule, abstracting away from the technicalities of delay declarations.

In this paper, we study termination of logic programs for input-consuming derivations with various *additional* assumptions about the selection rule, e.g. say-

B. Demoen and V. Lifschitz (Eds.): ICLP 2004, LNCS 3132, pp. 43–57, 2004.
© Springer-Verlag Berlin Heidelberg 2004

ing that the selected atom must be ground in its input positions. Some authors have considered termination under such strong assumptions [13–15, 17, 22], partly because certain programs do not terminate for input-consuming derivations, but also because termination for input-consuming derivations is so hard to show: termination proofs usually use *level mappings*, which measure the size of an atom; an atom is *bounded* if its level is invariant under instantiation. Now, the usual reasoning that there is a decrease in level mapping between a clause head and the clause body atoms does not readily apply to derivations where selected atoms are not necessarily bounded.

After intensive studies of the semantics [6], and restricting to a class of programs that is well-behaved wrt. the modes, we now have a sufficient and necessary criterion for termination of input-consuming derivations [7]. The key concept of that approach is a special notion of *model*, bottom-up computable by a variant of the well-known T_P-operator. The notion reflects the answer substitutions computed by input-consuming derivations. We build on this work here.

We consider additional assumptions in two dimensions. *Certain* additional assumptions about derivations, e.g. the one above, can be formulated in terms of the selected atoms alone. We do this abstractly by saying that each selected atom must have a property $\mathcal{P}$. There are some natural conditions on $\mathcal{P}$ mentioned later. It turns out that the approach of [7] can be easily adapted to give a *sufficient* criterion for termination of $\mathcal{P}$-derivations [20]. The semantic notions (model) of [7] could be used without change. In this paper we give a criterion that is also *necessary*. To this end, the approach of [7] required some small modifications in many places. More specifically, the model notion had to be modified.

Other additional assumptions about derivations cannot be expressed in terms of the selected atoms alone. We consider here one such assumption, that of derivations being *local*, meaning that in a resolution step, the most recently introduced atoms must be resolved first [14]. This is not a property of a single atom, but of atoms in the context of a derivation. To deal with local selection rules, we modify the model notion of [7] so that it reflects the substitutions computed by local derivations. Based on such models, we can give a sufficient criterion for termination of *local* derivations, parametrised by a $\mathcal{P}$ as before.

We thus present a framework for showing termination of logic programs with dynamic scheduling. The initial motivation for this work was our impression that while stronger assumptions than that of input-consuming derivations are sometimes required, *locality* is too strong. More specifically, by instantiating the framework appropriately, we can now make the following five points:

1. There is a class of recursive clauses, using a natural pattern of programming, that narrowly misses the property of termination for input-consuming derivations. Put simply, theses clauses have the form $p(\mathbf{X}) \leftarrow q(\mathbf{X}, \mathbf{Y}),\ p(\mathbf{Y})$, where the mode is $p(input)$, $q(input, output)$. Due to the variable in the head, it follows that an atom using p may always be selected, and hence we have non-termination. Sometimes, just requiring the argument of p to be at least non-variable is enough to ensure termination. This can be captured by setting (the relevant subset of) $\mathcal{P}$ to $\{p(t) \mid t$ is non-variable$\}$ (Ex. 17).

2. Some programs require for termination that selected atoms must be bounded wrt. a level mapping $|.|$. This is related to *speculative output bindings*, and the PERMUTE program is the standard example [17]. This can be captured in our approach by setting $\mathcal{P}$ to the set of bounded atoms (Ex. 14).
3. For some programs it is useful to consider "hybrid" selection rules, where differently strong assumptions are made for different predicates. For example, one might require ground input positions for some predicates but no additional assumptions for other predicates. This can be captured by setting $\mathcal{P}$ accordingly (Ex. 18).
4. A method for showing termination of programs with delay declarations has been proposed in [14], assuming local selection rules. In our opinion, this assumption is unsatisfactory. No implementation of local selection rules is mentioned. Local selection rules do not permit any coroutining. But most importantly, while "the class of local selection rules [...] supports simple tools for proving termination" [14], in practice, it does not seem to make programs terminate that would not terminate otherwise. In fact, we can show termination for PERMUTE without requiring local selection rules (Ex. 14).
5. In spite of point 4, there are programs that crucially rely on the assumption of local selection rules for termination. We are only aware of artificial examples, but our treatment of local selection rules helps to understand the role this assumption plays in proving termination and why this assumption is not required for more realistic examples (Ex. 23).

The rest of this paper is organised as follows. The next section gives some preliminaries. In Sec. 3, we adapt the semantics approach of [7] to $\mathcal{P}$-derivations. In Sec. 4, we study termination for such derivations. In Sec. 5, we adapt our approach to local selection rules. In Sec. 6, we conclude.

2   Preliminaries

We assume familiarity with the basic notions and results of logic programming [1]. For $m, n \in \mathbb{N}_0$, $m \leq n$, the set $\{m, \ldots, n\}$ is denoted by $[m..n]$. For any kind of object that we commonly denote with a certain letter, we use the same letter in boldface to denote a finite *sequence* of such objects [1].

We denote by *Term* and *Atom* the set of terms and atoms of the language in which the programs and queries in question are written. The arity n of a predicate symbol p is indicated by writing p/n. We use typewriter font for logical variables, e.g. X, Ys, and lower case letters for arbitrary terms, e.g. t, s, xs.

For any syntactic object o, we denote by *Vars*(o) the set of variables occurring in o. A syntactic object is **linear** if every variable occurs in it at most once.

A **substitution** is a finite mapping from variables to terms. The domain (resp., set of variables in the range) of a substitution σ is denoted as $Dom(\sigma)$ (resp., $Ran(\sigma)$). We denote by $\sigma_{|o}$ the restriction of a substitution σ to *Vars*(o). The result of the application of a substitution σ to a term t is called an **instance** of t and it is denoted by $t\sigma$. We say t is a **variant** of t' if t and t' are instances of each other. A substitution σ is a **unifier** of terms t and t' if $t\sigma = t'\sigma$. We denote by $mgu(t, t')$ any *most general unifier* (*mgu*) of t and t'.

A **query** is a finite sequence of atoms $A_1, \ldots, A_m$, denoted $\square$ when $m = 0$. A **clause** is a formula $H \leftarrow \mathbf{B}$ where H is an atom (the **head**) and $\mathbf{B}$ is a query (the **body**). $H \leftarrow \square$ is simply written $H \leftarrow$. A **program** is a finite set of clauses. We denote atoms by H, A, B, C, D, E, queries by $\mathbf{Q}, \mathbf{A}, \mathbf{B}, \mathbf{C}, \mathbf{D}, \mathbf{E}$, clauses by c, d and programs by P. We often suppress reference to P.

If $\mathbf{A}, B, \mathbf{C}$ is a query and $c = H \leftarrow \mathbf{B}$ is a fresh variant of a clause, and B and H unify with mgu σ, then $(\mathbf{A}, \mathbf{B}, \mathbf{C})\sigma$ is called a **resolvent of** $\mathbf{A}, B, \mathbf{C}$ **and** $H \leftarrow \mathbf{B}$ **with selected atom** B **and mgu** σ. We call $\mathbf{A}, B, \mathbf{C} \overset{\sigma}{\Longrightarrow}_c (\mathbf{A}, \mathbf{B}, \mathbf{C})\sigma$ a **derivation step**, in short: **step**. If c is irrelevant then we drop the reference. A sequence $\delta = \mathbf{Q}_0 \overset{\sigma_1}{\Longrightarrow}_{c_1} \mathbf{Q}_1 \overset{\sigma_2}{\Longrightarrow}_{c_2} \cdots$ is called a **derivation of** $P \cup \{\mathbf{Q}_0\}$.

If $\delta = \mathbf{Q}_0 \overset{\sigma_1}{\Longrightarrow}_{c_1} \cdots \overset{\sigma_n}{\Longrightarrow}_{c_n} \mathbf{Q}_n$ is a finite derivation, we also denote it as $\delta = \mathbf{Q}_0 \overset{\sigma}{\longrightarrow} \mathbf{Q}_n$ where $\sigma = \sigma_1 \cdots \sigma_n$. We call $len(\delta) = n$ the **length** of δ.

2.1 Moded Programs

For a predicate p/n, a **mode** is an atom $p(m_1, \ldots, m_n)$, where $m_i \in \{I, O\}$ for $i \in [1..n]$. Positions with I (O) are called **input** (**output**) positions of p. To simplify the notation, an atom $p(\mathbf{s}, \mathbf{t})$ means: $\mathbf{s}$ is the vector of terms filling in the input positions, and $\mathbf{t}$ is the vector of terms filling in the output positions.

We assume that the mode of each predicate is unique. One way of ensuring this is to rename predicates whenever multiple modes are desired.

Several notions of "modedness" have been proposed, e.g. *nicely-modedness* and *well-modedness* [1]. We assume here *simply* moded programs [2], a special case of nicely moded programs. Most practical programs are simply moded [7], although we will also give an example of a clause that is not.

Note that the use of the letters $\mathbf{s}$ and $\mathbf{t}$ is reversed for clause heads. We believe that this notation naturally reflects the data flow within a clause.

Definition 1. A clause $p(\mathbf{t}_0, \mathbf{s}_{n+1}) \leftarrow p_1(\mathbf{s}_1, \mathbf{t}_1), \ldots, p_n(\mathbf{s}_n, \mathbf{t}_n)$ is **simply moded** if $\mathbf{t}_1, \ldots, \mathbf{t}_n$ is a linear vector of variables and for all $i \in [1..n]$

$$Vars(\mathbf{t}_i) \cap Vars(\mathbf{t}_0) = \emptyset \quad \text{and} \quad Vars(\mathbf{t}_i) \cap \bigcup_{j=1}^{i} Vars(\mathbf{s}_j) = \emptyset.$$

A query $\mathbf{B}$ is **simply moded** if the clause $\mathtt{dummy} \leftarrow \mathbf{B}$ is simply moded. A program is **simply moded** if all of its clauses are simply moded.

Thus, a clause is simply moded if the output positions of body atoms are filled in by distinct variables, and every variable occurring in an output position of a body atom does not occur in an earlier input position.

As an example of a clause that is *not* simply moded, consider the clause

```
reverse([X|Xs],Ys) ← append(Zs,[X],Ys), reverse(Xs,Zs).
```

in mode $\mathtt{reverse}(O, I), \mathtt{append}(O, O, I)$: $[\mathtt{X}]$ is not a variable. In Ex. 16, we give a slightly modified version of the NAIVE_REVERSE program that is simply moded. *Robustly typed* programs [22] are in some sense a generalisation of simply moded programs, and include the above clause. However, the results of this paper have so far not been generalised to robustly typed programs.

2.2 Norms and Level Mappings

Proofs of termination usually rely on the notions of *norm* and *level mapping* for measuring the size of terms and atoms. These concepts were originally defined for ground objects [10], but here we define them for arbitrary objects (in [18], we call such norms and level mappings *generalised*). To show termination of moded programs, it is natural to use *moded* level mappings, where the level of an atom depends only on its input positions [7].

Definition 2. A **norm** is a function $|.| : Term \rightarrow \mathbb{N}_0$, and a **level mapping** is a function $|.| : Atom \rightarrow \mathbb{N}_0$, both invariant under renaming. A **moded level mapping** is a level mapping where for any $\mathbf{s}$, $\mathbf{t}$ and $\mathbf{u}$, $|p(\mathbf{s}, \mathbf{t})| = |p(\mathbf{s}, \mathbf{u})|$.

An atom A is **bounded** wrt. the level mapping $|.|$ if there exists $k \in \mathbb{N}$ such that for every substitution σ, we have $k > |A\sigma|$.

Our method of showing termination, following [7], inherently relies on measuring the size of atoms that are not bounded. In Def. 13, a decrease in level mapping must be shown (also) for such atoms. So it is important to understand that stating $|A| = k$ is different from stating that A is bounded by k.

One commonly used norm is the term size norm, defined as

$$|f(t_1, \dots, t_n)| = 1 + |t_1| + \dots + |t_n| \quad \text{if } n > 0,$$
$$|t| = 0 \quad \text{if } t \text{ constant/variable.}$$

Another widely used norm is the list-length function, defined as

$$|[t|ts]| = 1 + |ts|,$$
$$|t| = 0 \quad \text{if } t \neq [\_|\_] \text{ (in particular, if } t \text{ variable).}$$

For a nil-terminated list $[t_1, \dots, t_n]$, the list-length is n.

2.3 Selection Rules in the Literature

A selection rule is some rule stating which atom in a query may be selected in each step. We do not give any formal definition here; instead we define various kinds of derivations and state our formal results in terms of those.

The notion of *input-consuming derivation* was introduced in [19] as formalism for describing dynamic scheduling in an abstract way.

Definition 3. A derivation step $\mathbf{A}, p(\mathbf{s}, \mathbf{t}), \mathbf{C} \stackrel{\sigma}{\Longrightarrow} (\mathbf{A}, \mathbf{B}, \mathbf{C})\sigma$ is **input-consuming** if $\mathbf{s}\sigma = \mathbf{s}$. A derivation is **input-consuming** if all its steps are input-consuming.

Local derivations were treated in [14]. Consider a query, containing atoms A and B, in a derivation ξ. Then A is **introduced more recently** than B if the step introducing A comes after the step introducing B, in ξ.

Definition 4. A derivation is **local** if in each step, there is no more recently introduced atom in the current query than the selected atom.

Intuitively, in a local derivation, once an atom is selected, that atom must be resolved away completely before any of its siblings may be selected.

3   Input-Consuming $\mathcal{P}$-Derivations

We consider derivations restricted by some property $\mathcal{P}$ of the selectable atoms. There are two conditions on $\mathcal{P}$. Some of our results would hold without these conditions, but the conditions are so natural that we do not bother with this.

Definition 5. A **$\mathcal{P}$-derivation** is a derivation such that each selected atom is in $\mathcal{P}$, where

1. $\mathcal{P}$ is a set of atoms closed under instantiation;
2. for any $\mathbf{s}$, $\mathbf{t}$ and $\mathbf{u}$, $p(\mathbf{s}, \mathbf{t}) \in \mathcal{P}$ implies $p(\mathbf{s}, \mathbf{u}) \in \mathcal{P}$.

Note that the atoms of a simply moded query have variables in their output positions, and so it would clearly be pathological to require a particular instantiation of the output arguments of an atom for that atom to be selected.

This is the first published work introducing the concept of $\mathcal{P}$-derivations. Of course, a $\mathcal{P}$-derivation can be qualified further by saying *input-consuming* $\mathcal{P}$-derivation etc.

Input-consuming ($\mathcal{P}$-)derivations may end in a query where no atom can be selected. This situation is called **deadlock**. It is a form of termination.

We now define *simply-local* substitutions, which reflect the way simply moded clauses become instantiated in input-consuming derivations [7]. Given a clause $c = p(\mathbf{t}_0, \mathbf{s}_{n+1}) \leftarrow p_1(\mathbf{s}_1, \mathbf{t}_1), \dots, p_n(\mathbf{s}_n, \mathbf{t}_n)$, first $\mathbf{t}_0$ becomes instantiated, and the range of that substitution contains only variables from outside of c. Then, by resolving $p_1(\mathbf{s}_1, \mathbf{t}_1)$, $\mathbf{t}_1$ becomes instantiated, and the range of that substitution contains variables from outside of c and from $\mathbf{s}_1$. Continuing in the same way, finally, $\mathbf{t}_n$ becomes instantiated, and the range of that substitution contains variables from outside of c and from $\mathbf{s}_1 \dots \mathbf{s}_n$.

Definition 6. The substitution σ is **simply-local** wrt. the clause $c = p(\mathbf{t}_0, \mathbf{s}_{n+1}) \leftarrow p_1(\mathbf{s}_1, \mathbf{t}_1), \dots, p_n(\mathbf{s}_n, \mathbf{t}_n)$ if there exist substitutions $\sigma_0, \sigma_1 \dots, \sigma_n$ and disjoint sets $V_0, V_1, \dots, V_n$ consisting of fresh (wrt. c) variables such that $\sigma = \sigma_0 \sigma_1 \cdots \sigma_n$, where for $i \in [0..n]$,

- $Dom(\sigma_i) \subseteq Vars(\mathbf{t}_i)$,
- $Ran(\sigma_i) \subseteq Vars(\mathbf{s}_i \sigma_0 \sigma_1 \cdots \sigma_{i-1}) \cup V_i$ [1].

σ is **simply-local** wrt. a query $\mathbf{B}$ if σ is simply-local wrt. the clause $\mathsf{dummy} \leftarrow \mathbf{B}$.

In the case of a simply-local substitution wrt. a query, σ_0 is the identity.

Example 7. Consider DELETE in Fig. 1, with mode $\mathsf{delete}(I, O, O)$. The substitution $\sigma = \{\mathsf{Y}/\mathsf{V}, \mathsf{Zs}/[\mathsf{W}], \mathsf{Xs}/[], \mathsf{X}/\mathsf{W}\}$ is simply-local wrt. the recursive clause: let $\sigma_0 = \{\mathsf{Y}/\mathsf{V}, \mathsf{Zs}/[\mathsf{W}]\}$, $\sigma_1 = \{\mathsf{X}/\mathsf{W}, \mathsf{Xs}/[]\}$, and $\sigma_2 = \emptyset$; then $Dom(\sigma_0) \subseteq \{\mathsf{Y}, \mathsf{Zs}\}$, $Ran(\sigma_0) \subseteq V_0$ where $V_0 = \{\mathsf{V}, \mathsf{W}\}$, $Dom(\sigma_1) \subseteq \{\mathsf{Xs}, \mathsf{X}\}$, $Ran(\sigma_1) \subseteq Vars(\mathsf{Zs}\,\sigma_0)$.

---

[1] Note that $\mathbf{s}_0$ is undefined. By abuse of notation, $Vars(\mathbf{s}_0 \dots) = \emptyset$.

```
permute([],[]).                        delete([X|Xs],Xs,X).
permute(Ys,[X|Xs]) ←                   delete([Y|Zs],[Y|Xs],X) ←
    delete(Ys,Zs,X),                       delete(Zs,Xs,X), call_late.
    permute(Zs,Xs).                        call_late.
```

Fig. 1. PERMUTE (DELETE)

We can safely assume that all the mgu's employed in an input-consuming derivation of a simply moded program with a simply moded query are simply-local, that is to say: if $\mathbf{A}, B, \mathbf{C} \Longrightarrow (\mathbf{A}, \mathbf{B}, \mathbf{C})\sigma$ is an input-consuming step using clause $c = H \leftarrow \mathbf{B}$, then $\sigma = \sigma_0 \sigma_1$ and $\sigma_0 (= \sigma_{|H})$ is simply-local wrt. the clause $H \leftarrow$ and $\sigma_1 (= \sigma_{|B})$ is simply-local wrt. the atom[2] B [7, Lemma 3.8]. This assumption is crucial in the proofs of the results of this paper.

In [7], a particular notion of model is defined, which reflects the substitutions that can be computed by input-consuming derivations. According to this notion, a model is a set of *not necessarily ground* atoms. Here, we generalise this notion so that it reflects the substitutions that can be computed by input-consuming $\mathcal{P}$-derivations. This generalisation is crucial for the results in Subsec. 4.3.

Definition 8. Let $M \subseteq Atom$. We say that M is a **simply-local $\mathcal{P}$-model** of $c = H \leftarrow B_1, \ldots, B_n$ if for every substitution σ simply-local wrt. c,

$$\text{if } B_1\sigma, \ldots, B_n\sigma \in M \text{ and } H\sigma \in \mathcal{P} \text{ then } H\sigma \in M. \tag{1}$$

M is a **simply-local $\mathcal{P}$-model** of a program P if M is a simply-local $\mathcal{P}$-model of each clause of P.

We denote the set of all simply moded atoms[2] for the program P by SM_P.

Least simply-local $\mathcal{P}$-models, possibly containing SM_P, can be computed by a variant of the well-known T_P-operator [7].

Definition 9. Given a program P and $I \subseteq Atom$, we define

$$T_P^{sl\mathcal{P}}(I) = \{H\sigma \mid \exists\, c = H \leftarrow B_1, \ldots, B_n \text{ variant of a clause in } P,$$
$$\sigma \text{ is simply-local wrt. } c, \ B_1\sigma, \ldots, B_n\sigma \in I, \ H\sigma \in \mathcal{P}\},$$
$$T_P^{SL\mathcal{P}}(I) = I \cup T_P^{sl\mathcal{P}}(I).$$

We denote the least simply-local $\mathcal{P}$-model of P containing SM_P by $PM_P^{SL\mathcal{P}}$.

Example 10. Consider the program DELETE (see Fig. 1) ignoring the call_late predicate. Recall Ex. 7. Let $\mathcal{P}$ be the set containing *all* atoms using delete. SM_P consists of all atoms of the form delete(vs, Us, U) where Us, U $\notin$ $Vars(vs)$. To construct $PM_P^{SL\mathcal{P}}$, we iterate $T_P^{SL\mathcal{P}}$ starting from any atom in SM_P (the resulting atoms are written on the l.h.s. below) and the fact clause (r.h.s.). Each line below corresponds to one iteration of $T_P^{SL\mathcal{P}}$. We have $PM_P^{SL\mathcal{P}} =$

---

[2] We sometimes say "atom" for "query containing only one atom".

$$\{ \text{delete}(vs, \text{Us}, \text{U}),$$
$$\text{delete}([y_1|vs], [y_1|\text{Us}], \text{U}), \qquad \text{delete}([x_1|xs_1], xs_1, x_1),$$
$$\text{delete}([y_2, y_1|vs], [y_2, y_1|\text{Us}], \text{U}), \text{delete}([y_1, x_1|xs_1], [y_1|xs_1], x_1), \qquad (2)$$
$$\dots \qquad \qquad \dots$$
$$\mid vs, xs_1, x_1, y_1, y_2, \dots \text{ arbitrary where } \text{Us}, \text{U} \notin \text{Vars}(vs)\}.$$

Observe the variable occurrences of U, Us in the atoms on the l.h.s. In Ex. 14, we will see the importance of such variable occurrences.

In the above example, we assume that $\mathcal{P}$ is the set of *all* atoms, and so the simply-local $\mathcal{P}$-model is in fact a *simply-local model* [7]. In order to obtain a *necessary* termination criterion, the approach of [7] required some small modifications in many places, one of them being the generalisation of simply-local models to simply-local $\mathcal{P}$-models. However, we are not aware of a practical situation where one has to consider a simply-local $\mathcal{P}$-model that is not a simply-local model.

The model semantics given here is equivalent to the operational semantics. We do not formally state this equivalence here for lack of space, but it is used in the proofs of the termination results of the following sections [21].

4   Termination Without Requiring Local Selection Rules

4.1   Simply $\mathcal{P}$-Accceptable Programs

The following concept is adopted from Apt [1].

Definition 11. Let p, q be predicates in a program P. We say that p **refers to** q if there is a clause in P with p in its head and q in its body, and p **depends on** q (written $p \sqsupseteq q$) if (p, q) is in the reflexive, transitive closure of *refers to*. We write $p \sqsupset q$ if $p \sqsupseteq q$ and $q \not\sqsupseteq p$, and $p \simeq q$ if $p \sqsupseteq q$ and $q \sqsupseteq p$.

We extend this notation to *atoms*, e.g. $p(\mathbf{s}, \mathbf{t}) \simeq q(\mathbf{u}, \mathbf{v})$ if $p \simeq q$.

Definition 12. A program is **input $\mathcal{P}$-terminating** if all input-consuming $\mathcal{P}$-derivations starting in a simply-moded query are finite.

Previously, we had defined *input termination*, which is input $\mathcal{P}$-termination for $\mathcal{P}$ being the set of all atoms [7]. We now give a sufficient and necessary criterion for input $\mathcal{P}$-termination.

Definition 13. Let P be a simply moded program, $|.|$ a moded level mapping and M a simply-local $\mathcal{P}$-model of P containing SM_P. A clause $H \leftarrow B_1, \dots, B_n$ is **simply $\mathcal{P}$-acceptable by** $|.|$ **and** M if for every substitution σ simply-local wrt. it, for all $i \in [1..n]$,

$$B_1\sigma, \dots, B_{i-1}\sigma \in M \text{ and } H \simeq B_i \text{ and } H\sigma \in \mathcal{P} \text{ and } B_i\sigma \in \mathcal{P} \text{ imply } |H\sigma| > |B_i\sigma|. \tag{3}$$

The program P is **simply $\mathcal{P}$-acceptable by** $|.|$ **and** M if each clause of P is simply $\mathcal{P}$-acceptable by $|.|$ and M.

The difference to the definition of a *simply acceptable* clause [7] is in the conditions $B_i\sigma \in \mathcal{P}$ and $H\sigma \in \mathcal{P}$. The condition $B_i\sigma \in \mathcal{P}$ may seem more natural than the condition $H\sigma \in \mathcal{P}$, since σ, due to the model condition, reflects the degree of instantiation that B_i may have when it is selected. But for $i = 1$, σ reflects the degree of instantiation of the entire clause obtained by unification when the clause is used for an input-consuming $\mathcal{P}$-derivation step. Moreover, the condition $H\sigma \in \mathcal{P}$ is important for showing *necessity* (Subsec. 4.3).

Note that a decrease between the head and body atoms must be shown only for the atoms where $H \simeq B_i$. The idea is that termination is shown incrementally, so we assume that for the B_i where $H \sqsupset B_i$, termination has been shown already. One can go further and explicitly give *modular* termination results [7, 10], but this is a side issue for us and we refrain from it for space reasons.

The following is the standard example of a program that requires boundedness as additional condition on selected atoms (see point 2 in the introduction).

Example 14. Consider PERMUTE in mode permute(I, O), delete(I, O, O) (Fig. 1). Recall Ex. 10. As norm we take the list-length function, and we define the level mapping as $|\mathtt{permute}(zs, xs)| = |zs|$ and $|\mathtt{delete}(xs, zs, x)| = |xs|$. Now for all atoms delete(ys, zs, x) $\in PM_P^{SLP}$, we have $|ys| \geq |zs|$; for the ones on the r.h.s. even $|ys| > |zs|$. Let $\mathcal{P}$ be the set of bounded atoms wrt. $|.|$.

Now let us look at the recursive clause for permute. We verify that the second body atom fulfils the requirement of Def. 13, where M is PM_P^{SLP}. So we have to consider all simply-local substitutions σ such that delete(Ys, Zs, X)$\sigma \in PM_P^{SLP}$. For the atoms on the l.h.s. in (2), this means that

$$\sigma \supseteq \{\mathtt{Ys}/[y_n, \ldots, y_1|vs], \mathtt{Zs}/[y_n, \ldots, y_1|\mathtt{Us}], \mathtt{X}/\mathtt{U}\} \qquad (n \geq 0).$$

Clearly, permute(Zs, Xs)$\sigma \notin \mathcal{P}$, and hence no proof obligation arises. For the atoms on the r.h.s. in (2), this means that

$$\sigma \supseteq \{\mathtt{Ys}/[y_n, \ldots, y_1, x_1|xs_1], \mathtt{Zs}/[y_n, \ldots, y_1|xs_1], \mathtt{X}/x_1\} \qquad (n \geq 0).$$

But then $|\mathtt{permute}(\mathtt{Ys}, [\mathtt{X}|\mathtt{Xs}])\sigma| > |\mathtt{permute}(\mathtt{Zs}, \mathtt{Xs})\sigma|$.

The other clauses are trivial to check, and so PERMUTE is simply $\mathcal{P}$-acceptable. Observe that only the model of DELETE played a role in our argument, not the model of PERMUTE.

The atom call_late only serves the purpose of allowing for non-local derivations, to emphasise that locality is not needed for termination (see point 4 in Sec. 1). Without this atom, all $\mathcal{P}$-derivations would automatically be local.

The following infinite derivation (ignoring call_late), input-consuming but not a $\mathcal{P}$-derivation, demonstrates that the program does not input-terminate:

permute([1], W) $\Longrightarrow$ delete([1], Zs', X'), permute(Zs', Xs') $\Longrightarrow$
delete([], Xs'', X'), permute([1|Xs''], Xs') $\Longrightarrow$
delete([], Xs'', X'), delete([1|Xs''], Zs''', X'''), permute(Zs''', Xs') $\Longrightarrow$
delete([], Xs'', X'), delete(Xs'', Xs'''', X'''), permute([1|Xs''''], Xs') $\Longrightarrow \ldots$

```
reverse([X|Xs],Ys) ←              append_sing([X|Xs],Y,[X|Zs]) ←
    append_sing(Zs,X,Ys),             append_sing(Xs,Y,Zs).
    reverse(Xs,Zs).               append_sing([],Y,[Y]).
reverse([],[]).
```

Fig. 2. NAIVE_REVERSE

4.2 Sufficiency of Simply $\mathcal{P}$-Acceptability

In [7], we find a result stating that simply acceptable programs are input terminating. The following theorem generalises this result to $\mathcal{P}$-derivations. The proofs of all results of this paper can be found in [21].

Theorem 15. Let P be a simply moded program. Let M be a simply-local $\mathcal{P}$-model of P containing SM_P. Suppose that P is simply $\mathcal{P}$-acceptable by M and a moded level mapping $|.|$. Then P is input $\mathcal{P}$-terminating.

We give three further examples. The first supports point 2 in the introduction.

Example 16. The program NAIVE_REVERSE (Fig. 2) in mode $\texttt{reverse}(O, I)$, $\texttt{append\_sing}(O, O, I)$ is not input terminating, but it is input $\mathcal{P}$-terminating for $\mathcal{P}$ chosen in analogy to Ex. 14.

The next example illustrates point 1 in the introduction.

Example 17. Let PERMUTE2 be the program obtained from PERMUTE by replacing the recursive clause for delete by its *most specific variant* [17]:

$$\texttt{delete([Y,H|T],[Y|Xs],X)} \leftarrow \texttt{delete([H|T],Xs,X)}.$$

Assume $|.|$ and the modes as in Ex. 14. As in Ex. 10 we have

$$SM_P = \{\texttt{delete}(vs, \texttt{Us}, \texttt{U}) \mid vs \text{ arbitrary}\},$$

but when we start applying T_P^{SLP} to the atoms in SM_P, then due to the modified clause above, only the atoms of the form $\texttt{delete}([v|vs'], \texttt{Us}, \texttt{U})$ contribute; $\texttt{delete}([], \texttt{Us}, \texttt{U})$ does not contribute:

$$
\begin{aligned}
PM_P^{SLP} = \{&\texttt{delete}(vs, \texttt{Us}, \texttt{U}), \\
&\texttt{delete}([y_1, v, vs'], [y_1|\texttt{Us}], \texttt{U}), \qquad \texttt{delete}([x_1|xs_1], xs_1, x_1), \\
&\texttt{delete}([y_2, y_1, v|vs'], [y_2, y_1|\texttt{Us}], \texttt{U}), \texttt{delete}([y_1, x_1|xs_1], [y_1|xs_1], x_1), \\
&\cdots \qquad\qquad\qquad\qquad\qquad \cdots \\
&\mid vs, v, vs', xs_1, x_1, y_1, y_2, \ldots \text{arbitrary where } \texttt{Us}, \texttt{U} \notin \mathit{Vars}(vs, v, vs')\}.
\end{aligned}
$$

We show that the program is simply $\mathcal{P}$-acceptable by $|.|$ and PM_P^{SLP}, where $\mathcal{P}$ is the set of atoms that are at least non-variable in their input positions. As in Ex. 14, we focus on the second body atom of the recursive clause for permute. We have to consider all simply-local substitutions σ such that $\texttt{delete}(\texttt{Ys}, \texttt{Zs}, \texttt{X})\sigma \in PM_P^{SLP}$, and moreover $\texttt{permute}(\texttt{Zs}, \texttt{Xs})\sigma \in \mathcal{P}$. It is easy to see that for all such σ, we have $|\texttt{permute}(\texttt{Ys}, [\texttt{X}|\texttt{Xs}])\sigma| > |\texttt{permute}(\texttt{Zs}, \texttt{Xs})\sigma|$. The important point is that the atoms of the form $\texttt{delete}(vs, \texttt{Us}, \texttt{U}) \in PM_P^{SLP}$ do not give rise to a proof obligation since $\texttt{permute}(\texttt{Us}, \_) \notin \mathcal{P}$.

The following is an example of "hybrid" selection rules (point 3 in Sec. 1).

Example 18. For space reasons, we only sketch this example. A program for the well-known n-queens problem has the following main clause:

```
nqueens(N,Sol) ←
    sequence(N,Seq), permute(Seq,Sol), safe(Sol).
```

We could implement `permute` as in Ex. 14 or as in Ex. 17. In either case, we have a non-trivial $\mathcal{P}$. In contrast, $\mathcal{P}$ may contain *all* atoms using `safe`. In fact, for efficiency reasons, atoms using `safe` should be selected as early as possible.

Note that such a hybrid selection rule can be implemented by means of the *default left-to-right selection rule* [22]. To this end, the second and third atoms must be swapped. Since any results in this paper do not actually depend on the textual position of atoms, they still apply to the thus modified program.

4.3   Necessity of Simply $\mathcal{P}$-Acceptability

We now give the converse of Theorem 15, namely that our criterion for proving input $\mathcal{P}$-termination wrt. simply moded queries is also necessary. The level mapping is constructed as a kind of tree that reflects all possible input-consuming $\mathcal{P}$-derivations, following the approach of [7] which in turn is based on [5]. But for space reasons, we only state the main result.

Theorem 19. Let P be a simply moded program and $\mathcal{P}$ a set of atoms according to Def. 5. If P is input $\mathcal{P}$-terminating then P is $\mathcal{P}$-simply acceptable. In particular, P is $\mathcal{P}$-simply acceptable by $PM_P^{SL\mathcal{P}}$.

5   Local Selection Rules

In this section, we adapt the results of the two previous sections to local selection rules. First note that local derivations genuinely need special treatment, since one cannot express locality as a property $\mathcal{P}$ of the selected atoms. Note also that *local* [14] and *simply-local* [6, 7] are completely different concepts.

Assuming local selection rules is helpful for showing termination, since one can exploit model information almost in the same way as for LD derivations [4]. In fact, some arguments are simpler here than in the previous two sections, manifest in the proofs [21]. However, this is also due to the fact that we currently just have a sufficient termination criterion for local derivations. How this criterion must be adapted to become also necessary is a topic for future work.

A *simply-local model* [7] is a simply-local $\mathcal{P}$-model where $\mathcal{P}$ is the set of all atoms. Analogously, we write PM_P^{SL} instead of $PM_P^{SL\mathcal{P}}$ in this case. To reflect the substitutions that can be computed by local derivations, we need as model the union of a simply-local model (for the completely resolved atoms) and the set of simply moded atoms (for the unresolved atoms).

Let M be the least simply-local model of P (note: not the least simply-local model of P *containing* SM_P) We define $LM_P^{SL} := SM_P \cup M$. So LM_P^{SL} contains SM_P, but unlike PM_P^{SL}, does not involve applications of T_P^{SL} to atoms in SM_P.

Example 20. Let P be the following program in mode $\texttt{even}(I), \texttt{minus2}(I, O)$:

```
even(X) ← minus2(X,Y), even(Y).        minus2(X,s(X)) ← fail.
even(0).                               minus2(s(s(X)),X).
```

We have

$$SM_P = \{\texttt{even}(x), \texttt{minus2}(x, \texttt{Z}), \texttt{fail} \mid x \text{ arbitrary where } \texttt{Z} \notin \mathit{Vars}(x)\}$$
$$PM_P^{SL} = SM_P \cup \{\texttt{even}(0), \texttt{minus2}(\texttt{s}(\texttt{s}(x)), x), \texttt{minus2}(x, \texttt{s}(x)),$$
$$\texttt{even}(\texttt{s}(\texttt{s}(x))), \texttt{even}(x) \mid x \text{ arbitrary}\}.$$

The minimal simply-local model of P, not containing SM_P, is the following:

$$M = \{\texttt{even}(\texttt{s}^{2n}(0)), \texttt{minus2}(\texttt{s}(\texttt{s}(x)), x) \mid n \in \mathbb{N}_0, \ x \text{ arbitrary}\}.$$

Then $LM_P^{SL} = SM_P \cup M$. In contrast to PM_P^{SL} we have $\texttt{minus2}(x, \texttt{s}(x)) \notin LM_P^{SL}$. This reflects that in a local derivation, resolving an atom with the clause head $\texttt{minus2}(\texttt{X}, \texttt{s}(\texttt{X}))$ will definitely lead to finite failure. For this program, locality is crucial for termination (see point 5 in Sec. 1).

The example[3] is contrived since the first clause for $\texttt{minus2}$ is completely unnecessary, yet natural enough to suggest that there might be a "real" example.

We now proceed with the treatment of termination.

Definition 21. A program is **local $\mathcal{P}$-terminating** if all input-consuming local $\mathcal{P}$-derivations starting in a simply-moded query are finite.

We now give a sufficient criterion for local $\mathcal{P}$-termination.

Definition 22. Let P be a simply moded program, $|.|$ a moded level mapping and M a set such that $SM_P \subseteq M$ and for some simply-local model M' of P, $M' \subseteq M$. A clause $A \leftarrow B_1, \ldots, B_n$ is **local $\mathcal{P}$-acceptable by $|.|$ and M**[4] if for every substitution σ simply-local wrt. it, for all $i \in [1..n]$,

$$(B_1, \ldots, B_{i-1})\sigma \in M \text{ and } A \simeq B_i \text{ and } B_i\sigma \in \mathcal{P} \quad \text{implies} \quad |A\sigma| > |B_i\sigma|.$$

The program P is **local $\mathcal{P}$-acceptable by $|.|$ and M** if each clause of P is local $\mathcal{P}$-acceptable by $|.|$ and M.

Example 23. Consider again the program in Ex. 20, in particular the recursive clause. Let $\mathcal{P}$ be the set of atoms where all input arguments are non-variable and $|\texttt{even}(x)| = |\texttt{minus2}(x, y)| = |x|$ where $|.|$ is the term size norm. We verify that the second body atom fulfils the requirement of Def. 22, taking $M = LM_P^{SL}$. We have to consider all simply-local σ such that $\texttt{minus2}(\texttt{X}, \texttt{Y})\sigma \in LM_P^{SL}$. So

$$\sigma \supseteq \{\texttt{X}/x, \texttt{Y}/\texttt{Z}\} \quad \text{or} \quad \sigma \supseteq \{\texttt{X}/\texttt{s}(\texttt{s}(x)), \texttt{Y}/x\}.$$

---

[3] Thanks to Felix Klaedtke for inspiring the example!

[4] This terminology should be regarded as provisional. If a sufficient and *necessary* condition for local $\mathcal{P}$-termination different from the one given here is found eventually, then it should be called "local $\mathcal{P}$-acceptable" rather than inventing a new name.

In the first case, $\mathtt{even(Y)}\sigma \notin \mathcal{P}$ and hence no proof obligation arises. In the second case, $|\mathtt{even(X)}\sigma| > |\mathtt{even(Y)}\sigma|$. Hence the clause is local $\mathcal{P}$-acceptable. Note that the clause is not simply $\mathcal{P}$-acceptable (due to $\mathtt{minus2}(x, \mathtt{s}(x)) \in PM_P^{SL}$).

Observe that unlike [14], we do not require that the selected atoms must be bounded. In our formalism, the instantiation requirements of the selected atom and the locality issue are two separate dimensions.

Theorem 24. Let P be a simply moded program. Let M be a set such that $SM_P \subseteq M$ and for some simply-local model M' of P, $M' \subseteq M$. Suppose that P is local $\mathcal{P}$-acceptable by M and a moded level mapping $|.|$. Then P is local $\mathcal{P}$-terminating.

6 Conclusion

We have presented a framework for proving termination of logic programs with dynamic scheduling. We have considered various assumptions about the selection rule, in addition to the assumption that derivations must be input-consuming. On the one hand, derivations can be restricted by giving a property $\mathcal{P}$ that the selected atoms must fulfil. On the other hand, derivations may or may not be required to be local. These aspects can be combined freely. We now refer back to the five points in the introduction.

Some programs terminate under an assumption about the selection rule that is just slightly stronger than assuming input-consuming derivations (point 1). Others need what we call *strong* assumptions: the selected atom must be bounded wrt. a level mapping (point 2). Different versions of **PERMUTE**, which is the standard example of a program that tends to loop for dynamic scheduling [17], are representatives of these program classes. Then there are programs for which one should make hybrid assumptions about the selection rule: depending on the predicate, an atom should be bounded in its input positions or not (point 3). Considering our work together with [7], it is no longer true that "the termination behaviour of 'delay until nonvar' is poorly understood" [14].

The authors of [14] have assumed local selection rules. There are programs for which this assumption is genuinely needed. Abstractly, this is the case for a query $A_1, \ldots, A_n$ where for some atom A_i and some clause c, the subderivations associated with A_i and c all fail, but at the same time, the unification between A_i and c's head produces a substitution that may trigger an infinite derivation for some atom A_j, where $j > i$. In this case, locality ensures failure of A_i before the infinite derivation of A_j can happen. The comparison between our model notions (see Ex. 20) also clarifies the role of locality: substitutions obtained by *partial* resolution of an atom can be disregarded (point 5). But we are not aware of a *realistic* program where this matters (point 4). As an obvious consequence, we have no realistic program that we can show to terminate for local derivations and the method of [14] cannot. But the better understanding of the role of locality may direct the search for such an example.

For derivations that are not assumed to be local, we obtain a sufficient and necessary termination criterion. For local derivations, our criterion is sufficient but probably not necessary. Finding a necessary criterion is a topic for future work. This would be an important advance over [14], since the criterion given there is known not to be necessary.

The concepts of *input-consuming derivations* and $\mathcal{P}$-derivations are both meant to be abstract descriptions of dynamic scheduling. Delay declarations that check for arguments being at least non-variable, or at least non-variable in some sub-argument [12, 23], are often adequate for ensuring input-consuming derivations with $\mathcal{P}$ stating that the input arguments are at least non-variable (see Ex. 17). Delay declarations that check for groundness are adequate for ensuring boundedness of atoms (see Ex. 14). In general groundness is stronger than boundedness, but we are not aware of delay declarations that could check for boundedness, e.g., check for a list being nil-terminated. This deficiency has been mentioned previously [13]. Hybrid selection rules can be realised with delay declarations combined with the default left-to-right selection rule (see Ex. 18).

Concerning automation of our method, the problems are not so different from the ones encountered when proving left-termination: we have to reason about infinite models — to do so, abstract interpretation approaches, where terms are abstracted as their norms, may be useful [11, 16]. It seems that in our case automation is additionally complicated because we have to consider infinitely many simply-local substitutions. But looking at Ex. 10, we have terms $y_1, y_2, \ldots$ that are arbitrary and whose form does not affect the termination problem. Hence it may be sufficient to consider *most general* substitutions in applications of T_P^{SLP}.

Another topic for future work is, of course, a practical evaluation, looking at a larger program suite. In this context, it would be desirable to infer a $\mathcal{P}$, as unrestrictive as possible, automatically. Also, we should consider the following issues: (1) possible generalisations of the results in Sec. 5, leaving aside the assumption of input-consuming derivations; (2) a termination criterion that would capture programs that terminate for certain (intended) queries, but not for all queries; (3) relaxing the condition of simply moded programs.

References

1. K. R. Apt. *From Logic Programming to Prolog*. Prentice Hall, 1997.
2. K. R. Apt and S. Etalle. On the unification free Prolog programs. In A. Borzyszkowski and S. Sokolowski, editors, *Proc. of the 18th International Symposium on Mathematical Foundations of Computer Science*, volume 711 of *LNCS*, pages 1–19. Springer-Verlag, 1993.
3. K. R. Apt and I. Luitjes. Verification of logic programs with delay declarations. In V. S. Alagar and M. Nivat, editors, *Proc. of the 4th International Conference on Algebraic Methodology and Software Technology*, volume 936 of *LNCS*, pages 66–90. Springer-Verlag, 1995.
4. K. R. Apt and D. Pedreschi. Reasoning about termination of pure Prolog programs. *Information and Computation*, 106(1):109–157, 1993.

5. K. R. Apt and D. Pedreschi. Modular termination proofs for logic and pure Prolog programs. In G. Levi, editor, *Advances in Logic Programming Theory*, pages 183–229. Oxford University Press, 1994.
6. A. Bossi, S. Etalle, and S. Rossi. Properties of input-consuming derivations. *Theory and Practice of Logic Programming*, 2(2):125–154, 2002.
7. A. Bossi, S. Etalle, S. Rossi, and J.-G. Smaus. Semantics and termination of simply moded logic programs with dynamic scheduling. *Transactions on Computational Logic*, 2004. To appear in summer 2004.
8. D. De Schreye and S. Decorte. Termination of logic programs: The never-ending story. *Journal of Logic Programming*, 19/20:199–260, 1994.
9. N. Dershowitz, N. Lindenstrauss, Y. Sagiv, and A. Serebrenik. A general framework for automatic termination analysis of logic programs. *Applicable Algebra in Engineering, Communication and Computing*, 2001(1/2):117–156, 2001.
10. S. Etalle, A. Bossi, and N. Cocco. Termination of well-moded programs. *Journal of Logic Programming*, 38(2):243–257, 1999.
11. S. Genaim, M. Codish, J. Gallagher, and V. Lagoon. Combining norms to prove termination. In A. Cortesi, editor, *Proc. of the 3rd International Workshop on Verification, Model Checking, and Abstract Interpretation*, volume 2294 of *LNCS*, pages 126–138. Springer-Verlag, 2002.
12. P. M. Hill and J. W. Lloyd. *The Gödel Programming Language*. MIT Press, 1994.
13. S. Lüttringhaus-Kappel. Control generation for logic programs. In D. S. Warren, editor, *Proceedings of the 10th International Conference on Logic Programming*, pages 478–495. MIT Press, 1993.
14. E. Marchiori and F. Teusink. On termination of logic programs with delay declarations. *Journal of Logic Programming*, 39(1-3):95–124, 1999.
15. J. Martin and A. King. Generating efficient, terminating logic programs. In M. Bidoit and M. Dauchet, editors, *Proc. of the 7th International Conference on Theory and Practice of Software Development*, volume 1214 of *LNCS*, pages 273–284. Springer-Verlag, 1997.
16. F. Mesnard and U. Neumerkel. Applying static analysis techniques for inferring termination conditions of logic programs. In P. Cousot, editor, *Proc. of the 8th Static Analysis Symposium*, volume 2126 of *LNCS*, pages 93–110. Springer-Verlag, 2001.
17. L. Naish. Coroutining and the construction of terminating logic programs. Technical Report 92/5, Department of Computer Science, University of Melbourne, 1992.
18. D. Pedreschi, S. Ruggieri, and J.-G. Smaus. Classes of terminating logic programs. *Theory and Practice of Logic Programming*, 2(3):369–418, 2002.
19. J.-G. Smaus. Proving termination of input-consuming logic programs. In D. De Schreye, editor, *Proc. of the International Conference on Logic Programming*, pages 335–349. MIT Press, 1999.
20. J.-G. Smaus. Termination of logic programs for various dynamic selection rules. Technical Report 191, Institut für Informatik, Universität Freiburg, 2003.
21. J.-G. Smaus. Termination of logic programs using various dynamic selection rules. Technical Report 203, Institut für Informatik, Universität Freiburg, 2004.
22. J.-G. Smaus, P. M. Hill, and A. M. King. Verifying termination and error-freedom of logic programs with `block` declarations. *Theory and Practice of Logic Programming*, 1(4):447–486, 2001.
23. Swedish Institute of Computer Science. *SICStus Prolog User's Manual*, 2003. http://www.sics.se/isl/sicstuswww/site/documentation.html.

Improving Prolog Programs: Refactoring for Prolog

Tom Schrijvers[1,*] and Alexander Serebrenik[2,**]

[1] Department of Computer Science, K.U. Leuven
Celestijnenlaan 200A, B-3001, Heverlee, Belgium
Tom.Schrijvers@cs.kuleuven.ac.be
[2] Laboratory of Quality of Software (LaQuSo), T.U. Eindhoven
HG 5.91, Den Dolech 2, P.O. Box 513, 5600 MB Eindhoven, The Netherlands
a.serebrenik@laquso.com

Abstract. *Refactoring* is an established technique from the OO-community to restructure code: it aims at improving software readability, maintainability and extensibility. Although refactoring is not tied to the OO-paradigm in particular, its ideas have not been applied to Logic Programming until now.

This paper applies the ideas of refactoring to Prolog programs. A catalogue is presented listing refactorings classified according to scope. Some of the refactorings have been adapted from the OO-paradigm, while others have been specifically designed for Prolog. Also the discrepancy between intended and operational semantics in Prolog is addressed by some of the refactorings.

In addition, ViPReSS, a semi-automatic refactoring browser, is discussed and the experience with applying ViPReSS to a large Prolog legacy system is reported. Our main conclusion is that refactoring is not only a viable technique in Prolog but also a rather desirable one.

1 Introduction

Program changes take up a substantial part of the entire programming effort. Often changes are required to incorporate additional functionality or to improve efficiency. In both cases, a preliminary step of improving the design without altering the external behaviour is recommended. This methodology, called *refactoring*, emerged from a number of pioneer results in the OO-community [6, 13, 15] and recently came to prominence for functional languages [11]. More formally, refactoring is a source-to-source program transformation that changes program structure and organisation, but not program functionality. The major aim of refactoring is to improve readability, maintainability and extensibility of the existing software. While performance improvement is not considered as a crucial issue for refactoring, it can be noted that well-structured software is more amenable to performance tuning. We also observe that certain techniques that were developed in the context of program optimisation, such as dead-code elimination and redundant argument filtering, can improve program organisation and, hence, can

---

* Research Assistant of the Fund for Scientific Research-Flanders (Belgium) (F.W.O.-Vlaanderen).

** The research presented has been carried out during the second author's stay at Department of Computer Science, K.U. Leuven, Belgium and STIX, École Polytechnique, France.

B. Demoen and V. Lifschitz (Eds.): ICLP 2004, LNCS 3132, pp. 58–72, 2004.
© Springer-Verlag Berlin Heidelberg 2004

be considered refactoring techniques. In this paper we discuss additional refactoring techniques for Prolog programs.

To achieve the above goals two questions need to be answered: *where* and *how* transformations need to be performed. Unlike automated program transformations, neither of the steps aims at transforming the program fully automatically. The decision whether to transform is left to the program developer. However, providing automated support for refactoring is useful and an important challenge.

Deciding automatically *where* to apply a transformation can be a difficult task on its own. Several ways to resolve this may be considered. First, program analysis approaches can be used. For example, it is common practice while ordering predicate arguments to start with the input arguments and end with the output arguments. Mode information can be used to detect when this rule is violated and to suggest the user to reorder the arguments. Second, machine learning techniques can be used to predict further refactorings based on those already applied. Useful sequences of refactoring steps can be learned analogously to automated macro construction [9]. Following these approaches, automatic refactoring tools, so called *refactoring browsers*, can be expected to make suggestions on where refactoring transformations should be applied. These suggestions can then be either confirmed or rejected by the program developer.

Answering *how* the program should be transformed might also require the user's input. Consider for example a refactoring that renames a predicate: while automatic tools can hardly be expected to guess the new predicate name, they should be able to detect all program points affected by the change. Other refactorings require certain properties, like as absence of user-defined meta-predicates, that cannot be easily inferred. It is then up to the user to evaluate whether the properties hold.

The outline of this paper is as follows. We first illustrate the use of several refactoring techniques on a small example in Section 2. Then a more comprehensive catalogue of Prolog refactorings is given in Section 3. In Section 4 we introduce ViPReSS , our refactoring browser, currently implementing most of the refactorings of the catalogue. ViPReSS has been successfully applied for refactoring a 50,000 lines-long legacy system. Finally, in Section 5 we conclude.

2   Detailed Prolog Refactoring Example

We illustrate some of the techniques proposed by a detailed refactoring example. Consider the following code fragment borrowed from O'Keefe's "The Craft of Prolog" [12], p. 195. It describes three operations on a *reader* data structure used to sequentially read terms from a file. The three operations are make_reader/3 to initialise the data structure, reader_done/1 to check whether no more terms can be read and reader_next/3 to get the next term and advance the reader.

```
──────── O'Keefe's original version ────────
make_reader(File,Stream,State) :-
        open(File,read,Stream),
        read(Stream,Term),
        reader_code(Term,Stream,State).

reader_code(end_of_file,_,end_of_file) :- ! .
```

```
reader_code(Term,Stream,read(Term,Stream,Position)) :-
        stream_position(Stream,Position).

reader_done(end_of_file).

reader_next(Term,read(Term,Stream,Pos),State)) :-
        stream_position(Stream,_,Pos),
        read(Stream,Next),
        reader_code(Next,Stream,State).
```

We will now apply several refactorings to the above program to improve its readability.

First of all, we use if-then-else introduction to get rid of the ugly red cut in the reader_code/3 predicate:

```
───────────── Replace cut by if-then-else ─────────────
reader_code(Term,Stream,State) :-
        ( Term = end_of_file,
          State = end_of_file ->
                true
        ;
                State = read(Term,Stream,Position),
                stream_position(Stream,Position)
        ).
```

This automatic transformation reveals two malpractices, the first of which is producing output before the commit, something O'Keefe himself disapproves of (p. 97). This is fixed manually to:

```
───────────── Output after commit ─────────────
reader_code(Term,Stream,State) :-
        ( Term = end_of_file ->
                State = end_of_file
        ;
                State = read(Term,Stream,Position),
                stream_position(Stream,Position)
        ).
```

The second malpractice is a unification in the condition of the if-then-else where actually an equality test is meant. Consider that the Term argument is a variable. Then the binding is certainly unwanted behaviour. Manual change generates the following code:

```
───────────── Equality test ─────────────
reader_code(Term,Stream,State) :-
        ( Term == end_of_file ->
                State = end_of_file
        ;
                State = read(Term,Stream,Position),
                stream_position(Stream,Position)
        ).
```

Next, we notice that the sequence read/2, reader_code/3 occurs twice, either by simple observation or by computing common body subsequences. By applying predicate extraction of this common sequence, we get:

```
_____ Predicate extraction _____
make_reader(File,Stream,State) :-
        open(File,read,Stream),
        read_next_state(Stream,State).

reader_next(Term,read(Term,Stream,Pos),State)) :-
        stream_position(Stream,_,Pos),
        read_next_state(Stream,State).

read_next_state(Stream,State) :-
        read(Stream,Term),
        reader_code(Term,Stream,State).
```

Next we apply O'Keefe's own principle of putting the input argument first and the output arguments last (p. 14–15):

```
_____ Argument reordering _____
reader_next(read(Term,Stream,Pos),Term,State) :-
        stream_position(Stream,_,Pos),
        read_next_code(Stream,State).
```

Finally, we introduce less confusing and overlapping names for the read/3 functor, the stream_position/[2,3] built-ins and a more consistent naming for make_reader, more in line with the other two predicates in the interface. O'Keefe stresses the importance of consistent naming conventions (p. 213).

Note that direct renaming of built-ins such as stream_position is not possible, but a similar effect can be achieved by extracting the built-in into a new predicate with the desired name.

```
_____ Renaming _____
reader_init(File,Stream,State) :-
        open(File,read,Stream),
        reader_next_state(Stream,State).

reader_next(reader(Term,Stream,Pos),Term,State)) :-
        set_stream_position(Stream,Pos),
        reader_next_state(Stream,State).

reader_done(end_of_file).

reader_next_state(Stream,State) :-
        read(Stream,Term),
        build_reader_state(Term,Stream,State).

build_reader_state(Term,Stream,State) :-
        ( Term == end_of_file ->
                State = end_of_file
```

```
        ;
                State = reader(Term,Stream,Position),
                get_stream_position(Stream,Position)
        ).

set_stream_position(Stream,Position) :-
        stream_position(Stream,_,Position).
get_stream_position(Stream,Position) :-
        stream_position(Stream,Position).
```

While the above changes can be performed manually, a refactoring browser such as ViPReSS (see Section 4) guarantees consistency, correctness and furthermore can automatically single out opportunities for refactoring.

3   Comprehensive Catalogue of Prolog Refactorings

In this section we present a number of refactorings that we have found to be useful when Prolog programs are considered. A more comprehensive discussion of the presented refactorings can be found in [16].

We stress that the programs are not limited to pure logic programs, but may contain various built-ins such as those defined in the ISO standard [2]. The only exception are higher-order constructs that are not dealt with automatically, but manually. Automating the detection and handling of higher-order predicates is an important part of future work.

The refactorings in this catalogue are grouped by scope. The scope expresses the user-selected target of a particular refactoring. While the particular refactoring may affect code outside the selected scope, it is only because the refactoring operation detects a dependency outside the scope.

For Prolog programs we distinguish the following four scopes, based on the code units of Prolog: system scope (Section 3.1), module scope (Section 3.2), predicate scope (Section 3.3) and clause scope (Section 3.4).

3.1   System Scope Refactorings

The system scope encompasses the entire code base. Hence the user does not want to transform a particular subpart, but to affect the system as a whole.

Extract Common Code into Predicates. This refactoring looks for common functionality across the system and extracts it into new predicates. The common functionality consists of subsequences of goals that are called in different predicate bodies. By replacing these common subsequences with calls to new predicates the overall readability of the program improves. Moreover the increased sharing simplifies maintenance as now only one copy needs to be modified. User input is required to decide what common sequences form meaningful new predicates. Finding the common sequences and the actual replacing are handled automatically by ViPReSS.

Hide Predicates. This refactoring removes export declarations for predicates that are not imported in any other module. User input is required to confirm that a particular predicate is not meant for use outside the module in the future. This refactoring simplifies the program by reducing the number of entry points into modules and hence the intermodule dependencies.

Remove Dead Code. Dead code elimination is sometimes performed in compilers for efficiency reasons, but it is also useful for developers: dead code clutters the program.

We consider a predicate definition in its entirety as a code unit that can be dead, as opposed to a subset of clauses. While eliminating a subset of clauses can change the semantics of the predicate and hence lead to an erroneous use, this is not the case if the entire predicate is removed.

It is well-known that reachability of a certain program point (predicate) is, in general, undecidable. However, one can safely approximate the dead code by inspecting the *predicate dependency graph* (PDG) of the system. The PDG connects definitions of predicates to the predicates that use them in their own definition. This graph is useful for other refactorings, like *remove redundant arguments*. In the system one or more predicates should be declared as top-level predicates that are called in top-level queries and form the main entry points of the system. Now dead predicates are those predicates not reachable from any of the top-level predicates in the PDG.

User input is necessary whether a predicate can safely be removed or should stay because of some intended future use.

In addition to unused predicate definitions, redundant predicate import declarations should also be removed. This may enable the *hide predicate* refactoring to hide more predicates. Dead-code elimination is supported by ViPReSS.

Remove Duplicate Predicates. Predicate duplication or cloning is a well-known problem. One of the prominent causes is the practice known as "copy and paste". Another cause is unawareness of available libraries and exported predicates in other modules. The main problem with this duplicate code is its bad maintainability. Changes to the code need to be applied to all copies.

Looking for all possible duplications can be quite expensive. In practice in ViPReSS we limit the number of possibilities by only considering predicates with identical names in different modules as possible duplicates. The search proceeds stratum per stratum upwards in the stratified PDG. In each stratum the strongly connected components (SCCs) are compared with each other. If all the predicate definitions in an SCC are identical to those in the other component and they depend on duplicate components in lower strata, then they are considered duplicates as well.

It is up to the user to decide whether to throw away some of the duplicates or replace all the duplicate predicates by a shared version in a new module.

Remove Redundant Arguments. The basic intuition here is that parameters that are no longer used by a predicate should be dropped. This problem has been studied, among others, by Leuschel and Sørensen [10] in the context of program specialisation. They established that the redundancy property is undecidable and suggested two techniques to find safe and effective approximations: top-down goal-oriented RAF and bottom-up goal-independent FAR. In the context of refactoring FAR is the more useful technique. Firstly, FAR is the only possibility if exported predicates are considered. Secondly, refactoring-based software development regards the development process as a sequence of small "change - refactor - test" steps. These changes most probably will be local. Hence, FAR is the technique applied in ViPReSS.

FAR marks an argument position in the head of the clause as unused if it is occupied by a variable that appears exactly once in the argument position that has not been marked as unused. The marking process proceeds bottom-up per strongly connected component (SCC) of the predicate dependency graph.

The argument-removing technique should consist of two steps. First, unused argument positions are marked by FAR. Second, depending on user input, marked argument positions are dropped. Similarly to removing unused predicates (dead code elimination) by removing unused argument positions from predicates we improve readability of the existing code.

Rename Functor. This refactoring renames a term functor across the system. If the functor has several different meanings and only one should be renamed, it is up to the user to identify what use corresponds with what meaning. In a typed language, a meaning would correspond with a type and the distinction could be made automatically. Alternatively, type information can be inferred and the renaming can be based on it.

3.2 Module Scope Refactorings

The module scope considers a particular module. Usually a module is implementing a well-defined functionality and is typically contained in one file.

Merge Modules. Merging a number of modules in one can be advantageous in case of strong interdependency of the modules involved. Refactoring browsers are expected to discover interrelated modules by taking software metrics such as the number of mutually imported predicates into account. Upon user confirmation the actual transformation can be performed.

Remove Dead Code Intra-module. Similar to *dead code removal* for an entire system (see Section 3.1), this refactoring works at the level of a single module. It is useful for incomplete systems or library modules with an unknown number of uses. The set of top level predicates is extended with, or replaced by, the exported predicates of the module.

Rename Module. This refactoring applies when the name of the module no longer corresponds to the functionality it implements, e.g. due to other refactorings. It also involves updating import statements in the modules that depend on the module.

Split Module. This refactoring is the opposite of Merge Modules. By splitting a large module into separate modules, the code units become more manageable. Moreover, it is easier to reuse a particular functionality if it is contained in a separate module. Similarly to the previous refactoring, this one involves updating dependent import statements.

3.3 Predicate Scope Refactorings

The predicate scope targets a single predicate. The code that depends on the predicate may need updating as well. But this is considered an implication of the refactoring of which either the user is alerted or the necessary transformations are performed implicitly.

Add Argument. This refactoring should be applied when a callee needs more information from its (direct or indirect) caller. Our experience suggests that the situation is very common while developing Prolog programs. It can be illustrated by the following example:

```
_____ Original Code _____
compiler(Program,CompiledCode) :-
        translate(Program,Translated),
        optimise(Translated,CompiledCode).

optimise([assignment(Var,Expr)|Statements],CompiledCode) :-
        optimise_assignment(Expr,OptimisedExpr), ...
...
optimise([if(Test,Then,Else)|Statements],CompiledCode) :-
        optimise_test(Test,OptimisedTest), ...

optimise_test(Test,OptimisedTest) :- ...
```

Assume that a new analysis (analyse) of if-conditions has been implemented. Since this analysis requires the original program code as an input, the only place to plug the call to analyse is in the body of compiler:

```
_____ Extended Code _____
compiler(Program,CompiledCode) :-
        analyse(Program,AnalysisResults),
        translate(Program,Translated),
        optimise(Translated,CompiledCode).
```

In order to profit from the results of analyse the variable AnalysisResults should be passed all the way down to optimise_test. In other words, an extra argument should be added to optimise and optimise_test and its value should be initialised to AnalysisResults.

Hence, given a variable in the body of the caller and the name of the callee, the refactoring browser should propagate this variable along all possible computation paths from the caller to the callee. This refactoring is an important preliminary step preceding additional functionality integration or efficiency improvement.

Move Predicate. This refactoring corresponds to the "move method" refactoring of Fowler [5]. Moving predicate from one module to another can improve the overall structure of the program by bringing together interdependent or related predicates.

Rename Predicate. This is the counterpart of the "rename method" refactoring. It can improve readability and should be applied when the name of a predicate does not reveal its purpose. Renaming a predicate requires updating the calls to it as well as the interface between the defining and importing modules.

Reorder Arguments. Our experience suggests that while writing predicate definitions Prolog programmers tend to begin with the input arguments and to end with the output arguments. This methodology has been identified as a good practice and even further refined by O'Keefe [12] to more elaborate rules. Hence, to improve readability, argument reordering is recommended: given the predicate name and the intended order of the arguments, the refactoring browser should produce the code such that the arguments of the predicate have been appropriately reordered.

It should be noted that most Prolog systems use indexing on the first argument. Argument reordering can improve the efficiency of the program execution in this way.

Another efficiency improvement is possible. Consider the fact f(a_out,b_in). For the query ?- f(X,c_in), first the variable X is bound to a_out and then the unification of c_in with b_in fails. It is more efficient to first unify the input argument and only if that succeeds bind the output argument. This is somewhat similar to *produce output before commit* in the next section.

3.4 Clause Scope Refactorings

The clause scope affects a single clause in a predicate. Usually, this does not affect any code outside the clause directly.

Extract Predicate Locally. Similarly to the system-scope refactoring with the same name this technique replaces body subgoals with a call to a new predicate defined by these subgoals. Unlike for the system-scope here we do not aim to automatically discover useful candidates for replacement or to replace similar sequences in the entire system. The user is responsible for selecting the subgoal that should be extracted.

By restructuring a clause this refactoring technique can improve its readability. Suitable candidates for this transformation are clauses with overly large bodies or clauses performing several distinct subtasks. By cutting the bodies of clauses down to size and isolating subtasks, it becomes easier for programmers to understand their meaning.

Invert if-then-else. The idea behind this transformation is that while logically the order of the "then" and the "else" branches does not matter, it can be important for code readability. Indeed, an important readability criterion is to have an intuitive and simple condition. The semantics of the if-then-else construct in Prolog have been for years a source of controversy [1] until it was finally fixed in the ISO standard [2]. The main issue is that its semantics differ greatly from those of other programming languages. Restricting oneself to only conditions that do not bind variables but only perform tests[1], makes it easier to understand the meaning of the if-then-else.

To enhance readability it might be worth putting the shorter branch as "then" and the longer one as "else". Alternatively, the negation of the condition may be more readable, for example a double negation can be eliminated. This transformation might also disclose other transformations that simplify the code.

Hence, we suggest a technique replacing (P -> Q ; R) with (\+ P -> R ; P, Q). Of course, for a built-in P ViPReSS generates the appropriate negated built-in instead

---

[1] This is similar to the guideline in imperative languages not to use assignments or other side effects in conditions.

of \+ P. The call to P in the "else" branch is there to keep any bindings generated in P. If it can be inferred that P cannot generate any bindings, (e.g. because P is a built-in known not to generate any bindings) then P can be omitted from the "else" branch.

Replace Cut by if-then-else. This technique aims at improving program readability by replacing cuts (!) by if-then-else (-> ;). Despite the controversy on the use of cut inside the logic programming community, it is commonly used in practical applications both for efficiency and for correctness reasons. We suggest a transformation that replaces some uses of cut by the more declarative and potentially more efficient if-then-else.

Example 1. Figure 1 shows how this refactoring in ViPReSS transforms the program on the left to the program on the right.

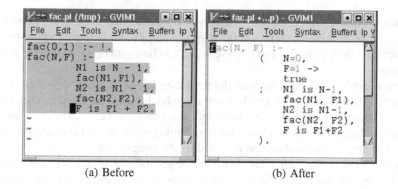

(a) Before   (b) After

Fig. 1. Replace cut by if-then-else in ViPReSS.

The right-hand side program shows that the refactoring preserves operational semantics. Moreover, assuming that N is the input and F the output of fac/2, the refactoring reveals hidden malpractices. These malpractices are discussed in more detail in the next two refactorings.

Replace Unification by (In)equality Test. The previous refactoring may expose a hidden malpractice: full unifications are used instead of equality or other tests.

O'Keefe in [12] advocates the importance of steadfast code: code that produces the right answers for all possible modes and inputs. A more moderate approach is to write code that works for the intended mode only.

Unification succeeds in several modes and so does not convey a particular intended mode. Equality (==, =:=) and inequality (\==, =\=) checks usually only succeed for one particular mode and fail or raise an error for other modes. Hence their presence makes it easier in the code and at runtime to see the intended mode. Moreover, if only a comparison was intended, then full unification may lead to unwanted behaviour in unforeseen cases.

The two versions of `fac/2` in Example 1 use unification to compare N to 0. This succeeds if N is variable by binding it, although this is not the intended mode of the predicate. By replacing `N = 0` with `N == 0` we indicate that N has to be instantiated to 0. This makes it easier for future maintenance to understand the intended mode of the predicate. A weaker check is `N =:= 0` which allows N to be any expression that evaluates to 0. It may be worthwhile to consider a slightly bigger change of semantics: `N =< 0` turns the predicate into a total function. Another way to avoid an infinite loop for negative input is to add `N > 0` to the recursive clause. These checks capture the intended meaning better than the original unification.

Note that equality tests are cheaper to execute in some Prolog systems, especially if they appear as the only goal in the condition of an if-then-else. Nevertheless, the main intent of this refactoring is to bring the operational semantics closer to the intended semantics of the programmer. If only a comparison is required, then full unification may lead to unwanted behaviour in unforeseen cases.

Produce Output After Commit. Another malpractice that may be revealed by the *replace cut by if-then-else* refactoring, is producing output before the commit. This malpractice is disapproved of by O'Keefe in [12], in line with his advocacy for steadfast predicates.

Now consider what happens with the predicate `fac/2` in Example 1 if is called as `?- fac(0,0)`. It does not fail. On the contrary, it backtracks into the second clause and goes into an infinite loop. On the other hand, the query `?- fac(0,F), F=0` does fail. Contrary to the intuition which holds for pure Prolog programs, it is not always valid to further instantiate a query than was intended by the programmer.

By producing output after the commit, the second clause can no longer be considered as an alternative for the first query. Hence, the following version of the first clause has better steadfastness properties: `fac(0,F) :- !, F = 1`. This refactoring may have an impact on the efficiency of the code. If the output is produced before a particular clause or case is committed to and this fails, other cases may be tried, which incurs an overhead. This is illustrated to the extreme with the non-terminating `fac(0,0)` query.

4   The ViPReSS Refactoring Browser

The refactoring techniques presented above have been implemented in the refactoring browser ViPReSS[2]. To facilitate acceptance of the tool ViPReSS by the developers community it has been implemented on the basis of VIM, a popular clone of the well-known VI editor. Techniques like *predicate duplication* provided are easy to implement with the text editing facilities of VIM.

Most of the refactoring tasks have been implemented as SICStus Prolog [7] programs inspecting source files and/or call graphs. Updates to files have been implemented either directly in the scripting language of VIM or, in the case many files had to be updated at once, through `ed` scripts. VIM functions have been written to initiate the refactorings and to get user input.

---

[2] Vi(m) P(rolog) Re(factoring) (by) S(chrijvers) (and) S(erebrenik)

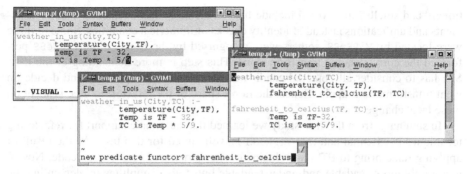

Fig. 2. Screenshot of ViPReSS in action: *extract predicate locally.*

Figure 2 shows a screenshot of *extract predicate locally* in VIM. The user selects the subgoals that are to be extracted into a predicate and then invokes the refactoring by hitting the appropriate key. Then the user enters the desired predicate name. Finally, the file is filtered through a Prolog program that generates the new predicate and replaces the original goals by a call to it.

ViPReSS has been successfully applied to a large (more than 53,000 lines) legacy system used at the Computer Science department of the Katholieke Universiteit Leuven to manage the educational activities. The system, called BTW, (Flemish for value-added tax) has been developed and extended since the early eighties by more than ten different programmers, many of whom are no longer employed by the department. The implementation has been done in the MasterProLog [8] system that, to the best of our knowledge, is no longer supported.

By using the refactoring techniques we succeeded in obtaining a better understanding of this real-world system, in improving its structure and maintainability, and in preparing it for further intended changes such as porting it to a state-of-the-art Prolog system and adapting it to new educational tasks the department is facing as a part of the unified Bachelor-Master system in Europe.

We started by removing some parts of the system that have been identified by the expert as obsolete, including out-of-fashion user interfaces and outdated versions of program files. The bulk of dead code was eliminated in this way, reducing the system size to a mere 20,000 lines.

Next, we applied most of the system-scope refactorings described above. Even after removal of dead code by the experts ViPReSS identified and eliminated 299 dead predicates. This reduced the size by another 1,500 lines. Moreover ViPReSS discovered 79 pairwise identical predicates. In most of the cases, identical predicates were moved to new modules used by the original ones. The previous steps allowed us to improve the overall structure of the program by reducing the number of files from 294 to 116 files with a total of 18,000 lines. Very little time was spent to bring the system into this state. The experts were sufficiently familiar with the system to immediately identify obsolete parts. The system-scope refactorings took only a few minutes each.

The second step of refactoring consisted of a thorough code inspection aimed at local improvement. Many malpractices have been identified: excessive use of cut combined with producing the output before commit being the most notorious one. Additional "bad smells" discovered include bad predicate names such as q, unused arguments and unifications instead of identity checks or numerical equalities. Some of these were located by ViPReSS , others were recognised by the users, while ViPReSS performed the corresponding transformations. This step is more demanding of the user. She has to consider all potential candidates for refactoring separately and decide on what transformations apply. Hence, the lion's share of the refactoring time is spent on these local changes.

In summary, from the case study we learned that automatic support for refactoring techniques is essential and that ViPReSS is well-suited for this task. As the result of applying refactoring to BTW we obtained better-structured lumber-free code. Now it is not only more readable and understandable but it also simplifies implementing the intended changes. From our experience with refactoring this large legacy system and the relative time investments of the global and the local refactorings, we recommend to start out with the global ones and then selectively apply local refactorings as the need occurs.

A version of ViPReSS to refactor SICStus programs can be downloaded from: http://www.cs.kuleuven.ac.be/~toms/vipress. The current version, 0.2.1, consists of 1,559 lines of code and can also refactor ISO Prolog programs. Dependencies on the system specific builtins and the module system have been separated as much as possible from the refactoring logic. This should make it fairly easy to refactor other Prolog variants as well.

5   Conclusions and Future Work

In this paper we have shown that the ideas of refactoring are applicable and important for logic programming. Refactoring helps bridging the gap between prototypes and real-world applications. Indeed, extending a prototype to provide additional functionality often leads to cumbersome code. Refactoring allows software developers both to clean up code after changes and to prepare code for future changes.

We have presented a catalogue of refactorings, at different scopes of a containing both previously known refactorings for object-oriented languages now adapted for Prolog and entirely new Prolog-specific refactorings. Although the presented refactorings do require human input as it is in the general spirit of refactoring, a large part of the work can be automated. Our refactoring browser ViPReSS integrates the automatable parts of the presented refactorings in the VIM editor.

Logic programming languages and refactoring have already been put together at different levels. Tarau [20] has refactored the Prolog language itself. However, this approach differs significantly from the traditional notion of refactoring as introduced by Fowler [6]. We follow the latter definition. Recent relevant work is [21] in the context of object oriented languages: a meta-logic very similar to Prolog is used to detect for instance obsolete parameters.

None of these papers, however, considers applying refactoring techniques to logic programs. In our previous work [18] we have emphasised the importance of refactoring for logic programming and discussed the applicability of the refactoring techniques developed for object-oriented languages to Prolog and CLP-programs. Seipel *et al.* [17]

include refactoring among the analysis and visualisation techniques that can be easily implemented by means of FNQUERY, a Prolog-inspired query language for XML. However, the discussion stays at the level of an example and no detailed study has been conducted.

In the logic programming community questions related to refactoring have been intensively studied in context of program transformation and specialisation [3, 4, 10, 14]. There are two important differences with this line of work. Firstly, refactoring does not aim at optimising performance but at improving readability, maintainability and extensibility. In the past these features where often sacrified to achieve efficiency. Secondly, user input is essential in the refactoring process while traditionally only automatic approaches were considered. Moreover, usually program transformations are part of a compiler and hence, they are "invisible" to the program developer. However, some of the transformations developed for program optimisation, e.g. *dead code elimination*, can be considered as refactorings and should be implemented in refactoring browsers.

To further increase the level of automation of particular refactorings additional information such as types and modes can be used. To obtain this information the refactoring system could be extended with type and mode analyses. On the other hand, it seems worthwhile to consider the proposed refactorings in the context of languages with type and mode declarations like Mercury [19], especially as these languages claim to be of greater relevance for programming in the large than traditional Prolog. Moreover, dealing with higher order features is essential for refactoring in a real world context. The above mentioned languages with explicit declarations for such constructs would facilitate the implementation of an industrial strength refactoring environment.

References

1. The `->` operator. *Association for Logic Programming Newsletter*, 4(2):10–12, 1991.
2. *Information technology–Programming languages–Prolog–Part 1: General core*. ISO/IEC, 1995. ISO/IEC 13211-1:1995.
3. Y. Deville. *Logic Programming: Systematic program development*. Addison-Wesley, 1990.
4. S. Etalle, M. Gabbrielli, and M. C. Meo. Transformations of CCP programs. *ACM Transactions on Programming Languages and Systems*, 23(3):304–395, May 2001.
5. M. Fowler. Refactorings in alphabetical order.
   Available at http://www.refactoring.com/catalog/, 2003.
6. M. Fowler, K. Beck, J. Brant, W. Opdyke, and D. Roberts. *Refactoring: improving the design of existing code*. Object Technology Series. Addison-Wesley, 1999.
7. Intelligent Systems Laboratory. *SICStus Prolog User's Manual*. PO Box 1263, SE-164 29 Kista, Sweden, October 2003.
8. IT Masters. MasterProLog Programming Environment. www.itmasters.com, 2000.
9. N. Jacobs and H. Blockeel. The learning shell : Automated macro construction. In *User Modeling 2001*, volume 2109 of *LNAI*, pages 34–43. Springer Verlag, 2001.
10. M. Leuschel and M. H. Sørensen. Redundant argument filtering of logic programs. In J. Gallagher, editor, *Proceedings of the 6th International Workshop on Logic Program Synthesis and Transformation*, volume 1207 of *LNCS*, pages 83–103. Springer Verlag, 1996.
11. H. Li, C. Reinke, and S. Thompson. Tool support for refactoring functional programs. In J. Jeuring, editor, *Haskell Workshop 2003*. Association for Computing Machinery, 2003.
12. R. A. O'Keefe. *The Craft of Prolog*. MIT Press, Cambridge, MA, USA, 1994.

13. W. F. Opdyke. *Refactoring object-oriented frameworks*. PhD thesis, University of Illinois at Urbana-Champaign, 1992.
14. A. Pettorossi and M. Proietti. Transformation of logic programs: Foundations and techniques. *Journal of Logic Programming*, 19/20:261–320, May/July 1994.
15. D. Roberts, J. Brant, and R. Johnson. A refactoring tool for Smalltalk. *Theory and Practice of ObjectSystems (TAPOS)*, 3(4):253–263, 1997.
16. T. Schrijvers, A. Serebrenik, and B. Demoen. Refactoring Prolog programs. Technical Report CW373, Department of Computerscience, K.U.Leuven, December 2003.
17. D. Seipel, M. Hopfner, and B. Heumesser. Analysing and visualizing Prolog programs based on XML representations. In F. Mesnard and A. Serebrenik, editors, *Proceedings of the 13th International Workshop on Logic Programming Environments*, pages 31–45, 2003. Published as technical report CW371 of Katholieke Universiteit Leuven.
18. A. Serebrenik and B. Demoen. Refactoring logic programs. Poster. Ninetheenth International Conference on Logic Programming, Mumbai, India, December 9-13, 2003.
19. Z. Somogyi, F. Henderson, and T. Conway. Mercury: an efficient purely declarative logic programming language. In *Australian Computer Science Conference*.
20. P. Tarau. Fluents: A refactoring of Prolog for uniform reflection an interoperation with external objects. In *Computational Logic, First International Conference, London, UK, July 2000, Proceedings*, volume 1861 of *LNAI*, pages 1225–1239. Springer Verlag, 2000.
21. T. Tourwé and T. Mens. Identifying refactoring opportunities using logic meta programming. In *7th European Conference on Software Maintenance and Reengineering, Proceedings*, pages 91–100. IEEE Computer Society, 2003.

Smodels with CLP and Its Applications:
A Simple and Effective Approach
to Aggregates in ASP

Islam Elkabani, Enrico Pontelli, and Tran Cao Son

Department of Computer Science
New Mexico State University
{ielkaban,epontell,tson}@cs.nmsu.edu

Abstract. In this work we propose a semantically well-founded extension of *Answer Set Programming (ASP)* with aggregates, which relies on the integration between answer set solvers and constraint logic programming systems. The resulting system is efficient, flexible, and supports form of aggregation more general than those previously proposed in the literature. The system is developed as an instance of a general framework for the embedding of arbitrary constraint theories within ASP.

1 Introduction

In recent years we witnessed the rapid development of alternative logical systems, called *non-monotonic logics* [2], which allow new axioms to retract existing theorems; these logical systems are particularly adequate for common-sense reasoning and modeling of dynamic and incomplete knowledge. In particular, in the last few years a novel *programming paradigm* based on non-monotonic logics, has arisen, called *Answer Sets Programming (ASP)* [12], which builds on the mathematical foundations of *logic programming (LP)* and *non-monotonic reasoning*. ASP offers novel and declarative solutions in well-defined application areas, such as intelligent agents, planning, and diagnosis.

Many practical systems have been recently proposed to support execution of *Answer Set Programming (ASP)* [15,6]. The logic-based languages provided by these systems offer a variety of syntactic structures, aimed at supporting the requirements arising from different application domains. *Smodels* and *DLV* have pioneered the introduction of language-level extensions, such as choice-literals, weight and cardinality constraints, weak constraints [15,6] to facilitate the declarative development of applications. Nevertheless, there are simple properties, commonly encountered in real-world applications, that cannot be conveniently handled within the current framework of ASP – such as properties dealing with arithmetic and aggregation. In particular, aggregations and other forms of set constructions have been shown [5,3,13,9] to be essential to reduce the complexity of software development and to improve the declarative level of the programming framework. In ASP, the lack of aggregation may lead to an exponential growth in the number of rules required for encoding a problem [1].

B. Demoen and V. Lifschitz (Eds.): ICLP 2004, LNCS 3132, pp. 73–89, 2004.

The objective of this work is to address some of these aspects within the framework of Answer Set Programming. In particular, the main concrete objective we propose to accomplish is to develop an extension of ASP which supports a semantically well-founded, flexible, and efficient implementation of aggregates. The model of aggregates we provide is more general than the form of aggregates currently present in the Smodels system [15] and those proposed in the A-Prolog system [7]. The *DLV* system has recently reported an excellent development to allow aggregates in ASP [3]; the DLV approach covers similar classes of aggregates as those described here, although our proposal follows a radically different methodology. The model we propose has the advantage of allowing developers to easily generalize to other classes of aggregates, to modify the strategies employed during evaluation, and even to accommodate for different semantics. A proposal for optimization of aggregate constraints have appeared in [14].

We follow a fairly general and flexible approach to address these issues. We start by offering a generic framework, called ASP-CLP, which provides a simple and elegant treatment of extensions of ASP w.r.t. *generic constraint domains*. We then instantiate this generic framework to the case of a constraint theory for aggregates. The resulting language, called ASP-CLP(Agg), is then implemented following the same strategy – i.e., by relying on the integration between a state-of-the-art ASP solver, specifically the Smodels system [15], and an external constraint solver. Instead of relying directly on an external constraint solver for aggregates, we make use of an external constraint solver for *Finite Domain* constraints (ECLiPSe [17]). The implementation is simple and elegant, and it supports easy modifications of aggregates and execution strategies.

2   ASP with CLP: A General Perspective

Let us consider a signature $\Sigma_C = \langle \mathcal{F}_C, \mathcal{V}, \Pi_C \rangle$, where $\mathcal{F}_C$ is a set of constants and function symbols, $\mathcal{V}$ is a denumerable set of variables, and Π_C is a collection of predicates. We will refer to Σ_C as the *constraint signature* and it will be used to build constraint formulae. A *primitive constraint* is an atom of the form $p(t_1, \ldots, t_n)$, where $p \in \Pi_C$ and $t_1, \ldots, t_n$ are terms built from symbols of $\mathcal{F}_C \cup \mathcal{V}$. A *C-constraint* is a conjunction of primitive constraints and their negation.

Let us also assume a separate signature $\Sigma_P = \langle \mathcal{F}_P, \mathcal{V}', \Pi_P \rangle$, where $\mathcal{F}_P$ is a collection of constants, $\mathcal{V}'$ is a denumerable collection of variables and Π_P is a collection of predicate symbols. We will refer to Σ_P as the *ASP signature* and we will denote with $\mathcal{H}_P$ the Herbrand universe built from the symbol of Σ_P and with $\mathcal{B}_P$ the Herbrand base. We will refer to an atom $p(t_1, \ldots, t_n)$, where $t_i \in \mathcal{F}_P \cup \mathcal{V}'$ and $p \in \Pi_P$, as an ASP-atom; an ASP-literal is either an ASP-atom or the negation (*not A*) of an ASP-atom. An ASP-clause is a formula $A :- B_1, \ldots, B_k$ where A is an ASP-atom and $B_1, \ldots, B_k$ are ASP-literals. An ASP-CLP clause is a formula of the form $A :- C \parallel B_1, \ldots, B_k$ where A is an ASP-atom, C is a *C-constraint*, and $B_1, \ldots, B_k$ are ASP-literals. A program is a finite collection of ASP-CLP clauses.

We assume that an interpretation structure $\mathcal{A}_C = \langle A, (\cdot)^C \rangle$ for the constraint signature is given, where A is the domain and $(\cdot)^C$ is a function mapping elements of $\mathcal{F}_C$ (Π_C) to functions (relations) over A. Given a primitive constraint c, we will use the notation $\mathcal{A}_C \models c$ iff $(c)^C$ is true; the notion can be easily generalized to constraints. Let P be a ground ASP-CLP program and let $M \subseteq \mathcal{B}_P$. We define the ASP-CLP-reduct of P w.r.t. M as the set of ground clauses

$$P_M^C = \left\{ A :- B_1, \ldots, B_n \;\middle|\; \begin{array}{l} A :- C \, [\![B_1, \ldots, B_n, not\, D_1, \ldots, not\, D_m \in P, \\ \qquad\qquad\qquad M \not\models D_i (1 \leq i \leq m), \\ \qquad\qquad\qquad\qquad \mathcal{A}_C \models C^M \end{array} \right\}$$

where C^M denotes the grounding of C w.r.t. the interpretation M. M is an ASP-CLP-stable model of P iff M is the least Herbrand model of P_M^C.

3   ASP with CLP: Aggregates in ASP

Our objective is to introduce different types of *aggregates* in ASP. Database query languages (e.g., SQL) use aggregate functions – such as *sum, count, max*, and *min* – to obtain summary information from a database. Aggregates have been shown to significantly improve the compactness and clarity of programs in various flavors of logic programming [11, 5, 3]. We expect to gain similar advantages from the introduction of different forms of aggregations in ASP.

Example 1 ([13]). Let $owns(X,Y,N)$ denote the fact that company X owns a fraction N of the shares of company Y. A company X *controls* a company Y if the sum of the shares it owns in Y together with the sum of the shares owned in Y by companies controlled by X is greater than half of the total shares of Y [1].

---

control(X, X, Y, N) :- owns(X,Y,N).
control(X, Z, Y, N) :- control(X,Z), owns(Z,Y,N).
fraction(X,Y,N)   *:- sum({{M: (control(X,Z,Y,M):company(Z)) }}) = N.*
control(X,Y)   *:- fraction(X,Y,N), N >0.5.*

A significant body of research has been developed in the database and in the constraint programming communities exploring the theoretical foundations and, in a more limited fashion, the algorithmic properties of aggregation constructs in logic programming (e.g. [11, 16, 13, 4]). More limited attention has been devoted to the more practical aspects related to computing in logic programming in presence of aggregates. In [1], it has been shown that aggregate functions can be encoded in ASP (e.g., example 1 above). The main disadvantage of this proposal is that the obtained encoding contains several intermediate variables, thus making the grounding phase quite expensive in term of space and time. Recently, a number of proposals to extend logic programming with aggregates have been developed, including work on the use of aggregates in ASET [7], work on sets and grouping in logic programming [5], and a recently proposed implementation of aggregates in the *DLV* system [3].

---

[1] For the sake of simplicity we omitted the domain predicates required by *Smodels*.

The specific approach proposed in this work accomplishes the same objectives as [3, 7]. The novelty of our approach lies in the technique adopted to support aggregates. We rely on the integration of different *constraint solving* technologies to support the management of different flavors of sets and aggregates. In this paper, we describe a back-end inference engine – obtained by integrating *Smodels* with a finite-domain constraint solver – capable of executing *Smodels* programs with aggregates. The back-end is meant to be used in conjunction with front-ends capable of performing high-level constraint handling of sets and aggregates (as in [5]). We will refer to the resulting system as ASP-CLP(Agg) hereafter.

4   The Language

Now we will give a formal definition of the syntax and semantics of the language accepted by the ASP-CLP(Agg) system. This language is an extension of the *Smodels* language, with the addition of aggregate functions.

Syntax. The input language accepted by our system is analogous to the language of *Smodels* with the exception of a new class of literals – *the aggregate literals*.

Definition 1. *An* extensional set (multiset) *is a set (multiset) of the form* $\{a_1, \ldots, a_k\}$ *(*$\{\!\{a_1, \ldots, a_k\}\!\}$*) where* a_i *are terms. An* intentional set *is a set of the form* $\{X : Goal[X, \bar{Y}]\}$*; an* intentional multiset *is a multiset of the form* $\{\!\{X : Goal[X, \bar{Y}]\}\!\}$*. In both definitions,* X *is the* grouping variable *while* $\bar{Y}$ *are* existentially quantified variables. *Following the syntactic structure of* Smodels, $Goal[X, \bar{Y}]$ *is an expression of the form:* $p(X)$ *(*$\bar{Y}$ *is empty), where* $p \in \Pi_P$*, or* $p(X, \bar{Y}) : q(\bar{Y})$*, where* $p, q \in \Pi_P$ *and* $q(\bar{Y})$ *is the domain predicate for* $\bar{Y}$ *[15]. An* intensional set (multiset) *is* ground *if* $vars(Goal[X, \bar{Y}]) = \{X, \bar{Y}\}$*. An* aggregate term *is of the form* $aggr(S)$*, where* S *is either an extensional or intensional set or multiset, and* $aggr$ *is a function. We will mostly focus on the handling of the "traditional" aggregate functions, i.e.,* count, sum, min, max, avg, times.

With respect to the generic syntax of Section 2, in ASP-CLP(Agg) we assume that $\mathcal{F}_C$ contains a collection of function symbols of the type $F^{\{\}}_{Goal[X, \bar{Y}]}$ and $F^{\{\!\{\}\!\}}_{Goal[X, \bar{Y}]}$. The arity of each such function symbol corresponds to the number of free variables different from the grouping variable and the existentially quantified variables present in $Goal[X, \bar{Y}]$ – i.e.,

$$arity\left(F^{\{\}}_{Goal[X, \bar{Y}]}\right) = |vars(Goal[X, \bar{Y}]) \setminus \{X, \bar{Y}\}| = arity\left(F^{\{\!\{\}\!\}}_{Goal[X, \bar{Y}]}\right)$$

Thus, $F(\{X : Goal[X, \bar{Y}]\})$ and $F(\{\!\{X : Goal[X, \bar{Y}]\}\!\})$ are syntactic sugars for the terms: $F^{\{\}}_{Goal[X, \bar{Y}]}(Z_1, \ldots, Z_n)$ and $F^{\{\!\{\}\!\}}_{Goal[X, \bar{Y}]}(Z_1, \ldots, Z_n)$, where $\{Z_1, \ldots, Z_n\} = vars(Goal[X, \bar{Y}]) \setminus \{X, \bar{Y}\}$. Similar definitions apply to the case of aggregate terms built using extensional sets.

Definition 2. Aggregate literals *are of the form* $aggr(S)$ op *Result, where* op *is a relation from the set* $\{=, \neq, <, >, \leq, \geq\}$ *and Result is a variable or a number.*

The assumption is that the language of Section 2 is instantiated with $\Pi_C = \{=,$ $\neq, \leq, \geq, >, <\}$. Observe that the variables $X, \bar{Y}$ are locally quantified within the aggregate. At this time, the aggregate literal cannot play the role of a domain predicate – thus other variables appearing in an aggregate literal (e.g., *Result*) are treated in the same way as variables appearing in a negative literal.

Definition 3. *An* ASP-CLP*(Agg) rule is in the form:* $A \leftarrow L_1, \ldots, L_n$ *where A is a positive literal and $L_1, \ldots, L_n$ are standard literals or aggregate literals[2]. An* ASP-CLP*(Agg) program is a set of* ASP-CLP*(Agg) rules.*

In ASP-CLP(Agg), we have opted for relaxing the stratification requirements proposed in [7], which prevent the introduction of recursion through aggregates. The price to pay is the presence of non-minimal models [5, 11]; on the other hand, the literature has highlighted situations where stratification of aggregates prevents natural solutions to problems [13, 4].

Semantics. Now we will provide the stable model semantics [8] of the language, based on the interpretation of the aggregate atoms. The construction is simply an appropriate instantiation of the general definition provided in Section 2. Let us start with some terminology. Given a set A, we denote with $\mathcal{M}(A)$ the set of all finite multisets composed of elements of A, and let us denote with $\mathcal{P}(A)$ the set of all finite subsets of A.

Given a ground intensional set (multiset) s term $\{X : Goal[X, \bar{Y}]\}$ ($\{\!\!\{X : Goal[X, \bar{Y}]\}\!\!\}$), and given an interpretation $M \subseteq \mathcal{B}_P$, the grounding of s w.r.t. M (denoted by s^M) is the ground extensional set (multiset) term: $\{a_1, \ldots, a_k\}$ ($\{\!\!\{a_1, \ldots, a_k\}\!\!\}$) where $\{(a_1, \bar{b}_1), \ldots, (a_k, \bar{b}_k)\} = \{(x, \bar{y}) \mid M \models Goal[x, \bar{y}]\}$.

As we have seen in Section 2, we assume the existence of a predefined interpretation structure $\mathcal{A}_C = \langle A, (\cdot)^C \rangle$ for the constraint part of the language. In our case, the interpretation is meant to describe the meaning of the aggregate function and relations of ASP-CLP(Agg).

Let us start by defining the interpretation for the function symbols F^a, where F is an aggregate operation (e.g., *sum*, *count*) and a is either $\{\}$ or $\{\!\!\{\}\!\!\}$. Intuitively, each aggregate function is interpreted as a function over sets or multisets of integers. In particular, we assume that standard aggregate functions are interpreted according to their usual meaning, e.g., (a is an element of $\{\{\}, \{\!\!\{\}\!\!\}\}$) $(sum^a)^C$ is the function that maps a set (multiset) of integers to their sum, $(count^a)^C$ is a function mapping a set (multiset) of integers to its cardinality, etc. If s is the extensional set (multiset) term $\{a_1, \ldots, a_k\}$ ($\{\!\!\{a_1, \ldots, a_k\}\!\!\}$), then $(F_s^{\{\}})^C$ ($(F_s^{\{\!\!\{\}\!\!\}})^C$) is simply defined as the element of $\mathbb{Z}$: $(F_s^{\{\}})^C = (F^{\{\}})^C(\{a_1^C, \ldots, a_k^C\})$ and $(F_s^{\{\!\!\{\}\!\!\}})^C = (F^{\{\!\!\{\}\!\!\}})^C(\{a_1^C, \ldots, a_k^C\})$.

Given an interpretation $M \subseteq \mathcal{B}_P$ and given $Goal[X, \bar{Y}]$ such that $vars(Goal[X, \bar{Y}]) = \{X, \bar{Y}\}$, for each $F^{\{\}}_{Goal[X,\bar{Y}]} \in \mathcal{F}_C$ and for each $F^{\{\!\!\{\}\!\!\}}_{Goal[X,\bar{Y}]} \in \mathcal{F}_C$ we assume that ($F^{\{\}}_{Goal[X,\bar{Y}]}$)^C = $(F^{\{\}}_{Goal[X,\bar{Y}]M})^C$ and ($F^{\{\!\!\{\}\!\!\}}_{Goal[X,\bar{Y}]}$)^C = $(F^{\{\!\!\{\}\!\!\}}_{Goal[X,\bar{Y}]M})^C$. Similarly, we assume that the constraint structure interprets the

---

[2] We do not distinguish between the constraint and non-constraint part of each rule.

various relational operators employed in the construction of aggregate atoms – i.e., $=, \neq, \leq, \geq, >, <$ – according to their intuitive meaning as comparisons between integer numbers. We can summarize the notion of satisfaction as follows:

Definition 4. *Given* $M \subseteq \mathcal{B}_P$ *and a ground aggregate* $F(\{X : Goal[X, \bar{Y}]\})$ *op* R, *then* $\mathcal{A}_C \models (F(\{X : Goal[X, \bar{Y}]\})$ *op* $R)^M$ *iff*

$$(F^{\{\}})^C (\{a \in \mathbb{Z} \mid \exists \bar{b} \in \mathcal{H}_P^*.\ M \models Goal[a, \bar{b}]\}) \ op \ R$$

is true w.r.t. $\mathcal{A}_C$. *Similarly, given a ground aggregate atom* $F(\{\!\{X : Goal[X, \bar{Y}]\}\!\})$ *op* R, *then* $\mathcal{A}_C \models (F(\{\!\{X : Goal[X, \bar{Y}]\}\!\})$ *op* $R)^M$ *iff* $(F^{\{\!\{\}\!\}})^C(\{a \in \mathbb{Z} \mid \exists \bar{b} \in \mathcal{H}_P^*.\ M \models Goal[a, \bar{b}]\})$ *op* R *is true w.r.t.* $\mathcal{A}_C$.

The remaining aspects of the notion of stable models are immediately derived from the definitions in Section 2, using the notion of entailment of constraints defined in Definition 4. Observe that in the case of aggregates, this semantics definition essentially coincides with the semantics proposed by a number of authors, e.g., [11, 7, 6]. Observe also that this semantics characterization has some drawbacks – in particular, there are situations where recursion through aggregates leads to non-minimal models [11, 4], as shown in the following example.

Example 2. Consider the following program:

$p(1).\qquad p(2).\qquad p(3).\qquad p(5) :- q.\qquad q :- sum(\{X : p(X)\}) > 10.$

This program contains recursion through aggregates, and has two answer sets: $A_1 = \{p(1), p(2), p(3)\}$ and $A_2 = \{p(1), p(2), p(3), p(5), q\}$. A_2 is not minimal.

5   Practical Integration of Aggregates in ASP

The overall design of the proposed ASP-CLP(Agg) system is illustrated in Figure 1. The structure resembles the typical structure of most ASP solvers – i.e., a preprocessing phase, which is employed to simplify the input program and produce an appropriate ground version, is followed by the execution of an actual solver to determine the stable models of the program. The preprocessor is enriched with a module used to determine dependencies between constraints present in the input program

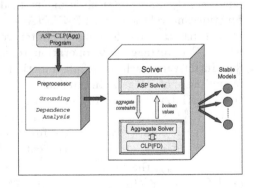

Fig. 1. Overall Design

and regular ASP atoms; in our case, the preprocessor detects the dependences between aggregates used in the program and the atoms that directly contribute to such aggregates. The result of the dependence analysis is passed to the solver (along with the ground program) to allow the creation of data structures to manage the constraints.

The solver is a combination of a traditional ASP solver – in charge of handling the program rules and controlling the flow of execution – and a constraint solver; the ASP solver sends the constraints to be evaluated to the external solver, which in turn returns instantiations of the boolean variables representing the components of the constraint. Intuitively, the constraint solver is employed to determine under what conditions (in terms of truth values of standard ASP atoms) a certain constraint will be satisfied. The result of the constraint processing will be used by ASP to modify the structure of the stable model under construction. Thus, the constraint solver is a "helper" in the computation of the stable models; at any point in time, relations between standard atoms exist within the data structures of *Smodels* while numerical relations expressed by aggregates exist within the constraint store. In the specific case of ASP-CLP(Agg), the solver used to handle aggregate constraints is implemented using a solver over finite domains.

5.1   Representing Aggregates as Finite Domain Constraints

As described in Figure 1, each aggregate constraint in a ASP-CLP(Agg) program is managed through a finite domain constraint solver. This section discusses the encoding of aggregate constraints as finite domain constraints.

First, each atom appearing in an aggregate is represented as a domain variable with domain 0..1; the whole aggregate is then expressed as a constraint involving such variables. The intuition behind this transformation is to take advantage of the powerful propagation capabilities of finite domain constraint solver to automatically test the satisfiability of an aggregate and prune alternatives from its solution search space. In this work we rely on the finite domain constraint solver provided by the ECLiPSe system [17]. Let us summarize the encoding of the most relevant forms of aggregates used in ASP-CLP(Agg):

- **Count Aggregate:** An aggregate atom in the form $count(\{\!\{X : Goal [X, \bar{Y}])\}\!\})$ op *Result* is represented as the finite domain constraint:

$$X[i_1] + X[i_2] + \ldots + X[i_n] \; con\_op \; Result$$

where the $X[i]$'s are finite domain constraint variables representing all the ground atoms of $Goal[X, \bar{Y}]$, the i's are the indices of the ground atoms in the atom table and con_op is the ECLiPSe operator corresponding to the relational operator op. E.g., given the atoms $p(1), p(2), p(3)$, the aggregate $count(\{\!\{A : p(A)\}\!\}) < 3$ will lead to the constraint

$$X[1]::0..1, \; X[2]::0..1, \; X[3]::0..1, \; X[1]+X[2]+X[3] \; \#< 3$$

where $X[1], X[2], X[3]$ are constraint variables corresponding to $p(1), p(2), p(3)$ respectively. The handling of the corresponding aggregate in presence of sets instead of multisets is very similar and it relies on the preprocessor identifying in advance atoms that provide the same contribution, and combine them with a logical or statement. E.g., assume that the extension of p contains the atoms $p(1, a), p(1, b), p(2, c)$ and we have an aggregate of the type $count(\{X : p(X, Y) : domain(Y)\}) \#> 1$ it will be encoded as

$$[X[i_1], X[i_2], X[i_3]] :: 0..1, (X[i_1]\#= 1\#\backslash/X[i_2]\#= 1)\# \Leftrightarrow B1, (B1 + X[i_3])\#> 1.$$

- **Sum Aggregate:** An aggregate atom in the form $sum(\{\!\!\{ X : Goal[X, \bar{Y}]\}\!\!\})$ op $Result$ is represented as a finite domain constraint in the form: $X[i_1] * v_{i_1} + X[i_2] * v_{i_2} + \ldots + X[i_n] * v_{i_n}$ con_op $Result$, where the $X[i]$'s are finite domain variables representing all the ground atoms of $Goal[X, \bar{Y}]$, the i's are the indices of the ground atoms in the atom table, v_i's are the values of X satisfying the atom $Goal[X, \bar{Y}]$ and con_op is the ECLiPSe operator corresponding to the relational op. E.g., given the atoms $p(1), p(2), p(3)$, the aggregate $sum(\{\!\!\{ A : p(A)\}\!\!\}) < 3$ will lead to the constraint

$$X[1]::0..1,\ X[2]::0..1,\ X[3]::0..1,\ X[1]*1+X[2]*2+X[3]*3 \ \#< 3$$

  The handling of the aggregates based on intensional sets instead of multisets follows the same strategy highlighted in the case of the *count* aggregate.

- **Max Aggregate:** An aggregate atom in the form $max(\{\!\!\{ X : Goal[X, \bar{Y}]\}\!\!\})$ op $Result$ is represented as the finite domain constraint:

$$maxlist([\ X[i_1] * v_{i_1},\ X[i_2] * v_{i_2}, \ldots, X[i_n] * v_{i_n}\ ])\ con\_op\ Result$$

  where the $X[i]$'s are finite domain constraint variables representing all the ground atoms of $Goal[X, \bar{Y}]$, the i's are the indices of the ground atoms in the atom table, v_i's are the constants instantiating the atom $Goal[X, \bar{Y}]$ and con_op is the ECLiPSe operator corresponding to the relational operator op. E.g., given the atoms $p(1), p(2), p(3)$, the aggregate $max(\{\!\!\{ A : p(A)\}\!\!\})<5$ will lead to the constraint $[X[1], X[2], X[3]]::0..1$, $maxlist([X[1] * 1, X[2] * 2, X[3] * 3])$ $\#< 5$. Observe that in this case there is no difference in the encoding if the aggregate is defined on intensional sets instead of multisets. Observe also that the contributions of the various atoms will have to be shifted to ensure that no negative contributions are present.

- **Min Aggregate:** It might seem that the representation of the $min(\{\!\!\{ X : Goal[X, \bar{Y}]\}\!\!\})opResult$ aggregate atom as a finite domain constraint is analogous to that of the max aggregate with the only difference of using $minlist/1$ instead of $maxlist/1$. This is not absolutely true. We have noticed a problem that might evolve when we represent the min aggregate in the same way as we did with the max aggregate. The problem is that we might have one or more values of the X_i's are set to 0, which are the X_i's that represent ground atoms having false truth values, this might lead to a wrong answer when we compute the minimum value in a list, since the result will be 0 all the time, although the real minimum value could be another value rather than 0 (the minimum value of the v_i's that correspond to the $X[i]$'s representing ground atoms having true truth values). E.g. , given the atoms $p(3), p(4), p(5)$, if we already knew that $p(3)$ and $p(4)$ are true, while $p(5)$ is false, in this case if we use the same representation as the max aggregate in representing the aggregate $min(\{\!\!\{ A : p(A)\}\!\!\})<2$ that will lead to the constraint

$$[X[1], X[2], X[3]]::0..1,\ minlist([X[1] * 3, X[2] * 4, X[3] * 5]) \ \#< 2$$

This representation is wrong, since in this case the result for this constraint will be true, since the result from applying minlist will be 0 and 0 is less than two, but the correct answer should be false, since the minimum of the values that correspond to ground atoms having true truth value is 3 which is not less than 2. In order to overcome this problem, we have suggested the following representation of the aggregate atom $min(\{X : Goal(X)\})$ op $Result$ as a finite domain constraint:

$$Y[i_1] \#= (X[i_1]*1)+1,$$
$$\vdots$$
$$Y[i_n] \#= (X[i_n]*n)+1,$$
$$element(Y[i_1],[M, v_{i_1},\ldots, v_{i_n}], Z[i_1]),$$
$$\vdots$$
$$element(Y[i_n],[M, v_{i_1},\ldots, v_{i_n}], Z[i_n]),$$
$$minlist([Z[i_1], Z[i_2],\ldots, Z[i_n]])\ con\_op\ Result$$

where M is a constant such that $M > v_i$, for all possible values of i, the Y_i's are selector indices that are used to select a value from the list $[M, v_{i_1},\ldots, v_{i_n}]$ to be assigned to the $Z[i]$'s by using the fd-library constraint $element/3$ and the $Z[i]$'s are the new list of $X[i]*v_i$ with the exception that each $X[i] * v_i$ that corresponds to an atom with a false truth value is changed to M. E.g. , by applying this to the previous example, we will find that $Z[1]$ is assigned 3, $Z[2]$ is assigned 4 and $Z[3]$ is assigned a large number. In this case the result of the constraint $minlist([Z[1], Z[2], Z[3]]) \#< 2$ is false, which is a correct answer (since $3 < 2$ is false).

5.2   Implementation

The implementation of ASP-CLP(Agg) has been realized by introducing localized modifications in the *Smodels* (V. 2.27) system [15] and by using the ECLiPSe system (V. 5.4) as a solver for finite domain constraints. In particular, the implementation makes use of both *Smodels* – i.e., the actual answer set solver – and *lparse* – the front-end used by *Smodels* to intelligently ground the input program. In this section we provide details regarding the structure of the implementation.

Preprocessing. The Preprocessing module is composed of three sequential steps. In the *first* step, a program – called *Pre-Analyzer* – is used to perform a number of simple syntactic transformations of the input program. The transformations are mostly aimed at rewriting the aggregate literals in a format acceptable by *lparse*. The *second* step executes the *lparse* program on the output of the pre-analyzer, producing a ground version of the program in the *Smodels* format – i.e., with a numerical encoding of rules and with an explicit atom table. The *third* step is performed by the *Post-Analyzer*, whose major activities are:

- Identification of the dependencies between aggregate literals and atoms contributing to such aggregates; these dependencies are explicitly represented.
- Generation of the constraints encoding the aggregate; e.g., an entry like
  "57 sum(x,use(8,x),3,multiset,greater)" in the atom table (describing the aggregate $sum(\{\!\{X : use(8, X)\}\!\}) > 3$) is converted to

*"57 sum(3,[16,32,48], "X16 * 2 + X32 * 1 + X48 * 4 + 0 #> 3")"* (16, 32, 48 are indices of *use(8,_)*).

Data Structures. Now we will describe in more details the modifications done to the *Smodels* system data structures, in order to extend it with aggregate functions and make it capable of communicating the ECLiPSe constraint solver. As in *Smodels*, each atom in the program has a separate internal representation – including aggregate literals. In particular, each aggregate literal representation maintains information regarding what program rules it appears in. The representation of each aggregate literal is similar to that of a standard atom, with the exception of some additional fields; these are used to store an ECLiPSe structure representing the constraint associated to the aggregate. Each standard atom includes a list of pointers to all the aggregate literals depending on such atom.

Atom: Most of the new data structures that have been added in the new ASP-CLP(Agg) system are extensions of the class Atom – used by *Smodels* to represent one atom. This is because we are introducing a new type of atoms (aggregate literals) which has its own properties. To represent these properties we have augmented the class Atom with the following fields:

- *Atom* ** **dependents**: If this atom is an aggregate constraint, *dependents* is the list of atoms this aggregate depends on.
- *Atom* ** **constraints** stores the aggregate literals depending on this atom.
- *int* **met_dependents**: If this atom is an aggregate constraint, *met_dependents* is the number of its dependent atoms that still have unknown truth value.
- *EC_word* **PosCon** (**NegCon**) is an ECLiPSe data structure that holds the positive (negative) constraint to be posted in the constraint store (certina aggregates require different constraints to assert true and false status).
- *EC_ref* **hook**: It is one domain variable, representing a reified version of the constraint associated to the current aggregate atom.

Finite Domain Variables: The communication between the *Smodels* system and the ECLiPSe is a two-way communication. The *Smodels* system is capable of posting constraints into the ECLiPSe constraint solver. On the other hand, ECLiPSe is communicating with *Smodels* by either sending the truth value of a posted completed aggregate constraint or by sending back values of labeled variables appearing in a constraint corresponding to a non-completed aggregate. These types of communication require *Smodels* to be able to directly access values of finite domain variables present in the constraint store managed by ECLiPSe. This can be done using the ECLiPSe data types *EC_refs / EC_ref*. We have added the following data structures in order to handle this situation:

- *EC_refs* * **X** is an ECLiPSe structure that holds n references to ECLiPSe variables, where n is the number of atoms in the ground program. Thus, each atom is represented in the constraint store by a separate domain variable – these variables are declared as domain variables with domain $0 \ldots 1$. The discovery of the truth value of an atom in *Smodels* can be communicated to the constraint store by binding the corresponding variable; constraints in the store can force variables to a selected value, which will be retrieved by *Smodels* and transformed in truth value assignment.

Execution Control. The main flow of execution is directed by *Smodels*. In parallel with the construction of the model, our system builds a *constraint store* within ECLiPSe. The constraint store maintains *one conjunction* of constraints, representing the level of aggregate instantiation achieved so far. The implementation of ASP-CLP(Agg) required localized changes to various modules of *Smodels*. During our description for the control of execution, we are going to highlight some of the main changes that have been applied to the *Smodels* modules.

Main: during the initialization of the data structures, an additional step is performed by ASP-CLP(Agg) related to the management of the aggregates. A collection of declarations and constraints are immediately posted to the ECLiPSe constraint store; these include:

- If i is the internal index of one atom in *Smodels*, then a domain variable $X[i]$ is created and the declaration $X[i] :: 0..1$ posted;

- If an aggregate is present in the program and the preprocessor has created the constraint c for such aggregate, then $B_i :: 0..1, c\# <=> B_i$ is posted in the store. The variable B_i is stored in the Atom structure for the aggregate.

These two steps are illustrated in the **post** operations (1) and (2) in Figure 2.

Expand: The goal of the *Smodels* **expand** module is to deterministically extend the set of atoms whose truth values are known. In our ASP-CLP(Agg) system we extend the expand module in such a way that, each time an aggregate dependent atom is made true or false, a new constraint is posted in the constraint store. If i is the index of such atom within *Smodels*, and the atom is made true (false), then the constraint $X[i]\#=1$ $(X[i]\#=0)$ is posted in the ECLiPSe constraint store. (Fig. 2, **post** operations (3) and (4)). If the ECLiPSe returns EC_fail this means that a conflict is detected (inconsistency), so the control returns to *Smodels* where the conflict is handled. Otherwise, ECLiPSe returns EC_succeed and the control returns to the **expand** module.

Since aggregate literals are treated by *Smodels* as standard program atoms, they can be made true, false, or guessed. The only difference is that, whenever their truth value is decided, a different type of constraint will be posted to the store – i.e., the constraint representation of the aggregate. For each aggregate, its constraint representation is reified and posted during the initialization. If the aggregate is determined to be true (false), then we simply need to post a constraint of the type $B_i\# = 1$ $(B_i\# = 0)$, where B_i is the variable reifying the constraint for the aggregate (Fig. 2, **post** operation (5)). Observe that the constraints posted to the store have an active role during the execution:

- Constraints can provide feedback to *Smodels* by forcing a truth value for previously uncovered atoms. This means that ECLiPSe can return an answer, in terms of instantiation of previously unbound variables, to *Smodels*. This instantiation is converted into a truth value for atoms in the *Smodels* and then the control returns to the expand module again. E.g., if the constraint $(X[12]*2+X[13]*4\#<5)\# <=> B$ is posted to the store during initialization (corresponding to the aggregate $sum(\{\!\{X : p(X)\}\!\})$<4) and $X[12]\#= 1$ has been previously posted (i.e., $p(2)$ is true), then requiring the aggregate to be true (by posting $B\#= 1$) will force $X[3]\#= 0$, i.e., $p(3)$ to be false (Fig. 2, post operation (5)). If there are more answers for the aggregate constraint, the control must return back to ECLiPSe for backtracking and generating another answer; this happens after *Smodels* computes the stable model containing the previous answer or fails to get a stable model containing the previous answer and backtracks.

- Inconsistencies in the constraint store have to be propagated to *Smodels*. E.g., if we have $(X[12] + X[13] + X[14]\# > 2)\# <=> B1$ (corresponding to $count(\{\!\{X : p(X)\}\!\}) > 2$) and $X[13]\#= 0$ (corresponding to $p(2)$ being false), and we finally request the aggregate to be true (posting $B1\#= 1$), then ECLiPSe will return a failure, that will activate backtracking in *Smodels*.

Check aggregate completion: An aggregate literal may become true/false not only as the result of the deductive closure computation of *Smodels* **expand** procedure, but also because enough evidence has been accumulated to prove its status. In this case, every time an aggregate dependent atom is made true or false, the aggregate literal it appears in should be checked for truth/falsity. The test can be simply performed by verifying the value of the variable B_i attached to the reification of the aggregate constraint. If the value of B_i is 1 (0), then the aggregate can be immediately evaluated to true (false), regardless of the still unknown truth values of the rest of its dependent atoms E.g., if the constraint $(X[16]*1 + X[17]*2 + X[14] * 3\#>2)\# <=> B2$ is posted to the store (corresponding to the aggregate $sum(\{\!\{X : q(X)\}\!\})$>2) and $X[14]\#= 1$ (i.e., $q(3)$ is true), then in this case ECLiPSe instantiates $B2$ to 1, which should be translated to a true value for the atom representing the aggregate in *Smodels* (while $q(1)$ and $q(2)$ are still unknown) (Fig. 2, check operation (7)).

Pick: The structure of the computation developed by *Smodels* is reflected in the structure of the constraints store (see Fig. 2). In particular, each time *Smodels* generates a choice point (e.g., as effect of guessing the truth value of an atom), a corresponding choice point has to be generated in the constraint store (see Fig. 2, post operation (6)). Similarly, whenever *Smodels* detects a conflict and initiates backtracking, a failure has to be triggered in the store as well. Observe that choice points and failures can be easily generated in the constraint store using the *repeat* and *fail* predicates of ECLiPSe. In our ASP-CLP(Agg) system, we have extended the *Smodels* pick module to allow aggregate atoms to be picked and its truth value is guessed in the same manner as in the case of non-aggregate atoms. Obviously, aggregate atoms that are picked are non-completed aggregate atoms since, as we mentioned previously, aggregate atoms are checked for their completion every time a dependent atom is made true or false. In this case, the picked aggregate atom is set to true (by simply posting the constraint $B\#= 1$, where B is the variable associated to the reification of the aggregate).

As mentioned, a choice point is generated (using the repeat predicate) into the ECLiPSe constraint store before posting the picked aggregate. If a conflict is detected, it is propagated to the ECLiPSe constraint store (by posting the

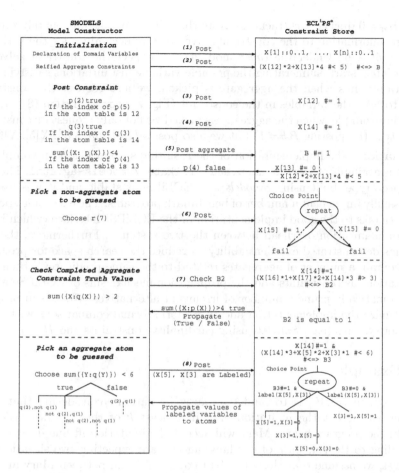

Fig. 2. Communication between *Smodels* and ECLiPSe

`fail` constraint to the constraint store) where a failure is generated to force backtracking to the choice point. Backtracking to a choice point will require posting the complementary constraint to the constraint store – e.g., if originally the constraint generated was $X[i]\#= 1$ $(B\#= 1)$ then upon backtracking the constraint $X[i]\#= 0$ $(B\#= 0)$ will be posted (see the `post` operation (6) in Fig. 2). If no conflicts were detected, then the *Smodels* will continue the computation of the model and a backtracking will take place for constructing a new model. At this point the control will return to ECLiPSe where a new answer is generated.

ASP-CLP(Agg) supports two modalities for picking aggregate atoms. Under the *lazy* modality, the truth value of an aggregate atom is guessed by simply instantiating the variable associated to the corresponding reification. E.g., if we want to guess the truth value of the aggregate $count(\{X : p(X)\}) < 2$, which was initially reified as $(X[3] + X[5] + X[6]\# < 2)\# <=> B$, then the pick operation will simply generate a choice point and post the constraint $B\#= 1$

(and $B\#= 0$ during backtracking). Note that this may not immediately provide enough information to the constraint solver to produce values for the variables $X[3], X[5], X[6]$. Under the *eager* modality, we expect the constraint solver to immediately start enumerating the possible variable instantiations satisfying the constraint; thus when the aggregate is picked, we also request the constraint store to *label* the variables in the constraint (Fig. 2, post operation (8)). In the previous example, when the aggregate is picked we not only request its constraint to be true (by posting $B\#= 1$) but we also post a *labeling*$([X[3], X[5], X[6]])$.

Evaluation. The implementation of the resulting system has been completed, and it is available at www.cs.nmsu.edu/~ielkaban/smodels-ag.html. The current prototype, built using *Smodels* and ECLiPSe is stable and it was used to successfully implement a number of benchmark programs. The execution speed is good, thanks to the good implementation of the ECLiPSe interface (which limits the communication overhead between the two systems). Furthermore, the system has demonstrated excellent ability to reduce the search space for programs that contain a number of aggregates related to the same predicates – their representations as constraints and the propagation mechanisms of ECLiPSe allows to automatically prune a number of irrelevant alternatives. Work is in progress to optimize the implementation and to perform formal comparisons with other relevant systems (e.g., *Smodels* using cardinality constraints and *DLV*).

6   Example

The problem [13, 10] is to send out party invitations, considering that some people will accept the invitation only if at least k of their friends accept it too. In the program below, Mary will accept the invitation iff Sue does as well. According to the semantic of our language we are expecting two situations. In the first, we assume that there is a bad communication between Mary and Sue and in this case a deadlock situation will occur and neither of them will accept the invitation. The other situation is that both of them simultaneously accept. The relation requires(X, K) is true when an invited person X requires at least K of her friends to accept.

```
requires(ann,0). requires(rose,0). requires(mary,1). requires(sue,1).
friend(mary,sue).          friend(sue,mary).
coming(X) :- requires(X,0).
coming(X) :- requires(X,K), count({{ Y: kc(X,Y)}}) >= K.
kc(X,Y) :- friend(X,Y), coming(Y).
```

Two models are returned, one containing coming(ann), coming(rose) and one containing coming(mary), coming(sue), coming(ann), coming(rose).

7   Discussion

Various proposals have been put forward to provide alternative semantics for logic programming with aggregates [4, 13]. A natural alternative semantics, which removes the presence of non-minimal models, can be defined as follows.

Definition 5. *Let us consider a ground aggregate literal α of the form $F\{\!\{X : Goal[X, \bar{Y}]\}\!\}$ op Result. Let us denote with $\mathcal{S}(\alpha)$ the following set:*

$$\mathcal{S}(\alpha) = \left\{ \{(a_1, \bar{b}_1), \ldots, (a_n, \bar{b}_n)\} \mid \begin{array}{l} a_i, \bar{b}_i \text{ are ground terms,} \\ \mathcal{A}_C \models (F\{\!\{a_1, \ldots, a_n\}\!\} \text{ op Result}) \end{array} \right\}$$

We will refer to $\mathcal{S}(\alpha)$ as the Aggregate Solution Set.

Definition 6 (Aggregate Unfolding). *Let α be the ground aggregate $F\{\!\{X : Goal[X, \bar{Y}]\}\!\}$ op Result. We define the unfolding of α (unfold(α)) as the set*

$$unfold(\alpha) = \left\{ \bigwedge_{(a, \bar{b}) \in S} Goal[a, \bar{b}] \wedge \bigwedge_{(a, \bar{b}) \notin S} not\, Goal[a, \bar{b}] \mid S \in \mathcal{S}(\alpha) \right\}$$

For a non-aggregate literal A, we have $unfold(A) = \{A\}$. The unfolding of a clause $H :- B_1, \ldots, B_n$ is defined as the set of clauses:
$unfold(H :- B_1, \ldots, B_n) = \{(H :- \beta_1, \ldots, \beta_n) \mid \beta_i \in unfold(B_i), 1 \le i \le n\}$
The unfolding of a program P (unfold(P)) is obtained by unfolding each clause.

Definition 7 (Alternative Stable Model Semantics for Aggregates). *Let M be an Herbrand interpretation and let P be a program with aggregates. M is a stable model of P iff M is a stable model of $unfold(P)$.*

Example 3. Consider the program of Example 2. The unfold of this program yields a program which is identical except for the last rule: q :- p(1), p(2), p(3), p(5). since $\{\!\{1, 2, 3, 5\}\!\}$ is the only multiset that satisfies the aggregate. The resulting program has a single answer set: $\{p(1), p(2), p(3)\}$, thus the non-minimal model accepted in the former semantic characterization (see Example 2) is no longer a stable model of the program.

This alternative semantics can be supported with minimal changes in the proposed system. The construction and handling of the constraints encoding aggregate computations is unchanged. The only changes are in the management of the declarative closure computation in presence of aggregates within *Smodels*. The presence of non-minimal models derives from true aggregates being treated as facts, loosing the dependencies between the aggregate and the atoms it depends on. These dependencies can be restored by dynamically introducing a rule upon satisfaction of an aggregate – where the body of the rules includes the true atoms satisfying the aggregates (readily available from the preprocessor).

8   Conclusions and Future Work

A prototype implementing these ideas has been completed and used on a pool of benchmarks. Performance is acceptable, but we expect significant improvements by refining the interface with ECLiPSe. Combining a constraint solver with *Smodels* brings many advantages:

- since we are relying on an external constraints solver to effectively handle the aggregates, the only step required to add new aggregates (e.g., *times*, *avg*) is the generation of the appropriate constraint formula during preprocessing;
- the constraint solvers are very flexible; e.g., using CHRs we can implement different strategies to handle constraints and new constraint operators;
- it is a straightforward extension to allow the user to declare aggregate instances as *eager*; in this case, instead of posting only the corresponding constraint to the store, we will also post a *labeling*, forcing the immediate resolution of the constraint store (i.e., guess the possible combinations of truth values of selected atoms involved in the aggregate). In this way, the aggregate will act as a generator of solutions instead of just a pruning mechanism.

We believe this approach has advantages over previous proposals. The use of a general constraint solver allows us to easily understand and customize the way aggregates are handled (e.g., allow the user to select eager vs. non-eager treatment); it also allows us to easily extend the system to include new form of aggregates, by simply adding new type of constraints. Furthermore, the current approach relaxes some of the syntactic restriction imposed in other proposals (e.g., stratification of aggregations). The implementation requires minimal modifications to *Smodels* and introduces insignificant overheads for regular programs. The prototype confirmed the feasibility of this approach.

In our future work, we propose to relax some of the syntactic restrictions – e.g., the use of labeling allows the aggregates to "force" solutions, so that the aggregate can act as a generator of values; this may remove the need for domain predicates for the result of the aggregate (e.g., the *safety* condition used in *DLV*).

Acknowledgments

The research is supported by NSF grants 0220590, 9810732.

References

1. C. Baral. *Knowledge Representation, reasoning, and problem solving*, Cambridge, 2003.
2. C. Baral and M. Gelfond. Logic Programming and Knowledge Representation. *JLP*, 19/20, 1994.
3. T. Dell'Armi et al. Aggregate Functions in DLV. *2nd Intl. ASP Workshop*, 2003.
4. M. Denecker et al. Ultimate well-founded and stable semantics for logic programs with aggregates. In *ICLP*, Springer. 2001.
5. A. Dovier et al. Intensional Sets in CLP. *ICLP*, Springer Verlag, 2003.
6. T. Eiter et al. The KR System dlv: Progress Report, Comparisons, and Benchmarks. *KRR*, 1998.
7. M. Gelfond. Representing Knowledge in A-Prolog. *Logic Programming&Beyond*, Springer, 2002.
8. M. Gelfond and V. Lifschitz. The Stable Model Semantics for Logic Programs. *ILPS*, MIT, 1988.

9. S. Greco. Dynamic Programming in Datalog with Aggregates. *TKDE*, 11(2), 1999.
10. D. Kemp et al. Efficient Recursive Aggregation and Negation in Deductive Databases. *TKDE*, 10(5), 1998.
11. D. Kemp and P. Stuckey. Semantics of Logic Programs with Aggregates. *ILPS*, MIT Press, 1991.
12. V. Marek and M. Truszczyński. Stable models and an alternative logic programming paradigm. *The Logic Programming Paradigm*, Springer Verlag, 1999.
13. K. A. Ross and Y. Sagiv. Monotonic Aggregation in Deductive Databases. *JCSS*, 54:79–97, 1997.
14. K. Ross et al. Foundations of Aggregation Constraints. *TCS*, 193(1-2), 1998.
15. P. Simons et al. Extending and Implementing the Stable Model Semantics. *AIJ*, 138(1–2), 2002.
16. A. Van Gelder. The Well-Founded Semantics of Aggregation. *ACM PODS*, 1992.
17. M. Wallace, S. Novello, J. Schimpf. ECLiPSe: a Platform for Constraint Logic Programming. IC-Parc, Imperial College, 1997.

The Refined Operational Semantics of Constraint Handling Rules

Gregory J. Duck[1], Peter J. Stuckey[1],
María García de la Banda[2], and Christian Holzbaur[3]

[1] Department of Computer Science and Software Engineering
The University of Melbourne, Vic. 3010, Australia
{gjd,pjs}@cs.mu.oz.au
[2] School of Computer Science and Software Engineering
Monash University, Vic. 3800, Australia
mbanda@csse.monash.edu.au
[3] holzbaur@chello.at

Abstract. Constraint Handling Rules (CHRs) are a high-level rule-based programming language commonly used to write constraint solvers. The theoretical operational semantics for CHRs is highly non-deterministic and relies on writing confluent programs to have a meaningful behaviour. Implementations of CHRs use an operational semantics which is considerably finer than the theoretical operational semantics, but is still non-deterministic (from the user's perspective). This paper formally defines this *refined* operational semantics and proves it implements the theoretical operational semantics. It also shows how to create a (partial) confluence checker capable of detecting programs which are confluent under this semantics, but not under the theoretical operational semantics. This supports the use of new idioms in CHR programs.

1 Introduction

Constraint Handling Rules (CHRs) are a high-level rule-based programming language commonly used to write constraint solvers. The theoretical operational semantics of CHRs is relatively high level with several choices, such as the order in which transitions are applied, left open. Therefore, only confluent CHR programs, where every possible execution results in the same result, have a guaranteed behaviour.

This paper looks at the *refined* operational semantics, a more specific operational semantics which has been implicitly described in [10, 11], and is used by every Prolog implementation of CHRs we know of. Although some choices are still left open in the refined operational semantics, both the order in which transitions are applied and the order in which occurrences are visited, is decided. Unsurprisingly, the decisions follow Prolog style and maximise efficiency of execution. The remaining choices, which matching partner constraints are tried first, and the order of evaluation of CHR constraints awoken by changes in variables they involve, are left as choices for two reasons. First it is very difficult to

B. Demoen and V. Lifschitz (Eds.): ICLP 2004, LNCS 3132, pp. 90–104, 2004.
© Springer-Verlag Berlin Heidelberg 2004

see how a CHR programmer will be able to understand a fixed strategy in these cases. And second implementing a fixed strategy will restrict the implementation to be less efficient, for example by disallowing hashing index structures.

It is clear that CHR programmers take the refined operational semantics into account when programming. For example, some of the standard CHR examples are non-terminating under the theoretical operational semantics.

Example 1. Consider the following simple program that calculates the greatest common divisor (*gcd*) between two integers using Euclid's algorithm:

```
gcd1 @ gcd(0)            <=> true.
gcd2 @ gcd(N) \ gcd(M) <=> M >= N | gcd(M-N).
```

Rule gcd1 is a simplification rule. It states that a fact gcd(0) in the store can be replaced by true. Rule gcd2 is a simpagation rule, it states that if there are two facts in the store gcd(n) and gcd(m) where $m \geq n$, we can replace the part after the slash gcd(m) by the right hand side gcd($m - n$)[1]. The idea of this program is to reduce an initial store of gcd(A), gcd(B) to a single constraint gcd(C) where C will be the *gcd* of A and B.

This program, which appears on the CHR webpage [6], is non-terminating under the theoretical operational semantics. Consider the constraint store gcd(3), gcd(0). If the first rule fires, we are left with gcd(3) and the program terminates. If, instead, the second rule fires (which is perfectly possible in the theoretical semantics), gcd(3) will be replaced with gcd(3-0) = gcd(3), thus essentially leaving the constraint store unchanged. If the second rule is applied indefinitely (assuming unfair rule application), we obtain an infinite loop.

In the above example, trivial non-termination can be avoided by using a *fair* rule application (i.e. one in which every rule that could fire, eventually does). Indeed, the theoretical operational semantics given in [7] explicitly states that rule application should be fair. Interestingly, although the refined operational semantics is not fair (it uses rule ordering to determine rule application), its unfairness ensures termination in the gcd example above. Of course, it could also have worked against it, since swapping the order of the rules would lead to non-termination.

The refined operational semantics allows us to use more programming idioms, since we can now treat the constraint store as a queryable data structure.

Example 2. Consider a CHR implementation of a simple database:

```
l1 @ entry(Key,Val) \ lookup(Key,ValOut) <=> ValOut = Val.
l2 @ lookup(_,_) <=> fail.
```

where the constraint lookup represents the basic database operations of key lookup, and entry represents a piece of data currently in the database (an entry in the database). Rule l1 looks for the matching entry to a lookup query and returns in ValOut the stored value. Rule l2 causes a lookup to fail if there is no matching entry. Clearly the rules are non-confluent in the theoretical operational semantics, since they rely on rule ordering to give the intended behaviour.

---

[1] Unlike Prolog, we assume the expression "$m - n$" is automatically evaluated.

The refined operational semantics also allows us to create more efficient programs and/or have a better idea regarding their time complexity.

Example 3. Consider the following implementation of Fibonacci numbers, fib(N,F), which holds if F is the Nth Fibonacci number:

```
f1 @ fib(N,F) <=> 1 >= N | F = 1.
f2 @ fib(N,F0) \ fib(N,F) <=> N >= 2 | F = F0.
f3 @ fib(N,F) ==> N >= 2 | fib(N-2, F1), fib(N-1,F2), F = F1 + F2.
```

Rule f3 is a propagation rule (as indicated by the ==> arrow), which is similar to a simplification rule except the matching constraint $fib(n, f)$ is not removed from the store.

The program is confluent in the theoretical operational semantics which, as we will see later, means it is also confluent in the refined operational semantics. Under the refined operational semantics it has linear complexity, while swapping rules f2 and f3 leads to exponential complexity. Since in the theoretical operational semantics both versions are equivalent, complexity is at best exponential.

We believe that Constraint Handling Rules under the refined operational semantics provide a powerful and elegant language suitable for general purpose computing. However, to make use of this language, authors need support to ensure their code is confluent within this context. In order to do this, we first provide a formal definition of the refined operational semantics of CHRs as implemented in logic programming systems. We then provide theoretical results linking the refined and theoretical operational semantics. Essentially, these results ensure that if a program is confluent under the theoretical semantics, it is also confluent under the refined semantics. Then, we provide a practical (partial) confluence test capable of detecting CHR programs which are confluent for the refined operational semantics, even though they are not confluent for the theoretical operational semantics. Finally, we study two CHR programs and argue our test is sufficient for real world CHR programs.

2   The Theoretical Operational Semantics ω_t

We begin by defining constraints, rules and CHR programs. For our purposes, a *constraint* is simply defined as an atom $p(t_1, ..., t_n)$ where p is some predicate symbol of arity $n \geq 0$ and $(t_1, ..., t_n)$ is an n-tuple of terms. A *term* is defined as either a variable X, or as $f(t_1, ..., t_n)$ where f is a function symbol of arity n and $t_1, ..., t_n$ are terms. Let $vars(A)$ return the variables occurring in any syntactic object A. We use $\bar{\exists}_A F$ to denote the formula $\exists X_1 \cdots \exists X_n F$ where $\{X_1, ... X_n\} = vars(F) - vars(A)$. We use $\bar{s} = \bar{t}$, where $\bar{s}$ and $\bar{t}$ are sequences, to denote the conjunction $s_1 = t_1 \wedge \cdots \wedge s_n = t_n$.

Constraints can be divided into either CHR constraints or *builtin* constraints in some constraint domain $\mathcal{D}$. While the former are manipulated by the CHR execution algorithm, the latter are handled by an *underlying* constraint solver. Decisions about rule matchings will rely on the underlying solver proving that the current constraint store for the underlying solver entails a *guard* (a conjunction of builtin constraints). We will assume the solver supports (at least) equality.

There are three types of rules: simplification, propagation and simpagation. For simplicity, we consider both simplification and propagation rules as special cases of a simpagation rules. The general form of a *simpagation* rule is:

$$r @ H_1 \setminus H_2 \Longleftrightarrow g \mid B$$

where r is the rule name, H_1 and H_2 are sequences of CHR constraints, g is a sequence of builtin constraints, and B is a sequence of constraints. If H_1 is empty, then the rule is a *simplification* rule. If H_2 is empty, then the rule is a *propagation* rule. At least one of H_1 and H_2 must be non-empty. Finally, a CHR program P is a sequence of rules.

We use $[H|T]$ to denote the first (H) and remaining elements (T) of a sequence, $+\!+$ for sequence concatenation, ϵ for empty sequences, and $\uplus$ for multiset union. We shall sometimes treat multisets as sequences, in which case we non-deterministically choose an order for the objects in the multiset.

Given a CHR program P, we will be interested in numbering the occurrences of each CHR constraint predicate p appearing in the head of the rule. We number the occurrences following the top-down rule order and right-to-left constraint order. The latter is aimed at ordering first the constraints after the backslash $(\setminus)$ and then those before it, since this gives the refined operational semantics a clearer behaviour.

Example 4. The following shows the gcd CHR program of Example 1, written using simpagation rules and with all its occurrences numbered:

```
gcd1 @ ε        \ gcd(0)₁ <=> true  | true.
gcd2 @ gcd(N)₃ \ gcd(M)₂ <=> M ≥ N  | gcd(M-N).
```

2.1   The ω_t Semantics

Several versions of the theoretical operational semantics have already appeared in the literature, e.g. [1, 7], essentially as a multiset rewriting semantics. This section presents our variation, which is equivalent to previous ones, but is close enough to our refined operational semantics to make proofs simple.

Firstly, we define an *execution state*, as the tuple $\langle G, S, B, T \rangle_n$ where each element is as follows. The *goal* G is the multiset (repeats are allowed) of constraints to be executed. The CHR constraint *store* S is the multiset of *identified* CHR constraints that can be matched with rules in the program P. An *identified* CHR constraint $c\#i$ is a CHR constraint c associated with some unique integer i. This number serves to differentiate among copies of the same constraint. We introduce functions $chr(c\#i) = c$ and $id(c\#i) = i$, and extend them to sequences and sets of identified CHR constraints in the obvious manner.

The *builtin constraint store* B contains any builtin constraint that has been passed to the underlying solver. Since we will usually have no information about the internal representation of B, we will model it as an abstract logical conjunction of constraints. The *propagation history* T is a set of sequences, each recording the identities of the CHR constraints which fired a rule, and the name of the rule itself. This is necessary to prevent trivial non-termination for propagation rules: a propagation rule is allowed to fire on a set of constraints only if the constraints have not been used to fire the rule before. Finally, the counter n represents the next free integer which can be used to number a CHR constraint.

Given an initial goal G, the *initial state* is: $\langle G, \emptyset, true, \emptyset \rangle_1$. The theoretical operational semantics ω_t is based on the following three transitions which map execution states to execution states:

1. Solve $\langle \{c\} \uplus G, S, B, T \rangle_n \rightarrowtail \langle G, S, c \wedge B, T \rangle_n$ where c is a builtin constraint.
2. Introduce $\langle \{c\} \uplus G, S, B, T \rangle_n \rightarrowtail \langle G, \{c\#n\} \uplus S, B, T \rangle_{(n+1)}$ where c is a CHR constraint.
3. Apply $\langle G, H_1 \uplus H_2 \uplus S, B, T \rangle_n \rightarrowtail \langle C \uplus G, H_1 \uplus S, \theta \wedge B, T' \rangle_n$ where there exists a (renamed apart) rule in P of the form

$$r \;@\; H_1' \setminus H_2' \iff g \mid C$$

and a matching substitution θ such that $chr(H_1) = \theta(H_1')$, $chr(H_2) = \theta(H_2')$ and $\mathcal{D} \models B \rightarrow \bar{\exists}_B(\theta \wedge g)$, and the tuple $id(H_1) \;+\!\!+\; id(H_2) \;+\!\!+\; [r] \notin T$. In the result $T' = T \cup \{id(H_1) \;+\!\!+\; id(H_2) \;+\!\!+\; [r]\}$ [2]. $\square$

The first rule tells the underlying solver to add a new builtin constraint to the builtin constraint store. The second adds a new identified CHR constraint to the CHR constraint store. The last one chooses a program rule for which matching constraints exist in the CHR constraint store, and whose guard is entailed by the underlying solver, and fires it. For readability, we usually apply the resulting substitution θ to all relevant fields in the execution state, i.e. G, S and B. This does not affect the meaning of the execution state, or its transition applicability, but it helps remove the build-up of too many variables and constraints.

The transitions are non-deterministically applied until either no more transitions are applicable (a successful derivation), or the underlying solver can prove $\mathcal{D} \models \neg \bar{\exists}_\emptyset B$ (a failed derivation). In both cases a *final state* has been reached.

Example 5. The following is a (terminating) derivation under ω_t for the query gcd(6), gcd(9) executed on the gcd program in Example 4. For brevity, B and T have been removed from each tuple.

$$\langle \{\mathrm{gcd}(6), \mathrm{gcd}(9)\}, \emptyset \rangle_1 \qquad (1)$$

	$\rightarrowtail_{introduce}$ $\langle \{\mathrm{gcd}(9)\}, \{\mathrm{gcd}(6)\#1\} \rangle_2$	(2)
	$\rightarrowtail_{introduce}$ $\langle \emptyset, \{\mathrm{gcd}(6)\#1, \mathrm{gcd}(9)\#2\} \rangle_3$	(3)
(gcd2 $N = 6 \wedge M = 9$)	$\rightarrowtail_{apply}$ $\langle \{\mathrm{gcd}(3)\}, \{\mathrm{gcd}(6)\#1\} \rangle_3$	(4)
	$\rightarrowtail_{introduce}$ $\langle \emptyset, \{\mathrm{gcd}(6)\#1, \mathrm{gcd}(3)\#3\} \rangle_4$	(5)
(gcd2 $N = 3 \wedge M = 6$)	$\rightarrowtail_{apply}$ $\langle \{\mathrm{gcd}(3)\}, \{\mathrm{gcd}(3)\#3\} \rangle_4$	(6)
	$\rightarrowtail_{introduce}$ $\langle \emptyset, \{\mathrm{gcd}(3)\#3, \mathrm{gcd}(3)\#4\} \rangle_5$	(7)
(gcd2 $N = 3 \wedge M = 3$)	$\rightarrowtail_{apply}$ $\langle \{\mathrm{gcd}(0)\}, \{\mathrm{gcd}(3)\#3\} \rangle_5$	(8)
	$\rightarrowtail_{introduce}$ $\langle \emptyset, \{\mathrm{gcd}(3)\#3, \mathrm{gcd}(0)\#5\} \rangle_6$	(9)
(gcd1)	$\rightarrowtail_{apply}$ $\langle \emptyset, \{\mathrm{gcd}(3)\#3\} \rangle_6$	(10)

No more transition rules are possible, so this is the final state.

---

[2] Note in practice we only need to keep track of tuples where H_2 is empty, since otherwise these CHR constraints are being deleted and the firing can not reoccur.

3   The Refined Operational Semantics ω_r

The *refined* operational semantics establishes an order for the constraints in G. As a result, we are no longer free to pick any constraint from G to either **Solve** or **Introduce** into the store. It also treats CHR constraints as procedure calls: each newly added *active* constraint searches for possible matching rules in order, until all matching rules have been executed or the constraint is deleted from the store. As with a procedure, when a matching rule fires other CHR constraints might be executed and, when they finish, the execution returns to finding rules for the current active constraint. Not surprisingly, this approach is used exactly because it corresponds closely to that of the language we compile to.

Formally, the execution state of the refined semantics is the tuple $\langle A, S, B, T \rangle_n$ where S, B, T and n, representing the CHR store, builtin store, propagation history and next free identity number respectively, are exactly as before. The *execution stack* A is a sequence of constraints, identified CHR constraints and occurrenced identified CHR constraints, with a strict ordering in which only the top-most constraint is active. An *occurrenced* identified CHR constraint $c\#i : j$ indicates that only matches with occurrence j of constraint c should be considered when the constraint is active. Unlike in the theoretical operational semantics, the same identified constraint may simultaneously appear in both the execution stack A and the store S.

Given initial goal G, the initial state is as before. Just as with the theoretical operational semantics, execution proceeds by exhaustively applying transitions to the initial execution state until the builtin solver state is unsatisfiable or no transitions are applicable. The possible transitions are as follows:

1. Solve $\langle [c|A], S_0 \uplus S_1, B, T \rangle_n \rightarrowtail \langle S_1 +\!\!\!+ A, S_0 \uplus S_1, c \wedge B, T \rangle_n$ where c is a builtin constraint, and $vars(S_0) \subseteq fixed(B)$, where $fixed(B)$ is the set of variables fixed by B [3]. This reconsiders constraints whose matches might be affected by c.

2. Activate $\langle [c|A], S, B, T \rangle_n \rightarrowtail \langle [c\#n : 1|A], \{c\#n\} \uplus S, B, T \rangle_{(n+1)}$ where c is a CHR constraint (which has never been active).

3. Reactivate $\langle [c\#i|A], S, B, T \rangle_n \rightarrowtail \langle [c\#i : 1|A], S, B, T \rangle_n$ where c is a CHR constraint (re-added to A by **Solve** but not yet active).

4. Drop $\langle [c\#i : j|A], S, B, T \rangle_n \rightarrowtail \langle A, S, B, T \rangle_n$ where $c\#i : j$ is an occurrenced active constraint and there is no such occurrence j in P (all existing ones have already been tried thanks to transition 7).

5. Simplify $\langle [c\#i : j|A], \{c\#i\} \uplus H_1 \uplus H_2 \uplus H_3 \uplus S, B, T \rangle_n \rightarrowtail \langle C +\!\!\!+ A, H_1 \uplus S, \theta \wedge B, T' \rangle_n$ where the jth occurrence of the CHR predicate of c in a (renamed apart) rule in P is

$$r @ H_1' \setminus H_2', d_j, H_3' \iff g \mid C$$

and there exists matching substitution θ is such that $c = \theta(d_j)$, $chr(H_1) = \theta(H_1')$, $chr(H_2) = \theta(H_2')$, $chr(H_3) = \theta(H_3')$, and $\mathcal{D} \models B \rightarrow \bar{\exists}_B(\theta \wedge g)$, and

---

[3] $v \in fixed(B)$ if $\mathcal{D} \models \bar{\exists}_v(B) \wedge \bar{\exists}_{\rho(v)}\rho(B) \rightarrow v = \rho(v)$ for arbitrary renaming ρ.

the tuple $id(H_1) \mathbin{+\!\!+} [i] \mathbin{+\!\!+} id(H_2) \mathbin{+\!\!+} id(H_3) \mathbin{+\!\!+} [r] \notin T$. In the result $T' = T \cup \{id(H_1) \mathbin{+\!\!+} id(H_2) \mathbin{+\!\!+} [i] \mathbin{+\!\!+} id(H_3) \mathbin{+\!\!+} [r]\}$.

6. Propagate $\langle [c\#i : j|A], \{c\#i\} \uplus H_1 \uplus H_2 \uplus H_3 \uplus S, B, T\rangle_n \rightarrowtail \langle C \mathbin{+\!\!+} [c\#i : j|A], \{c\#i\} \uplus H_1 \uplus H_2 \uplus S, \theta \wedge B, T'\rangle_n$ where the jth occurrence of the CHR predicate of c in a (renamed apart) rule in P is

$$r @ H'_1, d_j, H'_2 \setminus H'_3 \iff g \mid C$$

and there exists matching substitution θ is such that $c = \theta(d_j)$, $chr(H_1) = \theta(H'_1)$, $chr(H_2) = \theta(H'_2)$, $chr(H_3) = \theta(H'_3)$, and $\mathcal{D} \models B \rightarrow \bar{\exists}_B(\theta \wedge g)$, and the tuple $id(H_1) \mathbin{+\!\!+} [i] \mathbin{+\!\!+} id(H_2) \mathbin{+\!\!+} id(H_3) \mathbin{+\!\!+} [r] \notin T$. In the result $T' = T \cup \{id(H_1) \mathbin{+\!\!+} [i] \mathbin{+\!\!+} id(H_2) \mathbin{+\!\!+} id(H_3) \mathbin{+\!\!+} [r]\}$.

The role of the propagation histories T and T' is exactly the same as with the theoretical operational semantics, ω_t.

7. Default $\langle [c\#i : j|A], S, B, T\rangle_n \rightarrowtail \langle [c\#i : j+1|A], S, B, T\rangle_n$ if the current state cannot fire any other transition. $\square$

The refined operational semantics is still *non-deterministic*. Its first source of non-determinism is the **Solve** transition where the order in which constraints S_1 are added to the activation stack is still left open. The definition above (which considers all non-fixed CHR constraints) is weak. In practice, only constraints that may potentially cause a new rule to fire are re-added, see [5, 10] for more details.

The other source of non-determinism occurs within the **Simplify** and **Propagate** transitions, where we do not know which *partner* constraints (H_1, H_2 and H_3) may be chosen for the transition, if more than one possibility exists.

Both sources of non-determinism could be removed by further refining the operational semantics, however we use non-determinism to model implementation specific behaviour of CHRs. For example, different CHR implementations use different data structures to represent the store, and this may inadvertently affect the order partner constraints are matched against a rule. By leaving matching order non-deterministic, we capture the semantics of all current implementations. It also leave more freedom for optimization of CHR execution (see e.g. [12]).

Example 6. The following shows the derivation under ω_r semantics for the gcd program in Example 4 and the goal gcd(6),gcd(9). For brevity B and T have been eliminated and the substitutions θ applied throughout.

$$\langle [\text{gcd}(6), \text{gcd}(9)], \emptyset \rangle_1 \tag{1}$$

$\rightarrowtail_{activate}$ $\quad\langle [\text{gcd}(6)\#1 : 1, \text{gcd}(9)], \{\text{gcd}(6)\#1\}\rangle_2 \tag{2}$

$\rightarrowtail^{\times 3}_{default}$ $\quad\langle [\text{gcd}(6)\#1 : 4, \text{gcd}(9)], \{\text{gcd}(6)\#1\}\rangle_2 \tag{2}$

$\rightarrowtail_{drop}$ $\quad\langle [\text{gcd}(9)], \{\text{gcd}(6)\#1\}\rangle_2 \tag{2}$

$\rightarrowtail_{activate}\rightarrowtail_{default}$ $\langle [\text{gcd}(9)\#2 : 2], \{\text{gcd}(9)\#2, \text{gcd}(6)\#1\}\rangle_3 \tag{3}$

$\rightarrowtail_{simplify}$ $\quad\langle [\text{gcd}(3)], \{\text{gcd}(6)\#1\}\rangle_3 \tag{4}$

$\rightarrowtail_{activate}\rightarrowtail^{\times 2}_{default}$ $\langle [\text{gcd}(3)\#3 : 3], \{\text{gcd}(3)\#3, \text{gcd}(6)\#1\}\rangle_3 \tag{5}$

$\rightarrowtail_{propagate}$ $\quad\langle [\text{gcd}(3), \text{gcd}(3)\#3 : 3], \{\text{gcd}(3)\#3\}\rangle_4 \tag{6}$

$\rightarrowtail_{activate}\rightarrowtail_{default}$ $\langle [\text{gcd}(3)\#4 : 2, \text{gcd}(3)\#3 : 3], \{\text{gcd}(3)\#4, \text{gcd}(3)\#3\}\rangle_5 \tag{7}$

$\rightarrowtail_{simplify}$ $\quad\langle [\text{gcd}(0), \text{gcd}(3)\#3 : 3], \{\text{gcd}(3)\#3\}\rangle_5 \tag{8}$

$\rightarrowtail_{activate}$ $\quad\langle [\text{gcd}(0)\#5 : 1, \text{gcd}(3)\#3 : 3], \{\text{gcd}(0)\#5, \text{gcd}(3)\#3\}\rangle_6 \tag{9}$

$\rightarrowtail_{simplify}$ $\quad\langle [\text{gcd}(3)\#3 : 3], \{\text{gcd}(3)\#3\}\rangle_6 \tag{10}$

$\rightarrowtail_{default}\rightarrowtail_{drop}$ $\langle \epsilon, \{\text{gcd}(3)\#3\}\rangle_6 \tag{10}$

4   The Relationship Between the Two Semantics

Once both semantics are established, we can define an abstraction function α which maps execution states of ω_r to ω_t as follows:

$$\alpha(\langle A, S, B, T \rangle_n) = \langle no\_id(A), S, B, T \rangle_n$$

where $no\_id(A) = \{c \mid c \in A$ is not of the form $c\#i$ or $c\#i : j\}$.

Example 7. A state in Example 6 with number (N) is mapped to the state in Example 5 with the same number. For example, the state $\langle [\mathsf{gcd}(0), \mathsf{gcd}(3)\#3 : 3], \{\mathsf{gcd}(3)\#3\} \rangle_5$ corresponds to $\langle \{\mathsf{gcd}(0)\}, \{\mathsf{gcd}(3)\#3\} \rangle_5$ since both are numbered (8).

We now extend α to map a derivation D in ω_r to the corresponding derivation $\alpha(D)$ in ω_t, by mapping each state appropriately and eliminating adjacent equivalent states:

$$\alpha(S_1 \rightarrowtail D) = \begin{array}{ll} \alpha(D) & \text{if } D = S_2 \rightarrowtail D' \text{ and } \alpha(S_1) = \alpha(S_2) \\ \alpha(S_1) \rightarrowtail \alpha(D) & \text{otherwise} \end{array}$$

We can now show that each ω_r derivation has a corresponding ω_t derivation, and the final state of the ω_r corresponds to a final state in the ω_t derivation.

Theorem 1 (Correspondence). *Given a derivation D under ω_r then there exists a corresponding derivation $\alpha(D)$ under ω_t. If S is the final state in D then $\alpha(S)$ is a final state under ω_t.*

Theorem 1 shows that the refined operational semantics implements the theoretical operational semantics. Hence, the soundness and completeness results for CHRs under the theoretical operational semantics hold under the refined operational semantics ω_r.

4.1   Termination

Termination of CHR programs is obviously a desirable property. Thanks to Theorem 1, termination of ω_t programs ensures termination of ω_r.

Corollary 1. *If every derivation for G in ω_t terminates, then every derivation for G in ω_r also terminates.*

The converse is clearly not true, as shown in Example 1. In practice, proving termination for CHR programs under the theoretical operational semantics is quite difficult (see [8] for examples and discussion). It is somewhat simpler for the refined operational semantics but, just as with other programming languages, this is simply left to the programmer.

4.2   Confluence

Since both operational semantics of CHRs are non-deterministic, *confluence* of the program, which guarantees that whatever order the rules are applied in leads to the same result, is essential from a programmer's point of view. Without it the programmer cannot anticipate the answer that will arise from a goal.

Formally, a CHR program P is confluent under semantics ω if for any goal G and any two derivations $\langle G, \emptyset, true, \emptyset \rangle_1 \rightarrowtail^*_\omega \langle \_, S_1, B_1, \_ \rangle_-$ and $\langle G, \emptyset, true, \emptyset \rangle_1 \rightarrowtail^*_\omega \langle \_, S_2, B_2, \_ \rangle_-$ we have that $\mathcal{D} \models \bar{\exists}_G(S_1 \wedge B_1) \leftrightarrow \bar{\exists}_G(S_2 \wedge B_2)$. That is, the resulting constraints stores are equivalent.

Confluence of the theoretical operational semantics of CHR programs has been extensively studied [1, 2]. Abdennadher [1] provides a decidable confluence test for the theoretical semantics of terminating CHR programs. Essentially, it relies on computing critical pairs where two rules can possibly be used, and showing that each of the two resulting states lead to equivalent states.

Just as with termination, thanks to Theorem 1, confluence under ω_t implies confluence under ω_r.

Corollary 2. *If CHR program P is confluent with respect to ω_t, it is confluent with respect to ω_r.*

5   Checking Confluence for ω_r

One of the benefits of exposing the refined operational semantics is the ability to write and execute programs that are non-confluent with respect to the theoretical operational semantics, but are confluent with respect to the refined operational semantics. In order to take advantage of this, we need to provide a decidable test for confluence under ω_r. This test must be able to capture a reasonable number of programs which are confluent under ω_r but not under ω_t. However, this appears to be quite difficult.

Example 8. For example, consider the following CHR program

```
p1 @ p <=> true.
p2 @ q(_), p <=> true.
```

Rule p2 looks suspiciously non-confluent since, if it was the only rule present, the goal q(a),q(b),p could terminate with either q(a) or q(b) left in the store. However, when combined with p1, p2 will never fire since any active p constraint will be deleted by p1 before reaching p2. Thus, the program is ω_r confluent.

The example illustrates how extending the notion of critical pairs can be difficult, since many critical pairs will correspond to unreachable program states.

As mentioned before, there are two sources of non-determinism in the refined operational semantics. The first source, which occurs when deciding the order in which the CHR constraints are added to the activation stack while applying **Solve**, is hard to tackle. In practice, we will avoid re-activating most

CHR constraints in the store, by only considering those which might now cause a rule to fire when it did not fire before (see [5, 10] for more details). However, if re-activation actually occurs, the programmer is unlikely to have any control on what order re-activated constraints are re-executed. To avoid this non-determinism we will require S_1 to be empty in any **Solve** transition. This has in fact been the case for all the examples considered so far except fib, and all those in Section 6, since all CHR constraints added to the store had fixed arguments. Even for fib we could safely avoid reactivating the fib constraints whose second arguments are not fixed, since these arguments have no relationship with the guards.

For programs that really do interact with an underlying constraint solver, we have no better solution than relying on the confluence test of the theoretical operational semantics, for in this case it is very hard to see how the programmer can control execution sufficiently.

The second source of non-determinism occurs when there is more than one set of partner constraints in the CHR store that can be used to apply the **Simplify** and **Propagate** transitions. We formalise this as follows. A *matching* of occurrence j with active CHR constraint c in state $\langle [c\#i : j|A], S, B, T \rangle_n$ is the sequence of identified constraints $H_1 \mathbin{+\!\!+} H_2 \mathbin{+\!\!+} H_3 \mathbin{+\!\!+} [c\#i]$ used in transitions **Simplify** and **Propagate**. The *goal* of the matching is the right hand side of the associated rule with the matching substitution applied, i.e., $\theta(C)$.

Non-confluence arises when multiple matchings exist for a rule R, and R is not allowed to eventually try them all. This can happen if firing R with one matching results in the deletion of a constraint in another matching.

Definition 1. *An occurrence j in rule R is* matching complete *if for all reachable states $\langle [c\#i : j|A], S, B, T \rangle_n$ with $M_1, ..., M_m$ possible matchings and $G_1, ..., G_m$ corresponding goals, firing R for any matching M_l and executing G_l does not result in the deletion of a constraint occurring in a different matching $M_k, k \neq l$.*

Note that R itself may directly delete the active constraint. If so, R will only be matching complete if there is only one possible matching, i.e., $m = 1$.

Example 9. Consider the CHR program in Example 2. The occurrence of entry in rule 11 is matching complete since the lookup constraint is never stored (it is deleted before it becomes inactive). This is not however the case for the occurrence of lookup in 11. Goal entry(a,b),entry(a,c),lookup(a,V) will return V=b or V=c depending on which of the two matchings of the occurrence of lookup in 11 ([entry(a,b)#1,lookup(a,V)#3] or [entry(a,c)#2,lookup(a,V)#3]) is used, i.e., depending on which partner entry constraint is used for lookup(a,V) in 11. The code is matching complete if the database only contains one entry per key. Adding the rule

```
killdup @ entry(Key,Val1) \ entry(Key,Val2) <=> true.
```

which throws away duplicate entries for a key, provides a functional dependency from Key to Val in entry(Key,Val). This rule makes the occurrence matching complete, since only one matching will ever be possible.

Matching completeness can also be broken if the body of a rule deletes constraints from other matchings.

Example 10. Consider the following CHR program

```
r1 @ p, q(X) ==> r(X).
r2 @ p, r(a) <=> true.
```

The occurrence of p in r1 is not matching complete since the goal q(a),q(b),p, will obtain the final state q(a),q(b) or q(a),q(b),r(b) depending on which partner constraint (q(a) or q(b)) is used for the occurrence of p in r1. This is because the goal of the first matching (r(a)) deletes p.

A matching complete occurrence is guaranteed to eventually try all possible matchings for given execution state S. However, matching completeness is sometimes too strong if the user doesn't care which matching is chosen. This is common when the body does not depend on the matching chosen.

Example 11. For example, consider the following rule from a simple ray tracer.

```
shadow @ sphere(C,R,_) \ light_ray(L,P,_,_) <=> blocks(L,P,C,R) | true.
```

This rule calculates if point P is in shadow by testing if the ray from light L is blocked by a sphere at C with radius R. Consider an active light_ray constraint, there may be more than one sphere blocking the ray, however we don't care *which* sphere blocks, just *if* there is a sphere which blocks. This rule is not matching complete but, since the matching chosen does not affect the resulting state, it is matching independent.

Definition 2. *A matching incomplete occurrence j which is deleted by rule R is matching independent if for all reachable states $\langle [c\#i : j|A], S, B, T \rangle_n$ with $M_1, \ldots, M_m$ possible matchings and $G_1, \ldots, G_m$ corresponding goals, then all the final states for $\langle G_k, S_k, B, T_k \rangle_n, 1 \leq k \leq m$ are equivalent, where S_k is the store after firing on matching M_k and T_k is the resulting history.*

Suppose that a rule is matching complete, and there are multiple possible matchings. The ordering in which the matchings are tried is still chosen non-deterministically. Hence, there is still potential of non-confluence. For this reason we also require *order independence*, which ensures the choice of order does not affect the result.

Definition 3. *A matching complete occurrence j in rule R is order independent if for all reachable states $\langle [c\#i : j|A], S, B, T \rangle_n$ with $M_1, \ldots, M_m$ possible matchings and $G_1, \ldots, G_m$ corresponding goals, the execution of the state $\langle G_{\sigma(1)} +\!+ \cdots +\!+ G_{\sigma(m)}, S', B, T' \rangle_n$ where S' is the CHR store S where all constraints deleted by any matching are deleted, and T' has all sequences added by all matchings, for any permutation σ, leads to equivalent states.*

Note that, since j is matching complete, S' is well defined. Order independence is a fairly strong condition and, currently, we have little insight as to how to check it beyond a limited version of the confluence check for the theoretical operational semantics. Thus, we currently require user annotations about order independence. A matching complete occurrence, which may have more than one matching, only passes the confluence checker if all CHR constraints called by the body are annotated as order independent.

Example 12. Consider the following fragment for summing colors from a ray tracer.

```
add1 @ add_color(C1), color(C2) <=> C3 = C1 + C2, color(C3).
add2 @ add_color(C) <=> color(C).
```

All occurrences of `color` and `add_color` are matching complete. Furthermore, calling `add_color(C₁)`, ..., `add_color(Cₙ)` results in `color(C₁+...+Cₙ)`. Since addition is symmetric and associative, it does not matter in what order the `add_color` constraints are called. Consider the occurrence of `output` in

```
render @ output(P) \ light_ray(_,P,C,_) <=> add_color(C).
```

Here, calling `output(P)` calculates the (accumulated) color at point P where any `light_rays` (a ray from a light source) may intersect. If there are multiple light sources, then there may be multiple `light_ray` constraints. The order `add_color` is called does not matter, hence the occurrence is order independent.

We now have sufficient conditions for a simple confluence test.

Theorem 2 (Confluence Test). *Let P be a CHR program such that:*

1. *Starting from a fixed goal, any derived state is also fixed;*
2. *All occurrences in rules are matching complete or matching independent;*
3. *All matching complete occurrences in rules are order independent.*

Then P is ω_r confluent for fixed goals.

The HAL CHR confluence checker implements partial tests for fixedness of CHR constraints, matching completeness and matching independence, and relies on user annotation for determining order independence.

The confluence checker uses mode checking [9] to determine which CHR constraints are always fixed. A non-fixed constraint may also be safe, as long as it is never in the store when it is not active (such as `lookup` from Example 2). We call such constraints *never stored*.

The confluence checker uses information about never stored constraints and functional dependency analysis (see [12]) to determine how many possible matchings (0, 1 or many) there are for each occurence in a given rule. If there are multiple possible matchings for an occurence, it then checks that the removal of other matching constraints is impossible, by examining the rule itself and using a reachability analysis of the "call graph" for CHR rules, to determine if the constraints could be removed by executing the body of the rule.

The checker determines matching independence by determining which variables occuring in the body are functionally defined by the active occurence, making use of functional dependency analysis to do so. If all variables in the body and the deleted constraints are functionally defined by the active occurence, the occurence is matching independent.

Only bodies restricted to built-in constraints are considered as order independent by the current confluence checker. Otherwise, we rely on user annotation.

6   Case Studies: Confluence Test

This section investigates the confluence of two "real-life" CHR programs using our confluence checker. The programs are bounds – an extensible bounds propagation solver, and compiler – a new (bootstrapping) CHR compiler. Both were implemented with the refined operational semantics in mind, and simply will not work under the theoretical semantics.

6.1   Confluence of bounds

The bounds propagation solver is implemented in HAL and has a total of 83 rules, 37 CHR constraints and 113 occurences. An early version of a bounds propagation solver first appeared in [12]. The current version also implements simple dynamic scheduling (i.e. the user can delay goals until certain conditions hold), as well as supporting ask constraints. This program was implemented before the confluence checker.

The confluence checker finds 4 matching problems, and 3 order independence problems. One of the matching problems indicated a bug (see below), the others are attributed to the weakness in the compiler's analysis. We only had to annotate one constraint as order independent.

The confluence analysis complained that the following rule is matching incomplete and non-independent when kill(Id) is active since there are (potentially) many possible matchings for the delayed_goals partner.

```
kill @ kill(Id), delayed_goals(Id,X,_,...,_) <=> true.
```

Here delayed_goals(Id,X,_,...,_) represents the delayed goals for bounds solver variable X. The code should be

```
kill1 @ kill(Id) \ delayed_goals(Id,X,_,...,_) <=> true.
kill2 @ kill(_) <=> true.
```

This highlights how a simple confluence analysis can be used to discover bugs.

The confluence analysis also complains about the rules for bounds propagation themselves. The reason is that the constraint bounds(X,L,U) which stores the lower L and upper U bounds of variable X has complex self-interaction. Two bounds constraints for the same variable can interact using, for example,

```
b2b @ bounds(X,L1,U1), bounds(X,L2,U2)
         <=> bounds(X,max(L1,L2),min(U1,U2)).
```

Here, the user must annotate the matching completeness and order independence of bounds. In fact, the relevant parts of the program are confluent within the theoretical operational semantics, but this is currently beyond the capabilities of our confluence analysis (and difficult because it requires bounds reasoning).

6.2 Confluence of `compiler`

The bootstrapping compiler is implemented in SICStus Prolog (using the CHR library), including a total of 131 rules, 42 CHR constraints and 232 occurences. and performs most of the analysis and optimisations detailed in [12]. After bootstrapping it has similar speed to the original compiler written in Prolog and produces more efficient code due to the additional analysis performed. During the bootstrap, when compiling itself the first time, the new code outperformed the old code (the SICStus Prolog CHR compiler, 1100 lines of Prolog) by a factor of five. This comparison is rather crude, measuring the costs and effects of the optimisations based on the additional analysis and the improved runtime system at once. Yet it demonstrates the practicality of the bootstrapping approach for CHRs and that CHRs as a general purpose programming language under the refined semantics can be used to write moderately large sized verifiable programs.

Bootstrapping CHRs as such aims at easier portability to further host languages and as an internal reality check for CHRs as a general purpose programming system. To the best of our knowledge, the bootstrapping compiler is the largest single CHR program written by hand. (Automatic rule generators for constraint propagation algorithms [3] can produce large CHR programs too, but from the point of the compiler their structure is rather homogeneous in comparison to the compiler's own code).

The confluence checker finds 14 matching problems, and 45 order independence problems. 4 of the matching problems are removed by making functional dependencies explicit. The others are attributed to the weakness in the compiler's analysis. We had to annotate 18 constraints as order independent.

7 Conclusion

The refined operational semantics for Constraint Handling Rules provides a powerful and expressive language, ideal for applications such as compilers, since fixpoint computations and simple database operations are straightforward to program. In order to support programming for this language we need to help the author check the confluence of his program. In this paper we have defined a partial confluence checker that is powerful enough to check many idioms used in real programs. In the future we intend to extend this checker to better handle order independence, and to include the ability to check confluence with respect to the theoretical semantics.

References

1. S. Abdennadher. Operational semantics and confluence of constraint propagation rules. In Gert Smolka, editor, *Proceedings of the Third International Conference on Principles and Practice of Constraint Programming*, pages 252–266, 1997.
2. S. Abdennadher, T. Frühwirth, and H. Muess. Confluence and semantics of constraint simplification rules. *Constraints*, 4(2):133–166, 1999.

3. K. Apt and E. Monfroy. Automatic generation of constraint propagation algorithms for small finite domains. In *Principles and Practice of Constraint Programming*, pages 58–72, 1999.

4. B. Demoen, M. García de la Banda, W. Harvey, K. Marriott, and P.J. Stuckey. An overview of HAL. In *Proceedings of the Fourth International Conference on Principles and Practices of Constraint Programming*, pages 174–188, 1999.

5. G.J. Duck, P.J. Stuckey, M. García de la Banda, and C. Holzbaur. Extending arbitrary solvers with constraint handling rules. In D. Miller, editor, *Proceedings of the Fifth ACM SIGPLAN International Conference on Principles and Practice of Declarative Programming*, pages 79–90. ACM Press, 2003.

6. T. Frühwirth. http://www.pms.informatik.uni-muenchen.de/~webchr/.

7. T. Frühwirth. Theory and practice of constraint handling rules. *Journal of Logic Programming*, 37:95–138, 1998.

8. T. Frühwirth. Proving termination of constraint solver programs. In *New Trends in Contraints, Joint ERCIM/Compulog Net Workshop*, number 1865 in LNCS, pages 298–317. Springer-Verlag, 1999.

9. M. García de la Banda, P.J. Stuckey, W. Harvey, and K. Marriott. Mode checking in HAL. In J. LLoyd et al., editor, *Proceedings of the First International Conference on Computational Logic*, LNCS 1861, pages 1270–1284. Springer-Verlag, July 2000.

10. C. Holzbaur and T. Frühwirth. Compiling constraint handling rules into Prolog with attributed variables. In Gopalan Nadathur, editor, *Proceedings of the International Conference on Principles and Practice of Declarative Programming*, number 1702 in LNCS, pages 117–133. Springer-Verlag, 1999.

11. C. Holzbaur and T. Frühwirth. A Prolog constraint handling rules compiler and runtime system. *Journal of Applied Artificial Intelligence*, 14(4), 2000.

12. C. Holzbaur, P.J. Stuckey, M. García de la Banda, and D. Jeffery. Optimizing compilation of constraint handling rules. In P. Codognet, editor, *Logic Programming: Proceedings of the 17th International Conference*, LNCS, pages 74–89. Springer-Verlag, 2001.

Compiling Ask Constraints

Gregory J. Duck[1], María García de la Banda[2], and Peter J. Stuckey[1]

[1] Department of Computer Science and Software Engineering
The University of Melbourne, Vic. 3010, Australia
{gjd,pjs}@cs.mu.oz.au
[2] School of Computer Science and Software Engineering
Monash University, Vic. 3800, Australia
mbanda@csse.monash.edu.au

Abstract. In this paper we investigate how to extend a generic constraint solver that provides not only *tell* constraints (by adding the constraint to the store) but also *ask* tests (by checking whether the constraint is entailed by the store), with general ask constraints. Ask constraints are important for implementing constraint implication, extensible solvers using dynamic scheduling and reification. While the ask-test must be implemented by the solver writer, the compiler can extend this to provide ask behaviour for complex combinations of constraints, including constraints from multiple solvers. We illustrate the use of this approach within the HAL system.

1 Introduction

A constraint c of constraint domain $\mathcal{D}$ expresses relationships among variables of $\mathcal{D}$. All constraint programming frameworks (such as $CLP(\mathcal{D})$ [4,5]) use c as a *tell* constraint, allowing the programmer to add the relationship to the current constraint store C and check that the result is possible satisfiable, i.e., $\mathcal{D} \models \bar{\exists}(C \wedge c)$. However, some frameworks (such as $cc(\mathcal{D})$ [6]) also use c as an *ask* constraint, allowing the programmer to detect constraints stores C for which the relationship already holds, i.e., $\mathcal{D} \models C \rightarrow c$.

Ask constraints are often used to control execution by associating them to some goal, which is to be executed if and when the associated ask constraints succeed (i.e., become entailed by the constraint store).

Example 1. The following cc [6] definition of the constraint min(X,Y,Z)

```
min(X,Y,Z) :- X >= Y | Z = Y.
min(X,Y,Z) :- Y >= X | Z = X.
```

where Z is the minimum of X and Y is read as follows: when the min constraint is executed, wait until one of the ask constraints to the left of the bar | holds and then execute the tell constraint to the right of the bar. In the case of the cc framework the implementation also encodes a commit: once one ask constraint holds the other will never be reconsidered. The code implements a form of implication whose logical reading is:
$$min(x, y, z) \Leftrightarrow (x \geq y \rightarrow z = y) \wedge (y \geq x \rightarrow z = x)$$
□

B. Demoen and V. Lifschitz (Eds.): ICLP 2004, LNCS 3132, pp. 105–119, 2004.
© Springer-Verlag Berlin Heidelberg 2004

Note that it is not enough for the above framework to be able to test whether a constraint c is entailed by the current constraint store (this one-off test will be referred to in the future as the *ask-test*). It also needs to detect changes in the constraint store that might affect the entailment of c, so that the ask-test can be re-executed. Hence, ask constraints are strongly connected to logical implication. In fact, it is this connection that makes them so useful for implementing many important language extensions, such as those involving constraint solvers.

In this paper we consider a language that supports an ask construct of the form $(F_1 ==> G_1 \& \ldots \& F_n ==> G_n)$, where each F_i is a complex formula over constraints. The construct waits until some F_i is entailed by the store, and then executes its associated goal G_i. Several other languages, such as SICStus and ECLiPSe, implement related constructs for dynamic scheduling. However, they are typically hard-coded for a single solver, a pre-defined set of test conditions and do not support handling of (explicit) existential variables. Also, they usually only support formulas F made up of a single ask test condition. These restrictions considerably simplify the implementation of the construct.

This paper discusses the compilation of an ask construct with arbitrary ask-constraints, that allows the programmer to write code which closely resembles the logical specification. In particular, our contributions are as follows:

- We show how to extend an ask-test implemented by some underlying solver to a full *ask constraint* supporting dynamic scheduling.
- We show how to compile complex ask constraints which include existential variables and involve more than one solver, to the primitive ask-tests supported by the solvers.
- We show that the approach is feasible using an implementation in HAL [1].

2   Ask Constraints as High-Level Dynamic Scheduling

This section formalizes the syntax, logical semantics and operational semantics of our ask construct. Its basic syntax is as follows:

$$(\ <\text{ask-formula}>_1 \ ==> \ goal_1 \ \& \ \ldots \ \& \ \ <\text{ask-formula}>_n \ ==> \ goal_n \ )$$

where an $<\text{ask-formula}>_i$ is a formula made up of primitive ask constraints, disjunction, conjunction, and existential quantification. Formally:

$<\text{ask-formula}>$	:= $<\text{ask-constraint}>$	(*primitive constraint*)
$<\text{ask-formula}>$	:= $<\text{ask-formula}>$ ';' $<\text{ask-formula}>$	(*disjunction*)
$<\text{ask-formula}>$	:= $<\text{ask-formula}>$ ',' $<\text{ask-formula}>$	(*conjunction*)
$<\text{ask-formula}>$	:= exists $<\text{var-list}>$ $<\text{ask-formula}>$	(*existential quantification*)

where $<\text{ask-constraint}>$ represents some primitive ask constraint provided by a solver, $<\text{var-list}>$ is a list of variables, and each *ask-constraint/goal* pair is referred to as an *ask branch*.

The operational semantics of the above construct is as follows. As soon as the solver(s) determine that an ask-formula is entailed, the corresponding delayed goal is called. The remaining ask branches will then never be considered, thus effectively *committing* to one branch. This commit behaviour can be easily avoided by specifying separate ask constructs for each branch. Note that ask constraints are *monotonic*, i.e., once they hold at a point during a derivation, they will always hold for the rest of the derivation. The advantage of monotonicity is that delayed goals need only be executed once, as soon as the associated ask constraints are entailed.

The declarative semantics of an ask branch F==>G is simply logical implication $F \to G$. The semantics of the whole construct $(F_1$==>$G_1 \& \cdots \& F_n$==>$G_n)$ is a conjunction of implications, *but* in order to agree with the commit the programmer must promise that the individual implications agree. That is, that for program P:

$$\mathcal{D} \wedge P \models (F_i \wedge F_j) \to (G_i \leftrightarrow G_j)$$

In other words, if the ask construct wakes on the formula F_i causing G_i to execute, and later formula F_j is implied by the store, then G_j is already entailed by G_i and need not be executed. Note that under these conditions the commit is purely used for efficiency, it will not change the logical semantics of the program, although it may of course change the operational behaviour since the underlying solvers are likely to be incomplete.

Example 2. Consider the following implementation of the predicate either(X,Y) which holds iff X or Y are true:

```
either(X,Y) :- ( X = 0 ==> Y = 1  &    Y = 0 ==> X = 1).
```

The logical reading is $(X = 0 \to Y = 1) \wedge (Y = 0 \to X = 1)$ which is equivalent to $(X = 1 \vee Y = 1)$ in the Boolean domain. If both ask constraints are made true $(X = 0 \wedge Y = 0)$, the right hand sides are equivalent $(Y = 1 \leftrightarrow X = 1)$ to false. ⊡

The proposed ask construct is indeed quite versatile. The following examples show how to use it to implement reification constraints, build constraints that involve more than one solver, and implement negation.

Example 3. A reified constraint $b \leftrightarrow c$ constrains the Boolean variable b to be true if c is implied by the store, and b to be false if $\neg c$ is implied by the store, and vice versa. Consider defining a predicate $B \leftrightarrow \exists Y.X = [Y, Y]$ which "reifies" the right hand side. Note that the right hand side is equivalent to $\exists E1 \exists E2.X = [E1, E2], E1 = E2$. This can be implemented using ask constraints as

```
reifcomp(B,X) :-
    ( B=0, (exists [E1,E2] X = [E1,E2]) ==> X=[E1,E2], E1≠E2
    & B=1 ==> X=[Y,Y]
    & exists [Y] X=[Y,Y] ==> B=1
    & X=[] ; (exists [E1] X=[E1]) ;
            (exists [E1,E2,R] X=[E1,E2|R], (E1≠E2 ; R≠[])) ==> B=0)
```

These definitions assume X only takes on list values. ⊡

Example 4. The following program defines a length constraint which involves variables from a finite domain constraint solver, and from a Herbrand constraint solver for lists, and propagates information from one to the other:

```
length(L,N) :- ( N = 0 ; L = [] ==> N = 0, L = []
                 & N >= 1 ; (exists [U1,U2] L = [U1|U2]) ==>
                             L = [_|L1], N >= 1, length(L1,N-1)).        ⊡
```

Example 5. Consider the following definition of disequality

```
neq(X,Y) :- (X = Y ==> fail).
```

This (very weak) implementation of disequality waits until the arguments are constrained to be equal and then causes failure.   ⊡

3   Compiling Primitive Ask Constructs

Let us now examine how to compile a primitive ask construct (i.e., one in which the left hand side of every ask branch is a single ask constraint) to the low-level dynamic scheduling supported by HAL[1].

3.1   Low-Level Dynamic Scheduling in HAL

HAL [1] provides four low-level type class methods that can be combined to implement dynamic scheduling: `get_id(Id)` which returns an unused identifier for the delay construct; `delay(event_i, Id, goal_1)` which takes a solver event, an id and a goal, and stores the information in order to execute the goal whenever the solver event occurs; `kill(Id)` which causes all goals delayed for the input id to no longer wake up, and `alive(Id)` which succeeds if the input id is still alive. In order for a constraint solver in HAL to support delay, it must provide an implementation of the `delay/3` method. Implementations of `get_id/1`, `kill/1` and `alive/1` can either be given by the solver or be re-used from some other source (such as the built-in system implementations). For more details see e.g. [1].

There are three major differences between HAL's dynamic scheduling and our ask construct. First, solver events (*event_i*) are single predicates representing an event in the underlying solver, such as "the lower bound of variable X changes". No conjunction, disjunction or existential quantification of events is allowed. Second, solver events need not be monotonic. Indeed, the example event "lower bound has changed" is clearly not. And third, a delayed goal will be re-executed *every time* its associated solver event occurs, until its id is explicitly killed.

Example 6. A finite domain integer (`fdint`) solver in HAL supporting dynamic scheduling typically provides the following solver events:

`fixed(V)`	The domain of V reduces to a single value;
`lbc(V)`	The lower bound of V changes (increases);
`ubc(V)`	The upper bound of V changes (decreases);
`dc(V)`	The domain of V changes (reduces).

---

[1] The compilation scheme can be adapted straightforwardly to other dynamic scheduling systems supporting delay identifiers.

Note that solver events do not need to be mutually exclusive: if the domain $\{1,3,5\}$ of X changes to $\{1\}$, the events `fixed(X)`, `ubc(X)` and `dc(X)` all occur.

Using the above events, a bounds propagator for the constraint $X \geq Y$ can be written as

```
geq(X,Y) :- get_id(Id),delay(lbc(Y),Id,set_lb(X,max(lb(Y),lb(X)))),
            delay(ubc(X),Id,set_ub(Y,min(ub(X),ub(Y)))).
```

where `lb` (and `ub`) are functions returning the current lower (and upper) bound of their argument solver variable. Likewise, `set_lb` (and `set_ub`) set the lower (and upper) bound of their first argument solver variable to the second argument. The code gets a new delay id, and creates two delaying goals attached to this id. The first executes every time the lower bound of Y changes, enforcing X to be greater than this bound. The second implements the reverse direction.   ⊡

In addition to the four methods introduced above, HAL supports an "asks" declaration initially introduced into HAL to support the compilation of constraint handling rules that interact with arbitrary solvers [2]. The declaration allows constraints solvers to declare the relationship between a predicate implementing constraint c as a tell constraint, the predicate implementing c as an ask-test (a one-off test), and the list of solver events which might indicate the answer to the ask-test has changed and, therefore, the ask-test should be re-executed. Its syntax is as follows:

```
:- <ask-test> asks <tell-constraint> wakes <wakes-list>.
```

Example 7. The finite domain solver introduced in Example 6 might define the ask-test and declaration for the `geq` constraint as follows.

```
:- ask_geq(X,Y) asks geq(X,Y) wakes [lbc(X),ubc(Y)].
ask_geq(X,Y) :- lb(X) >= ub(Y).
```

The predicate `ask_geq` defines the ask-test for the `geq` constraint, and should be revisited when either the lower bound of X or the upper bound of Y change. ⊡

3.2   From Ask-Tests to Primitive Ask Constructs

The low-level dynamic scheduling of HAL allows us to compile the primitive ask construct:

$$(c_1(A_1^1,...,A_{m_1}^1) ==> Goal_1 \ \& \ ... \ \& \ c_n(A_1^n,...,A_{m_n}^n) ==> Goal_n)$$

if for each $c_i, 1 \leq i \leq n$, there exists the associated asks declaration:

```
:- ask_ci(X1,...,Xmi) asks ci(X1,...,Xmi) wakes [eventi1,...,eventin].
```

This is done by replacing the ask construct with:

```
get_id(Id),delay_c1(A11,...,A1m1,Id,Goal1),...,delay_c2(An1,...,Anmn,Id,Goaln)
```

and generating for each `delay_ci` the following code:

```
delay_c_i(X_1,...,X_{m_i},Id,Goal) :-
    ( alive(Id) -> ( ask_c_i(X_1,...,X_{m_i}) -> kill(Id), call(Goal)
                   ; Retest = retest_c_i(X_1,...,X_{m_i},Id,Goal)
                       delay(event_{i1},Id,Retest), ... delay(event_{in_i},Id,Retest))
    ;                  true ).
retest_c_i(X_1,...,X_{m_i},Id,Goal) :-
    ( ask_c_i(X_1,...,X_{m_i}) -> kill(Id), call(Goal) ; true).
```

The code for `delay_c_i` first checks if the `Id` is alive, and if so determines whether or not the constraint already holds by calling the ask-test ask_c_i/n. If so, the `Id` is killed, the `Goal` is immediately called, and no other action is necessary. If the constraint is not yet entailed, a closure for the retesting predicate `retest_c_i` is associated to each of the relevant solver events so that, each time a relevant solver event occurs, `retest_c_i` is executed. This predicates checks whether the ask-test now succeeds and, if so, kills the `Id` and executes the goal. Note that the `delay` predicate for each solver used in the ask construct must support the same delay id type.

Example 8. Consider the asks declaration of Example 7. The compilation of

```
min(X,Y) :- ( geq(X,Y) ==> Z = Y & geq(Y,X) ==> Z = X).
```

results in

```
min(X,Y) :- get_id(Id), delay_geq(X,Y,Id,Z = Y), delay_geq(Y,X,Id,Z = X).
delay_geq(X,Y,Id,Goal) :-
    (alive(Id) -> ( ask_geq(X,Y) -> kill(Id), call(Goal)
                  ; Retest = retest_geq(X,Y,Id,Goal),
                      delay(lbc(X),Id,Retest),delay(ubc(Y),Id,Retest))
    ;                 true ).
retest_geq(X,Y,Id,Goal):- ( ask_geq(X,Y) -> kill(Id), call(Goal) ; true).□
```

4   Compiling Disjunctions and Conjunctions

Conjunctions and disjunctions in ask formulae can be compiled away by taking advantage of the following logical identities:

1. Disjunctive implication: $(a \lor b) \to c$ is equivalent to $(a \to c) \land (b \to c)$; and
2. Conjunctive implication: $(a \land b) \to c$ is equivalent to $(a \to (b \to c))$.

Disjunctive implication is used to replace the branch
$$<ask\text{-}formula>_1 \; ; \; <ask\text{-}formula>_2 ==> \text{Goal}$$
in a construct, by the two branches
$$<ask\text{-}formula>_1 ==> \text{Goal} \; \& \; <ask\text{-}formula>_2 ==> \text{Goal}$$
The two programs are operationally equivalent: the delayed `Goal` will be called once, after either $<ask\text{-}formula>_1$ or $<ask\text{-}formula>_2$ (whichever is first) hold. Similarly, conjunctive implication is used to replace the construct
$$<ask\text{-}formula>_1 \; , \; <ask\text{-}formula>_2 ==> \text{Goal}$$
by the construct:

$$(\; <ask\text{-}formula>_1 \; ==> \; (\; <ask\text{-}formula>_2 \; ==> \; \texttt{Goal} \;) \;)$$

Again, the new code is operationally equivalent: the delayed goal `Goal` will only be called once, after both $<ask\text{-}formula>_1$ and $<ask\text{-}formula>_2$ hold.

Note that the above simple conjunctive transformation cannot be directly applied to a branch appearing in a construct with 2 or more branches, because of the interaction with commit (the entire construct would be killed as soon as $<ask\text{-}formula>_1$ held, even if $<ask\text{-}formula>_2$ never did). We can solve this problem by using a newly created (local) delay id (`LId`) representing the delay on $<ask\text{-}formula>_1$ while using the original (global) delay id (`GId`) for the internal delay (since if $<ask\text{-}formula>_2$ also holds, the whole ask construct can commit).

An added complexity is that, for efficiency, we should kill the local delay id `LId` whenever `GId` is killed (if, say, another branch commits) so that the low-level HAL machinery does not re-execute ($<ask\text{-}formula>_2$ ==> `Goal`) every time the events associated to $<ask\text{-}formula>_1$ become true. In order to do so we introduce the predicate `register(LId, GId)` which links `LId` to `GId`, so that if `GId` is ever killed, `LId` is also killed.

Example 9. Consider the compilation of

```
p(X,Y,Z,T) :- ( (X >= Y ; X >= Z) ==> Z = T & (Y >= X, Z >= X) ==> X = T).
```

The resulting code is

```
p(X,Y,Z,T) :- get_id(GId),
              delay_geq(X,Y,GId,Z = T), delay_geq(X,Z,GId,Z = T),
              get_Id(LId), register(LId,GId),
              delay_geq(Y,X,LId,delay_geq(Z,X,GId,X = T)).        ⊡
```

By iteratively applying these rules, we can remove all conjunctions and disjunctions from ask formulae (without existential quantifiers).

5   Normalization and Existential Quantification

One of the first steps performed by HAL during compilation is program normalization, which ensures that every function and predicate has variables as arguments. The normalization exhaustively applies the following rules:

1. Rewrite $\exists \bar{x}.C \wedge y = f(t_1, \ldots, t_i, \ldots, t_n)$ where f is an n-ary function and t_i is either a non-variable term or a variable equal to some other $t_j, j \neq i$, to $\exists \bar{x} \exists v.C \wedge v = t_i \wedge y = f(t_1, \ldots, v, \ldots, t_n)$, where v is a new variable.
2. Rewrite $\exists \bar{x}.C \wedge c(t_1, \ldots, t_i, \ldots, t_n)$ where c is an n-ary constraint symbol and t_i is either a non-variable term or a variable equal to some other $t_j, j \neq i$, to $\exists \bar{x} \exists v.C \wedge v = t_i \wedge c(t_1, \ldots, v, \ldots, t_n)$ where v is a new variable.

Example 10. Consider the following definition of a *before-or-after* constraint for two tasks with start times T1 and T2 and durations D1 and D2 implements $T2 \geq T1 + D1 \vee T1 \geq T2 + D2$ without creating a choice.

```
before_after(T1,D1,T2,D2) :- (T1 + D1 > T2 ==> T1 >= T2 + D2),
                             (T2 + D2 > T1 ==> T2 >= T1 + D1).
```

which will have the body normalized into:

```
(exists [U1] U1 = +(T1,D1), U1 > T2 ==> U2 = +(T2,D2), T1 >= U2),
(exists [U3] U3 = +(T2,D2), U3 > T1 ==> U4 = +(T1,D1), T2 >= U4).
```

thus adding the existentially quantified variables U1, ..., U4. While the explicit quantification can be omitted for the variables appearing in the *tell* constraints on the right hand side (U2 and U4), this is *not* true for the *ask* constraints, since the (implicit) existential quantifier escapes the negated context of the ask.   ⊡

Unfortunately, it is in general impossible to compile existential formulae down to primitive ask constraints. Only the solver can answer general questions about existential formulae.

Example 11. Consider an integer solver which supports the constraint X > Y and the function X = abs(Y) (which constrains X to be the absolute value of Y). The following ask construct (exists [N] abs(N) = 2, N > 1 ==> *Goal*)   will always hold. However, it is impossible to separate the two primitive constraints occurring in the ask formula. Instead, we would have to ask the solver to treat the entire conjunction at once.   ⊡

Thankfully, although normalization can lead to proliferation of existential variables in ask formulae, in many cases such existential variables can be compiled away without requiring extra help from the solver. Consider the expression

$$(\exists \bar{x} \exists v. v = f(y_1, \ldots, y_n) \wedge C) \to G$$

If f is a total function, such a v always exists and is unique. Thus, as long as none of the variables $y_1, \ldots, y_n$ are existentially quantified (i.e appear in $\bar{x}$) we can replace the above expression by the equivalent one

$$\exists v. v = f(y_1, \ldots, y_n) \wedge ((\exists \bar{x}.C) \to G)$$

Example 12. Returning to Example 10, we can transform the body code to

```
U1 = +(T1,D1), (U1 > T2 ==> U2 = +(T2,D2), T1 >= U2),
U3 = +(T2,D2), (U3 > T1 ==> U4 = +(T1,D1), T2 >= U4).
```

which does not require existential quantifiers in the ask-formula.   ⊡

There are other common cases that allow us to compile away existential variables, but require some support from the solver. Consider the expression

$$(\exists \bar{x} \exists v. v = f(y_1, \ldots, y_n) \wedge C) \to G$$

where f is a partial function and none of the variables $y_1, \ldots, y_n$ appears in $\bar{x}$. This is equivalent to

$$(\exists v. v = f(y_1, \ldots, y_n)) \to (\exists v. v = f(y_1, \ldots, y_n) \wedge (\exists \bar{x}.C \to G))$$

The result follows since if there exists a v of the form $f(y_1, \ldots, y_n)$, then it is unique. Hence, the function f in the context of this test is effectively total. This may not seem to simplify compilation, but if we provide an ask version of the constraint $\exists v, v = f(y_1, \ldots, y_n)$ then we can indeed simplify the resulting code.

Example 13. Assuming we are dealing with integers, the expression $(x + 2^y \geq 2 \to b = 1)$ is equivalent to $(\exists z'.z' = 2^y) \to (\exists z.z = 2^y \wedge (x + z \geq 2 \to b = 1))$. If the compiler knows that the constraint $\exists z'.z' = 2^y$ is equivalent to $y \geq 0$, compilation of the code

```
g(X,Y,B) :- (X + 2^Y ≥ 2 ==> B = 1)
```

results in `g(X,Y,B) :- (Y ≥ 0 ==> (Z = 2^Y, (X + Z ≥ 2 ==> B = 1))).`   ⊡

To use this simplification we need versions of the ask constraint for partial functions. These can be provided using the already introduced mechanisms for mapping tell constraints to ask constraints. For example, the mapping for $z = 2^y$ for a finite domain solver can be defined as

```
:- nonneg(Y) asks exists [Z] Z = 2^Y wakes [lbc(Y)].
nonneg(Y) :- lb(Y) >= 0.
```

To apply either of the simplifications above we also require information about total and partial functions. The HAL compiler already receives this information from the solver in terms of mode declarations. Example mode declarations that show the totality of + and the partialness of ^ are:

```
:- mode in + in ---> out is det.
:- mode in ^ in ---> out is semidet.
```

Partial functions are common in Herbrand constraints. Consider the constraint $x = f(y_1, \ldots, y_n)$, where f is a Herbrand constructor. This constraint defines, among others, a partial (deconstruct) function f_i^{-1} from x to each $y_i, 1 \leq i \leq n$. For this reason the compiler produces new ask tests bound_f(X) for each Herbrand constructor f, which check whether X is bound to the function f. Herbrand term deconstructions are then compiled as if the asks declaration

```
:- bound_f(X) asks exists [Y1,..,Yn] X = f(Y1,..,Yn) wakes [bound(X)]
```

appeared in the program. Note that in order to use this form of the ask constraint we may need to introduce further existential variables.

Example 14. Consider the compilation of the fragment (exists [Y] X = [Y|Z] ==> p(X,Z)). Although neither transformation seems directly applicable we can replace $\exists Y.X = [Y|Z]$ by the equivalent $\exists Y \exists V.X = [Y|V] \wedge V = Z$ and then use the partial function compilation to obtain

```
'bound_[|]'(X) ==> (X = [Y|V], (V = Z ==> p(X,Z)))
```
   ⊡

6   Compiling Equality

The general compilation scheme presented in previous sections assumes the existence of a simple mapping between an ask-test, and a set of solver events which indicate the answer to the ask-test may have changed. However, this is not always true, specially when dealing with structures that mix variables of different solvers. Consider testing the equality of lists of finite domain integers. To do so requires consulting both the Herbrand `list` solver and the `fdint` solver.

This problem is exacerbated by the fact that HAL supports polymorphic types, where some part of the type may only be known at run-time. Currently, the only solvers in HAL which include other solver types are Herbrand solvers and, thus, we will focus on them. However, the same issues arise if we wish to build sequence, multiset or set solvers over parametric types.

The problem of multiple types already arises when defining the ask-test version of equality (`==/2`). We can solve this problem in HAL by using type classes, i.e., by defining a type class for the `==/2` method and letting the compiler generate instances for this method for each Herbrand type.

Example 15. The code generated by the HAL compiler for the implementation of method `==/2` in the case of the `list(T)` type is as follows:

```
X == Y :- ( (var(X) ; var(Y)) -> X === Y
        ; X = [], Y = []     -> true
        ; X = [X1|X2], Y = [Y1|Y2], X1 == Y1, X2 == Y2 ).
```

where `===/2` succeeds if its arguments are (unbound) identical variables.   ⊡

Extending the above ask-test to an ask constraint has two problems. First the only solver events currently supported by a Herbrand solver are: `bound(X)`, which occurs if X is bound to a non-variable term; and `touched(X)`, which occurs if the variable X is bound or unified with another variable (which also has events of interest). The reason why these are the only events supported is because they are the only ones that are independent of the type of the subterms of X. Thus, the asks declaration can only be defined as:

```
:- X == Y asks X = Y wakes [touched(X),touched(Y)]
```

which results in a very weak behaviour since it only notices changes at the topmost level of X and Y. For example, the goal `?- neq(X,Y), X = f(U), Y = f(V), U = V.` will not fail since even though X and Y are in the end identical, the unification of U and V does not create a solver event to retest the equality.

It is possible, though complex, to use overloading to introduce a new overloaded solver event `changed(X)` which occurs if any subterm of X is changed in some way (including unification with a variable). We could then provide an asks declaration

```
:- X == Y asks X = Y wakes [changed(X),changed(Y)]
```

which does not suffer from the above problem. However, there is a second problem which affects both solutions: repeatedly calling `==/2` from the top of the term is inefficient for large terms. A more efficient solution is to only partially retest.

For this we introduce a new ask-test for Herbrand terms, and show how it can be used to implement an efficient ask-test version of `==/2`. The ask-test is `samefunctor(X,Y)` which holds if X and Y have the same top-level functor, and can be implemented in Prolog as follows:

```
samefunctor(X,Y) :- (var(X), X == Y -> true ;
                     nonvar(X), nonvar(Y), functor(X,F,A), functor(Y,F,A)).
```

The advantage of this simple ask-test is that it only needs to be re-tested when `touched(X)` or `bound(X)`, i.e., its asks declaration can be defined as :

```
:- samefunctor(X,Y) asks samefunctor(X,Y) wakes [touched(X),bound(Y)].
```

indicating that we need to recheck the ask-test if X is bound to another variable (which fires the `touched(X)` event), since it could have been bound to Y[2], and if X or Y is bound (the `touched(X)` event will fire if X is bound). Note that the ask-test has no corresponding tell version.

Let us now see how an efficient ask-test version for `==/2` can be written using `samefunctor`. Suppose the type of the Herbrand terms is $g(t_1, \ldots, t_n)$ where $t_1, \ldots t_n$ are types, and the type constructor g/n has $f_1/m_1, \ldots, f_k/m_k$ functor/arities. Then, the following implements (a high level view of) predicate '`delay_==_g_n`' which waits until two terms X and Y of type $g(t_1, \ldots, t_n)$ are equal to execute `Goal`. (`Id @ AskConstruct`) indicates the `Id` that should be given to the `delay` predicate resulting from each branch in `AskConstruct`.

```
'delay_==_g_n'(X,Y,GId,Goal) :-
    (alive(GId) -> get_id(LId), register(LId,GId),
       LId @ ( samefunctor(X,Y) ==>
          ( var(X) -> kill(GId), call(Goal)
          ; X = f₁(X₁,...,Xₘ₁), Y = f₁(Y₁,...,Yₘ₁),
             GId @ ( X₁ = Y₁, ..., Xₘ₁ = Yₘ₁ ==> kill(GId), call(Goal))
          ; ...
          ; X = fₖ(X₁,...,Xₘₖ), Y = fₖ(Y₁,...,Yₘₖ),
             GId @ ( X₁ = Y₁, ..., Xₘₖ = Yₘₖ ==> kill(GId), call(Goal))
    )) ; true ).
```

The code works as follows. If `GId` is alive, first a new local delay id `LId` is created for delay on `samefunctor`, and this is registered with `GId`. The whole body delays on the `samefunctor` ask constraint. When that holds, we test whether the variables are identical (true if either is a variable) and, if so, fire the goal. Otherwise, the two functors must be the same. Thus, we find the appropriate case and then delay on the conjunction of equality of the arguments. Here we can use the global delay identifier `GId` as the delay id for the ask formulae appearing for the arguments since at most one will be set up. The compilation of these conjunctions will, of course, introduce new local identifiers. When and if the arguments become equal, `Goal` will be called. Note that if the constructor f_i/m_i has arity zero (i.e. $m_i = 0$), then there are no arguments to delay until equal, and the goal will be immediately called.

The outermost ask construct code contains no explicit delay on equality, hence it can be compiled as described in the previous sections. The inner ask constructs do contain equality, and will be recursively handled in the same way.

---

[2] We do not need to delay on `touched(Y)`, since if `touched(Y)` occurs, causing X and Y to become identical variables then `touched(X)` must have also occurred.

Example 16. The generated code for the type list(T) is:

```
'delay_==_list_1'(X,Y,GId,Goal) :-
  (alive(Id) -> get_id(LId), register(LId,GId),
                delay_samefunctor(X,Y,LId,'delay_==_list_1_b'(X,Y,GId,Goal)
  ;             true).
'delay_==_list_1_b'(X,Y,GId,Goal) :-
  ( var(X) -> kill(GId), call(Goal)
  ;           X = [], Y = [], kill(GId), call(Goal)
  ;           X = [X1|X2], Y = [Y1|Y2], get_id(LId), register(LId,GId),
              'delay_=='(X1,X2,LId,'delay_=='(X2,Y2,GId,Goal))    ).     ⊡
```

In order for the solution to work for polymorphic types, the 'delay_==' predicate is defined as a method for a corresponding type class. HAL automatically generates the predicate 'delay_==_g_n' for every Herbrand type constructor g/n that supports delay and creates an appropriate instance. For non-Herbrand solver types, the instance must be created by the solver writer. Normal overloading resolution ensures that at runtime the appropriate method is called.

This solution kills two birds with one stone. Firstly, it resolves the problems of delaying on equality by generating specialized predicates for each type. Secondly, because the predicate 'delay_==' is overloaded, delay on equality is now polymorphic. Thus, it is possible to implement a truly polymorphic version of, for example, the neq/2 constraint. We can similarly implement a polymorphic ask constraint for disequality.

7   Experimental Results

The purpose of our experimental evaluation is to show that compiling ask constraints is practical, and to compare performance with hand-implemented dynamic scheduling where applicable. In order to do so, a simple prototype ask constraint compiler has been built into HAL. It does not yet handle existential quantifiers automatically. In the future we plan to extend the compiler to do this and also optimize the compilation where possible. All timings are the average over 10 runs on a Dual Pentium II 400MHz with 648M of RAM running under Linux RedHat 9 with kernel version 2.4.20 and are given in milliseconds.

The first experiment compares three versions of a Boolean solver written by extending a Herbrand constraint solver. The first, *hand*, is implemented using low-level dynamic scheduling (no compilation required). This is included as the ideal "target" for high-level compiled versions. The second, *equals*, implements the Boolean solver by delaying on equality, much like the **either** constraint in Example 2. Here, *equals* treats $X = t$ as a partial function and delays on the specialised **bound_t(X)**. Finally, *nonvar* implements the Boolean solver by delaying on the **nonvar(X)** ask-test (which holds if X is bound). Delaying on **nonvar** requires less delayed goals, since **nonvar(X)** subsumes both X=t and X=f. We believe an optimizing ask constraint compiler could translate *equals* to *nonvar* automatically.

Table 1(a) compares the execution times in milliseconds of the Boolean solvers on a test suite (details explained in [2]). Most of the overhead of *nonvar* compared to *hand* is due to the *nonvar* code retesting the **nonvar** ask-test

Table 1. Testing ask constraints: (a) Boolean benchmarks, (b) Sequence benchmarks

(a)

Prog	hand	equals	nonvar
pigeon(8,7)	524	988	618
pigeon(24,24)	157	338	167
schur(13)	7	11	5
schur(14)	57	87	65
queens(18)	4652	9333	5313
mycie(4)	1055	1988	1218
fulladder(5)	260	410	320
Geom. mean	237	179%	107%

(b)

Prog	poly	mono
neq(10000)	575	413
neq(20000)	1146	848
neq(40000)	2312	1676
neq(80000)	4592	3362
square(4)	414	219
square(5)	5563	2789
square(6)	2476	1213
square(7)	358	175
square(8)	12816	6168
triples(3)	88	70
triples(4)	535	436
triples(5)	4200	3526
Geom. mean	1349	64%

(which always holds if the retest predicate is woken up). The *equals* version adds overhead with respect to *nonvar* by using a greater number of (more specialised) ask constraints.

Our second experiment, shown in Table 1(b)), compares two versions of a sequence (Herbrand lists of finite domain integers) solver built using both a Herbrand solver for lists, and a finite domain (bounds propagation) solver. The resulting sequence solver provides three ask constraints over "complex" structures: length(Xs,L) (see Example 4), append(Xs,Ys,Zs) which constrains Zs to be the result of appending Xs and Ys (concatenation constraint), and neq(Xs,Ys) (see Example 5). The first benchmark neq(n) calls a single neq(Xs,Ys) constraint, then iteratively binds Xs and Ys to a list of length n (which eventually leads to failure). The second benchmark square(n) tries to find a $n \times n$ square of 1s and 0s such that no row/column/diagonal (in both directions) are equal. This is solved by first building the sequences for each row, column, diagonal and the reverse, then making each not equal to each other via the neq constraint, and then labeling. Here, square(4) has no solution, but square(5-8) do. The third benchmark triples(n) tries to find n triples of sequences of 1s and 0s such that (1) the length of each sequence is $\leq n$ (2) each sequence is not equal to any other sequence (from any triple); and (3) the concatenation for all triples must be equal. This example makes use of all three constraints, length, append and neq. All of triples(3-5) have solutions.

We use two versions of the sequence constraints. The first *poly* uses the polymorphic delay on equality for the neq constraints. The second, *mono* is a hand-edited version of *poly* where (1) all polymorphism has been specialised; and (2) a more efficient representation of the global id type is used. We can only use this more efficient global id type if we know in advance the types of the local ids, something not possible when using polymorphism. We see that, overall, *mono* is 36% faster than the more naïve *poly*.

Another interesting result is the linear behaviour of the neq(n) benchmarks with respect to n. As each list becomes more instantiated, we do not retest for equality over the entire list, rather we only retest the parts that have changed. If we retested the entire list, then we would expect quadratic behaviour.

8   Related Work and Conclusions

Ask constraints are closely related to dynamic scheduling, CHRs, reification and concurrent constraint programming.

The closest relation to this work is the when declarations of SICStus Prolog that allow a goal to delay until a test succeeds. These tests are similar to ask formulae (omitting existential quantification) over the primitive ask constraints nonvar(X), ground(X) and ?=(X,Y). The last succeeds when X and Y are either known to be equal or not equal. The SICStus compiler appears to do much the same translation of conjunctions and disjunctions as defined in Section 4, but does not allow (explicit) existential quantification. The ?=(X,Y) constraint includes the functionality of the ask equals defined in Section 6, but the SICStus implementation only deals with the a single constraint solver (Herbrand). The second difference is that the SICStus implementation does not break down testing of equality so that previous equal parts need not be retested.

CHRs are also closely related to this work, since an ask constraint is analogous to the guard of a CHR rule. We can consider the CHR rule $(H \texttt{<=>} G \,|\, B)$ as equivalent to $(H \texttt{<=>} (G \texttt{==>} B))$ using ask constraints. This translation is generally inefficient, as delayed goals will be set up for every possible matching of H against the CHR store, and it is incompatible with some CHR optimisations, e.g. join ordering [3] and wakeup specialisation [2]. Instead, the guards for all rules are considered as a whole, and delayed goals are set up which may check multiple rules if a solver event occurs (see [2] for more details). Another difference is that non-Herbrand existential variables are not yet handled by any CHR implementation we are aware of, this remains future work.

Reified constraints allow similar functionality to ask constraints, particularly when combined with delaying an arbitrary goal until a Boolean variable is true. Both SICStus Prolog and ECLiPSe support reification of various constraints in their finite domain (and finite set) solvers, including conjunction, disjunction and implication. Again they do not handle explicit existential quantification.

One of the advantages of ask constraints over reification is they allow us to implement reified complex constraints which cannot be implemented using reification alone due to the interaction with existential quantifiers, as in Example 3. In that sense the ask construct is strictly more expressive than reification alone.

In both SICStus and ECLiPSe existential variables arising through normalization appear to be treated using the total function simplification described in Section 5, this can lead to erroneous behaviour. For example, in ECLiPSe the goal ic:(Y < 0), ic:(B =:= (X + sqrt(Y) >= 2)) analogous to Example 13 incorrectly fails rather than set B = 0.

Guarded Horn Clauses [8] allows the programming of behaviour equivalent to ask formula for Herbrand constraints including conjunction, disjunction, and implicit existential quantifiers. The cc(FD) [9] language includes a blocking implication similar to ask constraints without commit, but only allows single constraints on the left hand side. However, one could use the cardinality constraint to mimic conjunction and disjunction. Both approaches treat a single solver, and do not handle explicit existential quantifiers.

Oz supports complex ask formula using constraint combinators [7]. Here ask constraints are executed in a separate constraint store which is checked for entailment by the original constraint store. This is a powerful approach which can handle examples that our approach cannot. However, its handling of existential variables is weaker than ours. For instance, the Oz equivalent to Example 13 will not set B to 1 when $X \geq 0$ and $Y \geq 1$. It would be interesting to extend Oz to handle existential variables better.

A constraint programming language supporting multiple solvers should support compilation of complex ask constraints. In this paper we have defined a solver-independent approach to this compilation, implemented it in HAL, and shown the resulting approach is practical and expressive. There is a significant amount of improvement that can be made to the naïve compilation strategy defined here, by transformations such as collecting calls for the same event. In the future we plan to investigate several optimizations.

References

1. M. García de la Banda, B. Demoen, K. Marriott, and P.J. Stuckey. To the gates of HAL: a HAL tutorial. In *Proceedings of the Sixth International Symposium on Functional and Logic Programming*, number 2441 in LNCS, pages 47–66. Springer-Verlag, 2002.
2. G.J. Duck, P.J. Stuckey, M. García de la Banda, and C. Holzbaur. Extending arbitrary solvers with constraint handling rules. In D. Miller, editor, *Proceedings of the Fifth ACM SIGPLAN International Conference on Principles and Practice of Declarative Programming*, pages 79–90. ACM Press, 2003.
3. C. Holzbaur, P.J. Stuckey, M. García de la Banda, and D. Jeffery. Optimizing compilation of constraint handling rules. In P. Codognet, editor, *Logic Programming: Proceedings of the 17th International Conference*, LNCS, pages 74–89. Springer-Verlag, 2001.
4. J. Jaffar and J.-L. Lassez. Constraint logic programming. In *Proc. Fourteenth ACM Symp. Principles of Programming Languages*, pages 111–119. ACM Press, 1987.
5. J. Jaffar, M. Maher, K. Marriott, and P.J. Stuckey. The semantics of constraint logic programs. *Journal of Logic Programming*, 37(1–3):1–46, 1998.
6. V. Saraswat. *Concurrent Constraint Programming Languages*. PhD thesis, Carnegie-Mellon University, 1989.
7. C. Schulte. Programming deep concurrent constraint combinators. In *Practical Aspects of Declarative Languages (PADL 2000)*, volume 1753 of *LNCS*, pages 215–229. Springer, 2000.
8. K. Ueda. Guarded horn clauses. In E. Shapiro, editor, *Concurrent Prolog: Collected Papers*, pages 140–156. MIT Press, 1987.
9. P. Van Hentenryck, V. Saraswat, and Y. Deville. Design, implementation, and evaluation of the constraint language cc(FD). *Journal of Logic Programming*, 37(1–3):139–164, 1998.

Constraint Handling Rules
and Tabled Execution

Tom Schrijvers[1],[*] and David S. Warren[2]

[1] Dept. of Computer Science, K.U.Leuven, Belgium
[2] Dept. of Computer Science, State University of New York at Stony Brook, USA

Abstract. Both Constraint Handling Rules (CHR) and tabling - as implemented in XSB - are powerful enhancements of Prolog systems, based on fix point computation. Until now they have only been implemented in separate systems. This paper presents the work involved in porting a CHR system to XSB and in particular the technical issues related to the integration of CHR with tabled resolution. These issues include call abstraction, answer projection, entailment checking, answer combination and tabled constraint store representations. Different optimizations related to tabling constraints are evaluated empirically. The integration requires no changes to the tabling engine. We also show that the performance of CHR programs without tabling is not affected. Now, with the combined power of CHR and tabling, it is possible to easily introduce constraint solvers in applications using tabling, or to use tabling in constraint solvers.

1 Introduction

XSB (see [19]) is a standard Prolog system extended with tabled resolution. Tabled resolution is useful for recursive query computation, allowing programs to terminate in many cases where Prolog does not.

Parsing, program analysis, model checking, data mining, diagnosis and many more applications benefit from tabled resolution. We refer the reader to [1] for a coverage of XSB's SLG execution strategy.

Constraint Handling Rules, or CHR for short, are a high level rule-based language (see [10]). As opposed to the top-down execution of XSB, it performs a bottom-up fixpoint computation. While CHR has currently many applications, it has been designed for writing constraint solvers in particular. Indeed, its compact and declarative syntax is excellent for prototyping succinct constraint solvers. Although its performance is not on par with constraint solvers written in lower-level languages, its flexibility and ease of use do favor a wider use. We refer the reader to [11] for an overview of CHR.

CHR is not a self-contained but an embedded language. Although versions of CHR for Haskell and Java do exist, Prolog is its original and natural host. Just as the traditional combination of Constraint and Logic Programming [14], the combination of CHR with Logic Programming seems to be the most powerful and expressive combination.

---

[*] Research Assistant of the Fund for Scientific Research - Flanders (Belgium) (F.W.O. - Vlaanderen)

B. Demoen and V. Lifschitz (Eds.): ICLP 2004, LNCS 3132, pp. 120–136, 2004.
© Springer-Verlag Berlin Heidelberg 2004

However, by integrating CHR with not just any standard Prolog system, but XSB with tabled resolution, we get an even more powerful and expressive system. This system integrates both the bottom-up and top-down fixpoint computations, the favorable termination properties of XSB and the constraint programming of CHR. This combined power enables programmers to easily write highly declarative programs that are easier to maintain and extend.

This proposed integration implies quite a number of implementation challenges that have to be dealt with. Firstly, a CHR system for non-tabled use in XSB is needed, as it does not come with one already. In Section 2 we explain how an existing CHR system was ported to XSB with minimal changes to that CHR system. The attributed variables implementation in XSB was extended to full functionality in the process. Benchmarks show that no performance overhead is incurred for non-tabled use and that it is even on par with the commercial SICStus Prolog system.

Secondly, the CHR system requires integration with tabled execution. In Section 3 we present the different interaction issues. We propose a solution to the conflict of the global CHR store with the required referential transparency of tabled predicates. Also two representations of tabled constraints are analyzed and a mechanism for answer constraint projection is presented. In addition, we study issues regarding answer entailment checking and advanced techniques for aggregate-like answer combination. The performance impact of tabling and several of the mentioned concepts are measured on a small constraint program. Throughout, we propose a declaration-based approach for enabling particular mechanisms that, in the spirit of both CHR and XSB, preserves the ease of use.

Finally, we conclude this paper in Section 4 and discuss related and possible future work.

2   The CHR System

Initially the CHR system described in this paper was written for the hProlog system. hProlog is based on dProlog (see [8]) and intended as an alternative backend to HAL (see [7]) next to the current Mercury backend. The initial intent of the implementation of a CHR system in hProlog was to validate the underlying implementation of dynamic attributes (see [6]).

The hProlog CHR system consists of a preprocessor and a runtime system:

- The preprocessor compiles embedded CHR rules in Prolog program files into Prolog code. The compiled form of CHR rules is very close to that of the CHR system by Christian Holzbaur, which is used in SICStus [13] and YAP [3]. The preprocessor allows for experimentation with optimized compilation of CHR rules, both through static inference and programmer declarations.
- The runtime system is nearly identical to that of Christian Holzbaur: suspended constraints are stored in a global constraint store. Variables in suspended constraints have attributes on them that function as indexes into this global store. Binding of these attributed variables causes the suspended constraints on them to trigger again.

Little difficulty was experienced while porting the preprocessor and runtime system from hProlog to XSB. The main problem turned out to be XSB's overly primitive interface for attributed variables: it did not support attributes in different modules. Moreover, the actual binding of attributed variables was not performed during the unification, but it was left up to the programmer of the interrupt handler. This causes unintuitive and unwanted behavior in several cases: while the binding is delayed from unification to interrupt handling, other code can be executed in between that relies on variables being bound, e.g. arithmetic. Due to these problems of the current XSB attributed variables, it was deemed acceptable to model the attributed variables interface and behavior more closely to that of hProlog. This facilitated the porting of the CHR system considerably.

2.1 Performance Evaluation

We have not adapted the compilation scheme of the CHR preprocessor in any way to accommodate the integration of CHR with tabling (see Section 3). We have only given in to a few minor changes for performance reasons, such as replacing calls to `once(G)` with `(G -> true)` as XSB does not inline the former.

Hence we show that the performance of CHR without tabling is not compromised in XSB. To do so we compare the results of eight benchmarks [17] in XSB with those in hProlog, the origin of the CHR preprocessor, and SICStus, the origin of the runtime system and one of the first systems to feature CHR.

The following causes for performance differences are to be expected:

- Firstly, we expect the outcome to be most heavily influenced by the relative performance difference on Prolog code as the CHR rules are compiled to Prolog: we have observed that plain Prolog in SICStus is on average 1.39 times faster than in XSB and hProlog is 1.85 times faster than XSB.
- Secondly, the results may be influenced by the slightly more powerful optimizations of the CHR preprocessor in hProlog and XSB. To eliminate these effects we have disabled all advanced optimizations not performed by the SICStus CHR compiler. In addition, the checking of guard bindings has been disabled in both systems. This does not affect the benchmarks, since no binding or instantiation errors occur in the guards. This increases the fairness of comparison since hProlog's analysis of redundant checks is more powerful and it does not intercept instantiation errors.
- Thirdly, the implementation and representation of attributed variables differs between the three systems. The global constraint store of CHR is represented as an attributed variable and it may undergo updates each time a new constraint is imposed or a constraint variable gets bound. Hence, the complexity and efficiency of accessing and updating attributed variables easily dominates the overall performance of a CHR program if care is not taken. Especially the length of reference chains has to be kept short, as otherwise accessing the cost of dereferencing the global store may easily grow out of bounds.

In hProlog much care has been taken in choosing a representation and corresponding implementation of the necessary operations, to take these considerations into account. SICStus and XSB have different low-level representations that do not allow to limit the cost of dereferencing equally well.

Table 1 shows the results for the benchmarks. All measurements have been made on an Intel Pentium 4 2.00 GHz with 512 MB of RAM. Timings are in milliseconds. The Prolog systems used are hProlog 2.4, SICStus 3.11.0 and our extension of XSB 2.6.

From the results we learn that hProlog is the fastest for CHR, as was the case for plain Prolog. Both SICStus and XSB are much slower than hProlog for CHR than for plain Prolog. However, on average XSB is SICStus's equal.

The huge difference between hProlog and the other two systems cannot simply be explained by the difference in runtimes of plain Prolog. The representation of attributed variables and the implementation of operations on them, seems to play a very important role in most of the benchmarks. The more efficient implementation of hProlog and XSB's CHR runtime and generated code mostly explains the smaller gap between SICStus and XSB.

All in all, XSB is not far behind SICStus in performance of CHR programs. This is quite remarkable considering that SICStus is clearly faster for plain Prolog programs. Future optimizations of the XSB CHR compiler may improve XSB's CHR performance even further. However, it is certainly worthwhile to consider changing the low-level implementation of attributed variables in XSB to follow more closely that of hProlog. Such a change would be orthogonal to the CHR system and other applications of attributed variables would benefit as well.

Table 1. Runtime performance of 8 CHR benchmarks in hProlog, SICStus and XSB.

Benchmark	hProlog		SICStus		XSB	
	runtime	relative	runtime	relative	runtime	relative
bool	870	100.0%	2,010	231.0%	1,729	198.7%
fib	1,240	100.0%	1,620	130.6%	2,509	202.3%
fibonacci	1,510	100.0%	4,260	282.1%	3,500	231.8%
leq	1,020	100.0%	1,250	122.5%	1,889	185.2%
primes	960	100.0%	1,870	194.8%	2,609	271.8%
ta	1,190	100.0%	2,240	188.2%	2,378	199.8%
wfs	850	100.0%	1,620	190.6%	2,039	239.9%
zebra	1,500	100.0%	7,050	470.0%	3,578	238.5%
average	-	100.0%	-	226.2%	-	221.0%

3   CHR and Tabled Execution

The main challenge of introducing CHR in XSB is integrating the forward chaining fixpoint computation of the CHR system with the backward chaining fixpoint computation of tabled resolution.

A similar integration problem has been solved in [4], which describes a framework for constraint solvers written with attributed variables for XSB. The name Tabled Constraint Logic Programming (TCLP) is coined in that publication.

The main difference for the programmer between CHR and attributed variables for developing constraint solvers, i.e. the fact that CHR is a much higher level language, should be carried over to the tabled context. Hence tabled CHR should be a more convenient paradigm for programming constraint solvers in than TCLP with attributed variables.

Indeed, the internals that are presented in the following can easily be hidden from the user. All the user then needs to supply is the following declaration:

```
:- table_chr f(_,_) with Options.
```

meaning that the predicate f/2 should be tabled and it involves CHR constraints. A list of additional options may be provided. The meaning of this declaration and the possible options are explained in the rest of this section.

In [4] the general framework specifies three operations to control the tabling of constraints: call abstraction, entailment checking of answers and answer projection. It is left up to the constraint solver programmer to implement these operations with respect to his solver implementation.

In the following we formulate these operations in terms of CHR. The operations are covered in significant detail as the actual CHR implementation and the representation of the global CHR constraint store are taken into account. Problems that have to be solved time and again for attributed variable constraint solvers are solved once and for all for CHR constraint solvers. Hence integrating a particular CHR constraint solver requires much less knowledge of implementation intricacies and decisions can be made on a higher level.

The different steps in handling a call to a tabled predicate are depicted in Figure 1. The different steps are explained in the rest of this section. Section 3.1 covers the representation of CHR constraint stores in tables. Next Section 3.2 explains how a call to a tabled predicate is abstracted and how the answer to the abstracted call is related to the original call. Section 3.3 proposes a high-level way of specifying projection and Section 3.4 discusses entailment. Finally, Section 3.5 finishes with an evaluation of tabling with several optimizations on a small shipment problem.

3.1   Tabled Store Representation

As constraints can be part of a call or an answer of a tabled predicate, some representation for them in call and answer tables is needed. In general, this representation should allow comparing the constraints in a call with all call patterns in the call table to select either a variant (under variant based tabling) or the most specific generalization (under subsumption based tabling). Furthermore, it should be possible to convert from the ordinary representation of the constraints and back, for insertion into the call table and retrieval from the answer table.

In the following we investigate two possible representations and discuss the complexity of variant checking.

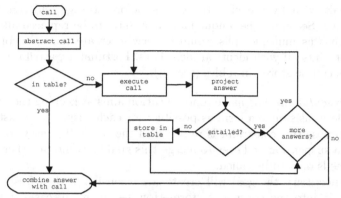

Fig. 1. Flowchart.

Two tabled CHR store representations. Before considering constraint store representations for tables, it is necessary to know a little about the ordinary representation of the CHR constraint store. The global CHR constraint store is an updatable term, containing suspended constraints grouped by functor. Each suspended constraint is represented as a suspension term, including the following information:

- the unique ID for sorting and equality testing
- the goal to execute when triggered, this goal contains the suspension itself as an argument, hence creating a cyclic term.
- the propagation history containing for each propagation rule the tuple of identifiers of other constraints that this constraint has interacted with

Furthermore, variables involved in the suspended constraints behave as indexes into the global store: they have the suspensions stored in them as attributes.

One piece of information that is not maintained during the normal CHR execution is the order in which constraints have been called. We will not do so for the sake of tabling either as this would overly complicate matters. Hence, we need to restrict ourselves to confluent[1] programs to avoid unpredictable behavior.

Two different tabled CHR store representations have been explored with: the *suspension* representation and the *naive* representation. A discussion of their respective merits and weaknesses as well as an evaluation follow.

Suspension representation. Here we aim to keep the tabled representation as close as possible to the ordinary representation. The idea here is to maintain the propagation history of the tabled constraints. In that way no unnecessary re-firing of propagation rules will occur after the constraints have been retrieved from the table.

However, it is not possible to just store the ordinary constraint suspensions in the table as they are. Firstly, the tables do not deal with cyclic terms. This

---

[1] A set of rules is confluent if the order in which the constraints are imposed does not matter for the final state of the constraint store.

can be dealt with by breaking the cycles before storage and resetting them after fetching. Secondly, the unique identifiers have to be replaced after fetching by fresh ones as multiple calls would otherwise create multiple copies of the same constraints all with identical identifiers. Fortunately, attributed variables themselves can be stored in tables (see [5]).

Naive representation. The naive representation aims at keeping the information in the table in as simple a form as possible: for each suspended constraint only the goal to pose this constraint is retained in the table. It is easy to create this goal from a suspension and easy to merge this goal back into another constraint store: it needs only to be called.

When necessary the goal will create a suspension with a fresh unique ID and insert it into the constraint store. However in many cases it may prove unnecessary to do so because of some simplification through interaction with constraints in the calling environment.

The only information that is lost in this representation is the propagation history. This may lead to multiple propagations for the same combination of head constraints. For this to be sound, a further restriction on the CHR rules is required: they should behave according to set semantics, i.e. the presence of multiple identical constraints should not lead to different answers modulo identical constraints.

Evaluation of both representations. To measure the relative performance of the two presented representations, consider the following two programs:

```
 ——————— prop ———————
:- constraints a/1.
  a(0) <=> true.
  a(N) ==> N > 0
      | M is N - 1, a(M).

  p(N) :- a(N).
```

```
 ——————— simp ———————
:- constraints a/1, b/1.
  b(0) <=> true.
  b(N) <=> N > 0
      | a(N), M is N - 1, b(M).

  p(N) :- b(N).
```

For both programs the predicate p(N) puts the constraints a(1)...a(N) in the constraint store. The prop program uses a propagation rule to achieve this while the simp program uses an auxiliary constraint b/1. The non-tabled version of the query p(N) or a(N) has time complexity $\mathcal{O}(N)$ for both the simp and the prop program.

The two possible representations for the answer constraint store can be specified in the tabling declaration as follows:

> :- table_chr p(_) with [representation(suspension)].

and

> :- table_chr p(_) with [representation(naive)].

Table 2 gives the results for the tabled query p(400) : runtime in milliseconds and space usage of the tables in bytes. For both programs the answer table contains the constraint store with the 400 a/1 constraints.

Table 2. Evaluation of the two tabled store representations.

program	representation(suspension)		representation(naive)	
	runtime	space	runtime	space
prop	150	2,153,100	1,739	270,700
simp	109	1,829,100	89	270,700

Most of the space overhead is due to the difference in representation: a suspension contains more information than a simple call. However, the difference is more or less a constant factor. The only part of a suspension in general that can have a size greater than $\mathcal{O}(1)$ is the propagation history, that for prop is limited to remembering that the propagation rule has been used. For the simp program the propagation history is always empty.

The runtime of the prop version with the suspension representation is considerably better than that of the version with the naive representation. In fact, there is a complexity difference. When the answer is retrieved from the table for the suspension representation, the propagation history prevents re-propagation. Hence answer retrieval is $\mathcal{O}(N)$. For the naive representation on the other hand, every constraint a(I) from the answer will start propagating and the complexity of answer retrieval becomes $\mathcal{O}(N^2)$.

On the other hand, for simp propagation history plays no role. The runtime overhead is mostly due to the additional overhead of the pre- and post-processing of the suspension representation as opposed to the simpler form of the naive representation.

Variant checking. The need to check whether two constraint stores are variants of each other may arise at two occasions:

- With no or only partial call abstraction (see Section 3.2) a constraint store is part of the call to the tabled predicate. The tabling system then needs to check whether a previous call with a variant of that constraint store appears in a table. If that is the case, the answer to the previous call can be reused.
- A limited form of entailment checking (see Section 3.4) is to check whether a new answer constraint store is a variant of any previous answer constraint store for the same call. In that case the new answer can be discarded.

We can consider this equality checking with the previously presented naive tabled representation of constraints. In that representation the tabled constraints are kept as a list of goals that impose the constraints. Any permutation of this list represents the same constraint store. If two constraint stores are identical modulo variable renaming, then they are variants.

In general, variant checking of constraint stores has exponential complexity. A naive algorithm would be to consider all permutations of one constraint store. If any one of the permutations equals the other constraint store, both are identical. With heuristics this algorithm could be improved and for particular constraints or even applications algorithms with a better complexity may exist. However further exploration falls outside of the scope of this paper. The problem can be ignored altogether, with possible duplication in tables as a consequence, or only partially tackled, e.g. by simple sorting and pattern matching.

3.2   Call Abstraction

Call abstraction replaces the called goal with a call to a more general goal followed by an operation that ensures that only the answer substitutions applicable to the particular call are retained. At the level of plain Prolog, abstraction means not passing certain bindings in to the call. E.g. p(q,A) can be abstracted to p(Q,A). This goal has then to be followed by Q = q to ensure that only the appropriate bindings for A are retained.

In XSB call abstraction is a means to control the number of tables. When a predicate is called with many different instantiation patterns, a table is generated for each such call instantiation pattern. Thus it is possible that the information for the same fully instantiated call is present many times in tables for different call instantiation patterns. However, this duplication in the tables can be avoided by using call abstraction to restrict to a small set of call instantiation patterns.

For constraint logic programming, call abstraction can be extended from bindings to constraints: abstraction means removing some of the constraints on the arguments. Consider for example the call p(Q,A) with constraint Q leq N on Q. This call can be abstracted to p(Q',A), followed by Q'=Q to reintroduce the constraint.

Abstraction is especially of value for those constraint solvers where the number of constraints on a variable can be much larger than the number of different bindings for that variable. Consider for example a finite domain constraint solver with constraint domain/2, where the first argument is a variable and the second argument the set of its possible values. If the variable can be bound to at most n values it can take as many as 2^n different domain/2 constraints, one for each subset of values. Thus many different tables would be needed to cover every possible call pattern.

Varying degrees of abstraction are possible and may depend on the particular constraint system or application. Full constraint abstraction, i.e. the removal of all constraints from the call, is generally more suitable for CHR for the following reasons:

- CHR rules do not require constraints to be on variables. They can be on ground terms or atoms as well. It is not straightforward to define abstraction for ground terms as these are not necessarily passed in as arguments but can just as well be created inside the call. Hence there is no explicit link with the call environment, while such a link is needed for call abstraction. As such, only no abstraction or full constraint abstraction seem suitable for CHR.
- Full constraint abstraction is preferable when the previously mentioned table blow-up is likely.
- As mentioned in the previous section, variant checking of constraint stores can have exponential complexity.

Moreover, it may be quite costly for certain constraint domains to sort out what constraints should be passed in to the call or abstracted away, involving transitive closure computations of reachability through constraints. Hence often full abstraction is cheaper than partial abstraction.

For CHR full abstraction requires the execution of the tabled predicate with an empty constraint store. If the call environment constraint store were used, interaction with new constraints would violate the assumption of full abstraction.

The code below shows how a predicate `p/1` that requires tabling:

```
:- table p/1.
p(X) :- ...
```

is transformed into two predicates, where the first one is called, takes care of the abstraction, calls the second predicate and afterwards combines the answer with the previously abstracted away constraints.

```
p(X) :-
        current_chr_store(CallStore)
        set_empty_chr_store,
        tabled_p(X1,AnswerStore),
        set_chr_store(CallStore),
        insert_answer_store(AnswerStore),
        X1 = X.

:- table tabled_p/2.
tabled_p(X,S_A) :- ...
```

The further implementation of `tabled_p` will be discussed in the next section. The given answer constraints are merged into the current global CHR constraint store by the predicate **insert_answer_store/1**. Given the naive representation discussed in the previous section, this boils down to calling a list of goals to impose the constraints.

The above transformation is not involved at all and can be easily automated, hiding the internals of the CHR-tabling integration from the user. All the user needs to supply is the arguments that are CHR constraint variables. We propose the following declaration:

```
:- table_chr f(_,chr) with Options.
```

meaning that the predicate `f/2` should be tabled, its first argument is an ordinary Prolog variable and its second argument is a CHR constraint variable of which all the constraints are abstracted away.

3.3   Answer Projection

Often one wants to project the answer constraint store on the non-local variables of the call. The usual motivation is that constraints on local variables are meaningless outside of the call. The constraint system should be complete so that no unsatisfiable constraints can be lost through projection.

For tabling there is an additional and perhaps even more pressing motivation for projection: a predicate with an infinite number of different answers may be turned into one with just a finite number of answers by throwing away the constraints on local and unreachable variables.

In some cases it may suffice to look at the constraints in the store separately and given a set of non-local variables to decide whether to keep the constraint or not. In those cases it may be convenient to exploit the operational semantics of CHR and implement projection as a `project/1` constraint with the list of variables on which to project as an argument. Simpagation rules can then be used to look at and decide what constraints to remove. A final simplification rule at the end can be used to remove the `project/1` constraint from the store.

The following example shows how to project away all leq/2 constraints that involve arguments not contained in a given set *Vars*:

```
project(Vars) \ leq(X,Y) <=> \+ (member(X,Vars),member(Y,Vars)) | true.
project(Vars)             <=> true.
```

Besides removal of constraints more sophisticated operations such as weakening are possible. E.g. consider a set solver with two constraints: `in/2` that requires an element to be in a set and `nonempty/1` that requires a set to be non-empty. The rules for projection could include the following weakening rule:

```
project(Vars) \ in(Elem,Set) <=>
             member(Set,Vars), \+ member(Elem,Vars) | nonempty(Set).
```

The predicate `tabled_p` would then look like:
```
                tabled_p(X,S_A) :- orig_p(X).
                             project([X]),
                             extract_store_representation(S_A).
```

Here the predicate `extract_store_representation/1` converts from the ordinary global store representation to the naive tabled store representation, discussed in Section 3.1.

This approach is of course not general in the sense that certain constraint domains may need more information than just the variables to project on, such as more intricate knowledge of the contents of the constraint store. In addition it relies on operational semantics and ordering of constraints. However, it is a rather compact and high level notation and as such it might be possible to infer conditions on its usage under which the technique is provably correct.

The `project/1` call could easily be added by the automatic transformation of the tabled predicate if the user supplies the `projection` option:

```
          :- table_chr p(chr) with [projection].
```

3.4   Entailment Checking and Other Answer Combinations

In some cases some of the answers computed for a tabled predicate are redundant and so need not be saved. Indeed there are cases in which for any tabled call only one answer needs to be maintained. Consider for example that the answer `p(a,X)` is already in the table of predicate p/2. Now a new answer, `p(a,b)` is found. This new answer is redundant as it is covered by the more general `p(a,X)` that is already in the table. Hence it is logically valid to not record this answer in the table, but to simply discard it. This does not affect the soundness or completeness of the procedure.

The idea of this answer subsumption technique is to reduce the number of answers in the table by replacing two (or more) answers by a single answer. Logically, the single new answer has to be equivalent to the disjunction of the replaced answers. For ordinary tabled Prolog, each answer H_i can be seen as a Herbrand constraint $Answer = Term$, e.g. $Answer = p(a, X)$. Now, for any two of these Herbrand constraints H_0 and H_1 the following two properties hold:

1. If the disjunction is equivalent to another constraint, that constraint is equivalent to one of the two constraints.

$$\exists H : H = H_0 \vee H_1 \iff \exists i \in \{0, 1\} : H = H_i$$

2. If the conjunction is equivalent to one of the two constraints, the disjunction is equivalent to the other.

$$\exists i \in \{0, 1\} : H_0 \wedge H_1 = H_j \iff H_0 \vee H_1 = H_{j-1}$$

These two properties suggest a possible strategy to compute the equivalent single answer of two answers: check whether the conjunction of two answers is equivalent to one of the two, then the other is the single equivalent answer. Otherwise, there is no single equivalent answer.

We can include CHR constraints in the same logically sound idea of answer subsumption. This path length computation will serve as an illustration:

```
dist(A,B,D) :- edge(A,B,D1), leq(D1,D).
dist(A,B,D) :- dist(A,C,D1), edge(C,B,D2), leq(D1 + D2, D).
```

Suppose appropriate rules for the `leq/2` constraint in the above program, where `leq` means less-than-or-equal. The semantics are that `dist(A,B,D)` holds if there is a path from A to B of length less than or equal to D. In other words, D is an upper bound on the length of a path from A to B.

If there is answer `dist(n1,n2,D) :- leq(d1, D)` already in the table and a new answer `dist(n1,n2,D) :- leq(d2, D)`, where `d1 =< d2`, is found, then this new answer is redundant. Hence it can be discarded. Again this does not affect the soundness, since logically the same answers are covered.

Operationally, the same strategy as proposed for ordinary Prolog can be used to reduce two answer constraint stores s_0 and s_1 to a single answer store s. At the end of the tabled predicate we merge a previous answer store s_0 with a new answer store s_1. After merging the store will be simplified and propagated to s by the available CHR rules. This combines the two answers into a new one. This mechanism can be used to check entailment of one of both answers by the other: if the combined answer store s is equal to one of the two, then that answer entails the other: $s_0 \wedge s_1 = s_i (i \in \{0, 1\}) \implies s_{1-i} = s_0 \vee s_1$.

The predicate `insert_answer_store/1`, mentioned in Section 3.2, can be used for the conjunction of two constraint stores. We assume that one store is the current global CHR constraint store.

When the above two answers of the `dist/3` predicate are merged, the following rule `leq/2` rule will simplify the constraint store to retain the more general answer:

```
leq(X,D1) \ leq(X,D2) <=> D1 =< D2 | true.
```

Note that the `dist/3` program would normally generate an infinite number of answers for a cyclic graph, logically correct but not terminating. However, if it is tabled with answer subsumption, it does terminate for non-negative weights. Not only does it terminate, it only produces one answer, namely `dist(n1,n2,D)` `:- leq(d,D)` with `d` the length of the shortest path. Indeed, the predicate only returns the optimal answer.

The above strategy is a sound approach to finding a single constraint store that is equivalent to two others. However, it is not complete: a single constraint store may be equivalent to the disjunction of two others, while it is not equivalent to one of the two. This is because, the first property for the Herbrand constraints does not hold for all constraint solvers, e.g. $leq(X,Y) \vee leq(Y,X) = true$. Nevertheless it is a rather convenient strategy, since it does not require any knowledge on the particularities of the used constraint solver. That makes it a good choice for the default strategy for CHR answer subsumption. Better strategies may be supplied for particular constraint solvers.

For some applications one can combine answers with answer generalization which does not preserve the logical correctness. An example in regular Prolog would be to have two answers `p(a,b)` and `p(a,c)` and to replace the two of them with one answer `p(a,X)`. This guarantees (for positive programs) that no answers are lost, but it may introduce extraneous answers. A similar technique is possible with constrained answers. While this approach is logically unsound, it may be acceptable for some applications if the overall correctness of the program is not affected. An example is the use of the least upper bound operator to combine answers in the tabled abstract interpretation setting of [2].

In summary, two additional options can be supplied to extend the automatic transformation:

- `canonical_form(PredName)` specifies the name of the predicate that should compute the (near) canonical form of the answer constraint store. This canonical form is used to check equivalence of two constraint stores.
- `answer_combination(PredName)` specifies the name of the predicate that should compute the combination of two answers, if they can be combined. The value `default` selects the above mentioned default strategy.

A subsumption-based optimization technique. The technique used in the `dist/3` program is to replace the computation of the exact distance of a path with the computation of an upper bound on the distance via constraints. Then, by tabling the predicate and performing answer subsumption, the defining predicate has effectively been turned into an optimizing one, computing the length of the shortest path. It is a straightforward yet powerful optimization technique that can be applied to other defining predicates as well, turning them into optimizing predicates with a minimum of changes. No meta-programming to iterate over all possible answers is required.

3.5   Evaluation of a Shipment Problem

Problem statement: *There are N packages available for shipping using trucks. Each package has a weight and some constraints on the time to be delivered. Each* *truck has a maximum load and a destination. Determine whether there is a subset of the packages that can fully load a truck destined for a certain place and all the packages in this subset are delivered on time.*

The problem is solved by the *truckload* program (see [17] for the source). Packages are represented by clauses of `pack/4`, e.g.

`pack(3,60,chicago,T) :- leq(4,T),leq(T,29).`

means this is the third package, it weights 60 pounds, is destined for Chicago and has to be delivered between the 4th and the 29th day. The `truckload/4` predicate computes the answer to the problem, e.g. `truckload(30,100,chicago,T)` computes whether a subset of the packages numbered 1 to 30 exists to fill up a truck with a maximum load of 100 pounds destined for Chicago. The time constraints are captured in the bound on the constraint variable T. There may be multiple answers to this query, if multiple subsets that satisfy it exist.

We have run the program in four different modes:

- Firstly, the program is run as is without tabling.
- Secondly, to avoid the recomputation of subproblems in recursive calls the `truckload/4` predicate is tabled with:

    `:- table_chr truckload(_,_,_,chr) with [representation(naive)].`

- In a third variant the answer store is canonicalized by simple sorting such that permutations are detected to be identical answers:

    `:- table_chr truckload(_,_,_,chr)`
    `          with [representation(naive),canonical_form(sort)].`

- Finally, in the fourth variant we apply a custom combinator to the answers: two answers with overlapping time intervals are merged into one answer with the union of the time intervals. For example the disjunction of the following two intervals on the left is equivalent to the interval on the right:

$$(1 \leq T \leq 3) \quad \vee \quad (2 \leq T \leq 4) \quad \Longleftrightarrow \quad (1 \leq T \leq 4)$$

This variant is declared as, with `interval_union/3` the custom answer combinator:

    `:- table_chr truckload(_,_,_,chr)`
    `          with [representation(naive),answer_combination(interval_union)].`

Table 3. Results for the `truckload` program

| | no tabling | tabling | | | | | | | | |
| | | plain | | | sorted | | | combinator | | |
load	runtime	runtime	space	answers	runtime	space	answers	runtime	space	answers
100	0	100	286	324	100	286	324	100	279	283
200	160	461	979	2,082	461	956	2,069	451	904	1,686
300	2,461	1,039	1,799	4,721	1,041	1,723	4,665	971	1,584	3,543
400	12,400	1,500	2,308	5,801	1.510	2,202	5,751	1,351	2,054	4,449
500	> 5 min.	1,541	2,449	4,972	1,541	2,365	4,935	1,451	2,267	4,017

Table 3 contains the results of running the program in the four different modes for different maximum loads. Runtime is in milliseconds and has been obtained on the same machine as in Section 2.1. For the modes with tabling the space usage, in kilobytes, of the tables and number of unique answers have been recorded as well.

It is clear from the results that tabling does have an overhead for small loads, but that it scales much better. Both the modes with the canonical form and the answer combination have a slight space advantage over plain tabling which increases with the total number of answers. There is hardly any runtime effect for the canonical form, whereas the answer combination mode is faster with increasing load.

In summary, tabling can be useful for certain programs with CHR constraints to considerably improve scalability. Canonicalization of the answer store and answer combination can have a favorable impact on both runtime and table space depending on the particular problem.

4   Related and Future Work

In this paper we have shown that it is possible to integrate the committed choice bottom-up execution of CHRs with the tabled top-down execution of XSB. In particular the issues related to the consistency of the global CHR store and tables have been established and solutions have been formulated for call abstraction, tabling constraint stores, answer projection, answer combination (e.g. for optimization), and answer entailment checking.

Several ad hoc approaches to using constraints in XSB exist, such as a meta-interpreter [15], interfacing with a solver written in C [9] and explicit constraint store management in Prolog [16]. However, these approaches are quite cumbersome and lack the ease of use and generality of CHR.

The main related work that this paper builds on is [4], which presents a framework for constraint solvers written with attributed variables. Attributed variables are a much cruder tool for writing constraint solvers though. Implementation issues such as constraint store representation and scheduling strategies that are hidden by CHR become the users responsibility when he programs with attributed variables. Also in the tabled setting, the user has to think through all the integration issues of his attributed variables solver. For CHR we have provided generic solutions that work for all CHR constraint solvers and more powerful features can be accessed through parametrized options.

Guo and Gupta propose a technique for dynamic programming with tabling ([12]) that is somewhat similar to the one proposed here. During entailment checking they compare a particular argument in a new answer with the value in the previous answer and keep either one based on whether that argument needs to be minimized or maximized. Their technique is specified for particular numeric arguments whereas ours is for constraint stores. Further investigation of our proposal is certainly necessary to establish the extent of its applicability.

In [18] we briefly discuss two applications of CHR with tabling in the field of model checking. The integration of CHR and XSB has shown to make the implementation of model checking applications with constraints a lot easier.

Indeed the next step in the search for applications is to explore more expressive models than are currently viable with traditional approaches.

We still have to look at how to implement partial abstraction and the implications of variant and subsumption based tabling. Partial abstraction and subsumption are closely related. The former transforms a call into a more general call while the latter looks for answers to more general calls, but if none are available still executes the actual call.

Finally, we would like to mention that an XSB release with the presented CHR system will soon be publicly available (see http://xsb.sf.net).

References

1. W. Chen and D. S. Warren. Tabled evaluation with delaying for general logic programs. *Journal of the ACM*, 43(1):20–74, 1996.
2. M. Codish, B. Demoen, and K. Sagonas. Semantic-based program analysis for logic-based languages using XSB. *International Journal of Software Tools for Technology Transfer*, 2(1):29–45, jan 1998.
3. V. S. Costa, L. Damas, R. Reis, and R. Azevedo. *YAP User's Manual*.
4. B. Cui and D. S. Warren. A System for Tabled Constraint Logic Programming. In *Computational Logic*, pages 478–492, 2000.
5. B. Cui and D. S. Warren. Attributed Variables in XSB. In I. Dutra et al., editors, *Electronic Notes in Theoretical Computer Science*, volume 30. Elsevier, 2000.
6. B. Demoen. Dynamic attributes, their hProlog implementation, and a first evaluation. Report CW 350, Department of Computer Science, K.U.Leuven, oct 2002.
7. B. Demoen, M. G. de la Banda, W. Harvey, K. Marriott, and P. J. Stuckey. An Overview of HAL. In *Principles and Practice of Constraint Programming*, pages 174–188, 1999.
8. B. Demoen and P.-L. Nguyen. So many WAM variations, so little time. In J. Lloyd et al., editors, *Computational Logic - CL2000, First International Conference, London, UK, July 2000, Proceedings*, volume 1861 of *LNAI*, pages 1240–1254, 2000.
9. X. Du, C. R. Ramakrishnan, and S. A. Smolka. Tabled Resolution + Constraints: A Recipe for Model Checking Real-Time Systems. In *IEEE Real Time Systems Symposium*, Orlando, Florida, November 2000.
10. T. Frühwirth. Constraint Handling Rules. In A. Podelski, editor, *Constraint Programming: Basics and Trends*, number 910 in LNCS, pages 90–107. Springer Verlag, March 1995.
11. T. Frühwirth. Theory and Practice of Constraint Handling Rules. In P. Stuckey and K. Marriot, editors, *Special Issue on Constraint Logic Programming*, volume 37, October 1998.
12. H.-F. Guo and G. Gupta. Simplifying Dynamic Programming via Tabling. In R. Lopes and M. Ferreira, editors, *Proceedings of CICLOPS 2003. Technical Report DCC-2003-05, DCC - FC & LIACC, University of Porto*.
13. Intelligent Systems Laboratory. *SICStus Prolog User's Manual*. PO Box 1263, SE-164 29 Kista, Sweden, October 2003.
14. J. Jaffar and J.-L. Lassez. Constraint Logic Programming. In *Proceedings of the 14th ACM SIGACT-SIGPLAN symposium on Principles of programming languages*, pages 111–119. ACM Press, 1987.

15. M. Mukund, C. R. Ramakrishnan, I. V. Ramakrishnan, and R. Verma. Symbolic Bisimulation using Tabled Constraint Logic Programming. In *International Workshop on Tabulation in Parsing and Deduction*, Vigo, Spain, September 2000.
16. G. Pemmasani, C. R. Ramakrishnan, and I. V. Ramakrishnan. Efficient Model Checking of Real Time Systems Using Tabled Logic Programming and Constraints. In *International Conference on Logic Programming*, LNCS, Copenhagen, Denmark, July 2002. Springer.
17. T. Schrijvers. CHR benchmarks and programs, January 2004. Available at http://www.cs.kuleuven.ac.be/~toms/Research/chr.html.
18. T. Schrijvers, D. S. Warren, and B. Demoen. CHR for XSB. In R. Lopes and M. Ferreira, editors, *Proceedings of CICLOPS 2003. Technical Report DCC-2003-05, DCC - FC & LIACC, University of Porto*, pages 7–20, December 2003.
19. D. S. Warren et al. The XSB Programmer's Manual: version 2.5, vols. 1 and 2, 2001.

Possible Worlds Semantics
for Probabilistic Logic Programs

Alex Dekhtyar[1] and Michael I. Dekhtyar[2]

[1] Department of Computer Science, University of Kentucky
dekhtyar@cs.uky.edu
[2] Department of Computer Science, Tver State University
Michael.Dekhtyar@tversu.ru

Abstract. In this paper we consider a logic programming framework
for reasoning about imprecise probabilities. In particular, we propose a
new semantics, for the Probabilistic Logic Programs (p-programs) of Ng
and Subrahmanian. P-programs represent imprecision using probability
intervals. Our semantics, based on the possible worlds semantics, considers all point probability distributions that satisfy a given p-program.
In the paper, we provide the exact characterization of such models of a
p-program. We show that the set of models of a p-program cannot, in
general case, be described by single intervals associated with atoms of
the program. We provide algorithms for efficient construction of this set
of models and study their complexity.

1 Introduction

Probabilities quantize our knowledge about possibilities. Imprecise probabilities
represent our uncertainty about such quantization. They arise from incomplete
data or from human unsureness. They occur in the analyses of survey responses,
in the use of GIS data, and risk assessment, to cite a few application domains.
The importance of imprecise probabilities has been observed by numerous researchers in the past 10-15 years [14, 3] and lead to the establishment of the
Imprecise Probabilities Project [6]. The appeal of standard, or point, probability theory is its clarity. Given the need for imprecision, there are many models:
second-order distributions, belief states or lower envelopes, intervals, and others. Among them, probability intervals as the means of representing imprecision
are the simplest extension of the traditional probability models. Even then, a
variety of different explanations of what it means for a probability of an event
e to be expressed as an interval $[a, b] \subseteq [0, 1]$ have been proposed in the past
decade and a half [14, 2, 15, 3]. Among them, the possible worlds approach introduced for probability distributions by De Campos, Huete and Moral [3] and
extended to Kolmogorov probability theory by Weichselberger [15] is, probably,
the most appealing from the point of view of the origins of imprecision. According to [3, 15], there is a single true *point* probability distribution underlying a
collection of random variables or events. The imprecision, expressed in terms of

B. Demoen and V. Lifschitz (Eds.): ICLP 2004, LNCS 3132, pp. 137–148, 2004.

probability intervals stems from our inability to establish what this true distribution *is*. Thus, interval probabilities are constraints on the set of possible point probability distributions that can be true.

Previous logic programming frameworks addressing the issue of imprecision in known probabilities [8, 7, 9, 4, 5] had taken similar approaches to interpreting probability intervals, but have stopped short of considering *precise descriptions* of sets of point probabilities as the semantics of probabilistic logic programs. In this paper, we seek to extend one such logic programming framework, Probabilistic Logic Programs (p-programs), introduced by Ng and Subrahmanian[9], to capture the exact set of point probabilities that satisfy a p-program.

The main contributions of this paper are as follows. First, we describe the possible worlds semantics for a simple logic programming language in which probability intervals are associated with each atom in a program (simple p-programs) (Section 2). The syntax of the language and its model theory are from [9], however, we show that the fixpoint semantics described there does not capture precisely the set of all point probability models of a program (Section 2.2). We then proceed to describe this set of models formally (Section 3.1), and provide an explicit construction for it (Section 3.2), complete with algorithms for implementing this constructions. We show that associating single intervals with atoms of p-programs is not sufficient to capture their model-theoretic semantics: one has to consider unions of open, closed and semi-closed intervals. We also show that while the size of such description of the set of models of a simple p-program can be, in the worst case exponential in the size of the program, our algorithm GenModT for its construction, works in an efficient manner.

2   Probabilistic Logic Programs

In this section we describe a simplified version of the Probabilistic Logic Programs of Ng and Subrahmanian [9]. Let L be some first order language containing infinitely many variable symbols, finitely many predicate symbols and no function symbols. Let $B_L = \{A_1, \ldots, A_N\}$ be the Herbrand base of L. A *p-annotated* atom, is an expression $A : \mu$ where $A \in B_L$, and $\mu = [\alpha, \beta] \subseteq [0, 1]$.

P-annotated atoms represent probabilistic information. Every atom in B_L is assumed to represent an (uncertain) event or statement. A *p-annotated atom* $A : [\alpha, \beta]$ is read as "the probability of the event corresponding to A to occur (have occurred) lies in the interval $[\alpha, \beta]$". Probabilistic Logic Programs (p-programs) are constructed from *p-annotated* formulas as follows. Let $A, A_1, \ldots A_n$ be some atoms and $\mu, \mu_1, \ldots, \mu_n$ be subintervals of $[0, 1]$ (also called *annotations*). Then, a simple *p-clause* is an expression of the form $A : \mu \longleftarrow A_1 : \mu_1 \wedge \ldots \wedge A_n : \mu_n$ (if $n = 0$, as usual, the *p-clause* $A : \mu \longleftarrow$ is referred to as a *fact*). A simple Probabilistic Logic Program (*p-program*) is a finite collection of simple *p-clauses*.

2.1   Model Theory and Fixpoint Semantics

The model theory assumes that in real world each atom from B_L is either true or false. However, the observer does not have exact information about the real world, and expresses his/her uncertainty in a form of a probability range. Given B_L, a world probability density function KI is defined as $KI : 2^{B_L} \to [0,1]$, $\sum_{W \subseteq B_L} KI(W) = 1$. Each subset W of B_L is considered to be a *possible world* and KI associates a point probability with it. A *probabilistic interpretation (p-interpretation)* I is defined on B_L as follows: $I : B_L \to [0,1]$, $I(A) = \sum_{A \in W} KI(W)$. P-interpretations assign probabilities to individual atoms of B_L by adding up the probabilities of all worlds in which a given atom is true. P-interpretations specify the model-theoretic semantics of p-programs. Given a p-interpretation I, the following definitions of satisfaction are given:

- $I \models A : \mu$ **iff** $I(A) \in \mu$;
- $I \models A_1 : \mu_1 \wedge \ldots \wedge A_n : \mu_n$ **iff** $(\forall 1 \leq i \leq n)(I \models A_i : \mu_i)$;
- $I \models A : \mu \longleftarrow A_1 : \mu_1 \wedge \ldots \wedge A_n : \mu_n$ **iff** either $I \models A : \mu$ or $I \not\models A_1 : \mu_1 \wedge \ldots \wedge A_n : \mu_n$.

Now, given a p-program P, $I \models P$ iff for all p-clauses $C \in P$ $I \models C$. Let $Mod(P)$ denote the set of all p-interpretations that satisfy p-program P. It is convenient to view a single p-interpretation I as a point $(I(A_1), \ldots, I(A_N))$ in N-dimensional unit cube E^N. Then, $Mod(P)$ can be viewed as a subset of E^N. P is called *consistent* iff $Mod(P) \neq \emptyset P$, otherwise P is called *inconsistent*.

Fixpoint semantics of simple p-programs is defined in terms of functions that assign intervals of probability values to atoms of B_L. An *atomic function* is a mapping $f : B_L \longrightarrow \mathcal{C}[0,1]$ where $\mathcal{C}[0,1]$ denotes the set of all closed subintervals of $[0,1]$. Generally, an atomic function f describes a closed parallelepiped in N-dimensional space: a family of p-interpretations $\mathcal{I}(f) = \{I | (\forall A \in B_L)(I(A) \in f(A))\}$ is associated.

The set of all atomic functions over B_L forms a complete lattice $\mathcal{FF}$ w.r.t. the subset inclusion: $f_1 \leq f_2$ iff $(\forall A \in B_L)(f_1(A) \supseteq f_2(A))$. The bottom element $\perp$ of this lattice is the atomic function that assigns $[0,1]$ interval to all atoms, and the top element $\top$ is the atomic function that assigns $\emptyset$ to all atoms.

Given a simple p-program P the fixpoint operator $T_P : \mathcal{FF} \longrightarrow \mathcal{FF}$ is defined as $T_P(f)(A) = \cap M_A$, where $M_A = \{\mu | A : \mu \longleftarrow B_1 : \mu_1 \wedge \ldots \wedge B_n : \mu_n \in P$ and $(\forall 1 \leq i \leq n)(f(B_i) \subseteq \mu_i)\}$. Ng and Subrahmanian show that this operator is monotonic [9]. The iterations of T_P are defined in a standard way: (i) $T_P^0 = \perp$; (ii) $T_P^{\alpha+1} = T_P(T_P^\alpha)$, where $\alpha + 1$ is the successor ordinal whose immediate predecessor is α; (iii) $T_P^\lambda = \sqcup\{T_P^\alpha | \alpha \leq \lambda\}$, where λ is a limit ordinal. Ng and Subrahmanian show that, the least fixpoint $lfp(T_P)$ of the T_P operator is reachable after a finite number of iterations ([9], Lemma 4). They also show that if a p-program P is consistent, then $\mathcal{I}(lfp(T_P))$ contains $Mod(P)$ ([9] Theorem 5, Claim (i)).

2.2   Fixpoint Is Not Enough

At the same time, the inverse of the last statement, is not true, as evidenced by the following examples. First, consider p-program P_1 shown in Figure 1.

Proposition 1. *There exists a p-interpretation I s. t. $I \in \mathcal{I}(lfp(T_{P_1}))$ but $I \not\models P_1$.*

$a : [0.2, 0.4] \longleftarrow .$	(1)
$b : [0.2, 0.5] \longleftarrow .$	(2)
$b : [0.2, 0.3] \longleftarrow a : [0.2, 0.3].$	(3)
$b : [0.4, 0.5] \longleftarrow a : [0.3, 0.4].$	(4)

Program P_1

$a : [0.2, 0.4] \longleftarrow .$	(1)
$b : [0.3, 0.5] \longleftarrow .$	(2)
$b : [0.6, 0.7] \longleftarrow a : [0.2, 0.3].$	(3)
$b : [0.6, 0.7] \longleftarrow a : [0.3, 0.4].$	(4)

Program P_2

Fig. 1. Sample P-programs.

Proof. It is easy to see that neither rule (3) nor rule (4) will fire during the computation of the least fixpoint. Indeed, $T_{P_1}^1(a) = [0.2, 0.4]$ and $T_{P_1}^1(b) = [0.2, 0.5]$ based on clauses (1) and (2). However, at the next step, as $[0.2, 0.4] \not\subseteq [0.2, 0.3]$, rule (3) will not fire and as $[0.2, 0.4] \not\subseteq [0.3, 0.4]$, rule (4) will not fire. Therefore, $lfp(T_{P_1}) = T_{P_1}^1$.

Now, consider p-interpretation I, such that $I(a) = 0.2$ and $I(b) = 0.35$. Clearly, $I \in \mathcal{I}(lfp(T_{P_1}))$. However, $I \not\models P_1$. Indeed, as $I(a) = 0.2 \in [0.2, 0.3]$, I satisfies the body of rule (3). Then I must satisfy its head, i.e., $I(b) \in [0.2, 0.3]$. However, $I(b) = 0.35 \notin [0.4, 0.5]$, and therefore rule (3) is not satisfied by I. ∎

We note that the fixpoint of P_1 is defined but it is not *tight* enough to represent exactly the set of satisfying p-interpretations. It is also possible for a p-program to have a well-defined fixpoint but be inconsistent. Consider p-program P_2 from Figure 1.

Proposition 2. *1. $lfp(T_{P_2}) = T_{P_2}^1$. In particular, $lfp(T_{P_2})(a) = [0.2, 0.4]$ and $lfp(T_{P_2})(b) = [0.3, 0.5]$.*
2. $Mod(P_2) = \emptyset$

Proof. The first part is similar to the proof of Proposition 1. To show that $Mod(P_2) = \emptyset$ consider some p-interpretation I such that $I \models P_2$. Let $I(a) = p$. As $p \in lfp(T_{P_2})(a) = [0.2, 0.4]$ then $p \in [0.2, 0.3]$, or $p \in [0.3, 0.4]$. In either case, the body of at least one of the rules (3),(4) will be satisfied by I and therefore, $I(b) \in [0.6, 0.7]$. However, we know that $I(b) \in lfp(T_{P_2})(b) = [0.3, 0.5]$, which leads to a contradiction. ∎

Note that the $lfp(T_P)$ specifies the semantics of a p-program as the set of p-interpretations inside a single N-dimensional parallelepiped whose borders are defined by $lfp(T_P)(A_1), \ldots, lfp(T_P)(A_N)$. Unfortunately, this is not always the case, i.e., $Mod(P)$ need not be a single N-dimensional parallelepiped, as evidenced by the following proposition.

Proposition 3. *If the atoms in B_L for P_1 (Figure 1) are ordered as a, b, then $Mod(P_3) = [0.2, 0.3) \times [0.2, 0.3] \cup (0.3, 0.4] \times [0.4, 0.5]$.*

Proof. First, we show that $Mod(P_1) \subseteq [0.2, 0.3) \times [0.2, 0.3] \cup (0.3, 0.4] \times [0.4, 0.5]$.

Let $I \models P_1$. As $lfp(T_P(P_1))(A) = [0.2, 0.4]$ (by rule (1)), three cases are possible.

1. $I(A) \in [0.2, 0.3)$. Consider rules (3) and (4). As $I(A) \in [0.2, 0.3)$, the body of rule (3) will be true, and the body of rule (4) will be false. Thus, I must satisfy the head of (3), i.e., $I(B) \in [0.2, 0.3]$. Therefore $I \in [0.2, 0.3) \times [0.2, 0.3]$.

2. $I(A) = 0.3$. In this case, the bodies of both rule (3) and rule (4) are satisfied, and therefore I must satisfy both heads of these rules, i.e., $I(B) \in [0.2, 0.3]$ and $I(B) \in [0.4, 0.5]$. But as $[0.2, 0.3] \cap [0.4, 0.5] = \emptyset$, we arrive to a contradiction. Therefore, for any p-interpretation $I \models P_1$, $I(A) \neq 0.3$.
3. $I(A) \in (0.3, 0.4]$. Here, the body of rule (3) will not be true, but the body of rule (4) will, therefore, I must satisfy the head of rule (4), i.e., $I(B) \in [0.4, 0.5]$. Then, $I \in (0.3, 0.4] \times [0.4, 0.5]$.

Combining the results of all three cases together we get $I \in [0.2, 0.3) \times [0.2, 0.3] \cup (0.3, 0.4] \times [0.4, 0.5]$, which proves the inclusion. It is easy to verify that any $I \in [0.2, 0.3) \times [0.2, 0.3] \cup (0.3, 0.4] \times [0.4, 0.5]$, is the model of P_1. ■

We note, here, that, in general, the problem of determining if a simple p-program P is consistent is hard. We define the set CONS-P= $\{P | Mod(P) \neq \emptyset\}$.

Theorem 1. *The set CONS-P is NP-complete.*

3 Semantics of PLPs Revisited

As shown in Section 2.2, even for the simplest p-programs, the set of their models may have a more complex structure than the one prescribed by the fixpoint procedure of [9]. In this section we study the problem of exact description and explicit computation of $Mod(P)$ given program P. We show that in general case, $Mod(P)$ is a union of a finite number of N-dimensional[1] open, closed, or semi-closed parallelepipeds within the N-dimensional unit hypercube $[0, 1]^N$. In Section 3.1 we characterize $Mod(P)$ as the set of solutions of a family of systems of inequalities constructed from P. In Section 3.2 we propose a way of computing $Mod(P)$ using special transformations of P.

3.1 Characterization of Models

Definition 1. *Let P be a simple p-program over the Herbrand base $B_L = \{A_1, \ldots, A_N\}$. With each atom $A \in B_L$ we will associate a real variable x_A with domain [0,1]. Let $C \equiv A : [l, u] \longleftarrow B_1 : [l_1, u_1] \wedge \ldots \wedge B_k : [l_k, u_k]$, $k \geq 0$ be a clause of P.*

The family of systems of inequalities induced by C, denoted $INEQ(C)$ is defined as follows:

- *$k = 0$ (C is a fact). $INEQ(C) = \{\{l \leq x_A \leq u\}\}$*
- *$k \geq 1$ (C is a rule).*
  $INEQ(C) = T(C) \cup F(C)$;
  $T(C) = \{\{l \leq x_A \leq u, l_i \leq x_{B_i} \leq u_i | 1 \leq i \leq k\}\}$;
  $F(C) = \{\{x_{B_i} < l_i\} | 1 \leq i \leq k\} \cup \{\{x_{B_i} > u_i\} | 1 \leq i \leq k\}$.

The family $INEQ(P)$ of systems of inequalities is defined as
$INEQ(P) = \{\alpha_1 \cup \ldots \cup \alpha_m | \alpha_i \in INEQ(C_i), 1 \leq i \leq k\}$.

---

[1] Whenever we are writing about N-dimensional parallelepipeds representing the set of models of a p-program, we implicitly assume the possibility that the true dimensionality of some of them can be less than N due to the fact that with certain atoms of B_L exact point probabilities, rather than intervals may be associated.

Note that all inequalities in all systems from the definition above involve only one variable. Given a system α of such inequalities, we denote the set of its solutions as $Sol(\alpha)$. For $A \in B_L$ let $l_A^\alpha = \max\{0 \cup \{l|(x_A \leq l) \in \alpha\}\}$ and $u_A^\alpha = \min\{1 \cup \{u|x_A \geq u \in \alpha\}\}$. Then it it easy to see that

$$Sol(\alpha) = \begin{cases} \emptyset & \text{if for some } A,\ l_A^\alpha > u_A^\alpha; \\ [l_{A_1}^\alpha, u_{A_1}^\alpha] \times \ldots \times [l_{A_N}^\alpha, u_{A_N}^\alpha] & \text{otherwise.} \end{cases}$$

Informally, the set $INEQ(P)$ represents all possible systems of restrictions on probabilities of atoms of B_L whose solutions satisfy every clause of P. Of course, not all individual systems of inequalities have solutions, but $INEQ(P)$ *captures all the systems that do*, as shown in the following lemma and theorem.

Lemma 1. *Let C be a p-clause and I be a p − interpretation (both over the same Herbrand Base B_L). Then $I \models C$ iff $\{x_A = I(A)\} \in Sol(\alpha)$ for some $\alpha \in INEQ(C)$.*

Theorem 2. *A p-interpretation I is a model of a simple p-program P **iff** there exists a system of inequalities $\alpha \in INEQ(P)$ such that $X = \{x_A = I(A)\} \in Sol(\alpha)$.*

This leads to the following description of $Mod(P)$:

Corollary 1. $Mod(P) = \bigcup_{\alpha \in INEQ(P)} Sol(\alpha)$

We denote as $Facts(P)$ and $Rules(P)$ the sets of p-clauses with empty and non-empty bodies in a p-program P, and as $f(P)$ and $r(P)$ - their respective sizes. Let also $k(P)$ be the maximum number of atoms in a body of a rule in P. Then, we can obtain the following bound on the size of $Mod(P)$.

Corollary 2. *The set of all p-interpretations I that satisfy a simple p-program P is a union of at most $M(P)$ (not necessarily disjoint) N-dimensional parallelepipeds, where $M(P) = (2k(P) + 1)^{r(P)}$.*

This Corollary provides an exponential, in the size of the p-program, upper bound on the number of disjoint parallelepipeds in the set $Mod(P)$. We can show that this bound cannot be substantially decreased in the general case. Consider p-program P_3 over the set of atoms $\{a, b_1, \ldots, b_n\}$:

$$a : [1, 1] \longleftarrow . \tag{1}$$
$$b_i : [0, 1] \longleftarrow .\ i = 1, \ldots, n \tag{2i}$$
$$a : [0, 0] \longleftarrow b_i : [0.2, 0.3].\ i = 1, \ldots, n \tag{3i}$$

Here, $INEQ(1)$ consists of a single equality $x_a = 1$; each of $INEQ(2i)$ includes trivial inequalities $0 \leq x_{b_i} \leq 1$, and each of $INEQ(3i)$ consists of three systems of inequalities: $\alpha_i^1 = \{0 \leq x_{b_i} < 0.2\}$, $\alpha_i^2 = \{0.3 < x_{b_i} \leq 1\}$, and $\alpha_i^3 = \{0.2 \leq x_{b_i} < 0.3; x_a = 0\}$. Since α_i^3 is inconsistent with $INEQ(1)$, each consistent set of inequalities in $INEQ(P_3)$ can be represented as $\{x_a = 1\} \cup \bigcup_{i=1}^n \alpha_i^{j_i}$ for some $j_i \in \{1, 2\}, i = 1, \ldots, n$. It is easy to see that for any two different α and α' of such form in $INEQ(P_3)$ sets $Sol(\alpha)$ and $Sol(\alpha')$ are disjoint. So, $Mod(P_3)$ consists of 2^n disjoint n-dimensional parallelepipeds. At the same time $f(P_3) = n+1$, $r(P_3) = n$, $k(P_3) = 1$ and a bitwise representation of P_3 takes only $O(n \log n)$ bits.

3.2   Explicit Computation of Models

In this section we will address the following problem: given a simple p-program P, output the description of the set $Mod(P)$ as a union of N-dimensional paral-lelepipeds.

The construction from previous section gives one algorithm for computing $Mod(P)$: given a program P construct explicitly the set of systems of inequal-ities $INEQ(P)$ and then solve each system from this set. This algorithm has exponential worst case complexity in the size of the program and as program P_3 illustrates the worst case cannot be avoided. However, it not hard to see that the algorithm based on solving individual systems of inequalities from $INEQ(P)$ can be quite inefficient in its work. Indeed, as the solution sets of individual systems of inequalities are not necessarily disjoint, this algorithm may wind up comput-ing parts of the final solution over and over. In this section, we propose a different approach to direct computation of the set of models of a simple p-program, which breaks the solution space into *disjoint* components and individually computes each such component.

Consider a simple p-program P over the Herbrand base $B_L = \{A_1, \ldots A_N\}$. As $AT(P)$ we denote the multiset of all p-annotated atoms found in all heads and bodies of clauses in P. Given $A \in B_L$ Let $AT(P)[A]$ be the set of all p-annotated atoms of the form $A : \mu$ from $AT(P)$. Define for each $A \in B_L$ a set $Prb_P(A_i)$ of all possible bounds of probability intervals used in P for A_i as follows $Prb_P(A) = \{\langle l, -\rangle | A : [l, u] \in AT(P)[A]\} \cup \{\langle u, +\rangle | A : [l, u] \in AT(P)[A]\} \cup \{<0, ->, <1, +>\}$. Thus with each occurrence of a probability bound for A in P, we are also storing (encoded as "$-$" or "$+$") whether it is a lower or upper bound.

We order the elements of $Prb_P(A)$ as follows. $\langle a, *\rangle < \langle b, *\rangle$ whenever $a \leq b$, and $\langle a, -\rangle < \langle a, +\rangle$. Consider now $Prb_P(A) = \{\beta_1 =< 0, ->, \beta_2, \ldots, \beta_m =< 1, +>\}$ where sequence $\beta_1, \ldots, \beta_m$ is in ascending order. Using the set $Prb_P(A)$ we will now construct the set of segments $SEG_P(A)$ as follows.

Let $\beta_i = \langle a_i, \lambda_i \rangle$ and $\beta_{i+1} = \langle a_{i+1}, \lambda_{i+1} \rangle$, $1 \leq i \leq m - 1$. We define the segment s_i associated with the pair β_i, β_{i+1} as shown in the table on the left side of Figure 2. Now, $SEG_P(A) = \{s_1, s_2, \ldots, s_{m-1}\}$.

Notice that if $a_i = a_{i+1}$ then, λ_i is a "$-$" and λ_{i+1} is a "$+$" (it follows from our order on β_is) and the interval $[a_i, a_{i+i}] = [a_i, a_i]$ will be added to $SEG_P(A)$. The following proposition establishes basic properties of the segment sets.

Proposition 4. *Let P be a simple p-program, $A \in B_L$ and $SEG_P(A) = \{s_1, \ldots, s_{m-1}\}$.*

1. *$SEG_P(A)$ is a partition of $[0, 1]$, in particular,. if $i \neq j$ then $s_i \cap s_j = \emptyset$.*
2. *Consider some $1 \leq i \leq m - 1$. Let $x, y \in s_i$ and let I_1 and I_2 be p-interpretations such that $I_1(A) = x$ and $I_2(A) = y$. Then for all $A : \mu \in AT(P)[A]$, $I_1 \models A : \mu$ iff $I_2 \models A : \mu$.*
3. *Consider some $1 \leq i \leq m - 2$. Let $x \in s_i$ and $y \in s_{i+1}$ and let I_1 and I_2 be p-interpretations such that $I_1(A) = x$ and $I_2(A) = y$. Then*

$$\{A : \mu \in AT(P)[A] \mid I_1 \models A : \mu\} \neq \{A : \mu \in AT(P)[A] \mid I_2 \models A : \mu\}.$$

λ_i	λ_{i+1}	s_i
$-$	$-$	$[a_i, a_{i+1})$
$-$	$+$	$[a_i, a_{i+1}]$
$+$	$-$	(a_i, a_{i+1})
$+$	$+$	$(a_i, a_{i+1}]$

> (1) Compute $SEG(P)$.
> (2) **for each** $J \in SEG(P)$ **do**
> (3)   Choose some interpretation (point) $I \in J$;
> (4)   **if** $I \models P$ **then** add J to $Mod(P)$ **end if**
> (5) **end do**

Fig. 2. Determination of segments in $SEG(A)$ (left) and algorithm GenMod for computing $Mod(P)$. (right).

Given a simple p-program P over the Herbrand base $B_L = \{A_1, \ldots, A_N\}$, the segmentation of P, denoted $SEG(P)$ is defined as follows

$$SEG(P) = \{s^1 \times s^2 \times \ldots \times s^N \mid s^j \in SEG_P(A_j), 1 \le j \le N\}.$$

Basically, $SEG(P)$ is a segmentation of the N-dimensional unit hypercube into a number of "bricks". Recall that each point inside the N-dimensional unit hypercube represents a p-interpretation. The following theorem shows that the set of all p-interpretations satisfying P can be constructed from some "bricks" of $SEG(P)$.

Theorem 3. *1. Any two different parallelepipeds of $SEG(P)$ do not intersect.*
2. For any parallelepiped $J \in SEG(P)$ either $J \subseteq Mod(P)$, or $J \cap Mod(P) = \emptyset$.
3. There exists such subset $S \subseteq SEG(P)$ that $Mod(P) = \bigcup_{J \in S} J$.

Consider again program P_1 (Fig. 1). Atom a has the set of probability bounds $Prb_{P_1}(a) = \{\langle 0, -\rangle, \langle 0.2, -\rangle, \langle 0.3, -\rangle, \langle 0.3, +\rangle, \langle 0.4, +\rangle, \langle 1, +\rangle\}$ and atom b has the set of bounds $Prb_{P_1}(b) = \{\langle 0, -\rangle, \langle 0.2, -\rangle, \langle 0.3, +\rangle, \langle 0.4, -\rangle, \langle 0.5, +\rangle, \langle 1, +\rangle\}$. The corresponding sets of the segments are
$SEG_{P_1}(a) = \{[0, 0.2], [0.2, 0.3), [0.3, 0.3], (0.3, 0.4], (0.4, 1]\}$ and
$SEG_{P_1}(b) = \{[0, 0.2), [0.2, 0.3], (0.3, 0.4), [0.4, 0.5], (0.5, 1]\}$.
Then $SEG(P_1)$ consists of 25 rectangles of the form $s^1 \times s^2$ where $s^1 \in SEG_{P_3}(a)$ and $s^2 \in SEG_{P_1}(b)$ (in fact, 5 of them with $s^1 = [0.3, 0.3]$ are linear segments). As is shown in Proposition 3 only 2 of them consist of models of P_3: $Mod(P_1) = [0.2, 0.3) \times [0.2, 0.3] \cup (0.3, 0.4] \times [0.4, 0.5]$.

Theorem 3 suggests that $Mod(P)$ can be constructed using the algorithm *GenMod* described in Figure 2. We note that steps (3) and (4) of this algorithm can be processed efficiently. In particular, if $J = s^1 \times \ldots \times s^N$ and each s^i is a segment with the lower bound l^i and the upper bound u^i, $i = 1, \ldots, N$, then for each i the value $I(A_i)$ on step (3) can be chosen to be equal to $(l^i + u^i)/2$. So, the runtime of *GenMod* is bounded by a polynomial of the size of $SEG(P)$. The size of $SEG(P)$ is, in its turn, exponential of the size of the set B_L of all atoms of P. Of course, it can be a case when some "bricks" in $SEG(P)$ can be united into one larger "brick", so that $Mod(P)$ is represented by a smaller number of bricks than $SEG(P)$. But the program P_3 shows that in the general case even minimal number of "non-unitable" bricks in $Mod(P)$ can be exponential in $|B_L|$. Therefore, the worst case running time of algorithm *GenMod* can not be

---

Algorithm GenModT(P:program, $\{A_1, \ldots, A_n\}$:atoms)
if $n = 1$ **and** $P = \bigcup_{j=1}^{k} \{A_1 : \mu_j \leftarrow .\}$ **then** $Sol := \bigcap_{j=1}^{k} \mu_j$
else // P includes at least two different atoms
    $Sol := \emptyset$;
    $S := NS(P)$;   // compute Ng-Subrahmanian T_P operator
    if $S = \emptyset$ **then** return($\emptyset$)
    else // if NS(P) is not empty, proceed with computations
        // reduce P wrt $S = \times_{i=1}^{n} sg_i$
        for $i = 1$ **to** n **do** $P := Reduct(P, A_i : sg_i)$ **end_do**
        $Seg := SEG(P, A_1) \cap sg_1$;   // the segmentation of A_1 inside
                                   // the T_P operator
// main loop
        for each $s = \langle a, b \rangle \in Seg$ **do**
            $P' := Reduct(P, A_1 : s)$;
            if P' is empty **then** $Sol := Sol \cup (s \times (\times_{i=2}^{n}[0, 1]))$
            else // find the solution for the reduct
                $RSol := GenModT(P', \{A_2, \ldots, A_n\})$;
                if $RSol \neq \emptyset$ **then** $Sol := Sol \cup (s \times RSol)$ **end if**
            end if   **end do**
    end if   **end if**
return Sol;

Fig. 3. Algorithm GenModT for computing $Mod(P)$.

improved. At the same time, we can improve on *GenMod*, by being more careful at how the N-dimensional "bricks" are considered.

We fix an ordering $A_1, \ldots, A_N$ of B_L. Given a simple p-program P, let $lfp(T_P(A_i)) = sg_i$ and $NS(P) = \times_{i=1}^{N} sg_i$. From [9] we know that $Mod(P) \in NS(P)$. We observe, that it is sufficient, to segment $NS(P)$ rather than the unit N-dimensional hypercube to compute $Mod(P)$. For a set of segments S and a segment μ let us denote by $S \cap \mu$ the set $\{s | s \in S \text{ and } s \subseteq \mu\}$.

Given a simple p-program P, an atom $A \in B_L$ and an interval $\nu \subseteq [0, 1]$, we denote by $Reduct(P, A : \nu)$ a reduced program which results from P as follows: (i) Delete from P any clause C with the head $A : \mu$ such that $\nu \subseteq \mu$. (ii) Delete from P any clause C whose body includes an atom $A : \mu$ such that $\mu \cap \nu = \emptyset$. (ii) Delete from the body of any other rule each atom $A : \mu$ such that $\nu \subseteq \mu$. It is easy to see that $Mod(Reduct(P, A : \nu)) = Mod(P \cup \{A : \nu \leftarrow .\})$.

Figure 3 contains the pseudocode for the algorithm GenModT, designed to intelligently execute all steps of the algorithm GenMod. The algorithm works as follows. On the first step, we compute $NS(P)$, reduce P wrt $NS(P)$ and construct segmentation of A_1. Then for each segment, we construct a reduced program P' and recursively run GenModT on P' and set $\{A_2, \ldots, A_n\}$ of atoms, and combine the solution returned by the recursive call with the segment of A_1 for which it was obtained. The union of solutions computed this way is returned at the end of each call to GenModT. The stopping conditions are either an empty reduct program, meaning that the segmentation leading to this reduct yields a part of the final solution, or a contradiction during the computation of $NS(P)$, meaning that current segmentation does not yield models of P. The theorem below states that Algorithm GenModT is correct.

Theorem 4. *Given a simple p-program P and an ordering $A_1, \ldots, A_N$ of B_L, algorithm GenModT returns the set $Mod(P)$.*

Apart from using $NS(.)$ as starting points for segmentation on every step, Algorithm GenModT improves over a naive implementation of GenMod in two ways. First, it may turn out that one of the stopping conditions for GenModT holds before the recursion has exhausted all atoms from P. In this case, it means that either an entire sub-space is part of the solution or is not part of the solution, but we no longer need to check each "brick" inside that sub-space. Second, on each step of the recursion after the first one, segmentation of the current atom occurs with respect to the current program, which is a reduct of P w.r.t. all previously considered atoms. This reduct has a simpler structure, and, in many cases, would have fewer and shorter rules. This means that the segmentation of the current atom w.r.t. the reduct may contain fewer segments than the segmentation w.r.t. original program P. Another convenient feature of GenModT is that it structures $Mod(P)$ in a form of a tree, corresponding to the way it recursively enumerates the solutions.

The advantages of GenModT over naive implementation of GenMod are demonstrated in the example of program P_1 (Fig. 1). It was shown that $NS(P_1)=$ $[0.2, 0.4] \times [0.2, 0.5]$ and that

$SEG_{P_1}(a) = \{[0, 0.2], [0.2, 0.3), [0.3, 0.3], (0.3, 0.4], (0.4, 1]\}$ and
$SEG_{P_1}(b) = \{[0, 0.2), [0.2, 0.3], (0.3, 0.4), [0.4, 0.5], (0.5, 1]\}$.

So, at the first step of GenModT $Seg = SEG_{P_1}(a) \cap (0.2, 0.4] = \{[0.2, 0.3), [0.3, 0.3], (0.3, 0.4]\}$ and the main loop will proceed three times as follows:

1) $s = [0.2, 0.3)$, $P' = \{b : [0.2, 0.3] \longleftarrow .\}$, $Sol = \{[0.2, 0.3) \times [0.2, 0.3]\}$;
2) $s = [0.3, 0.3]$, $P' = \{b : [0.2, 0.3] \longleftarrow .; \ b : [0.4, 0.5] \longleftarrow .\}$, $Sol := Sol \cup \emptyset$;
3) $s = (0.3, 0.4]$, $P' = \{ b : [0.4, 0.5] \longleftarrow .\}$, $Sol := Sol \cup \{(0.3, 0.4] \times [0.4, 0.5]\}$.

The result will be $Sol = [0.2, 0.3) \times [0.2, 0.3] \cup (0.3, 0.4] \times [0.4, 0.5]$ which is equal to $Mod(P_1)$ (see Proposition 3). Thus, GenModT tries only 3 bricks while GenMod will check all 25 bricks.

4   Related Work and Conclusions

There has been a number of logic programming frameworks for uncertainty proposed in the past 15 years (see [4] for a detailed survey), most concentrating on point probabilities. The work of Poole [13] and Ngo and Haddawy [12] treated the "$\longleftarrow$" as conditional dependence and used logic programming to model Bayesian Networks. In more recent work, Baral et al.[1] present an elegant way to incorporate probabilistic reasoning into an answer set programming framework, in which they combine probabilistic reasoning with traditional non-monotonic reasoning. At the same time,some work [8–11, 4, 5] looked at interval probabilities as the means of expressing imprecision in probability assessment. tics of the original In all those frameworks, the underlying semantics allowed for expression of the possible probability of an atom in a program as a single closed interval. Our work is the first to consider a harder problem of describing the semantics of interval-based probabilistic logic programs with sets of point probability assessments (p-interpretations), based on the semantics of interval probabilities proposed by De Campos et. al [3] and Weichselberger[15]. As shown in this paper, even for fairly simple syntax, such descriptions become more complex than single intervals and their computation is much more strenuous. Our next step is to study our semantics in the full language of p-programs of [9] and hybrid probabilistic programs [4]. We are also interested in investigating the relationship between the p-programs with possible worlds semantics and constraint logic programs.

References

1. Chitta Baral, Michael Gelfond, J. Nelson Rushton. (2004) Probabilistic Reasoning With Answer Sets, in *Proc. LPNMR-2004*, pp. 21-33.
2. V. Biazzo, A. Gilio. (1999) A Generalization of the Fundamental Theorem of de Finetti for Imprecise Conditional Probability Assessments, *Proc. 1st. Intl. Symposium on Imprecise Probabilities and Their Applications.*
3. Luis M. de Campos, Juan F. Huete, Serafin Moral (1994). Probability Intervals: A Tool for Uncertain Reasoning, *International Journal of Uncertainty, Fuzziness and Knowledge-Based Systems (IJUFKS)*, Vol. 2(2), pp. 167 – 196.
4. A. Dekhtyar and V.S. Subrahmanian (2000) Hybrid Probabilistic Programs. *Journal of Logic Programming*, Volume 43, Issue 3, pp. 187 – 250 .
5. M.I.. Dekhtyar, A. Dekhtyar and V.S. Subrahmanian (1999) Hybrid Probabilistic Programs: Algorithms and Complexity in Proc. of 1999 Conf. on Uncertainty in AI (UAI), pp 160 – 169.
6. H.E. Kyburg Jr. (1998) Interval-valued Probabilities, in *G. de Cooman, P. Walley and F.G. Cozman (Eds.), Imprecise Probabilities Project*, http://ippserv.rug.ac.be/documentation/interval_prob/interval_prob.html.
7. V.S. Lakshmanan and F. Sadri. (1994) *Modeling Uncertainty in Deductive Databases*, Proc. Int. Conf. on Database Expert Systems and Applications, (DEXA'94), September 7-9, 1994, Athens, Greece, Lecture Notes in Computer Science, Vol. 856, Springer (1994), pp. 724-733.
8. V.S. Lakshmanan and F. Sadri. (1994) *Probabilistic Deductive Databases*, Proc. Int. Logic Programming Symp., (ILPS'94), November 1994, Ithaca, NY, MIT Press.
9. R. Ng and V.S. Subrahmanian. (1993) Probabilistic Logic Programming, INFORMATION AND COMPUTATION, 101, 2, pps 150–201, 1993.
10. R. Ng and V.S. Subrahmanian. A Semantical Framework for Supporting Subjective and Conditional Probabilities in Deductive Databases, JOURNAL OF AUTOMATED REASONING, 10, 2, pps 191–235, 1993.
11. R. Ng and V.S. Subrahmanian. (1995) *Stable Semantics for Probabilistic Deductive Databases*, INFORMATION AND COMPUTATION, 110, 1, pps 42-83.

12. L. Ngo, P. Haddawy (1995) Probabilistic Logic Programming and Bayesian Networks, in *Proc. ASIAN-1995*, pp. 286-300.
13. D. Poole (1993). Probabilistic Horn Abduction and Bayesian Networks. *Artificial Intelligence*, Vol. 64(1), pp. 81-129.
14. Walley, P. (1991). Statistical Reasoning with Imprecise Probabilities. Chapman and Hall, 1991.
15. Weichselberger, K. (1999). The theory of interval-probability as a unifying concept for uncertainty. *Proc. 1st International Symp. on Imprecise Probabilities and Their Applications.*

Limiting Resolution:
From Foundations to Implementation

Patrick Caldon and Eric Martin

The University of New South Wales, Sydney, 2052, Australia
patc,emartin@cse.unsw.edu.au

Abstract. We present a generalization of SLD-resolution, Limiting Resolution (LR) which embeds concepts from the field of inductive inference into logic programming. This paper describes the development of
LR from theoretical underpinnings through to demonstrating a practical
implementation. LR is designed to represent and solve problems which
are not purely deductive more easily than current logic programming
formalisms. It is based on the notion of identification in the limit, where
successful computations produce a non-halting converging sequence of
outputs as opposed to computations which produce a single output and
halt. The queries of LR are of the form $\exists \overline{x}(\psi(\overline{x}) \wedge \forall \overline{y} \neg \chi(\overline{x}, \overline{y}))$, with some
restrictions on the occurrence of negation in ψ and χ. The programs are
divided into background knowledge and a potentially infinite stream of
data which drives the construction of the converging sequence of outputs.
In some problems true negation can be applied to data in this stream. We
describe the logical foundations of LR, where the notions of induction,
deduction and identification in the limit are unified in a common framework. The programs, queries, and proof procedure of LR are precisely
defined, and a completeness result is stated. Furthermore we present a
Prolog-style system, RichProlog, which implements LR, and provide an
extended example of RichProlog's execution. This example shows that it
is possible to solve genuine problems in polynomial time and also illustrates RichProlog's utility, conciseness, and declarative nature.

1 Introduction

1.1 Motivation and Background

Many problems encountered in AI have a significant inductive component, making application of deductive logic difficult and requiring recourse to nonmonotonic reasoning formalisms. Many AI problems require reasoning from only part
of the total possible data set, when not all the data are currently available. This
entails the possibility of a mind change when new data appear. It has been argued
that current nonmonotonic reasoning formalisms do not account satisfactorily
for common-sense reasoning of the kind needed to solve AI problems, particularly
as the formalisms do not account for how tentative solutions may subsequently
be contradicted[19]. The field of inductive inference deals with subsequent contradiction to a hypothesis in a not explicitly logical framework[9], which has

B. Demoen and V. Lifschitz (Eds.): ICLP 2004, LNCS 3132, pp. 149–164, 2004.
© Springer-Verlag Berlin Heidelberg 2004

recently been extended to a logical formalism[15, 16]. This paper outlines the theoretical underpinnings of a logic programming system, Limiting Resolution (LR), based on inductive inference, describes LR itself and demonstrates a practical implementation.

We remind the reader of the fundamental concepts of inductive inference. A system is said to identify or learn some set of countable nonempty sets $\mathcal{L}$ in the limit[6, 9] if, given an unknown member L of $\mathcal{L}$ with an infinite enumeration e of the members of L (possibly with repetitions), it produces a correct description of L in response to all but a finite number of initial segments of e. Visualize this scenario as playing a game where you must guess a set that we have in mind. Suppose we decide to play with $\mathcal{L}$ as the set of sets consisting of all the numbers greater than some natural number (an example member of $\mathcal{L}$ would be $\{4, 5, 6, \dots\}$). Having first chosen (for example) $L = \{2, 3, 4, \dots\}$, we then proceed through the game in rounds of guesses, as follows. Suppose we tell you 4 is in the set; you might guess $\{4, 5, 6, \dots\}$ as the set. If we tell you 7 is in the set, then presumably you would decide to stick with your guess. If however we tell you next that 2 is in the set, you might want to change your mind and revise your guess to $\{2, 3, 4, \dots\}$. As from this point on we will never mention the number 1, you'll always be happy with this guess of $\{2, 3, 4, \dots\}$ – however since you've only ever seen a finite initial sequence, it will appear to you that you *may* have to revise your guess at any time, and for this set L there's no finite collection of data which allows you to be sure that your guess is correct, and so you will not have a property analogous to compactness in classical logic. It is clear, however that the strategy of "guess the set whose least element is the lowest number thus far presented" will *in the limit* produce the correct hypothesis, that is after at most a finite number of mind changes on your part.

Parametric logic is a novel logic which encompasses notions from classical logic and inductive inference[15, 16]. It has a generalized notion of logical consequence intended to capture more comprehensively the logical nature of many problems currently encountered in AI. Parametric logic has a number of key properties which distinguish it from classical logic: it is related to the field of inductive inference, since some proofs can be considered as identifying in the limit from a set of data; it has an explicit idea of intended model; furthermore under some constraints exploited in LR it is sound and complete *in the limit*, meaning some finite number of incorrect answers may first be produced, but after these incorrect answers (which will require finite computation) only correct answers will be produced with no subsequent mind change. Many nonmonotonic reasoning formalisms have been proposed; however Parametric logic in general foregoes compactness, in contrast to those frameworks examined in [10], which all satisfy the compactness property. Several nonmonotonic logics including Reiter's default logic and Moore's auto-epistemic logic have close correspondence with negation-as-failure semantics for logic programming. Therefore in a logic programming context it is more appropriate to examine the relationships with nonmonotonic reasoning by analysing negation-as-failure semantics, discussed below.

LR is a generalization of resolution based on Parametric logic, with a well defined program and query syntax over which it is sound and complete. The queries in LR are particular examples of Σ_2 sentences, that is sentences of the form $\exists \bar{x} \forall \bar{y} \varphi(\bar{x}, \bar{y})$, where $\varphi(\bar{x}, \bar{y})$ is quantifier free[1]. A LR program is more general than a definite logic program and consists of background knowledge together with a potentially infinite stream of data that represent evidence or results of experiments. At any time, the system has access to the background knowledge plus some finite initial segment of the stream of data (the data observed or the results of experiments obtained so far). The completeness result guarantees that when sufficient data have been collected, the program will output a correct candidate, and the same candidate will be output again and again as more data become available. Although convergence to this correct candidate is guaranteed, usually it is not possible to know in advance how many data will be needed for convergence. RichProlog[2] is our implementation of this system. A preliminary version has been presented in [14]. The current version has a number of differences and improvements: there is no longer a confidence threshold for the correctness of an answer, there is a theoretically grounded notion of negation built into the system, a type system has been added allowing for the enumeration of terms, and it has a clearly defined syntax which is directly related to the completeness of LR.

Many AI problems are optimization problems, and so have a natural expression as a Σ_2 query; i.e. discovering the existence of some x which for all y, x is preferable to y. A more general example is: does there exists a rule x such that for all possible data y, x predicts y if and only if y can and will be observed. Matroids, a class of problems solved by greedy algorithms have a convenient expression as a LR query and program, and a natural expression of the minimum spanning tree problem is shown later in this paper. In particular, solutions to matroid problems of polynomial time complexity can be implemented with polynomial cost, and the example provided demonstrates this in a natural style.

1.2 Comparison with Existing Formalisms

Inductive Logic Programming (ILP)[17] systems have been proposed and constructed to learn theories inductively from collections of data; however these systems do not attempt to construct a proof in the conventional sense, as the computation is some kind of theory construction procedure, *e.g.* inverse entailment, and not some kind of Tarskian logical inference which we employ. A similar consideration applies to abductive logic programming. Also, our approach is quite distinct from that of answer-set programming, where the objective is to discover some stable model under a 3-valued semantics, rather than find a computed answer substitution in a 2-valued semantics. Furthermore, unlike belief revision systems, we know that any inconsistency that arises from the program, the available data and the tentative solution $\bar{t}$ of the query, has to be resolved by dismissing $\bar{t}$, as opposed to allowing revision anywhere in the program.

---

[1] We use $\bar{x}$ to denote a tuple of variables or terms of appropriate length.
[2] See: **http://www.cse.unsw.edu.au/~patc/richprolog**

Several resolution-style systems have been proposed which incorporate negation, including SLDNF[3], SLS[20], SLG[4], and constructive negation. The semantics for these systems are more complex than that for SLD-resolution, requiring in different cases 3-valued interpretations, restrictions to stratified programs, stable model semantics and other more complex constructions; Apt and Bol[2] provide a good summary. The proof technique of LR has some similarities to SLDNF, but the semantics are quite different. In particular, SLDNF queries are existentially quantified, whereas LR has both existential and universal quantification, LR permits the selection of non-ground literals, and its semantics are defined with respect to the program itself rather than its completion. SLS-resolution has a negation as (not necessarily) finite failure rule but is not an effective proof procedure as it does not identify a condition analogous to convergence in the limit. SLG solves the problems in SLS via a tabling mechanism but is characterized in terms of a 3-valued stable model semantics, and so is quite distinct from our work. SLDNFE[21] also has some similarities in proof theory in delaying non-ground literals prior to selection, but again with respect to a 3-valued semantics. Further differences between our formalism and others include: the weakening of the compactness property, use of Herbrand interpretations for intended interpretations as opposed to 3-valued interpretations (*e.g.*, stable and well-founded interpretations) and inclusion of a form of true negation. Universal quantification has been examined in a logic programming context. Voronkov proposes bounding universal quantifiers[22] with finite sets. Unlike this and similar systems, we use unbounded quantification in queries.

2   Parametric Logic

The semantics of LR programs is based on Parametric logic. An overview is provided here, but see [16] for a more complete exposition. Parametric logic has a set of parameters, namely, a countable *possible vocabulary* V, a class of *possible worlds* W (a class of V-structures), a *possible language* L (a set of V-sentences, *e.g.*, the set of first-order V-sentences), a set D of *possible data* and a set A of *possible assumptions* with $D, A \subseteq L$ and $D \cap A = \emptyset$. We set

$$P = (V, W, L, D, A)$$

and call P a *logical paradigm*. LR is based on settings of the parameters such that V contains at least one constant, W is a nonempty set of Herbrand interpretations, and D is a set of ground literals (*i.e.* atomic or negation of atomic sentences). The choice of D depends on the application, and corresponds to the simple observations one can make. Members of A on the other hand are the formulas which can be used to express some background knowledge. Suppose for instance that we have a data collector for tide heights; then assuming a reasonable choice of V, D could be defined as formulas of the form tide_height(*time*, *location*) > *low* or ¬(tide_height(*time*, *location*) > *high*) (where *time*, *location*, *low* and *high* are V-terms, whereas A could contain some facts and rules about arithmetic).

The set of possible data true in a possible world $\mathfrak{M}$ is called the $\mathcal{D}$-*diagram* of $\mathfrak{M}$, and is denoted by $\mathrm{Diag}_{\mathcal{D}}(\mathfrak{M})$; hence $\mathrm{Diag}_{\mathcal{D}}(\mathfrak{M}) = \{\varphi \in \mathcal{D} : \mathfrak{M} \models \varphi\}$. A useful starting point for logical investigation is a generalization of the consistent theories of classical logic; it is a *possible knowledge base*, defined as a set of the form $\mathrm{Diag}_{\mathcal{D}}(\mathfrak{M}) \cup A$ where $\mathfrak{M}$ is a possible world and A is a set of possible assumptions (formulas in $\mathcal{A}$) true in $\mathfrak{M}$. We denote by $\mathcal{B}$ the set of possible knowledge bases. Hence $\mathcal{B}$ is a derived parameter of the logical paradigm $\mathcal{P}$ and

$$\mathcal{B} = \{\mathrm{Diag}_{\mathcal{D}}(\mathfrak{M}) \cup A : \mathfrak{M} \in \mathcal{W}, \ A \subseteq \mathcal{A}, \ \mathfrak{M} \models A\}.$$

Intuitively, all possible data true in $\mathfrak{M}$ will eventually be observed, or measured, and some extra background knowledge about $\mathfrak{M}$ can be added to any 'natural' theory that (partially) describes $\mathfrak{M}$. Therefore, the intended models of a possible knowledge base (member of $\mathcal{B}$) T are the possible worlds $\mathfrak{M}$ such that $\mathrm{Diag}_{\mathcal{D}}(\mathfrak{M}) = T \cap \mathcal{D}$ and $\mathfrak{M} \models T \cap \mathcal{A}$. Both conditions imply that $\mathfrak{M}$ is a model of T, but a closed world assumption is applied to the possible data: a possible datum (member of $\mathcal{D}$) that does not belong to T has to be false in every intended model of T, whereas a possible assumption (member of $\mathcal{A}$) that does not belong to T can be either true or false (unless it is implied by the other members of T) in T's intended models. This notion of intended model is at the root of the generalized notion of logical consequence of Parametric logic, defined next:

Definition 1 *Let $T \in \mathcal{B}$ and $\varphi \in \mathcal{L}$ be given. We say that φ is a logical consequence of T in $\mathcal{P}$, and we write $T \models_{\mathcal{W}}^{\mathcal{D}} \varphi$, just in case for all $\mathfrak{M} \in \mathcal{W}$, if $\mathfrak{M} \models T$ and $\mathrm{Diag}_{\mathcal{D}}(\mathfrak{M}) = T \cap \mathcal{D}$ then $\mathfrak{M} \models \varphi$.*

Intuitively, the class of possible interpretations is restricted and a closed world assumption is applied to possible data but not to assumptions which has the effect of selecting a class of intended models. When $\mathcal{P}$ is the paradigm of classical first-order logic (*i.e.*, $\mathcal{W}$ = class of all $\mathcal{V}$-structures, $\mathcal{L}$ is the set of first-order $\mathcal{V}$-sentences, $\mathcal{D} = \emptyset$, and $\mathcal{A} = \mathcal{L}$), $\models_{\mathcal{W}}^{\mathcal{D}}$ is nothing but $\models$, but for other choices of values of the parameters – in particular, the values selected for LR– logical consequence in $\mathcal{P}$ is stronger than classical logical consequence; it is not compact, and accounts for various kinds of inference. We define three kinds of inference: deductive, inductive, and limiting inference. Deductive inferences in $\mathcal{P}$ are characterized by the compactness property: they are conclusive inferences on the basis of a finite subset of the underlying knowledge base.

Definition 2 *Let $T \in \mathcal{B}$ and $\varphi \in \mathcal{L}$ be such that $T \models_{\mathcal{W}}^{\mathcal{D}} \varphi$. We say that φ is a deductive consequence of T in $\mathcal{P}$ iff there exists a finite subset D of T such that for all $T' \in \mathcal{B}$, if $D \subseteq T'$ then $T' \models_{\mathcal{W}}^{\mathcal{D}} \varphi$.*

When $\mathcal{P}$ is the paradigm of first-order logic, '$T \models \varphi$' and 'φ is a deductive consequence of T in $\mathcal{P}$' are equivalent notions. More generally, for any logical paradigm $\mathcal{P}$, if $T \models \varphi$ then φ is a deductive consequence of T in $\mathcal{P}$, but the converse is not always true; this is an instance of the universal query problem [11]. Inductive inferences in $\mathcal{P}$ are characterized by a property of weak compactness: they are not conclusive inferences, but they can be conclusively refuted.

Definition 3 *Let $T \in \mathcal{B}$ and $\varphi \in \mathcal{L}$ be such that $T \models^{\mathcal{D}}_{\mathcal{W}} \varphi$. We say that φ is an inductive consequence of T in $\mathcal{P}$ iff there exists a finite $D \subseteq T$ such that for all $T' \in \mathcal{B}$, if $D \subseteq T'$ and $T' \not\models^{\mathcal{D}}_{\mathcal{W}} \varphi$ then $\neg\varphi$ is a deductive consequence of T' in $\mathcal{P}$.*

Note that in the definition above, the discovery of $\neg\varphi$ from T' is a refutation of φ from T' (from some finite subset D' of T' which might be different from D).

Definition 4 *Let $T \in \mathcal{B}$ and $\varphi \in \mathcal{L}$ be such that $T \models^{\mathcal{D}}_{\mathcal{W}} \varphi$. We say that φ is a limiting consequence of T in $\mathcal{P}$ iff there exists a finite subset D of T and a member ψ of $\mathcal{L}$ such that ψ is an inductive consequence of T in $\mathcal{P}$ and for all $T' \in \mathcal{B}$, if $D \subseteq T'$ and $T' \models^{\mathcal{D}}_{\mathcal{W}} \psi$ then $T' \models^{\mathcal{D}}_{\mathcal{W}} \varphi$.*

This more complex inference corresponds to an inductive inference followed by a deductive inference. Intuitively, in Definition 4, φ is a conclusive inference from a formula ψ which represents an inductive leap. Links with inductive inference can be established: deductive consequences in $\mathcal{P}$ can be discovered with no mind change, inductive consequences in $\mathcal{P}$ can be discovered with at most one mind change, and limiting consequences in $\mathcal{P}$ can be discovered in the limit [16]. Essential to LR is the relationship between limiting consequences in $\mathcal{P}$ and identification in the limit; this relationship is expressed in Proposition 7 below. Further, we can show the existence of a whole hierarchy of inferences with less than β mind changes where β is a non-null ordinal; deductive and inductive inferences are the particular case where $\beta = 1$ and $\beta = 2$, respectively. Under some assumptions, given a sentence φ, φ is a limiting consequence in $\mathcal{P}$ of any $T \in \mathcal{B}$ where $T \models^{\mathcal{D}}_{\mathcal{W}} \varphi$ if and only if φ is a Σ_2 sentence of a particular form, which yields precisely the syntax of the queries for LR.

For example, assume that $\mathcal{V}$ consists of constant $\overline{0}$, unary function s, and binary predicate R. For all $n \in \mathbb{N}$, let $\overline{n}$ denote the numeral ($\mathcal{V}$-term) that represents n. Assume that $\mathcal{W}$ is the set of Herbrand models of: 'R is a strict total ordering.' Finally, assume that $\mathcal{D}$ is the set of all atomic sentences of the form $R(\overline{m}, \overline{n})$, for $m, n \in \mathbb{N}$. Consider the possible world $\mathfrak{M}$ whose domain is $\mathbb{N}$ and such that $R^{\mathfrak{M}}$ is the strict total ordering $(\overline{1}, \overline{3}, \overline{5} \ldots \overline{0}, \overline{2}, \overline{4} \ldots)$ (a copy of $2\mathbb{N} + 1$ followed by a copy of $2\mathbb{N}$). The $\mathcal{D}$-diagram of $\mathfrak{M}$ contains $R(\overline{4}, \overline{8})$ and $R(\overline{5}, \overline{2})$, but neither $R(\overline{7}, \overline{3})$ nor $R(\overline{8}, \overline{3})$. Set $\varphi_1 = \exists x R(\overline{2}, x)$, $\varphi_2 = \forall y \neg R(y, \overline{1})$, and $\varphi_3 = \exists x \forall y \neg R(y, x)$. Then $\mathrm{Diag}_{\mathcal{D}}(\mathfrak{M})$ is a possible knowledge base and one can immediately verify that φ_1 is a deductive consequence of $\mathrm{Diag}_{\mathcal{D}}(\mathfrak{M})$ in $\mathcal{P}$, φ_2 is an inductive consequence of $\mathrm{Diag}_{\mathcal{D}}(\mathfrak{M})$ in $\mathcal{P}$, and φ_3 is a limiting consequence of $\mathrm{Diag}_{\mathcal{D}}(\mathfrak{M})$ in $\mathcal{P}$, taking $\psi = \varphi_2$ in Definition 4. The solution $x = \overline{1}$ to φ_3 viewed as a query can be computed in the limit, for instance by hypothesizing that $\overline{0}$ is the least element, before this wrong hypothesis is refuted and it is correctly conjectured that $\overline{1}$ is the least element. For this particular $\mathfrak{M}$, only 1 mind change is needed, but note that up to n mind changes might be needed if $\overline{n}$ is the least element, and if numerals are conjectured in their natural order.

Most problems allow the extraction of a background knowledge K, with the property that $\mathcal{W}$ is the set of Herbrand models of K. With the previous example, we would define K as a set of sentences expressing that R is a strict total ordering. For most problems, K is finite whereas the $\mathcal{D}$-diagram of a possible world is infinite. LR has access to K and a finite subset of $\text{Diag}_\mathcal{D}(\mathfrak{M})$, for some member $\mathfrak{M}$ of $\mathcal{W}$; the key point is that only a finite (though unknown) subset of $\text{Diag}_\mathcal{D}(\mathfrak{M})$ is necessary to make a correct inference, with larger subsets of $\text{Diag}_\mathcal{D}(\mathfrak{M})$ yielding the same result.

3 Limiting Resolution

3.1 Limiting Definite Programs and Queries

Limiting Resolution, described below, is a previously unpublished resolution-style system for perfoming inference according to Parametric Logic semantics. Let us define a *general rule* as a formula that can be represented as $\varphi \leftarrow \psi$, where φ is atomic and ψ is quantifier free and in negation normal form (*i.e.*, is built from the set of literals using disjunction and conjunction), using the standard logic programming abbreviations. The basic parts of a formula ψ are the literals that occur in ψ [3]. Given two sets X and Y of literals, we say that X *underlies* Y iff all closed instances of all members of X belong to Y. Intuitively, X underlies Y if the set X is syntactically more general than Y. Let a literal φ and a set X of literals be given. Let ψ denote the atomic formula such that $\varphi = \psi$ or $\varphi = \neg\psi$. We say that φ is *related* to X iff there exists an atomic formula ξ such that ψ and ξ unify, and ξ or $\neg\xi$ belongs to X. This is a particular case of a notion that has been considered in the literature on relevant logics [1]. Intuitively, if φ is not related to X then φ and X cannot interact.

A limiting definite program is to LR what a definite logic program is to SLD-resolution, and hence is more general. In the context of Parametric logic, limiting definite programs are a particular kind of possible knowledge base, in a logical paradigm $\mathcal{P}$ satisfying the following:

- $\mathcal{V}$ contains at least one constant.
- $\mathcal{D}$ is a set of ground literals; it might consist of nothing but ground atoms (for problems where only positive data are available), or ground literals (for problems where both positive and negative data are available).
- $\mathcal{A}$ is a set of general rules such that:
  - for all $\varphi \in \mathcal{A}$, the head of φ is not related to $\mathcal{D}$;
  - for all $\varphi \in \mathcal{A}$ and for all basic parts ψ of the body of φ, ψ is not related to $\mathcal{D}$ and ψ is atomic, or ψ is related to $\mathcal{D}$ and ψ underlies $\mathcal{D}$.
- $\mathcal{W}$ is the class of Herbrand models of $\mathcal{A}$.

Hence we consider the very particular case of a logical paradigm $\mathcal{P}$ where all possible assumptions are true in all possible worlds. This means that the whole of $\mathcal{A}$ can play the role of background knowledge. Though the set $\mathcal{B}$ of possible knowledge bases is equal to $\{\text{Diag}_\mathcal{D}(\mathfrak{M}) \cup A : \mathfrak{M} \in \mathcal{W}, \ A \subseteq \mathcal{A}\}$, we focus on the particular knowledge bases T where $T \cap \mathcal{A}$ is maximal, hence equal to $\mathcal{A}$:

---

[3] Of course, if α is an atomic formula and all occurrences of α in ψ are preceded by negation, then α is not a basic part of ψ.

Definition 5 *A* limiting definite program (in $\mathcal{P}$) *is a member of* $\mathcal{B}$ *of the form* $\mathcal{A} \cup \text{Diag}_{\mathcal{D}}(\mathfrak{M})$, *for some* $\mathfrak{M} \in \mathcal{W}$.

For instance, assume that $\mathcal{V}$ contains unary predicate symbols p_1, p_2, q_1, q_2, q_3. Suppose that $\mathcal{D} = \{q_1(t), q_2(t), \neg q_2(t), \neg q_3(t) : \text{ground terms } t\}$. Then:

- $p_1(X) \leftarrow q_1(X), p_2(Z), q_2(X), \neg q_2(Z), \neg q_3(Y)$ can be a member of $\mathcal{A}$.
- $p_1(X) \leftarrow q_1(X), \neg p_2(Z), q_2(X), \neg q_2(Z), q_3(Y)$ cannot be a member of $\mathcal{A}$ (because of either $\neg p_2(Z)$ or $q_3(Y)$).

The heads of the members of $\mathcal{A}$, and the basic parts in the bodies of the members of $\mathcal{A}$ that are not related to $\mathcal{D}$, should be thought of as *theoretical atoms*. The other formulas that occur in the bodies of the members of $\mathcal{A}$ are formulas such that all their closed instances are possible data. Note that singleton clauses can be either theoretical atoms, or literals all of whose closed instances are members of $\mathcal{D}$. A simple mechanism to ensure that theoretical atoms and members of the set $\mathcal{D}$ of possible data cannot interact is to partition the set of predicate symbols in $\mathcal{V}$ into two classes, evidential and theoretical predicate symbols, and require that a member of $\mathcal{D}$ (or resp. member of $\mathcal{A}$) be built from an evidential (or resp. theoretical) predicate symbol. LR solves limiting definite queries in the context of limiting definite programs. *Limiting definite queries* are more general than definite queries since they are Σ_2 sentences of a particular form. To define them we need a preliminary concept. A literal α is $\mathcal{D}$-*simple* iff:

- α is positive and not related to $\mathcal{D}$, or
- α underlies $\mathcal{D}$.

Definition 6 *A sentence* φ *is a* limiting definite query (in $\mathcal{P}$) *iff it is of the form* $\exists \overline{x}(\psi(\overline{x}) \wedge \forall \overline{y} \neg \chi(\overline{x}, \overline{y}))$ *where* ψ *and* χ *are quantifier free and in negation normal form, and all basic parts of* ψ *and* χ *are* $\mathcal{D}$-*simple*.

Assume that $\mathcal{V}$ and $\mathcal{D}$ are defined after Definition 5. Then in Definition 6, ψ cannot be $\neg p_1(X_1) \wedge q_3(X_1)$ (because of either $\neg p_1(X_1)$ or $q_3(X_1)$) and χ cannot be $(\neg p_2(Y_1) \vee \neg q_1(Y_2)) \wedge (q_2(Y_2) \vee \neg q_3(Y_2))$ (because of either $\neg p_2(Y_1)$ or $\neg q_1(Y_2)$). For a more complex example, if $\mathcal{D}$ is defined as $\{\text{observed}(t) : \text{ground terms } t\}$

$$Q = \exists P \exists L [\text{pattern}(P) \wedge \text{list}(L) \wedge \text{same\_length}(P, L) \wedge \text{match}(P, L) \wedge$$
$$\forall W \neg (\text{word}(W) \wedge \text{observed}(W) \wedge (\text{smaller\_length}(P, W) \vee \text{mismatch}(P, W)))]$$

is a limiting definite query. Solving Q means computing a witness for (P, L) that makes the query a logical consequence in $\mathcal{P}$ of the union of $\mathcal{A}$ (not shown here) with a possibly infinite set of sentences of the form $\text{observed}(t)$.

3.2   Limiting Resolution

The following result shows that we can discover in the limit whether a limiting definite query is a logical consequence in $\mathcal{P}$ of a limiting definite program.

Proposition 7 *Assume that* $\mathcal{P}$ *satisfies the conditions stated in Section 3.1. There exists a computable function* f *that maps finite subsets of* $\mathcal{D}$ *into* $\{0, 1\}$ *such that for all limiting definite queries* φ *and for all* $\mathfrak{M} \in \mathcal{W}$, *the following are equivalent.*

- $\mathcal{A} \cup \mathrm{Diag}_{\mathcal{D}}(\mathfrak{M}) \models^{\mathcal{D}}_{\mathcal{W}} \varphi$ [4];
- for all enumerations $(e_i)_{i \in \mathbb{N}}$ of $\mathrm{Diag}_{\mathcal{D}}(\mathfrak{M}) \cup \{\sharp\}$, $f(\{e_0, \ldots, e_i\} \setminus \{\sharp\}) = 1$ for all but finitely many $i \in \mathbb{N}$ [5].

Proposition 7 is a very particular case of a much more general result of Parametric logic. LR is a particular proof procedure that discovers in the limit whether a limiting definite query φ is a logical consequence in $\mathcal{P}$ of a limiting definite program, and that computes in the limit witnesses to the existentially quantified variables of φ.

LR proofs are constructed in a similar manner to SLD and negation-as-failure formalisms by constructing trees or forests whose nodes are labelled with formulas. We describe the system under the constraint that programs are restricted to clauses, and queries are in the form $\exists \overline{x}(\psi(\overline{x}) \wedge \forall \overline{y} \neg \chi(\overline{x}, \overline{y}))$ with ψ and χ being conjunctions of $\mathcal{D}$-simple literals. This description can be extended to the programs and queries of Definitions 5 and 6 respectively (which includes disjunction) by using a mechanism similar to the Lloyd-Topor transformation[13]. There is no conceptual difference between the simplified and more general version.

Take some possible world $\mathfrak{M}$, and consider $\Delta \subseteq \mathrm{Diag}_{\mathcal{D}}(\mathfrak{M})$. Assume that $\mathcal{A}$ is some set of clauses over $\mathcal{D}$-simple literals. Now $P = \Delta \cup \mathcal{A}$ is a fragment of the limiting definite program $\mathrm{Diag}_{\mathcal{D}}(\mathfrak{M}) \cup \mathcal{A}$. Let Q be a limiting definite query restricted to conjunctions. We define a *LR triple* for (P, Q) as a triple $\mathcal{F} = (T, I, s)$, with the following properties: T is a tree, called the *deductive tree* of the LR triple whose nodes are labelled with finite sets containing $\mathcal{D}$-simple literals and at most one negation of a conjunction of $\mathcal{D}$-simple literals; I is a collection of trees called the *inductive trees* of the LR triple with finite sets of $\mathcal{D}$-simple literals labelling the nodes; and s is a partial mapping from leaves in T to trees in I. Given a LR triple $\mathcal{F}$, a LR triple $\mathcal{F}'$ which *extends* $\mathcal{F}$ is defined inductively as follows. Take a leaf N from $\mathcal{F}$, with label M and select via some selection rule a $\mathcal{D}$-simple literal C in M; if no $\mathcal{D}$-simple literal is present then, if available, the negation of the conjunction of $\mathcal{D}$-simple literals will be selected as C. We attach a new component to $\mathcal{F}$ to create $\mathcal{F}' = (T', I', s')$, where T' extends T, I' expands I (*i.e.* by extending trees in I or adding new trees to I), and s' expands s depending on the following rules:

- If C is a $\mathcal{D}$-simple literal in some tree in $\{T\} \cup I$, and there is some rule $C' \leftarrow \bigwedge L \in P$, with L possibly empty, such that C and C' unify – create a new node labelled with $((M \setminus \{C\}) \cup L)\theta$ below N for every appropriate $C' \leftarrow \bigwedge L \in P$ where θ is the mgu of C and C'. The mapping s' is updated appropriately.
- If C is a negation of a conjunction of $\mathcal{D}$-simple literals and $s(C)$ is not defined
  - add a new single node tree U to I to create I' with the conjuncts in C labelling the root of U and expand s to s' by setting $s'(C) = U$.
- If neither rule applies – then $\mathcal{F}' = \mathcal{F}$.

---

[4] Since all members of $\mathcal{A}$ are assumed to be true in all members of $\mathcal{W}$, it is clear that $\mathcal{A} \cup \mathrm{Diag}_{\mathcal{D}}(\mathfrak{M}) \models^{\mathcal{D}}_{\mathcal{W}} \varphi$ is equivalent to $\mathrm{Diag}_{\mathcal{D}}(\mathfrak{M}) \models^{\mathcal{D}}_{\mathcal{W}} \varphi$.

[5] We denote by $\sharp$ an extra symbol, whose intended meaning is 'no datum provided,' that is necessary for the particular case where $\mathrm{Diag}_{\mathcal{D}}(\mathfrak{M}) = \emptyset$.

We then define a *LR forest* for (P, Q) as a sequence of LR triples for (P, Q) $(\mathcal{F}_0, \mathcal{F}_1, \mathcal{F}_2, \dots)$ where:

- the deductive tree of $\mathcal{F}_0$ is a root labelled with the original query and the set of inductive trees of $\mathcal{F}_0$ is empty;
- for all $i \in \mathbb{N}$, $\mathcal{F}_{i+1}$ is an extension of $\mathcal{F}_i$;
- whenever $i \in \mathbb{N}$ and a leaf N in one of the inductive trees of $\mathcal{F}_i$ is not either a success or a failure node in the sense of SLD-resolution, there exists some $j > i$ such that N is an interior node in all the inductive trees of $\mathcal{F}_j$.

A *maximal LR triple* is defined as a LR triple to which no non-identity extension applies. A LR triple is *successful* iff either its deductive tree contains a node labelled with the empty clause or the LR triple contains at least one inductive tree for which no node is labelled with the empty clause. A LR forest $(\mathcal{F}_i)_{i \in \mathbb{N}}$

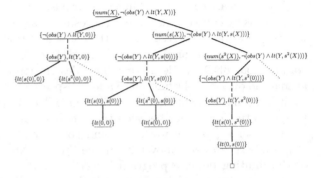

Fig. 1. Limiting Resolution Forest

is *successful* iff cofinitely many of its LR triples are successful. The system calculates computed answer substitutions on successful LR triples identically to SLD-resolution on the deductive trees, with the additional condition that negated conjunctions which label leaves of the deductive tree are considered successful with the empty answer substitution. The computed answer substitutions of a successful LR forest are defined as the substitutions that are the computed answer substitutions of cofinitely many successful LR triples.

For example, consider the set of formulas $\mathcal{A} = \{num(0), num(s(X)) \leftarrow num(X), lt(0, s(X)), lt(s(X), s(Y)) \leftarrow lt(X, Y)\}$ where $\mathcal{D} = \{obs(s^n(0)) : n \in \mathbb{N}\}$, and $\Delta = \{obs(s^n(0)) : n \geq 1\} = \mathrm{Diag}_{\mathcal{D}}(\mathfrak{M})$, and the program $P = \mathcal{A} \cup \Delta$. We ask the query, $\exists X(num(X) \wedge \forall Y \neg(obs(Y) \wedge lt(Y, X)))$. Figure 1 shows a diagrammatic representation of the computation, which has solutions $X = 0$ and $X = s(0)$. This diagram is infinite – for building practical systems we need the following key result:

Proposition 8 *Let a limiting definite query* $Q = \exists \overline{x}(\psi(\overline{x}) \wedge \forall \overline{y} \neg \chi(\overline{x}, \overline{y}))$, *a tuple of terms* $\overline{t}$, *and* $\mathfrak{M} \in W$ *be such that* $\mathrm{Diag}_{\mathcal{D}}(\mathfrak{M}) \cup \mathcal{A} \models_W^{\mathcal{D}} \psi(\overline{t}) \wedge \forall \overline{y} \neg \chi(\overline{t}, \overline{y})$. *Then there exists a successful LR forest* $(\mathcal{F}_i)_{i \in \mathbb{N}}$ *for* $(\mathrm{Diag}_{\mathcal{D}}(\mathfrak{M}) \cup \mathcal{A}, Q)$, *a tuple of terms* $\overline{t'}$, *and a finite subset* Δ *of* $\mathrm{Diag}_{\mathcal{D}}(\mathfrak{M})$ *with the following properties:*

- $\overline{t'}$ *is a computed answer substitution of* $(\mathcal{F}_i)_{i \in \mathbb{N}}$ *at least as general as* $\overline{t}$.
- *Let* Δ' *be such that* $\Delta \subseteq \Delta' \subseteq \mathrm{Diag}_{\mathcal{D}}(\mathfrak{M})$. *For all* $i \in \mathbb{N}$, *let* $\mathcal{F}'_i$ *be the maximal LR triple for* $(\Delta' \cup \mathcal{A}, Q)$ *such that* $\mathcal{F}_i$ *extends* $\mathcal{F}'_i$. *Then* $(\mathcal{F}'_i)_{i \in \mathbb{N}}$ *is a successful LR forest for* $(\Delta' \cup \mathcal{A}, Q)$ *having* $\overline{t'}$ *as a computed answer substitution.*

This construction and proposition provide a logic programming analogue to the formula f discussed in Proposition 7 above. Discovery of $\overline{t'}$ from some finite $\Delta \subseteq \mathrm{Diag}_{\mathcal{D}}(\mathfrak{M})$ corresponds to eventually finding some witness which remains a witness for the existentially quantified query variables as Δ is progressively extended to $\mathrm{Diag}_{\mathcal{D}}(\mathfrak{M})$. Assume that the members of $\mathrm{Diag}_{\mathcal{D}}(\mathfrak{M})$ are enumerated one by one. LR will then be run on the background knowledge $\mathcal{A}$ plus some finite initial segment of the enumeration of $\mathrm{Diag}_{\mathcal{D}}(\mathfrak{M})$. At the start of our computation $\mathrm{Diag}_{\mathcal{D}}(\mathfrak{M})$ is unknown, however the computation will necessarily converge in the limit to one of the same witnesses that $\mathrm{Diag}_{\mathcal{D}}(\mathfrak{M})$ would have produced. Consequently it is not necessary to traverse the entire (generally infinite) forest for $(\mathrm{Diag}_{\mathcal{D}}(\mathfrak{M}) \cup \mathcal{A}, Q)$, but only some finite portion of the forest. Usually, it is not possible to know in advance how many data will be necessary for LR to converge to the right answer.

To consider the relation with conventional logic programming semantics, consider the case where $\mathcal{A}$ is a set of definite clauses, all members of $\mathcal{D}$ are atomic, and T is a limiting definite program in $\mathcal{P}$. For all definite (as opposed to limiting definite) queries φ, $T \models \varphi$ iff $T \models_{\mathcal{W}}^{\mathcal{D}} \varphi$. But when φ is a limiting definite query, $T \models \varphi$ is generally not equivalent to $T \models_{\mathcal{W}}^{\mathcal{D}} \varphi$. LR is a system that targets formulas higher than Σ_1 in the arithmetical hierarchy, but w.r.t. to the *generalized* notion of logical consequence $\models_{\mathcal{W}}^{\mathcal{D}}$ rather than w.r.t. the *classical* notion of logical consequence $\models$. This is in contrast with extensions of Prolog proposed by [12].

4 Implementation

4.1 Implementation Details

RichProlog is our implementation of LR. Its execution proceeds by performing a depth-first search on the LR forest, attempting first to generate some tentative witness or directly find a contradiction in the deductive tree of the forest, and subsequently attempting to construct some refutation of the tentative witness in an inductive tree of the forest. Failed tentative witnesses cause backtracking to other tentative witnesses. In the course of the execution there is an opportunity for users to enter new members of $\mathcal{D}$, at every stage when a computed answer substitution is proffered to the user. RichProlog converges in the limit to a correct witness (actually a most general unifier) for the existentially quantified variables in the query should one exist, and otherwise reports a failure. RichProlog programs and queries are practical extensions of limiting definite programs and queries, in a similar manner to Prolog programs and queries being practical extensions of SLD-resolution (with the exception of negation-as-failure, since negation is already part of LR). The system is supported by the completeness result of LR, but note that it uses an incomplete left-to-right depth-first-search selection rule, and only optionally uses an occurs check on account of the worst-case exponential cost.

In the present implementation of RichProlog, the set $\mathcal{D}$ is defined implicitly. Evidential predicate symbols are those preceded with the quote symbol ‘, and

$\mathcal{D}$ will be derived from these predicates. The kind of (true) negation introduced in RichProlog programs is indicated by preceding the atom to negate with **rnot**. Note that $\mathcal{D}$ might not contain every ground atom built from an evidential predicate symbol. The list of evidential predicate symbols can be determined automatically by examining the program. Formulas built from an evidential predicate symbol can use any terms as arguments, but a type system described below may present additional restrictions on $\mathcal{D}$. Unlike Prolog, any solution presented by RichProlog is tentative and can possibly be contradicted as a result of later data being discovered.

Using a type system we can increase the scope of RichProlog queries. We permit queries of the form $\exists(\overline{x} \in T)\forall\overline{y}\varphi(\overline{x},\overline{y})$, where T defines some type, which can be rewritten as $\exists\overline{x}(\overline{x} \in T \wedge \forall\overline{y}\varphi(\overline{x},\overline{y}))$. This effectively constructs a generate-and-test strategy for the existentially quantified variables, and is convenient in practice. Many type systems have been proposed for logic programming languages. Among those, many only type variables, as we do, using the justification in [18], and here the syntax and unification rules we use are derived from this. The only notable departure is the addition of a type **@var**, to represent a variable in the enumeration of types. In general the variable type is required for completeness (since any constant in $\mathcal{V}$ can be replaced by a variable in an enumeration of all terms over $\mathcal{V}$), but it can be convenient to exclude this on occasion. Given that the type system exists primarily to define $\mathcal{V}$ we have used the most limited type system available. We anticipate extending this to a more substantial type system with more static checking and stronger capabilities for type inference. The type system is based on a very simple constraint system, allowing variables to be unified only with terms having the same type as variable. The current implementation is made simple by use of attributed variables[7].

4.2   Example

One might posit that the implementation of any complex algorithm will necessarily require exponential time on account of the implicit RichProlog "generate-and-test" strategy. We present a program for finding minimum spanning trees (MSTs) in RichProlog based on Kruskal's algorithm[5] which executes in polynomial time on finite graphs. The MST problem was chosen for being one of the more complex problems possible to present thoroughly in a short paper which demonstrates RichProlog features. This problem when restricted to finite graphs has a well known $O(E \log E)$ upper bound on complexity, E being the number of edges. If $\mathrm{Diag}_{\mathcal{D}}(\mathfrak{M})$ is finite, this problem corresponds to the conventional MST problem, however this implementation will also work for infinite cases. This MST problem asks "does there exist some finite spanning tree S of a (possibly infinite) graph G, such that for all spanning trees S', $l(S) < l(S')$ where l is the sum of the weights of edges in the graph". Solving this query directly appears to be intractable however. Kruskal's algorithm provides a tractable method, and can be quickly summarized: sort the edges into ascending order of weights, and set the partial MST $S := \emptyset$. Then for each edge e in the list, update $S := S \cup \{e\}$ iff $S \cup \{e\}$ is acyclic.

```
                                    % E - edge of graph; G - graph
                                    % T - candidate MST
exists - G ::: exists - T :::       % TP - transformed MST
  ordered_graph(G) , subgraph(G,T), kruskal_invariant(E,T) :-
  forall - E :::                        transform(E,T,TP),
    rnot (edge_of(E,G),                 acyclic(TP).
    ( edge_of_subgraph(E,T),     not_kruskal_invariant(E,T) :-
      not_kruskal_invariant(E,T)        transform(E,T,TP),
    ; not_edge_of_subgraph(E,T),        cyclic(TP).
      kruskal_invariant(E,T)
    )).
                                    'edge(n1-n2-3,1).'edge(n1-n3-1,2).
                                    'edge(n1-n4-2,3).'edge(n2-n3-7,4).
```

Fig. 2. Query and Program Fragment for Kruskal's Algorithm

It is easy to construct a RichProlog query corresponding to this algorithm: does there exist some subgraph S of G such that for all edges $e \in G$, e belongs to S iff (e, S) satisfies the invariant of Kruskal's algorithm, that is, $T(e, S) = \{e' \in S : l(e') < l(e)\} \cup \{e\}$ is acyclic. The translation from this informal description to a RichProlog query is straightforward (an excerpt is shown in Figure 2), using predicates to represent $e \in S$, $e \notin S$, "S is cyclic" and "S is acyclic". Each subgraph of G is represented by a list where, for example, [in,out,in] would represent that the subgraph contains the first and third edges of G but that the second edge is absent. This allows for a simple implementation of a `transform/3` predicate in negation-free Prolog, which given some subgraph $S \subseteq G$ and edge $e \in G$ produces the set $T(e, S)$ described above. The `subgraph/2` predicate produces an enumeration of all subgraphs of a graph. The `edge_of/2` predicate is similar to a pure Prolog `member/2` predicate, and `edge_of_subgraph/2` and `not_edge_of_subgraph/2` are simple tests to determine whether an edge is present in a subgraph or not. The predicates `cyclic/1` and `acyclic/1` are conventional depth first search checks for whether some subgraph is cyclic or not. It is easy to verify that all these predicates can be expressed as definite clauses enriched with a \= test. The data are presented in the `'edge/2` predicate, which is a two place predicate to allow the easy implementation of `ordered_graph/1`, which has the task of assembling an ordered graph from the edges.

Some key areas should be noted where the implementation is impure – these occur in the body of the program which is elided for brevity. The program conducts several does-not-unify (i.e. \=) tests. Since the vocabulary is known and finite, and the intended interpretations are Herbrand, this can be replaced with an explicit does-not-unify predicate for this vocabulary. As these are used to check either the non-unification of two ground variables, or the non-unification of a variable and [], asymptotically there will be no cost difference between a logical implementation and \=, given a good predicate indexing system in the underlying Prolog. The `sort/2` predicate is used, which is avoidable by choosing an order on atoms, and Prolog-style arithmetic is also employed, which could be replaced by Peano arithmetic or a constraint system. To simplify the implementation and subsequent argument we require that all edges be of different length; this is an inessential restriction. We suggest that all of these impure aspects of the implementation are straightforwardly overcome.

4.3   Cost

While it would appear that this implementation has exponential running time as presented, due to the exhaustive enumeration of subgraphs in the `subgraph/2` predicate, a tabling-based technique can dramatically reduce the search space. If any inductive tree succeeds (i.e. its calling query in the deductive phase fails), then any query subsumed by the label of the root of this inductive tree will also cause a failure. If the implementation ensures that the traversal of the deductive tree finds more general nodes before less general nodes, and tables or memoizes these more general nodes upon failure, then the traversal of the less general nodes in the tree can be avoided. There is a cost: at each inference step involving variables which appear in the nodes mapped to inductive trees, we need to test if the variables are subsumed by the table. This technique resembles the tabling technique of SLG resolution and other similar systems[4]. RichProlog tables n-tuples of terms (with n the number of existentially quantified variables) rather than subgoals, and makes a tabling check at each unification operation which concerns these variables rather than at each subgoal. This is of course more expensive, but seems to work well in practice.

We give a sketch of a proof that this implementation has polynomial time cost, even allowing for the additional tabling overheads. This sketch covers the key points of a formal proof, omitting the precise details of the underlying machine formalism. Consider first the cost of the negated part of the query inside the `rnot` statement. The selection of an edge from a list of edges of size E and the check for absence of an edge from such a list in `edge_of`, `edge_of_subgraph` and `not_edge_of_subgraph` is in $O(E)$, and the depth first searches in `cyclic/acyclic` can traverse each edge at most once, so these will again be in $O(E)$. The `transform/3` predicate can also be performed by conducting a linear scan of a subgraph and so has a bound in $O(E)$. Thus this part of the algorithm has a worst case bound in $7 \cdot O(E) = O(E)$. This is the time to consider a single edge being present or absent given a particular subgraph. The `subgraph/2` predicate produces subgraphs in the following order: [...,in|_],[...,out|_], in a general to specific ordering. Call the set of all list terms with i ground terms followed by a variable list element or the empty list T_i, so for example [in,out|_] is in T_2. Assume that all lists which are not initial segments of the list representation of some MST which are shorter than i already have a tabled term which will cause them to fail. Assume that the start of the list L just constructed by `subgraph/2` is a subgraph of the MST. Exactly one of L + [in] and L + [out] will be a subpart of some MST given all edges have distinct lengths; Kruskal's algorithm guarantees that the correct list is chosen. The other list will be tabled, and so all terms of length T_{i+1} which are not sublists of the MST will have some element in the table which will cause unification against them to fail. Furthermore, the empty list, the only member of T_0 will be a subgraph of every MST. Thus the program supplemented with tabling will consider at most 2 terms in T_i for each i. By performing this operation repeatedly, the program will determine the presence or absence of each edge in turn, which will require in the worst case $2 \cdot O(E) = O(E)$ attempts at the negated part of the query. For each T_i, of which there are E, there will be a check of the negated part of the query which requires $O(E)$ unifications. This entails a $O(E^2)$ upper bound on the number of unifications.

Tabling modifies the unification operation, making it more expensive and no longer an atomic operation for a cost analysis. In the worst case, the number of tabled elements is E (as each negated part of the query could contain a failure case), and the elements of the table have maximum size in $O(E)$ making the cost of a subsumption check $O(E)$ on account of the linear bound on a unification check without an occurs check, and so the worst case cost of a unification with tabling check is $O(E^2)$. The number of unifications involving a tabling check will be less than or equal to the number of unifications required in the execution of the entire program. In the normal execution of the algorithm, it is possible for a unification to occur at each point in the execution, which gives a simple upper bound on cost of $O(E^4)$, inside polynomial time.

5   Conclusion

Unlike most formalisms, Parametric logic accounts for logical consequence relationships that are not compact. Some of the developments from this are the construction of a resolution framework as well as a Prolog-like system which can both account for tentative solutions and the requirement for subsequent mind changes. LR is designed to tackle computation in the limit, and guarantees that after some finite computation a correct answer is constructed should one exist, however the system cannot necessarily determine when this point is reached. LR is sound and complete with respect to a natural 2-valued semantics, and incorporates a notion of true negation. It is possible to build a system which implements real algorithms in polynomial time, which goes some way to demonstrating the practicality of the system. RichProlog is upwards compatible with existing Prolog systems, and so we can expect that existing Prolog compiler technology will be usable in a RichProlog setting.

This work has several possible extensions. The relationships between existing nonmonotonic reasoning formalisms need to be more precisely characterized; particularly the precise relationship between existing negation-as-failure formalisms needs to be described beyond noting that LR is distinct from these formalisms. Also it may be fruitful to describe these formalisms in terms of mind change bounds. LR programs are currently restricted to positive theoretical literals, and finding an appropriate formalism to deal with these would be profitable. We have shown that RichProlog is useful in an example, and our aim is to apply it to more complex problems relevant to AI.

References

1. Anderson, A. and Belnap, N.: *Entailment: The Logic of Relevance and Necessity.* Princeton University Press. (1975)
2. Apt, K. R. and Bol, R.: *Logic Programming and Negation: A Survey.* J. of Logic Programming. **19/20** (1994) 9–71
3. Clark, K.: *Negation as Failure* In H. Gallaire and J. Minker, eds., *Logic and Databases.* Plenum Press, New York. (1978) 293–322
4. Chen, W. and Warren, D. S., *Tabled Evaluation with Delaying for General Logic Programs.* J. of the ACM. **43**:1 (1996) 20–74
5. Cormen, T. H., Leiserson, C. E., and Rivest, R. L.: *Introduction to Algorithms.* M.I.T. Press. (1990)
6. Gold, E.: *Language Identification in the Limit.* Information and Control. **10** (1967)
7. Holzbaur, C.: *Metastructures vs. attributed variables in the context of extensible unification.* In M. Bruynooghe and M. Wirsing, ed., 4th Int. Work. Program. Lang. Implementation and Logic Programming, LNCS 631. Springer. (1992)
8. Israel, D.J.: *What's wrong with nonmonotonic logic?* In Proc. of the First National Conference on Artificial Intelligence. (1980) 99-101
9. Jain, S., Osherson, D., Royer, J., and Sharma, A.: *Systems that Learn.* Second Edition. M.I.T. Press, Cambridge MA. (1999)
10. Kraus, S., Lehmann, D., and Magidor, M.: *Nonmonotonic Reasoning, Preferential Models and Cumulative Logics.* Artificial Intelligence. **44** (1990) 167–207
11. Kunen, K.: *Negation in logic programming.* J. of Logic Prog. **4** (1987) 289-308
12. Le, T.: *A general scheme for representing negative and quantified queries for deductive databases.* Proc. of the First Int. Conf. on Information and Knowledge Management. Baltimore, Maryland. (1992)
13. Lloyd J. W. and Topor, R. W.: *Making Prolog more expressive.* J. of Logic Programming. **1**:3 (1984) 225–240
14. Martin, E., Nguyen, P., Sharma, A., and Stephan, F.: *Learning in Logic with RichProlog.* Proc. of the 18th Int. Conf. on Logic Prog. Springer, LNCS 2401. (2002)
15. Martin, E., Sharma, A., and Stephan, F.: *A General Theory of Deduction, Induction, and Learning.* In Jantke, K., Shinohara, A.: Proc. of the Fourth International Conference on Discovery Science. Springer, LNAI 2226. (2001)
16. Martin, E., Sharma, A., and Stephan, F.: *Logic, Learning, and Topology in a Common Framework.* In Cesa-Bianchi, N., Numao, M., Reischuk, R.: Proc. of the 13th Intern. Conf. on Algorithmic Learning Theory. Springer, LNAI 2533. (2002).
17. Muggleton, S. and de Raedt, L.: *Inductive Logic Programming: Theory and Methods.* J. of Logic Programming. **19/20** (1994) 629–679
18. Mycroft, A. and O'Keefe, R. A.: *A Polymorphic Type System for Prolog.* Artificial Intelligence. **23** (1983) 295–307
19. Perlis, D.: *On the Consistency of Commonsense Reasoning.* Computational Intelligence. **2** (1986) 180–190
20. Przymusinski, T. C.: *On the declarative and procedural semantics of logic programs.* J. of Automated Reasoning. **5** (1989) 167–205
21. Shepherdson, J.C.: *A sound and complete semantics for a version of negation as failure.* Theoretical Computer Science. **65** (1989) 343–371
22. Voronkov, A.: *Logic programming with bounded quantifiers.* Proc. LPAR, Springer, LNCS 592. (1992) 486–514

Generalised Kernel Sets for Inverse Entailment

Oliver Ray, Krysia Broda, and Alessandra Russo

Department of Computing, Imperial College London,
180 Queen's Gate, London SW7 2BZ
{or,kb,ar3}@doc.ic.ac.uk

Abstract. The task of inverting logical entailment is of central importance to the disciplines of Abductive and Inductive Logic Programming
(ALP & ILP). Bottom Generalisation (BG) is a widely applied approach
for Inverse Entailment (IE), but is limited to deriving single clauses from
a hypothesis space restricted by Plotkin's notion of C-derivation. Moreover, known practical applications of BG are confined to Horn clause
logic. Recently, a hybrid ALP-ILP proof procedure, called HAIL, was
shown to generalise existing BG techniques by deriving multiple clauses
in response to a single example, and constructing hypotheses outside the
semantics of BG. The HAIL proof procedure is based on a new semantics,
called Kernel Set Subsumption (KSS), which was shown to be a sound
generalisation of BG. But so far KSS is defined only for Horn clauses.
This paper extends the semantics of KSS from Horn clause logic to general clausal logic, where it is shown to remain a sound extension of BG. A
generalisation of the C-derivation, called a K*-derivation, is introduced
and shown to provide a sound and complete characterisation of KSS.
Finally, the K*-derivation is used to provide a systematic comparison of
existing proof procedures based on IE.

1 Introduction

Abduction and induction are of great interest to those areas of *Artificial Intelligence* (AI) concerned with the tasks of explanation and generalisation, and
efforts to analyse and mechanise these forms of reasoning are gaining in importance. In particular, the disciplines of *Abductive Logic Programming (ALP)* [4]
and *Inductive Logic Programming (ILP)* [8] have developed semantics and proof
procedures of theoretical and practical value. Fundamentally, both ALP and ILP
are concerned with the task, called *Inverse Entailment (IE)*, of constructing a
hypothesis that logically entails a given example relative to a given background
theory. In practice, the main difference between ALP and ILP is that whereas
abductive hypotheses are normally restricted to sets of ground atoms, inductive
hypotheses can be general clausal theories.

To date, the inference method of *Bottom Generalisation (BG)* [6, 15] is one of
the most general approaches for IE to have resulted in the development of high-
performance tools of wide practical application. Central to this success has been
the use of Muggleton's notion of *Bottom Set (BS)* [6] to bound a search space
that would otherwise be intractable. However, methods based *directly* on BG

B. Demoen and V. Lifschitz (Eds.): ICLP 2004, LNCS 3132, pp. 165–179, 2004.
© Springer-Verlag Berlin Heidelberg 2004

are subject to several key limitations. By definition they can only hypothesise a single clause in response to a given example, and Yamamoto [14] has shown they are further limited to deriving a class of hypotheses characterised by Plotkin's notion of *C-derivation* [10]. In practice, known proof procedures for BG are limited to Horn clause logic; as evidenced, for example, by the state-of-the-art ILP system Progol [6].

Recently, Ray *et al.* [12] proposed a hybrid ALP-ILP proof procedure, called *HAIL*, that extends the Progol approach by hypothesising multiple clauses in response to a single example, and by constructing hypotheses outside the semantics of BG. Also in [12], a semantics for HAIL called *Kernel Set Subsumption (KSS)* was presented and shown to subsume that of BG. So far, this new semantics is defined only for Horn clause logic and, as yet, no corresponding characterisation of KSS has been found to generalise the relationship between BG and C-derivations. It was conjectured in [12], however, that a natural extension of the C-derivation, called a *K-derivation*, could be used to obtain such a characterisation of KSS.

In this paper, the semantics of KSS is extended from Horn clauses to general clauses, where it is shown to remain a sound generalisation of BG. A new derivation is defined, called a *K*-derivation*, that both refines the K-derivation and generalises the C-derivation. The K*-derivation is shown to give a sound and complete characterisation of KSS, thereby resolving the conjecture above. The paper is structured as follows. Section 2 reviews the relevant background material. Section 3 lifts the semantics of KSS to general clausal logic. Section 4 introduces the K*-derivation and shows how it characterises the generalised KSS. Section 5 uses the K*-derivation as a means of comparing related approaches. The paper concludes with a summary and directions for future work.

2 Background

This section reviews the necessary background material. After a summary of notation and terminology, the notions of ALP and ILP are briefly described in order to motivate the underlying task of IE. Relevant definitions and results are recalled concerning the semantics of BG and KSS.

Notation and Terminology. A *literal* L is an atom A or the (classical) negation of an atom $\neg A$. A *clause* C is a set of literals $\{L_1, ..., L_n\}$ that for convenience will be represented as a disjunction $L_1 \vee ... \vee L_n$. Any atom that appears negated in C is called a *negative* or *body* atom, and any atom that appears unnegated in C is called a *positive* or *head* atom. A *Horn clause* is a clause with at most one head atom. The *empty clause* is denoted $\square$. An *expression* is a term, a literal, or a clause. A *theory* T is a set of clauses $\{C_1, ..., C_m\}$ that for convenience will be represented as a conjunction $\{C_1 \wedge ... \wedge C_m\}$. This paper assumes a given first-order language $\mathfrak{L}$ that includes Skolem constants. An expression or theory is said to be *Skolem-free* whenever it contains no Skolem constant. The symbols $\top$ and $\bot$ will denote the logical constants for truth and falsity. The symbol $\models$ will denote classical first-order logical entailment. The equivalence $X \wedge Y \models Z$ iff $X \models \neg Y \vee Z$

will be called the *Entailment Theorem*. Whenever a clause is used in a logical formula, it is read as the universal closure of the disjunction of its literals. Whenever a theory is used in a logical formula, it is read as the conjunction of its clauses. In general, the symbols L, M will denote literals; λ, μ will denote ground literals; P, N will denote atoms; α, δ will denote ground atoms; S, T will denote theories; and C, D, E will denote clauses. Symbols B, H will denote Skolem-free theories representing background knowledge and hypotheses, respectively. Symbols e, h will denote Skolem-free clauses representing examples and hypotheses, respectively. A substitution σ is called a *Skolemising substitution for* a clause C whenever σ binds each variable in C to a *fresh* Skolem constant. A clause C is called a *factor* of a clause D whenever $C = D\phi$ and ϕ is a *most general unifier (mgu)* of one or more literals in D. A clause C is said to θ-*subsume* a clause D, written $C \succeq D$, whenever $C\theta \subseteq D$ for some substitution θ. A theory S is said to θ-*subsume* a theory T, written $S \sqsupseteq T$, whenever each clause in T is θ-subsumed by at least one clause in S. If L is a literal, then the *complement* of L, written $\overline{L}$, denotes the literal obtained by negating L if it is positive, and unnegating L if it is negative. If $C = L_1 \vee \dots \vee L_n$ is a clause and σ is a Skolemising substitution for C, then the *complement of C (using σ)*, written $\overline{C}$, is defined as the theory $\overline{C} = \{\overline{L_1}\sigma \wedge \dots \wedge \overline{L_n}\sigma\}$. The standard definition of *resolvent* is assumed, as defined for example in [2]. A *resolution derivation* of clause C from theory T is a finite non-empty sequence of clauses $\mathcal{R} = (R_1, \dots, R_n{=}C)$ such that each clause $R_i \in (R_1, \dots, R_n)$ is either a *fresh* variant of some clause $D \in T$, or a resolvent of two preceding clauses $P, Q \in (R_1, \dots, R_{i-1})$. In the first case, R_i is called an *input clause*, and D is called the *generator* of R_i. In the second case, R_i is called a *resolvent*, and P and Q are called the *parents* of R_i. A *tree derivation* of C from T is a resolution derivation of C from T in which each clause except the last is the parent of exactly one child. A derivation of $\square$ from T will also be called a *refutation from T*. The *composition* of two tree derivations $\mathcal{R}_1$ and $\mathcal{R}_2$, written $\mathcal{R}_1 + \mathcal{R}_2$, is the tree derivation obtained by concatenating the sequence $\mathcal{R}_2$ on to the sequence $\mathcal{R}_1$, taking care to rename any variables that may clash. The *Subsumption Theorem* states if a theory T logically entails a clause C then either C is a tautology or else there exists a tree derivation from T of a clause D that θ-subsumes C, as shown for example in [9].

Abductive and Inductive Logic Programming (ALP & ILP) [4,8] formalise in a logic programming context the notions of *explanation* and *generalisation*. With respect to a given theory, ALP constructs explanations for given observations, while ILP computes generalisations of given examples. Many ALP and ILP techniques are incremental in that they focus on one observation or example at a time and try to construct a partial hypothesis, H, that entails this one example, e, relative to the background theory, B. This fundamental problem, which is known as the task of *Inverse Entailment (IE)*, is formally defined as follows. Given a theory B and a clause e, find a theory H such that $B \cup H \models e$. For reasons of efficiency, some form of search bias is normally imposed on the process used to find H, and one such method is discussed next.

Bottom Generalisation (BG) [6, 15] is an important approach for IE that is based on the construction and generalisation of a particular clause called a *Bottom Set*. Formally, as shown in Definition 1 below, the Bottom Set of B and e, denoted $Bot(B, e)$, contains the set of ground literals μ whose complements are entailed by B and the complement of e. As shown in Definition 2, the hypotheses derivable by BG are those clauses h that θ-subsume $Bot(B, e)$. It is worth emphasising that B, h and e are all assumed to be Skolem-free.

Definition 1 (Bottom Set). *Let B be a theory, let e be a clause, let σ be a Skolemising substitution for e, and let $\overline{e}$ be the complement of e using σ. Then the Bottom Set of B and e (using σ), denoted $Bot(B, e)$, is the clause $Bot(B, e) = \{\mu \mid B \cup \overline{e} \models \overline{\mu}\}$ where the μ are ground literals.*

Definition 2 (BG). *Let B be a theory, and let e and h be clauses. Then h is said to be derivable by BG from B and e iff $h \succeq Bot(B, e)$.*

The key point is that instead of exploring the entire IE hypothesis space, which is intractable, BG only considers a sub-space that is both smaller and better structured than the original. Formally, this sub-space is the θ-subsumption lattice bounded by the Bottom Set and the empty set. But, as described below, the advantage of a more tractable search space comes at the price of incompleteness. This incompleteness can be characterised by Plotkin's notion of C-derivation [10], which is formalised in Definition 3.

Definition 3 (C-derivation). *Let T be a theory, and C and D be clauses. Then a C-derivation of D from T with respect to C is a tree derivation of D from $T \cup \{C\}$ such that C is the generator of at most one input clause. A clause D is said to be C-derivable from T with respect to C, denoted $(T, C) \vdash_c D$, iff there exists a C-derivation of D from T with respect to C.*

Informally, a C-derivation is a tree derivation in which some given clause C may be used at most once. The important result, as shown in [15], is that a hypothesis h is derivable by BG from B and e if and only if there is a C-refutation from $B \cup \overline{e}$ with respect to h. Therefore C-derivations characterise the restrictions on the hypotheses derivable by BG. In order to (partially) overcome these restrictions, the semantics of KSS was introduced, as described next.

Kernel Set Subsumption (KSS) [12] can be seen as extending BG to derive multiple clause hypotheses drawn from a larger hypothesis space. Like BG, KSS considers only a bounded lattice based sub-space of the full IE hypothesis space. But, whereas BG uses a single clause Bottom Set to bound its search space, KSS uses instead a *set* of clauses called a Kernel Set. The relevant notions are now recalled for the Horn clause case in Definitions 4, 5 and 6 below.

As shown in Definition 4, before a Kernel Set is formed, the inputs B and e are first normalised by Skolemising e and transferring the body atoms as facts to B. Formally, the normalised example ϵ is the clause containing the Skolemised head atom of e, while the normalised background knowledge $\mathcal{B}$ is the original theory B augmented with the Skolemised body atoms of e. In all of these definitions negative clauses are formally treated as if they had the head atom '$\perp$'.

Definition 4 (Horn Normalisation). *Let B be a Horn theory, let $e = P \vee \neg N_1 \vee ... \vee \neg N_m$ be a Horn clause, and let σ be a Skolemising substitution for e. Then the normalisation of B and e (using σ), consists of the theory $\mathcal{B} = B \cup \{N_1\sigma \wedge ... \wedge N_m\sigma\}$, and the clause $\epsilon = P\sigma$.*

Definition 5 (Horn Kernel Set). *Let $\mathcal{B}$ and ϵ be the result of normalising a Horn theory B and a Horn clause e, and let $\mathcal{K} = \{k_1 \wedge ... \wedge k_n\}$ be a set of ground Horn clauses $k_i = \alpha_i \vee \neg\delta_i^1 \vee ... \vee \neg\delta_i^{m_i}$. Then $\mathcal{K}$ is called a Kernel Set of B and e iff $\mathcal{B} \cup \{\alpha_1 \wedge ... \wedge \alpha_n\} \models \epsilon$, and $\mathcal{B} \models \delta_i^j$ for all $1 \leq i \leq n$ and $1 \leq j \leq m_i$.*

Definition 6 (Horn KSS). *Let B and H be Horn theories, and let e be a Horn clause. Then H is said to be derivable by KSS from B and e iff $H \sqsupseteq \mathcal{K}$ for some Kernel Set $\mathcal{K}$ of B and e.*

As shown in Definition 5 above, a Horn Kernel Set of a Horn theory B and Horn clause e is a Horn theory $\mathcal{K}$ whose head atoms $\alpha_1, ..., \alpha_n$ collectively entail the normalised example ϵ with respect to $\mathcal{B}$, and whose body atoms δ_i^j are individually entailed by the normalised background $\mathcal{B}$. Here, $n \geq 1$ denotes the (non-zero) number of clauses in $\mathcal{K}$, and $m_i \geq 0$ denotes the (possibly-zero) number of body atoms in the ith clause k_i. As shown in Definition 6, a theory H is derivable by KSS whenever it θ-subsumes a Kernel Set $\mathcal{K}$ of B and e.

So far KSS is defined only for the Horn clause subset of clausal logic. In this context it has been shown in [12] that KSS is sound with respect to IE and complete with respect to BG. However, as yet, no exact characterisation of the class of hypotheses derivable by KSS has been established. Such a task clearly requires a more general notion than the C-derivation. For this purpose, the concept of K-derivation, formalised in Definition 7 below, was introduced in [12] and conjectured to provide such a characterisation.

Definition 7 (K-derivation). *Let T and K be theories, and let D be a clause. Then a K-derivation of D from T with respect to K is a tree derivation of D from $T \cup K$ such that each clause $k \in K$ (but not in T) is the generator of at most one input clause, which is called a k-input clause. Clause D is said to be K-derivable from T with respect to K, denoted $(T, K) \vdash_k D$, iff there exists a K-derivation of D from T with respect to K.*

The notion of K-derivation generalises that of C-derivation in the following way. Whereas the C-derivation refers to a clause C that may be used at most once, in a K-derivation there are a *set of clauses* K each of which may be used at most once. A C-derivation is therefore a special case of a K-derivation, in which this set $K = \{C\}$ is a singleton.

In the next two sections, the semantics of KSS is extended to general clausal logic and a refinement of the K-derivation, called a K*-derivation, is introduced in order to provide a precise characterisation of KSS in the general case. The soundness and completeness results mentioned above are also lifted to the general case and the conjecture is proved.

3   Kernel Set Semantics for General Clausal Logic

In this section the semantics of KSS is generalised from Horn clauses to arbitrary clauses. It is shown in this general case that KSS remains sound with respect to IE and continues to subsume the semantics of BG. First the notion of normalisation is generalised in Definition 8, and two key properties are shown in Lemma 1. Then the generalised notion of Kernel Set is formalised in Definition 9.

Definition 8 (Normalisation). *Let B be a theory, let $e = P_1 \vee ... \vee P_n \vee \neg N_1 \vee ... \vee \neg N_m$ be a clause, and let σ be a Skolemising substitution for e. Then the normalisation of B and e (using σ), consists of the theory $\mathcal{B} = B \cup \{N_1\sigma \wedge ... \wedge N_m\sigma\}$, and the clause $\epsilon = P_1\sigma \vee ... \vee P_n\sigma$.*

Lemma 1. *Let $\mathcal{B}$ and ϵ be the result of normalising a theory B and a clause $e = P_1 \vee ... \vee P_n \vee \neg N_1 \vee ... \vee \neg N_m$ using σ. Let $\overline{e}$ denote the complement of e, also using σ. Then (1) $\mathcal{B} \cup T \models \epsilon$ iff $B \cup \overline{e} \cup T \models \square$ for all theories T, and (2) $\mathcal{B} \cup H \models \epsilon$ iff $B \cup H \models e$ for all (Skolem-free) theories H.*

Proof. Taking each case in turn:

1. $\mathcal{B} \cup T \models \epsilon$ iff $B \cup \{N_1\sigma \wedge ... \wedge N_m\sigma\} \cup T \models P_1\sigma \vee ... \vee P_n\sigma$ (by Definition 8), iff $B \cup \{N_1\sigma \wedge ... \wedge N_m\sigma \wedge \neg P_1\sigma \wedge ... \wedge \neg P_n\sigma\} \cup T \models \square$ (by the Entailment Theorem), iff $B \cup \overline{e} \cup T \models \square$ (by properties of complementation).
2. $\mathcal{B} \cup H \models \epsilon$ iff $B \cup \{N_1\sigma \wedge ... \wedge N_m\sigma\} \cup H \models P_1\sigma \vee ... \vee P_n\sigma$ (by Definition 8), iff $B \cup H \models P_1\sigma \vee ... \vee P_n\sigma \vee \neg N_1\sigma \vee ... \vee \neg N_m\sigma$ (by the Entailment Theorem), iff $B \cup H \models e\sigma$ (by properties of substitution), iff $B \cup H \models e$ (the forward direction uses the fact σ binds each variable in e to a constant not in B, H or e, the reverse direction uses the fact $e\sigma$ is an instance of e).

Definition 9 (Kernel Set). *Let $\mathcal{B}$ and ϵ be the result of normalising a theory B and a clause e. A Kernel Set of B and e is a ground theory $\mathcal{K}$ that can be written in the form:*

$$\mathcal{K} = \left\{ \begin{array}{c} \lambda_1^0 \vee \lambda_1^1 \vee \cdots\cdots\cdots \vee \lambda_1^{m_1} \\ \vdots \\ \lambda_i^0 \vee \lambda_i^1 \vee \cdots \lambda_i^j \cdots \vee \lambda_i^{m_i} \\ \vdots \\ \lambda_n^0 \vee \lambda_n^1 \vee \cdots\vdots\cdots \vee \lambda_n^{m_n} \end{array} \right\}$$

where $\mathcal{B} \cup \{\lambda_1^0 \wedge ... \wedge \lambda_n^0\} \models \epsilon$, and $\mathcal{B} \cup \{\lambda_i^j\} \models \epsilon$ for all $1 \leq i \leq n$ and $1 \leq j \leq m_i$. In this case, the literals $\lambda_1^0, ..., \lambda_n^0$ are called the key literals of $\mathcal{K}$.

In moving from the Horn case to the general case, the role previously played by the head atoms α_i is now played by the so-called *key literals* λ_i^0. Although any literal in a clause can be chosen as the key literal, for notational convenience it will be assumed that the key literal of a kernel clause k_i will always be denoted λ_i^0. As shown in Definition 9 above, for $\mathcal{K}$ to be a Kernel Set of B and e the key literals $\lambda_1^0, ..., \lambda_n^0$ must *collectively* entail ϵ with respect to $\mathcal{B}$, and the non-key literals λ_i^j must *individually* entail ϵ with respect to $\mathcal{B}$.

It is straightforward to show any Horn theory $\mathcal{K}$ that is a Kernel Set by Definition 5 is also a Kernel Set by Definition 9. From Definition 5 it holds $\mathcal{B} \cup \{\alpha_1 \wedge \ldots \wedge \alpha_n\} \models \epsilon$ and $\mathcal{B} \models \delta_i^j$. From the latter it follows $\mathcal{B} \cup \{\neg \delta_i^j\} \models \bot \models \epsilon$. Upon identifying each key literal λ_i^0 with the head atom α_i and each non-key literal λ_i^j with the negated body atom $\neg \delta_i^j$ it follows that $\mathcal{B} \cup \{\lambda_1^0 \wedge \ldots \wedge \lambda_n^0\} \models \epsilon$ and $\mathcal{B} \cup \{\lambda_i^j\} \models \epsilon$. Hence $\mathcal{K}$ is also a Kernel Set by Definition 9.

As formalised in Definition 10 below, the notion of KSS is the same in the general case as in Horn case. As before, a hypotheses H is derivable by KSS from B and e whenever it θ-subsumes a Kernel Set of B and e. The only difference is that general clauses are now used in place of Horn clauses, and the general Kernel Set replaces the Horn Kernel Set. As shown in Theorems 1 and 2, the key results from the Horn clause case apply also in the general case.

Definition 10 (KSS). *Let B and H be theories, and e be a clause. Then H is derivable by KSS from B and e iff $H \sqsupseteq \mathcal{K}$ for some Kernel Set $\mathcal{K}$ of B and e.*

Theorem 1 (Soundness of KSS wrt IE). *Let B and H be theories, let e be a clause, and let $\mathcal{K} = \{k_1 \wedge \ldots \wedge k_n\}$ be a Kernel Set of B and e. Then $H \sqsupseteq \mathcal{K}$ implies $B \cup H \models e$.*

Proof. By Definition 9 it holds that $\mathcal{B} \cup \{\lambda_1^0 \wedge \ldots \wedge \lambda_n^0\} \models \epsilon$. Therefore $B \cup \overline{e} \cup \{\lambda_1^0 \wedge \ldots \wedge \lambda_n^0\} \models \square$ by Lemma 1. Hence $B \cup \overline{e} \models \neg \lambda_1^0 \vee \ldots \vee \neg \lambda_n^0$ by the Entailment Theorem. If $\mathcal{M}$ is any model of $B \cup \overline{e}$ then for some $1 \leq i \leq n$ it follows $\mathcal{M}$ falsifies the key literal λ_i^0. But, by an analogous argument, it also follows from Definition 9 and Lemma 1 that $B \cup \overline{e} \models \neg \lambda_1^j$ for all $1 \leq i \leq n$ and $1 \leq j \leq m_i$. Hence $\mathcal{M}$ also falsifies all of the non-key literals $\lambda_i^1, \ldots, \lambda_i^{m_i}$. Therefore $\mathcal{M}$ falsifies the Kernel clause $k_i = \lambda_i^0 \vee \lambda_i^1 \vee \ldots \vee \lambda_i^{m_i}$ and also, therefore, the Kernel theory $\mathcal{K} = \{k_1 \wedge \ldots \wedge k_n\}$. Consequently, $B \cup \overline{e} \cup \mathcal{K} \models \square$. Since $H \sqsupseteq \mathcal{K}$, it follows $H \models \mathcal{K}$ and so $B \cup \overline{e} \cup H \models \square$. Therefore $\mathcal{B} \cup H \models \epsilon$ by Lemma 1 part (1) and hence $B \cup H \models e$ by Lemma 1 part (2).

Theorem 2 (KSS Extends BG). *Let B be a theory, let $e = P_1 \vee \ldots \vee P_n \vee \neg N_1 \vee \ldots \vee \neg N_m$ be a clause, let $Bot(B,e)$ be the Bottom Set of B and e using σ, and let $h = L_0 \vee \ldots \vee L_p$ be a clause. Then a clause h is derivable by BG from B and e only if the theory $H = \{h\}$ is derivable by KSS from B and e.*

Proof. Suppose h is derivable by BG from B and e. Then $h \succcurlyeq Bot(B,e)$ by Definition 2, and so $h\theta \subseteq Bot(B,e)$ for some θ. By Definition 1 it holds $B \cup \overline{e} \models \overline{L_i}\theta$ for all $0 \leq i \leq p$. Since $L_i\theta$ is a ground atom, $\overline{L_i}\theta = \neg L_i\theta$ and so $B \cup \overline{e} \cup \{L_i\theta\} \models \square$ by the Entailment Theorem. Consequently, $\mathcal{B} \cup \{L_i\theta\} \models \epsilon$ by Lemma 1. By Definition 9 the theory $\mathcal{K} = \{L_0\theta \vee L_1\theta \vee \ldots \vee L_p\theta\}$ is a single clause Kernel Set of B and e. By construction $\{h\} \sqsupseteq \mathcal{K}$ and hence it follows by Definition 10 that $H = \{h\}$ is derivable by KSS from B and e.

To show KSS is stronger than BG, simply let $B = \{p \vee \neg q(a) \vee \neg q(b)\}$ and $e = p$. In this case the three hypotheses $\{q(x)\}$ and $\{q(a) \wedge q(b)\}$ and $\{p\}$ are all derivable by KSS, but only the last one is derivable by BG from B and e. In order to illustrate the ideas presented above and to show how KSS can also derive non-Horn theories, this section now concludes with Example 1 below.

Example 1. Let the background theory B represent the knowledge that anyone in a *bar* may be served a *drink* unless he is a *child*, and that anyone in a *cafe* may be served a *drink*. Let the example e denote the fact that all *adults* may be served a *drink*.

$$B = \left\{ \begin{array}{l} drink \vee child \vee \neg bar \\ drink \vee \neg cafe \end{array} \right\} \qquad\qquad e = drink \vee \neg adult$$

Then the hypothesis H shown below, which states that an *adult* will go either to the *cafe* or to the *bar*, and that no one is both an *adult* and a *child*, is correct with respect to IE since it can be verified that $B \cup H \models e$.

$$H = \left\{ \begin{array}{l} bar \vee cafe \vee \neg adult \\ \neg child \vee \neg adult \end{array} \right\}$$

Using the abbreviations $a = adult, b = bar, c = child, d = drink, f = cafe$ it can be verified that the result of normalising B and e consists of the theory $\mathcal{B}$ and the clause ϵ shown below, and that the following sequents are true.

$$\mathcal{B} = \left\{ \begin{array}{l} d \vee c \vee \neg b \\ d \vee \neg f \\ a \end{array} \right\} \qquad \epsilon = d \qquad \begin{array}{l} \mathcal{B} \cup \{b \wedge \neg c\} \models \epsilon \\ \mathcal{B} \cup \{f\} \models \epsilon \\ \mathcal{B} \cup \{\neg a\} \models \epsilon \end{array}$$

Therefore, by Definitions 9 and 10, theory H is a Kernel Set of B and e, with key literals b and $\neg c$, and H is derivable by KSS from B and e. But note $Bot(B, e) = drink \vee cafe \vee \neg adult$ and so neither clause in H is derivable by BG.

4   Characterisation in Terms of K*-Derivations

This section provides a sound and complete characterisation of Kernel Sets in terms of a new derivation, called a *K*-derivation*. The K*-derivation is at the same time a generalisation of the C-derivation and a refinement of the K-derivation. Where a K-derivation requires that each clause in a set K is used at most once, a K*-derivation imposes one additional restriction on the way such clauses are used. The basis of this restriction is a new notion, called *T-reduction*, formalised in Definition 11 below and illustrated in Fig 1.

Definition 11 (T-reduction). *Let T be a theory, and let C and D be clauses. Then a T-reduction of C to D is a C-derivation $\mathcal{R}$ of D from T with respect to C such that $\mathcal{R} = \mathcal{R}^1 + ... + \mathcal{R}^m + (C=C^0, ..., C^m=D)$ where for all $1 \leq i \leq m$ each $\mathcal{R}^i$ is a tree derivation of a clause E^i from T, and C^i is a resolvent of C^{i-1} with a unit factor of E^i. The clause C is said to be reduced to D by T in $\mathcal{R}$.*

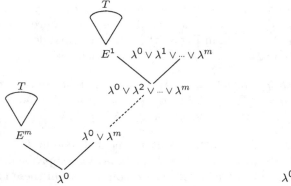

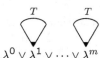

Fig. 1. T-reduction   **Fig. 2.** Abbreviation of Fig 1

Informally, T-reduction is the process of progressively resolving a clause C with clauses derived from a theory T. Fig 1 illustrates the T-reduction of a ground clause $C = C^0 = \lambda^0 \vee \lambda^1 \vee ... \vee \lambda^m$ to the ground literal $\lambda^0 = C^m = D$. Each descendent $C^i = \lambda^0 \vee \lambda^{i+1} \vee ... \vee \lambda^m$ of C differs from predecessor C^{i-1} in the removal of a literal λ^i, which is 'resolved away' by a clause E^i derived from T. Each wedge denotes the tree derivation $\mathcal{R}^i$ of the clause E^i shown at the base of the wedge, from the theory T shown at the top.

To simplify the representation of the T-reduction of a ground clause to a single literal, it is convenient to introduce the graphical abbreviation shown in Fig 2. Just as in Fig 1, the wedges denote the tree derivations $\mathcal{R}^i$ of the clauses E^i. But now, instead of the clause E^i, the complementary literal λ^i appears at the base each wedge. The black tip of each wedge emphasises that it is not the literal λ^i which is derived, but the clause E^i that resolves away λ^i. Intuitively, this graphic shows the literals of C being resolved away until only λ^0 remains.

The notion of T-reduction is now used to define the concept of K*-derivation. As formalised in Definition 12, a K*-derivation consists of a *principal derivation*, which is a tree derivation of some clause C_0 from T, and zero or more *reduction trees*, in each of which a k-input clause k_i is reduced to a clause D_i by T. Clause C_0 is then reduced to D in the 'tail' $(C_1, ..., C_n)$ of the derivation, by resolving with each of the D_i in turn. For an example, the reader is referred to Fig 5.

Definition 12 (K*-derivation). *Let T and K be theories, and let D be a clause. Then a K*-derivation of D from T with respect to K is a K-derivation $\mathcal{R}$ of D from T with respect to K such that $\mathcal{R} = \mathcal{R}_0 + \mathcal{R}_1 + ... + \mathcal{R}_n + (C_1, ..., C_n = D)$ where $\mathcal{R}_0$ is a tree derivation, called the* principal derivation, *of a clause C_0 from T, and for all $1 \leq i \leq n$ each $\mathcal{R}_i$ is a T-reduction, called a* reduction tree, *of a k-input clause $k_i \in K$ to a clause D_i, and each C_i is the resolvent of C_{i-1} with a unit factor of D_i. The clause D is said to be K*-derivable from T with respect to K, denoted $(T, K) \vdash_{k*} D$, whenever such a derivation exists.*

The rest of this section shows how the K*-derivation provides a sound and complete characterisation of KSS. First, Lemma 2 demonstrates an important relationship between abduction and K*-derivations. Informally, this result states that all of the ground facts used in a refutation, need be used just once, at the very end. Such a refutation $\mathcal{R}$ is shown in Fig 3, where the principal derivation $\mathcal{R}_0$ is denoted by the wedge, and $\lambda'_1, \ldots, \lambda'_p$ are the ground facts used.

Lemma 2. *Let T be a theory, and let $\Delta = \{\lambda_1 \wedge \ldots \wedge \lambda_n\}$ be a ground unit theory. Then $T \cup \Delta \models \square$ implies $(T, \Delta) \vdash_{k*} \square$ with a K*-derivation of the form $\mathcal{R} = \mathcal{R}_0 + (\lambda'_1, \ldots, \lambda'_p) + (C_1, \ldots, C_p{=}\square)$ for some $\{\lambda'_1 \wedge \ldots \wedge \lambda'_p\} \subseteq \Delta$.*

Proof. Suppose that $T \cup \Delta \models \square$. Then by the Entailment Theorem $T \models D$ where $D = \overline{\lambda}_1 \vee \ldots \vee \overline{\lambda}_n$. If D is a tautology, then Δ contains two complementary unit clauses, which means there is a trivial tree derivation of $\square$ from these two unit clauses, and so $(T, \Delta) \vdash_{k*} \square$ by Definition 12. If D is not a tautology, then by the Subsumption Theorem there is a tree derivation $\mathcal{R}_0$, from the theory T of a clause C_0 such that $C_0 \theta \subseteq D$ for some substitution θ. Now, define the set $\Delta' = \{\lambda'_1, \ldots, \lambda'_p\}$ such that $\Delta' = \overline{C_0} \theta \cap \Delta$. (i.e. Δ' is the subset of Δ whose literals are complementary to those in C_0 under θ). Next, let $(C_1, \ldots, C_p{=}\square)$ be the (unique) sequence of clauses $C_i = M_i^0 \vee M_i^1 \vee \ldots \vee M_i^{q_i}$ such that each clause $C_{i+1} \in (C_1, \ldots, C_p)$ is the resolvent of C_i and λ'_{i+1} on the factor $C_i \phi_i$ of C_i where ϕ_i is the mgu of the set $S_i = \{M_i^j \in C_i \mid M_i^j \theta = \lambda'_{i+1}\}$. (i.e. S_i is the subset of C_i whose literals are complementary to λ'_{i+1} under θ). Then, by Definition 12, it follows $\mathcal{R} = \mathcal{R}_0 + (\lambda'_1, \ldots, \lambda'_p) + (C_1, \ldots, C_p{=}\square)$ is a K*-refutation from T with respect to Δ, with principal derivation $\mathcal{R}_0$ and trivial reduction trees where each $\mathcal{R}_i = (\lambda'_i)$ simply contains the unit clause $\lambda'_i \in \Delta$ (see Fig 3).

Lemma 2 is now used in Theorem 3 to show that a theory $\mathcal{K}$ is a Kernel Set of B and e if and only if there exists a K*-refutation from $B \cup \overline{e}$ with respect to $\mathcal{K}$. Informally, as illustrated in Fig 4, a K*-derivation can always be constructed in which (zero or more) Kernel clauses are reduced by the theory $B \cup \overline{e}$ to their key literals. The key literals are then used one by one in the tail of the derivation to resolve away the clause C_0 derived in the principal derivation.

Theorem 3 (K*-derivations characterise Kernel Sets). *Let $\mathcal{B}$ and ϵ be the result of normalising a theory B and clause e using σ. Let $\overline{e}$ be the complement of e, also using σ. Let $\mathcal{K} = \{k_1 \wedge \ldots \wedge k_n\}$ be a theory of ground clauses written $k_i = \lambda_i^0 \vee \lambda_i^1 \vee \ldots \vee \lambda_i^{m_i}$, and let $\Delta = \{\lambda_1^0 \wedge \ldots \wedge \lambda_n^0\}$. Then the theory $\mathcal{K}$ is a Kernel Set of B and e iff $(B \cup \overline{e}, \mathcal{K}) \vdash_{k*} \square$*

Proof. Taking the "if" and "only if" cases individually:

1. Suppose $(B \cup \overline{e}, \mathcal{K}) \vdash_{k*} \square$. Then by Definition 12 for some $0 \leq p \leq n$ there is a K*-derivation $\mathcal{R} = \mathcal{R}_0 + \mathcal{R}_1 + \ldots + \mathcal{R}_p + (C_1, \ldots, C_p{=}\square)$ with principal derivation $\mathcal{R}_0$ and reduction trees $\mathcal{R}_1, \ldots, \mathcal{R}_p$. By Definition 11 it follows for all $1 \leq i \leq p$ that $\mathcal{R}_i = \mathcal{R}_i^1 + \ldots + \mathcal{R}_i^{m_i} + (k_i{=}C_i^0, \ldots, C_i^{m_i}{=}\lambda'_i)$ is a T-reduction of a ground k-input clause $k_i \in \mathcal{K}$ to single literal $\lambda'_i \in k_i$ by the theory $B \cup \overline{e}$. Without loss of generality, assume $\mathcal{K}$ has been written so $\mathcal{K} = \{k_1 \wedge \ldots \wedge k_p \wedge \ldots \wedge k_n\}$ and $k_i = \lambda_i^0 \vee \lambda_i^1 \vee \ldots \vee \lambda_i^{m_i}$ with $\lambda'_i = \lambda_i^0$ for all

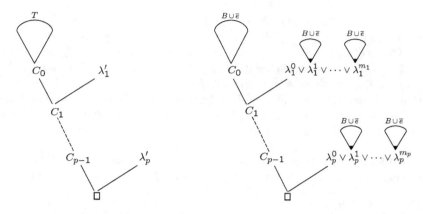

Fig. 3. Abductive Derivation   **Fig. 4.** K*-derivation

$1 \leq i \leq p$. Therefore $\mathcal{R}' = \mathcal{R}_0 + (\lambda_1^0, ..., \lambda_p^0) + (C_1, ..., C_p{=}\square)$ is a tree refutation from $B \cup \overline{e} \cup \Delta$. Hence $B \cup \overline{e} \cup \Delta \models \square$ by the soundness of resolution, and so $B \cup \Delta \models \epsilon$ by Lemma 1. Now, by Definition 11 each $\mathcal{R}_i^j$ with $1 \leq i \leq p$ and $1 \leq j \leq m_i$ is a tree derivation of a clause D_i^j from $B \cup \overline{e}$ such that D_i^j resolves away λ_i^j. Therefore $\mathcal{R}_i^j + (\lambda_i^j) + (\square)$ is a tree refutation from $B \cup \overline{e} \cup \{\lambda_i^j\}$. Hence $B \cup \overline{e} \cup \{\lambda_i^j\} \models \square$ by soundness of resolution, and so $B \cup \{\lambda_i^j\} \models \epsilon$ by Lemma 1. Since $B \cup \Delta \models \epsilon$ and $B \cup \{\lambda_i^j\} \models \epsilon$ it follows by Definition 9 that $\mathcal{K}$ is a Kernel Set of B and e with key literals Δ.

2. Suppose $\mathcal{K}$ is a Kernel Set of B and e with key literals Δ. By Definition 9 it follows $B \cup \Delta \models \epsilon$. Consequently, $B \cup \overline{e} \cup \Delta \models \square$ by Lemma 1. By Lemma 2 there is a K*-refutation $\mathcal{R} = \mathcal{R}_0 + (\lambda_1', ..., \lambda_p') + (C_1, ..., C_p{=}\square)$ from $B \cup \overline{e}$ for some $\{\lambda_1' \wedge ... \wedge \lambda_p'\} \subseteq \Delta$ (see Fig 3). Without loss of generality, assume $\mathcal{K}$ has been written so $\mathcal{K} = \{k_1 \wedge ... \wedge k_p \wedge ... \wedge k_n\}$ and $k_i = \lambda_i^0 \vee \lambda_i^1 \vee ... \vee \lambda_i^{m_i}$ with $\lambda_i' = \lambda_i^0$ for all $1 \leq i \leq p$. By Definition 9 for each $1 \leq j \leq m_i$ it follows $B \cup \{\lambda_i^j\} \models \epsilon$. Consequently $B \cup \overline{e} \cup \{\lambda_i^j\} \models \square$ by Lemma 1. By Lemma 2 there is a K*-refutation $\mathcal{R}_i^j + (\lambda_i^j) + (\square)$ in which λ_i^j may or may not be used. If λ_i^j is not used, then by Definition 12 it trivially follows $(B \cup \overline{e}, \mathcal{K}) \vdash_{k*} \square$ and the theorem is proved. If λ_i^j is used, then by Definition 12 it follows $\mathcal{R}_i^j$ is a tree derivation from $B \cup \overline{e}$ of a clause E_i^j that resolves away λ_i^j. Now, for all $1 \leq i \leq p$ and $0 \leq j \leq m_i$ define the clause $C_i^j = \lambda_i^0 \vee ... \vee \lambda_i^j$ and the derivation $\mathcal{R}_i = \mathcal{R}_i^1 + ... + \mathcal{R}_i^{m_i} + (k_i{=}C_i^{m_i}, ..., C_i^1, C_i^0{=}\lambda_i^j)$. Then by Definition 11 it follows $\mathcal{R}_i$ is a tree derivation in which k_i is T-reduced to λ_i^j by $B \cup \overline{e}$. Hence by Definition 11 the tree derivation $\mathcal{R}' = \mathcal{R}_0 + \mathcal{R}_1 + ... + \mathcal{R}_p + (C_1, ..., C_p{=}\square)$ is a K*-refutation from $B \cup \overline{e}$ with respect to $\mathcal{K}$ (see Fig 4). Thus $(B \cup \overline{e}, \mathcal{K}) \vdash_{k*} \square$ by Definition 12.

To characterise the *hypotheses* derivable by KSS in terms of K*-derivations, one complication must be addressed. Given that $H \sqsupseteq \mathcal{K}$, it is possible for one clause $h \in H$ to θ-subsume more than one clause in $\mathcal{K}$, so that more than one instance of h is needed to derive $\square$ from $B \cup \overline{e}$ and H. For example, let

$B = \{p \vee \neg q(a) \vee \neg q(b)\}$ and $e = p$. Then hypothesis $H = p(X)$ subsumes the Kernel Set $\mathcal{K} = \{q(a) \wedge q(b)\}$, and *two* instances of H are required.

One way of handling this complication is by treating the hypothesis H as a *multi-set*, and treating the relation $H \sqsupseteq \mathcal{K}$ as an *injection* that maps each clause k in set $\mathcal{K}$ to a clause h in multi-set H such that $h \succcurlyeq k$. Then it can be shown that a theory H is derivable by KSS from a theory B and a clause e, if and only if there is a K*-refutation from $B \cup \overline{e}$ with respect to H. For completeness the proof of this result is sketched in Corollary 1 below.

Corollary 1. *Let B be a set of clauses, let e be a clause, and let H be a multi-set of clauses. Then H is derivable by KSS from B and e iff $(B \cup \overline{e}, H) \vdash_{k*} \square$*

Proof. (Sketch)

1. Suppose H is derivable by KSS from B and e. Then there is a theory $\mathcal{K}$ such that $H \sqsupseteq \mathcal{K}$ and $\mathcal{K}$ is a Kernel Set of B and e. By Theorem 3 there is a K*-refutation from $B \cup \overline{e}$ with respect to $\mathcal{K}$. Now replace each reduction tree of a k-input clause k by the reduction tree of a fresh variant of the clause h to which k is mapped by $\sqsupseteq$. After appropriate syntactic changes, the result is a K*-refutation from $B \cup \overline{e}$ with respect to H.
2. Suppose such a K*-derivation exists. Replace each reduction tree of a k-input clause h by the reduction tree of a ground instance of k of h consistent with the substitutions in the derivation. After appropriate syntactic changes, the result is a K*-refutation from $B \cup \overline{e}$ with respect to the clauses k. By Theorem 3 this set of clauses is a Kernel Set of B and e, and by construction it is θ-subsumed by H. Therefore H is derivable by KSS from B and e.

In order to illustrate the concepts introduced above, this section concludes by presenting a full K*-derivation for Example 1. As shown in Fig 5, the reduction trees of the two underlined hypothesis clauses to the literals b and $\neg c$ are indicated by the dashed triangles. The principal derivation of the clause $c \vee \neg b$ containing the complements of these literals is marked by the dashed rectangle. The tail of the derivation is shown by the dashed ellipse. Finally, Fig 6 shows how this derivation is abbreviated using the compact notation introduced in Fig 2.

5   Related Work

The semantics of KSS is aimed ultimately at extending the principles of BG in order to provide a more general context for developing practical proof procedures for IE. However, it can also be used as a means of systematically comparing existing methods for BG and KSS. In particular, as shown in the previous section, independently of how a hypothesis H is actually computed from B and e, there will always be an associated K*-refutation from $B \cup \overline{e}$ with respect to H. Consequently, existing methods can be classified in terms of the restrictions needed on the principal and reduction derivations in order to characterise the class of derivable hypotheses. Several methods are now compared in this way.

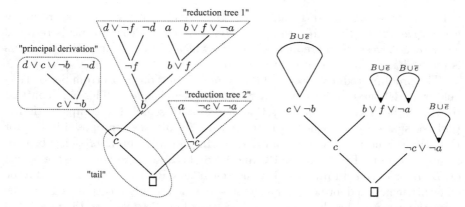

Fig. 5. K*-derivation of Example 1   **Fig. 6.** Abbreviation of Fig 5

Progol4 [6] is one of the best known and widely applied systems in ILP. This procedure uses a methodology called *Mode Directed Inverse Entailment (MDIE)* that efficiently implements BG the use of user-specified language bias. A subset of the Bottom Set is constructed by an SLD procedure and is then generalised by a lattice based search routine. Like all BG approaches, Progol4 induces only a single clause for each example, and like most existing procedures it is restricted to Horn clause logic. The hypotheses derivable by Progol4 are associated with K*-derivations of a simple form. The principal derivation always consists of a single unit clause containing the (unique) negative literal from $\overline{e}$; and this literal is always resolved away by a single reduction tree in which the (only) hypothesis clause is reduced to an instance of its head atom.

Progol5 [7] is the latest member of the Progol family. This proof procedure realises a technique called *Theory Completion by Inverse Entailment (TCIE)* that augments MDIE with a reasoning mechanism based on *contrapositive locking* [13]. Although the principal derivations associated with Progol5 hypotheses also result in a negative unit clause, unlike Progol4 they may involve the nontrivial derivation of a negative literal distinct from that in $\overline{e}$. However, due to an incompleteness of the contrapositive reasoning mechanism identified in [12], no *merging* of literals may occur within the principal derivation. In the corresponding reduction tree, the single hypothesis clause is reduced to an instance of its head atom.

HAIL [11] is a recently proposed proof procedure that extends TCIE with the ability to derive multiple clause hypotheses within the semantics of KSS. This procedure is based on an approach called *Hybrid Abductive-Inductive Learning* that integrates explicit abduction, deduction and induction, within a cycle of learning that generalises the mode-directed approach of Progol5. Key literals of the Kernel Set are computed using an ALP proof procedure [5], while non-key literals are computed using the same SLD procedure used by Progol. Like Progol5, HAIL is currently restricted to Horn clause logic, but unlike Progol, the hypotheses derivable by HAIL can give rise to K*-derivations in which there is no restriction on merging, and where the principal derivation may result in a negative clause with more than one literal. Each of these literals is resolved away by a corresponding reduction tree, in which one of the hypothesis clauses is reduced to an instance of its head atom.

The proof procedures discussed above use the notions of Bottom Set or Kernel Set to deliberately restrict their respective search spaces. This is in contrast to some other recent approaches that attempt to search the complete IE hypothesis space. A technique based on *Residue Hypotheses* is proposed in [16] for Hypothesis Finding in general clausal logic. In principle, this approach subsumes all approaches for IE - including BG and KSS - because no restrictions are placed on B, H or e. But, in practice, it is not clear how Residue Hypotheses may be efficiently computed, or how language bias may be usefully incorporated into the reasoning process. An alternative method, based on *Consequence Finding* in full clausal logic, is proposed in [3] that supports a form of language bias called a *production field* and admits pruning strategies such as *clause ordering*. However, this procedure is still computationally expensive and has yet to achieve the same degree of practical success as less complete systems such as Progol.

6   Conclusion

In this paper the semantics of KSS has been extended from Horn clauses to general clausal logic. It was shown in the general case that KSS remains sound with respect to the task of IE and that it continues to subsume the semantics of BG. In addition, an extension of Plotkin's C-derivation, called a K*-derivation, was introduced and shown to provide a sound and complete characterisation of the hypotheses derivable by KSS in the general case. These results can be seen as extending the essential principles of BG in order to enable the derivation multiple clause hypotheses in general clausal logic and thereby enlarging the class of soluble problems.

The aim of this work is to provide a general context in which to develop practical proof procedures for IE. It is believed such procedures can be developed for KSS through the integration ALP and ILP methods and the efficient use of language bias. A hybrid ALP-ILP proof procedure has been proposed in [12] for computing multiple clause hypotheses, but currently this procedure is restricted to Horn clauses and has not been implemented. To address these issues, efficient abductive and inductive procedures are required for general clausal logic. One promising approach would be to adapt the work already begun by [1] and [3] in the context of semantic tableaux and to apply them in the context of KSS.

References

1. A. Aliseda. *Seeking Explanations: Abduction in Logic, Philosophy of Science and Artifical Intelligence.* PhD thesis, Institute for Logic, Language and Computation (ILLC), University of Amsterdam, 1997.

2. C. Chang and R.C. Lee. *Symbolic Logic and Mechanical Theorem Proving.* Academic Press, 1973.
3. K. Inoue. Induction, Abduction, and Consequence-Finding. In C. Rouveirol and M. Sebag, editors, *Proceedings 11th International Conference on Inductive Logic Programming*, volume 2157 of *Lecture Notes in AI*, pages 65–79. Springer Verlag, 2001.
4. A.C. Kakas, R.A. Kowalski, and F. Toni. Abductive Logic Programming. *Journal of Logic and Computation*, 2(6):719–770, 1992.
5. A.C. Kakas and P. Mancarella. Database Updates through Abduction. In *16th International Conference on Very Large Databases (VLDB)*, pages 650–661. Morgan Kaufmann, 1990.
6. S.H. Muggleton. Inverse Entailment and Progol. *New Generation Computing, Special issue on Inductive Logic Programming*, 13(3-4):245–286, 1995.
7. S.H. Muggleton and C.H. Bryant. Theory Completion Using Inverse Entailment. *Lecture Notes in Computer Science*, 1866:130–146, 2000.
8. S.H. Muggleton and L. De Raedt. Inductive Logic Programming: Theory and Methods. *Journal of Logic Programming*, 19,20:629–679, 1994.
9. S.H. Nienhuys-Cheng and R. de Wolf. *Foundations of Inductive Logic Programming*, volume 1228 of *Lecture Notes in Artificial Intelligence*. Springer, first edition, 1997.
10. G.D. Plotkin. *Automatic Methods of Inductive Inference.* PhD thesis, Edinburgh University, 1971.
11. O. Ray. HAIL: Hybrid Abductive-Inductive Learning. Technical Report 2003/6, Department of Computing, Imperial College London, 2003.
12. O. Ray, K. Broda, and A. Russo. Hybrid Abductive Inductive Learning: a Generalisation of Progol. In T. Horváth and A. Yamamoto, editors, *13th International Conference on Inductive Logic Programming*, volume 2835 of *Lecture Notes in AI*, pages 311–328. Springer Verlag, 2003.
13. M.E. Stickel. A Prolog technology theorem prover: Implementation by an extended Prolog compiler. In J. H. Siekmann, editor, *Journal of Automated Reasoning*, volume 4(4), pages 353–380, 1988.
14. A. Yamamoto. Which Hypotheses Can Be Found with Inverse Entailment? In S. Džeroski and N. Lavrač, editors, *Proceedings of the 7th International Workshop on Inductive Logic Programming*, volume 1297, pages 296–308. Springer-Verlag, 1997.
15. A. Yamamoto. An Inference Method for the Complete Inverse of Relative Subsumption. *New Generation Computing*, 17(1):99–117, 1999.
16. A. Yamamoto and B. Fronhöfer. Hypothesis Finding via Residue Hypotheses with the Resolution Principle. In *Proceedings of the 11th International Conference on Algorithmic Learning Theory*, volume 1968 of *Lecture Notes in Computer Science*, pages 156–165. Springer-Verlag, 2000.

On Programs with Linearly Ordered
Multiple Preferences

Davy Van Nieuwenborgh*, Stijn Heymans, and Dirk Vermeir**

Dept. of Computer Science
Vrije Universiteit Brussel, VUB
Pleinlaan 2, B1050 Brussels, Belgium
{dvnieuwe,sheymans,dvermeir}@vub.ac.be

Abstract. The extended answer set semantics for logic programs allows for the defeat of rules to resolve contradictions. We propose a refinement of these semantics based on a preference relation on extended literals. This relation, a strict partial order, induces a partial order on extended answer sets. The preferred answer sets, i.e. those that are minimal w.r.t. the induced order, represent the solutions that best comply with the stated preference on extended literals. In a further extension, we propose linearly ordered programs that are equipped with a linear hierarchy of preference relations. The resulting formalism is rather expressive and essentially covers the polynomial hierarchy. E.g. the membership problem for a program with a hierarchy of height n is Σ_{n+1}^{P}-complete. We illustrate an application of the approach by showing how it can easily express hierarchically structured weak constraints, i.e. a layering of "desirable" constraints, such that one tries to minimize the set of violated constraints on lower levels, regardless of the violation of constraints on higher levels.

1 Introduction

In *answer set programming* (see e.g. [3, 22]) one uses a logic program to modularly describe the requirements that must be fulfilled by the solutions to a problem. The solutions then correspond to the models (answer sets) of the program, which are usually defined through (a variant of) the stable model semantics[19]. The technique has been successfully applied in problem areas such as planning[22, 13, 14], configuration and verification [27, 28], diagnosis[12, 31], game theory[11], updates[15] and database repairs[2, 29].

The traditional answer set semantics is not universal, i.e. programs may not have any answer sets at all. While natural, this poses a problem in cases where, although there is no exact solution, one would appreciate to obtain an approximate one, even if it violates some of the rules. E.g. in an over-constrained timetabling problem, an approximate solution that ignores some demands of some users may be preferable to having no schedule at all.

* Supported by the FWO.
** This work was partially funded by the Information Society Technologies programme of the European Commission, Future and Emerging Technologies under the IST-2001-37004 WASP project.

B. Demoen and V. Lifschitz (Eds.): ICLP 2004, LNCS 3132, pp. 180–194, 2004.
© Springer-Verlag Berlin Heidelberg 2004

The extended answer set semantics from [29, 30] achieves this by allowing for the *defeat* of problematic rules. Consider for example the rules $a \leftarrow$, $b \leftarrow$ and $\neg a \leftarrow b$. Clearly, these rules are inconsistent and have no classical answer set, while both $\{a, b\}$ and $\{\neg a, b\}$ will be recognized as extended answer sets. In $\{a, b\}$, $\neg a \leftarrow b$ is defeated by $a \leftarrow$ while in $\{\neg a, b\}$, $a \leftarrow$ is defeated by $\neg a \leftarrow b$.

In this paper, we extend the above semantics by equipping programs with a preference relation over extended literals (outcomes). Such a preference relation can be used to induce a partial order on the extended answer sets, the minimal elements of which will be preferred. In this way, the proposed extension allows one to select the more appropriate approximate solutions of an over-constrained problem.

Consider for example a news redaction that has four different news items available that are described using the following extended answer sets:

$$N_1 = \{local, politics\}$$
$$N_2 = \{local, sports\}$$
$$N_3 = \{national, economy\}$$
$$N_4 = \{international, economy\} \ .$$

The redaction wishes to order them according to their preferences. Assuming that, regardless of the actual subject, local news is preferred over national or international items, the preference could be encoded as[1]

$$local < national < international < \{economy, politics, sports\} \ .$$

Intuitively, using the above preference relation, N_1 and N_2 should be preferred upon N_3, which should again be preferred upon N_4, i.e. $N_1, N_2 \sqsubseteq N_3 \sqsubseteq N_4$.

In the above example, only one preference relation is used, corresponding to one point of decision in the news redaction. In practice, different journalists may have conflicting preferences, and different authorities. E.g., the editor-in-chief will have the final word on which item comes first, but she will restrict herself to the selection made by the journalists. Suppose the editor-in-chief has the following preference

$$economy < politics < sports < \{local, national, international\} \ .$$

Applying this preference to the preferred items N_1 and N_2 presented by the journalists yields the most preferred item N_1.

Such hierarchies of preference relations are supported by *linearly ordered programs*, where a program is equipped with an ordered list $\langle <_i \rangle_{i=1,\dots n}$ of preference relations on extended literals, representing the hierarchy of user preferences ($<_i$ has a higher priority than $<_{i+1}$). Semantically, preferred extended answer sets for such programs will result from first optimizing w.r.t. $<_1$, then selecting from the result the optimal sets w.r.t. $<_2$ etc. Obviously, the order in which the preference relations are applied is important, e.g. exchanging the priorities of the preference relations in the example would yield N_3 as the preferred news item.

---

[1] We use $a < X$, with X a set, as an abbreviation for $\{a < x \mid x \in X\}$.

It turns out that such hierarchically layered preference relations are very expressive. More specifically, we show that such programs can solve arbitrary complete problems of the polynomial hierarchy.

In [8], weak constraints are introduced as a type of constraint[2] that is "desirable" but may be violated if there are no other options, i.e. violations of weak constraints should be minimized. The framework also supports hierarchically structured weak constraints, where constraints on the lower levels are more important than constraints on higher levels. Mirroring the semantics for linearly ordered programs, solutions minimizing the violation of constraints on the lowest level are first selected, and, among those, the solutions that minimize the constraints on the second level are retained, continuing up to the highest level. Weak constraints are useful in areas such as planning, abduction and optimizations from graph theory[16, 10]. It will be shown that hierarchically structured weak constraints can be easily captured by linearly ordered programs.

The remainder of the paper is organized as follows. In Section 2, we present the extended answer set semantics together with a preference relation on extended literals and illustrate how it can be used to elegantly express common problems. Section 3 introduces linearly ordered programs, the complexity of the proposed semantics is discussed in Section 4. Before concluding and giving directions for further research in Section 6, we show in Section 5 how weak constraints can be implemented using linearly ordered programs.

2 Ordered Programs

We use the following basic definitions and notation. A *literal* is an *atom* a or a negated atom $\neg a$. For a set or literals X, $\neg X$ denotes $\{\neg a \mid a \in X\}$ where $\neg\neg a = a$. X is *consistent* if $X \cap \neg X = \emptyset$. An interpretation I is a consistent set of (ordinary) literals.

An *extended literal* is a literal or a *naf-literal* of the form *not* l where l is a literal. The latter form denotes negation as failure. For a set of extended literals X, we use X^- to denote the set of ordinary literals underlying the naf-literals in X, i.e. $X^- = \{l \mid not\ l \in X\}$. An extended literal l is true w.r.t. an interpretation I, denoted $I \models l$ if $l \in I$ in case l is ordinary, or $a \notin I$ if $l = not\ a$ for some ordinary literal a. As usual, $I \models X$ for some set of (extended) literals l iff $\forall l \in X \cdot I \models l$.

An *extended rule* is a rule of the form $\alpha \leftarrow \beta$ where $\alpha \cup \beta$ is a finite set of extended literals[3] and $|\alpha| \leq 1$. An extended rule $r = \alpha \leftarrow \beta$ is *satisfied* by I, denoted $I \models r$, if $I \models \alpha$ and $\alpha \neq \emptyset$, whenever $I \models \beta$, i.e. if r is *applicable* ($I \models \beta$), then it must be *applied* ($I \models \alpha \cup \beta \land \alpha \neq \emptyset$). Note that this implies that a *constraint*, i.e. a rule with empty head ($\alpha = \emptyset$), can only be satisfied if it is not applicable ($I \not\models \beta$).

A countable set of extended rules is called an *extended logic program* (ELP). The *Herbrand base* $\mathcal{B}_P$ of an ELP P contains all atoms appearing in P. Further, we use $\mathcal{L}_P$ and $\mathcal{L}_P^*$ to denote the set of literals (resp. extended literals) that can be constructed from $\mathcal{B}_P$, i.e. $\mathcal{L}_P = \mathcal{B}_P \cup \neg\mathcal{B}_P$ and $\mathcal{L}_P^* = \mathcal{L}_P \cup \{not\ l \mid l \in \mathcal{L}_P\}$. For an ELP P and an interpretation I we use $P_I \subseteq P$ to denote the *reduct* of P w.r.t. I, i.e. $P_I = \{r \in P \mid$

---

[2] A constraint is a rule of the form $\leftarrow \alpha$, i.e. with an empty head. Any answer set should therefore not contain α.

[3] As usual, we assume that programs have already been grounded.

$I \models r\}$, the set of rules satisfied by I. We call an interpretation I a model of a program P if $P_I = P$, i.e. I satisfies all rules in P. It is a minimal model of P if there is no model J of P such that $J \subset I$.

A *simple program* is a program without negation as failure. For simple programs P, we define an answer set of P as the minimal model of P. On the other hand, for a program P containing negation as failure, we define the *GL-reduct*[19] for P w.r.t. I, denoted P^I, as the program consisting of those rules $(\alpha \setminus not\ \alpha^-) \leftarrow (\beta \setminus not\ \beta^-)$ where $\alpha \leftarrow \beta$ is in P, $I \models not\ \beta^-$ and $I \models \alpha^-$.

Note that all rules in P^I are free from negation as failure, i.e. P^I is a simple program. An interpretation I is then an *answer set* of P iff I is a minimal model of the GL-reduct P^I. An extended rule $r = \alpha \leftarrow \beta$ is *defeated* w.r.t. P and I iff there exists an applied *competing rule* $r' = \alpha' \leftarrow \beta'$ such that $\{\alpha, \alpha'\}$ is inconsistent. An *extended answer set* for P is any interpretation I such that I is an answer set of P_I and each unsatisfied rule in $P \setminus P_I$ is defeated.

Example 1. Consider the ELP P shown below. The program describes a choice between speeding or not. Sticking to the indicated limit guarantees not getting a fine while speeding, when it is known that the police are carrying out checks, will definitely result in a fine. Finally, if nothing is known about checks, there is still a chance for a fine.

$$
\begin{aligned}
speeding &\leftarrow & fine &\leftarrow speeding, check \\
\neg speeding &\leftarrow & maybe\_fine &\leftarrow speeding, not\ check \\
check &\leftarrow & \neg fine &\leftarrow \neg speeding \\
not\ check &\leftarrow & fine &\leftarrow maybe\_fine \\
not\ fine &\leftarrow maybe\_fine
\end{aligned}
$$

The above program has five possible extended answer sets, which are $M_1 = \{speeding, check, fine\}$, $M_2 = \{speeding, maybe\_fine\}$, $M_3 = \{\neg speeding, check, \neg fine\}$, $M_4 = \{\neg speeding, \neg fine\}$ and $M_5 = \{speeding, maybe\_fine, fine\}$.

Unlike traditional answer sets, extended answer sets are, in general, not subset minimal, i.e. an ELP P can have extended answer sets M and N with $M \subset N$, as witnessed by M_3 and M_4 in Example 1. Moreover, a program can have both answer sets and extended answer sets (that are not answer sets). E.g. the ELP $\{a \leftarrow;\ not\ a \leftarrow not\ a\}$, has two extended answer sets $I = \{a\}$, which is also a traditional answer set, and $J = \emptyset$, which is not.

Often, certain extended answer sets are preferable over others. E.g., in Example 1, one would obviously prefer not to get fined, which can be represented as a strict partial order $<_1$ on literals: $<_1 = \neg fine < \mathcal{L}_P^* \setminus \{\neg fine\}$. However, in an emergency, one may prefer to ignore the speed limit, resulting in an alternative preference relation $<_2 = \{speeding < \neg speeding < C;\ maybe\_fine < fine < C\}$, where $C = \mathcal{L}_P^* \setminus \{speeding, \neg speeding, maybe\_fine, fine\}$.

In general, we introduce, for an ELP P, a strict partial order[4] $<$ on extended literals, such that, for two extended literals l_1 and l_2, $l_1 < l_2$ expresses that l_1 is more preferred

---

[4] A strict partial order $<$ on a set X is a binary relation on X that is antisymmetric, anti-reflexive and transitive. The relation $<$ is well-founded if every nonempty subset of X has a $<$-minimal element.

than l_2. This preference relation induces a partial order[5] $\sqsubseteq$ on the extended answer sets of P.

Definition 1. *An **ordered program** is a pair $\langle P, < \rangle$ where P is an ELP and $<$ is a strict well-founded[6] partial order on $\mathcal{L}_P^*$. For subsets $M, N \subseteq \mathcal{L}_P$, we define $M \sqsubseteq N$ iff $\forall n \in \{l \in \mathcal{L}_P^* \mid N \models l \wedge M \not\models l\} \cdot \exists m \in \{l \in \mathcal{L}_P^* \mid M \models l \wedge N \not\models l\} \cdot m < n$. A **preferred answer set** of $\langle P, < \rangle$ is an extended answer set of P that is minimal w.r.t. $\sqsubseteq$ among the set of extended answer sets of P.*

Intuitively, M is preferable over N, i.e. $M \sqsubseteq N$, if every literal n from $N \setminus M$ is "countered" by a "better" literal $m < n$ from $M \setminus N$.

Applying the above definition on Example 1 with $<_1$ as described above, yields both M_3 and M_4 as preferred answer sets, while M_2 is the only preferred answer set w.r.t. $<_2$, which fits our intuition in both cases.

In the sequel, we will specify a strict partial order over a set X using an expression of the form

$$L = \{x_1 < y_1, \ldots, x_n < y_n, z_1, \ldots, z_m\}$$

which stands, unless explicitly stated otherwise, for the strict partial order defined by

$$
\begin{aligned}
& \{x_i < y_i \mid 1 \leq i \leq n\} \\
\cup\ & \{x_i < u \mid 1 \leq i \leq n \wedge u \in U\} \\
\cup\ & \{y_i < u \mid 1 \leq i \leq n \wedge u \in U\} \\
\cup\ & \{z_j < u \mid 1 \leq j \leq m \wedge u \in U\}
\end{aligned}
$$

with U the set of elements not occurring in L, i.e. $U = X \setminus K$ with $K = \{x_i \mid 1 \leq i \leq n\} \cup \{y_i \mid 1 \leq i \leq n\} \cup \{z_j \mid 1 \leq j \leq m\}$.

This notation implies that extended literals outside of L are least preferred and thus cannot influence the preference among extended answer sets. E.g. if $L = \{a < b\}$ then both $\{a, c\} \sqsubseteq \{b\}$ and $\{a\} \sqsubseteq \{b, c\}$ (where $M \sqsubset N$ iff $M \sqsubseteq N$ and $M \neq N$).

Example 2. The program below offers a choice between a large and a small drink to go with spicy or mild food.

$$
\begin{aligned}
large\_drink &\leftarrow not\ small\_drink \\
small\_drink &\leftarrow not\ large\_drink \\
spicy &\leftarrow not\ mild \\
mild &\leftarrow not\ spicy \\
large\_drink &\leftarrow spicy
\end{aligned}
$$

There are three extended answer sets: $M_1 = \{large\_drink, spicy\}$, $M_2 = \{large\_drink, mild\}$ and $M_3 = \{small\_drink, mild\}$.

A smaller drink is preferred and there is no particular preference between $mild$ and $spicy$, yielding $\{small\_drink < large\_drink,\ mild,\ spicy\}$ to describe the preferences. The preference for a small drink causes $M_3 \sqsubseteq M_2$ while M_1 is incomparable with both M_2 and M_3. Thus both M_1 and M_3 are preferred.

---

[5] That $\sqsubseteq$ is a partial order follows from Theorem 6 in [29].

[6] It is easy to verify that, if $<$ is empty, then $M \sqsubseteq N$ iff $\{l \mid N \models l\} \subseteq \{l \mid M \models l\}$ which reduces to $N = M$, i.e. all extended answer sets are preferred.

There is no "one true way" to induce a preference relation $\sqsubseteq$ over extended answer sets from a particular ordering $<$ over extended literals. E.g. [26], which deals with traditional answer sets of extended disjunctive programs, proposes a different method which is shown below, adapted to the current framework.

Definition 2. *For an **ordered program** $\langle P, < \rangle$ and subsets $M, N \subseteq \mathcal{L}_P$, we define $M \sqsubseteq_s N$ iff*

- $M = N$ *(reflexive), or*
- $\exists L \cdot M \sqsubseteq_s L \wedge L \sqsubseteq_s N$ *(transitive), or*
- $\exists e_1 \in \{l \in \mathcal{L}_P^* \mid M \models l \wedge N \not\models l\}$ *such that*

$$\exists e_2 \in \{l \in \mathcal{L}_P^* \mid N \models l \wedge M \not\models l\} \cdot e_1 < e_2$$
$$\wedge \neg \exists e_3 \in \{l \in \mathcal{L}_P^* \mid N \models l \wedge M \not\models l\} \cdot e_3 < e_1 .$$

Obviously, $\sqsubseteq_s$ is also a partial order.

Theorem 1. *Let $\langle P, < \rangle$ be an ordered program and let M and N be two extended answer sets of P. Then $M \sqsubseteq N$ implies that $M \sqsubseteq_s N$.*

The other direction is in general not true, as appears from the following example.

Example 3. Consider the program P depicted below.

$$shares \leftarrow not\ cash \qquad cash \leftarrow not\ shares$$
$$\$100 \leftarrow shares \qquad \$1000 \leftarrow cash$$
$$stock\_options \leftarrow shares$$

This program has two extended answer sets, i.e. $M_1 = \{cash, \$1000\}$ and $M_2 = \{shares, \$100, stock\_options\}$.

The preference $<= \{\$1000 < \$100\}$, where we take $<$ as is, i.e. without applying the expansion from the previous page, expresses no preference between cash, shares and stock options, except that, obviously, a larger amount of cash is preferred over a smaller amount. Using the $\sqsubseteq_s$ preference relation, we get $M_1 \sqsubseteq_s M_2$ and $M_2 \not\sqsubseteq_s M_1$, while for the $\sqsubseteq$ relation both $M_1 \not\sqsubseteq M_2$ and $M_2 \not\sqsubseteq M_1$ holds. This makes M_1 preferred w.r.t. $\sqsubseteq_s$, while both M_1 and M_2 are preferred w.r.t. $\sqsubseteq$. Note that, e.g. $M_1 \not\sqsubseteq M_2$ because M_1 cannot counter the $stock\_options$ of M_2 by something more preferred.

In general, $\sqsubseteq$ makes no decision between extended answer sets containing unrelated literals in their differences, while $\sqsubseteq_s$ is more credulous, preferring e.g. $1000 over $100 and some "unknown" $stock\_options$.

In the next section, the skeptical approach of $\sqsubseteq$ will turn out to be useful since it allows for new information to refine an earlier result. E.g., if, in the above example, it is later learned that the stock options provide great value, $stock\_options < \$1000$, might be added, possibly in a different preference relation, and used to prefer M_2 among the earlier "best choices" M_1 and M_2.

From Theorem 1, the following is immediate.

Corollary 1. *Let $R = \langle P, < \rangle$ be an ordered program. Then, the preferred answer sets of R w.r.t. $\sqsubseteq_s$ are also preferred w.r.t. $\sqsubseteq$.*

3   Linear n-Ordered Programs

A strict partial order on literals, as defined in the previous section, is a powerful and flexible tool to express a wide range of preferences. However, in practice, it is sometimes useful to have different layers of preferences, each applied in turn. As an example, consider the staff selection procedure of a company. Job applicants are divided into certain profiles, e.g. either female or male, old or young, experienced or not. Further, it is believed that inexperienced applicants tend to be ambitious, which is captured by the following program.

$$
\begin{array}{ll}
female \leftarrow not\ male & male \leftarrow not\ female \\
old \leftarrow not\ young & young \leftarrow not\ old \\
experienced \leftarrow not\ inexperienced & inexperienced \leftarrow not\ experienced \\
ambitious \leftarrow inexperienced &
\end{array}
$$

The decision to hire a new staff member goes through a chain of decision makers. On the lowest, and most preferred, level, company policy is implemented. It stipulates that experienced persons are to be preferred over inexperienced and ambitious persons, i.e. $<_1 = \{experienced < \{inexperienced, ambitious\}\}$. On the second level, the financial department prefers young and inexperienced employees, since they tend to cost less, i.e. $<_2 = \{young < old, inexperienced < experienced\}$. On the last, weakest, level, the manager prefers a woman to enforce her largely male team, i.e. $<_3 = \{female < male\}$.

In this example, any preferred extended answer set should be preferred w.r.t. $\sqsubseteq_1$ (induced by $<_1$) among all extended answer sets and, furthermore, among the $\sqsubseteq_1$-preferred sets, it should also be $\sqsubseteq_2$-preferred (where $\sqsubseteq_2$ is induced by $<_2$). Finally, the preferred answer sets of the complete problem are the $\sqsubseteq_2$-preferred sets which are also $\sqsubseteq_3$-preferred (where $\sqsubseteq_3$ is induced by $<_3$).

Formally, we extend ordered programs, by allowing a linearly ordered set of preference relations $<_1, \ldots, <_n$ for an ELP P, where $<_1$ is the order with the highest priority.

Definition 3. *A **linearly ordered program** (LOLP) is a pair $\langle P, \langle <_i \rangle_{i=1,\ldots,n} \rangle$ where P is an ELP and $\langle <_i \rangle_{i=1,\ldots,n}$ is a sequence of (strict partial order) preference relations $<_1, \ldots, <_n$. Each of these orders $<_i$ induces a preference relation $\sqsubseteq_i$ between extended answer sets, as in Definition 1.*

We define the preference up to a certain order of extended answer sets by induction.

Definition 4. *Let $\langle P, \langle <_i \rangle_{i=1,\ldots,n} \rangle$ be a LOLP. An extended answer M set is preferable up to $<_i$, $1 \leq i \leq n$, iff*

- *$i = 1$ and M is preferred w.r.t. $\sqsubseteq_i$, or*
- *$i > 1$, M is preferable up to $<_{i-1}$, and there is no N, preferable up to $<_{i-1}$, such that $N \sqsubset_i M$.*

*An extended answer set M of P is **preferred** if it is preferable up to $<_n$.*

Continuing the above example, we have eight extended answer sets for the program, which are all preferable up to $<_0$. After applying $<_1$, only four of them are left, i.e. $M_1 = \{experienced, old, female\}$, $M_2 = \{experienced, young, female\}$, $M_3 = \{experienced, male, young\}$ and $M_4 = \{experienced, old, male\}$, which fits the company policy to drop inexperienced ambitious people. When $<_2$ is applied on these four remaining extended answer sets, only M_2 and M_3 are kept as preferable up to $<_2$. Finally, the manager will select M_2 as the only extended answer set preferable up to $<_3$.

Note that rearranging the chain of orders gives, in general, different results. E.g., interchanging $<_1$ with $<_2$ yields $\{young, female, ambitious, inexperienced\}$ as the only extended answer set preferable up to $<_3$.

4 Complexity

We first recall briefly some relevant notions of complexity theory (see e.g. [24, 3] for a nice introduction). The class P (NP) represents the problems that are deterministically (nondeterministically) decidable in polynomial time, while $coNP$ contains the problems whose complement are in NP.

The polynomial hierarchy, denoted PH, is made up of three classes of problems, i.e. Δ_k^P, Σ_k^P and Π_k^P, $k \geq 0$, which are defined as follows:

1. $\Delta_0^P = \Sigma_0^P = \Pi_0^P = P$; and
2. $\Delta_{k+1}^P = P^{\Sigma_k^P}$, $\Sigma_{k+1}^P = NP^{\Sigma_k^P}$, $\Pi_{k+1}^P = co\Sigma_{k+1}^P$.

The class $P^{\Sigma_k^P}$ ($NP^{\Sigma_k^P}$) represents the problems decidable in deterministic (nondeterministic) polynomial time using an oracle for problems in Σ_k^P, where an oracle is a subroutine capable of solving Σ_k^P problems in unit time. Note that $\Delta_1^P = P, \Sigma_1^P = NP$ and $\Pi_1^P = coNP$. Further, it is obvious that $\Sigma_k^P \subseteq \Sigma_k^P \cup \Pi_k^P \subseteq \Delta_{k+1}^P \subseteq \Sigma_{k+1}^P$, but for $k \geq 1$ any equality is considered unlikely. Further, the class PH is defined by $PH = \bigcup_{k=0}^{\infty} \Sigma_k^P$.

A language L is called complete for a complexity class C if both L is in C and L is hard for C. Showing that L is hard is normally done by reducing a known complete decision problem into a decision problem in L. For the classes Σ_k^P and Π_k^P with $k > 0$ a known complete, under polynomial time transformation, problem is checking whether a quantified boolean formula (QBF) ϕ is valid. Note that this does not hold for the class PH for which no complete problem is known unless $P = NP$.

Quantified boolean formulas are expressions of the form $Q_1 X_1 Q_2 X_2 \ldots Q_k X_k \cdot G$, where $k \geq 1$, G is a Boolean expression over the atoms of the pairwise nonempty sets of variables $X_1, \ldots, X_k$ and the Q_i's, for $i = 1, \ldots, k$ are alternating quantifiers from $\{\exists, \forall\}$. When $Q_1 = \exists$, the QBF is k-existential, when $Q_1 = \forall$ we say it is k-universal. We use $QBF_{k,\exists}$ ($QBF_{k,\forall}$) to denote the set of all valid k-existential (k-universal) QBFs.

Deciding, for a given k-existential (k-universal) QBF ϕ, whether $\phi \in QBF_{k,\exists}$ ($\phi \in QBF_{k,\forall}$) is a Σ_k^P-complete (Π_k^P-complete) problem.

The following results shed some light on the complexity of the preferred answer set semantics for linear n-ordered logic programs.

First of all, checking whether an interpretation I is an extended answer set of an ELP P is in P, because (a) checking if each rule in P is either satisfied or defeated w.r.t. I, (b) applying the GL-reduct on P_I w.r.t. I, i.e. computing $(P_I)^I$, and (c) checking whether the positive program $(P_I)^I$ has I as its unique minimal model, can all be done in polynomial time.

On the other hand, the complexity of checking whether an extended answer set M is not preferable up to a certain $<_n$ depends on n, as shown in the next lemma.

Lemma 1. *Let $\langle P, \langle <_i \rangle_{i=1,...,n} \rangle$ be a LOLP, and let M be an extended answer set of P. Checking whether M is not preferable up to $<_n$ is in Σ_n^P.*

Proof. The proof is by induction on n.

The base case, i.e. $n = 0$, holds vacuously as checking whether M is an extended answer set is in $P = \Sigma_0^P$.

For the induction step, checking that M is not preferable up to $<_n$ can be done by (a) checking that M is (or is not) preferable up to $<_{n-1}$, which is in Σ_{n-1}^P due to the induction hypothesis; and (b) guessing, if M is preferable up to $<_{n-1}$, an interpretation $N \sqsubset_n M$ and checking that it is not the case that N is not preferable up to $<_{n-1}$, which is again in Σ_{n-1}^P due to the induction hypothesis. As a result, at most two calls are made to a Σ_{n-1}^P oracle and at most one guess is made, yielding that the problem itself is in $NP^{\Sigma_{n-1}^P} = \Sigma_n^P$.   □

Using the above yields the following theorem about the complexity of LOLPs.

Theorem 2. *Let $\langle P, \langle <_i \rangle_{i=1,...,n} \rangle$ be a LOLP and l a literal. Deciding whether there is a preferred answer set containing l is in Σ_{n+1}^P.*

Proof. The task can be performed by an NP-algorithm that guesses an interpretation $M \ni l$ and checks that it is not the case that M is not preferable up to level n. Due to Lemma 1, the latter is in Σ_n^P, so the former is in $NP^{\Sigma_n^P} = \Sigma_{n+1}^P$.   □

Theorem 3. *Let $\langle P, \langle <_i \rangle_{i=1,...,n} \rangle$ be a LOLP and l a literal. Deciding whether every preferred answer set contains l is in Π_{n+1}^P.*

Proof. Due to Theorem 2, finding a preferred answer set M not containing l, i.e. $l \notin M$, is in Σ_{n+1}^P. Hence, the complement of the problem is in Π_{n+1}^P.   □

To prove hardness, we provide a reduction of deciding validity of QBFs by means of LOLPs.

Theorem 4. *The problem of deciding, given a LOLP $\langle P, \langle <_i \rangle_{i=1,...,n} \rangle$ and a literal l, whether there exists a preferred answer set containing l is Σ_{n+1}^P-hard.*

Proof. (Sketch). Let $\phi = \exists X_1 \forall X_2 \ldots Q X_{n+1} \cdot G \in QBF_{n+1,\exists}$, where $Q = \forall$ if n is odd and $Q = \exists$ otherwise. We assume, without loss of generality, that G is in disjunctive normal form, i.e. $G = \vee_{c \in C} C$ where C is a set of sets of literals over $X_1 \cup \ldots \cup X_{n+1}$ and each $c \in C$ has to be read as a conjunction. In what follows, we will write $l <_i X_{p...q}$ to denote the longer $\{l <_i x \; ; \; l <_i \neg x \mid x \in X_j \wedge p \leq j \leq q\}$.

The LOLP $\langle P_\phi, \langle <_i \rangle_{i=1,\ldots,n}\rangle$ corresponding to ϕ is defined by the ELP P_ϕ:

$$P_1 : \{x \leftarrow ; \ \neg x \leftarrow |\ x \in X_i \wedge 1 \le i \le n+1\}$$
$$P_2 : \qquad\qquad \{g \leftarrow c \mid c \in C\}$$
$$P_3 : \qquad\qquad\qquad sat \leftarrow g$$
$$P_4 : \qquad\qquad\qquad \neg sat \leftarrow not\ g$$

and the sequence $\langle <_i \rangle_{i=1,\ldots,n}$ of orders defined by

$$\{\neg sat <_n sat, g <_n X_{2\ldots n+1}, \ X_1\}$$
$$\{sat, g <_{n-1} \neg sat <_{n-1} X_{3\ldots n+1}, \ X_1, \ X_2\}$$
$$\ldots$$
$$\{w <_1 w' <_1 X_{n+1\ldots n+1}, \ X_1, \ \ldots, \ X_n\}$$

where $w = \neg sat$ and $w' = sat, g$ if n is odd; and $w = sat, g$ and $w' = \neg sat$ otherwise.

Obviously, the construction can be done in polynomial time. Intuitively, the rules in P_1 are used to guess a truth assignment for $X_1 \cup \ldots \cup X_{n+1}$. For each such truth assignment, the rules in P_2, P_3 and P_4 will decide whether the formula G is valid or not. The intuition behind the orders is to prefer those extended answer sets of P_ϕ that give a counterexample to the validity of ϕ. Only when such an example does not exist, i.e. ϕ is valid, an extended answer set containing the literal sat will be preferred.

First note that an order relation $<_k = w < w' < X_{n-k+2\ldots n+1}$ can only prefer an extended answer set M_1 upon M_2, i.e. $M_1 \sqsubseteq_k M_2$, if $M_1 \cap (X_1 \cup \ldots \cup X_{n-k+1}) = M_2 \cap (X_1 \cup \ldots \cup X_{n-k+1})$; otherwise we have both $M_1 \not\sqsubseteq_k M_2$ and $M_2 \not\sqsubseteq_k M_1$. Further, when $<_k = sat, g < \neg sat < X_{n-k+2\ldots n+1}$ (respectively $<_k = \neg sat < sat, g < X_{n-k+2\ldots n+1}$), then the $(n - k + 2)^{th}$ quantifier, denoted Q_{n-k+2} in ϕ is $\exists$ ($\forall$ respectively).

In the sequel we use $\mathcal{M}^k$, with $0 \le k \le n$ to denote the set of extended answer sets of P_ϕ that are preferable up to $<_k$. We will show by induction that $\mathcal{M}^k$ only contains extended answer sets $M \in \mathcal{M}^k$ with $sat \in M$ iff $Q_{n-k+2} \cdots Q_{n+1} \cdot G$ is valid using $x_M^{1\ldots n-k+1}$, i.e. the truth combination over $X_1 \cup \cdots \cup X_{n-k+1}$ in M.

The base case, i.e. $k = 0$, holds vacuously, as we have, for each possible truth combination over $X_1 \cup \cdots \cup X_{n+1}$, an extended answer set $M \in \mathcal{M}^0$ containing $sat \in M$ if G is valid and $\neg sat \in M$ if G is not.

For the induction step, suppose the claim holds for $\mathcal{M}^{k-1}$ and consider $<_k$ and Q_{n-k+2}. When $Q_{n-k+2} = \exists$, $<_k$ will prefer those extended answer sets in $\mathcal{M}^{k-1}$ containing sat for a fixed truth combination X over $X_1 \cup \ldots \cup X_{n-k+1}$. By the induction hypothesis, we have that $M \in \mathcal{M}^{k-1}$ with $sat \in M$ iff $Q_{n-k+3} \cdots Q_{n+1} \cdot G$ is valid for $x_M^{1\ldots n-k+2}$. Clearly, $Q_{n-k+2} \cdots Q_{n+1} \cdot G$ is then valid for $x_M^{1\ldots n-k+1}$ iff $\mathcal{M}^k$ contains an extended answer set M with $sat \in M$.

On the other hand, when $Q_{n-k+2} = \forall$, $<_k$ will prefer those extended answer sets in $\mathcal{M}^{k-1}$ containing $\neg sat$ for a fixed truth combination X over $X_1 \cup \ldots \cup X_{n-k+1}$. By the induction hypothesis, we have that $M \in \mathcal{M}^{k-1}$ with $\neg sat \in M$ iff $Q_{n-k+3} \cdots Q_{n+1} \cdot G$ is not valid for $x_M^{1\ldots n-k+2}$. Clearly, only when $Q_{n-k+3} \cdots Q_{n+1} \cdot G$ holds for every combination of X_{n-k+2} with X, no extended answer sets with $\neg sat$ will be in $\mathcal{M}^{k-1}$ for X, and all those with sat will be passed to $\mathcal{M}^k$, yielding that $Q_{n-k+2} \cdots Q_{n+1} \cdot G$ holds for x_M iff $M \in \mathcal{M}^k$ with $sat \in M$.

Finally, by induction the above yields for $\mathcal{M}^n$, i.e. the preferred answer sets, which implies that ϕ is valid iff $\mathcal{M}^n$ contains a preferred answer set M containing sat, i.e. $\exists M \in \mathcal{M}^n \cdot sat \in M$, from which the theorem readily follows. $\square$

Theorem 5. *The problem of deciding, given a LOLP $\langle P, \langle <_i \rangle_{i=1,\ldots,n} \rangle$ and a literal l, whether every preferred answer set contains l is Π_{n+1}^P-hard.*

Proof. Reconsider the LOLP in the proof of Theorem 4. Let l be a fresh atom not occurring in P_ϕ and define P'_ϕ as P_ϕ with two extra rules $l \leftarrow$ and $\neg l \leftarrow$. Clearly, showing that l does not occur in every preferred answer set is the same as showing that $\neg l$ occurs in any preferred answer set. Deciding the latter is Σ_{n+1}^P-hard by Theorem 4; thus deciding the complement of the former is Π_{n+1}^P-hard. $\square$

The following is immediate from Theorem 2, 3, 4 and 5.

Corollary 2. *The problem of deciding, given an arbitrary LOLP $\langle P, \langle <_i \rangle_{i=1,\ldots,n} \rangle$ and a literal l, whether there is a preferred answer set containing l is Σ_{n+1}^P-complete. On the other hand, deciding whether every preferred answer set contains l is Π_{n+1}^P-complete.*

5   Weak Constraints

Weak constraints were introduced in [8] as a relaxation of the concept of a constraint. Intuitively, a weak constraint is allowed to be violated, but only as a last resort, meaning that one tries to minimize the set of violated constraints. Here minimization is typically interpreted as either *subset minimality* or *cardinality minimality*. In the former, we prefer a solution that violates a set of weak constraints C_1 over one that violates a set C_2 iff $C_1 \subset C_2$, while in the latter, we would only need that C_1 contains less violated constraints than C_2, i.e. $|C_1| < |C_2|$.

Subset minimality is obviously less controversial since, for cardinality minimality, it may happen that, while $|C_1| < |C_2|$, C_1 contains more important constraints than C_2[7].

In [8] a semantics for hierarchies of weak constraints is defined, where one minimizes constraints on lower levels, before minimizing, among the results of the previous levels, constraints on higher levels. Formally, weak constraints have the same syntactic form as constraints, i.e. $\leftarrow \beta$ with β a set of extended literals. We then assign the weak constraints for a certain level i to a set W_i, similar to [8], and define a *weak logic program* as consisting of a program and a hierarchy of sets of weak constraints.

Definition 5. *A weak logic program (WLP) is a pair $\langle P, W \rangle$ where P is a program and W is a set $\{W_1, \ldots, W_n\}$, with each W_i, $1 \leq i \leq n$, a set of weak constraints.*

To enhance readability of the following definition, we assume an empty dummy set W_0 of weak constraints.

---

[7] A similar preference for subset minimality over cardinality minimality is also common in, for example, the domain of *diagnosis* [25, 31], where one tries to minimize the set of causes responsible for certain failures.

Definition 6. *Let $\langle P, W \rangle$ be a WLP. The extended answer sets of P are **preferable up to** W_0. An extended answer set M of P set is preferable up to W_i, $1 \le i \le n$, if*

- *M is preferable up to W_{i-1}, and*
- *there is no N, preferable up to W_{i-1}, such that $W_N^i \subset W_M^i$, where $W_N^i = \{c \mid c \in W_i \wedge N \not\models c\}$, i.e. the constraints in W_i that are violated by N.*

*An extended answer set of P is a **preferred** answer set of a WLP $\langle P, W \rangle$ if it is preferable up to W_n.*

LOLPs can easily implement weak constraints. Intuitively, each order $<_i$ in the hierarchy will try to minimize the violation of weak constraints in W_i.

For a WLP $\langle P, \{W_1, \ldots, W_n\} \rangle$, define the LOLP $\langle P \cup WC, \langle <_i \rangle_{i=1,\ldots,n} \rangle$ with $WC = \{c \leftarrow \beta \mid c = (\leftarrow \beta) \in W_i, 1 \le i \le n\}$ representing the weak constraints by rules with new atoms c, one for each constraint $\leftarrow \beta$, and each order $<_i$ in $\langle <_i \rangle_{i=1,\ldots,n}$ defined by

$$\{not\ c_i <_i c_i \mid c_i \in W_i\}.$$

The orders prefer extended answer sets that do not contain c since c can only be obtained by applying $c \leftarrow \beta$, corresponding to a violation of the corresponding original constraint $\leftarrow \beta$.

Theorem 6. *An extended answer set M of a WLP $\langle P, W \rangle$ is preferred iff $M \cup \{c \mid c \in W, M \not\models c\}$ is a preferred answer set of the LOLP $\langle P \cup WC, \langle <_i \rangle_{i=1,\ldots,n} \rangle$.*

The other approach to minimize the violation of weak constraints, is to take into account the cardinality of the sets of violated weak constraints, as in [8]. The following definition formalizes the notion of cardinality preferred, or c-preferred for short, answer sets.

Definition 7. *Let $\langle P, W \rangle$ be a WLP. The extended answer sets of P are **c-preferable up to** W_0. An extended answer M of P set is c-preferable up to W_i, $1 \le i \le n$, if*

- *M is c-preferable up to W_{i-1}, and*
- *there is no N, c-preferable up to W_{i-1}, such that $|W_N^i| < |W_M^i|$.*

*An extended answer set of P is a **c-preferred** answer set of an WLP $\langle P, W \rangle$ if it is c-preferable up to W_n.*

In the special case that the preferable answer sets on a level are c-preferable we have that, on the next level, the c-preferable answer sets are preferable. Denote the set of extended answer sets that are c-preferable up to W_i as $\mathcal{M}_c^i$ and the set of extended answer sets preferable up to W_i as $\mathcal{M}^i$.

Theorem 7. *Let $\langle P, W \rangle$ be a WLP and let $\mathcal{M}_c^{i-1} = \mathcal{M}^{i-1}$ for some $1 \le i \le n$. Then $\mathcal{M}_c^i \subseteq \mathcal{M}^i$.*

The pre-condition that every extended answer set, preferable up to W_{i-1}, has to be c-preferable is necessary, as can be seen from the following example, where we have a c-preferred answer set that is not preferred.

Example 4. Take a WLP $\langle P, \{W_1, W_2\} \rangle$ with P the program

$$\neg a \leftarrow$$
$$a \leftarrow$$
$$b \leftarrow a$$

and the weak constraints $W_1 = \{c_1 :\leftarrow \neg a \;;\; c_2 :\leftarrow a \;;\; c_3 :\leftarrow b\}$ and the second level $W_2 = \{c_4 :\leftarrow \neg a, not\ b\}$. The program P has two extended answer sets $M = \{\neg a\}$ and $N = \{a, b\}$. This leads to the following sets of violated constraints: $W_M^1 = \{c_1\}$, $W_N^1 = \{c_2, c_3\}$, $W_M^2 = \{c_4\}$, and $W_N^2 = \emptyset$. Then, M is c-preferable up to W_1, while N is not. Both M and N are preferable up to W_1. However, M is c-preferable up to W_2, since there are no other extended answer sets that are c-preferable up to W_1, while M is not preferable up to W_2.

If there is only one level of weak constraints we have the attractive property that c-preferred answer sets are preferred.

Corollary 3. *Let $\langle P, \{W_1\} \rangle$ be a WLP with one level of weak constraints. A c-preferred answer set of $\langle P, \{W_1\} \rangle$ is preferred.*

In this case, if the preferred answer sets are already computed, and one decides later on that c-preferred answer sets are needed, the search space can be restricted to just the preferred answer sets instead of all extended answer sets.

6   Conclusions and Directions for Further Research

Equipping logic programs with a preference relation on the rules has a relatively long history [21, 20, 18, 9, 7, 5, 32, 1, 29]. Also approaches that consider a preference relation on (extended) literals have been considered: [26] proposes explicit preferences while [4, 6] encodes dynamic preferences within the program.

In this paper, we applied such preferences on the extended answer set semantics, thus allowing the selection of preferred "approximate" answer sets for inconsistent programs. We also considered a natural extension, linearly ordered programs, where there are several preference relations. This extension increases the expressiveness of the resulting formalism to cover the polynomial hierarchy.

Such preference hierarchies occur naturally in several application areas such as timetabling. As an application of the approach, we have shown that hierarchically structured weak constraints can be considered as a special case of linearly ordered programs.

Future work may generalize the structure of the preference relations, e.g. to arbitrary partial orders or to cyclic structures, where the latter may provide a natural model for agent communication.

A brute force prototype implementation for LOLPs is available which uses an existing answer set solver to generate all extended answer sets, and then filters out the preferred ones taking into account the given preference levels. A dedicated implementation, using existing answer set solvers, could, similarly to [6], compute preferred answer sets more directly by generating one extended answer set and then trying to generate a better one using an augmented program, which, when applied in a fixpoint computation, results in a preferred answer set.

References

1. José Júlio Alferes and Luís Moniz Pereira. Updates plus preferences. In Ojeda-Aciego et al. [23], pages 345–360.
2. Marcelo Arenas, Leopoldo Bertossi, and Jan Chomicki. Specifying and querying database repairs using logic programs with exceptions. In *Proceedings of the 4th International Conference on Flexible Query Answering Systems*, pages 27–41, Warsaw, Octobre 2000. Springer-Verlag.
3. Chitta Baral. *Knowledge Representation, Reasoning and Declarative Problem Solving*. Cambridge Press, 2003.
4. G. Brewka. Logic programming with ordered disjunction. In *Proceedings of the 18th National Conference on Artificial Intelligence and Fourteenth Conference on Innovative Applications of Artificial Intelligence*, pages 100–105, Edmonton, Canada, July 2002. AAAI Press.
5. Gerhard Brewka and Thomas Eiter. Preferred answer sets for extended logic programs. *Artificial Intelligence*, 109(1-2):297–356, April 1999.
6. Gerhard Brewka, Ilkka Niemela, and Tommi Syrjanen. Implementing ordered disjunction using answer set solvers for normal programs. In Flesca et al. [17], pages 444–455.
7. Francesco Buccafurri, Wolfgang Faber, and Nicola Leone. Disjunctive logic programs with inheritance. In Danny De Schreye, editor, *Logic Programming: The 1999 International Conference*, pages 79–93, Las Cruces, New Mexico, December 1999. MIT Press.
8. Francesco Buccafurri, Nicola Leone, and Pasquale Rullo. Strong and weak constraints in disjunctive datalog. In *Proceedings of the 4th International Conference on Logic Programming (LPNMR '97)*, pages 2–17, 1997.
9. Francesco Buccafurri, Nicola Leone, and Pasquale Rullo. Disjunctive ordered logic: Semantics and expressiveness. In Anthony G. Cohn, Lenhard K. Schubert, and Stuart C. Shapiro, editors, *Proceedings of the 6th International Conference on Principles of Knowledge Representation and Reasoning*, pages 418–431, Trento, June 1998. Morgan Kaufmann.
10. Francesco Buccafurri, Nicola Leone, and Pasquale Rullo. Enhancing disjunctive datalog by constraints. *Knowledge and Data Engineering*, 12(5):845–860, 2000.
11. Marina De Vos and Dirk Vermeir. Choice Logic Programs and Nash Equilibria in Strategic Games. In Jörg Flum and Mario Rodríguez-Artalejo, editors, *Computer Science Logic (CSL'99)*, volume 1683 of *Lecture Notes in Computer Science*, pages 266–276, Madrid, Spain, 1999. Springer Verslag.
12. Thomas Eiter, Wolfgang Faber, Nicola Leone, and Gerald Pfeifer. The diagnosis frontend of the dlv system. *AI Communications*, 12(1-2):99–111, 1999.
13. Thomas Eiter, Wolfgang Faber, Nicola Leone, Gerald Pfeifer, and Axel Polleres. Planning under incomplete knowledge. In John W. Lloyd, Verónica Dahl, Ulrich Furbach, Manfred Kerber, Kung-Kiu Lau, Catuscia Palamidessi, Luís Moniz Pereira, Yehoshua Sagiv, and Peter J. Stuckey, editors, *Proceedings of the First International Conference on Computational Logic (CL2000)*, volume 1861 of *Lecture Notes in Computer Science*, pages 807–821. Springer, 2000.
14. Thomas Eiter, Wolfgang Faber, Nicola Leone, Gerald Pfeifer, and Axel Polleres. The DLV^k planning system. In Flesca et al. [17], pages 541–544.
15. Thomas Eiter, Michael Fink, Giuliana Sabbatini, and Hans Tompits. Considerations on updates of logic programs. In Ojeda-Aciego et al. [23], pages 2–20.
16. Wolfgang Faber, Nicola Leone, and Gerald Pfeifer. Representing school timetabling in a disjunctive logic programming language. In *Proceedings of the 13th Workshop on Logic Programming (WLP '98)*, 1998.

17. Sergio Flesca, Sergio Greco, Nicola Leone, and Giovambattista Ianni, editors. *Logic in Artificial Intelligence*, volume 2424 of *Lecture Notes in Artificial Intelligence*, Cosenza, Italy, September 2002. Springer Verlag.
18. D. Gabbay, E. Laenens, and D. Vermeir. Credulous vs. Sceptical Semantics for Ordered Logic Programs. In J. Allen, R. Fikes, and E. Sandewall, editors, *Proceedings of the 2nd International Conference on Principles of Knowledge Representation and Reasoning*, pages 208–217, Cambridge, Mass, 1991. Morgan Kaufmann.
19. Michael Gelfond and Vladimir Lifschitz. The stable model semantics for logic programming. In Robert A. Kowalski and Kenneth A. Bowen, editors, *Logic Programming, Proceedings of the Fifth International Conference and Symposium*, pages 1070–1080, Seattle, Washington, August 1988. The MIT Press.
20. Robert A. Kowalski and Fariba Sadri. Logic programs with exceptions. In David H. D. Warren and Peter Szeredi, editors, *Proceedings of the 7th International Conference on Logic Programming*, pages 598–613, Jerusalem, 1990. The MIT Press.
21. Els Laenens and Dirk Vermeir. A logical basis for object oriented programming. In Jan van Eijck, editor, *European Workshop, JELIA 90*, volume 478 of *Lecture Notes in Artificial Intelligence*, pages 317–332, Amsterdam, The Netherlands, September 1990. Springer Verlag.
22. Vladimir Lifschitz. Answer set programming and plan generation. *Journal of Artificial Intelligence*, 138(1-2):39–54, 2002.
23. Manual Ojeda-Aciego, Inma P. de Guzmán, Gerhard Brewka, and Luíz Moniz Pereira, editors. *Logic in Artificial Intelligence*, volume 1919 of *Lecture Notes in Artificial Intelligence*, Malaga, Spain, September–October 2000. Springer Verlag.
24. Christos H. Papadimitriou. *Computational Complexity*. Addison Wesley, 1994.
25. Raymond Reiter. A theory of diagnosis from first principles. *Artificial Intelligence*, 32(1):57–95, 1987.
26. Chiaki Sakama and Katsumi Inoue. Representing priorities in logic programs. In Michael J. Maher, editor, *Proceedings of the 1996 Joint International Conference and Symposium on Logic Programming*, pages 82–96, Bonn, September 1996. MIT Press.
27. T. Soininen and I. Niemelä. Developing a declarative rule language for applications in product configuration. In *Proceedings of the First International Workshop on Practical Aspects of Declarative Languages (PADL '99)*, Lecture Notes in Computer Science, San Antonio, Texas, 1999. Springer Verslag.
28. T. Soininen, I. Niemelä, J. Tiihonen, and R. Sulonen. Representing configuration knowledge with weight constraint rules. In *Proceedings of the AAAI Spring 2001 Symposium on Answer Set Programming: Towards Efficient and Scalable Knowledge*, Stanford, USA, 2001.
29. Davy Van Nieuwenborgh and Dirk Vermeir. Preferred answer sets for ordered logic programs. In Flesca et al. [17], pages 432–443.
30. Davy Van Nieuwenborgh and Dirk Vermeir. Order and negation as failure. In Catuscia Palamidessi, editor, *Proceedings of the International Conference on Logic Programming*, volume 2916 of *Lecture Notes in Computer Science*, pages 194–208. Springer, 2003.
31. Davy Van Nieuwenborgh and Dirk Vermeir. Ordered diagnosis. In *Proceedings of the 10th International Conference on Logic for Programming, Artificial Intelligence, and Reasoning (LPAR2003)*, volume 2850 of *Lecture Notes in Artificial Intelligence*, pages 244–258. Springer Verlag, 2003.
32. Kewen Wang, Lizhu Zhou, and Fangzhen Lin. Alternating fixpoint theory for logic programs with priority. In *Proceedings of the International Conference on Computational Logic (CL2000)*, volume 1861 of *Lecture Notes in Computer Science*, pages 164–178. Springer, 2000.

Splitting an Operator

An Algebraic Modularity Result and Its Application to Logic Programming

Joost Vennekens, David Gilis, and Marc Denecker

Department of Computer Science, K.U. Leuven
Celestijnenlaan 200A
B-3001 Leuven, Belgium

Abstract. It is well known that, under certain conditions, it is possible to *split* logic programs under stable model semantics, i.e. to divide such a program into a number of different "levels", such that the models of the entire program can be constructed by incrementally constructing models for each level. Similar results exist for other non-monotonic formalisms, such as auto-epistemic logic and default logic. In this work, we present a general, algebraic splitting theory for programs/theories under a fixpoint semantics. Together with the framework of *approximation theory*, a general fixpoint theory for arbitrary operators, this gives us a uniform and powerful way of deriving splitting results for each logic with a fixpoint semantics. We demonstrate the usefulness of these results, by generalizing Lifschitz and Turner's splitting theorem to other semantics for (non-disjunctive) logic programs.

1 Introduction

An important aspect of human reasoning is that it is often incremental in nature. When dealing with a complex domain, we tend to initially restrict ourselves to a small subset of all relevant concepts. Once these "basic" concepts have been figured out, we then build another, more "advanced", layer of concepts on this knowledge. A quite illustrative example of this can be found in most textbooks on computer networking. These typically present a seven-layered model of the way in which computers communicate. First, in the so-called physical layer, there is only talk of hardware and concepts such as wires, cables and electronic pulses. Once these low-level issues have been dealt with, the resulting knowledge becomes a *fixed* base, upon which a new layer, the data-link layer, is built. This no longer considers wires and cables and so on, but rather talks about packages of information travelling from one computer to another. Once again, after the workings of this layer have been figured out, this information is taken "for granted" and becomes part of the foundation upon which a new layer is built. This process continues all the way up to a seventh layer, the application layer, and together all of these layers describe the operation of the entire system.

In this paper, we investigate a formal equivalent of this method. More specifically, we address the question of whether a formal theory in some non-monotonic

B. Demoen and V. Lifschitz (Eds.): ICLP 2004, LNCS 3132, pp. 195–209, 2004.
© Springer-Verlag Berlin Heidelberg 2004

language can be *split* into a number of different levels or *strata*, such that the formal semantics of the entire theory can be constructed by succesively constructing the semantics of the various strata. (We use the terms "stratification" and "splitting" interchangeably to denote a division into a number of different levels. This is a more general use of both these terms, than in literature such as [Gel87].) Such stratifications are interesting from both a practical and a more theoretical, knowledge representational point of view. For instance, computing models of a stratified version of a theory is often significantly faster than computing models of the original theory. Furthermore, in order to be able to build and maintain large knowledge bases, it is crucial to know which parts of a theory can be analysed or constructed independently and, conversely, whether combining several correct theories will have any unexpected side-effects.

It is therefore not surprising that this issue has already been intensively studied. Indeed, splitting results have been proven for auto-epistemic logic under the semantics of expansions [GP92,NR94] default logic under the semantics of extensions [Tur96] and various kinds of logic programs under the stable model semantics [LT94,EL04]. In all of these works, stratification is seen as a syntactical property of a theory in a certain language under a certain formal semantics.

In this work, we take a different approach to studying this topic. The semantics of several (non-monotonic) logics can be expressed through fixpoint characterizations in some lattice of semantic structures. In such a semantics, the meaning of a theory is described by an operator, which revises proposed "states of affairs". The models of a theory are those states which no longer have to be revised. Knowing such a revision operator for a theory, should suffice to know whether it is stratifiable: this will be the case if no higher levels are ever used to revise the state of affairs for lower-level concepts. This motivates us to study the stratification of these revision operators themselves. As such, we are able to develop a general theory of stratification at an abstract, algebraic level and apply its results to each formalism which has a fixpoint semantics.

This approach is especially powerful when combined with the framework of *approximation theory*, a general fixpoint theory for arbitrary operators, which has already proved highly useful in the study of non-monotonic reasoning. It naturally captures, for instance, (most of) the common semantics of logic programming [DMT00], auto-epistemic logic [DMT03] and default logic [DMT03]. As such, studying stratification within this framework, allows our abstract results to be directly and easily applicable to logic programming, auto-epistemic logic and default logic.

Studying stratification at this more *semantical* level has three distinct advantages. First of all, it avoids duplication of effort, as the same algebraic theory takes care of stratification in logic programming, auto-epistemic logic, default logic and indeed any logic with a fixpoint semantics. Secondly, our results can be used to easily extend existing results to other (fixpoint) semantics of the aforementioned languages. Finally, our work also offers greater insight into the general principles underlying various known stratification results, as we are able to study this issue in itself, free of being restricted to a particular syntax or semantics.

This papers is structured in the following way. In section 2, some basic notions from lattice theory are introduced and a brief introduction to the main concepts of approximation theory is given. Section 3 is the main part of this work, in which we present our algebraic theory of stratifiable operators. In section 4, we then show how these results can be applied to logic programming. We would like stress that, although space restrictions prevent us from demonstrating this here, a similar treatment exists for both auto-epistemic logic and default logic.

2   Preliminaries

2.1   Orders and Lattices

A binary relation $\leq$ on a set S is a *partial order* if it is reflexive, transitive and anti-symmetric. An element $x \in S$ is a *central element* if it is comparable to each other element of S, i.e. $x \leq y$ or $x \geq y$ for each $y \in S$. For each subset R of S, an element l of S, such that $l \leq r$ for all $r \in R$ is a *lower bound* of R. An element g in S such that g is a lower bound of R and for each other lower bound l of R, $l \leq g$, is called the *greatest lower bound*, denoted $glb(R)$, of R. Similarly, an element u such that for each $r \in R$, $u \geq r$ is an *upper bound* of R and if one such upper bound is less or equal to each other upper bound of R, it is the *least upper bound* $lub(R)$ of R.

A partial order $\leq$ on a set S is *well-founded* if each subset R of S has a minimal element; it is *total* if every two elements $x, y \in S$ are comparable, i.e. $x \leq y$ or $x \geq y$.

A pair $\langle L, \leq \rangle$ is a *lattice* if $\leq$ is a partial order on a non-empty set L, such that each two elements x, y of L have a greatest lower bound $glb(x, y)$ and a least upper bound $lub(x, y)$. A lattice $\langle L, \leq \rangle$ is *complete* if each subset L' of L has a greatest lower bound $glb(L')$ and least upper bound $lub(L')$. By definition, such a lattice has a minimal (or *bottom*) element $\bot$ and a maximal (or *top*) element $\top$. Often, we will not explicitly mention the partial order $\leq$ of a lattice $\langle L, \leq \rangle$ and simply speak of the lattice L.

An operator O is a function from a lattice to itself. An operator on a lattice L is monotone if for each $x, y \in L$, such that $x \leq y$, $O(x) \leq O(y)$. An element x in L is a *fixpoint* of O if $O(x) = x$. We denote the set of all fixpoint of O by $fp(O)$. A fixpoint x of L, such that for each other fixpoint y of L, $x \leq y$, is *the least fixpoint $lfp(O)$* of O. It can be shown [Tar55] that each monotone operator has such a unique least fixpoint.

2.2   Approximation Theory

Approximation theory is a general fixpoint theory for arbitrary operators, which generalizes ideas found in, among others, [BS91] and [Fit89]. Our presentation of this theory is based on [DMT00].

Let $\langle L, \leq \rangle$ be a lattice. An element (x, y) of the square L^2 of the domain of such a lattice, can be seen as denoting an interval $[x, y] = \{z \in L \mid x \leq z \leq y\}$.

Using this intuition, we can derive a *precision* order $\leq_p$ on the set L^2 from the order $\leq$ on L: for each $x, y, x', y' \in L, (x, y) \leq_p (x', y')$ iff $x \leq x'$ and $y' \leq y$. Indeed, if $(x, y) \leq_p (x', y')$, then $[x, y] \supseteq [x', y']$. It can easily be shown that $\langle L^2, \leq_p \rangle$ is also a lattice, which we will call the *bilattice* corresponding to L. Moreover, if L is complete, then so is L^2. As an interval $[x, x]$ contains precisely one element, namely x itself, elements (x, x) of L^2 are called *exact*. The set of all exact elements of L^2 forms a natural embedding of L in L^2. A pair (x, y) only corresponds to a non-empty interval if $x \leq y$. Such pairs are called *consistent*.

Approximation theory is based on the study of operators on bilattices L^2 which are monotone w.r.t. the precision order $\leq_p$. Such operators are called *approximations*. For an approximation A and $x, y \in L$, we denote by $A^1(x, y)$ and $A^2(x, y)$ the unique elements of L, for which $A(x, y) = (A^1(x, y), A^2(x, y))$. An approximation *approximates* an operator O on L if for each $x \in L$, $A(x, x)$ contains $O(x)$, i.e. $A^1(x, x) \leq O(x) \leq A^2(x, x)$. An *exact* approximation is one which maps exact elements to exact elements, i.e. $A^1(x, x) = A^2(x, x)$ for all $x \in L$. Similarly, a *consistent* approximation maps consistent elements to consistent elements, i.e. if $x \leq y$ then $A^1(x, y) \leq A^2(x, y)$. An inconsistent approximation cannot approximate any operator. Each exact approximation is consistent and approximates a unique operator O on L, namely that which maps each $x \in L$ to $A^1(x, x)$. An approximation is *symmetric* if for each pair $(x, y) \in L^2$, if $A(x, y) = (x', y')$ then $A(y, x) = (y', x')$. Each symmetric approximation is also exact.

For an approximation A on L^2, the following two operators on L can be defined: the function $A^1(\cdot, y)$ maps an element $x \in L$ to $A^1(x, y)$, i.e. $A^1(\cdot, y) = \lambda x . A^1(x, y)$, and the function $A^2(x, \cdot)$ maps an element $y \in L$ to $A^2(x, y)$, i.e. $A^2(x, \cdot) = \lambda y . A^2(x, y)$. As all such operators are monotone, they all have a unique least fixpoint. We define an operator $C_A^\downarrow$ on L, which maps each $y \in L$ to $lfp(A^1(\cdot, y))$ and, similarly, an operator $C_A^\uparrow$, which maps each $x \in L$ to $lfp(A^2(x, \cdot))$. $C_A^\downarrow$ is called the *lower stable operator* of A, while $C_A^\uparrow$ is the *upper stable operator* of A. Both these operators are anti-monotone. Combining these two operators, the operator C_A on L^2 maps each pair (x, y) to $(C_A^\downarrow(y), C_A^\uparrow(x))$. This operator is called the *partial stable operator* of A. Because the lower and upper partial stable operators $C_A^\downarrow$ and $C_A^\uparrow$ are anti-monotone, the partial stable operator C_A is monotone. Note that if an approximation A is symmetric, its lower and upper partial stable operators will always be equal, i.e. $C_A^\downarrow = C_A^\uparrow$.

An approximation defines a number of different fixpoints: its least fixpoint is called its *Kripke-Kleene fixpoint*, fixpoints of its partial stable operator C_A are *stable fixpoints* and the least fixpoint of C_A is called the *well-founded fixpoint* of A. As shown in [DMT00] and [DMT03], these fixpoints correspond to various semantics of logic programming, auto-epistemic logic and default logic.

Finally, it should be noted that the concept of an approximation as defined in [DMT00] corresponds to our definition of a *symmetric* approximation.

3   Stratification of Operators

In this section, we develop a theory of stratifiable operators. We will, in section 3.2, investigate operators on a special kind of lattice, namely *product lattices*, which will be introduced in section 3.1. In section 3.3, we then return to approximation theory and discuss stratifiable approximations on product lattices.

3.1   Product Lattices

We begin by defining the notion of a *product set*, which is a generalization of the well-known concept of cartesian products.

Definition 3.1.1. *Let I be a set, which we will call the* index set *of the product set, and for each $i \in I$, let S_i be a set. The product set $\bigotimes_{i \in I} S_i$ is the following set of functions:* $\bigotimes_{i \in I} S_i = \{f \mid f : I \to \bigcup_{i \in I} S_i \text{ such that } \forall i \in I : f(i) \in S_i\}$

Intuitively, a product set $\bigotimes_{i \in I} S_i$ contains all ways of selecting one element from each set S_i. As such, if I is a set with n elements, e.g. the set $\{1, \ldots, n\}$, the product set $\bigotimes_{i \in I} S_i$ is simply (isomorphic to) the cartesian product $S_1 \times \cdots \times S_n$.

Definition 3.1.2. *Let I be a set and for each $i \in I$, let $\langle S_i, \leq_i \rangle$ be a partially ordered set. The* product order $\leq_\otimes$ *on the set $\bigotimes_{i \in I} S_i$ is defined as:* $\forall x, y \in \bigotimes_{i \in I} S_i : x \leq_\otimes y$ *iff* $\forall i \in I : x(i) \leq_i y(i)$.

It can easily be shown that if all of the partially ordered sets S_i are (complete) lattices, the product set $\otimes_{i \in I} S_i$, together with its product order $\leq_\otimes$, is also a (complete) lattice. We therefore refer to the pair $\langle \otimes_{i \in I} S_i, \leq_\otimes \rangle$ as the *product lattice* of lattices S_i.

From now on, we will only consider product lattices with a *well-founded* index set, i.e. index sets I with a partial order $\preceq$ such that each non-empty subset of I has a $\preceq$-minimal element. This will allow us to use inductive arguments in dealing with elements of product lattices. Most of our results, however, also hold for index sets with an arbitrary partial order; if a certain proof depends on the well-foundedness of I, we will always explicitly mention this.

In the next sections, the following notations will be used. For a function $f : A \to B$ and a subset A' of A, we denote by $f|_{A'}$ the restriction of f to A', i.e. $f|_{A'} : A' \to B : a' \mapsto f(a')$. For an element x of a product lattice $\otimes_{i \in I} L_i$ and an $i \in I$, we abbreviate $x|_{\{j \in I \mid j \preceq i\}}$ by $x|_{\preceq i}$. We also use similar abbreviations $x|_{\prec i}$, $x|_i$ and $x|_{\not\preceq i}$. If i is a minimal element of the well-founded set I, $x|_{\prec i}$ is defined as the empty function. For each index i, the set $\{x|_{\preceq i} \mid x \in L\}$, ordered by the appropriate restriction $\leq_\otimes|_{\preceq i}$ of the product order, is also a lattice. Clearly, this sublattice of L is isomorphic to the product lattice $\otimes_{j \preceq i} L_j$. We denote this sublattice by $L|_{\preceq i}$ and use a similar notation $L|_{\prec i}$ for $\otimes_{j \prec i} L_j$.

If f, g are functions $f : A \to B$, $g : C \to D$ and the domains A and C are disjoint, we denote by $f \sqcup g$ the function from $A \cup C$ to $B \cup D$, such that for all $a \in A$, $(f \sqcup g)(a) = f(a)$ and for all $c \in C$, $(f \sqcup g)(c) = g(c)$. Furthermore, for any g whose domain is disjoint from the domain of f, we call $f \sqcup g$ an *extension* of f. For each element x of a product lattice L and each index $i \in I$, the extension $x|_{\prec i} \sqcup x|_i$ of $x|_{\prec i}$ is clearly equal to $x|_{\preceq i}$. For ease of notation, we sometimes simply write $x(i)$ instead of $x|_i$ in such expressions, i.e. we identify an element a

of the ith lattice L_i with the function from $\{i\}$ to L_i which maps i to a. Similarly, $x|_{\prec i} \sqcup x(i) \sqcup x|_{\npreceq i} = x$.

We will use the symbols x, y to denote elements of an entire product lattice L; a, b to denote elements of a single level L_i and u, v to denote elements of $L|_{\prec i}$.

3.2   Operators on Product Lattices

Let $\langle I, \preceq \rangle$ be a well-founded index set and let $L = \otimes_{i \in I} L_i$ be the product lattice of lattices $\langle L_i, \leq_i \rangle_{i \in I}$. Intuitively, an operator O on L is stratifiable over the order $\preceq$, if the value $(O(x))(i)$ of $O(x)$ in the ith stratum only depends on values $x(j)$ for which $j \preceq i$. This is formalized in the following definition.

Definition 3.2.1. *An operator O on a product lattice L is* stratifiable *iff* $\forall x, y \in L, \forall i \in I$: *if* $x|_{\preceq i} = y|_{\preceq i}$ *then* $O(x)|_{\preceq i} = O(y)|_{\preceq i}$.

It is possible to characterize stratifiablity in a more constructive manner. The following theorem shows that stratifiablity of an operator O on a product lattice L is equivalent to the existence of a family of operators on each lattice L_i (one for each $u \in L|_{\prec i}$), which mimics the behaviour of O on this lattice.

Proposition 3.2.1. *Let O be an operator on a product lattice L. O is stratifiable iff for each $i \in I$ and $u \in L|_{\prec i}$ there exists a unique operator O_i^u on L_i, such that for all $x \in L$: If $x|_{\prec i} = u$ then $(O(x))(i) = O_i^u(x(i))$.*

Proof. To prove the implication from left to right, let O be a stratifiable operator, $i \in I$ and $u \in L|_{\prec i}$. We define the operator O_i^u on L_i as $O_i^u : L_i \to L_i : a \mapsto (O(y))(i)$, with y some element of L extending $u \sqcup a$. Because of the stratifiability of O, this operator is well-defined and it trivially satisfies the required condition.

To prove the other direction, suppose the right-hand side of the equivalence holds and let x, x' be elements of L, such that $x|_{\preceq i} = x'|_{\preceq i}$. Then for each $j \preceq i$,

$$(O(x))(j) = O_j^{x|_{\prec j}}(x(j)) = O_j^{x'|_{\prec j}}(x'(j)) = (O(x'))(j).$$

The operators O_i^u are called the *components* of O. Their existence allows us to already prove one of the main theorems of this paper, which states that is possible to construct the fixpoints of a stratifiable operator in a bottom-up manner w.r.t. the well-founded order $\preceq$ on the index set.

Theorem 3.2.1. *Let O be a stratifiable operator on a product lattice L. Then for each $x \in L$: x is a fixpoint of O iff $\forall i \in I$: $x(i)$ is a fixpoint of $O_i^{x|_{\prec i}}$.*

Proof. Follows immediately from proposition 3.2.1.

If O is a monotone operator on a complete lattice, we are often interested in its *least* fixpoint. This can also be constructed by means of the least fixpoints of the components of O. Such a construction of course requires each component to actually have a least fixpoint as well. We will therefore first show that the components of a monotone operator are also monotone.

Proposition 3.2.2. *Let O be a stratifiable operator on a product lattice L, which is monotone w.r.t. the product order $\leq_\otimes$. Then for each $i \in I$ and $u \in L|_{\prec i}$, the component $O_i^u : L_i \to L_i$ is monotone w.r.t. to the order $\leq_i$ of the ith lattice L_i of L.*

Proof. Let i be an index in I, u an element of $L|_{\prec i}$ and a, b elements of L_i, such that $a \leq_i b$. Let $x, y \in L$, such that x extends $u \sqcup a$, y extends $u \sqcup b$ and for each $j \not\preceq i$, $x(j) = y(j)$. Because of the definition of $\leq_\otimes$, clearly $x \leq_\otimes y$ and therefore $\forall j \in I : O_j^{x|_{\prec j}}(x(j)) = (O(x))(j) \leq_j (O(y))(j) = O_j^{y|_{\prec j}}(y(j))$, which, taking $j = i$, implies $O_i^u(a) \leq_i O_i^u(b)$.

Now, we can prove that the least fixpoints of the components of a monotone stratifiable operator indeed form the least fixpoint of the operator itself. We will do this, by first proving the following, slightly more general theorem, which we will be able to reuse later on.

Proposition 3.2.3. *Let O be a monotone operator on a complete product lattice L and let for each $i \in I$, $u \in L|_{\prec i}$, P_i^u be a monotone operator on L_i (not necessarily a component of O), such that:*

$$x \text{ is a fixpoint of } O \quad iff \quad \forall i \in I : x(i) \text{ is a fixpoint of } P_i^{x|_{\prec i}}.$$

Then the following equivalence also holds:

$$x \text{ is the least fixpoint of } O \quad iff \quad \forall i \in I : x(i) \text{ is the least fixpoint of } P_i^{x|_{\prec i}}.$$

Proof. To prove the implication from left to right, let x be the least fixpoint of O and let i be an arbitrary index in I. We will show that for each fixpoint a of $P_i^{x|_{\prec i}}$, $a \geq x(i)$. So, let a be such a fixpoint. We can inductively extend $x|_{\prec i} \sqcup a$ to an element y of L by defining for all $j \not\preceq i$, $y(j)$ as $lfp(P_j^{y|_{\prec j}})$. Because of the well-foundedness of $\preceq$, y is well defined. Furthermore, y is clearly also a fixpoint of O. Therefore $x \leq y$ and, by definition of the product order on L, $x(i) \leq_i y(i) = a$.

To prove the other direction, let x be an element of L, such that, for each $i \in I$, $x(i)$ is the least fixpoint of $P_i^{x|_{\prec i}}$. Now, let y be the least fixpoint of O. To prove that $x = y$, it suffices to show that for each $i \in I$, $x|_{\preceq i} = y|_{\preceq i}$. We will prove this by by induction on the well-founded order $\preceq$ of I. If i is a minimal element of I, the proposition trivially holds. Now, let i be an index which is not the minimal element of I and assume that for each $j \prec i$, $x|_{\preceq j} = y|_{\preceq j}$. It suffices to show that $x(i) = y(i)$. Because y is a fixpoint of O, $y(i)$ is fixpoint of $P_i^{y|_{\prec i}}$. As the induction hypothesis implies that $x|_{\prec i} = y|_{\prec i}$, $y(i)$ is a also fixpoint of $P_i^{x|_{\prec i}}$ and therefore $x(i) \leq y(i)$. However, because x is also a fixpoint of O and therefore must be greater than the least fixpoint y of O, the definition of the product order on L implies that $x(i) \geq y(i)$ as well. Therefore $x(i) = y(i)$.

It is worth noting that the condition that the order $\preceq$ on I should be well-founded is necessary for this proposition to hold. Indeed, consider for example the product lattice $L = \bigotimes_{z \in \mathbb{Z}} \{0, 1\}$, with $\mathbb{Z}$ the integers ordered by their usual, non-well-founded order. Let O be the operator mapping each $x \in L$ to $y : \mathbb{Z} \to \{0, 1\}$ of L, which maps each $z \in \mathbb{Z}$ to 0 if $x(z - 1) = 0$ and to 1 otherwize. This operator is stratifiable over the order $\leq$ of $\mathbb{Z}$ and its components are the family of operators O_z^u, with $z \in \mathbb{Z}$ and $u \in L|_{\leq z}$, which are defined as mapping both 0 and 1 to 0 if $u(z - 1) = 0$ and to 1 otherwize. Clearly, the bottom element $\perp_L$ of L, which maps each $z \in \mathbb{Z}$ to 0, is the least fixpoint of O. However, the element $x \in L$ which maps each $z \in \mathbb{Z}$ to 1 satisfies the condition that for each $z \in \mathbb{Z}$, $x(z)$ is the least fixpoint of $P_z^{x|<z}$, but is not the least fixpoint of O.

Together with theorem 3.2.1 and proposition 3.2.2, this proposition implies that for each stratifiable operator O on a product lattice L, an element $x \in L$ is the least fixpoint of O iff $\forall i \in I$, $x(i)$ is the least fixpoint of $O_i^{x|_{\prec i}}$. In other words, the least fixpoint of a stratifiable operator can also be incrementally constructed.

3.3   Approximations on Product Lattices

In section 2.2, we introduced several concepts from approximation theory, pointing out that we are mainly interested in studying Kripke-Kleene, stable and well-founded fixpoints of approximations. Similar to our treatment of general operators in the previous section, we will in this section investigate the relation between these various fixpoints of an approximation and its components. In doing so, it will be convenient to switch to an alternative representation of the bilattice L^2 of a product lattice $L = \otimes_{i \in I} L_i$. Indeed, this bilattice is clearly isomorphic to the structure $\otimes_{i \in I} L_i^2$, i.e. to a product lattice of bilattices. From now on, we will not distinguish between these two representations. More specifically, when viewing A as a stratifiable operator, it will be convenient to consider its domain equal to $\otimes_{i \in I} L_i^2$, while when viewing A as an approximation, the representation $(\otimes_{i \in I} L_i)^2$ is more natural.

Obviously, this isomorphism and the results of the previous section already provide a way of constructing the Kripke-Kleene fixpoint of a stratifiable approximation A, by means of its components A_i^u. Also, it is clear that if A is both exact and stratifiable, the unique operator O approximated by A is stratifiable as well. Indeed, this is a trivial consequence of the fact that $A(x, x) = (O(x), O(x))$ for each $x \in L$.

These results leave only the stable and well-founded fixpoints of A to be investigated. We will first examine the operators $A^1(\cdot, y)$ and $A^2(x, \cdot)$, and then move on to the lower and upper stable operators $C_A^{\downarrow}$ and $C_A^{\uparrow}$, before finally getting to the partial stable operator $\mathcal{C}_A$ itself.

Proposition 3.3.1. *Let L be a product lattice and let $A : L^2 \to L^2$ be a stratifiable approximation. Then, for each $x, y \in L$, the operators $A^1(\cdot, y)$, $A^2(x, \cdot)$ are also stratifiable. Moreover, for each $i \in I$, $u \in L|_{\prec i}$, the components of these operators are:*

$$(A^1(\cdot, y))_i^u = (A_i^{(u, y|_{\prec i})})^1(\cdot, y(i)),$$
$$(A^2(x, \cdot))_i^u = (A_i^{(x|_{\prec i}, u)})^2(x(i), \cdot),$$

Proof. Let x, y be elements of L, i an element of I. Then, because A is stratifiable, $(A(x,y))(i) = (A_i^{(x,y)|_{\prec i}})(x(i), y(i))$. From this, the two equalities follow.

In the previous section, we showed that the components of a monotone operator are monotone as well (proposition 3.2.2). This result implies that the components A_i^u of a stratifiable approximation are also approximations. Therefore, such a component A_i^u also has a lower and uppers stable operator $C_{A_i^u}^{\downarrow}$ and $C_{A_i^u}^{\uparrow}$. It turns out that the lower and upper stable operators of the components of A, characterize the components of the lower and upper stable operators of A.

Proposition 3.3.2. *Let L be a product lattice and let A be a stratifiable approximation on L^2. Then the operators $C_A^{\downarrow}$ and $C_A^{\uparrow}$ are also stratifiable. Moreover, for each $x, y \in L$,*

$$x = C_A^{\downarrow}(y) \qquad \text{iff} \qquad \text{for each } i \in I, x(i) = C_{A_i^{(x,y)|_{\prec i}}}^{\downarrow}(y(i));$$

$$y = C_A^{\uparrow}(x) \qquad \text{iff} \qquad \text{for each } i \in I, y(i) = C_{A_i^{(x,y)|_{\prec i}}}^{\uparrow}(x(i)).$$

Proof. Let x, y be elements of L. Because $A^1(\cdot, y)$ is stratifiable (proposition 3.3.1), the corollary to proposition 3.2.3 implies that $x = C_A^{\downarrow}(y) = lfp(A^1(\cdot, y))$ iff for each $i \in I$, $x(i) = lfp((A^1(\cdot, y))_i^{x|_{\prec i}})$. Because of proposition 3.3.1, this is in turn equivalent to for each $i \in I$, $x(i) = lfp((A_i^{(x,y)|_{\prec i}})^1(\cdot, y(i))) = C_{A_i^{(x,y)|_{\prec i}}}^{\downarrow}(y(i))$. The proof of the second equivalence is similar.

This proposition shows how, for each $x, y \in L$, $C_A^{\downarrow}(y)$ and $C_A^{\uparrow}(x)$ can be be constructed incrementally from the upper and lower stable operators corresponding to the components of A. This result also implies a similar property for the partial stable operator C_A of an approximation A.

Proposition 3.3.3. *Let L be a product lattice and let $A : L^2 \to L^2$ be a stratifiable approximation. Then the operator C_A is also stratifiable. Moreover, for each $x, x', y, y' \in L$, the following equivalence holds:*

$$(x', y') = C_A(x, y) \qquad iff \qquad \forall i \in I : \begin{cases} x' = C_{A_i^{(x',y)|_{\prec i}}}^{\downarrow}(y(i)), \\ y' = C_{A_i^{(x,y')|_{\prec i}}}^{\uparrow}(x(i)). \end{cases}$$

Proof. Follows immediately from proposition 3.3.2.

It should be noted that the components $(C_A)_i^{(u,v)}$ of the partial stable operator of a stratifiable approximation A are not equal to the partial stable operators $C_{A_i^{(u,v)}}$ of the components of A. Indeed, $(C_A)_i^{(u,v)} = ((C_A^{\downarrow})_i^v, (C_A^{\uparrow})_i^u))$, whereas $C_{A_i^{(u,v)}} = (C_{A_i^{(u,v)}}^{\downarrow}, C_{A_i^{(u,v)}}^{\uparrow})$. Clearly, these two pairs are, in general, not equal, as $(C_A^{\downarrow})_i^v$ ignores the argument u, which does appear in $C_{A_i^{(u,v)}}^{\downarrow}$. We can, however, characterize the fixpoints of C_A, i.e. the partial stable fixpoints of A, by means of the partial stable fixpoints of the components of A.

Theorem 3.3.1. *Let L be a product lattice and let $A : L^2 \to L^2$ be a stratifiable approximation. Then for each element (x, y) of L^2:*

$$(x, y) \text{ is a fixpoint of } \mathcal{C}_A \qquad iff \qquad \forall i \in I : (x, y)(i) \text{ is a fixpoint of } \mathcal{C}_{A_i^{(x,y)|_{\prec i}}}.$$

Proof. Let x, y be elements of L, such that $(x, y) = \mathcal{C}_A(x, y)$. By proposition 3.3.3, this is equivalent to $\forall i \in I$, $x = C^{\downarrow}_{A_i^{(x,y)|_{\prec i}}}(y(i))$ and $y = C^{\uparrow}_{A_i^{(x,y)|_{\prec i}}}(x(i))$.

By proposition 3.2.3, this theorem has the following corollary:

Corollary 1. *Let L be a product lattice and let $A : L^2 \to L^2$ be a stratifiable approximation. Then for each element (x, y) of L^2: $(x, y) = lfp(\mathcal{C}_A)$ iff $\forall i \in I$: $(x, y)(i) = lfp(\mathcal{C}_{A_i^{(x,y)|_{\prec i}}})$.*

Putting all of this together, the main results of this section can be summarized as follows. If A is a stratifiable approximation on a product lattice L, then a pair (x, y) is a fixpoint, Kripke-Kleene fixpoint, stable fixpoint or well-founded fixpoint of A iff for each $i \in I$, $(x(i), y(i))$ is a fixpoint, Kripke-Kleene fixpoint, stable fixpoint or well-founded fixpoint of the component $A_i^{(x,y)|_{\prec i}}$ of A. Moreover, if A is exact then an element $x \in L$ is a fixpoint of the unique operator O approximated by A iff for each $i \in I$, $(x(i), x(i))$ is a fixpoint of the component $A_i^{(x,x)|_{\prec i}}$ of A. These characterizations give us a way of incrementally constructing each of these fixpoints.

4   Application to Logic Programming

The general, algebraic framework of stratifiable operators developed in the previous section, allows us to easily and uniformly prove splitting theorems for all fixpoint semantics of non-monotonic reasoning formalisms. We will demonstrate this by applying the previous results to logic programming.

4.1   Syntax and Semantics

For simplicity, we will deal with propositional logic programs. Let Σ be an alphabet, i.e. a collection of symbols which are called *atoms*. A *literal* is either an atom p or the negation $\neg q$ of an atom q. A logic program is a set of *clauses* the form $h \leftarrow b_1, \ldots, b_n$. Here, h is an atom and all b_i are literals. For such a clause r, we denote h by $head(r)$ and the set $\{b_1, \ldots, b_n\}$ by $body(r)$.

Logic programs can be interpreted in the lattice $\langle 2^\Sigma, \subseteq \rangle$, i.e. the powerset of Σ. This set of *interpretations* of Σ is denoted by $\mathcal{I}_\Sigma$. Following the framework of approximation theory, we will, however, interpret programs in the bilattice $B_\Sigma = \mathcal{I}_\Sigma^2$. In keeping with the intuitions presented in section 2.2, for such a pair (X, Y), the interpretation X can be seen as representing an *under*estimate of the set of true atoms, while Y represents an *over*estimate. Or, to put it another way, X contains all atoms which are *certainly* true, while Y contains atoms which are *possibly* true. These intuitions lead naturally to the following definition of the truth value of a propositional formula.

Definition 4.1.1. *Let φ, ψ be propositional formula in an alphabet Σ, a an atom of Σ and let $(X, Y) \in B_\Sigma$. We define*

- $H_{(X,Y)}(a) = \mathbf{t}$ *iff $a \in X$;*
- $H_{(X,Y)}(\varphi \wedge \psi) = \mathbf{t}$ *iff $H_{(X,Y)}(\varphi) = \mathbf{t}$ and $H_{(X,Y)}(\psi) = \mathbf{t}$;*
- $H_{(X,Y)}(\varphi \vee \psi) = \mathbf{t}$ *iff $H_{(X,Y)}(\varphi) = \mathbf{t}$ or $H_{(X,Y)}(\psi) = \mathbf{t}$;*
- $H_{(X,Y)}(\neg\varphi) = \mathbf{t}$ *iff $H_{(Y,X)}(\varphi) = \mathbf{f}$;*

Note that to evaluate the negation of a formula $\neg\varphi$ in a pair (X, Y), we actually evaluate φ in (Y, X). Indeed, the negation of a formula will be certain if the formula itself is not possible and vice versa. Using this definition, we can now define the following operator on B_Σ.

Definition 4.1.2. *Let P be a logic program with an alphabet Σ. The operator $\mathcal{T}_P$ on B_Σ is defined as: $\mathcal{T}_P(X, Y) = (U_P(X, Y), U_P(Y, X))$, with $U_P(X, Y) = \{p \in \Sigma \mid \exists r \in P : head(r) = p, H_{(X,Y)}(body(r)) = \mathbf{t}\}$.*

When restricted to consistent pairs of interpretation, this operator $\mathcal{T}_P$ is the well known 3-valued Fitting operator [Fit85]. In [DMT00], $\mathcal{T}_P$ is shown to be a symmetric approximation. Furthermore, it can be used to define most of the "popular" semantics for logic programs: the operator which maps an interpretation X to $U_P(X, X)$ is the well known (two-valued) T_P-operator [Llo87]; the partial stable operator of $\mathcal{T}_P$ is the Gelfond-Lifschitz operator $\mathcal{GL}$ [VRS91]. Fixpoints of $\mathcal{T}_P$ are *supported* models of P, the least fixpoint of $\mathcal{T}_P$ is the Kripke-Kleene model of P, fixpoints of $\mathcal{GL}$ are (four-valued) stable models of P and its least fixpoint is the well-founded model of P.

4.2   Stratification

Our discussion of the stratification of logic programs will be based on the dependecies between atoms, which are expressed by a logic program. These induce the following partial order on the alphabet of the program.

Definition 4.2.1. *Let P be a logic program with alphabet Σ. The dependency order $\leq_{dep}$ on Σ is defined as: for all $p, q \in \Sigma$: $p \leq_{dep} q$ iff $\exists r \in P : q = head(r), p \in body(r)$.*

To illustrate this definition, consider the following small program:

$$E = \left\{ \begin{array}{l} p \leftarrow \neg q, \neg r. \\ q \leftarrow \neg p, \neg r. \\ s \leftarrow p, q. \end{array} \right\}$$

The dependency order of this program can be graphically represented as:

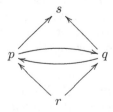

In other words, $r \leq_{dep} p, r \leq_{dep} q, p \leq_{dep} q, q \leq_{dep} p, s \leq_{dep} p$ and $s \leq_{dep} q$.

Based on this dependency order, the concept of a *splitting* of the alphabet of a logic program can be defined.

Definition 4.2.2. *Let P be a logic program with alphabet Σ. A splitting of P is a partition $(\Sigma_i)_{i \in I}$ of Σ, such that the well-founded order $\preceq$ on I agrees with the dependency order $\leq_{dep}$ of P, i.e. if $p \leq_{dep} q$, $p \in \Sigma_i$ and $q \in \Sigma_j$, then $i \preceq j$.*

For instance, the following partition is a splitting of the program E: $\Sigma_0 = \{r\}$, $\Sigma_1 = \{p, q\}$ and $\Sigma_2 = \{s\}$ (with the totally ordered set $\{0, 1, 2\}$ as index set).

If $(\Sigma_i)_{i \in I}$ is a partition of a logic program P with alphabet Σ, the product lattice $\otimes_{i \in I} 2^{\Sigma_i}$ is isomorphic to the powerset 2^Σ. We can therefore view the operator $\mathcal{T}_P$ of such a program as being an operator on the bilattice of this product lattice, instead of on the original lattice B_Σ. Moreover, if such a partition is a splitting of P, the $\mathcal{T}_P$-operator on this product lattice is stratifiable.

Theorem 4.2.1. *Let P be a logic program and let $(\Sigma_i)_{i \in I}$ be a splitting of this program. Then the operator $\mathcal{T}_P$ on the bilattice of the product lattice $\otimes_{i \in I} 2^{\Sigma_i}$ is stratifiable.*

Proof. Let $\Sigma_j \in S$ and $(X, Y), (X', Y') \in B_\Sigma$, s.t. $X|_{\preceq i} = X'|_{\preceq i}$ and $Y|_{\preceq i} = Y'|_{\preceq i}$. It suffices to show that for each clause with an atom from Σ_j in its head, $H_{(X,Y)}(body(c)) = H_{(X',Y')}(body(c))$. By definition 4.2.2, this is trivially so.

By theorem 3.3.1, this theorem implies that, for a stratifiable program P, it is possible to stratify the operators $\mathcal{T}_P, \mathcal{T}_P$ and $\mathcal{GL}$. In other words, it is possible to split logic programs w.r.t. supported model, Kripke-Kleene, stable model and well-founded semantics. Moreover, the supported, Kripke-Kleene, stable and well-founded models of P can be computed from, respectively, the supported, Kripke-Kleene, stable and well-founded models of the components of $\mathcal{T}_P$.

In order to be able to perform this construction in practice, however, we also need a more precise characterization of these components. We will now show how to construct new logic programs from the original program, such that these components correspond to an operator associated with these new programs. First, we will define the restriction of a program to a subset of its alphabet.

Definition 4.2.3. *Let P be a logic program with a splitting $(\Sigma_i)_{i \in I}$. For each $i \in I$, the program P_i consists of all clauses with an atom from Σ_i in their head.*

In the case of our example, the program E is partitioned in $\{E_0, E_1, E_2\}$ with $E_0 = \{\}$, $E_1 = \{p \leftarrow \neg q, \neg r.\ q \leftarrow \neg p, \neg r.\}$ and $E_2 = \{s \leftarrow p, q.\}$.

If P has a splitting $(\Sigma_i)_{i \in I}$, then clearly such a program P_i contains, by definition, only atoms from $\bigcup_{j \preceq i} \Sigma_j$. When given a pair (U, V) of interpretations of $\bigcup_{j \prec i} \Sigma_j$, we can therefore construct a program containing only atoms from Σ_i by replacing each other atom by its truth-value according to (U, V).

Definition 4.2.4. *Let P be a logic program with a splitting $(\Sigma_i)_{i \in I}$. For each $i \in I$ and $(U, V) \in B_\Sigma|_{\prec i}$, we define $P_i \langle (U, V) \rangle$ as the new logic program P', which results from replacing each literal l whose atom is in $\bigcup_{j \prec i} \Sigma_j$ by $H_{(U,V)}(\{l\})$.*

Of course, one can further simplify such a program by removing all clauses containing **f** and just omitting all atoms **t**. Programs constructed in this way are now precisely those which characterize the components of the operator $\mathcal{T}_P$.

Theorem 4.2.2. *Let P be a logic program with a splitting $(\Sigma_i)_{i \in I}$. For each $i \in I$, $(U, V) \in B_{\Sigma|_{\prec i}}$ and $(A, B) \in B_{\Sigma_i}$:*

$$(\mathcal{T}_P)_i^{(U,V)}(A, B) = (U_{P_i \langle\langle (U,V) \rangle\rangle}(A, B), U_{P_i \langle\langle (V,U) \rangle\rangle}(B, A)).$$

Proof. Let i, U, V, A and B be as above. Then because the order $\preceq$ on I agrees with the dependency order of P, $(\mathcal{T}_P)_i^{(U,V)}(A, B) = (A', B')$, with

$$A' = \{p \in \Sigma_i \mid \exists r \in P : head(r) = p, H_{(U \sqcup A, V \sqcup B)}(body(r)) = \mathbf{t}\}$$
$$B' = \{p \in \Sigma_i \mid \exists r \in P : head(r) = p, H_{(V \sqcup B, U \sqcup A)}(body(r)) = \mathbf{t}\}$$

We will show that $A' = \mathcal{T}_{P_i \langle\langle (U,V) \rangle\rangle}(A, B)$; the proof that $B' = \mathcal{T}_{P_i \langle\langle (V,U) \rangle\rangle}(B, A)$ is similar. Let r be a clause of P, such that $head(r) \in \Sigma_i$. Then $H_{(U \sqcup A, V \sqcup B)}(body(r)) = \mathbf{t}$ iff $H_{(U,V)}(l) = \mathbf{t}$ for each literal l with an atom from $\bigcup_{j \prec i} \Sigma_j$ and $H_{(A,B)}(l') = \mathbf{t}$ for each literal $'l$ with an atom from Σ_i. Because for each literal l with an atom from $\bigcup_{j \prec i} \Sigma_j$), $H_{(U,V)}(l) = \mathbf{t}$ precisely iff l was replaced by $\mathbf{t}$ in $P_i \langle\langle (U, V) \rangle\rangle$, this is in turn equivalent to $H_{(A,B)}(r\langle\langle (U, V) \rangle\rangle) = \mathbf{t}$ (by $r\langle\langle (U, V) \rangle\rangle$ we denote the clause which replaces r in $P_i \langle\langle (U, V) \rangle\rangle$).

It is worth noting that this theorem implies that a component $(\mathcal{T}_P)_i^{(U,V)}$ is, in contrast to the operator $\mathcal{T}_P$ itself, not necessarily exact.

With this final theorem, we can now incrementally compute the various fixpoints of the operator $\mathcal{T}_P$. We will illustrate this by computing the well-founded model of our example E. Recall that this program is partitioned into the programs $E_0 = \{\}$, $E_1 = \{p \leftarrow \neg q, \neg r.\ q \leftarrow \neg p, \neg r.\}$ and $E_2 = \{s \leftarrow p, q.\}$. The well-founded model of E_0 is $(\{\}, \{\})$. Replacing the atom r in E_1 by its truth-value according to this interpretation, yields the new program $E_1 \langle\langle (\{\}, \{\}) \rangle\rangle = \{p \leftarrow \neg q.\ q \leftarrow \neg p.\}$. The well-founded model of this program is $(\{\}, \{p, q\})$. Replacing the atoms p and q in E_2 by their truth-value according to the pair of interpretations $(\{\}, \{p, q\})$, gives the new program $E_2' = E_2 \langle\langle (\{\}, \{p, q\}) \rangle\rangle = \{\}$. Replacing these by their truth-value according to the pair of interpretations $(\{p, q\}, \{\})$, gives the new program $E_2'' = E_2 \langle\langle (\{p, q\}, \{\}) \rangle\rangle = \{s\}$. The well-founded fixpoint of $(U_{E_2'}, U_{E_2''})$ is $(\{\}, \{s\})$. Therefore, the well-founded model of the entire program E is $(\{\} \cup \{\} \cup \{\}, \{\} \cup \{p, q\} \cup \{s\}) = (\{\}, \{p, q, s\})$.

Of course, it also possible to apply these results to more complicated programs. Consider for instance the following program in the natural numbers:

$$Even = \left\{ \begin{array}{c} even(0). \\ odd(X + 1) \leftarrow even(X). \\ even(X + 1) \leftarrow odd(X). \end{array} \right\}$$

which can be seen as an abbreviation of the infitine propositional logic program: $\{even(0).\quad odd(1) \leftarrow even(1).\quad even(1) \leftarrow odd(1).\quad \cdots\}$. Clearly, the operator

$\mathcal{T}_{Even}$ is stratifiable w.r.t. to the partition $(\{even(n), odd(n)\})_{n \in \mathbb{N}}$ (using the standard order on the natural numbers) of the alphabet $\{even(n) \mid n \in \mathbb{N}\} \cup \{odd(n) \mid n \in \mathbb{N}\}$. The component $(\mathcal{T}_{Even})_0$ of this operator corresponds to the program $Even_0 = \{even(0).\}$, which has $\{even(0)\}$ as its only fixpoint. Let $n \in \mathbb{N}$ and $U_n = \{even(i) \mid i < n, i \text{ is even}\} \cup \{odd(i) \mid i < n, i \text{ is odd}\}$. Clearly, if n is even, the component $(\mathcal{T}_{Even})_n^{(U_n, U_n)}$ corresponds to the program $\{even(n).\}$, while if n is odd $(\mathcal{T}_{Even})_n^{(U_n, U_n)}$ corresponds to the program $\{odd(n).\}$. This proves that the supported, Kripke-Kleene, stable and well-founded models of $Even$ all contain precisely those atoms $even(n)$ for which n is an even natural number and those atoms $odd(n)$ for which n is an odd natural number.

4.3 Related Work

In [LT94], Lifschitz and Turner proved a splitting theorem for logic programs under stable model semantics. They, however, considered logic programs in an extended syntax, which allows disjunction in the head of clauses and two kinds of negation (negation-as-failure and classical negation). When considering only programs in the syntax described here, our results generalize their results to include supported model, Kripke-Kleene and well-founded semantics as well. While we have not done so here, the fact that the stable model semantics for such extended programs can also be characterized as a fixpoint semantics [LRS95], seems to suggest that our approach could be used to obtain similar results for this extended syntax as well. In future work, we plan to investigate this further.

5   Conclusion

Stratification is, both theoretically and practically, an important concept in knowledge representation. We have studied this issue at a general, algebraic level by investigating stratification of *operators* and *approximations* (section 3). This gave us a small but very useful set of theorems, which can be used to easily and uniformly prove splitting results for all fixpoint semantics of logic programs, auto-epistemic logic theories and default logic theories, thus generalizing existing results. In section 4, we demonstrated this for the case of logic programming.

As such, the importance of the work presented here is threefold. Firstly, there are the concrete, applied results of section 4 themselves. Secondly, and more importantly, there is the general, algebraic framework for the study of stratification, which can be applied to every formalism with a fixpoint semantics. Finally, on a more abstract level, our work offers greater insight into the principles underlying various existing splitting results, as we are able to "look beyond" purely syntactical properties of a certain formalism.

References

[BS91]   C. Baral and V. Subrahmanian. Duality between alternative semantics of logic programs and nonmonotonic formalisms. In A. Nerode, W. Marek, and V. Subrahmanian, editors, *Intl. Workshop on Logic Programming and Nonmonotonic Reasoning*, pages 69–86, Washington DC., 1991. MIT Press.

[DMT00]   M. Denecker, V. Marek, and M. Truszczynski. Approximating operators, stable operators, well-founded fixpoints and applications in non-monotonic reasoning. In *Logic-based Artificial Intelligence*, The Kluwer International Series in Engineering and Computer Science, pages 127–144. 2000.

[DMT03]   M. Denecker, V. Marek, and M. Truszczynski. Uniform semantic treatment of default and autoepistemic logics. *Artificial Intelligence*, 143(1):79–122, 2003.

[EL04]   S.T. Erdoğan and V. Lifschitz. Definitions in Answer Set Programming. In *Proc. Logic Programming and Non Monotonic Reasoning, LPNMR'04*, volume 2923 of *LNAI*, pages 185–197. Springer-Verlag, 2004.

[Fit85]   M. Fitting. A Kripke-Kleene Semantics for Logic Programs. *Journal of Logic Programming*, 2(4):295–312, 1985.

[Fit89]   M. Fitting. Bilattices and the semantics of logic programming. *Journal of Logic Programming*, 1989.

[Gel87]   M. Gelfond. On Stratified Autoepistemic Theories. In *Proc. of AAAI87*, pages 207–211. Morgan Kaufman, 1987.

[GP92]   M. Gelfond and H. Przymusinska. On consistency and completeness of autoepistemic theories. *Fundamenta Informaticae*, 16(1):59–92, 1992.

[Llo87]   J.W. Lloyd. *Foundations of Logic Programming*. Springer-Verlag, 1987.

[LRS95]   N. Leone, P. Rullo, and F. Scarcello. Declarative and fixpoints characterizations of disjunctive stable models. In *Proc. of International Logic Programming Ssymposium-ILPS'95*, pages 399–413. MIT Press, 1995.

[LT94]   V. Lifschitz and H. Turner. Splitting a logic program. In *International Conference on Logic Programming*, pages 23–37, 1994.

[NR94]   I. Niemelä and J. Rintanen. On the impact of stratification on the complexity of nonmonotonic reasoning. *Journal of Applied Non-Classical Logics*, 4(2), 1994.

[Tar55]   A. Tarski. Lattice-theoretic fixpoint theorem and its applications. *Pacific Journal of Mathematics*, 5:285–309, 1955.

[Tur96]   H. Turner. Splitting a default theory. In *Proc. Thirteenth National Conference on Artificial Intelligence and the Eighth Innovative Applications of Artificial Intelligence Conference*, pages 645–651. AAAI Press, 1996.

[VRS91]   A. Van Gelder, K.A. Ross, and J.S. Schlipf. The Well-Founded Semantics for General Logic Programs. *Journal of the ACM*, 38(3):620–650, 1991.

Simplifying Logic Programs
Under Answer Set Semantics

David Pearce*

Department of Informatics, Statistics and Telematics
Universidad Rey Juan Carlos, Madrid, Spain
d.pearce@escet.urjc.es

Abstract. Now that answer set programming has emerged as a practical tool
for knowledge representation and declarative problem solving there has recently
been a revival of interest in transformation rules that allow for programs to be simplified and perhaps even reduced to programs of 'lower' complexity. Although it
has been known for some that there is a maximal monotonic logic, denoted by
N_5, with the property that its valid (equivalence preserving) inference rules provide valid transformations of programs under answer set semantics, with few exceptions this fact has not really been exploited in the literature. The paper studies
some new transformation rules using N_5-inference to simplify extended disjunctive logic programs known to be strongly equivalent to programs with nested
expressions.

1 Introduction

With the emergence of answer set solvers such as DLV [20], GnT [18], and smodels [33], answer set programming (ASP) now provides a practical and viable environment for tasks of knowledge representation and declarative problem solving. Applications of this paradigm include planning and diagnosis, as exemplified in a prototype decision support system for the space shuttle [2], the management of heterogenous data in
information systems, as performed in the INFOMIX project[1], the representation of on-
tologies in the semantic web allowing for default knowledge and inference, as discussed
in [5], as well as compact and fully declarative representations of hard combinatorial
problems such as n-Queens, Hamiltonian paths, and so on[2].

Following the rise of ASP as a practical tool, there has recently been a revival of interest in transformation rules that allow for a program to be simplified and perhaps even
reduced to a program of 'lower' complexity, eg reducing a disjunctive program to a normal program. Recent studies have included [4, 25, 31, 11]. Although it has been known
since [27] that there is a maximal monotonic logic, denoted by N_5, with the property
that all of its valid (equivalence preserving) inference rules provide valid transformations of programs under answer set semantics, with few exceptions this fact has not

---

* Partially supported by CICyT project TIC-2003-9001-C02, URJC project PPR-2003-39 and
WASP (IST-2001-37004).
[1] http://sv.mat.unical.it/infomix/
[2] For these and other examples as well as a general introduction to ASP, see [3].

B. Demoen and V. Lifschitz (Eds.): ICLP 2004, LNCS 3132, pp. 210–224, 2004.

really been exploited in the literature. In this paper we explore several ways in which inference in N_5 can be used for program simplification and other computational purposes. The main contributions of the paper, in order of presentation, are as follows. In §2 we give an informal account of how the logic N_5 can be employed as tool for program transformations in ASP. §3 provides the logical background and summarises the main known results showing how N_5 provides a suitable logical foundation for ASP. In §4 we illustrate how N_5 can be used to check that a given transformation rule preserves semantic equivalence of the programs concerned and we discuss new rules for program simplification based on deriving literals (and their negations) from the program in N_5. Continuing this theme, in §5 we show how other kinds of N_5-derivability may yield computationally useful metatheoretic properties. Some brief remarks on the complexity of these methods follows in §6 and in §7 we conclude with some remarks on related work and on future research topics.

2   Monotonic vs. Nonmonotonic Semantic Transformation Rules

Since 1995, (published as [27]), it has been known that the nonclassical logic of here-and-there with strong negation, N_5, provides a suitable logical foundation for the study of programs and theories under answer set semantics. One property of N_5 is basic here: answer sets of logic programs correspond to simple kinds of minimal N_5-models, called *equilibrium* models. It was at once apparent that this property could be useful in evaluating putative transformation rules for logic programs, in particular to check the property that a rule is valid under answer set semantics, ie preserves the answer sets of the program being transformed. In particular, any transformation of a program that proceeds according to a valid, given or derived, inference rule of N_5 will lead to a logically equivalent program having the same models and therefore the same (minimal) equilibrium models and the same answer sets. It is evident that there are two immediate applications for this property: it may be used to give rather simple proofs that certain known transformation rules are valid for answer set semantics, and it may prove useful in helping to find new rules that preserve the semantics. This was pointed out in [27] but not systematically exploited at the time. More recently this fact was used by others, notably Osorio et al [25], to verify the validity of certain rules such as TAUT, RED-, NONMIN and others considered by Brass and Dix [4]. It is interesting to note that while this shows that answer sets are preserved under any transformations valid in intuitionistic logic, besides some stronger ones, the same is not true of the weaker well-founded semantics, WFS. There are intuitionistically valid transformations that do not preserve the well-founded semantics of a program[3].

In fact it is easy to see that transformations of programs that are valid in N_5, ie that take a program Π to an N_5-equivalent program Π', have a still stronger property. Not only are the programs equivalent under answer set semantics, they must be equivalent for all possible extensions $\Pi \cup \Sigma$, $\Pi' \cup \Sigma$, for the obvious reason that these extended

---

[3] Consider the program Π consisting of two rules (written as logical formulas) $\neg a \rightarrow a$; $\neg a \rightarrow b$. Since in intuitionistic logic, $\neg a \rightarrow a \vdash \neg a \rightarrow b$, the second rule can be eliminated without loss. However the WFS of the resulting program $\neg a \rightarrow a$ is different from that of Π.

programs are also logically equivalent. This, stronger form of equivalence of programs has subsequently been studied under the rubric *strong equivalence* ([22]).

There has been considerable study in the literature of rules respecting ordinary equivalence under answer sets or WFS. Generally speaking, in the case of answer sets we can distinguish two kinds of rules: those that are valid monotonically (ie. correspond to valid inferences in $\mathbf{N_5}$), and those that we might term *nonmonotonic*. This terminology is justified by the following observation. Any transformation valid in $\mathbf{N_5}$ is certainly monotonic and preserves answer sets, while there are transformations valid in classical logic which do not; more precisely it can be shown that there is *no proper monotonic strengthening of* $\mathbf{N_5}$ *with the property that all of its valid rules will preserve answer sets*[4]. Therefore if a rule nonvalid in $\mathbf{N_5}$ has the property of preserving answer sets, this is not say because it is a valid rule of classical logic or some other stronger monotonic system, but rather that it goes beyond ordinary monotonic logic. An example is the rule RED+ (see [4]) which states that if an atom A does not appear in the head of any rule of Π, then any occurrence of $\neg A$ in Π can be deleted without affecting the answer sets of Π. This rule is clearly not monotonic and is neither classically sound nor sound in $\mathbf{N_5}$. It relies rather on the fact that answer sets correspond to certain minimal models and obey the supportedness principle.

A second basic property of the logic $\mathbf{N_5}$ was proven in [22]: two programs are strongly equivalent if and *only if* they are logically equivalent viewed as propositional theories in $\mathbf{N_5}$. This fact has an obvious but nonetheless interesting corollary: while transformation rules preserving ordinary equivalence may be monotonic or nonmonotonic, as just noted, rules preserving strong equivalence *must be monotonic*. The argument is immediate: any transformation that takes Π to a program Π' that is not $\mathbf{N_5}$-equivalent does not preserve strong equivalence[5].

3   Logical Background

We work in the nonclassical logic of here-and-there with strong negation $\mathbf{N_5}$ and its nonmonotonic extension, equilibrium logic [27], which generalises answer set semantics for logic programs to arbitrary propositional theories, see eg [22]. We give an overview of the logic here; for more details see [27, 22, 28] and the logic texts cited.

Formulas of $\mathbf{N_5}$ are built-up in the usual way using the logical constants: $\wedge$, $\vee$, $\rightarrow$, $\neg$, $\sim$, standing respectively for conjunction, disjunction, implication, weak (or intu-

---

[4] While there are infinitely many logics between intuitionistic and classical logic, there are none at all between here-and-there and classical. Adding strong negation does produce two nontrivial strengthenings of $\mathbf{N_5}$ but these are easily seen to be 'stronger' than answer set inference.

[5] Though answer set semantics was often criticised in the past for failing certain principles of nonmonotonic reasoning, such as cumulativity and relevance, this shows that answer set inference does have one very nice property from the logical point of view. Not only does it have a greatest deductive base logic ($\mathbf{N_5}$), but this logic exactly captures the equivalence classes of strongly equivalent programs. It is not known whether the same is true for well-founded semantics. Though we know by a result of Dietrich [8] that since WFS is cumulative it must have a greatest deductive base, it is not known what that base is and whether it captures strong equivalence for WFS in a similar way.

itionistic) negation and strong negation. The axioms and rules of inference for $\mathbf{N}_5$ are those of intuitionistic logic (see eg [6]) together with:

1. the axiom schema $(\neg\alpha \to \beta) \to (((\beta \to \alpha) \to \beta) \to \beta)$, which characterises the 3-valued here-and-there logic of Heyting [15], and Gödel [13] (hence it is sometimes known as Gödel's 3-valued logic).
2. the following axiom schemata involving strong negation taken from the calculus of Vorob'ev [36, 37] (where '$\alpha \leftrightarrow \beta$' abbreviates $(\alpha \to \beta) \wedge (\beta \to \alpha)$):

N1. $\sim (\alpha \to \beta) \leftrightarrow \alpha \wedge \sim\beta$ **N2.** $\sim(\alpha \wedge \beta) \leftrightarrow \sim\alpha \vee \sim \beta$

N3. $\sim(\alpha \vee \beta) \leftrightarrow \sim\alpha \wedge \sim\beta$ **N4.** $\sim \sim\alpha \leftrightarrow \alpha$

N5. $\sim\neg\alpha \leftrightarrow \alpha$ **N6.** (for atomic α) $\sim\alpha \to \neg\alpha$

The inference relation of $\mathbf{N}_5$ is denoted by $\vdash$. The model theory of $\mathbf{N}_5$ is based on the usual Kripke semantics for Nelson's constructive logic $\mathbf{N}$ (see eg. [14, 6]), but $\mathbf{N}_5$ is complete for Kripke frames $\mathcal{F} = \langle W, \leq \rangle$ (where as usual W is the set of point or worlds and $\leq$ is a partial-ordering on W) having exactly two worlds say h ('here') and t ('there') with $h \leq t$. As usual a *model* is a frame together with an assignment i that associates to each element of W a set of *literals*[6], such that if $w \leq w'$ then $i(w) \subseteq i(w')$. An assignment is then extended inductively to all formulas via the usual rules for conjunction, disjunction, implication and (weak) negation in intuitionistic logic, viz.

$$\varphi \wedge \psi \in i(w) \quad \text{iff} \qquad \varphi \in i(w) \quad \text{and} \quad \psi \in i(w)$$
$$\varphi \vee \psi \in i(w) \quad \text{iff} \qquad \varphi \in i(w) \quad \text{or} \quad \psi \in i(w)$$
$$\varphi \to \psi \in i(w) \quad \text{iff} \qquad \varphi \in i(w') \quad \text{implies} \quad \psi \in i(w'), \forall w' \geq w$$
$$\neg\varphi \in i(w) \quad \text{iff} \quad \varphi \notin i(w'), \forall w' \geq w$$

together with the following rules governing strongly negated formulas:

$$\sim (\varphi \wedge \psi) \in i(w) \quad \text{iff} \quad \sim\varphi \in i(w) \quad \text{or} \quad \sim\psi \in i(w)$$
$$\sim(\varphi \vee \psi) \in i(w) \quad \text{iff} \quad \sim \varphi \in i(w) \quad \text{and} \quad \sim\psi \in i(w)$$
$$\sim(\varphi \to \psi) \in i(w) \quad \text{iff} \quad \varphi \in i(w) \quad \text{and} \quad \sim\psi \in i(w)$$
$$\sim \neg\varphi \in i(w) \quad \text{iff} \quad \varphi \in i(w)$$
$$\sim\sim\varphi \in i(w) \quad \text{iff} \quad \varphi \in i(w)$$

It is convenient to represent an $\mathbf{N}_5$-model as an ordered pair $\langle H, T \rangle$ of sets of literals, where $H = i(h)$ and $T = i(t)$ under a suitable assignment i. By $h \leq t$, it follows that $H \subseteq T$. Again, by extending i inductively we know what it means for an arbitrary formula φ to be true in a model $\langle H, T \rangle$.

A formula φ is true in a here-and-there model $\mathcal{M} = \langle H, T \rangle$ in symbols $\mathcal{M} \models \varphi$, if it is true at each world in $\mathcal{M}$. A formula φ is said to be *valid* in $\mathbf{N}_5$, in symbols $\models \varphi$, if it is true in all here-and-there models. Logical consequence for $\mathbf{N}_5$ is understood as follows: φ is said to be an $\mathbf{N}_5$-consequence of a set Π of formulas, written $\Pi \models \varphi$, iff for all models $\mathcal{M}$ and any world $w \in \mathcal{M}$, $\mathcal{M}, w \models \Pi$ implies $\mathcal{M}, w \models \varphi$. Equivalently this can be expressed by saying that φ is true in all models of Π. By strong completeness, we have $\Pi \models \varphi \Leftrightarrow \Pi \vdash \varphi$, for all Π, φ. Further properties of $\mathbf{N}_5$ are studied in

---

[6] We use the term 'literal' to denote an atom, or atom prefixed by strong negation.

[19]. By adding to N_5 the axiom schema $\neg\neg\alpha \to \alpha$ we obtain a 3-valued logic, called *classical logic with strong negation*, denoted by N_3. This logic is complete for total models consisting of a single world. It was studied in the first-order case by Gurevich [14] and independently in the propositional case by Vakarelov [35] who showed that it is equivalent, via a suitable translation, to Lukasiewicz's 3-valued logic. Tableau calculi for both N_5 and N_3 can be found in [28]. For the logic of here-and-there, ie N_5 without strong negation, a tableau calculus is presented in [1].

Equilibrium models are special kinds of minimal N_5 Kripke models. We first define a partial ordering $\trianglelefteq$ on N_5 models.

Definition 1. *Given any two models* $\langle H, T \rangle$, $\langle H', T' \rangle$, *we set* $\langle H, T \rangle \trianglelefteq \langle H', T' \rangle$ *if* $T = T'$ *and* $H \subseteq H'$.

Definition 2. *Let* Π *be a set of* N_5 *formulas and* $\langle H, T \rangle$ *a model of* Π.

1. *$\langle H, T \rangle$ is said to be* total *if* $H = T$.
2. *$\langle H, T \rangle$ is said to be an* equilibrium *model of* Π *if it is minimal under* $\trianglelefteq$ *among models of* Π, *and it is total.*

In other words a model $\langle H, T \rangle$ of Π is in equilibrium if it is total and there is no model $\langle H', T \rangle$ of Π with $H' \subset H$. Equilibrium logic is the logic determined by the equilibrium models of a theory, ie a set of N_5 sentences. A formula φ is said to be an equilibrium consequence of a theory Π, in symbols $\Pi \hspace{0.5pt}\vdash\hspace{-6pt}\sim \varphi$, if φ is true in each equilibrium model of Π; if Π has no equilibrium models, we set $\hspace{0.5pt}\vdash\hspace{-6pt}\sim\, = \models$. Two theories Π and Π' are said to be *logically equivalent*, in symbols $\Pi \equiv \Pi'$, if they have the same (N_5) models; by completeness they are therefore inter-derivable. They are said to be simply *equivalent* if they have the same equilibrium models and *strongly equivalent*, in symbols $\Pi \equiv_s \Pi'$, if $\Pi \cup \Sigma$ and $\Pi' \cup \Sigma$ have the same equilibrium models, for any set of sentences Σ. If the latter equivalence holds where Σ is restricted to being a set of atoms, then Π and Π' are said to be *uniform equivalent* [10].

Equilibrium logic generalises answer set semantics in the following sense. For all the usual classes of logic programs, including normal, extended, disjunctive and nested programs, equilibrium models correspond to answer sets [27, 22]. The 'translation' from the syntax of programs to N_5 propositional formulas is the trivial one, eg. a ground rule of an disjunctive program of the form

$$K_1 \vee \ldots \vee K_k \leftarrow L_1, \ldots, L_m, not\, L_{m+1}, \ldots, not\, L_n,$$

where the L_i and K_j are literals, corresponds to the N_5 sentence

$$L_1 \wedge \ldots \wedge L_m \wedge \neg L_{m+1} \wedge \ldots \wedge \neg L_n \to K_1 \vee \ldots \vee K_k$$

Proposition 1 ([27, 22]). *For any logic program* Π, *an* N_5 *model* $\langle T, T \rangle$ *is an equilibrium model of* Π *if and only if* T *is an answer set of* Π.

In this paper we shall for the most part consider not arbitrary theories but an extension of the usual syntax of disjunctive programs. Specifically we allow, besides strong negation, also weak negation to occur in the heads of program rules. So program formulas, also called *rules*, are of the form

$$L_1 \ldots \wedge \ldots L_m \wedge \neg L_{m+1} \wedge \ldots \wedge \neg L_n \rightarrow K_1 \vee \ldots \vee K_k \vee \neg K_{k+1} \vee \ldots \neg K_l \quad (1)$$

We call such programs *extended disjunctive programs*. They were introduced and studied under answer set semantics in [21]. As shown by [23], every nested logic program is strongly equivalent to a program of this kind. When needed, we abbreviate rules of form (1) in the following way. The set of literals $L_1, \ldots, L_m$ comprising the positive body of r is denoted by $B^+(r)$ and the set of literals $L_{m+1}, \ldots, L_n$ comprising the negative body of r is denoted by $B^-(r)$. Likewise, we set $H^+(r) = K_1, \ldots, K_k$ and $H^-(r) = K_{k+1}, \ldots, K_l$, for the positive and negative heads, respectively. With a slight abuse of notation we can then re-write a rule r of form (1) as

$$B^+(r) \wedge \neg B^-(r) \rightarrow H^+(r) \vee \neg H^-(r) \quad (2)$$

As mentioned already, N_5 captures strong equivalence between theories, hence between logic programs under answer set semantics, as follows.

Proposition 2 ([22]). *Any two theories Π and Π' are strongly equivalent iff they are logically equivalent, ie. $\Pi \equiv_s \Pi'$ iff $\Pi \equiv \Pi'$.*

Other characterisations of strong equivalence can be found in [34, 16]; uniform equivalence is characterised in [10, 32]

We shall not formalise here the notion of transformation rule (see [4] for a more detailed account). For our purposes, any set of operations that can be applied systematically to a program or theory to yield another program or theory can be regarded as a transformation rule. In answer set programming one is mainly interested in rules that transform a program Π into a program Π' equivalent to Π in one of the above senses. Let us say that a transformation rule is N_5-*valid* if it takes a theory or program Π to a theory or program Π' that is logically equivalent to Π. An immediate corollary of Proposition 2 is that a transformation rule preserves strong equivalence if and only if it is N_5-valid. It is interesting to note that N_5 is a maximal logic with this property.

4   Program Simplification

Eiter *et al* [11] consider several syntactic and semantic transformation rules which may allow disjunctive logic programs to be simplified under strong or uniform equivalence. In other words, by applying such rules one transforms a program Π to a program Π' that is either uniformly or strongly equivalent to Π. As they observe, the rules TAUT, RED-, NONMIN, WGPPE, CONTRA and S-IMP preserve strong equivalence. They do not mention, however, that each of these rules is easily seen to be valid in the logic N_5, which thus guarantees preservation of strong equivalence. This is essentially the method by which [25] demonstrates the validity of TAUT, RED- and NONMIN in the case of programs without strong negation[7].

---

[7] In [25] the authors actually make use of a weaker intermediate logic, that of weak excluded middle, WEM. This is an inessential difference because, as [16] have shown, all logics between WEM and here-and-there characterise strong equivalence for programs up to the syntax of nested expressions.

To illustrate how the method works, let us consider the rule S-IMP, due to Wang and Zhou [38] and discussed in [11]. As in the case of NONMIN this is a kind of subsumption rule allowing one to eliminate a rule that is less specific than another rule belonging to the program. As [11] points out, if a rule r of Π stands in the S-IMP relation to a rule r' of Π, then $\Pi \equiv_s \Pi \backslash \{r'\}$. Viewed in more logical terms one is here applying the principle:

$$r \vdash r' \ \& \ r, r' \in \Pi \Rightarrow \Pi \equiv \Pi \backslash \{r'\}.$$

By definition, r stands in the S-IMP relation to r', in symbols $r > r'$, iff there exists a set $A \subseteq B^-(r')$ such that (i) $H(r) \subseteq H(r') \cup A$; (ii) $B^-(r) \subseteq B^-(r') \backslash A$; (iii) $B^+(r) \subseteq B^+(r')$.

Proposition 3 ([11]). *The rule S-IMP preserves strong equivalence.*

Proof. To verify validity we need only show that if $r > r'$, then $r \vdash r'$. By (i) we can write r in the form $r = B^+(r) \wedge \neg B^-(r) \rightarrow H_1(r) \vee H_2(r)$ where $H_1(r) \subseteq H(r')$ and $H_2(r) \cap H(r') = \emptyset$. It follows that $H_2(r) \subseteq A$. Then clearly $r \vdash B^+(r) \wedge \neg B^-(r) \wedge \neg H_2(r) \rightarrow H_1(r)$. Since $H_2(r) \subseteq A$, we have $r \vdash B^+(r) \wedge \neg B^-(r) \wedge \neg A \rightarrow H_1(r)$ and so by (ii) also $r \vdash B^+(r) \wedge \neg B^-(r') \rightarrow H_1(r)$. Applying (i) and (iii), strengthening the antecedent and weakening the consequent, we have $r \vdash B^+(r') \wedge \neg B^-(r') \rightarrow H(r')$, ie. $r \vdash r'$.

Eiter et al [11] also mention the following semantic rule SUPRA of supraclassicality, discussed by [4]:

$$\Pi \models_c A \Rightarrow \Pi \equiv_e \Pi \cup \{A\},$$

where $\models_c$ is classical consequence and A is an atom. It is easy to see that this rule is not generally valid where say $\equiv_e$ is equivalence under stable models or WFS. A simple counterexample is the program Π comprising the single rule $\neg a \rightarrow a$ which classically derives a. But the stable model and well-founded semantics of $\Pi \cup \{a\}$ are clearly different from those of Π [8]. Thus [11] make no further use of SUPRA; yet this deprives them of a powerful tool for simplifying programs. First note that SUPRA is valid for answer set semantics in the following restricted form:

$$\Pi \models_c \neg A \Rightarrow \Pi \equiv_s \Pi \cup \{\neg A\}.$$

Second, already [26] pointed out that SUPRA is perfectly valid if classical consequence is replaced by the weaker consequence relation of intuitionistic logic, or its strong negation extension, Nelson's constructive logic. By the later results of [27] it follows immediately that SUPRA is valid in the following stronger form:

$$\Pi \models \varphi \Rightarrow \Pi \equiv \Pi \cup \{\varphi\} \text{ hence also } \Pi \models \varphi \Rightarrow \Pi \equiv_s \Pi \cup \{\varphi\}.$$

Note too that $\models$ is a maximal consequence relation with this property. In this form SUPRA can be used as a basis to transform and simplify programs according to a

---

[8] For ordinary, but not strong, equivalence under stable model semantics SUPRA holds in the restricted case that Π has a stable model. But clearly it cannot be used to simplify a program if the existence of a stable model is not guaranteed.

straighforward set of derived rules. The key idea is that if $\Pi \models \varphi$ we transform Π to a simpler program Π' with the property

$$\Pi \equiv \Pi' \cup \{\varphi\}.$$

We consider two kinds of rules, which we denote by $\mathbf{DEC}^+$ and $\mathbf{DEC}^-$, according to whether the formula φ is a literal L or its negation $\neg L$. In each case we let L range over literals and we consider the transformation of Π to Π'. We denote the complement of a literal L by L^* (ie for an atom A, $A^* = \sim A$, $(\sim A)^* = A$). We assume that an extended disjunctive program Π is grounded and r ranges over rules in Π.
$\mathbf{DEC}^+$. Suppose that $\Pi \vdash L$. (a) Let

$$\Sigma = \{r : L^* \in B^+(r)\} \cup \{r : \neg L^* \in H(r)\} \cup \{r : \neg L \in B(r)\} \cup \{r : L \in H(r)\}.$$

Set $\Pi' = \Pi \backslash \Sigma \cup \{L\}$.
    (b) Π' can be further simplified by removing from it all other remaining occurrences of L in the bodies of its rules, all occurrences of $\neg L$ in heads as well as all occurrences of L^* and $\neg L^*$.
$\mathbf{DEC}^-$. Suppose $\Pi \vdash \neg L$ (but $\Pi \not\vdash \sim L$ - note that the case that Π derives $\neg L$ and the complement of L falls under case $\mathbf{DEC}^+$). (a) Let

$$\Sigma = \{r \in \Pi : L \in B^+(r)\} \cup \{r \in \Pi : \neg L \in H(r)\}.$$

Set $\Pi' = \Pi \backslash \Sigma \cup \{L \rightarrow \sim L\}$. Note that adding $L \rightarrow \sim L$ is the same as adding the integrity constraint $\leftarrow L$ or the formula $\neg L$, one can choose one or other according to preferred syntax.
    (b) Π' can be further simplified by deleting from it all remaining occurrences of $\neg L$ except for the newly added constraint and all positive occurrences of L (not in the scope of $\sim$).

Proposition 4. *Applications   of   each   of   the   transformations $\mathbf{DEC}^+(a),(b)$, $\mathbf{DEC}^-(a),(b)$ preserve strong equivalence. In particular we have $\Pi \equiv \Pi' \equiv_s \Pi$.*

Proof. Assume the pre-condition of $\mathbf{DEC}^+$. Suppose r is a rule such that $L^* \in B^+(r)$. Since for any C, we have $L \vdash \sim L \rightarrow C$, we must also have $L \vdash L^* \wedge \varphi \rightarrow C \vee \psi$ for arbitrary φ, ψ; so $L \vdash r$. Suppose on the other hand that $\neg L$ appears in the body of a rule r. Again by the $\mathbf{N}_5$ axioms, $L \vdash \neg L \rightarrow C$ for any C, so by strengthening the antecedent and weakening the consequent, clearly $L \vdash r$. Now, if r contains an occurrence of L in its head, then immediately $L \vdash r$. Similarly, since $L \vdash \neg L^*$, for any any rule r with an occurrence of $\neg L^*$ in its head, we also have $L \vdash r$. So in each of the four cases r can be eliminated and $\Pi \equiv \Pi'$.
    Now consider any rule of Π' that contains an occurrence of L in its body. The only possibility is that $L \in B^+(r)$. Then r is of the form $L \wedge \varphi \rightarrow \psi$ and it is clear that if r' is the result of deleting L from r, then $L \cup r \vdash r'$ and $r' \vdash r$. Likewise, if $L^* \in B^-(r)$ then r must be of the form $\neg \sim L \wedge \varphi \rightarrow \psi$, and the same argument applies. So any remaining occurrences of $\neg L^*$ can be eliminated. Now, suppose r contains $\neg L$ in its head, ie is of the form $\varphi \rightarrow \neg L \vee \psi$, and let r' be the corresponding rule $\varphi \rightarrow \psi$ where L is eliminated. Then clearly $r' \vdash r$ and $r \cup L \vdash r'$ by applying disjunctive syllogism.

Since $L^* \vdash \neg L$, the same argument applies to any remaining occurence of L^* which must be in the (positive) head of a rule r.

Assume that the condition of **DEC**$^-$ holds and let r be a rule such that $L \in B^+(r)$. For arbitrary C we have $\neg L \vdash \neg\neg L \rightarrow C$, hence $\neg L \vdash L \rightarrow C$, hence $\neg L \vdash L \wedge \varphi \rightarrow C \vee \psi$, for any φ, ψ. On the other hand, let r be such that $\neg L \in H(r)$. $\neg L \vdash r$ follows immediately. So by construction $\Pi' \equiv \Pi$. Clearly the only possible remaining occurrences of $\neg L$ are in the bodies of rules r, ie where r is of the form $\neg L \wedge \varphi \rightarrow \psi$. Let $r' = \varphi \rightarrow \psi$. Then clearly $r' \vdash r$ and $r \cup \neg L \vdash r'$. Now consider any occurrence of L in a rule r that is not in the scope of $\sim$. Then clearly $L \in H(r)$ and r has the form $\varphi \rightarrow L \vee \psi$. Deleting L to form the rule $r' = \varphi \rightarrow \psi$, we see that $r' \vdash r$ and $r \cup \neg L \vdash r'$. $\square$

Rules **DEC**$^+$(a) and **DEC**$^-$(a) correspond to what in [11] is called removing redundant rules (once simple additions have been made to the program), while rules **DEC**$^+$(b) and **DEC**$^-$(b) correspond to rule simplification or condensation, where literals are removed from a given rule. Notice that the condition for applying **DEC**$^-$, that a literal L is decided negatively, ie. $\Pi \vdash \neg L$, holds if and only if $\neg L$ is classically derivable from Π, or more correctly if $\Pi \models_{\mathbf{N}_3} \neg L$.

The following example shows how the above rules may be applied in practice. Consider the program Π consisting of the following numbered rules:

r1.	$c \vee \neg d$	**r2.**	$\sim a$
r3.	$b \rightarrow a$	**r4.**	$e \wedge \neg b \rightarrow d \vee \neg c$
r5.	$\neg a \rightarrow e$	**r6.**	$c \wedge d \rightarrow a$
r7.	$a \wedge f \rightarrow g$	**r8.**	$\neg c \wedge \neg f \rightarrow g \vee a$
r9.	$\neg d \wedge \neg g \rightarrow f \vee \neg e$	**r10.**	$h \rightarrow \neg d$
r11.	$h \wedge c \rightarrow j.$		

It is natural to start by applying transformation rule **DEC**$^+$(a) to any literal that holds as a fact in the program. In this case the literal $\sim a$. This produces the following simplifications. Rule **r5** becomes just e. **r6** becomes

$$c \wedge d \rightarrow \bot.$$

r7 is deleted, and **r8** becomes

$$\neg c \wedge \neg f \rightarrow g.$$

Next we apply the transformation using the fact that e is derivable. Rule **r4** now simplifies to

$$\neg b \rightarrow d \vee \neg c$$

and **r9** simplifies to $\neg d \wedge \neg g \rightarrow f$. Since no further literals have emerged as facts we may now check whether some weakly negated literal is derivable. It is easily seen that rules **r2**, **r3** yield that $\neg b$ is derivable. This further simplifies **r4** to $d \vee \neg c$. So at this stage Π' looks as follows.

r1.	$c \vee \neg d$	**r2.**	$\sim a$
r3.	$b \rightarrow \sim b$	**r4.**	$d \vee \neg c$
r5.	e	**r6.**	$c \wedge d \rightarrow \bot$
r8.	$\neg c \wedge \neg f \rightarrow g$	**r9.**	$\neg d \wedge \neg g \rightarrow f$
r10.	$h \rightarrow \neg d$	**r11.**	$h \wedge c \rightarrow j$

In this program, **r1,r4,r6** resolve to $\neg c, \neg d$. So applying **DEC⁻** to these formulas, the program now becomes

$$\sim a \qquad\qquad e$$
$$b \to \sim b \qquad c \to \sim c$$
$$d \to \sim d \qquad \neg f \to g$$
$$\neg g \to f$$

whose answer sets are readily seen to be $\{\sim a, e, f\}$ and $\{\sim a, e, g\}$.

5 Decidable, Stable and Safe Literals

In this section we explore some further uses for $\mathbf{N_5}$-derivability. For any program Π a literal L is said to be *decidable* if either of the pre-conditions of **DEC⁺** or **DEC⁻** obtain, in other words if either $\Pi \vdash L$ or $\Pi \vdash \neg L$, otherwise L is said to be *undecidable*. Let $Und(\Pi)$ be the set of undecidable literals L in the language of Π and let $Neg(\Pi)$ be the set of literals L such that $\neg L$ appears in some rule in Π other than the degenerate rule $\neg L$. Then we have shown in particular the following:

Corollary 1 ([27]). [9] *Any program Π is strongly equivalent to a program Π' such that $Neg(\Pi') \subseteq Und(\Pi')$; in other words a program in which all decidable literals in $Neg(\Pi)$ are eliminated.*

Proof. Apply rules **DEC⁺** and **DEC⁻** to all decidable literals to form a strongly equivalent program Π'. Let L be any decidable literal such that $\neg L$ appears in some rule r in Π. Rule **DEC⁺**(a) deletes r if $\neg L \in B(r)$ and **DEC⁺**(b) deletes an occurrence of $\neg L$ if $\neg L \in H(r)$. On the other hand, rule **DEC⁻**(a) deletes a rule r such that $\neg L \in H(r)$ and **DEC⁻**(b) deletes any remaining occurrence of $\neg L$. Hence all decidable occurrences of L that appear in the scope of $\neg$ are eliminated. $\square$

We have seen that L might be decidable (negatively) without $\sim L$ being decidable. This is precisely case **DEC⁻**. In this case although we eliminate occurrences of $\neg L$ and positive occurrences of L, the method does not license us to eliminate any remaining occurrences of L in the scope of strong negation, nor equivalently occurrences of L^* in the case that L is already a negative literal.

The set $Neg(\Pi)$ of the weakly negated literals of a program clearly plays a fundamental role in answer set semantics. The above corollary ensures that by monotonic means we can essentially eliminate all occurrences of negation except those that are in a sense genuinely 'nonmonotonic'. In fact, in the limit where all literals in $Neg(\Pi)$ are decidable, Π behaves purely monotonically, as the following shows:

Proposition 5. *Suppose that each literal $L \in Neg(\Pi)$ is decidable. Then for all φ, $\Pi \vdash \varphi \Leftrightarrow \Pi \models \varphi$.*

A different but related notion is that of *stability*, a concept due to van Dantzig [7], see also Dummett [9]. Originally introduced in the context of intuitionistic mathematics, it is applicable to any superintuitionistic logic (we state it for $\mathbf{N_5}$):

---

[9] In [27] this result is stated without proof for the case of ordinary disjunctive programs and ordinary equivalence.

Definition 3. *A formula φ is said to be* stable *in a theory Π if $\Pi \vdash \neg\neg\varphi \to \varphi$.*

Obviously a decidable literal is stable, but the converse need not hold. While the decidable literals in a program are relevant for determining the composition of its answer sets, the stable literals are relevant for guaranteeing the existence of answer sets. Again what is important here is not the collection of all literals of the program but those that are prefixed by weak negation.

Proposition 6. *A consistent program Π has an answer set if each literal in $Neg(\Pi)$ is stable in Π.*

Proof. Assume that each $L \in Neg(\Pi)$ is stable. We will show that Π has an equilibrium model. Suppose not. Then for any t-minimal total model $\langle T, T \rangle$ of Π, there is an $H \subset T$ such that $\langle H, T \rangle \models \Pi$. So for each rule $r \in \Pi$ of form (1), we have $\langle H, T \rangle \models r$. In particular by the truth conditions for r at world h, this means

$$B^+(r) \subseteq H \ \& \ B^-(r) \cap T = \emptyset \Rightarrow H^+(r) \cap H \neq \emptyset \ or \ H^-(r) \not\subseteq T$$

By assumption each weakly negated literal L in r is stable, so $\langle H, T \rangle \models \neg\neg L \to L$. Therefore $L \in H \Leftrightarrow L \in T$ for each $L \in Neg(\Pi)$. So the above truth condition can be re-written as

$$B^+(r) \subseteq H \ \& \ B^-(r) \cap H = \emptyset \Rightarrow H^+(r) \cap H \neq \emptyset \ or \ H^-(r) \not\subseteq H$$

But this implies that $\langle H, H \rangle \models r$, which is impossible by the minimality of $\langle T, T \rangle$. This contradicts the initial assumption. □

It is easy to see that the condition of stability is quite different from purely syntactic conditions such as signings, stratifications etc. The reader may readily construct simple examples that satisfy the condition of Proposition 6 but which do not possess signings or stratifications. Proposition 6 provides an unexpected link between two historically distinct and apparently quite independent concepts of stability. Not surprisingly, we cannot strengthen Proposition 6 so as to provide also a necessary condition for the existence of an answer set. Any attempt is bound to fail on purely complexity-theoretic grounds. Deciding whether a literal is stable is a co-NP complete problem, while deciding whether a nested or disjunctive logic program has an answer set is Σ_2^p-complete, [12, 29, 30].

Any literal L that is decidable positively in a program Π, ie $\Pi \vdash L$, not only belongs to every answer set of Π but enjoys the stronger property of belonging to every answer set of any extension of Π (providing it has an answer set). We may call such a literal *safe* for Π, since it cannot be defeated by extending Π in any consistent way. Conversely we may call a literal *defeasible* if in some extension of Π it is no longer nonmonotonically derivable. The following definition makes this precise.

Definition 4. *Let φ be a formula such that $\Pi \hspace{0.5mm}\vdash\hspace{-2.2mm}\sim\hspace{0.5mm} \varphi$. φ is said to be* safe *for Π if for any Σ, $\Pi \cup \Sigma \hspace{0.5mm}\vdash\hspace{-2.2mm}\sim\hspace{0.5mm} \varphi$, whenever $\Pi \cup \Sigma$ has an equilibrium model or answer set; otherwise φ is said to be* defeasible *in Π.*

Now, in order to be safe a literal L need not be monotonically derivable from Π in $\mathbf{N_5}$. In fact it is easy to see that it suffices that $\Pi \vdash \neg\neg L$, since then $\neg\neg L$ must be derivable in every extension of Π and so L must be true in any answer sets possessed by such an extension. So L is safe in Π if $\Pi \vdash \neg\neg L$ (or equivalently $\Pi \vdash_{N_3} L$). Further reflection shows that this condition is also necessary, as the following makes clear (we state it for arbitrary theories in equilibrium logic):

Proposition 7. *Let Π be any theory possessing an equilibrium model. A literal L is safe for Π iff $\Pi \vdash \neg\neg L$.*

Proof. It remains to check necessity. Thus, suppose that $\Pi \not\vdash \neg\neg L$. We need to show that there is an extension Σ of Π such that $\Sigma \not\vdash L$. By the assumption $\Pi \cup \{\neg\neg\neg L\}$ ($\equiv \Pi \cup \{\neg L\}$) is consistent so it has an N_5-model say $\langle H, T \rangle$ in which L is false, ie $L \notin T$. Clearly also $\langle T, T \rangle \models \Pi$ and is an equilibrium model of $\Pi \cup \{T\}$. Hence there is an extension $\Pi \cup \{T\}$ of Π such that $\Pi \cup \{T\} \not\vdash L$. $\square$

To illustrate the above concepts, consider the program Π comprising the following rules:

$$\sim a; \neg b \rightarrow a; \neg c \rightarrow b; \neg d \rightarrow e; \neg q \rightarrow p; q \rightarrow \neg p$$

whose single answer set is $\{\sim a, b, e, p\}$. Evidently $\sim a$ is decidable (hence stable and safe). It is easy to check that p is stable but is undecidable and defeasible, b is safe but unstable, while e is defeasible and unstable.

6   Some Complexity and Implementation Issues

Complexity results for reasoning in ASP are well-discussed in the literature. For disjunctive logic programs (with strong negation) deciding whether a program has an answer set is, as mentioned above, Σ_2^p-complete, [12]. Deciding for some φ whether $\Pi \vdash \varphi$ is Π_2^p-complete. The corresponding complexity classes for programs with nested expressions [23] and for propositional theories in equilibrium logic are the same, [29, 30]. So complexity does not alter when the syntax is extended in this way. We already observed that each nested logic program is strongly equivalent to an extended disjunctive program, as shown in [23]. The transformation that performs this reduction is not generally polynomial, however [31]. In [31] a polynomial reduction of this kind is presented, where however new atoms are added to the language. This method has been implemented in a compiler, nlp, publicly available as a front-end to the disjunctive logic programming system DLV[10]. In [17] it was shown how extended disjunctive programs can be polynomially reduced to ordinary disjunctive programs, again using a similar extension of the language with new atoms.

Deciding whether a formula φ is an N_5-consequence of a theory Π is of lower complexity: this problem is coNP-complete [29, 30], see also [24]. Therefore the preconditions for applying the rules $\mathbf{DEC^+}$ and $\mathbf{DEC^-}$ are of this complexity, as are the problems of checking whether a literal is stable or safe. Clearly, once the pre-condition of a rule has been verified for some literal, the algorithm executing the rule is linear for that literal, hence quadratic if repeated for all literals. As noted, a tableaux system for checking N_5-consequence was presented in [29]. Since this system can also be used to the verify strong equivalence of programs, a workable implementation is desirable. Currently a prototype implementation is under construction at the University of Málaga.

---

[10] See http://www.cs.uni-potsdam.de/torsten/nlp

7 Related Work and Conclusions

A standard reference for the study of transformation rules in logic programs with default negation and disjunction is the work of Brass and Dix [4] who consider the behaviour of a number of transformation rules with respect to the main types of logic programming semantics. Brass and Dix are concerned mainly with simplifying rules preserving (ordinary) equivalence of programs; in some cases the rules are strong enough actually to compute the semantics of a program. In [27] it was observed for the first time that a nonclassical logic, that of here-and-there with strong negation, $\mathbf{N_5}$, could be useful to discover or check the validity of transformation rules preserving equivalence under answer set semantics; the present paper pursues this idea further. We already noted that some simplification rules for ASP were discussed by [25] making use of the weaker superintutionistic logic of *weak excluded middle*. [25] also consider extended disjunctive programs, but without the presence of strong negation. In [11] Eiter *et al* discuss simplifying rules preserving strong equivalence as well as some rules preserving uniform equivalence (in special cases). However, while they employ a chacterisation of strong equivalence essentially equivalent to Proposition 2 above, they make no further use of $\mathbf{N_5}$-inference as a means to test the validity of existing rules and search for new ones. The logic $\mathbf{N_5}$ without strong negation (ie the logic of here-and-there) *is* used in [31] to verify strong equivalence preserving rules. However the main aim there is to show how arbitrary nested programs can be reduced to disjunctive ones.

In this paper, we have considered several new ways in which inference in the nonclassical logic $\mathbf{N_5}$ of here-and-there with strong negation can be useful for program simplification under answer set semantics. First, for any kind of program it provides a simple check to verify whether a putative transformation rule preserves strong equivalence in answer set semantics or equilibrium logic, as illustrated here for the rule S-IMP. Secondly, we discussed two new transformation rules $\mathbf{DEC^+}$ and $\mathbf{DEC^-}$ based on $\mathbf{N_5}$ inference that can be used to simplify extended disjunctive programs. One feature, in particular, is that they eliminate all decidable occurrences of literals in the scope of weak negation (negation-as-failure). Third, we showed how varying the kinds of formulas to be tested for $\mathbf{N_5}$-derivability from a program can provide further information that is useful from a computational point of view: for example we may carry out a partial check for the existence of an answer set as well as distinguish between the defeasible and non-defeasible literals in a program.

Several lines of work lay open for future investigation. First, it seems that further study of inference in $\mathbf{N_5}$ is likely to result in discovering new ways of simplifying programs in ASP. Secondly, since uniform equivalence is also characterised by a simple structural condition on $\mathbf{N_5}$-models ([10, 32]), we may hope to use this to extend the work of [11] on transformation rules preserving uniform equivalence. Thirdly, once an efficient implementation of an $\mathbf{N_5}$ theorem prover is available, we would like to experiment with adding this, extended with an implementation of the $\mathbf{DEC^+}$ and $\mathbf{DEC^-}$ rules, as a pre-processor to systems such as DLV; specifically as a module fitting between the program grounding and the model generation processes. Fourthly, and more ambitiously, it would be desirable to have a full first-order version of equilibrium logic, based on a suitable first-order version of the logic $\mathbf{N_5}$ and which is sound and complete with respect to current ASP solvers. In this case one could search for simplifying transformation rules that apply *prior to* grounding and perhaps thereby achieve more extensive efficiency gains.

References

1. A. Avellone, M. Ferrari and P. Miglioli. Duplication-Free Tableau Calculi and Related Cut-Free Sequent Calculi for the Interpolable Propositional Intermediate Logics. *Logic Journal of the IGPL* 7(4): 447-480 (1999).
2. M. Balduccini, M. Gelfond, R. Watson and M. Noguiera. The USA-Advisor: A case study in answer set planning. In *Logic Programming and Nonmonotonic Reasoning*, LPNMR 2001, Springer LNAI 2173, 2001.
3. C. Baral *Knowlewdge Representation, Reasoning and Declarative Problem Solving* Cambridge University Press, 2003.
4. S. Brass and J. Dix. Semantics of (Disjunctive) Logic Programs Based on Partial Evaluation. *Journal of Logic Programming*, 40 (1): 1-46, 1999.
5. F. Calimeri, S. Galizia, M. Ruffolo, P. Rullo Enhancing Disjunctive Logic Programming for Ontology Specification. Proceedings AGP 2003
6. D. van Dalen. Intuitionistic logic. In *Handbook of Philosophical Logic, Volume III: Alternatives in Classical Logic*, Dordrecht, 1986. D. Reidel Publishing Co.
7. D. van Dantzig. On the Principles of Intuitionistic and Affirmative Mathematics. Indagationes Mathematicae 9, 1947: 429-440; 506-517.
8. J. Dietrich *Inferenzframes*. Doctoral Dissertation, University of Leipzig, 1995.
9. M. Dummett *Elements of Intuitionism*. Clarendon Press, Oxford, 1977.
10. T. Eiter and M. Fink. Uniform equivalence of logic programs under the stable model semantics. In *Int. Conf. in Logic Programming, ICLP'03*, Mumbay, India. Springer, 2003.
11. T. Eiter, M. Fink, H. Tompits and S. Woltran. Simplifying Logic Programs under Uniform and Strong Equivalence V Lifschitz & I Niemela (eds.), *Proceedings LPNMR 2004*, Springer, LNAI 2923, 2004.
12. T. Eiter and G. Gottlob. On the Computational Cost of Disjunctive Logic Programming: Propositional Case. *Annals of Mathematics and Artificial Intelligence*, 15 (3-4), 1995, 289-323.
13. K. Gödel. Zum intuitionistischen aussagenkalkül. *Anzeiger der Akademie der Wissenschaften Wien, mathematisch, naturwissenschaftliche Klasse*, 69:65–66, 1932.
14. Y. Gurevich. Intuitionistic logic with strong negation. *Studia Logica*, 36(1–2):49–59, 1977.
15. A. Heyting. Die formalen regeln der intuitionistischen logik. *Sitzungsberichte der Preussischen Akademie der Wissenschaften, Physikalisch-mathematische Klasse*, pages 42–56, 1930.
16. D. De Jongh and L. Hendriks. Characterization of strongly equivalent logic programs in intermediate logics. *Theory and Practice of Logic Programming*, 3(3):259–270, 2003.
17. T. Janhunen. On the Effect of Default Negation on the Expressiveness of Disjunctive Rules. In T. Eiter et al (eds) *Proceedings LPNMR 2001*, Springer LNCS 2173, 2001: 93-106.
18. T. Janhumen, I. Niemelä, D. Seipel, P. Simons, and J.-H. You. Unfolding partiality and disjunctions in stable model semantics. CoRR: cs.AI/0303009, March, 2003.
19. M. Kracht. On extensions of intermediate logics by strong negation. *Journal of Philosophical Logic*, 27(1):49–73, 1998.
20. N. Leone, G. Pfeifer, W. Faber, T. Eiter, G, Gottlob, S. Perri and F. Scarcello. The DLV System for Knowledge Representation and Reasoning. CoRR: cs.AI/0211004, September, 2003.
21. V. Lifschitz. Foundations of Logic Programming. in G. Brewka (ed) *Principles of Knowledge Representation*, CSLI Publications, 1996, 69–128.

22. V. Lifschitz, D. Pearce, and A. Valverde. Strongly equivalent logic programs. *ACM Transactions on Computational Logic*, 2(4):526–541, 2001.
23. V. Lifschitz, L. Tang and H. Turner. Nested Expressions in Logic Programs. *Annals of Mathematics and Artificial Intelligence*, 25(3-4): 369-389, 1999.
24. D. Mundici. Satisfiability in Many-Valued Sentential Logic is NP-complete. *Theoretical Computer Science*, 52(1-2): 145-153, 1987.
25. M. Osorio, J. Navarro and J. Arrazola. Equivalence in Answer Set Programming. In *Proc. LOPSTR 2001*, LNCS 2372, Springer, 2001, 57-75.
26. D. Pearce. Nonmonotonicity and Answer Set Inference. In *Proc. LPNMR 1995*, LNAI 928, pages 372–387, Springer, 1995.
27. D. Pearce. A new logical characterization of stable models and answer sets. In *Non-Monotonic Extensions of Logic Programming, NMELP 96*, LNCS 1216, pages 57–70. Springer, 1997.
28. D. Pearce, I.P. de Guzmán, and A. Valverde. A tableau calculus for equilibrium entailment. In *Automated Reasoning with Analytic Tableaux and Related Methods, TABLEAUX 2000*, LNAI 1847, pages 352–367. Springer, 2000.
29. D. Pearce, I.P. de Guzmán, and A. Valverde. Computing Equilibrium Models Using Signed Formulas. In John W. Lloyd et al (eds) *Computational Logic - CL 2000, First International Conference. Proceedings*, LNAI 1861, pages 688-702, Springer, 2000.
30. D. Pearce, H. Tompits and S. Woltran. Encodings for Equilibrium Logic and Logic Programs with Nested Expressions. In *Proceedings EPIA '01*, LNAI , pages 306–320. Springer, 2001.
31. D. Pearce, V. Sarsakov, T. Schaub, H. Tompits and S. Woltran. A Polynomial Translation of Logic Programs with Nested Expressions into Disjunctive Logic Programs: Preliminary Report. In P. J. Stuckey (Ed.): *Logic Programming, 18th International Conference, ICLP 2002*, Lecture Notes in Computer Science 2401, Springer 200, pages 405-420.
32. D. Pearce and A. Valverde. Uniform Equivalence for Equilibrium Logic and Logic Programs. In V. Lifschitz and I. Niemelaä (eds) *Logic Programming and Nonmonotonic Reasoning*, LPNMR 2004, Springer LNAI 2923, 2004.
33. P. Simons, I. Niemelä, and T. Soininen. Extending and implementing the stable model semantics. *Artificial Intellingence*, 138(1–2):181–234, 2002.
34. H. Turner. Strong equivalence for logic programs and default theories (made easy). In *Proc. of the Logic Programming and Nonmonotonic Reasoning, LPNMR'01*, LNAI 2173, pages 81–92. Springer, 2001.
35. D. Vakarelov Notes on N-Lattices and Constructive Logic with Strong Negation. *Studia Logica*, 36(1–2):109–125, 1977.
36. N. N. Vorob'ev. A constructive propositional calculus with strong negation (in Russian). *Doklady Akademii Nauk SSR*, 85:465–468, 1952.
37. N. N. Vorob'ev. The problem of deducibility in constructive propositional calculus with strong negation (in Russian). *Doklady Akademii Nauk SSR*, 85:689–692, 1952.
38. K. Wang and L. Zhou. Comparisons and Computation of Well-founded Semantics for Disjunctive Logic Programs. *ACM Transactions on Computational Logic*, to appear.

On Acyclic and Head-Cycle Free
Nested Logic Programs[*]

Thomas Linke[1], Hans Tompits[2], and Stefan Woltran[2]

[1] Institut für Informatik, Universität Potsdam,
Postfach 90 03 27, D-14439 Potsdam, Germany
linke@cs.uni-potsdam.de
[2] Institut für Informationssysteme 184/3, Technische Universität Wien,
Favoritenstraße 9–11, A-1040 Vienna, Austria
{tompits,stefan}@kr.tuwien.ac.at

Abstract. We define the class of head-cycle free nested logic programs, and its
proper subclass of acyclic nested programs, generalising similar classes originally
defined for disjunctive logic programs. We then extend several results known for
acyclic and head-cycle free disjunctive programs under the stable-model semantics to the nested case. Most notably, we provide a propositional semantics for
the program classes under consideration. This generalises different extensions
of Fages' theorem, including a recent result by Erdem and Lifschitz for tight
logic programs. We further show that, based on a shifting method, head-cycle free
nested programs can be rewritten into normal programs in polynomial time and
space, extending a similar technique for head-cycle free disjunctive programs. All
this shows that head-cycle free nested programs constitute a subclass of nested
programs possessing a lower computational complexity than arbitrary nested programs, providing the polynomial hierarchy does not collapse.

1 Introduction

This paper deals with generalisations and refinements of several reducibility results for
nested logic programs (NLPs) under the stable-model semantics. This class of programs
is characterised by the condition that arbitrarily nested formulas, formed from atoms using negation as failure, conjunction, and disjunction, serve as bodies and heads of rules,
extending the well-known classes of *normal logic programs* (nLPs), *disjunctive logic
programs* (DLPs), and *generalised disjunctive logic programs* (GDLPs). Nested logic
programs under the stable-model semantics (or rather under the answer-set semantics,
by allowing also strong negation) were introduced by Lifschitz, Tang, and Turner [18],
and currently receive increasing interest in the literature, both from a logical as well as
from a computational point of view.

In complexity theory, a frontier is identified having DLPs, GDLPs and NLPs on
the one side, and nLPs and so-called *nested normal programs* (NnLPs), for which only

---

[*] This work was partially supported by the Austrian Science Fund (FWF) under projects Z29-
N04 and P15068-INF, by the German Science Foundation (DFG) under grants FOR 375/1 and
SCHA 550/6, TP C, as well as by the European Commission under projects FET-2001-37004
WASP and IST-2001-33570 INFOMIX.

B. Demoen and V. Lifschitz (Eds.): ICLP 2004, LNCS 3132, pp. 225–239, 2004.

positive literals are allowed as heads of rules (cf. Table 1 below), on the other side. For the former program classes, the main reasoning tasks lie at the second level of the polynomial hierarchy [9, 26], while for the latter classes, the main reasoning tasks have NP complexity [24, 2][1]. There are various translatability results between the different syntactic subclasses of programs. Among them, there are translations between nested programs and GDLPs [18], and between DLPs and nLPs [8], both requiring exponential space in the worst case. Additionally, there exist linear-time constructible translations between NLPs and DLPs [25], and between GDLPs and DLPs [14, 15]. Note that, unless the polynomial hierarchy collapses, the above mentioned complexity gap does not allow for polynomial translations between, e.g., nested logic programs and normal logic programs. However, one can seek for subclasses of NLPs where such a translation is possible.

In this paper, we identify non-trivial subclasses of nested programs for which we establish two forms of reductions:

1. reductions to classical propositional logic; and
2. reductions to normal logic programs.

More specifically, we introduce the classes of *head-cycle free* (*HCF*) *nested programs* and its proper subclass of *acyclic nested programs*. Both program classes are defined as generalisations of similar kinds of programs originally introduced as syntactic subclasses of disjunctive logic programs a decade ago by Ben-Eliyahu and Dechter [1]. Moreover, the reductions we provide here are, on the one hand, *extensions* of previous results, established for more restricted kinds of programs, and, on the other hand, with respect to head-cycle free and acyclic nested programs, *optimisations* of general translatability results developed in [26, 25]. We detail the main aspects of our results in the following.

Concerning the reduction to classical propositional logic, we construct mappings, $T[\cdot]$ and $T^*[\cdot]$, assigning to each program a propositional theory such that

1. given an acyclic nested program Π, the stable models of Π are given by the models of the classical theory $T[\Pi]$; and
2. given a head-cycle free nested program Π, the stable models of Π are given by sets of form $I \cap V$, where I is a model of the classical theory $T^*[\Pi]$ and V is the set of atoms occurring in Π.

In both cases, the size of the assigned classical theory is *polynomial* in the size of the input program. Moreover, the translation $T^*[\cdot]$ is defined using newly introduced auxiliary variables, whereas for $T[\cdot]$, no new variables are required.

These results are generalisations of similar characterisations given by Ben-Eliyahu and Dechter [1] for acyclic and head-cycle free DLPs. Moreover, our results generalise results relating the stable-model semantics to *Clark's completion* [5]. Recall that Clark's completion was one of the first semantics proposed for programs containing default negation, in which a normal logic program Π is associated with a propositional theory, COMP[Π], called the *completion of* Π. Although every stable model of Π is also a

---

[1] The NP-completeness for NnLPs can be derived from a translation from NnLPs to nLPs due to You, Yuan, and Zhang [29].

model of the completion of Π, the converse does not always hold. In fact, Fages [12] showed that the converse holds providing Π satisfies certain syntactic restrictions. Our results generalise Fages' characterisation in the sense that, if Π is a normal program, then both $T[\Pi]$ and $T^*[\Pi]$ coincide with $\text{COMP}[\Pi]$.

Fages' theorem was generalised in several directions: Erdem and Lifschitz [10, 11] extended it for NnLPs, providing the given programs are *tight*. We extend the notion of tightness to *arbitrary* nested programs and refine our results by showing that

> if a nested program Π is HCF and tight on an interpretation I, then I is a stable model of Π iff I is a model of $T[\Pi]$.

Other generalisations of Fages' theorem drop the syntactic proviso but add instead additional so-called *loop formulas* guaranteeing equivalence between the stable models of the given program and the classical models of the resultant theory. This idea was pursued by Lin and Zhao [19] for normal programs and subsequently extended by Lee and Lifschitz [17] for disjunctive programs with nested formulas in rule bodies. In contrast to Clark's completion for normal programs, the size of the resultant theories in these approaches is in the worst case *exponential* in the size of the input programs. We further note that, for the sort of programs dealt with in [17], the notion of completion defined there coincides with our transformation $T[\cdot]$.

The reductions to classical propositional logic allow us also to draw immediate complexity results for acyclic and HCF nested programs. As noted above, the main reasoning tasks associated with arbitrary nested programs lie at the second level of the polynomial hierarchy [26], whereas our current results imply that analogous tasks for acyclic and HCF nested programs have NP or co-NP complexity (depending on the specific reasoning task). Thus, providing the polynomial hierarchy does not collapse, acyclic and HCF programs are computationally simpler than arbitrary nested programs.

Let us now turn to our results concerning the reductions to normal logic programs. As was shown by Ben-Eliyahu and Dechter [1], HCF disjunctive programs can be transformed into equivalent normal programs by shifting head atoms into the body (cf. also [6, 13]). For instance, a rule of form $p \vee q \leftarrow r$ is replaced by this method by the two rules $p \leftarrow r, \neg q$ and $q \leftarrow r, \neg p$ (where "$\neg$" denotes the negation-as-failure operator). We generalise this method for HCF nested programs, obtaining a polynomial reduction from HCF nested programs (and thus, in particular, also from acyclic nested programs) into nLPs. Note that applying such a shifting technique for programs which are not HCF does in general not retain the stable models.

Previous to our work, Inoue and Sakama [14] already defined the notions of acyclicity and head-cycle freeness for *generalised disjunctive programs*, extending the respective notions introduced in [1]. They showed that GDLPs satisfying either of these extended notions can likewise be transformed to nLPs by shifting head atoms to the bodies of rules and thus have the same worst-case complexity as normal programs. However, their notions of acyclicity and head-cycle freeness are more restrictive than ours, with respect to GDLPs, and hence our results hold for a larger class of programs.

We finally note that, at first glance, one may attempt to construct a polynomial translation from acyclic or head-cycle free NLPs into normal programs or into classical propositional logic by first applying the polynomial translation from NLPs to DLPs due to Pearce *et al.* [25], and afterwards by transforming the resultant programs into either normal programs or into classical logic using the results of Ben-Eliyahu and Dechter [1]. However, since the translation of [25] does neither preserve acyclicity nor head-cycle freeness, such an approach does not work in general.

The paper is organised as follows. The next section supplies some background on logic programs and the stable-model semantics. In Section 3, we introduce acyclic and head-cycle free nested programs and show some invariance theorems. Section 4 discusses the reductions to classical propositional logic, and Section 5 deals with the generalised shifting technique for reducing HCF programs into nLPs. Section 6 is devoted to tight nested programs, and Section 7 concludes the paper.

2   Preliminaries

We deal with propositional languages and use the logical symbols $\top$, $\bot$, $\neg$, $\vee$, $\wedge$, $\rightarrow$, and $\leftrightarrow$ to construct formulas over propositional variables (or atoms) in the usual way. A formula using only $\wedge$, $\vee$, or $\neg$ as its sentential connectives is called an *expression*. *Literals* are formulas of form v or $\neg v$, where v is some variable, or one of $\top$, $\bot$. We refer to a literal of form v (where v is as before) as a *positive literal* and to a literal of form $\neg v$ as a *negative literal*. Disjunctions of form $\bigvee_{i \in I} \phi_i$ are assumed to stand for the logical constant $\bot$ whenever $I = \emptyset$, and, likewise, conjunctions of form $\bigwedge_{i \in I} \phi_i$ with $I = \emptyset$ stand for $\top$. The set of all atoms occurring in a formula ϕ is denoted by $Atm(\phi)$.

By an interpretation, I, we understand a set of variables. Informally, a variable v is true under I iff $v \in I$. Interpretations induce truth values (in the sense of classical logic) of arbitrary formulas in the usual way. The set of models of a formula ϕ is denoted by $Mod(\phi)$. Two formulas, ϕ and ψ, are *(logically) equivalent*, iff $Mod(\phi) = Mod(\psi)$. For a set V and a family of sets S, by $S|_V$ we denote the family $\{I \cap V \mid I \in S\}$.

The fundamental objects of our investigation are *nested logic programs* (NLPs), introduced by Lifschitz, Tang, and Turner [18]. NLPs are characterised by the condition that the bodies and heads of rules are given by arbitrary expressions as defined above. For reasons of simplicity, we deal here only with languages containing one kind of negation, corresponding to default negation. Therefore, $\neg$ refers to default negation, whenever used in logic programs.

In more formal terms, a *rule*, r, is a pair of form

$$H(r) \leftarrow B(r),$$

where $B(r)$ and $H(r)$ are expressions. $B(r)$ is called the *body* of r and $H(r)$ is the *head* of r. If $B(r) = \top$, then r is a *fact*, and if $H(r) = \bot$, then r is a *constraint*. A nested logic program, or simply a *program*, is a finite set of rules.

We associate to every program Π the propositional formula

$$c(\Pi) = \bigwedge_{r \in \Pi} \big(B(r) \rightarrow H(r)\big).$$

Furthermore, $Atm(\Pi)$ denotes the set of all atoms occurring in program Π.

Let Π be a program and I an interpretation. Then, the *reduct*, Π^I, of Π with respect to I is obtained from Π by replacing every occurrence of an expression $\neg\psi$ in Π which

Table 1. Classes of programs.

Class	Heads	Bodies
NLP	expression	expression
GDLP	disjunction of literals	conjunction of literals
DLP	disjunction of atoms	conjunction of literals
NnLP	positive literal	expression
nLP	positive literal	conjunction of literals

is not in the scope of any other negation by $\perp$ if ψ is true under I, and by $\top$ otherwise. I is an *answer set* (or *stable model*) *of* Π iff it is a minimal model (with respect to set inclusion) of $c(\Pi^I)$. The collection of all answer sets of Π is denoted by $AS(\Pi)$. Two logic programs, Π_1 and Π_2, are *equivalent* iff $AS(\Pi_1) = AS(\Pi_2)$.

By restricting the syntactic form of bodies and heads of rules, different classes of programs are identified. Besides NLPs, for our purposes, the following classes are of interest: *generalised disjunctive logic programs* (GDLPs), *disjunctive logic programs* (DLPs), *nested normal logic programs* (NnLPs), and *normal logic programs* (nLPs). Table 1 summarises the defining attributes of these classes.

Following Lloyd and Topor [23] (cf. also [11]), we define the completion of an NnLP Π as the propositional formula

$$\text{COMP}[\Pi] = \bigwedge_{p \in A} \left(p \leftrightarrow \bigvee_{r \in \Pi, H(r) = p} B(r) \right),$$

where $A = Atm(\Pi) \cup \{\perp\}$.

Finally, we recall some graph-theoretical notations. A *(directed) graph*, G, is a pair (V, E) such that V is a finite set of *nodes* and $E \subseteq V \times V$ is a set of *edges*. A *path from* v *to* v' in G is a sequence $P_{v,v'} = (v_1, \ldots, v_n)$ of nodes such that $v = v_1$, $v' = v_n$, and $(v_i, v_{i+1}) \in E$, for each $1 \leq i < n$. A graph $G = (V, E)$ is *acyclic* iff, for each node $v \in V$, there is no path from v to itself. A *strongly connected component* (or *component*, for short) of a graph G is a maximal set S of nodes such that, for any two nodes p and q in S, there is a path from p to q in G. Strongly connected components can be identified in linear time [28]. The *size* of a component is the length (i.e., number of edges) of the longest acyclic path in it.

3   Acyclic and Head-Cycle Free Nested Programs

We start our formal elaboration by recalling the notion of a dependency graph for nested logic programs. Based on this, we define acyclic and head-cycle free nested programs, and show that these notions are invariant with respect to rewritings into DLPs.

We commence with the following auxiliary notions.

Definition 1. *Let p be an atom and φ an expression. Then, the* polarity *of a specific occurrence of p in φ is* positive *iff it is not in the scope of a negation, and* negative *otherwise. The set of atoms having a positive occurrence in φ is denoted by $Atm^+(\varphi)$. For a program Π, we define $Atm^+(\Pi) = \bigcup_{r \in \Pi}(Atm^+(H(r)) \cup Atm^+(B(r)))$.*

With this notation at hand, we are able to define the concept of dependency graphs for NLPs, following Lee and Lifschitz [17].

Definition 2. *The* (positive) dependency graph *of a program Π is given by $G_\Pi = (Atm(\Pi), E_\Pi)$, where $E_\Pi \subseteq Atm(\Pi) \times Atm(\Pi)$ is defined by the condition that $(p, q) \in E_\Pi$ iff there is some $r \in \Pi$ such that $p \in Atm^+(B(r))$ and $q \in Atm^+(H(r))$.*

Our first category of programs is then introduced as follows:

Definition 3. *A* nested logic program *Π is* acyclic *iff its dependency graph G_Π is acyclic.*

It is a straightforward matter to check that this definition generalises acyclic DLPs as introduced by Ben-Eliyahu and Dechter [1], i.e., a DLP Π is acyclic in the sense of Definition 3 iff it is acyclic in the sense of [1].

Example 1. Consider the following two programs:

$$\Pi_1 = \{p \vee q \leftarrow; p \leftarrow q; q \leftarrow p\}; \qquad \Pi_2 = \{p \vee q \leftarrow; p \leftarrow \neg\neg q; q \leftarrow \neg\neg p\}.$$

Programs Π_1 and Π_2 have dependency graphs $G_{\Pi_1} = (\{p, q\}, \{(p, q), (q, p)\})$ and $G_{\Pi_2} = (\{p, q\}, \emptyset)$, respectively. Thus, Π_1 is not acyclic, whereas Π_2 is. One may verify that both programs have the same stable models, viz. $AS(\Pi_1) = AS(\Pi_2) = \{\{p, q\}\}$.

Next, we generalise the notion of a head-cycle free DLP to the class of NLPs. To this end, we need the following definition.

Definition 4. *Two distinct atoms, p and q, are* joint-positive *in an expression ϕ iff there exists a subformula $\phi_1 \vee \phi_2$ of ϕ with $p \in Atm^+(\phi_1)$ and $q \in Atm^+(\phi_2)$, or vice versa. Moreover, p and q are called* head-sharing *in a program Π iff p and q are joint-positive in $H(r)$, for some $r \in \Pi$.*

From this, the class of head-cycle free NLPs is characterised in the following way:

Definition 5. *A* nested program *Π is* head-cycle free *(HCF) iff its dependency graph G_Π does not contain a directed cycle going through two head-sharing atoms in Π.*

Again, it can be shown that a DLP Π is HCF in the above sense iff it is HCF in the sense of [1]. Thus, the class of HCF NLPs is a proper generalisation of the class of HCF DLPs. Furthermore, it is easy to see that every acyclic NLP is HCF.

Example 2. Consider the programs Π_1 and Π_2 from Example 1. Observe that p and q are head-sharing in both Π_1 and Π_2. Hence, Π_1 is not HCF, since there is a cycle in G_{Π_1} involving p and q. On the other hand, Π_2 is HCF, and, as we already know from the above, acyclic.

In what follows, we review the translations introduced by Lifschitz, Tang, and Turner [18] and Janhunen [15], which, jointly applied, allow for translating any nested program into a DLP via the substitutions (L1)–(L12) and (J) from Table 2. Observe that

Table 2. Replacements in logic programs. It is assumed that ϕ, ψ, and φ are expressions, A is a set of atoms, p is an atom, L and L_p are new atoms, and $\circ \in \{\wedge, \vee\}$.

Name	Occurrence α	Replaced by β
(L1)	$\phi \circ \psi$	$\psi \circ \phi$
(L2)	$(\phi \circ \psi) \circ \varphi$	$\phi \circ (\psi \circ \varphi) \circ \in \{\wedge, \vee\}$
(L3)	$\phi \circ \phi$	ϕ
(L4)	$(\phi \wedge \psi) \vee \varphi$	$(\phi \vee \varphi) \wedge (\psi \vee \varphi)$
(L5)	$(\phi \vee \psi) \wedge \varphi$	$(\phi \wedge \varphi) \vee (\psi \wedge \varphi)$
(L6)	$\neg(\phi \vee \psi)$	$(\neg\phi \wedge \neg\psi)$
(L7)	$\neg(\phi \wedge \psi)$	$(\neg\phi \vee \neg\psi)$
(L8)	$\neg\neg\neg\phi$	$\neg\phi$
(L9)	$\phi \leftarrow \psi \vee \varphi$	$\phi \leftarrow \psi; \; \phi \leftarrow \varphi$
(L10)	$\phi \wedge \psi \leftarrow \varphi$	$\phi \leftarrow \varphi; \; \psi \leftarrow \varphi$
(L11)	$\phi \leftarrow \psi \wedge \neg\neg\varphi$	$\phi \vee \neg\varphi \leftarrow \psi$
(L12)	$\neg\neg\phi \vee \psi \leftarrow \varphi$	$\psi \leftarrow \varphi \wedge \neg\phi$
(J)	$\neg p \vee \psi \leftarrow \phi$	$L_p \vee \psi \leftarrow \phi; \; \bot \leftarrow p \wedge L_p; \; L_p \leftarrow \neg p$
(S)[1]	$\phi \vee \psi \leftarrow \varphi$	$\phi \leftarrow \varphi \wedge \neg\psi; \; \psi \leftarrow \varphi \wedge \neg\phi$
(T*)[2]	$\phi \leftarrow \psi$	$\{\phi[(A \setminus \{p\})/\top] \leftarrow \psi[p/\bot]; \; \phi[p/\top] \leftarrow \psi[(A \setminus \{p\})/\bot] \mid p \in A\}$
(D)	$\phi \vee \psi \leftarrow \varphi$	$\phi \vee L \leftarrow \varphi; \; \psi \leftarrow L$
(Y1)	$p \leftarrow \psi \wedge (\phi \vee \varphi)$	$p \leftarrow \psi \wedge L; \; L \leftarrow \phi \vee \varphi$
(Y2)	$p \leftarrow \psi \wedge \neg\neg q;$	$p \leftarrow \psi \wedge \neg L; \; L \leftarrow \neg q$
(C)	$\phi \wedge \psi \leftarrow \varphi$	$L \leftarrow \varphi; \; \phi \leftarrow L; \; \psi \leftarrow L$

[1] applicable only if $Atm^+(\phi) \cap Atm^+(\psi) = \emptyset$.
[2] applicable only for non-empty $A \subseteq Atm^+(\phi) \cap Atm^+(\psi)$.

the DLPs obtained in this way may be exponential in the size of the respective input programs. Our goal is to show that our notions of acyclicity and head-cycle freeness for NLPs are invariant with respect to the applications of these substitutions.

Any substitution σ from Table 2 is applied as follows: We say that a program Π' is *obtained from Π via σ* by replacing[2] an occurrence of an expression, or a single rule α, by β, which itself is an expression, a rule, or a set of rules. Moreover, $\theta[p/x]$ denotes the replacement of *all positive* occurrences of an atom p in θ by expression x. Accordingly, for a set of atoms S, $\theta[S/x]$ denotes the replacement of all positive occurrences of $p \in S$ in θ by x. Thus, $\theta[S/x] = \theta$ whenever $S \cap Atm^+(\theta)$ is empty. We sometimes use a substitution σ in the reverse way, i.e., replacing β by α. This is made explicit by writing $\sigma^{\leftarrow}$. We note that in this section we require only a part of the translations given in Table 2; the remaining ones are needed later on.

We start with the translation from NLPs to GDLPs due to Lifschitz, Tang, and Turner [18]. This translation is based on substitutions (L1)–(L12) from Table 2.

Proposition 1 ([18]). *Let Π be a nested program.*

Then, for every program Π' obtained from Π via any substitution from (L1)–(L12), it holds that $AS(\Pi) = AS(\Pi')$. Moreover, there is a program Π'' obtained from Π

---

[2] For (L11), (L12), (J), (Y1), and (Y2), we allow the component ψ in α to be vacuous; in this case, for β, ψ is set to $\top$ in (L11) and to $\bot$ in (L12).

via a sequence of substitutions from (L1)–(L12) such that Π'' is a GDLP and $AS(\Pi) = AS(\Pi'')$.

Next, we close the gap between GDLPs and DLPs. To this end, we require the substitution rule (J) of Table 2, which is a generalised stepwise variant of a labeling technique discussed in [15], introducing a globally new atom L_p, for any atom p. Observe that acyclicity and head-cycle freeness are invariant with respect to applications of substitutions (L1)–(L12) and (J). More precisely, (L1)–(L12) preserve both the dependency graph and the pairs of head-sharing atoms. An application of Substitution (J), however, changes the dependency graph $G_\Pi = (Atm(\Pi), E_\Pi)$, for a given program Π, to $G'_\Pi = (Atm(\Pi) \cup \{L_p\}, E_\Pi \cup \{(q, L_p) \mid q \in Atm^+(\phi)\})$ and yields additional pairs q and L_p of head-sharing atoms, for any $q \in Atm^+(\psi)$ (cf. Table 2), but no additional cycles are introduced in G'_Π. This gives us the desired result.

Theorem 1. *Let Π be a nested program, and let Π' be obtained from Π by applying any sequence of substitutions from (L1)–(L12) and (J).*

Then, the following properties hold:

1. $AS(\Pi) = AS(\Pi')|_{Atm(\Pi)}$;
2. Π is acyclic iff Π' is acyclic; and
3. Π is HCF iff Π' is HCF.

This theorem states that the properties of being acyclic and of being HCF are invariant with respect to any sequence of substitutions from (L1)–(L12) and (J). The next theorem demonstrates that substitutions (L1)–(L12) and (J) are sufficient to transform a given NLP into a corresponding DLP.

Theorem 2. *For any nested program Π, there is a program Π' obtained from Π via a sequence of substitutions from (L1)–(L12) and (J) obeying the conditions from Theorem 1 and such that Π' is a DLP.*

Example 3. For Π_2 from Example 1, we derive the following DLP by applying substitutions (L11) and (J) to both of the last two rules of Π_2:

$$\Pi' = \{p \vee q \leftarrow; p \vee L_q \leftarrow; q \vee L_p \leftarrow\} \cup \{\bot \leftarrow v \wedge L_v; v \leftarrow \neg L_v \mid v \in \{p, q\}\}.$$

The dependency graph of this program is $(\{p, q, L_p, L_q\}, \emptyset)$, and thus it is still HCF and acyclic. As well, the only stable model of Π' is $\{p, q\}$.

4   Reductions to Classical Propositional Logic

We now proceed with assigning a propositional semantics to acyclic and head-cycle free nested programs, in the sense that a program Π is transformed into a propositional formula ϕ such that the answer sets of Π are given by the models of ϕ. Observing that these encodings yield propositional formulas whose sizes are *polynomial* in the sizes of the input programs, we also draw some immediate complexity results.

We have the following building blocks. Let Π be a nested program. For any $p \in Atm^+(\Pi)$ occurring in a strongly connected component of size $l > 1$ in G_Π, we introduce globally new variables $p_1, \ldots, p_k$, where $k = \lceil \log_2(l-1) \rceil$. For two atoms p, q occurring in the same component of size $l > 1$ of the dependency graph, we define

$$prec_\Pi[q, p] = \bigwedge_{i=1}^{k}(q_i \rightarrow \bigvee_{j=i}^{k} p_j) \wedge \neg \bigwedge_{i=1}^{k}(p_i \rightarrow q_i).$$

Informally, $prec_\Pi[\cdot, \cdot]$ assigns a strict partial order to the atoms in Π, based on a binary encoding technique.

Now we are ready to define our two main transformations, $T[\cdot]$ and $T^*[\cdot]$, from nested logic programs into formulas of propositional logic.

Definition 6. *Let Π be a nested program, and let Π_p be the program resulting from Π by taking those rules $r \in \Pi$ where $p \in Atm^+(H(r))$ and replacing each positive occurrence of p in a head by $\bot$. Furthermore, let Π_p^* be the program resulting from Π_p by replacing each positive occurrence of an atom $q \neq p$ in a body by the formula $q \wedge prec_\Pi[q, p]$, providing q is in the same component as p in G_Π.*
Then, define

$$T[\Pi] = c(\Pi) \wedge \bigwedge_{p \in Atm(\Pi)} (p \rightarrow \neg c(\Pi_p)) \quad \text{and}$$

$$T^*[\Pi] = c(\Pi) \wedge \bigwedge_{p \in Atm(\Pi)} (p \rightarrow \neg c(\Pi_p^*)).$$

Note that both the size of $T[\Pi]$ as well as the size of $T^*[\Pi]$ is polynomial in the size of Π. Furthermore, if Π is an NnLP, then $T[\Pi]$ is equivalent to the completion COMP$[\Pi]$, and if Π is an acyclic NLP, then $T^*[\Pi] = T[\Pi]$. Moreover, it can be shown that, for any DLP Π, the theories $T[\Pi]$ and $T^*[\Pi]$ are equivalent to the encodings given by Ben-Eliyahu and Dechter [1] for acyclic and HCF DLPs, respectively. The main characterisations of [1] can thus be paraphrased as follows:

Proposition 2 ([1]). *For any DLP Π,*

1. *if Π is acyclic, then $I \in AS(\Pi)$ iff $I \in Mod(T[\Pi])$, for all $I \subseteq Atm(\Pi)$; and*
2. *if Π is HCF, then $AS(\Pi) = Mod(T^*[\Pi])|_{Atm(\Pi)}$.*

The restriction in the second result is used to "hide" the newly introduced variables in formulas $prec_\Pi[\cdot, \cdot]$ in $T^*[\Pi]$.

With the next results, we generalise Proposition 2 to HCF and acyclic nested programs. To begin with, we have the following theorem.

Theorem 3. *Let Π be a HCF nested logic program.*
Then, $AS(\Pi) = Mod(T^*[\Pi])|_{Atm(\Pi)}$.

This theorem is proved by showing that models of $T^*[\cdot]$ are invariant (modulo the introduction of new atoms) under substitution rules (L1)–(L12) and (J).

As an immediate consequence, we obtain the following corollary for acyclic nested programs.

Corollary 1. *Let Π be an acyclic nested logic program, and let $I \subseteq Atm(\Pi)$.*
Then, $I \in AS(\Pi)$ iff $I \in Mod(T[\Pi])$.

Let us briefly mention that our encodings easily extend to typical reasoning tasks associated to logic programs. Following [1], we define the following inference operators. Let Π be a logic program and S a finite set of atoms.

1. *Brave consequence*: $\Pi \vdash_b S$ iff S is contained in some answer set of Π.
2. *Skeptical consequence*: $\Pi \vdash_s S$ iff S is contained in all answer sets of Π.
3. *Disjunctive entailment*: $\Pi \vdash_d S$ iff, for each answer set I of Π, there is some $p \in S$ such that $p \in I$.

We then obtain the following straightforward encodings:

Theorem 4. *Let S be a finite set of atoms.*

1. *For any acyclic NLP Π, we have that*
   (a) $\Pi \vdash_b S$ iff $T[\Pi] \wedge \bigwedge_{p \in S} p$ *is satisfiable;*
   (b) $\Pi \vdash_s S$ iff $T[\Pi] \rightarrow \bigwedge_{p \in S} p$ *is valid; and*
   (c) $\Pi \vdash_d S$ iff $T[\Pi] \rightarrow \bigvee_{p \in S} p$ *is valid.*
2. *For any HCF NLP Π, we have that*
   (a) $\Pi \vdash_b S$ iff $T^*[\Pi] \wedge \bigwedge_{p \in S} p$ *is satisfiable;*
   (b) $\Pi \vdash_s S$ iff $T^*[\Pi] \rightarrow \bigwedge_{p \in S} p$ *is valid; and*
   (c) $\Pi \vdash_d S$ iff $T^*[\Pi] \rightarrow \bigvee_{p \in S} p$ *is valid.*

Observing that the above encodings are clearly constructible in polynomial time, we derive the following immediate complexity results:

Theorem 5. *Checking whether $\Pi \vdash_b S$ holds, for a given acyclic or HCF NLP Π and a given finite set S of atoms, is NP-complete. Furthermore, checking whether $\Pi \vdash_s S$ or whether $\Pi \vdash_d S$ holds, given Π and S as before, is co-NP-complete.*

Note that the upper complexity bounds follow from the complexity of classical propositional logic, and the lower complexity bounds are inherited from the complexity of normal logic programs.

5   A Generalised Shifting Approach

The result that HCF nested programs have NP or co-NP complexity motivates to seek a polynomial translation from HCF programs to NnLPs and furthermore to nLPs. We do this by introducing a generalised variant of the well-known shifting technique [1, 6]. Recall that shifting for DLPs is defined as follows: Let $r \in \Pi$ be a disjunctive rule in a HCF DLP Π. Then, following [1], Π is equivalent to the program resulting from Π by replacing r by the following set of rules[3]:

$$\{p \leftarrow B(r) \wedge \neg(Atm(H(r)) \setminus \{p\}) \mid p \in Atm(H(r))\}. \tag{1}$$

---

[3] For a finite set S of atoms, $\neg S$ denotes $\bigwedge_{s \in S} \neg s$.

For generalising this shifting technique to nested programs, we introduce the substitution rule (S), depicted in Table 2, which allows the replacement of $\phi \vee \psi \leftarrow \varphi$ by the two rules $\phi \leftarrow \varphi \wedge \neg\psi$ and $\psi \leftarrow \varphi \wedge \neg\phi$, where ϕ and ψ are arbitrary expressions, providing $Atm^+(\phi) \cap Atm^+(\psi) = \emptyset$. Observe that (S) preserves head-cycle freeness.

In view of its proviso, (S) is not always applicable, even if a given program is HCF. But this problem is already apparent in the case of disjunctive programs. Indeed, in (1), we used the set $Atm(H(r))$ rather than the disjunction $H(r)$ explicitly, otherwise we would have run into problems: For instance, the DLP $\{p \vee p \leftarrow\}$ is clearly not equivalent to $\{p \leftarrow \neg p\}$.

We can establish the following property:

Lemma 1. *Let Π be a HCF nested program, and let Π' be obtained from Π via (S). Then, $AS(\Pi) = AS(\Pi')$.*

This lemma follows from the property that models of $\mathcal{T}^*[\cdot]$ are preserved under application of (S), together with Theorem 3.

Theorem 6. *Let Π be a nested program.*

Then, there is a program $\mathcal{S}_{exp}[\Pi]$ obtained from Π via a finite sequence of substitutions from (L1)–(L4), (L6)–(L8), (L10), (L11)$^\leftarrow$, (L12), and (S), such that (i) $\mathcal{S}_{exp}[\Pi]$ is an NnLP, and (ii) if Π is HCF, then $AS(\Pi) = AS(\mathcal{S}_{exp}[\Pi])$.

The "strategy" to obtain $\mathcal{S}_{exp}[\Pi]$ from Π is as follows: First, we translate Π into a program where all heads are disjunctions of atoms. Then, via (L1), (L2), and (L3), we can easily eliminate repeated occurrences of an atom p in a head. Finally, we then apply (S) to replace each (proper) disjunctive rule into a set of nested normal rules.

Observe that the subscript "exp" in $\mathcal{S}_{exp}[\cdot]$ indicates that the size of $\mathcal{S}_{exp}[\Pi]$ may be exponential in the size of Π in the worst case. The reason is the use of substitution rule (L4). We can circumvent the application of (L4), and thus the exponential blow-up, if we could use (S) more directly. To this end, we introduce the two substitution rules (D) and (T*), as given in Table 2. Observe that (T*) is a generalisation of an optimisation rule called (TAUT) due to Brass and Dix [3]. In fact, we want to apply (D) instead of (S), but (D) may introduce new head cycles according to its definition. In particular, this situation occurs whenever an atom occurs positively in both the body and the head of the considered rule. Hence, the strategy is then as follows: If (S) is not applicable, we first use (T*) to eliminate all atoms which occur positively in both the body and the head of the considered rule. After applying (D), we are clearly allowed to apply (S) to the resulting rules of form $\phi \vee L \leftarrow \varphi$, since L is a new atom not occurring in ϕ. In order to apply (S) after (D) and (T*), it is required that acyclicity and head-cycle freeness are invariant under application of (D) and (T*), which is indeed the case. Given that both substitutions can be shown to be answer-set preserving for HCF programs as well, we obtain the following theorem.

Theorem 7. *Let Π be a nested program.*
Then, there is a program $\mathcal{S}_{poly}[\Pi]$ obtained from Π via a polynomial sequence of substitutions from (L1)–(L3), (L6)–(L8), (L10), (L11)$^\leftarrow$, (L12), (S), (T*), and (D) such that (i) $\mathcal{S}_{poly}[\Pi]$ is an NnLP, and (ii) if Π is HCF, then $AS(\Pi) = AS(\mathcal{S}_{poly}[\Pi])|_{Atm(\Pi)}$.

Note that $\mathcal{S}_{poly}[\Pi]$ is polynomial in the size of Π, since the distributivity rule (L4) is not included. Indeed, new atoms are only introduced by (D).

So far, we showed how to translate HCF nested programs into NnLPs in polynomial time. In order to obtain a reduction to nLPs, we consider two additional rules, (Y1) and (Y2), depicted in Table 2. The following result holds:

Proposition 3 ([29]). *Let Π be an NnLP, and let Π' be obtained from Π via (Y1) or (Y2).*
Then, $AS(\Pi) = AS(\Pi')|_{Atm(\Pi)}$.

Putting the previous results together, the following property can be shown:

Theorem 8. *Let Π be a nested program.*
Then, there is a program $\mathcal{S}[\Pi]$ obtained from Π via a polynomial sequence of substitutions from (L1)–(L3), (L6)–(L9), (L10), (L11)$^{\leftarrow}$, (L12), (S), (T*), (D), (Y1), and (Y2), such that (i) $\mathcal{S}[\Pi]$ is normal, and (ii) if Π is HCF, then $AS(\Pi) = AS(\mathcal{S}[\Pi])|_{Atm(\Pi)}$.

Example 4. Observe that program Π_2 from Example 1 can be translated into the nLP

$$\mathcal{S}[\Pi] = \{p \leftarrow \neg q; \ q \leftarrow \neg p; \ p \leftarrow \neg L_1; \ L_1 \leftarrow \neg q; \ q \leftarrow \neg L_2; \ L_2 \leftarrow \neg p\}.$$

6   Tight Nested Logic Programs

It is well known that every stable model of an NnLP Π is a model of COMP$[\Pi]$ (cf., e.g., [11]). However, the converse holds only providing certain syntactic restrictions are enforced. Such conditions were first given by Fages [12] for nLPs, and subsequently extended by Erdem and Lifschitz [11] for NnLPs. In the latter work, the notion of *tight nested normal logic programs* is introduced. In this section, we extend tightness to general nested logic programs and show that HCF NLPs which satisfy tightness can be reduced to theories of classical propositional logic by means of translation $T[\cdot]$. That is, the resultant theories are equivalent to COMP$[\Pi]$ in case of an NnLP Π.

Following [11], we define the *positive conjunctive components* of an expression ϕ, denoted $cc(\phi)$, as follows: First, every expression ϕ can be written in the form $\phi_1 \land \cdots \land \phi_n$ ($n \geq 1$), where each ϕ_i is not a conjunction. The formulas $\phi_1, \ldots, \phi_n$ are called the *conjunctive components* of ϕ. Then, $cc(\phi)$ is the conjunction of all those conjunctive components of ϕ such that at least one atom occurs positively in it. Note that, e.g., $cc(\neg p) = \top$, where p is some atom.

Definition 7. *A nested program Π is tight on an interpretation I iff there exists a function λ from $Atm(\Pi)$ to ordinals such that, for each rule $r \in \Pi$, if $I \in Mod(H(r) \land B(r))$, then $\lambda(p) < \lambda(q)$, for each $p \in Atm(cc(B(r)))$ and each $q \in Atm^+(H(r))$.*

Obviously, this definition generalises the one in [11]. Using our translation $T[\cdot]$, we can reformulate the main theorem in [11] as follows:

Proposition 4 ([11]). *Let Π be an NnLP, and let $I \subseteq Atm(\Pi)$ be an interpretation such that Π is tight on I.*
Then, $I \in AS(\Pi)$ iff $I \in Mod(T[\Pi])$.

We generalise this proposition by showing that $T[\Pi]$ is applicable to tight HCF nested programs as well. To this end, we make partly use of the results discussed in the previous section showing how nested programs can be reduced to NnLPs. Note that, whenever such a translation simultaneously retains tightness and models of $T[\cdot]$, we directly get the desired generalisation, according to Proposition 4.

Lemma 2. *Let Π be a nested program, let I be an interpretation, and let Π' be obtained from Π via any substitution from (L1)–(L8), (L12), (L11)$^\leftarrow$, or (S).*
Then, Π' is tight on I whenever Π is tight on I.

Lemma 3. *Let Π be a nested program, and let Π' be obtained from Π via any substitution from (L1)–(L12), (L11)$^\leftarrow$, or (S).*
Then, $Mod(T[\Pi]) = Mod(T[\Pi'])$.

Observe that not all substitution rules from Table 2 used in Theorem 6 to obtain NnLPs are included in Lemma 2. In fact, there is some problem with (L10). Consider the program $\Pi = \{a \leftarrow b; b \wedge c \leftarrow a\}$, which is tight on interpretation $I = \{a, b\}$, since only for the first rule $r = a \leftarrow b$ the condition $I \in Mod(H(r) \wedge B(r))$ from Definition 7 holds. Applying (L10), we obtain $\Pi' = \{a \leftarrow b; b \leftarrow a; c \leftarrow a\}$ which is not tight on $\{a, b\}$ anymore, because now, both $I \in Mod(H(r) \wedge B(r))$ and $I \in Mod(H(r') \wedge B(r'))$ holds, for $r = a \leftarrow b$ and $r' = b \leftarrow a$. We therefore replace (L10) by the new rule (C) from Table 2, which can be shown to retain tightness, models of $T[\cdot]$ (modulo newly introduced atoms), and head-cycle freeness.

By these invariance results, we get the main result of this section.

Theorem 9. *Let Π be a HCF nested program, and let $I \subseteq Atm(\Pi)$ be an interpretation such that Π is tight on I.*
Then, $I \in AS(\Pi)$ iff $I \in Mod(T[\Pi])$.

7   Conclusion

In this paper, we introduced the classes of acyclic and head-cycle free nested programs as generalisations of similar classes originally introduced for disjunctive logic programs. We furthermore extended several results related to Clark's completion to our classes of programs, by introducing the polynomial reductions $T[\cdot]$ and $T^*[\cdot]$ to classical propositional logic. Moreover, we extended the notion of tightness to nested programs, and we constructed a polynomial translation of HCF nested programs into normal programs by applying a generalised shifting technique. We also derived immediate complexity results, showing that acyclic and HCF nested programs have a lower complexity than arbitrary NLPs, providing the polynomial hierarchy does not collapse.

Transformations $T[\cdot]$ and $T^*[\cdot]$ can also be viewed as optimisations of a translation studied in [26], in which (arbitrary) nested programs are efficiently mapped to *quantified Boolean formulas* such that the stable models of the former are given by the models of the latter. Hence, the present results show that, in case of acyclic and HCF programs, a reduction to classical formulas suffices instead of a reduction to the more expressive class of quantified Boolean formulas.

The translation of acyclic and HCF nested programs to nLPs optimises a polynomial translation presented in [25] from arbitrary nested programs into disjunctive logic programs, in the sense that our current method (i) introduces in general fewer additional variables, and (ii) translates a subclass of NLPs into a (presumably) less complex subclass of DLPs, viz. normal programs.

Furthermore, our translation extends and optimises also a recent result due to Eiter *et al.* [8] which discusses a general method to eliminate disjunctions from a given DLP under different notions of equivalence. To wit, under ordinary equivalence (i.e., preservance of stable models), the aforementioned method allows to transform a given DLP into an nLP by applying the usual shifting technique [1] and by adding suitable rules in order to retain equivalence between the programs. However, in general, the size of the resultant programs is exponential in the size of the input programs. Hence, for HCF programs, we obtain not only a generalisation of this general result to the nested case but also a *polynomial* method to achieve a transformation to nLPs.

Following the remarks in [29], our polynomial transformations from HCF nested programs into normal programs can be used to utilise extant answers-set solvers, like DLV [7], Smodels [27], or ASSAT [19], for computing answer sets of HCF nested programs. Furthermore, the present results indicate how to compute answer sets of HCF NLPs directly by generalising graph based methods as described in [4, 20, 16]. More precisely, we may define $Atm^-(\varphi)$ as the set of atoms having negative occurrences in φ, which enables us to express positive as well as negative dependencies between atoms in expressions. Therefore, graph coloring techniques as described in [16, 21], and used as basis of the noMoRe system [22], may be generalised to HCF NLPs. Hence, our approach offers different ways for answer-set computation of nested programs.

Although our current results are established for programs containing only one kind of negation, viz. default negation, they can be extended to programs allowing strong negation as well. Furthermore, another issue is the lifting of the notions of acyclic and head-cycle free nested programs to the first-order case, which can be done along the lines of [14].

References

1. R. Ben-Eliyahu and R. Dechter. Propositional Semantics for Disjunctive Logic Programs. *Annals of Mathematics and Artificial Intelligence*, 12:53–87, 1994.
2. N. Bidoit and C. Froidevaux. Negation by Default and Unstratifiable Logic Programs. *Theoretical Computer Science*, 78:85–112, 1991.
3. S. Brass and J. Dix. Semantics of (Disjunctive) Logic Programs Based on Partial Evaluation. *Journal of Logic Programming*, 38(3):167–213, 1999.
4. G. Brignoli, S. Costantini, O. D'Antona, and A. Provetti. Characterizing and Computing Stable Models of Logic Programs: The Non-stratified Case. In *Proc. of the 2nd International Conference on Information Technology (CIT-99)*, pp. 197–201, 1999.
5. K. L. Clark. Negation as Failure. In *Logic and Databases*, pp. 293–322. Plenum, 1978.
6. J. Dix, G. Gottlob, and V. Marek. Reducing Disjunctive to Non-Disjunctive Semantics by Shift-Operations. *Fundamenta Informaticae*, XXVIII(1/2):87–100, 1996.
7. T. Eiter, W. Faber, N. Leone, and G. Pfeifer. Declarative Problem-Solving Using the DLV System. In *Logic-Based Artificial Intelligence*, pp. 79–103. Kluwer, 2000.

8. T. Eiter, M. Fink, H. Tompits, and S. Woltran. On Eliminating Disjunctions in Stable Logic Programming. In *Proc. KR-04*, 2004. To appear.

9. T. Eiter and G. Gottlob. On the Computational Cost of Disjunctive Logic Programming: Propositional Case. *Annals of Mathematics and Artificial Intelligence*, 15(3–4):289–323, 1995.

10. E. Erdem and V. Lifschitz. Fages' Theorem for Programs with Nested Expressions. In *Proc. ICLP-01*, LNCS 2237, pp. 242–254, Springer, 2001.

11. E. Erdem and V. Lifschitz. Tight Logic Programs. *Theory and Practice of Logic Programming*, 3(4–5):499–518, 2003.

12. F. Fages. Consistency of Clark's Completion and Existence of Stable Models. *Methods of Logic in Computer Science*, 1:51–60, 1994.

13. M. Gelfond, V. Lifschitz, H. Przymusinska, and M. Truszczyński. Disjunctive Defaults. In *Proc. KR-91*, pp. 230–237. Morgan Kaufmann, 1991.

14. K. Inoue and C. Sakama. Negation as Failure in the Head. *Journal of Logic Programming*, 35(1):39–78, 1998.

15. T. Janhunen. On the Effect of Default Negation on the Expressiveness of Disjunctive Rules. In *Proc. LPNMR-01*, LNCS 2173, pp. 93–106, Springer, 2001.

16. K. Konczak, T. Linke, and T. Schaub. Graphs and Colorings for Answer Set Programming: Abridged Report. In *Proc. LPNMR-04*, LNCS 2923, pp. 127–140. Springer, 2004.

17. J. Lee and V. Lifschitz. Loop Formulas for Disjunctive Logic Programs. In *Proc. ICLP-03*, LNCS 2916, pp. 451–465, Springer, 2003.

18. V. Lifschitz, L. Tang, and H. Turner. Nested Expressions in Logic Programs. *Annals of Mathematics and Artificial Intelligence*, 25(3-4):369–389, 1999.

19. F. Lin and Y. Zhao. ASSAT: Computing Answer Sets of a Logic Program by SAT Solvers. In *Proc. AAAI-02*, pp. 112–117, 2002.

20. T. Linke. Graph Theoretical Characterization and Computation of Answer Sets. In *Proc. IJCAI-01*, pp. 641–645. Morgan Kaufmann, 2001.

21. T. Linke. Suitable Graphs for Answer Set Programming. In *Proc. ASP-03*, pp. 15–28. CEUR Workshop Proceedings, volume 78, 2003.

22. T. Linke, C. Anger, and K. Konczak. More on noMoRe. In *Proc. JELIA-02*, LNCS 2424, pp. 468–480, Springer, 2002.

23. J. Lloyd and R. Topor. Making Prolog More Expressive. *Journal of Logic Programming*, 3:225–240, 1984.

24. W. Marek and M. Truszczyński. Autoepistemic Logic. *Journal of the ACM*, 38:588–619, 1991.

25. D. Pearce, V. Sarsakov, T. Schaub, H. Tompits, and S. Woltran. A Polynomial Translation of Logic Programs with Nested Expressions into Disjunctive Logic Programs: Preliminary Report. In *Proc. ICLP-02*, LNCS 2401, pp. 405–420. Springer, 2002.

26. D. Pearce, H. Tompits, and S. Woltran. Encodings for Equilibrium Logic and Logic Programs with Nested Expressions. In *Proc. EPIA-01*, LNCS 2285, pp. 306–320. Springer, 2001.

27. P. Simons, I. Niemelä, and T. Soininen. Extending and Implementing the Stable Model Semantics. *Artificial Intelligence*, 138:181–234, 2002.

28. R. Tarjan. Depth-first Search and Linear Graph Algorithms. *SIAM Journal on Computing*, 1:146–160, 1972.

29. J. You, L. Yuan, and M. Zhang. On the Equivalence Between Answer Sets and Models of Completion for Nested Logic Programs. In *Proc. IJCAI-03*, pp. 859–865, 2003.

Fast Query Evaluation
with (Lazy) Control Flow Compilation

Remko Tronçon, Gerda Janssens, and Henk Vandecasteele

K.U.Leuven – Department of Computer Science
{remko,gerda,henkv}@cs.kuleuven.ac.be

Abstract. Learning algorithms such as decision tree learners dynamically generate a huge amount of large queries. Because these queries
are executed often, the trade-off between meta-calling and compiling &
running them has been in favor of the latter, as compiled code is faster.
This paper presents a technique named *control flow compilation*, which
improves the compilation time of the queries by an order of magnitude
without reducing the performance of executing the queries. We exploit
the technique further by using it in a just-in-time manner. This improves
performance in two ways: it opens the way to incremental compilation
of the generated queries, and also gives potentially large gains by never
compiling dynamically unreachable code. Both the implementation of
(lazy) control flow compilation and its experimental evaluation in a real
world application are reported on.

1 Introduction

In previous work, *query packs* [5] were introduced as an efficient method for
executing a set of similar queries. A query pack is basically the body of a rule
with no arguments, with a huge number of literals and disjunctions. The query
pack execution mechanism deals with the disjunctions in a special way, namely
by avoiding a branch which already succeeded before. Query packs are interesting
in the context of several types of learners, including first order decision trees [4,
8], first order pattern discovery [7], and rule-based learners [9–11]. These query
packs can be executed in ilProlog [1], a WAM [17] based Prolog algorithm with
special support for Inductive Logic Programming (ILP). They are generated
dynamically by the ILP algorithm, compiled by the underlying Prolog system,
after which the compiled code is executed on a dataset (which is actually a large
collection of different logic programs). This is not an unreasonable approach,
and we have indeed measured large speedups in ILP systems based on this
approach [5].

However, measurements indicate that the compilation of a complete query
pack is a very costly operation, and sometimes causes more overhead than what
is gained later when executing the compiled version (instead of meta-calling the
query pack). Also, some goals of a generated query pack fail on each example,
meaning that the part of the query following that goal was compiled in vain.
Therefore, we started investigating *control flow compilation* [14] as a more flexible and faster alternative to classical compilation. This is basically a hybrid

B. Demoen and V. Lifschitz (Eds.): ICLP 2004, LNCS 3132, pp. 240–253, 2004.
© Springer-Verlag Berlin Heidelberg 2004

between compilation and meta-call. While classical WAM code for a compiled query contains both instructions encoding the calls to predicates and instructions dealing with the control flow (e.g. selection of clauses/branches), control flow compilation only generates the control flow instructions and uses meta-call to deal with the calls. The resulting compilation is much less expensive, and the generated code is as fast as classical compiled code. Moreover, this technique allows a *lazy* compilation scheme, which only compiles a part of a query when it is actually executed. Not only does this avoid redundant compilation, lazy compilation is also a first step towards supporting the incremental generation of queries and query packs. Introducing laziness in the full WAM compiler is not straightforward, because its variable classification and allocation scheme is optimized towards the situation where all the code is known. Moreover, because query packs are very large, specialized techniques for dealing with its variables are needed [16], which complicates matters even further. On the other hand, the control flow compiler does not have to deal with the variables in the query packs, and can therefore compile an increment to a query almost independently of the previous query.

In this paper, we present control flow compilation and its lazy variant as an innovative way to deal with compilation overhead and to achieve faster execution of queries. We illustrate its advantages with real life examples. Lazy control flow compilation is also an enabling technology for incrementality in the ILP process of query (pack) generation and execution. In principle, any application depending on an efficient meta-call could benefit from this technique. Nevertheless, the focus of this work is on ILP.

Control flow compilation is described and evaluated in Section 3. Based on control flow compilation, we develop a lazy compilation scheme for queries containing conjunctions and disjunctions in Section 4. (Lazy) control flow compilation is extended to query packs in Section 5. We evaluate our approaches using both artificial and real world experiments. Finally, Section 6 concludes and discusses future work.

We assume that the reader is familiar with the WAM [2].

2   Background: Queries in ILP

We start by sketching a particular setting in which our work is relevant, namely the execution of queries in Inductive Logic Programming. The goal of Inductive Logic Programming is to find a theory that best explains a large set of data (or examples). In the ILP setting at hand, each example is a logic program, and the logical theory is represented as a set of logical queries. The ILP algorithm searches for these queries using generate-and-test: generated queries are run on sets of examples; based on the failure or success of these queries, only the ones with the 'best' results[1] are kept and are extended (e.g. by adding literals). These

---

[1] Which queries are best depends on the ILP algorithm. In the case of classification, the information gain can be used as a criterium, whereas in the case of regression, the reduction of variance is often used.

extended queries are in turn tested on each example, and this process continues until a satisfactory query (or set of queries) describing the examples has been found.

At each iteration of the algorithm, a set of queries is executed on a large set of logic programs (the examples). Since these queries are the result of adding different literals to the end of another query, the queries in this set have a lot of common prefixes. To avoid repeating the common parts by executing each query separately, the set of queries is transformed into a special kind of disjunction: a *query pack* [5]. For example, the set of queries

```
?- a, b, c, d.
?- a, b, c, e.
?- a, b, f, g.
```

is transformed into the query

```
?- a, b, ( (c,(d;e)) ; f,g ).
```

by applying left factoring on the initial set of queries. However, because only the success of a query on an example is measured, the normal Prolog disjunction might still cause too much backtracking. So, for efficiency reasons the ';'/2 is given a slightly different semantics in query packs: it cuts away branches from the disjunction as soon as they succeed. Since each query pack is run on a large set of examples, a query pack is first compiled, and the compiled code is executed on the examples. This compiled code makes use of dedicated WAM instructions for the query pack execution mechanism. More details can be found in [5].

3 Control Flow Compilation

3.1 Technology

Executing compiled queries instead of meta-calling them results in considerable speedups. However, compilation of a query can take as much time as the execution of the query on all examples. Moreover, classical compilation makes it very difficult to exploit the incremental nature of query generation in the ILP setting. It would require a tight coupling between the generation of the queries and their compilation. Also, assignment of variables to environment slots uses a classification of variables which assumes that all the code is known at compile time. This motivated the preliminary study of alternatives for compile & run in [14]. The most interesting alternative is *control flow compilation*, which is a hybrid between meta-calling and compiling a query. In this section, we introduce control flow compilation for queries whose bodies consist of conjunctions and disjunctions. Control flow compilation for query packs is discussed in Section 5.

The essential difference between classical compilation and control flow compilation is the sequence of instructions generated for setting up and calling a goal. Instead of generating the usual WAM put and call instructions, the latter generates one new cf_call instruction, whose argument points to a heap data structure (the goal) that is meta-called. Hence, control flow code only contains the control flow instructions (`try`, `retry`, ...) and `cf_call` (and `cf_deallex`) instructions.

For example, control flow compiling the query

$$q \text{ :- } a(X,Y), \text{ (} b(Y,Z) \text{ ; } c(Y,Z), d(Z,U); e(a,Y) \text{).}$$

results in the code in the left part of Figure 1. Note that the query itself is a term on the heap, and that we use &a(X,Y) to represent the pointer to its subterm a(X,Y). On the right of Figure 1 is the classical compiled code for the same query. Before calling each goal, the compiled code first sets up the arguments to

q :- a(X,Y), (b(Y,Z) ; c(Y,Z), d(Z,U); e(a,Y)).

Control flow code	Compiled code
allocate 2	allocate 4
	bldtvar A1
	putpvar Y2 A2
cf_call &a(X,Y)	call a/2
trymeorelse L1	trymeorelse L1
	putpval Y2 A1
	bldtvar A2
cf_deallex &b(Y,Z)	deallex b/2
L1: retrymeorelse L2	retrymeorelse L2
	putpval Y2 A1
	putpvar Y3 A2
cf_call &c(Y,Z)	call c/2
	putpval Y3 A1
	bldtvar A2
cf_deallex &d(Z,U)	deallex d/2
L2: trustmeorelsefail	trustmeorelsefail
	putpval Y2 A2
	put_atom A1 a
cf_deallex &e(a,Y)	deallex e/2

Fig. 1. Control flow compiled code vs. classical compiled code.

the goal, whereas the control flow compiled code uses a reference to the subterm of the query to indicate the goal that is called. One important aspect is that the control flow code saves emulator cycles, because it contains no instructions related to the arguments of the goals that are called. Moreover, the absence of this kind of instructions is very interesting for the lazy compilation we have in mind. Suppose that we want to extend a query by adding a disjunction after its last call (e.g. refining e(a,Y) into e(a,Y),(f(Y,Z);g(Y,U),h(U,V))); within the control flow compilation scheme, it is possible to extend the existing code just by adding more control flow instructions at the end, without the usual compilation issues concerning the variables.

Contrary to compiled code, control flow code cannot exist on its own, since it contains external references to terms on the heap. This introduces some memory management issues: (1) these terms have to be kept alive as long as the control flow compiled code exists; (2) when these terms are moved to another place in memory (e.g. by the garbage collector), the references in the code must be adapted as well.

3.2   Evaluation

For evaluating our approach, we added control flow compilation to the ilProlog system [1]. During the experiments, the heap garbage collector was deactivated, as it does not yet take into account the control flow code. The experiments were run on a Pentium III 1.1 GHz with 2 GB main memory running Linux under a normal load.

Two kinds of experiments are discussed: the benchmarks in Table 1 show the potential gain in an artificial setting, whereas the results in Table 2 are obtained from a real world application.

Table 1. Experiments for artificial disjunctions. (timings in milliseconds).

	(5,5,4)		(10,5,4)		(5,10,4)		(10,10,4)		(5,5,6)	
	comp	exec	comp	exec	comp	exec	comp	exec	comp	exec
control flow	25	0.13	52	0.25	390	4.07	735	7.73	682	7.03
compile & run	322	0.28	663	0.48	4676	5.49	11856	9.18	11099	9.32
meta-call	-	2.1	-	3.79	-	31.73	-	58.83	-	58.43

The artificially generated queries in Table 1 have the following parameters:

- g: the number of goals in a branch,
- b: the branching factor in a disjunction,
- d: the nesting depth of disjunctions.

For example, for the values (2,3,1) for (g,b,d) we generate the query $a(A,B,C)$, $a(C,D,E)$, $(a(E,F,G)$, $a(G,H,I)$; $a(E,J,K)$, $a(K,L,M)$; $a(E,N,O)$, $a(O,P,Q))$. For (1,2,2), the generated query has nested disjunctions: $a(A,B,C)$, $(a(C,D,E)$, $(a(E,F,G)$; $a(E,H,I))$; $a(C,J,K)$, $(a(K,L,M)$; $a(K,N,O)))$. The definition for $a/3$ is simply $a(\_,\_,\_)$. These queries have the same structure as query packs: disjunctions obtained from left factoring a set of conjunctions. The different values of (g,b,d) can be found in the upper row of the table. We report on the following three alternatives:

- *control flow*: the query is compiled using the control flow approach before it is executed.
- *compile & run*: the query is compiled using the classical WAM before it is executed.
- *meta-call*: the query is meta-called (no compilation at all).

The *comp* column gives the compilation time, while the *exec* column gives the execution time of a single execution of a query.

The control flow compilation is definitely better than compile & run: the compilation times are improved by one order of magnitude, while the execution times are also better. The compilation in the control flow approach is much faster because it does not need to perform expensive tasks such as assigning variables to environment slots. The better execution times are explained by the fact that only one emulation cycle per call is needed as no arguments have to be put in registers. Doubling the g parameter more or less doubles the timings. For larger queries, namely for (10,10,4) and (5,5,6), control flow compilation becomes a factor 15 faster than compile & run. If the query is executed a number of times, meta-call is outperformed by control flow compilation (e.g. for (5,5,4), this number is 13). Since in ILP, each query is run on a significant number of examples, these results are very promising.

Table 2. Experiments for conjunctions from a real world application.

	ACE:muta		ACE:bongard		ACE:carcino	
	Timings (seconds)					
	comp	exec	comp	exec	comp	exec
control flow	0.11	0.17	0.7	19.88	2.91	46.52
compile & run	0.24	0.24	3.13	19.46	16.81	44.45
meta-call	-	0.26	-	22.41	-	83.74
	Benchmark Characteristics					
number of queries	2021		9335		48399	
average runs/query	69.51		244.77		103.07	

The real world experiment consists in running the TILDE algorithm [4] from the ILP system ACE [1] on three well-known datasets from the ILP community: Mutagenesis [13], Bongard [6] and Carcinogenesis [12]. During the execution of TILDE, queries are subsequently generated, and every query needs to be run on a subset of the examples. These queries contain only conjunctions; disjunctions are dealt with as query packs in Section 5. Table 2 compares again control flow compilation with compile & run and meta-call. Times are given in seconds. For each data set, *comp* gives the total compilation time (namely the time for compiling all the queries generated by TILDE) and *exec* the total execution time (namely the time to execute all the (compiled) queries). For each dataset, the lower part of Table 2 also gives the number of queries generated and the average number of runs per query.

In the TILDE runs, control flow compilation gains a factor 2 to 6 with respect to usual compilation. Control flow compiled code outperforms classical compiled code for the Mutagenesis dataset, but is about 5% slower for Carcinogenesis (which is still acceptable). When we consider the total time (namely *comp* + *exec*), control flow compilation is clearly the best alternative out of the three for Carcinogenesis. For Bongard, control flow compilation is slightly faster than the other two, which are comparable. Because Mutagenesis has relatively small queries which are run infrequently, meta-call performs best for this dataset.

The results are more pronounced for the artificial benchmarks than for the TILDE ones for several reasons. The artificial queries are longer than the typical TILDE queries; making the artificial queries shorter makes the timings unreliable. During the artificial benchmarks, the time spent in the called goals is very small (only `proceed`), whereas in the TILDE experiments much more time is spent in the predicates, and as such the effect of control flow on the *exec* timing decreases. Another observation is that control flow code uses pointers to the heap, and as the heap garbage collection is currently deactivated, the heap contains all the queries ever generated. This is bad for locality: we have indeed observed that locality can have a large impact on the execution time in the case of control flow compilation. We expect that as soon as the heap garbage collector is adapted and is activated again, the execution times will improve. This line of reasoning is compatible with the fact that the number of queries in Mutagenesis is relatively small, such that locality is better and thus the control flow *exec* timing is better than for normal compilation. Finally, it is important to note that, while meta-call outperforms the other approaches for one of the datasets, its speedup will have to be sacrificed when we want to benefit from removing branches that already succeeded in the query packs approach.

The main goal of control flow compilation was to have a flexible scheme for introducing lazy compilation for query packs, without slowing down execution itself. Our experiments prove that control flow compilation achieves this goal: if the execution times are slower, it is within an acceptable range of 5%, and in all our benchmarks the loss is compensated by the order of magnitude that can be gained for the compilation.

4   Lazy Control Flow Compilation

4.1   Technology

In [3], *lazy compilation* is identified as a kind of *just-in-time* (JIT) compilation or *dynamic compilation*, which is characterized as translation which occurs after a program begins execution. In this paper, we present lazy variants of control flow compilation. The requirement in [3] that the compiler used for JIT compilation should be fast enough is satisfied by our control flow compiler. Our lazy variant implicitly calls the control flow compiler when execution reaches a part of the query that is not yet compiled. As before, we restrict the discussion in this section to queries with conjunctions and disjunctions; the extension to query packs is presented in Section 5.

As with normal control flow compilation, the query is represented by a term on the heap. We introduce a new WAM instruction `lazy_compile`, whose argument is a pointer to the term on the heap that needs compiling when execution reaches this instruction.

Consider the query q :- a(X,Y), b(Y,Z). The initial lazy compiled version of q is

```
allocate 2
lazy_compile &(a(X,Y),b(Y,Z))
```

The `lazy_compile` instruction points to a conjunction: its execution replaces itself by the compiled code for the first conjunct, namely a `cf_call`, and adds for the second conjunct another `lazy_compile` instruction, resulting in:

```
allocate 2
cf_call &a(X,Y)
lazy_compile &b(Y,Z)
```

The execution continues with the newly generated `cf_call` instruction as is expected. After the next execution of `lazy_compile`, the compiled code is equal to code generated without laziness:

```
allocate 2
cf_call &a(X,Y)
cf_deallex &b(Y,Z)
```

Note that lazy compilation overwrites the `lazy_compile` instruction with a `cf_` instruction, and that once we have executed the query for the first time completely, the resulting code is the same as the code produced by non-lazy control flow compilation.

Now, consider the lazy compilation of the query from Figure 1:

```
q :- a(X,Y), ( b(Y,Z) ; c(Y,Z), d(Z,U); e(a,Y) ).
```

Initially, the code is

```
allocate 2
lazy_compile &(a(X,Y),(b(Y,Z);c(Y,Z),d(Z,U);e(a,Y)))
```

The `lazy_compile` changes the code to:

```
allocate 2
cf_call &a(X,Y)
lazy_compile &(b(Y,Z);c(Y,Z),d(Z,U);e(a,Y))
```

Now, `lazy_compile` will compile a disjunction. Where normal (control flow) compilation would generate a `trymeorelse` instruction, we generate a lazy variant of this. The `lazy_trymeorelse` instruction has as its argument the second part of the disjunction, which will be compiled upon failure of the first branch. The instruction is immediately followed by the code of the first branch, which is initially again a `lazy_compile`:

```
allocate 2
cf_call &a(X,Y)
lazy_trymeorelse &(c(Y,Z),d(Z,U);e(a,Y))
lazy_compile &b(Y,Z)
```

Execution continues with the `lazy_trymeorelse`: a special choice point is created such that on backtracking the remaining branches of the disjunction will be compiled in a lazy way. To achieve this, the failure continuation of the choice point is set to a new `lazy_disj_compile` instruction, which behaves similarly to `lazy_compile`. Then, execution continues with the first branch:

```
allocate 2
cf_call &a(X,Y)
lazy_trymeorelse &(c(Y,Z),d(Z,U);e(a,Y))
cf_deallex &b(Y,Z)
```

Upon backtracking to the special choice point created in `lazy_trymeorelse`, the `lazy_disj_compile` instruction continues compilation, and replaces the corresponding `lazy_trymeorelse` by a `trymeorelse` instruction with as argument the address of the code to be generated:

```
    allocate 2
    cf_call &a(X,Y)
    trymeorelse L1
    cf_deallex &b(Y,Z)
L1: lazy_retrymeorelse &(e(a,Y))
    lazy_compile &(c(Y,Z),d(Z,U))
```

Here, `lazy_retrymeorelse` – the lazy variant of `retrymeorelse` – behaves similar to `lazy_trymeorelse`, but instead of creating a special choice point, it alters the existing choice point. It is immediately followed by the code of the next part of the disjunction, which after execution looks as follows:

```
    allocate 2
    cf_call &a(X,Y)
    trymeorelse L1
    cf_deallex &b(Y,Z)
L1: lazy_retrymeorelse  &(e(a,Y))
    cf_call &c(Y,Z)
    cf_deallex &d(Z,U)
```

Upon backtracking, `lazy_retrymorelse` is overwritten, and a `trustmeorelse` is generated for the last branch of the disjunction, followed by a `lazy_compile` for this branch:

```
    allocate 2
    cf_call &a(X,Y)
    trymeorelse L1
    cf_deallex &b(Y,Z)
L1: retrymeorelse L2
    cf_call &c(Y,Z)
    cf_deallex &d(Z,U)
L2: trustmeorelsefail
    lazy_compile &e(a,Y)
```

After the execution of the last branch, we end up with the full control flow code.

The lazy compilation as we described it proceeds from goal to goal. Other granularities have been implemented and evaluated as well (see Table 3):

- *Per conjunction:* All the goals in a conjunction are compiled at once. This avoids constant switching between the compiler and the execution by compiling bigger chunks.
- *Per disjunction:* All the branches of a disjunction are compiled at once up to the point where a new disjunction occurs. This approach is reasonable, because all branches of a disjunction will by tried (and thus compiled) eventually.

Besides the overhead of switching between compiler and execution, these approaches might also generate different code depending on the execution itself. When a goal inside a disjunction fails, the next branch of the conjunction is executed, and newly compiled code is inserted at the end of the existing code. When in a later stage the same goal succeeds, the rest of the branch is compiled and added to the end of the code, and a jump to the new code is generated. These jumps cost extra emulator cycles and decrease locality of the code. Lazy compilation per goal can in the worst case have as many jumps as there are goals in the disjunctions. Compiling per conjunction can have as many jumps as there are disjunctions. If a disjunction is completely compiled in one step, each branch of the disjunction ends in a jump to the next disjunction.

4.2   Evaluation

The experiments of Table 3 use some of the artificial benchmarks from Table 1. Timings (in milliseconds) are given for the different settings of the lazy compilation. The timings report the time needed for one execution of the query, thus including the time of its lazy compilation. The last line gives the times for the non-lazy control flow compilation[2]. Lazy compilation per goal clearly has a substantial overhead, whereas the other settings have a small overhead. We also measured the execution times for the three lazy alternatives once they are compiled: they were all equal, and are therefore not included in the table.

Table 3. Lazy compilation for several kinds of disjunctions. (timings in milliseconds).

| | (5,5,4) | (10,5,4) |
	cexec	cexec
per goal	55	111
per conj	34	60
per disj	32	59
control flow	28	59

The main message here is that the introduction of laziness in the control flow compilation does not degrade performance much, and that it opens perspectives

---

[2] Note that these timings are slightly higher than the sum of *comp* and *exec* in Table 1. This is probably due to the fact that both experiments are run in different circumstances with different locality.

for query packs compilation: (1) lazy compilation is fast; (2) in non-artificial benchmarks, some branches will never have to be compiled due to failure of goals, whereas in our artificial setting all goals in the queries succeed; (3) in the long run, it allows incremental compilation: if we would allow open ended queries (queries that end with an uninstantiated call), the ILP system can refine the query later by further instantiating the open end, and lazy compilation will automatically compile the new part of the query when it is reached.

5   Lazy Control Flow Compilation for Query Packs

5.1   Technology

So far, we restricted our (lazy) control flow compilation approach to queries containing conjunctions and 'ordinary' disjunctions. However, the main motivation for this work was optimizing the execution of *query packs* [5]. These query packs represent a set of (similar) queries which are to be executed, laid out in a disjunction. The semantics of this disjunction is implemented by dedicated WAM instructions [5], as explained in Section 2. These instructions replace the instructions generated for encoding ordinary disjunctions.

Extending control flow compilation to handle these query packs is rather straightforward. The difference between the compilation of disjunctions handled so far and the disjunctions of a query pack is that the dedicated WAM instructions have to be generated as control flow instructions for the disjunctions. Introducing laziness in control flow compilation for query packs requires more changes. Originally, query packs used static data structures which were allocated once, since all the information on the size and contents of these data structures was known at compile time. However, when laziness is introduced, only parts of the query pack are analyzed, and so the data structures need to be dynamic and expandable.

To facilitate the implementation of lazy control flow compilation for query packs, we chose to implement only one of the lazy variants described in Section 4. Since the experiments showed little difference between all the variants (except for lazy compilation per goal), this seems like a reasonable decision. We chose to compile one complete disjunction at a time, because this makes integration with the existing query pack data structures easier.

5.2   Experiments

The experiments are again performed with the real world applications from Table 2. Instead of a set of queries (the conjunctions of Table 2), TILDE now generates query packs. These query packs are then compiled and finally executed for a subset of the examples. The use of query packs allows us to set up a larger experiment (in ILP terms: we now use a lookahead of 3 instead of 2), which results in more and longer queries.

The timings in Table 4 are in seconds: for compile & run and control flow, we give the sum of the total compilation time and the total execution time; for

Table 4. Experiments for query packs from a real world application.

	ACE:muta	ACE:bongard	ACE:carcino
	Timings (seconds)		
	(comp + exec = cexec)		
control flow	0.13+0.08 = 0.21	1.02 +23.75 = 24.77	2.92+7.07 = 9.99
lazy control flow	0.24	24.0	8.15
compile & run	0.69+0.11 = 0.80	12.27+22.48 = 34.75	47.97+5.24 = 53.21
	Query Pack Characteristics		
Nb. of packs	50	4	28
Nb. of queries	6010	63668	204527
Avg. runs/pack	61.52	723.50	134.67
	Code size reduction with lazy compilation		
Reduction	17.0 %	57.2 %	61.4 %

lazy control flow compilation, no distinction can be made, and so the total time for compilation and execution is given.

First, we compare control flow compilation with compile & run. For query packs, control flow compilation is also up to an order of magnitude faster than classical compilation, even though the ilProlog system already has a compiler that is optimized for dealing with large disjunctions [16] (in particular for the classification of variables in query packs). The execution times show the same characteristics as in the experiments with the conjunctions in Table 2: control flow has a faster execution in the case of Mutagenesis, whereas in the other two cases it is a bit slower. For the ILP application, the total time must be considered: the total time of control flow is up to a factor 4 faster than compile & run.

Next, Table 3 shows that lazy compilation has some overhead, but we hoped that it would be compensated by avoiding the compilation of failing parts in the query packs. For Bongard and Carcinogenesis, lazy control flow timings are indeed better than for the plain control flow. The information about the code size reduction in the case of the lazy variant confirms the idea that we gain by avoiding the compilation of parts of the query packs that fail for all the examples. Also, the locality is better when less code is generated. Mutagenesis is a smaller benchmark with less code reduction, and so the compilation/execution ratio is large. This explains why the overhead of interleaved compilation with execution is not compensated for.

The resulting timings confirm that lazy control flow compilation is the best approach for query packs.

6   Conclusion and Future Work

This paper presents a new method for faster compilation and execution of dynamically generated queries: control flow compilation is up to an order of magnitude faster than classical compilation, while the execution times are similar. To our knowledge, this is also the first time that lazy compilation (as an instance of just-in-time compilation [3]) is used in the context of logic programming, in particular for queries.

The benefits of control flow compilation versus classical compilation are clear and are confirmed in the context of real world applications from the ILP community. For larger benchmarks, the lazy variant gives the best results in combination with query packs.

For control flow compilation itself, the main future work will consist in extending the garbage collector of the ilProlog system to support control flow compiled code. This extension can be realized within the current garbage collector, and mainly requires a coding effort. We expect that garbage collection improves the locality and the execution times of queries. It also has to be investigated whether it is interesting to put the control flow code on the heap, thus making code garbage collection of queries a part of the heap garbage collection process.

We also plan to adapt (lazy) control flow compilation to extensions of query packs reported in [15]. We expect control flow compilation to yield the same speedups for these execution mechanisms as for query packs. However, the impact of laziness needs to be investigated.

Finally, this work allows us to investigate how incremental generation and compilation of queries can be supported in an ILP system.

Acknowledgments

Remko Tronçon is supported by the Institute for the Promotion of Innovation by Science and Technology in Flanders (I.W.T.). This work is partially supported by the GOA 'Inductive Knowledge Bases'. We are indebted to Bart Demoen for his significant contributions to the achievements presented in this paper.

References

1. The ACE data mining system. http://www.cs.kuleuven.ac.be/~dtai/ACE/.
2. H. Ait-Kaci. The WAM: a (real) tutorial. Technical Report 5, DEC Paris Research Report, 1990. See also: http://www.isg.sfu.ca/~hak/documents/wam.html.
3. J. Aycock. A brief history of just-in-time. *ACM Computing Surveys*, 35(2):97–113, 2003.
4. H. Blockeel and L. De Raedt. Top-down induction of first order logical decision trees. *Artificial Intelligence*, 101(1-2):285–297, June 1998.
5. H. Blockeel, L. Dehaspe, B. Demoen, G. Janssens, J. Ramon, and H. Vandecasteele. Improving the efficiency of Inductive Logic Programming through the use of query packs. *Journal of Artificial Intelligence*, 16:135–166, 2002.
6. L. De Raedt and W. Van Laer. Inductive constraint logic. In K. P. Jantke, T. Shinohara, and T. Zeugmann, editors, *Proceedings of the Sixth International Workshop on Algorithmic Learning Theory*, volume 997 of *Lecture Notes in Artificial Intelligence*, pages 80–94. Springer-Verlag, 1995.

7. L. Dehaspe and H. Toivonen. Discovery of frequent datalog patterns. *Data Mining and Knowledge Discovery*, 3(1):7–36, 1999.
8. S. Kramer. Structural regression trees. In *Proceedings of the Thirteenth National Conference on Artificial Intelligence*, pages 812–819, Cambridge/Menlo Park, 1996. AAAI Press/MIT Press.
9. S. Muggleton. Inverse entailment and Progol. *New Generation Computing, Special issue on Inductive Logic Programming*, 13(3-4):245–286, 1995.
10. J. Quinlan. Learning logical definitions from relations. *Machine Learning*, 5:239–266, 1990.
11. A. Srinivasan. The Aleph manual. http://web.comlab.ox.ac.uk/oucl/research/ areas/machlearn/Aleph/.
12. A. Srinivasan, R. King, and D. Bristol. An assessment of ILP-assisted models for toxicology and the PTE-3 experiment. In *Proceedings of the Ninth International Workshop on Inductive Logic Programming*, volume 1634 of *Lecture Notes in Artificial Intelligence*, pages 291–302. Springer-Verlag, 1999.
13. A. Srinivasan, S. Muggleton, M. Sternberg, and R. King. Theories for mutagenicity: A study in first-order and feature-based induction. *Artificial Intelligence*, 85(1,2):277–299, 1996.
14. R. Tronçon, G. Janssens, and B. Demoen. Alternatives for compile & run in the WAM. In *Proceedings of CICLOPS 2003: Colloquium on Implementation of Constraint and LOgic Programming Systems*, pages 45–58. University of Porto, 2003. Technical Report DCC-2003-05, DCC - FC & LIACC, University of Porto, December 2003. http://www.cs.kuleuven.ac.be/cgi-bin-dtai/publ_info.pl?id=41065.
15. R. Tronçon, H. Vandecasteele, J. Struyf, B. Demoen, and G. Janssens. Query optimization: Combining query packs and the once-tranformation. In *Inductive Logic Programming, 13th International Conference, ILP 2003, Szeged, Hungary, Short Presentations*, pages 105–115, 2003. http://www.cs.kuleuven.ac.be/cgi-bin-dtai/publ_info.pl?id=40938.
16. H. Vandecasteele, B. Demoen, and G. Janssens. Compiling large disjunctions. In I. de Castro Dutra, E. Pontelli, and V. S. Costa, editors, *First International Conference on Computational Logic : Workshop on Parallelism and Implementation Technology for (Constraint) Logic Programming Languages*, pages 103–121. Imperial College, 2000. http://www.cs.kuleuven.ac.be/cgi-bin-dtai/publ_info.pl?id=32065.
17. D. H. D. Warren. An abstract Prolog instruction set. Technical Report 309, SRI, 1983.

Speculative Computations
in Or-Parallel Tabled Logic Programs

Ricardo Rocha[1], Fernando Silva[1], and Vítor Santos Costa[2]

[1] DCC-FC & LIACC
University of Porto, Portugal
{ricroc,fds}@ncc.up.pt
[2] COPPE Systems & LIACC
Federal University of Rio de Janeiro, Brazil
vitor@cos.ufrj.br

Abstract. Pruning operators, such as *cut*, are important to develop efficient logic programs as they allow programmers to reduce the search space and thus discard unnecessary computations. For parallel systems, the presence of pruning operators introduces the problem of *speculative computations*. A computation is named speculative if it can be pruned during parallel evaluation, therefore resulting in wasted effort when compared to sequential execution. In this work we discuss the problems behind the management of speculative computations in or-parallel tabled logic programs. In parallel tabling, not only the answers found for the query goal may not be valid, but also answers found for tabled predicates may be invalidated. The problem here is even more serious because to achieve an efficient implementation it is required to have the set of valid tabled answers released as soon as possible. To deal with this, we propose a strategy to deliver tabled answers as soon as it is found that they are safe from being pruned, and present its implementation in the OPTYap parallel tabling system.

1 Introduction

Logic programming is a programming paradigm based on Horn Clause Logic, a subset of First Order Logic. Given a theory (or program) and a query, execution of logic programs uses a simple theorem prover that performs refutation in order to search for alternative ways to satisfy the query. Prolog implements a refutation strategy called SLD resolution. Further, subgoals in a query are always solved from left to right, and that clauses that match a subgoal are always applied in the textual order as they appear in the program.

In order to make Prolog an useful programming language, Prolog designers were forced to introduce features not found within First Order Logic. One such feature is the cut operator. The cut operator adds a limited form of control to the execution by pruning alternatives from the computation. Cut is an asymmetric pruning operator because it only prunes alternatives to the right. Some Prolog systems also implement symmetric pruning operators, with a generic name of

B. Demoen and V. Lifschitz (Eds.): ICLP 2004, LNCS 3132, pp. 254–268, 2004.

commit. In practice, pruning operators are almost always required when developing actual programs, because they allow programmers to reduce the search space and thus discard unnecessary computation.

Because their semantics are purely operational, pruning operators cause difficulties when considering alternative execution strategies for logic programs. The implementation of or-parallel systems is one example [1–4]. Namely, it has been observed that the presence of pruning operators during parallel execution introduces the problem of *speculative computations*. Ciepielewski defines speculative computations as *work which would not be done in a system with one processor* [5]. Alternatives picked for parallel execution, may later be pruned away by a cut. Earlier execution of such computations results in wasted effort when compared to sequential execution.

Pruning operators also raise questions in the context of tabling based execution models for Prolog. The basic idea behind tabling is straightforward: programs are evaluated by storing newly found answers of current subgoals in an appropriate data space, called the *table space*. New calls to a predicate check this table to verify whether they are repeated. If they are, answers are recalled from the table instead of the call being re-evaluated against the program clauses.

We can consider two types of cut operations in a tabling environment: cuts that do not prune alternatives in tabled predicates – *inner cut* operations, and cuts that prune alternatives in tabled predicates – *outer cut* operations. Inner cuts can be easily implemented in sequential systems. On the other hand, because tabling intrinsically changes the left-to-right semantics of Prolog, outer cuts present major difficulties, both in terms of semantics and of implementation.

In this work we address the problem of how to do inner pruning on systems that combine tabling with or-parallelism. Our interest stems from our work in the OPTYap system [6], to our knowledge the first available system that can exploit parallelism from tabled programs. Our experience has shown that many applications do require support for inner pruning. In contrast, outer pruning is not widely used in current tabling systems. Unfortunately, new problems arise even when performing inner pruning in parallel systems. Namely, speculative answers found for tabled predicates may later be invalidated. In the worst case, tabling such speculative answers may allow them to be consumed elsewhere in the tree, generating in turn more speculative computation and eventually cause wrong answers to occur. Answers for tabled predicates *can only be tabled when they are safe from being pruned.* On the other hand, finding and consuming answers is the natural way to get a tabled computation going forward. Delaying the consumption of valid answers too much may compromise such flow. Therefore, tabled answers *should be released as soon as it is found that they are not speculative.*

The main contribution of this paper is a design that allows the correct and efficient implementation of inner pruning in an or-parallel tabling system. To do so, we generalise Ali and Karlsson cut scheme [3], which prunes useless work as early as possible, to tabling systems. Our design allows speculative answers to be stored in advance into the table, but its availability is delayed. Answers will only be made available when proved to be not speculative.

The remainder of the paper is organised as follows. First, we discuss speculative computations in or-parallel systems and introduce the cut scheme currently implemented in OPTYap. Next, we discuss the problems arising with speculative tabled computations. Initially, we introduce the basic tabling definitions and the inner and outer cuts operations. After that, we present the support actually implemented in OPTYap to deal with speculative tabled computations. We end by outlining some conclusions.

2   Cut Within the Or-Parallel Environment

Cut is a system built-in predicate that is represented by the symbol "!". Its execution results in pruning all the alternatives to the right of the current branch up to the scope of the cut. In a sequential system, cut only prunes alternatives whose exploitation has not been started yet. This does not hold for or-parallel systems, as cut can prune alternatives that are being exploited by other workers or that have already been completely exploited. Therefore, the cut semantics in a parallel environment introduces new problems. First, a pruning operation cannot always be completely performed if the branch executing the cut is not leftmost, because the operation itself may be pruned by the execution of other pruning operation in a branch to the left. Similarly, an answer for the query goal in a non-leftmost branch may not be valid. Last, when pruning we should stop the workers exploiting the pruned branches.

Ali showed that speculative computations can be completely banned from a parallel system if proper rules are applied [1]. However, such rules severely restrict parallelism. Hence, most parallel systems allow speculative computations. Speculative computations can be controlled more or less tightly. Ideally, we would prune all computations as soon as they become useless. In practice, deciding if a computation is still speculative or already useless can be quite complex when nested cuts with intersecting scopes are considered. We next discuss how cut executes in OPTYap (later we will discuss how cut affects the table).

2.1   Cut in OPTYap

The OPTYap system builds on the or-parallel system YapOr [7] and on the tabling engine YapTab [8]. YapOr is based on the environment copying model for shared memory machines [9]. YapTab is a sequential tabling engine that extends Yap's execution model to support tabled evaluation for definite programs. YapTab's design is largely based on the ground-breaking XSB logic programming system [10], which implements the SLG-WAM [11]. OPTYap's execution model considers tabling as the base component of the system. Each computational worker behaves as a full sequential tabling engine. The or-parallel component of the system is triggered to allow synchronised access to the shared part of the search space or to schedule work.

OPTYap currently implements a cut scheme based on the ideas presented by Ali and Karlsson [3], designed to prune useless work as early as possible. The guiding rule is: *we cannot prune branches that would not be pruned if our own branch will be pruned by a branch to the left.* Thus, a worker executing cut must go up in the tree until it reaches either the *scope of the cut*, or, a node with *workers executing in branches to the left.* A worker may not be able to complete a cut if there are workers in branches to the left, because such workers can themselves prune the current cut. Such incomplete cuts are called *left pending.* In OPTYap, a cut is left pending on the youngest node $\mathcal{N}$ that has left branches. A pending cut can only be resumed when all workers to the left backtrack to $\mathcal{N}$. It will then be the responsibility of the last worker backtracking to $\mathcal{N}$ to continue the execution of the pending cut.

While going up, a worker may also find workers in branches to the right. If so, it sends them a signal informing that their branches have been pruned. Such workers must backtrack to the shared part of the tree and start searching for new work. Note that even if a cut is left pending in a node $\mathcal{N}$, there may be branches, older than $\mathcal{N}$, that correspond to useless work. OPTYap prunes these branches immediately. To illustrate how these branches can be detected we present in Fig. 1 a small example taken from [3]. For simplicity, the example ignores indexing and assumes that a node is always allocated for predicates defined by more than one clause. To better understand the example, we index the repeated calls to the same predicate by call order. For instance, the node representing the first call to predicate p is referred as p_1, the second as p_2 and successively. We also write $p_n^{(i)}$ to denote the *ith* alternative of node p_n. Note also that we use the symbol ! to mark the alternatives corresponding to clauses with cuts.

Figure 1(a) shows the initial configuration, where a worker $\mathcal{W}$ is computing the branch corresponding to $[p_1^{(1)}, q_1^{(1)}, p_2^{(1)}, q_2^{(2)}, p_3^{(2)}]$. Its current goal is "$!(p_2), !(p_1)$", where $!(p_2)$ means a cut with the scope p_2 and $!(p_1)$ means a cut with the scope p_1. There are only two branches to the left, corresponding to alternatives $p_3^{(1)}$ and $q_2^{(1)}$. If there are workers within alternative $p_3^{(1)}$, then $\mathcal{W}$ cannot execute any pruning at all because $p_3^{(1)}$ is marked as containing cuts. A potential execution of a pruning operation in $p_3^{(1)}$ will invalidate any cut executed in $p_3^{(2)}$ by $\mathcal{W}$. Therefore, $\mathcal{W}$ saves a cut marker in p_3 to indicate a pending cut operation (Fig. 1(b)). A cut marker is a two field data structure containing information about the scope of the cut and about the alternative of the node which executed the cut.

Let's now assume that there are no workers in alternative $p_3^{(1)}$, but there are in alternative $q_2^{(1)}$. Alternative $q_2^{(1)}$ is not marked as containing cuts, but the continuation of q_2 contains two pruning operations, $!(p_2)$ and $!(p_1)$. The worker $\mathcal{W}$ first executes $!(p_2)$ in order to prune $q_2^{(3)}$ and $p_2^{(2)}$. This is a safe pruning operation because any pruning from $q_2^{(1)}$ will also prune $q_2^{(3)}$ and $p_2^{(2)}$. At the same time $\mathcal{W}$ stores a cut marker in q_2 to signal the pruning operation done. As we will see, for such cases, the cut marker is used to prevent unsafe future pruning operations from the same branch. Consider the continuation of the situation, $\mathcal{W}$

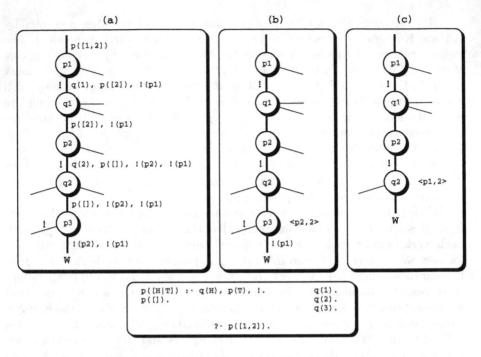

Fig. 1. Pruning in the or-parallel environment

tries to execute $!(p_1)$ in order to prune $q_1^{(2)}$, $q_1^{(3)}$ and $p_1^{(2)}$. However, this is a dangerous operation. A worker in $q_2^{(1)}$ may execute the previous pruning operation, $!(p_2)$, pruning $\mathcal{W}$'s branch but not $q_1^{(2)}$, $q_1^{(3)}$ or $p_1^{(2)}$. Hence, there is no guarantee that the second pruning, $!(p_1)$, is safe. The cut marker stored in q_2 is a warning that this possibility exists. So, instead of doing pruning immediately, $\mathcal{W}$ updates the cut marker stored in q_2 to indicate the new pending cut operation (Fig. 1(c)).

2.2 Tree Representation

To represent the shared part of the search tree, OPTYap follows the Muse approach [9] and uses *or-frames*. When sharing work, an or-frame is added per choice point being shared, in such a way that the complete set of or-frames form a tree that represents the shared part of the search tree. Or-frames are used to synchronise access to the unexploited alternatives in a shared choice point, and to store scheduling data. By default, an or-frame contains the following fields: the OrFr_lock field supports a busy-wait locking mutex mechanism that guarantees atomic updates to the or-frame data; the OrFr_alt field stores the pointer to the next unexploited alternative in the choice point; the OrFr_members field is a bitmap that stores the set of workers sharing the choice point; the OrFr_node field is a back pointer to the correspondent choice point; and the OrFr_next field is a pointer to the parent or-frame on the current branch.

Identifying workers on left branches or checking whether a branch is leftmost requires a mechanism to represent the relative positions of workers in the search tree. Our implementation uses a $branch()$ matrix, where each entry $branch(w, d)$ corresponds to the alternative taken by worker w in the shared node with depth d of its current branch. Figure 2 shows a small example that clarifies the correspondence between a particular search tree and its matrix representation. Note that we only need to represent the shared part of a search tree in the matrix. This is due to the fact that the position of each worker in the private part of the search tree is not relevant when computing relative positions.

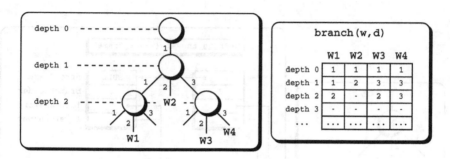

Fig. 2. Search tree representation

To correctly consult or update the branch matrix, we need to know the depth of each shared node. We thus introduced a new data field in the or-frame data structure, the OrFr_depth field, that holds the depth of the corresponding node. By using the OrFr_depth field and the OrFr_members bitmap of each or-frame to consult the branch matrix, we can easily identify the workers in a node that are in branches at the left or at the right the current branch of a given worker.

Let us suppose that a worker W wants to check whether it is leftmost or at which node it ceases from being leftmost. W should start from the youngest shared node $\mathcal{N}$ on its branch, read the OrFr_members bitmap from the or-frame associated with $\mathcal{N}$ to determine the workers sharing the node, and investigate the branch matrix to determine the alternative number taken by each worker sharing $\mathcal{N}$. If W finds an alternative number less than its own, then W is not leftmost. Otherwise, W is leftmost in $\mathcal{N}$ and will repeat the same procedure at the next upper node on branch and so on until reaching the root node or a node where it is not leftmost.

2.3 Pending Answers

OPTYap also builds on a mechanism originally designed for a problem in or-parallel systems: an answer for the query goal may not be valid, if the branch where the answer was found may be pruned. At the end of the computation, only valid answers should be seen.

OPTYap addresses this problem by storing a new answer in the youngest node where the current branch is not leftmost. A new data field was therefore introduced in the or-frame data structure, the OrFr_qg_answers field. This field allows access to the set of pending answers stored in the corresponding node. Also, new data structures store the pending answers that are being found for the query goal in hand. Figure 3 details the data structures used to efficiently keep track of pending answers. Answers from the same branch are grouped into a common top data structure. The top data structures are organised by reverse branch order. This organisation simplifies the pruning of answers that became invalid in consequence of a cut operation to the left.

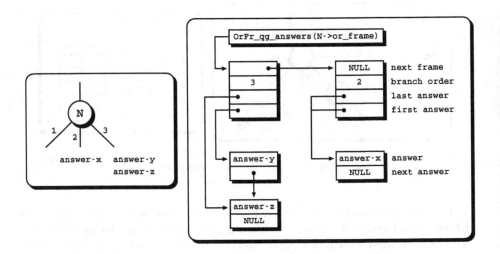

Fig. 3. Dealing with pending answers

When a node $\mathcal{N}$ is fully exploited and its corresponding or-frame is being deallocated, the whole set of pending answers stored in $\mathcal{N}$ can be easily linked together and moved to the next node where the current branch is not leftmost. At the end, the set of answers stored in the root node are the set of valid answers for the given query goal.

3   Cut Within the Or-Parallel Tabling Environment

Extending the or-parallel system to include tabling introduces further complexity into cut's semantics. Dealing with speculative tabled computations and guaranteeing the correctness of tabling semantics, without compromising the performance of the or-parallel tabling system, requires very efficient implementation mechanisms. In this section, we present the OPTYap's approach. Before we start, we provide a brief overview of the basic tabling definitions and distinguish the two types of cut operations in a tabling environment: inner cuts and outer cuts.

3.1   Basic Tabling Definitions

Tabling is about storing intermediate answers for subgoals so that they can be reused when a repeated subgoal appears. Whenever a tabled subgoal S is first called, an entry for S is allocated in the table space. This entry will collect all the answers found for S. Repeated calls to *variants* of S are resolved by consuming the answers already stored in the table. Meanwhile, as new answers are generated, they are inserted into the table and returned to all variant subgoals. Within this model, the nodes in the search space are classified as either *generator nodes*, corresponding to first calls to tabled subgoals, *consumer nodes*, corresponding to variant calls to tabled subgoals, and *interior nodes*, corresponding to non-tabled subgoals.

Tabling evaluation has four main types of operations for definite programs. The *tabled subgoal call* operation checks if the subgoal is in the table and if not, inserts it and allocates a new generator node. Otherwise, allocates a consumer node and starts consuming the available answers. The *new answer* operation verifies whether a newly generated answer is already in the table, and if not, inserts it. The *answer resolution* operation consumes the next unconsumed answer from the table, if any. The *completion* operation determines whether a tabled subgoal is completely evaluated, and if not, schedules a possible resolution to continue the execution.

The table space can be accessed in different ways: to look up if a subgoal is in the table, and if not insert it; to verify whether a newly found answer is already in the table, and if not insert it; and to pick up answers to consumer nodes. Hence, a correct design of the algorithms to access and manipulate the table data is a critical issue to obtain an efficient implementation. Our implementation uses tries as the basis for tables, as proposed by Ramakrishnan *et al.* in [12].

Figure 4 shows the general table structure for a tabled predicate. Table lookup starts from the *table entry* data structure. Each table predicate has one such structure, which is allocated at compilation time. Calls to the predicate will always access the table starting from this point.

The table entry points to a tree of trie nodes, the *subgoal trie structure*. More precisely, each different call to the tabled predicate in hand corresponds to a unique path through the subgoal trie structure. Such a path always starts from the table entry, follows a sequence of subgoal trie data units, the *subgoal trie nodes*, and terminates at a leaf data structure, the *subgoal frame*.

Each subgoal frame stores information about the subgoal, namely an entry point to its *answer trie structure*. Each unique path through the answer trie data units, the *answer trie nodes*, corresponds to a different answer to the entry subgoal. To obtain the set of available answers for a tabled subgoal, the leaf answer nodes are chained in a linked list in insertion time order, so that we can recover answers in the same order they were inserted. The subgoal frame points to the first and last answer in this list. Thus, a consumer node only needs to point at the leaf node for its last consumed answer, and consumes more answers just by following the chain. To load an answer, the trie nodes are traversed in bottom-up order and the answer is reconstructed.

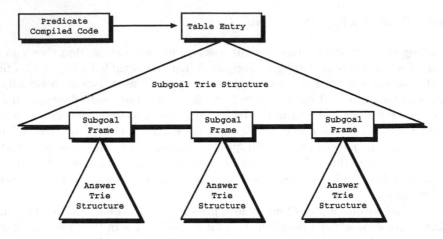

Fig. 4. Using tries to organise the table space

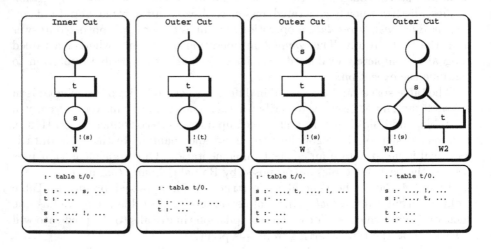

Fig. 5. The two types of cut operations in a tabling environment

3.2   Inner and Outer Cut Operations

We consider two types of pruning in a tabling environment: cuts that do not prune alternatives in tabled predicates – *inner cut* operations, and cuts that prune alternatives in tabled predicates – *outer cut* operations. In Fig. 5 we illustrate four different situations corresponding to inner and outer cut operations. Below each illustration we present a block of Prolog code that may lead to such situations. For simplicity, we assume that t is the unique tabled predicate defined and that the "..." parts do not include t. Note that the rightmost situation only occurs if a parallel tabling environment is considered, as otherwise t will only be called if the cut operation in the first alternative of s is not executed.

Cut semantics for outer cut operations is still an open problem. A major problem is that of pruning generator nodes. Pruning generator nodes cancels its further completion and puts the table space in an inconsistent state. For sequential tabling, a simple approach is to delete the whole table data structures related with the pruned subgoal and recompute it from the beginning when it reappears. This can be safely done because when a generator is pruned all variant consumers are also pruned. On the other hand, for parallel tabling, it is possible that generators will execute earlier, and in a different branch than in sequential execution. In fact, different workers may execute the generator and the consumer goals. Workers may have consumer nodes while not having the corresponding generator nodes in their branches. Conversely, the owner of a generator node can have consumer nodes being executed by several different workers.

The intricate dependencies in a parallel tabled evaluation makes pruning a very complex problem. A possible solution to this problem can be moving the generator's role to a non-pruned dependent consumer node, if any, in order to allow further exploitation of the generator's unexploited branches. Such a solution will require that the other non-pruned consumer nodes recompute and update their dependencies relatively to the new generator node. Otherwise, if all dependent consumer nodes are also pruned, we can suspend the execution stacks and the table data structures of the pruned subgoal and try to resume them when the next variant call takes place. Further research is still necessary in order to study the combination of pruning and parallel tabling. Currently, OPTYap still does not support outer cut operations and for such cases execution is aborted. Outer cut operations are detected when a worker moves up in the tree either because it is executing a cut operation or it has received a signal informing that its branch have been pruned away by another worker.

3.3 Detecting Speculative Tabled Answers

As mentioned before, a main goal in the implementation of speculative tabling is to allow storing valid answers immediately. We would like to maintain the same performance as for the programs without cut operators. In this subsection, we introduce and describe the data structures and implementation extensions required to efficiently detect if a tabled answer is speculative or not.

We introduced a global bitmap register named GLOBAL_pruning_workers to keep track of the workers that are executing branches that contain cut operators and that, in consequence, may prune the current goal. Additionally, each worker maintains a local register, LOCAL_safe_scope, that references the youngest node that cannot be pruned by any pruning operation executed by itself.

The correct manipulation of these new registers is achieved by introducing a new instruction clause_with_cuts to mark the blocks of code that include cut instructions. During compilation, the code generated for the clauses containing cut operators is extended to include the clause_with_cuts instruction so that it is the first instruction to be executed for such clauses. When a worker loads a clause_with_cuts instruction, it executes the clause_with_cuts() procedure.

Figure 6 details the pseudo-code that implements the clause_with_cuts() procedure. It sets the worker's bit in the GLOBAL_pruning_workers register and, if the LOCAL_safe_scope register is younger than the current node, it updates the LOCAL_safe_scope register to refer to the current node. The current node is the resulting top node if a pruning operation takes place in the clause in hand.

```
clause_with_cuts() {
    if (LOCAL_safe_scope == NULL) {                    // first time here
        insert_into_bitmap(GLOBAL_pruning_workers, WORKER_id)
        LOCAL_safe_scope = B  // B is a pointer to the current choice point
    } else if (LOCAL_safe_scope is younger than B) {
        LOCAL_safe_scope = B
    }
}
```

Fig. 6. Pseudo-code for clause_with_cuts()

When a worker finds a new answer for a tabled subgoal, it first inserts it into the table space and then checks if the answer is safe from being pruned. When this is the case, the answer is inserted at the end of the list of available answers, as usual. Otherwise, if it is found that the answer can be pruned by another worker, its availability is delayed. Figure 7 presents the pseudo-code that implements the checking procedure.

```
speculative_tabled_answer(generator node G) {    // G is the generator...
    prune_wks = GLOBAL_pruning_workers  // ...for the answer being checked
    delete_from_bitmap(prune_wks, WORKER_id)
    if (prune_wks is not empty) {          // there are workers that may...
        or_fr = youngest_or_frame()        // ...execute pruning operations
        depth = OrFr_depth(or_fr)
        scope_depth = OrFr_depth(G->or_frame)
        while (depth > scope_depth) {          // check the branch till...
            alt_number = branch(WORKER_id, depth)        // ...the generator
            for (w = 0; w < number_workers; w++) {
                if (w is in prune_wks && w is in OrFr_members(or_fr) &&
                    branch(w, depth) < alt_number &&
                    OrFr_node(or_fr) is younger than LOCAL_safe_scope(w))
                    return or_fr       // the answer can be pruned by worker w
            }
            or_fr = OrFr_next(or_fr)
            depth = OrFr_depth(or_fr)
        }
    }
    return NULL                         // the answer is safe from being pruned
}
```

Fig. 7. Pseudo-code for speculative_tabled_answer()

The procedure starts by determining if there are workers that may execute pruning operations. If so, it checks the safeness of the branch where the tabled answer was found. The branch only needs to be checked until the corresponding generator node, as otherwise it would be an outer cut operation. A branch is found to be safe if it is leftmost, or if the workers in the branches to the left cannot prune it. If it is found that the answer being checked can be speculative, the procedure returns the or-frame that corresponds to the youngest node where the answer can be pruned by a worker in a left branch. That or-frame is where the answer should be *left pending*. Otherwise, if it is found that the answer is safe, the procedure returns NULL.

3.4   Pending Tabled Answers

Tabled answers are inserted in advance into the table space. However, if a tabled answer is found to be speculative, its insertion in the list of available answers is delayed and the answer is left pending. This prevents unsafe answers to be consumed elsewhere in the tree. Only when it is found that a pending answer is safe from being pruned, it is released as a valid answer and inserted at the end of the list of available answers for the subgoal. Dealing with pending tabled answers requires efficient support to allow that the operations of pruning or releasing pending answers are efficiently performed.

Remember that speculative tabled answers are left pending in nodes. To allow access to the set of pending answers for a node, a new data field was introduced in the or-frame data structure, the OrFr_tg_answers field. New data structures were also introduced to efficiently keep track of the pending answers being found for the several tabled subgoals. Figure 8 details that data structure organisation.

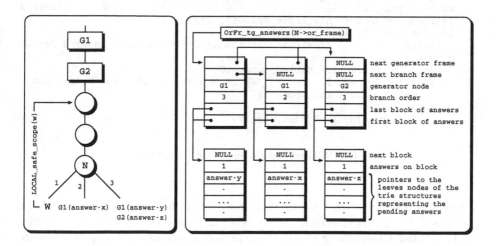

Fig. 8. Dealing with pending tabled answers

The figure shows a situation where three tabled answers, answer-x, answer-y and answer-z, were found to be speculative and therefore have all been left pending in a common node $\mathcal{N}$. $\mathcal{N}$ is the youngest node where a worker in a left branch, $\mathcal{W}$ in the figure, holds a LOCAL_safe_scope register pointing to a node older than $\mathcal{N}$.

Pending answers found for the same subgoal and from the same branch are addressed by a common top data structure. As the answers in the figure were found in different subgoal/branch pairs, three top data structures were required. answer-x, answer-y and answer-z were found, respectively, in branches 2, 3 and 3 for the subgoals corresponding to generator nodes $\mathcal{G}_1$, $\mathcal{G}_1$ and $\mathcal{G}_2$. These data structures are organised in older to younger generator order and by reverse branch order when they are for the same generator. Hence, each data structure contains two types of pointers to follow the chain of structures, one points to the structure that corresponds to the next younger generator node, while the other points to the structure that corresponds to the next branch within the same generator.

Blocks of answers address the set of pending answers for a subgoal/branch pair. Each block points to a fixed number of answers. By linking the blocks we can have a large number of answers for the same subgoal/branch pair. Note that the block data structure does not hold the representation of a pending answer, only a pointer to the leaf node of the answer trie structure representing the pending answer. As we will see, with this simple scheme, we can easily differentiate between occurrences of the same speculative answer in different branches. Figure 9 shows the procedure that OPTYap executes when a tabled answer is found.

```
tabled_answer(answer A, generator node G) {      // G is the generator...
    sf = subgoal_frame(G)                         // ...for the answer A
    leaf_node = insert_into_table_space(A, sf)
    if (leaf_node is a valid answer) {
        fail()            // already in the list of available answers for sf
    } else {
        or_fr = speculative_tabled_answer(G)
        if (or_fr == NULL)           // the answer is safe from being pruned
            valid_answer(leaf_node, sf)
        else
            left_pending(leaf_node, or_fr)
    }
}
```

Fig. 9. Pseudo-code for tabled_answer()

The procedure starts by inserting the answer in the table space. Then, it verifies if the answer is already tabled as a valid answer and, if so, the execution fails as usual. Otherwise, it checks if the answer is safe from being pruned. Being this the case, the answer is tabled as a valid answer. Otherwise, it is left pending.

Suppose now that we have an answer $\mathcal{A}$ left pending in a node $\mathcal{N}$ and that a new occurrence of $\mathcal{A}$ is found elsewhere. Two situations may happen: the new occurrence of $\mathcal{A}$ is also speculative or it is safe from being pruned. In the first case, $\mathcal{A}$ is left pending in a node of the current branch. This is necessary because there is no way to know beforehand in which branch $\mathcal{A}$ will be proved first to be not speculative, if in any. In the second case, $\mathcal{A}$ is released as a valid answer and inserted in the list of available answers for the subgoal in hand. Note that in this case, $\mathcal{A}$ still remains left pending in node $\mathcal{N}$. In any case, $\mathcal{A}$ is only represented once in the table space.

With this scheme, OPTYap implements the following algorithm in order to release answers as soon as possible: the last worker W leaving a node $\mathcal{N}$ with pending tabled answers, determines the next node $\mathcal{M}$ on its branch that can be pruned by a worker to the left. The pending answers from $\mathcal{N}$ that correspond to generator nodes equal or younger than $\mathcal{M}$ are made available (if an answer is already valid, nothing is done), while the remaining are moved from $\mathcal{N}$ to $\mathcal{M}$. Note that W only needs to check for the existence of $\mathcal{M}$ up to the oldest generator node for the pending answers stored in $\mathcal{N}$. To simplify finding the oldest generator node we organised the top data structures in older to younger generator order (please see Fig. 8).

On the other hand, when a node $\mathcal{N}$ is pruned, its pending tabled answers can be in one of three situations: only left pending in $\mathcal{N}$; also left pending in other nodes; or already valid answers. Note that for all situations no interaction with the table space is needed and $\mathcal{N}$ can simply be pruned away. Even for the first situation, we may keep the answers in the table and wait until completion, as in the meantime such answers can still be generated again in other branches. So, only when a subgoal is completed evaluated, it is required that the answer trie nodes representing speculative answers are removed from the table. As this requires traversing the whole answer trie structure, for simplicity and efficiency, this is only done in the first call to the tabled subgoal after it has been completed.

4   Conclusions

In this paper we discussed the management of speculative computations in or-parallel tabled logic programs. Our approach deals with inner pruning at a first step and we address speculative tabled computations by delaying the point at which their answers are made available in the table. With this support, OPTYap is now able to execute a wider range of applications without introducing significant overheads (less than 1%) for applications without cuts.

Support for outer cuts is a delicate issue. To our knowledge, the first proposal on outer cuts for sequential tabling was presented by Guo and Gupta in [13]. They argue that cuts in tabling systems are most naturally interpreted as a commit, and they define the cut operator in terms of the operational semantics of their tabling strategy [14], which is based on recomputation of so-called looping alternatives. In more recent work, Castro and Warren propose the demand-based *once* pruning operator [15], whose semantics are independent of the operational semantics for tabling, but which does not fully support cut. We believe that a complete design for outer cut operations in sequential tabling is still an open and, arguably, a controversial problem.

To fully support pruning in parallel tabling, further work is also required. We need to do it *correctly*, that is, in such a way that the system will not break but instead produce sensible answers according to the proposed sequential semantics, and *well*, that is, allow useful pruning with good performance.

Acknowledgments

This work has been partially supported by APRIL (POSI/SRI/40749/2001) and by funds granted to LIACC through the Programa de Financiamento Plurianual, Fundação para a Ciência e Tecnologia and Programa POSI.

References

1. Ali, K.: A Method for Implementing Cut in Parallel Execution of Prolog. In: Proceedings of the International Logic Programming Symposium, IEEE Computer Society Press (1987) 449–456
2. Hausman, B.: Pruning and Speculative Work in OR-Parallel PROLOG. PhD thesis, The Royal Institute of Technology (1990)
3. Ali, K., Karlsson, R.: Scheduling Speculative Work in MUSE and Performance Results. International Journal of Parallel Programming 21 (1992) 449–476
4. Beaumont, A., Warren, D.H.D.: Scheduling Speculative Work in Or-Parallel Prolog Systems. In: Proceedings of the 10th International Conference on Logic Programming, The MIT Press (1993) 135–149
5. Ciepielewski, A.: Scheduling in Or-parallel Prolog Systems: Survey and Open Problems. International Journal of Parallel Programming 20 (1991) 421–451
6. Rocha, R., Silva, F., Santos Costa, V.: On a Tabling Engine that Can Exploit Or-Parallelism. In: Proceedings of the 17th International Conference on Logic Programming. Number 2237 in LNCS, Springer-Verlag (2001) 43–58
7. Rocha, R., Silva, F., Santos Costa, V.: YapOr: an Or-Parallel Prolog System Based on Environment Copying. In: Proceedings of the 9th Portuguese Conference on Artificial Intelligence. Number 1695 in LNAI, Springer-Verlag (1999) 178–192
8. Rocha, R., Silva, F., Santos Costa, V.: YapTab: A Tabling Engine Designed to Support Parallelism. In: Proceedings of the 2nd Conference on Tabulation in Parsing and Deduction. (2000) 77–87
9. Ali, K., Karlsson, R.: Full Prolog and Scheduling OR-Parallelism in Muse. International Journal of Parallel Programming 19 (1990) 445–475
10. Sagonas, K., Swift, T., Warren, D.S.: XSB as an Efficient Deductive Database Engine. In: Proceedings of the ACM SIGMOD International Conference on the Management of Data, ACM Press (1994) 442–453
11. Sagonas, K., Swift, T.: An Abstract Machine for Tabled Execution of Fixed-Order Stratified Logic Programs. ACM Transactions on Programming Languages and Systems 20 (1998) 586–634
12. Ramakrishnan, I.V., Rao, P., Sagonas, K., Swift, T., Warren, D.S.: Efficient Access Mechanisms for Tabled Logic Programs. Journal of Logic Programming 38 (1999) 31–54
13. Guo, H.F., Gupta, G.: Cuts in Tabled Logic Programming. In: Proceedings of the Colloquium on Implementation of Constraint and LOgic Programming Systems. (2002)
14. Guo, H.F., Gupta, G.: A Simple Scheme for Implementing Tabled Logic Programming Systems Based on Dynamic Reordering of Alternatives. In: Proceedings of the 17th International Conference on Logic Programming. Number 2237 in LNCS, Springer-Verlag (2001) 181–196
15. Castro, L.F., Warren, D.S.: Approximate Pruning in Tabled Logic Programming. In: Proceedings of the 12th European Symposium on Programming. Volume 2618 of LNCS., Springer Verlag (2003) 69–83

αProlog: A Logic Programming Language with Names, Binding and α-Equivalence

James Cheney[1] and Christian Urban[2]

[1] Cornell University
jcheney@cs.cornell.edu
[2] University of Cambridge
cu200@cl.cam.ac.uk

Abstract. There are two well-known approaches to programming with names, binding, and equivalence up to consistent renaming: representing names and bindings as concrete identifiers in a first-order language (such as Prolog), or encoding names and bindings as variables and abstractions in a higher-order language (such as λProlog). However, both approaches have drawbacks: the former often involves stateful name-generation and requires manual definitions for α-equivalence and capture-avoiding substitution, and the latter is semantically very complicated, so reasoning about programs written using either approach can be very difficult. Gabbay and Pitts have developed a new approach to encoding abstract syntax with binding based on primitive operations of name-swapping and freshness. This paper presents αProlog, a logic programming language that uses this approach, along with several illustrative example programs and an operational semantics.

1 Introduction

Names, binding, α-equivalence, and capture-avoiding substitution are endemic phenomena in logics and programming languages. The related concepts of name freshness, fresh name generation and equivalence up to consistent renaming also appear in many other domains, including state identifiers in finite automata, nonces in security protocols, and channel names in process calculi. Dealing with names is therefore an important practical problem in meta-programming, and there are a variety of approaches to doing so, involving different tradeoffs [3, 4, 9, 12, 15, 18, 21, 24] . The following are important desiderata for such techniques:

- *Convenience*: Basic operations including substitution, α-equivalence, and fresh name generation should be built-in.
- *Simplicity*: The semantics of the meta-language should be as simple as possible in order to facilitate reasoning about programs.
- *Abstraction*: Low-level implementation details concerning names should be taken care of by the meta-language and hidden from the programmer.
- *Faithfulness/Adequacy*: Object terms should be in bijective correspondence with the values of some meta-language type.

In *first-order abstract syntax* (FOAS), object languages are encoded using first-order terms (e.g. Prolog terms or ML datatypes). Names are encoded using a

B. Demoen and V. Lifschitz (Eds.): ICLP 2004, LNCS 3132, pp. 269–283, 2004.

concrete datatype *var* such as strings, and binders are encoded using first-order function symbols like *lam* : *var* × *exp* → *exp*. FOAS has several disadvantages: the encoding does not respect α-equivalence, damaging adequacy; fresh names are often generated using side-effects, complicating the semantics; and operations like α-equivalence and substitution must be implemented manually (and painstakingly). Nameless encodings like de Bruijn indices [3] ameliorate some, but not all, of these problems.

In *higher-order abstract syntax* (HOAS) [18], object languages are encoded using higher-order terms (e.g. λ-terms in λProlog [16]). In HOAS, names are encoded as meta-language variables and binders are encoded with meta-language λ-abstraction using higher-order function symbols like *lam* : (*exp* → *exp*) → *exp*. Capture-avoiding substitution and α-equivalence need only be implemented once, in the meta-language, and can be inherited by all object languages. However, because of the presence of types like *exp* that are defined via negative recursion, the semantics of HOAS is complex [10] and induction principles are difficult to develop. Moreover, HOAS cannot deal with open object terms, that is terms containing free variables. In *weak HOAS* [4], induction principles are recovered by encoding names using a concrete type *var*, and encoding binders encoded as λ-abstractions using constructors like *lam* : (*var* → *exp*) → *exp*. In this approach, α-equivalence is still built-in, but substitution must be defined. Also, weak HOAS encodings may not be adequate because of the presence of *exotic* terms, or closed terms of type *exp* which do not correspond to any object term; additional well-formedness predicates are needed to recover adequacy.

Recently, Gabbay and Pitts developed a novel approach to encoding names and binding [8], based on taking *name-swapping* and *freshness* as fundamental operations on names. This approach has been codified by Pitts as a theory of first-order logic called *nominal logic* [19], in which names are a first-order abstract data type admitting only swapping, binding, and equality and freshness testing operations. Object language variables and binding can be encoded using names x, y and *name-abstractions* x.t, which are considered equal up to α-equivalence. For example, object variables x and binders $\lambda x.t$ can be encoded as nominal terms *var*(x) and abstractions *lam*(x.t) where *var* : *id* → *exp* and *lam* : ⟨*id*⟩*exp* → *exp*.

We refer to this approach to programming with names and binding as *nominal abstract syntax* (NAS). NAS provides α-equivalence and fresh name generation for free, while remaining semantically simple, requiring neither recursive types nor stateful name-generation. Furthermore, names are sufficiently abstract that the low-level details of name generation can be hidden from the programmer, and exotic terms are not possible in NAS encodings. However, names are still sufficiently concrete that there is no problem working with open terms. Therefore NAS makes possible a distinctive new style of meta-programming.

This paper presents αProlog, a logic programming language based on the Horn clause fragment of nominal logic which supports nominal abstract syntax. In the rest of this paper, we describe αProlog, and discuss its unification and constraint solving algorithm (due to Urban, Pitts, and Gabbay [25]) and operational semantics. We also discuss an important open issue: our current implementation is incomplete, because complete proof search in αProlog requires solving *equivariant unification* problems, which are **NP**-complete in general [2]. However, this problem can often be avoided, and we give several examples of interesting languages and relations that can be encoded using NAS in αProlog. We conclude with a discussion of related languages and future work.

2   Syntax

The term language of αProlog consists of *(nominal) terms*, constructed according to the grammar

$$t ::= X \mid \mathsf{n} \mid \mathsf{n}.t \mid (\mathsf{n}\ \mathsf{m}) \cdot t \mid f(\bar{t})$$

where X is a *(logic) variable*, f is a *function symbol* (we write $\bar{t}$ to denote a (possibly empty) sequence $(t_1, \ldots, t_n)$), and n, m are *names*. By convention, function symbols are lower case, logic variables are capitalized, and names are printed using the sans-serif typeface. We shall refer to a term of the form $f(\bar{t})$ as an atomic term. Terms of the form $\mathsf{n}.t$ are called *abstractions*, and terms of the form $(\mathsf{n}\ \mathsf{m}) \cdot t$ are called *swapping*, which intuitively denote the result of swapping names n, m within t. Swapping takes higher precedence than abstraction, i.e., $(\mathsf{a}\ \mathsf{b}) \cdot \mathsf{c}.t = ((\mathsf{a}\ \mathsf{b}) \cdot \mathsf{c}).t$. Variables cannot be used to form abstractions and transpositions, i.e., $X.t$ and $(X\ Y) \cdot t$ are not legal terms.

αProlog has a ML-like polymorphic type system. Types are classified into two *kinds*: **type**, the kind of all types, and **name_type**, the kind of types inhabited only by names. Types classify terms, and include atomic type constructor applications $c(\sigma_1, \ldots, \sigma_n)$ as well as type variables α and abstraction types $.\nu\sigma$. In an abstraction, the kind of ν must be **name_type**. Type constructor and uninterpreted function symbol declarations are of the form as $c : (\bar{\kappa}) \to \kappa'$ and $f : (\bar{\sigma}) \to \sigma'$, where κ and σ indicate kinds and types respectively. The result type of an uninterpreted function symbol may not be a built-in type or a **name_type**. Relation symbols are declared as **pred** $p(\bar{\sigma})$ and interpreted function symbols as **func** $f(\bar{\sigma}) = \sigma'$. Type abbreviations can be made with the declaration **type** $c(\bar{\alpha}) = \sigma$. The latter three declaration forms are loosely based on Mercury syntax [23]. We assume built-in and self-explanatory type and function symbols for pairs $((x, y) : \sigma \times \sigma')$ and lists $([], x :: y, [x|y] : [\sigma])$.

Atomic formulas A are terms of the form $p(t_1, \ldots, t_n)$, where p is a *relation symbol*. *Constraints* C include freshness formulas $t \# u$, and equality formulas $t = u$. In $t \# u$, the term t must be of some name type $\nu : $ **name_type**, whereas u may be of any type; in $t = u$, both t and u must be of the same type. *Goals* G consist of sequences of constraints and atomic formulas. *Program clauses* include Horn clauses of the form $A :- G$ and function-definition clauses of the form $f(\bar{t}) = t' :- G$, which introduce a (conditional) rewrite rule for an atomic term with an interpreted head symbol f.

By convention, constant symbols are function symbols applied the empty argument list; we write c instead of $c()$, and $c : \tau$ instead of $c : () \to \tau$. This also applies to propositional and type constants. We abbreviate clauses $A :- ()$ and

$f(\bar{t}) = t' :- ()$, where $()$ denotes the empty sequence, as A and $f(\bar{t}) = t'$. We write $V(\cdot)$ and $N(\cdot)$ for the variables or names of a term or formula. Observe that $N(\cdot)$ includes all occurrences of names in t, even abstracted ones, hence $N(\mathsf{x}.\mathsf{x}) = \{\mathsf{x}\}$. We say a nominal term e is *ground* when $V(e) = \emptyset$; names may appear in ground terms, so $f(X,Y)$ is not ground but $f(\mathsf{x},\mathsf{y})$ is. We write $VN(t)$ for $V(t) \cup N(t)$.

3   Semantics

In this section we present an operational semantics for αProlog programs. We describe the equality and freshness theory of nominal logic, nominal unification, and αProlog's execution algorithm, emphasizing the main novelties relative to standard unification and logic programming execution.

3.1   Equality, Freshness, and Unification

Figure 1 shows the axioms of equality and freshness for ground nominal terms (based on [19, 25]). The swapping axioms (S_1)–(S_5) describe the behavior of swapping. From now on, we assume that all terms are normalized with respect to these axioms (read right-to-left as rewrite rules), so that swaps are not present in ground terms and are present only surrounding variables in non-ground terms.

The next two axioms (A_1), (A_2) define equality for abstractions. The first axiom is a simple congruence property. The second guarantees that abstractions are equal "up to renaming". Two abstractions of different names $\mathsf{x}.t$, $\mathsf{y}.u$ are equal just in case their bodies are equal up to swapping the names (i.e., $t = (\mathsf{x}\,\mathsf{y})\cdot u$) and x does not appear free in u (i..e., $\mathsf{x} \mathbin{\#} u$) Symmetrically, it suffices to check $\mathsf{y} \mathbin{\#} t$; the two conditions are equivalent if $t = (\mathsf{x}\,\mathsf{y}) \cdot u$. For example, $\mathsf{x}.g(\mathsf{x}) = \mathsf{y}.g(\mathsf{y})$ and $\mathsf{x}.f(\mathsf{x},\mathsf{y}) = \mathsf{z}.f(\mathsf{z},\mathsf{y})$, but $\mathsf{x}.f(\mathsf{x},\mathsf{y}) \neq \mathsf{y}.f(\mathsf{y},\mathsf{x})$ because $\mathsf{x} \mathbin{\#} f(\mathsf{y},\mathsf{x})$ fails.

The freshness axioms (F_1)–(F_5) describe the freshness relation. Intuitively, $\mathsf{x} \mathbin{\#} t$ means "name x does not appear unbound in t". For example, it is never the case that $\mathsf{x} \mathbin{\#} \mathsf{x}$, whereas any two distinct names are fresh $(\mathsf{x} \neq \mathsf{y} \Rightarrow \mathsf{x} \mathbin{\#} \mathsf{y})$. Moreover, freshness passes through function symbols (in particular, any name is fresh for any constant). The abstraction freshness rules are more interesting: $\mathsf{x} \mathbin{\#} \mathsf{x}.t$ is unconditionally valid because any name is fresh for a term in which it is immediately abstracted, whereas if x and y are different names, then $\mathsf{x} \mathbin{\#} \mathsf{y}.t$ just in case $\mathsf{x} \mathbin{\#} t$.

(S_1) $(\mathsf{n}\,\mathsf{m}) \cdot \mathsf{n} = \mathsf{m}$ (S_2) $(\mathsf{n}\,\mathsf{m}) \cdot \mathsf{m} = \mathsf{n}$ (S_3) $\mathsf{x} \mathbin{\#} \mathsf{n}, \mathsf{x} \mathbin{\#} \mathsf{m} \Rightarrow (\mathsf{n}\,\mathsf{m}) \cdot \mathsf{x} = \mathsf{x}$

(S_4) $(\mathsf{n}\,\mathsf{m}) \cdot f(\bar{t}) = f((\mathsf{n}\,\mathsf{m}) \cdot \bar{t})$ (S_5) $(\mathsf{n}\,\mathsf{m}) \cdot (\mathsf{x}.t) = (\mathsf{n}\,\mathsf{m}) \cdot \mathsf{x}.(\mathsf{n}\,\mathsf{m}) \cdot t$

(A_1) $t = u \Rightarrow \mathsf{n}.t = \mathsf{n}.u$ (A_2) $t = (\mathsf{n}\,\mathsf{m}) \cdot u \wedge \mathsf{n} \mathbin{\#} u \Rightarrow \mathsf{n}.t = \mathsf{m}.u$

(F_1) $\mathsf{n} \neq \mathsf{m} \Rightarrow \mathsf{n} \mathbin{\#} \mathsf{m}$ (F_2) $\neg(\mathsf{n} \mathbin{\#} \mathsf{n})$ (F_3) $\bigwedge_{i=1}^{n} \mathsf{n} \mathbin{\#} t_i \Rightarrow \mathsf{n} \mathbin{\#} f(\bar{t})$

(F_4) $\mathsf{n} \mathbin{\#} \mathsf{n}.t$ (F_5) $\mathsf{n} \mathbin{\#} \mathsf{m} \wedge \mathsf{n} \mathbin{\#} t \Rightarrow \mathsf{n} \mathbin{\#} \mathsf{m}.t$

Fig. 1. Ground equational and freshness theory

Nominal unification is unification of nominal terms up to α-equivalence (as formalized by the axioms of Figure 1). For ground terms, nominal unification coincides with α-equivalence: for example, the term n.n unifies with m.m, but n.m and n.n do not unify. However, non-ground terms such as n.X and m.X unify only subject to the *freshness constraints* n # X and m # X. A freshness constraint of the form n # X states that X may not be instantiated with a term containing a free occurrence of n. The problem n.X ≈? m.Y is unified by substitution $X = (\text{n m}) \cdot Y$ subject to the constraint n # X; that is, X must be identical to Y with n and m swapped, and n must be fresh for X. The nominal unification algorithm therefore also must solve freshness (or *disunification*) subproblems of the form t #? u, where t is of name type.

Urban, Pitts, and Gabbay [25] developed an algorithm for solving nominal unification and freshness constraint problems of the form encountered in αProlog. A modified form of this algorithm is used in our current implementation. For space reasons, we omit a fuller discussion of the details of the algorithm, and note that any other constraint solving procedure for nominal equality and freshness constraints could be used instead.

3.2 Operational Semantics

We now present the operational semantics of αProlog programs. This semantics is based loosely on that of *constraint logic programming* [11], over the domain of nominal terms as axiomatized in Figure 1. A *program* is a set $\mathcal{P}$ of program clauses, closed under permutative renaming of names and variables. A *program state* consists a goal G and a set ∇ of equality and freshness constraints; we shall write $\langle G \mid \nabla \rangle$ for such a state. An *answer* to this query is a set of constraints ∇'. We define the operational semantics of an αProlog query using transitions of the form $\langle G \mid \nabla \rangle \longrightarrow \langle G' \mid \nabla' \rangle$ and write $G \dashrightarrow \nabla$ if $\langle G \mid \emptyset \rangle \longrightarrow^* \langle \emptyset \mid \nabla \rangle$. The rules for the transitions are as follows:

$$\langle C, G \mid \nabla \rangle \;\; \longrightarrow \langle G \mid \{C\} \cup \nabla \rangle \quad \text{if } \{C\} \cup \nabla \text{ satisfiable}$$
$$\langle p(\bar{t}), G \mid \nabla \rangle \longrightarrow \langle \bar{t} = \bar{u}, G', G \mid \nabla \rangle \text{ if } (p(\bar{u}) :- G') \in \mathcal{P}$$
$$\text{and } VN(p(\bar{u}) :- G') \cap VN(p(\bar{t}), G, \nabla) = \emptyset$$
$$\langle G \mid \nabla \rangle \qquad \longrightarrow \langle G \mid \nabla' \rangle \qquad \text{if } \nabla' \vdash \nabla$$

In the last rule, $\nabla' \vdash \nabla$ is constraint entailment in the theory of Figure 1; this rule permits constraint simplification via unification. In αProlog, as usual in logic programming, variables in program clauses or rewriting rules are renamed to new variables during backchaining; in addition, names are freshened to new names. Rewriting rules $f(\bar{t}) = u :- G$ defining function symbols are translated to a clausal form $p_f(\bar{t}, u) :- G'$ via *flattening*, as in many Prolog systems.

It is straightforward to show that our operational semantics is sound with respect to an appropriate variant of nominal logic. The proof of this fact relies on the soundness of nominal unification for nominal equational satisfiability ([25, Thm. 2]). However, completeness fails, because we have not taken into account *equivariance*, an important property of nominal logic that guarantees that validity is preserved by name-swapping [19]. Formally, the equivariance axiom asserts that $p(\bar{t}) \Rightarrow p((n\ m) \cdot \bar{t})$ is valid in nominal logic for any atomic formula $p(\bar{t})$ and names n, m. For example, for any binary relation **pred** $p(\nu, \nu)$ for $\nu : \textbf{name\_type}$, we have $p(x, y) \iff p(y, z)$ valid in both directions because the swapping $(x\ y)(y\ z)$ translates between them. But many-to-one renamings may not preserve validity: for example, $x \mathbin{\#} y \Rightarrow z \mathbin{\#} z$ is not valid.

Because of equivariance, backchaining based on nominal unification is incomplete. For example, given program clause $p(n)$ where n is a name, the goal $p(n)$ cannot be solved. Even though $p(n) \Rightarrow p(n)$ is obviously valid, proof search fails because the program clause $p(n)$ must be freshened to $p(n')$, and $p(n')$ and $p(n)$ do not unify. However, by equivariance these formulas are equivalent in nominal logic, since $p(n') \Rightarrow p((n\ n') \cdot n') \Rightarrow p(n) \Rightarrow p((n\ n') \cdot n) \Rightarrow p(n')$.

This can be fixed by adding a transition rule

$$\langle p(\bar{t}), G \mid \nabla \rangle - \quad \rightarrow\!\!p((a\ b) \cdot \bar{t}), G \mid \nabla \rangle .$$

However, this rule introduces nondeterminism. To perform goal-directed proof search, it seems preferable to replace the naive backchaining rule above with one based on unifying up to nominal equality modulo a permutation:

$$\langle p(\bar{t}), G \mid \nabla \rangle - \quad \rightarrow\!\!\pi\langle \cdot \bar{t} = \bar{u}, G', G \mid \nabla \rangle$$
$$\text{if } (p(\bar{u}) :- G') \in \mathcal{P} \text{ and } VN(p(\bar{u}) :- G') \cap VN(p(\bar{t}), G, \nabla) = \emptyset$$

where π is a sequence of transpositions $(a_1\ b_1) \cdots (a_n\ b_n)$. We use the term *equivariant unification* for the problem of unifying up to nominal equality modulo a permutation. However, even deciding whether an equivariant unification problem has a solution is **NP**-complete [2]. This does not necessarily mean that equivariant unification is impractical. Developing a practical approach to equivariant unification or constraint solving is the subject of current research, however, and the current version of αProlog opts for efficiency over completeness. We have experimented with brute-force search and more advanced techniques for equivariant unification but have yet to find a satisfactory solution.

Nevertheless, our incomplete implementation of αProlog is still useful. Equivariant unification does not seem necessary for many interesting αProlog programs, including all purely first-order programs and all the example programs in this paper (capture-avoiding substitution, typing, etc.). In fact, the semantics we have presented is complete for such programs. In a separate paper, we identify (and prove correct) a condition on program clauses that ensures that nominal unification-based backchaining is complete [26].

4   Example: The λ-Calculus

The prototypical example of a language with variable binding is the λ-calculus. In αProlog, the syntax of λ-terms may be described with the following type and constructor declarations:

$id : \textbf{name\_type}.$ $exp : \textbf{type}.$
$var : id \rightarrow exp.$ $app : (exp, exp) \rightarrow exp.$ $lam : \langle id \rangle exp \rightarrow exp.$

We make the simplifying assumption that the variables of object λ-terms are constants of type *id*. Then we can translate λ-terms as follows:

$$\ulcorner x \urcorner = var(x) \qquad \ulcorner e_1\, e_2 \urcorner = app(\ulcorner e_1 \urcorner, \ulcorner e_2 \urcorner) \qquad \ulcorner \lambda x.e \urcorner = lam(x.\ulcorner e \urcorner)$$

It is not difficult to verify that e is a λ-term if and only if $\ulcorner e \urcorner$ is a *closed* nominal term, i.e. $FV(\ulcorner e \urcorner) = \emptyset$, and we have that $e \equiv_\alpha e'$ if and only if $\ulcorner e \urcorner \approx \ulcorner e' \urcorner$.

Example 1 (Typechecking and inference). First, we consider the problem of type-checking λ-terms. The syntax of types can be encoded as follows:

$$tid : \textbf{name\_type}. \qquad ty : \textbf{type}. \qquad tvar : tid \rightarrow ty. \qquad arr : (ty, ty) \rightarrow ty.$$

We define contexts *ctx* as lists of pairs of identifiers and types, and the 3-ary relation *typ* relating a context, term, and type:

> **type** $ctx = [id \times ty]$.
> **pred** $typ(ctx, tm, ty)$.
> $typ(C, var(X), T) \qquad\qquad :- mem((X, T), C).$
> $typ(C, app(E_1, E_2), T') \qquad :- typ(C, E_1, arr(T, T')), typ(C, E_2, T).$
> $typ(C, lam(x.E), arr(T, T')) :- x \# C, typ([(x, T)|C], E, T').$

The predicate $mem(\alpha, [\alpha])$ is the usual predicate for testing list membership. The side-condition $x \notin Dom(\Gamma)$ is translated to the freshness constraint $x \# C$.

Consider the query $?- typ([], lam(x.lam(y.var(x))), T)$. We can reduce this goal by backchaining against the suitably freshened rule

$$typ(C_1, lam(x_1.E_1), arr(T_1, U_1)) :- x_1 \# C_1, typ([(x_1, T_1)|C_1], E_1, U_1)$$

which unifies with the goal with $[C_1 = [], E_1 = lam(y.var(x_1)), T = arr(T_1, U_1)]$. This yields subgoal $x_1 \# [], typ([(x_1, T_1)|C_1], E_1, U_1)$. The first conjunct is trivially valid since C_1 is a constant. The second is solved by backchaining against the third *typ*-rule again, producing unifier $[C_2 = [(x_1, T_1)], E_2 = var(x_1), U_1 = arr(T_2, U_2)]$ and subgoal $x_2 \# [(x_1, T_1)], typ([(x_2, T_2), (x_1, T_1)], var(x_1), U_2)$. The freshness subgoal reduces to the constraint $x_2 \# T_1$, and the *typ* subgoal can be solved by backchaining against

$$typ(C_3, var(X_3), T_3) :- mem((X_3, T_3), C_3)$$

using unifier $[C_3 = [(x_2, T_2), (x_1, T_1)], X_3 = x_1, T_3 = U_2]$. Finally, the remaining subgoal $mem((x_1, U_2), [(x_2, T_2), (x_1, T_1)])$ clearly has most general solution $[U_2 = T_1]$. Solving for T, we have $T = arr(T_1, U_1) = arr(T_1, arr(T_2, U_2)) = arr(T_1, arr(T_2, T_1))$. This solution corresponds to the principal type of $\lambda x.\lambda y.x$.

Example 2 (Capture-avoiding substitution). Although capture-avoiding substitution is not a built-in operator in αProlog, it is easy to define via the clauses:

> **func** $subst(exp, exp, id) = exp$.
> $subst(var(X), E, X) \qquad = E$.
> $subst(var(Y), E, X) \qquad = var(Y) :- X \# Y$.
> $subst(app(E_1, E_2), E, X) = app(subst(E_1, E, X), subst(E_2, E, X))$.
> $subst(lam(y.E'), E, X) \quad = lam(y.subst(E', E, X)) :- y \# (X, E)$.

Note the two freshness side-conditions: the constraint $X \# Y$ prevents the first and second clauses from overlapping; the constraint $y \# (X, E)$ ensures capture-avoidance, by restricting the application of the fourth clause to when y is fresh for X and E. Despite these side-conditions, this definition is total and deterministic. Determinism is immediate: no two clauses overlap. Totality follows because, by nominal logic's *freshness principle*, the bound name y in $lam(y.E')$ can always be renamed to a fresh z chosen so that $z \# (X, E)$. It is straightforward to prove that $subst(\ulcorner t \urcorner, \ulcorner t' \urcorner, x)$ coincides with the traditional capture-avoiding substitution on λ-terms $t[t'/x]$.

Consider the goal $X = subst(lam(x.var(y)), var(x), y)$. The substitution on the right-hand side is in danger of capturing the free variable $var(x)$. How is capture avoided in αProlog? First, note that function definitions are translated to a flattened clausal form in αProlog, so we must solve the equivalent goal $subst'(lam(x.var(y)), var(x), y, X)$ subject to an appropriately translated definition of $subst'$. The freshened, flattened clause

$$subst'(lam(y_1.E_1'), E_1, X_1, lam(y_1, E_1'')) :- y_1 \# E_1, subst'(E_1', E_1, X_1, E_1'')$$

unifies with substitution $[E_1' = var(y), X_1 = y, E_1 = var(x), X = lam(y_1.E_1'')]$. The freshness constraint $y_1 \# var(x)$ guarantees that $var(x)$ cannot be captured. It is easily verified, so the goal reduces to $subst'(var(y), var(x), y, E_1'')$. Using the freshened rule $subst'(var(X_2), E_2, X_2, E_2)$ with unifying substitution $[X_2 = y, E_2 = var(x), E_1'' = var(x)]$, we obtain the solution $X = lam(y_1.var(x))$.

Example 3 (Parsing). Logic programming languages often provide advanced support for parsing using definite clause grammars (DCGs). DCG parsing can be implemented in αProlog by translating DCG rules $h - \rightarrow t$ to ordinary αProlog programs. We assume familiarity with DCG syntax in this example. We assume that $v(string), ws\_opt, ws, token(string)$ are predefined nonterminals recognizing variable names, (optional) whitespace, and string tokens. Here is a small example of parsing λ-terms from strings. (Here, $mem1(S, X, M)$ holds when S, X is the first binding of S in M.)

$$
\begin{array}{ll}
\textbf{type } map = [(string, id)] & \\
ltm(M, var(X)) & - \rightarrow v(S), \{mem1(S, X, M)\}. \\
ltm(M, app(E_1, E_2)) & - \rightarrow token(``("), ws\_opt, ltm(M, E_1), ws, \\
& \quad ltm(M, E_2), ws\_opt, token(``)") \\
ltm(M, lam(x.E)) & \longrightarrow \{x \# M\}, token(``\backslash"), ws\_opt, v(X), ws\_opt, \\
& \quad token(``."), ws\_opt, ltm([(S, x)|M], E).
\end{array}
$$

This program parses "$\backslash x.\backslash y.x$" to $lam(x.lam(y.x))$.

4.1   Extending to the $\lambda\mu$-Calculus

The $\lambda\mu$-calculus, invented by Parigot [17], extends the λ-calculus with *continuations* α; terms may be "named" by continuations ($[\alpha]e$) and continuations may be introduced with μ-binding ($\mu\alpha.e$). Intuitively, $\lambda\mu$-terms are proof terms

Terms, Types, and Contexts

$$e ::= x \mid (e\ e') \mid \lambda x.e \mid [\alpha]e \mid \mu\alpha.e$$
$$\tau ::= b \mid \tau \to \tau' \mid \bot$$
$$\Gamma ::= \cdot \mid \Gamma, x : \tau \mid \Gamma, \alpha : \bar{\tau}$$

Replacement Operation

$$x\{e/\alpha\} = x$$
$$(e_1\ e_2)\{t/\alpha\} = (e_1\{e/\alpha\}\ e_2\{e/\alpha\})$$
$$(\lambda y.e')\{e/\alpha\} = \lambda y.e'\{e/\alpha\}$$
$$([\alpha]e')\{e/\alpha\} = [\alpha](e'\{e/\alpha\}\ e)$$
$$([\beta]e')\{e/\alpha\} = [\beta](e'\{e/\alpha\}) \quad (\beta \ne \alpha)$$
$$(\mu\beta.e')\{e/\alpha\} = \mu\beta.e'\{e/\alpha\} \quad (\beta \notin FN(e,\alpha))$$

Some Typing-Rules

$$\frac{\alpha:\bar{\tau} \in \Gamma \quad \Gamma \vdash e : \tau}{\Gamma \vdash [\alpha]e : \bot} \qquad \frac{\Gamma \vdash e_1 : \bot \quad \Gamma \vdash e_2 : \tau}{\Gamma \vdash (e_1\ e_2) : \bot} \qquad \frac{\Gamma, \alpha:\bar{\tau} \vdash e : \bot \quad (\alpha \notin Dom(\Gamma))}{\Gamma \vdash \mu\alpha.e : \tau}$$

Fig. 2. A slight variant of Parigot's $\lambda\mu$-calculus

for classical natural deduction, and μ-abstractions represent proofs by double negation. In addition to capture-avoiding substitution of terms for variables, the $\lambda\mu$-calculus introduces a capture-avoiding *replacement* operator $e'\{e/\alpha\}$ which replaces each occurrence of the pattern $[\alpha]e_0$ in e' with $[\alpha](e_0\ e)$. We give a variant of the $\lambda\mu$-calculus in Figure 2. In contexts Γ, the bar over the type of α indicates that it is not a value of type τ, but a continuation accepting the type τ.

We may extend the λ-calculus encoding with a new name type *con* for continuations and term constructors for $\lambda\mu$-terms:

$$con : \textbf{name\_type} \qquad pass : (con, exp) \to exp \qquad mu : \langle con \rangle exp \to exp$$

and encoding $\ulcorner[\alpha]t\urcorner = pass(\alpha, \ulcorner t\urcorner)$ and $\ulcorner\mu\alpha.t\urcorner = mu(\alpha.\ulcorner t\urcorner)$. Again, it is easy to show that ground *exp*-terms are in bijective correspondence with $\lambda\mu$-terms.

The standard approach to typechecking $\lambda\mu$-terms is to use two contexts, Γ and Δ, for variable- and continuation-bindings respectively. We instead consider a single context with variable-bindings $x : \tau$ and continuation-bindings $\alpha : \bar{\tau}$. Therefore we modify the encoding of contexts slightly as follows:

$$bind : \textbf{type}. \quad vb : (id, ty) \to bind \quad cb : (con, ty) \to bind \quad \textbf{type } ctx = [bind].$$

Then the typechecking rules from the previous section may be adapted by replacing bindings (x, T) with $vb(x, T)$, and adding three new rules:

$$typ(C, pass(X, E), bot) :- mem(cb(X, T), C), typ(C, E, T).$$
$$typ(C, app(E, E'), bot) :- typ(C, E, bot), typ(C, E', T).$$
$$typ(C, mu(a.E), T) \quad :- a\ \#\ C, typ([cb(a, T)|C], E, bot).$$

The following query illustrates the typechecking for the term $\lambda x.\mu\alpha.(x\ (\lambda y.[\alpha]y))$ whose principal type corresponds to the classical double negation law.

$$?\text{--}\ typ([], lam(x.mu(a.app(var(x), lam(y.pass(a, var(y)))))), T).$$
$$T = arr(arr(arr(T_{162}, bot), bot), T_{162})$$

Capture-avoiding substitution can be extended to $\lambda\mu$-terms easily. For replacement, we show the interesting cases for continuation applications and μ-abstractions:

$$\textbf{func } repl(exp, exp, con) = exp.$$
$$repl(pass(A, E'), E, A) = pass(A, app(repl(E', E, A), E)).$$
$$repl(pass(B, E'), E, A) = pass(B, repl(E', E, A)) :\!- A \mathop{\#} B.$$
$$repl(mu(\mathsf{b}.E'), E, A) = mu(\mathsf{b}.repl(E', E, A)) :\!- \mathsf{b} \mathop{\#} (A, E).$$

This first-order NAS encoding is quite different in flavor from a HOAS encoding of the $\lambda\mu$-calculus due to Abel [1]. There, $\mu\alpha.t$ is encoded as $mu(\lambda\ulcorner\alpha\urcorner.\ulcorner t\urcorner)$, where $mu : ((tm\ A \to nam) \to nam) \to tm\ A$, and $tm\ A$ is the type of terms of type A and nam the type of named terms. Continuations are encoded as variables $\ulcorner\alpha\urcorner : (tm\ A \to nam)$ and named terms $[\alpha]t$ are encoded as applications $\ulcorner\alpha\urcorner\ulcorner t\urcorner$. While elegant, this third-order encoding is semantically complex, making proofs of interesting properties difficult.

5   Example: The π-Calculus

The π-calculus is a calculus of concurrent, mobile processes. Its syntax (following Milner, Parrow, and Walker [14]) is described by the grammar rules shown in Figure 3. The symbols $x, y, \ldots$ are *channel names*. The inactive process 0 is inert. The $\tau.p$ process performs a *silent action* τ and then does p. Parallel composition is denoted $p|q$ and nondeterministic choice by $p + q$. The process $x(y).p$ inputs a channel name from x, binds it to y, and then does p. The process $\bar{x}y.p$ outputs y to x and then does p. The match operator $[x = y]p$ is p provided $x = y$, but is inactive if $x \neq y$. The restriction operator $(y)p$ restricts y to p. Parenthesized names (e.g. y in $x(y).p$ and $(y)p$) are binding, and $fn(p)$, $bn(p)$ and $n(p)$ denote the sets of free, bound, and all names occurring in p. Capture-avoiding renaming is written $t\{x/y\}$.

Milner et al.'s original operational semantics (shown in Figure 3, symmetric cases omitted) is a labeled transition system with relation $p -\!\!\stackrel{a}{\to}\!\!q$ indicating "p

Process terms $p ::= 0 \mid \tau.p \mid p|q \mid p + q \mid x(y).p \mid \bar{x}y.p \mid [x = y]p \mid (x)p$
Actions $\qquad a ::= \tau \mid x(y) \mid \bar{x}y \mid \bar{x}(y)$

$$\frac{}{\tau.p -\!\!\stackrel{\tau}{\to}\!\! p} \qquad \frac{p -\!\!\stackrel{a}{\to}\!\! p' \quad bn(a) \cap fn(q) = \emptyset}{p|q -\!\!\stackrel{a}{\to}\!\! p'|q} \qquad \frac{p -\!\!\stackrel{\bar{x}y}{\to}\!\! p' \quad q -\!\!\stackrel{x(z)}{\to}\!\! q'}{p|q -\!\!\stackrel{\tau}{\to}\!\! p'|q'\{y/z\}}$$

$$\frac{p -\!\!\stackrel{a}{\to}\!\! p'}{p + q -\!\!\stackrel{a}{\to}\!\! p'} \qquad \frac{}{\bar{x}y.p -\!\!\stackrel{\bar{x}y}{\to}\!\! p} \quad \frac{w \notin fn((z)p)}{x(z).p -\!\!\stackrel{x(w)}{\to}\!\! p\{w/z\}} \quad \frac{p -\!\!\stackrel{a}{\to}\!\! p'}{[x = x]p -\!\!\stackrel{a}{\to}\!\! p'}$$

$$\frac{p -\!\!\stackrel{\bar{x}(w)}{\to}\!\! p' \quad q -\!\!\stackrel{x(w)}{\to}\!\! q'}{p|q -\!\!\stackrel{\tau}{\to}\!\! (w)(p'|q')} \quad \frac{p -\!\!\stackrel{a}{\to}\!\! p' \quad y \notin n(a)}{(y)p -\!\!\stackrel{a}{\to}\!\! (y)p'} \quad \frac{p -\!\!\stackrel{\bar{x}y}{\to}\!\! p' \quad y \neq x \quad w \notin fn((y)p)}{(y)p -\!\!\stackrel{\bar{x}(w)}{\to}\!\! p'\{w/y\}}$$

Fig. 3. The π-calculus

$\textbf{func } ren\_p(proc, chan, chan) = proc.$ (* definition omitted *)
$\textbf{pred } safe(act, pr).$ (* tests $bn(A) \cap fn(P) = \emptyset$ *)
$safe(tau\_a, P).$
$safe(fout\_a(X, Y), P).$
$safe(bout\_a(X, Y), P) \;:- Y \,\#\, P.$
$safe(in\_a(X, Y), P) \quad:- Y \,\#\, P.$
$\textbf{pred } step(pr, act, pr).$ (* encodes $p \overset{a}{-\!\!\!\rightarrow} p'$ *)
$step(tau(P), tau\_a, P).$
$step(par(P, Q), A, par(P', Q)) \qquad\qquad:- step(P, A, P'), safe(A, Q).$
$step(par(P, Q), tau\_a, par(P', Q'')) \qquad:- step(P, fout\_a(X, Y), P'),$
$\qquad\qquad\qquad\qquad\qquad\qquad\qquad\qquad\quad step(Q, in\_a(X, Z), Q'),$
$\qquad\qquad\qquad\qquad\qquad\qquad\qquad\qquad\quad Q'' = ren\_p(Q', Y, Z).$
$step(sum(P, Q), A, P') \qquad\qquad\qquad\;\;:- step(P, A, P').$
$step(out(X, Y, P), fout\_a(X, Y), P).$
$step(in(X, z.P), in\_a(X, W), P') \qquad\;\;:- W \,\#\, z.P, P' = ren\_p(P, W, z).$
$step(match(X, X, P), A, P') \qquad\qquad:- step(P, A, P').$
$step(par(P, Q), tau\_a, res(z.par(P', Q'))) :- step(P, bout\_a(X, z), P'),$
$\qquad\qquad\qquad\qquad\qquad\qquad\qquad\qquad\quad step(Q, in\_a(X, z), Q').$
$step(res(y.P), A, res(y.P')) \qquad\qquad:- y \,\#\, A, step(P, A, P').$
$step(res(y.P), bout\_a(X, W), P'') \qquad:- step(P, fout\_a(X, y), P'), y \,\#\, X,$
$\qquad\qquad\qquad\qquad\qquad\qquad\qquad\qquad\quad W \,\#\, y.P, P'' = ren\_p(P', W, y).$

Fig. 4. π-calculus transitions in αProlog

steps to q by performing action a". Actions τ, $\overline{x}y$, $x(y)$, $\overline{x}(y)$ are referred to as *silent, free output, input,* and *bound output* actions respectively; the first two are called *free* and the second two are called *bound* actions. For an action a, $n(a)$ is the set of all names appearing in a, and $bn(a)$ is empty if a is a free action and is $\{y\}$ if a is a bound action $x(y)$ or $\overline{x}(y)$. Processes and actions can be encoded using the following syntax:

$chan : \textbf{name\_type}. \quad proc : \textbf{type}. \quad ina : proc. \quad tau : proc \rightarrow proc.$
$par, sum : (proc, proc) \rightarrow proc. \qquad\quad in : (chan, \langle chan \rangle proc) \rightarrow proc.$
$out, match : (chan, chan, proc) \rightarrow proc. \quad res : (\langle chan \rangle proc) \rightarrow proc.$
$act : \textbf{type}. \quad tau\_a : act. \quad in\_a, fout\_a, bout\_a : (chan, chan) \rightarrow act.$

Much of the complexity of the rules is due to the need to handle *scope extrusion*, which occurs when restricted names "escape" their scope because of communication. In $((x)\overline{a}x.p)|(a(z).z(x).0) \overset{\tau}{-\!\!\!\rightarrow} (x')(p|x'(x).0))$, for example, it is necessary to "freshen" x to x' in order to avoid capturing the free x in $a(z).z(x).0$. Bound output actions are used to lift the scope of an escaping name out to the point where it is received. The rules can be translated directly into αProlog (see Figure 4). The function $ren\_p(P, Y, X)$ performing capture-avoiding renaming is not shown, but easy to define.

We can check that this implementation of the operational semantics produces correct answers for the following queries:

$$?-\ step(res(\mathsf{x}.par(res(\mathsf{y}.out(\mathsf{x},\mathsf{y},ina))),in(\mathsf{x},\mathsf{z}.out(\mathsf{z},\mathsf{x},ina)))),A,P).$$
$$A = tau\_a, P = res(\mathsf{y}_{58}.res(\mathsf{z}_{643}.par(ina,out(\mathsf{z}_{643},\mathsf{y}_{58},ina))))$$
$$?-\ step(res(\mathsf{x}.out(\mathsf{x},\mathsf{y},ina)),A,P).$$
$$No.$$

This αProlog session shows that $(x)((y)\overline{x}y.0 \mid x(y).\overline{y}x.0) \xrightarrow{\tau} (x)(y)(0 \mid \overline{y}x.0)$, but $(x)(x(y).0)$ cannot make any transition. Moreover, the answer to the first query is unique (up to renaming).

Röckl [20] and Gabbay [6] have also considered encodings of the π-calculus using nominal abstract syntax. Röckl considered only modeling the syntax of terms up to α-equivalence using swapping, whereas Gabbay went further, encoding transitions and the bisimulation relation and proving basic properties thereof. By [6, Thm 4.5], Gabbay's version of the π-calculus is equivalent to our conventional representation. In fact, Gabbay's presentation is a bit simpler and easier to reason about, but we have chosen Milner et al.'s original presentation to emphasize that informal "paper" presentations (even for fairly complicated calculi) can be translated directly to αProlog programs.

6 Concluding Remarks

6.1 Related Work

FreshML [22]: an extension of the ML programming language with Gabbay-Pitts names, name-binding with pattern matching, and fresh name generation. αProlog is related to FreshML in many ways, and it is fair to say that αProlog is to logic programming what FreshML is to functional programming. We believe however that the differences between FreshML and αProlog are more than cosmetic. αProlog lends itself to a declarative style of nameful programming which is refreshingly close to informal declarative presentations of operational semantics, type systems and logics, in contrast to FreshML which remains procedural (and effectful) at heart. There are also major differences from a technical point of view: in FreshML much research went into designing an expressive type-system, while the problems we face in αProlog concern the design of an efficient proof search procedure (see [26]).

Qu-Prolog [24]: an extension of Prolog with built-in names, binding, and explicit capture-avoiding substitutions and unification up to both α-equivalence and substitution evaluation. Qu-Prolog includes "not free in" constraints corresponding to our freshness constraints. Nevertheless, there are significant differences; αProlog is not a reinvention of Qu-Prolog. First, αProlog is a strongly typed polymorphic language, in contrast to Qu-Prolog, which is untyped in the Prolog tradition. Second, αProlog is based on a simpler unification algorithm that unifies up to α-equivalence but not up to substitution. Finally, Qu-Prolog lacks a logical semantics, and because of its internalized treatment of capture-avoiding substitution, developing one would likely be difficult. In contrast, nominal logic [19] provides a solid semantic foundation for αProlog.

Logic Programming with Binding Algebras: Hamana [9] has formalized a logic programming language based on Fiore, Turi, and Plotkin's *binding algebras* [5]. No implementation of this language appears to be available. However, since binding algebras are a formalization of HOAS, we believe that this approach will also share the semantic complexity of HOAS.

L_λ: Miller [12] discovered a restricted form of higher-order logic programming called L_λ in which unification is efficiently decidable and HOAS encodings are possible, but built-in capture-avoiding substitution is not available. There are several interesting parallels between L_λ and αProlog (and nominal unification and L_λ unification); relating these languages is future work.

Delphin: Schürmann et al. [21] are developing a functional programming language called Delphin which supports advanced meta-programming with recursion over higher-order abstract syntax. This approach seems very powerful, but also very complex because it is based on HOAS.

6.2   Status and Future Work

We have implemented an interpreter for αProlog based on nominal unification as outlined in this paper, along with many additional example programs, such as translation to a small typed assembly language, evaluation for a core object calculus, and modeling a cryptographic authentication protocol. The implementation is available online[1]. Some additional applications of interest, such as type inference for a small ML-like language and translations from regular expressions to finite automata, do not work properly because of αProlog's current incomplete implementation. Therefore we are very interested in developing techniques for equivariant unification and resolution.

Following Miller et al. [13], we have formulated a uniform proof theoretic semantics for *nominal hereditary Harrop formulas* based on a sequent calculus for nominal logic [7]. A more traditional model-theoretic semantics is in development. We also plan to develop mode and determinism analyses for αProlog. Another interesting direction is the possibility of integrating αProlog's constraint domain into an existing constraint logic programming system.

One deficiency of αProlog relative to HOAS systems and Qu-Prolog is that capture-avoiding substitution is not built-in, but must be written by hand when needed. We are currently experimenting with an operation $\cdot\{\cdot/\cdot\} : (\alpha, \beta, \beta) \to \alpha$, such that $t\{u/v\}$ denotes the result of replacing the term v with u everywhere in t, renaming abstractions to avoid capture. Thus, $subst(t, u, \mathsf{x})$ for λ or $\lambda\mu$-terms can be written as $t\{u/var(\mathsf{x})\}$, and $ren\_p(p, \mathsf{a}, \mathsf{b})$ as $p\{\mathsf{a}/\mathsf{b}\}$. Currently there are *ad hoc* restrictions such as that t and v must be ground when $t\{u/v\}$ is evaluated. Also, this does not help with unusual substitution-like operations

---

[1] http://www.cs.cornell.edu/People/jcheney/aprolog/

such as $\lambda\mu$-calculus replacement. Developing a logical account of substitution in nominal logic and αProlog is an important area for future work.

6.3 Summary

Though still a work in progress, αProlog shows great promise. Although αProlog is not the first language to include special constructs for dealing with variable binding, αProlog allows programming much closer to informal "paper" definitions than any other extant system. We have given several examples of languages that can be defined both declaratively and concisely in αProlog. We have also described the operational semantics for core αProlog, which is sound with respect to nominal logic, but complete only for a class of well-behaved programs. Additional work is needed to develop practical techniques for *equivariant unification* necessary for complete nominal resolution, and to develop static analyses and other forms of reasoning about αProlog programs. More broadly, we view αProlog as a modest first step toward a *nominal logical framework* for reasoning about programming languages, logics, and type systems encoded in nominal abstract syntax.

References

1. Andreas Abel. A third-order representation of the $\lambda\mu$-calculus. In S.J. Ambler, R.L. Crole, and A. Momigliano, editors, *MERLIN 2001: Mechanized Reasoning about Languages with Variable Binding*, volume 58(1) of *Electronic Notes in Theoretical Computer Science*. Elsevier, 2001.
2. James Cheney. The complexity of equivariant unification. In *Proceedings of the 31st International Colloquium on Automata, Languages and Programming (ICALP 2004)*, 2004. To appear.
3. N. G. de Bruijn. Lambda-calculus notation with nameless dummies, a tool for automatic formula manipulation. *Indag. Mat.*, 34(5):381–392, 1972.
4. Joëlle Despeyroux, Amy Felty, and André Hirschowitz. Higher-order abstract syntax in Coq. In M. Dezani-Ciancaglini and G. Plotkin, editors, *Proc. Int. Conf. on Typed Lambda Calculi and Applications*, pages 124–138, Edinburgh, Scotland, 1995. Springer-Verlag LNCS 902.
5. M. P. Fiore, G. D. Plotkin, and D. Turi. Abstract syntax and variable binding. In *Proc. 14th Symp. on Logic in Computer Science (LICS 1999)*, pages 193–202. IEEE, 1999.
6. M. J. Gabbay. The π-calculus in FM. In Fairouz Kamareddine, editor, *Thirty-five years of Automath*. Kluwer, 2003.
7. M. J. Gabbay and J. Cheney. A proof theory for nominal logic. In *Proceedings of the 19th Annual IEEE Symposium on Logic in Computer Science (LICS 2004)*, 2004. To appear.
8. M. J. Gabbay and A. M. Pitts. A new approach to abstract syntax with variable binding. *Formal Aspects of Computing*, 13:341–363, 2002.
9. Makoto Hamana. A logic programming language based on binding algebras. In *Proc. Theoretical Aspects of Computer Science (TACS 2001)*, number 2215 in Lecture Notes in Computer Science, pages 243–262. Springer-Verlag, 2001.

10. Martin Hofmann. Semantical analysis of higher-order abstract syntax. In *Proc. 14th Symp. on Logic in Computer Science*, pages 204–213. IEEE, July 1999.
11. Joxan Jaffar, Michael J. Maher, Kim Marriott, and Peter J. Stuckey. The semantics of constraint logic programs. *Journal of Logic Programming*, 37(1-3):1–46, 1998.
12. Dale Miller. A logic programming language with lambda-abstraction, function variables, and simple unification. *J. Logic and Computation*, 1(4):497–536, 1991.
13. Dale Miller, Gopalan Nadathur, Frank Pfenning, and Andre Scedrov. Uniform proofs as a foundation for logic programming. *Annals of Pure and Applied Logic*, 51:125–157, 1991.
14. Robin Milner, Joachim Parrow, and David Walker. A calculus of mobile processes, I-II. *Information and Computation*, 100(1):1–77, September 1992.
15. A. Momigliano, S. J. Ambler, and R. L. Crole. A comparison of formalizations of the meta-theory of a language with variable bindings in Isabelle. In *Informatics Research Report EDI-INF-RR-0046, Supplemental Proceedings of TPHOLs 2001*, pages 267–282. University of Edinburgh, 2001.
16. G. Nadathur and D. Miller. Higher-order logic programming. In D. M. Gabbay, C. J. Hogger, and J. A. Robinson, editors, *Handbook of Logic in Artificial Intelligence and Logic Programming*, volume 5, chapter 8, pages 499–590. Oxford University Press, 1998.
17. Michel Parigot. Lambda-mu-calculus: An algorithmic interpretation of classical natural deduction. In A. Voronkov, editor, *Proceedings of the 1992 International Conference on Logic Programming and Automated Reasoning (LPAR '92)*, number 624 in LNAI, pages 190–201, 1992.
18. Frank Pfenning and Conal Elliott. Higher-order abstract syntax. In *Proc. ACM SIGPLAN Conf. on Programming Language Design and Implementation (PLDI '89)*, pages 199–208. ACM Press, 1989.
19. A. M. Pitts. Nominal logic, a first order theory of names and binding. *Information and Computation*, 183:165–193, 2003.
20. Christine Röckl. A first-order syntax for the pi-calculus in isabelle/hol using permutations. In S.J. Ambler, R.L. Crole, and A. Momigliano, editors, *MERLIN 2001: Mechanized Reasoning about Languages with Variable Binding*, volume 58(1) of *Electronic Notes in Theoretical Computer Science*. Elsevier, 2001.
21. C. Schürmann, R. Fontana, and Y. Liao. Delphin: Functional programming with deductive systems. Available at http://cs-www.cs.yale.edu/homes/carsten/, 2002.
22. M. R. Shinwell, A. M. Pitts, and M. J. Gabbay. FreshML: Programmming with binders made simple. In *Proc. 8th ACM SIGPLAN Int. Conf. on Functional Programming (ICFP 2003)*, pages 263–274, Uppsala, Sweden, 2003. ACM Press.
23. Zoltan Somogyi, Fergus Henderson, and Thomas Conway. The execution algorithm of Mercury: an efficient purely declarative logic programming language. *J. Logic Programming*, 29(1–3):17–64, October-December 1996.
24. J. Staples, P. J. Robinson, R. A. Paterson, R. A. Hagen, A. J. Craddock, and P. C. Wallis. Qu-prolog: An extended prolog for meta level programming. In Harvey Abramson and M. H. Rogers, editors, *Meta-Programming in Logic Programming*, chapter 23. MIT Press, 1996.
25. C. Urban, A. M. Pitts, and M. J. Gabbay. Nominal unification. In M. Baaz, editor, *Computer Science Logic and 8th Kurt Gödel Colloquium (CSL'03 & KGC)*, volume 2803 of *Lecture Notes in Computer Science*, pages 513–527, Vienna, Austria, 2003. Springer-Verlag.
26. Christian Urban and James Cheney. Avoiding equivariant unification. Submitted.

Implementation Results
in Classical Constructive Negation

Susana Muñoz-Hernández and Juan José Moreno-Navarro

LSIIS, Facultad de Informática
Universidad Politécnica de Madrid
Campus de Montegancedo s/n Boadilla del Monte
28660 Madrid, Spain*
{susana,jjmoreno}@fi.upm.es

Abstract. Logic Programming has been advocated as a language for system
specification, especially for those involving logical behaviours, rules and knowledge. However, modeling problems involving negation, which is quite natural in
many cases, is somewhat limited if Prolog is used as the specification / implementation language. These restrictions are not related to theory viewpoint, where
users can find many different models with their respective semantics; they concern practical implementation issues. The negation capabilities supported by current Prolog systems are rather constrained, and there is no a correct and complete
implementation available. In this paper, we refine and propose some extensions
to the classical method of constructive negation, providing the complete theoretical algorithm. Furthermore, we also discuss implementation issues providing a
preliminary implementation and also an optimized one to negate predicates with
a finite number of solutions.

Keywords: Constructive Negation, Negation in Logic Programming, Constraint
Logic Programming, Implementations of Logic Programming, Optimization.

1 Introduction

From its very beginning Logic Programming has been advocated to be both a programming language and a specification language. It is natural to use Logic Programming for
specifying/programming systems involving logical behaviours, rules and knowledge.
However, this idea has a severe limitation: the use of negation. Negation is probably the
most significant aspect of logic that was not included from the outset. This is due to the
fact that dealing with negation involves significant additional complexity. Nevertheless,
the use of negation is very natural and plays an important role in many cases, for instance, constraints management in databases, program composition, manipulation and
transformation, default reasoning, natural language processing, etc.

Although this restriction cannot be perceived from the theoretical point of view
(because there are many ways to understand and incorporate negation into Logic Programming), the problems really start at the semantic level, where the different proposals (negation as failure -*naf*-, stable models, well-founded semantics, explicit negation,

---

* This work was partly supported by the Spanish MCYT project TIC2003-01036.

B. Demoen and V. Lifschitz (Eds.): ICLP 2004, LNCS 3132, pp. 284–298, 2004.
© Springer-Verlag Berlin Heidelberg 2004

etc.) differ not only as to expressiveness but also as to semantics. However, the negation techniques supported by current Prolog[1] compilers are rather limited, restricted to negation as failure under Fitting/Kunen semantics [13] (sound only under some circumstances usually not checked by compilers) which is a built-in or library in most Prolog compilers (Quintus, SICStus, Ciao, BinProlog, etc.), and the "delay technique" (applying negation as failure only *when* the variables of the negated goal become ground, which is sound but incomplete due to the possibility of floundering), which is present in Nu-Prolog, Gödel, and Prolog systems that implement delays (most of the above).

Of all the proposals, constructive negation [8, 9] (that we will call *classical* constructive negation) is probably the most promising because it has been proven to be sound and complete, and its semantics is fully compatible with Prolog's. Constructive negation was, in fact, announced in early versions of the Eclipse Prolog compiler, but was removed from the latest releases. The reasons seem to be related to some technical problems with the use of coroutining (risk of floundering) and the management of constrained solutions. We are trying to fill a long time open gap in this area (remember that the original papers are from late 80s) facing the problem of providing a correct implementation.

The goal of this paper is to give an algorithmic description of constructive negation, i.e. explicitly stating the details needed for an implementation. We also intend to discuss the pragmatic ideas needed to provide a concrete and real implementation. We are combining several different techniques: implementation of disequality constraint, program transformation, efficient management of constraints on the Herbrand universe, etc. While many of them are relatively easy to understand (and the main inspiration are, of course, in papers on theoretical aspects of constructive negation including Chan's ones) the main novelty of this work is the way we combine by reformulating constructive negation aspect in an implementation oriented way. In fact, results for a concrete implementation extending the Ciao Prolog compiler are presented. Due to space limitations, we assume some familiarity with constructive negation techniques [8, 9].

On the side of related work, unfortunately we cannot compare our work with any existing implementation of classical constructive negation in Prolog (even with implementations of other negation techniques, like intensional negation [3, 6, 16] or negation as instantiation [20] where many papers discuss the theoretical aspects but not implementation details) because we have not found in the literature any reported practical realization. However, there are some very interesting experiences: notably XSB prototypes implementing well-founded semantics ([1]). Less interesting seem to be the implementation of constructive negation reported in [5] because of the severe limitations in source programs (they cannot contain free variables in clauses) and the prototype sketched in [2] where a botton-up computation of literal answers is discussed (no execution times are reported but it is easy to deduce innefficiency both in terms of time and memory).

The remainder of the paper is organized as follows. Section 2 details our constructive negation algorithm. It explains how to obtain the *frontier* of a goal (Section 2.1), how to prepare the goal for negation (Section 2.2) and, finally, how to negate the goal

---

[1] We understand Prolog as depth-first, left to right implementation of SLD resolution for Horn clause programs, ignoring, in principle, side effects, cuts, etc.

(Section 2.3). Section 3 discusses implementation issues: code expansion (Section 3.1), required disequality constraints (Section 3.2) and optimizations (Section 3.3). Section 4 provides some experimental results and Section 5 talks about a variant of our implementation for negating goals that have a finite number of solutions. Finally, we conclude and outline some future work in Section 6.

2   Constructive Negation

Most of the papers addressing constructive negation deal with semantic aspects. In fact, only the original papers by Chan gave some hints about a possible implementation based on coroutining, but the technique was only outlined. When we tried to reconstruct this implementation we came across several problems, including the management of constrained answers and floundering (which appears to be the main reason why constructive negation was removed from recent versions of Eclipse). It is our belief that these problems cannot be easily and efficiently overcome. Therefore, we decided to design an implementation from scratch. One of our additional requirements is that we want to use a standard Prolog implementation to enable that Prolog programs with negation could reuse libraries and existing Prolog code. Additionaly, we want to maintain the efficiency of these Prolog programs, at least for the part that does not use negation. In this sense we will avoid implementation-level manipulations that would delay simple programs without negations.

We start with the definition of a frontier and how it can be managed to negate the respective formula.

2.1   Frontier

Firstly, we present Chan's definition of frontier (we actually owe the formal definition to Stuckey [23]).

Definition 1. Frontier
A frontier of a goal G is the disjunction of a finite set of nodes in the derivation tree such that every derivation of G is either finitely failed or passes through exactly one frontier node.

What is missing is a method to generate the frontier. So far we have used the simplest possible frontier: the frontier of depth 1 obtained by taking all the possible single SLD resolution steps. This can be done by a simple inspection of the clauses of the program[2]. Additionally, built-in based goals receive a special treatment (moving conjunctions into disjunctions, disjunctions into conjunction, eliminating double negations, etc.)

Definition 2. Depth-one frontier

– *If $G \equiv (G_1; G_2)$ then $Frontier(G) \equiv Frontier(G_1) \vee Frontier(G_2)$.*

---

[2] Nevertheless, we plan to generate the frontier in a more efficient way by using abstract interpretation over the input program for detecting the degree of evaluation of a term that will be necesary at execution time.

- *If $G \equiv (G_1, G_2)$ then $Frontier(G) \equiv Frontier(G_1) \wedge Frontier(G_2)$ and then we have to apply DeMorgan's distributive property to retain the disjunction of conjunctions format.*
- *If $G \equiv p(\overline{X})$ and predicate p/m is defined by N clauses:* $\quad p(\overline{X}^1) : -C'_1.$

$$p(\overline{X}^N) : -C'_N.$$

The frontier of the goal has the format: $Frontier(G) \equiv C_1 \vee C_2 \vee \ldots \vee C_N$, where each C_i is the union of the conjunction of subgoals C'_i plus the equalities that are needed to unify the variables of $\overline{X}$ and the respective terms of $\overline{X}^i$.

The definition is an easy adaptation of Chan's one, but it is also a simple example of the way we attack the problem, reformulating yet defined concepts in an implementation oriented way.
Consider, for instance, the following code:

```
odd(s(0)).
odd(s(s(X))) :- odd(X).
```

The frontier for the goal $odd(Y)$ is as follows:

$$Frontier(odd(Y)) = \{(Y = s(0)) \vee (Y = s(s(X)) \wedge odd(X))\}$$

To get the negation of G it suffices to negate the frontier formula. This is done by negating each component of the disjunction of all implied clauses (that form the frontier) and combining the results. That is, $\neg G \equiv \neg Frontier(G) \equiv \neg C_1 \wedge \ldots \wedge \neg C_N$.

Therefore, the solutions of $cneg(G)$ are the result of the combination (conjunction) of one solution of each $\neg C_i$. So, we are going to explain how to negate a single conjunction C_i. This is done in two phases: *Preparation* and *Negation of the formula*.

2.2 Preparation

Before negating a conjunction obtained from the frontier, we have to simplify, organize, and normalize this conjunction. The basic ideas are present in [8] in a rather obscure way. In Chan's papers, and then in Stuckey's one, it is simply stated that the conjunction is negated using logic standard techniques. Of course, it is true but it is not so easy in the middle of a Prolog computation because we have not access to the whole formula or predicate we are executing[3].

- **Simplification of the conjunction.** If one of the terms of C_i is trivially equivalent to *true* (e.g. $X = X$), we can eliminate this term from C_i. Symmetrically, if one of the terms is trivially *fail* (e.g. $X \neq X$), we can simplify $C_i \equiv fail$. The simplification phase can be carried out during the generation of frontier terms.
- **Organization of the conjunction.** Three groups are created containing the components of C_i, which are divided into equalities ($\overline{I}$), disequalities ($\overline{D}$), and other subgoals ($\overline{R}$). Then, we get $C_i \equiv \overline{I} \wedge \overline{D} \wedge \overline{R}$.

---

[3] Unless we use metaprogramming techniques that we try to avoid for efficiency reasons.

- **Normalization of the conjunction.** Let us classify the variables in the formula. The set of variables of the goal, G, is called *GoalVars*. The set of free variables of $\overline{R}$ is called *RelVars*.

  - **Elimination of redundant variables and equalities.** If $I_i \equiv X = Y$, where $Y \notin GoalVars$, then we now have the formula $(I_1 \wedge \ldots \wedge I_{i-1} \wedge I_{i+1} \wedge \ldots \wedge I_{NI} \wedge \overline{D} \wedge \overline{R})\sigma$, where $\sigma = \{Y/X\}$, i.e. the variable Y is substituted by X in the entire formula.

  - **Elimination of irrelevant disequalities.** *ImpVars* is the set of variables of *GoalVars* and the variables that appear in $\overline{I}$. The disequalities D_i that contain any variable that was neither in *ImpVars* nor in *RelVars* are irrelevant and should be eliminated.

2.3 Negation of the Formula

It is not feasible, to get all solutions of C_i and to negate their disjunction because C_i can have an infinite number of solutions. So, we have to use the classical constructive negation algorithm.

We consider that *ExpVars* is the set of variables of $\overline{R}$ that are not in *ImpVars*, i.e. *RelVars*, except the variables of $\overline{I}$ in the normalized formula.

First step: **Division of the formula**
C_i is divided into: $C_i \equiv \overline{I} \wedge \overline{D}_{imp} \wedge \overline{R}_{imp} \wedge \overline{D}_{exp} \wedge \overline{R}_{exp}$
where $\overline{D}_{exp}$ are the disequalities in $\overline{D}$ with variables in *ExpVars* and $\overline{D}_{imp}$ are the other disequalities, $\overline{R}_{exp}$ are the goals of $\overline{R}$ with variables in *ExpVars* and $\overline{R}_{imp}$ are the other goals, and $\overline{I}$ are the equalities.

Therefore, the constructive negation of the divided formula is:
$$\neg\, C_i \equiv \neg\, \overline{I} \vee (\overline{I} \wedge \neg\, \overline{D}_{imp}) \vee (\overline{I} \wedge \overline{D}_{imp} \wedge \neg\, \overline{R}_{imp}) \vee \overline{I} \wedge \overline{D}_{imp} \wedge \overline{R}_{imp} \wedge \neg\, (\overline{D}_{exp} \wedge \overline{R}_{exp}))$$

It is not possible to separate $\overline{D}_{exp}$ and $\overline{R}_{exp}$ because they contain free variables and they cannot be negated separately. The answers of the negations will be the answers of the negation of the equalities, the answers of the negation of the disequalities without free variables, the answers of the negation of the subgoals without free variables and the answers of the negation of the other subgoals of the conjunctions (the ones with free variables). Each of them will be obtained as follows:

Second step: **Negation of subformulas**

- **Negation of $\overline{I}$.** We have $\overline{I} \equiv I_1 \wedge \ldots \wedge I_{NI} \equiv \exists\, \overline{Z}_1\, X_1 = t_1 \wedge \ldots \wedge \exists\, \overline{Z}_{NI}\, X_{NI} = t_{NI}$ where $\overline{Z}_i$ are the variables of the equality I_i that are not included in *GoalVars* (i.e. that are not quantified and are therefore free variables). When we negate this conjunction of equalities we get the constraint $\underbrace{\forall\, \overline{Z}_1\, X_1 \neq t_1}_{\neg\, I_1} \vee \ldots \vee \underbrace{\forall\, \overline{Z}_{NI}\, X_{NI} \neq t_{NI}}_{\neg\, I_{NI}} \equiv$

  $\bigvee_{i=1}^{NI} \forall\, \overline{Z}_i X_i \neq t_i$ This constraint is the first answer of the negation of C_i that contains NI components.

- **Negation of $\overline{D}_{imp}$.** If we have $N_{D_{imp}}$ disequalities $\overline{D}_{imp} \equiv D_1 \wedge \ldots \wedge D_{N_{D_{imp}}}$ where $D_i \equiv \forall\, \overline{W}_i\, \exists\, \overline{Z}_i\, Y_i \neq s_i$ where Y_i is a variable of *ImpVars*, s_i is a term without variables in *ExpVars*, $\overline{W}_i$ are universally quantified variables that are neither in the equalities[4], nor in the other goals of $\overline{R}$ because otherwise $\overline{R}$ would be a disequality of $\overline{D}_{exp}$. Then we will get $N_{D_{imp}}$ new solutions with the format:

$$\overline{I} \wedge \neg D_1$$
$$\overline{I} \wedge D_1 \wedge \neg D_2$$
$$\ldots$$
$$\overline{I} \wedge D_1 \wedge \ldots \wedge D_{N_{D_{imp}}-1} \wedge \neg D_{N_{D_{imp}}}$$

where $\neg D_i \equiv \exists \overline{W}_i\ Y_i = s_i$. The negation of a universal quantification turns into an existential quantification and the quantification of free variables of $\overline{Z}_i$ gets lost, because the variables are unified with the evaluation of the equalities of $\overline{I}$. Then, we will get $N_{D_{imp}}$ new answers.

- **Negation of $\overline{R}_{imp}$.** If we have $N_{R_{imp}}$ subgoals $\overline{R}_{imp} \equiv R_1 \wedge \ldots \wedge R_{N_{R_{imp}}}$. Then we will get new answers from each of the conjunctions:

$$\overline{I} \wedge \overline{D}_{imp} \wedge \neg R_1$$
$$\overline{I} \wedge \overline{D}_{imp} \wedge R_1 \wedge \neg R_2$$
$$\ldots$$
$$\overline{I} \wedge \overline{D}_{imp} \wedge R_1 \wedge \ldots \wedge R_{N_{R_{imp}}-1} \wedge \neg R_{N_{R_{imp}}}$$

where $\neg R_i \equiv cneg(R_i)$. Constructive negation is again applied over R_i recursively using this operational semantics.

- **Negation of $\overline{D}_{exp} \wedge \overline{R}_{exp}$.** This conjunction cannot be separated because of the negation of $\exists \overline{V}_{exp}\ \overline{D}_{exp} \wedge \overline{R}_{exp}$, where $\overline{V}_{exp}$ gives universal quantifications: $\forall \overline{V}_{exp}\ cneg(\overline{D}_{exp} \wedge \overline{R}_{exp})$. The entire constructive negation algorithm must be applied again. Notice the recursive application of constructive negation. However, the previous steps could have generated an answer for the original negated goal. Of course it is possible to produce infinitely many answer to a negated goal.

Note that the new set *GoalVars* is the former set *ImpVars*. Variables of $\overline{V}_{exp}$ are considered as free variables. When solutions of $cneg(\overline{D}_{exp} \wedge \overline{R}_{exp})$ are obtained some can be rejected: solutions with equalities with variables in $\overline{V}_{exp}$. If there is a disequality with any of these variables, e.g. V, the variable will be universally quantified in the disequality. This is the way to obtain the negation of a goal, but there is a detail that was not considered in former approaches and that is necessary to get a sound implementation: the existence of universally quantified variables in $\overline{D}_{exp} \wedge \overline{R}_{exp}$ by the iterative application of the method. That is, we are really negating a subgoal of the form: $\exists \overline{V}_{exp}\ \overline{D}_{exp} \wedge \overline{R}_{exp}$. Its negation is $\forall \overline{V}_{exp}\ \neg(\overline{D}_{exp} \wedge \overline{R}_{exp})$ and therefore, we will provide the last group of answers that comes from:

$$\overline{I} \wedge \overline{D}_{imp} \wedge \overline{R}_{imp} \wedge \forall \overline{V}_{exp}\ \neg (\overline{D}_{exp} \wedge \overline{R}_{exp})$$

3   Implementation Issues

Having described the theoretical algorithm, including important details, we now discuss important aspects for a practical implementation, including how to compute the frontier and manage answer constraints.

---
[4] There are, of course, no universally quantified variables in an equality.

3.1   Code Expansion

The first issue is how to get the frontier of a goal. It is possible to handle the code of clauses during the execution thanks to the Ciao package system [7], which allows the code to be expanded at run time. The expansion is implemented in the *cneg.pl* package which is included in the declaration of the module that is going to be expanded (i.e. where there are goals that are negations).

Note that a similar, but less efficient, behaviour can be emulated using metaprogramming facilities, available in most Prolog compilers.

3.2   Disequality Constraints

An instrumental step for managing negation is to be able to handle disequalities between terms such as $t_1 \neq t_2$. The typical Prolog resources for handling these disequalities are limited to the built-in predicate /== /2, which needs both terms to be ground because it always succeeds in the presence of free variables. It is clear that a variable needs to be bound with a disequality to achieve a "constructive" behaviour. Moreover, when an equation $X = t(\overline{Y})$ is negated, the free variables in the equation must be universally quantified, unless affected by a more external quantification, i.e. $\forall \overline{Y} \; X \neq t(\overline{Y})$ is the correct negation. As we explained in [17], the inclusion of disequalities and constrained answers has a very low cost. From the theoretical point of view, it incorporates negative normal form constraints (in the form of conjuntion of equalities plus conjunction of disjunctions of possibly universally quantified disequations) instead of simple bindings as the decomposition step can produce disjunctions. In the implementation side, attributed variables are used which associate a data structure, containing a normal form constraint, to any variable:

$$\underbrace{(\bigwedge_j \forall \overline{Z}_j^1 \; (Y_j^1 \neq s_j^1) \vee \ldots \vee \bigwedge_l \forall \overline{Z}_l^n \; (Y_l^n \neq s_l^n))}_{\text{negative information}}$$

Additionaly, a Prolog predicate =/= /2 has been defined, used to check disequalities, similarly to explicit unification (=). Each constraint is a disjunction of conjunctions of disequalities. A universal quantification in a disequality (e.g., $\forall Y \; X \neq c(Y)$), is represented with a new constructor fA/1 (e.g., X =/= c(fA(Y))). Due to the lack of space, we refer the interested reader to check the details in [17].

3.3   Optimizing the Algorithm and the Implementation

Our constructive negation algorithm and the implementation techniques admit some additional optimizations that can improve the runtime behaviour of the system. Basically, the optimizations rely on the compact representation of information, as well as the early detection of successful or failing branches.

Compact information. In our system, negative information is represented quite compactly thanks to our constraint normal form, providing fewer solutions from the negation of $\overline{I}$ and $\overline{D}_{imp}$. The advantage is twofold. On the one hand constraints contain more information and failing branches can be detected earlier (i.e. the search space could be smaller). On the other hand, if we ask for all solutions using backtracking, we are cutting the search tree by offering all the solutions together in a single answer. For example, we can offer a simple answer for the negation of a predicate p (the code for p is skipped because it is no relevant for the example):

```
?- cneg(p(X,Y,Z,W)).
(X=/=0, Y=/=s(Z)) ; (X=/=Y) ; (X=/=Z) ;
(X=/=W) ; (X=/=s(0), Z=/=0) ? ;
no
```

(which is equivalent to the formula $(X \neq 0 \wedge Y \neq s(Z)) \vee X \neq Y \vee X \neq Z \vee X \neq W \vee (X \neq s(0) \wedge Z \neq 0)$ that can be represented in our constraint normal form and, therefore, managed by attributes to the involved variables), instead of returning the six equivalent answers upon backtracking:

```
?- cneg(p(X,Y,Z,W)).
X=/=0, Y=/=s(Z) ? ;
X=/=Y ? ;
X=/=Z ? ;
X=/=W ? ;
X=/=s(0), Z=/=0 ? ;
no
```

In this case we get the whole disjunction at once instead of getting it by backtraking step by step. The generation of compact formulas in the negation of subformulas (see above Second step) is used whenever possible (in the negation of $\bar{I}$ and the negation of $\bar{D}_{imp}$). The negation of $\bar{R}_{imp}$ and the negation of $(\bar{D}_{exp} \vee \bar{R}_{exp})$ can have infinite solutions whose disjunction would be impossible to compute. So, for these cases we construct incrementally the solutions using backtracking.

Pruning subgoals. The frontiers generation search tree can be cut with a double action over the ground subgoals: removing the subgoals whose failure we are able to detect early on, and simplifying the subgoals that can be reduced to true. Suppose we have a predicate $p/2$ defined as

```
p(X,Y):- greater(X,Y), q(X,Y,Z), r(Z).
```

where $q/3$ and $r/1$ are predicates defined by several clauses with a complex computation. To negate the goal $p(s(0), s(s(0)))$, its frontier is computed:

$$Frontier(p(s(0), s(s(0)))) \equiv$$

Step 1 $X = s(0) \wedge Y = s(s(0)) \wedge greater(X,Y) \wedge q(X,Y,Z) \wedge r(Z) \equiv$

Step 2 $greater(s(0), s(s(0))) \wedge q(s(0), s(s(0)), Z) \wedge r(Z) \equiv$

Step 3 $fail \wedge q(s(0), s(s(0)), Z) \wedge r(Z) \equiv$

Step 4 $fail$

The first step is to expand the code of the subgoals of the frontier to the combination of the code of all their clauses (disjunction of conjunctions in general but only one conjunction in this case because $p/2$ is defined by one only clause), and the result will be a very complicated and hard to check frontier. However, the process is optimized by evaluating ground terms (Step 2). In this case, $greater(s(0), s(s(0)))$ fails and, therefore, it is not necessary to continue with the generation of the frontier, because the result is reduced to fail (i.e. the negation of $p(s(0), s(s(0)))$ will be trivially true). The opposite example is a simplification of a successful term in the third step:

$$Frontier(p(s(s(0)), s(0))) \equiv$$

Step 1 $X = s(s(0)) \wedge Y = s(0) \wedge greater(X,Y) \wedge q(X,Y,Z) \wedge r(Z) \equiv$

Step 2 $greater(s(s(0)),s(0)) \wedge q(s(s(0)),s(0),Z) \wedge r(Z) \equiv$
Step 3 $true \wedge q(s(s(0)),s(0),Z) \wedge r(Z) \equiv$
Step 4 $q(s(s(0)),s(0),Z) \wedge r(Z)$

Constraint simplification. During the whole process for negating a goal, the frontier variables are constrained. In cases where the constraints are satisfiable, they can be eliminated and where the constraints can be reduced to fail, the evaluation can be stopped with result *true*.

We focus on the negative information of a normal form constraint F:

$$F \equiv \bigvee_i \bigwedge_j \forall \overline{Z}^i_j \, (Y^i_j \neq s^i_j)$$

Firstly, the Prenex form [21] can be obtained by extracting the universal variables with different names to the head of the formula, applying logic rules:

$$F \equiv \forall \overline{x} \bigvee_i \bigwedge_j (Y^i_j \neq s^i_j)$$

and using the distributive property (notice that subindexes are different):

$$F \equiv \forall \overline{x} \bigwedge_k \bigvee_l (Y^k_l \neq s^k_l)$$

The formula can be separated into subformulas that are simple disjunctions of disequalities :

$$F \equiv \bigwedge_k \forall \overline{x} \bigvee_l (Y^k_l \neq s^k_l) \equiv F_1 \wedge ... \wedge F_n$$

Each single formula F_k can be evaluated. The first step will be to substitute the existentially quantified variables (variables that do not belong to $\overline{x}$) by Skolem constants that will keep the equivalence without losing generality:

$$F_k \equiv \forall \overline{x} \bigvee_l (Y^k_l \neq s^k_l) \equiv \forall \overline{x} \bigvee_l (Y^k_{Skl} \neq s^k_{Skl})$$

Then it can be transformed into:

$$F_k \equiv \neg \exists \, \overline{x} \neg (\bigvee_l (Y^k_{Skl} \neq s^k_{Skl})) \equiv \neg Fe_K$$

The meaning of F_k is the negation of the meaning of Fe_k;

$$Fe_k \equiv \exists \, \overline{x} \neg (\bigvee_l (Y^k_{Skl} \neq s^k_{Skl}))$$

Solving the negations, the result is obtained through simple unifications of the variables of $\overline{x}$:

$$Fe_k \equiv \exists \, \overline{x} \bigwedge \neg (Y^k_{Skl} \neq s^k_{Skl}) \equiv \exists \, \overline{x} \bigwedge (Y^k_{Skl} = s^k_{Skl})$$

Therefore, we get the truth value of F_k from the negation of the value of Fe_k and, finally, the value of F is the conjunction of the values of all F_k. If F succeeds, then the constraint is removed because it is redundant and we continue with the negation process. If it fails, then the negation directly succeeds.

4   Experimental Results

Our prototype is a simple library that is added to the set of libraries of Ciao Prolog. Indeed, it is easy to port the library to other Prolog compilers. The only requirement is that attributed variables should be available.

This section reports some experimental results from our prototype implementation. First of all, we show the behaviour of the implementation in some simple examples.

4.1   Examples

The interesting side of this implementation is that it returns constructive results from a negative question. Let us start with a simple example involving predicate *boole*/1.

```
boole(0).
boole(1).
```
```
?- cneg(boole(X)).
X=/=1, X=/=0 ? ;
no
```

Another simple example obtained from [23] gives us the following answers:
```
p(a,b,c).
p(b,a,c).
p(c,a,b).
proof1(X,Y,Z):-
    X =/= a, Z = c,
    cneg(p(X,Y,Z)).
```
```
?- proof1(X,Y,Z).
Z = c, X=/=b, X=/=a ? ;
Z = c, Y=/=a, X=/=a ? ;
no
```

[23] contains another example showing how a constructive answer $(\forall T\ X \neq s(T))$ is provided for the negation of an undefined goal in Prolog:

```
p(X):- X = s(T), q(T).
q(T):- q(T).
r(X):- cneg(p(X)).
```
```
?- r(X).
X=/=s(fA(_A)) ?
yes
```

Notice that if we would ask for a second answer, then it will loop according to the Prolog resolution. An example with an infinite number of solutions is more interesting.

```
positive(0).
positive(s(X)):-
            positive(X).
```
```
?- cneg(positive(X)).
X=/=s(fA(_A)), X=/=0 ? ;
X = s(_A),
(_A=/=s(fA(_B)), _A=/=0) ? ;
X = s(s(_A)),
(_A=/=s(fA(_B)), _A=/=0) ? ;
X = s(s(s(_A))),
(_A=/=s(fA(_B)), _A=/=0) ?
yes
```

4.2 Implementation Measures

We have firstly measured the execution times in milliseconds for the above examples when using negation as failure ($naf/1$) and constructive negation ($cneg/1$). A '-' in a cell means that negation as failure is not applicable. Some goals were executed a number of times to get a significant measurement. All of them were made using Ciao Prolog[5] 1.5 on a Pentium II at 350 MHz. The results are shown in Table 1. We have added a first column with the runtime of the evaluation of the positive goal that is negated in the other columns and a last column with the ratio that measures the speedup of the *naf* technique w.r.t. constructive negation.

Using **naf** instead of **cneg** results in small ratios around 1.06 on average for ground calls with few recursive calls. So, the possible slow-down for constructive negation is not so high as we might expect for these examples. Furthermore, the results are rather similar. But the same goals with data that involve many recursive calls yield ratios near 14.69 on average w.r.t **naf**, increasing exponentially with the number of recursive calls.

---

[5] The negation system is coded as a library module ("package" [7]), which includes the respective syntactic and semantic extensions (i.e. Ciao's attributed variables). Such extensions apply locally within each module which uses this negation library.

Table 1. Runtime comparation

goals	Goal	naf(Goal)	cneg(Goal)	ratio
boole(1)	2049	2099	2069	0.98
boole(8)	2070	2170	2590	1.19
positive(s(s(s(s(s(s(0)))))))	2079	1600	2159	1.3
positive(s(s(s(s(s(0))))))	2079	2139	2060	0.96
greater(s(s(s(0))),s(0))	2110	2099	2100	1.00
greater(s(0),s(s(s(0))))	2119	2129	2089	0.98
average				1.06
positive(500000)	2930	2949	41929	14.21
positive(1000000)	3820	3689	81840	22.18
greater(500000,500000)	3200	3339	22370	7.70
average				14.69
boole(X)	2080	-	3109	
positive(X)	2020	-	7189	
greater(s(s(s(0))),X)	2099	-	6990	
greater(X,Y)	7040	-	7519	
queens(s(s(0)),Qs)	6939	-	9119	

There are, of course, many goals that cannot be negated using the *naf* technique and that are solved using constructive negation.

5   Finite Constructive Negation

The problem with the constructive negation algorithm is of course efficiency. It is the price that it has to be paid for a powerful mechanism that negates any kind of goal. Thinking of Prolog programs, many goals have a finite number of solutions (we are considering also that this can be discovered in finite time, of course). There is a simplification of the constructive negation algorithm that we use to negate these goals. It is very simple in the sense that if we have a goal $\neg G$ where the solution of the positive subgoal G is a set of n solutions like $\{S_1, S_2, ..., S_n\}$, then we can consider these equivalences: $\neg G \equiv \neg(S_1 \vee S_2 \vee ... \vee S_n) \equiv (\neg S_1 \wedge \neg S_2 \wedge ... \wedge \neg S_n)$

Of course, these solutions are a conjunction of unifications (equalities) and disequality constraints. As described in section 3.2, we know how to handle and negate this kind of information. The implementation of the predicate $cnegf/1$ is something akin to

```
cnegf(Goal):-
    varset(Goal,GVars), % Getting variables of the Goal
    setof(GVars,Goal,LValores),!, % Getting the solutions
    cneg_solutions(GVars,LValores). % Negating solutions
cnegf(_Goal). % Without solutions, the negation succeeds
```

where *cneg_solutions*/2 is the predicate that negates the disjunction of conjunctions of solutions of the goal that we are negating. It works as described in section 2.3, but it is simpler, because here we are only negating equalities and disequalities.

We get the set of variables, *GVars*, of the goal, *Goal*, that we want to negate (we use the predicate *varset*/2). Then we use the *setof*/3 predicate to get the values of the variables of *GVars* for each solution of *Goal*. For example, if we want to evaluate $cnegf(boole(X))$, then we get $varset(boole(X),[X])$, $setof([X],boole(X),[[0],[1]])$ (i.e. $X = 0 \vee X = 1$) and $cneg\_solutions/2$ will return $X \neq 0 \wedge X \neq 1$.

If we have the goal $p(X,Y)$, which, has two solutions $X = a$, $Y = b$ and $X = c$, $Y = d$, then, in the evaluation of $cnegf(p(X,Y))$, we will get $varset(p(X,Y),[X,Y])$, $setof([X,Y],p(X,Y),[[a,b],[c,d]])$ (i.e. $(X = a \wedge Y = b) \vee (X = c \wedge Y = d)$) and $cneg\_solutions/2$ will return the four solutions $(X \neq a \wedge X \neq c) \vee (X \neq a \wedge Y \neq d) \vee (Y \neq b \wedge X \neq c) \vee (Y \neq b \wedge Y \neq d)$.

5.1   Analysis of the Number of Solutions

The optimization below is very intuitive but, perhaps, the main problem is to detect when a goal is going to have a finite number of solutions. To get sound results, we are going to use this technique (finite constructive negation) just to negate the goals that, we are sure do not have infinite solutions. So, our analysis is conservative.

We use a combination of two analyses to determine if a goal G can be negated with $cnegf/2$: the non-failure analysis (if G does not fail) and the analysis of upper cost [14] (if G has an upper cost inferior to infinite). Both are implemented in the Ciao Prolog precompiler [12]. Indeed, finite constructive negation can handle the negation of failure that is success. So the finite upper cost analysis is enough in practice. We test these analyses at compilation time and then, when possible, we directly execute the optimized version of constructive negation at compilation time.

It is more complicated to check this at execution time although we could provide a rough approximation. First, we get a maximun number N of solutions of G (we can use the library predicate *findnsols*/4) and then we check the number of solutions that we have obtained. If it is less than N, we can assure that G has a finite number of solutions and otherwise we do not know.

5.2   Experimental Results

We have implemented a predicate $cnegf/1$ to negate the disjunction of all the solutions of its argument (a goal). The implementation of this predicate takes advantage of backtracking to obtain only the information that we need to get the first answer. Then, if the user asks for another answer, the backtracking gets information enough to provide it. Accordingly, we avoid the complete evaluation of the negation of all the solutions first time round. We negate the subterms only when we need to provide the next solution. In this sense, if we have the goal G (where each S_i is the conjunction of Ni equalities or disequalities) $G \equiv S_1 \vee ... \vee S_n \equiv (S_1^1 \wedge ... \wedge S_1^{N1}) \vee ... \vee (S_n^1 \wedge ... \wedge S_n^{Nn})$
and we then want to obtain $\neg G$, then we have $\neg G \equiv \neg(S_1 \vee S_2 \vee ... \vee S_n) \equiv (\neg S_1 \wedge \neg S_2 \wedge ... \wedge \neg S_n) \equiv \neg(S_1^1 \wedge ... \wedge S_1^{N1}) \wedge ... \wedge \neg(S_n^1 \wedge ... \wedge S_n^{Nn}) \equiv (\neg S_1^1 \vee ... \vee \neg S_1^{N1}) \wedge ... \wedge (\neg S_n^1 \vee ... \vee \neg S_n^{Nn}) \equiv (\neg S_1^1 \wedge ... \wedge \neg S_n^1) \vee ... \vee (\neg S_1^{N1} \wedge ... \wedge \neg S_n^{Nn})$
we begin calculating just the first answer of the negation that will be $(\neg S_1^1 \wedge ... \wedge \neg S_n^1)$, and the rest will be calculated if necessary using backtracking.

Table 2. Runtime comparison of finite constructive negation

goals	Goal	cneg(Goal)	cnegf(Goal)	ratio
boole(1)	821	831	822	1,01
positive(s(s(s(0))))	811	1351	860	1,57
greater(s(0),s(s(0)))	772	1210	840	1,44
positive(s^{500000}(0))	1564	8259	3213	2,57
positive($s^{7500000}$(0))	2846	12445	3255	3,82
greater(s^{50000}(0),s^{50000}(0))	1240	66758	30112	2,21
boole(X)	900	1321	881	1,49
greater(s(s(0)),X)	990	1113	1090	1,02
queens(s(s(s(0))),Qs)	1481	50160	1402	35,77

Let us present a simple example:

```
?- member(3,[X,Y,Z]).          ?- cnegf(member(3,[X,Y,Z])).
X = 3 ? ;                       X=/=3, Y=/=3, Z=/=3 ?;
Y = 3 ? ;                       no
Z = 3 ? ;
no
```

We get the symmetric behavior for the negation of the negation of the initial query

```
?- cnegf(cnegf(member(3,[X,Y,Z]))).
X = 3 ? ;
Y = 3 ? ;
Z = 3 ? ;
no
```

We checked some time results in Table 2. The results are much more significant for more complicated goals. Indeed, the more complicated the code of a predicate is, the more inefficient its classical constructive negation (*cneg*) is. However, finite constructive negation (*cnegf*) is independent of code complexity. Finite constructive negation depends on the complexity of the solutions obtained for the positive goal and, of course, the number of solutions of this goal.

6   Conclusion and Future Work

After running some preliminary experiments with the classical constructive negation technique following Chan's description, we realized that the algorithm needed some additional explanations and modifications.

Having given a detailed specification of the algorithm in a detailed way we proceed to provide a real, complete and consistent implementation. To our knowledge it is the first reported work of a running implementation of constructive negation in Prolog from its definition in 1988. The results we have reported are very encouraging, because we have proved that it is possible to extend Prolog with a constructive negation module relatively inexpensively and overall without any delay in Prolog programs that are not using this negation. Nevertheless, it is quite important to address possible optimizations, and we are working to improve the efficiency of the implementation. These include a more accurate selection of the frontier based on the demanded form of argument in the vein of [15]). The full version of the paper will provide more details as well as these additional optimizations. Another possible future work is to incorporate our algorithm at the WAM machine level.

In any case, we will probably not be able to provide an efficient enough implementation of constructive negation, because the algorithm is inherently inefficient. This is why we do not intend to use it either for all cases of negation or for negating goals directly.

Our goal is to design and implement a practical negation operator and incorporate it into a Prolog compiler. In [17, 18] we systematically studied what we understood to be the most interesting existing proposals: negation as failure (*naf*) [10], use of delays to apply *naf* securely [19], intensional negation [3, 4], and constructive negation [8, 9, 11, 22, 23]. As none of them can satisfy our requirements of completeness and efficiency, we propose to use a combination of these techniques, where the information from static program analyzers could be used to reduce the cost of selecting techniques [18]. So, in many cases, we avoid the inefficiency of classical constructive negation. However, we still need it because it is the only method that is sound and complete for any kind of goals. For example, looking at the goals in Table 1, the strategy will obtain all ground negations using the *naf* technique and it would only use classical constructive negation for the goals with variables where it is impossible to use *naf*. Otherwise, the strategy will use finite constructive negation (*cnegf*) for the three last goals of Table 2 because the positive goals have a finite number of solutions.

We are testing the implementation and trying to improve the code, and our intention is to include it in the next version of Ciao Prolog[6].

References

1. J. J. Alferes, C. V. Damásio, and L. M. Pereira. A logic programming system for non-monotonic reasoning. In *Journal of Automated Reasoning*, volume 14(1), pages 93–147, 1995.
2. J. Alvez, P. Lucio, F. Orejas, E. Pasarella, and E. Pino. Constructive negation by bottom-up computation of literal answers,. In *Proceedings of the 2004 ACM Symposium on Applied Computing*, volume 2 of *ACM*, pages 1468–1475, Nicosia (Cyprus), 2004.
3. R. Barbuti, D. Mancarella, D. Pedreschi, and F. Turini. Intensional negation of logic programs. *LNCS*, 250:96–110, 1987.
4. R. Barbuti, D. Mancarella, D. Pedreschi, and F. Turini. A transformational approach to negation in logic programming. *JLP*, 8(3):201–228, 1990.
5. R. Barták. Constructive negation in clp(h). Tech. Report 98/6, Department of Theoretical Computer Science, Charles University, Prague, July 1998.
6. P. Bruscoli, F. Levi, G. Levi, and M. C. Meo. Compilative Constructive Negation in Constraint Logic Programs. In Sophie Tyson, editor, *Proc. of the 19th International CAAP '94*, volume 787 of *LNCS*, pages 52–67, Berlin, 1994. Springer-Verlag.
7. D. Cabeza and M. Hermenegildo. A New Module System for Prolog. In *CL2000*, number 1861 in LNAI, pages 131–148. Springer-Verlag, July 2000.

---

[6] http://www.clip.dia.fi.upm.es/Software

8. D. Chan. Constructive negation based on the complete database. In *Proc. Int. Conference on LP'88*, pages 111–125. The MIT Press, 1988.

9. D. Chan. An extension of constructive negation and its application in coroutining. In *Proc. NACLP'89*, pages 477–493. The MIT Press, 1989.

10. K. L. Clark. Negation as failure. In H. Gallaire and J. Minker, editors, *Logic and Data Bases*, pages 293–322, New York, NY, 1978. Plenum Press.

11. W. Drabent. What is a failure? An approach to constructive negation. *Acta Informatica.*, 33:27–59, 1995.

12. M. Hermenegildo, F. Bueno, G. Puebla, and P. López-García. Program Analysis, Debugging and Optimization Using the Ciao System Preprocessor. In *1999 ICLP*, pages 52–66, Cambridge, MA, November 1999. MIT Press.

13. K. Kunen. Negation in logic programming. *JLP*, 4:289–308, 1987.

14. P. López-García, M. Hermenegildo, S. Debray, and N. W. Lin. Lower bound cost estimation for logic programs. In *1997 International Logic Programming Symposium*. MIT Press, 1997.

15. J. J. Moreno-Navarro. Extending constructive negation for partial functions in lazy narrowing-based languages. *ELP*, 1996.

16. S. Muñoz, J. Mariño, and J. J. Moreno-Navarro. Constructive intensional negation. In *Proceedings of the 7th International Symposiun in Functional and Logic Programming, FLOPS'04*, number 2998 in LNCS, pages 39–54, Nara, Japan, 2004.

17. S. Muñoz and J. J. Moreno-Navarro. How to incorporate negation in a prolog compiler. In E. Pontelli and V. Santos Costa, editors, *2nd International Workshop PADL'2000*, volume 1753 of *LNCS*, pages 124–140, Boston, MA (USA), 2000. Springer-Verlag.

18. S. Muñoz, J. J. Moreno-Navarro, and M. Hermenegildo. Efficient negation using abstract interpretation. In R. Nieuwenhuis and A. Voronkov, editors, *LPAR 2001*, number 2250 in LNAI, pages 485–494, La Habana (Cuba), 2001.

19. L. Naish. *Negation and control in Prolog*. Number 238 in Lecture Notes in Computer Science. Springer-Verlag, New York, 1986.

20. A. Di Pierro and W. Drabent. On negation as instantiation. *Proceedings of The Fifth International Conference on Algebraic and Logic Programming ALP'96*, 1996.

21. J. R. Shoenfield. *Mathematical Logic*. Association for Symbolic Logic, 1967.

22. P. Stuckey. Constructive negation for constraint logic programming. In *Proc. IEEE Symp. on Logic in Computer Science*, volume 660. IEEE Comp. Soc. Press, 1991.

23. P. Stuckey. Negation and constraint logic programming. In *Information and Computation*, volume 118(1), pages 12–33, 1995.

On Hybridization of Local Search and Constraint Propagation

Eric Monfroy[1], Frédéric Saubion[2], and Tony Lambert[1,2]

[1] LINA, Université de Nantes, France
eric.monfroy@lina.univ-nantes.fr
[2] LERIA, Université d'Angers, France
{frederic.saubion,tony.lambert}@univ-angers.fr

Abstract. Hybridization of local search and constraint programming techniques for solving Constraint Satisfaction Problems is generally restricted to some kind of master-slave combinations for specific classes of problems. In this paper we propose a theoretical model based on K.R. Apt's chaotic iterations for hybridization of local search and constraint propagation. Hybrid resolution can be achieved as the computation of a fixpoint of some specific reduction functions. Our framework opens up new and finer possibilities for hybridization/combination strategies. We also present some combinations of techniques such as tabu search, node and bound consistencies. Some experimental results show the interest of our model to design such hybridization.

1 Introduction

Constraint Satisfaction Problems (CSP) [15] provide a general framework for the modeling of many practical applications (planning, scheduling, time tabling,...). A CSP is usually defined by a set of variables associated to domains of possible values and by a set of constraints. We only consider here CSP over finite domains. Constraints can be understood as relations over some variables and therefore, solving a CSP consists in finding tuples that belong to each constraint (an assignment of values to the variables that satisfies these constraints). To this end, many resolution algorithms have been proposed and we may distinguish at least two classes of general methods: 1) *complete methods* aim at exploring the whole search space in order to find all the solutions or to detect that the CSP is not consistent. Among these methods, we find methods based on constraint propagation, one of the most common techniques from constraint programming [4] (CP) for solving CSP; and 2) *incomplete methods* (such as Local Search [1] (LS)) mainly rely on the use of heuristics providing a more efficient exploration of interesting areas of the search space in order to find some solutions.

A common idea is to build more efficient and robust algorithms by combining several resolution paradigms in order to take advantage of their respective assets (e.g., [5] presents an overview of possible uses of LS in CP). The benefit of the hybridization LS+CP is well-known and does not have to be proven (see e.g., [8, 13, 12, 14]). Most of the previous works are either algorithmic approaches which

B. Demoen and V. Lifschitz (Eds.): ICLP 2004, LNCS 3132, pp. 299–313, 2004.
© Springer-Verlag Berlin Heidelberg 2004

define a kind of master-slave combination (e.g., LS to guide the search in CP, or CP to reduce interesting area of the search space explored in LS), or ad-hoc realizations of systems for specific classes of problems.

In this paper, we are concerned with a model for hybridization in which local search [1] and constraint propagation [4] are broken up into their component parts. These basic operators can then be managed at the same level by a single mechanism. In this framework, properties concerning solvers (e.g., termination, solutions) can be easily expressed and established. This framework also opens up new and finer possibilities of combination strategies.

Our model is based on K.R. Apt's chaotic iterations [2] which define a mathematical framework for iteration of a finite set of functions over "abstract" domains with partial ordering. This framework is well-suited for solving CSPs with constraint propagation: domains are instantiated with variable domains (possible values of variables), and functions with domain reduction functions to remove inconsistent (w.r.t. constraints) values of domain variables (reduction functions abstract the notion of constraint in this mechanism).

Moreover, to get a complete solver (a solver which is always able to determine whether a CSP has some solutions), constraint propagation is generally associated with a splitting mechanism (a technique such as enumeration or bisection) to cut the search space into some smaller search spaces from which one can hope to perform more propagation. Propagation and splitting are interleaved until the solutions are reached.

In our model, Local Search [1] is based on 3 notions: samples which are particular points or sets of points of the search space, neighborhood that defines which samples can be reached from a specific sample, and a fitness function that defines the "quality" of a sample. Then, LS explores the search space by moving from sample to sample guided by the fitness function in order to reach a local optimum.

For our purpose, we introduce in our model the notion of sCSP (sampled CSP) which is an extension of CSP with a path (list) of samples (generally points of the search space). We also integrate the splitting as some reduction functions. This way, the "abstract" domains of chaotic iteration are instantiated with union of sCSPs. Usual domain reduction functions (used for constraint propagation) are extended to fit this new domain. Some new functions (the LS functions) are also introduced to jump from samples to samples: these functions have the sufficient properties required to be used in the chaotic iteration algorithm.

Thus, in the chaotic iteration framework, constraint propagation functions, local search moves, and splitting functions are considered at the same level and all apply to unions of sCSPs. Since interleaving and order of applications of these functions are totally free, this framework enables one to design finer strategies for hybridization than the usual master-slave combinations. Moreover, termination of the realized solvers is straight forward, i.e., fixpoint of the reduction functions.

In order to illustrate our framework, we realized some hybrid solvers using some well-known techniques and strategies such as tabu search (for LS), node and arc consistencies (for propagation), and bisection functions (for splitting).

We obtained some experimental results that show the interest of combination strategies compared to a single use of these methods. Moreover, the combination strategies can easily be designed and specified, and their properties can be proven in our model.

This paper is organized as follows. Section 2 describes constraint propagation and local search in terms of basic operators. We present our framework for hybridization in Section 3. Some experiments are given in Section 4 before concluding in Section 5.

2   Constraint Satisfaction Problems

In this section we recall basic notions related to Constraint Satisfaction Problems (CSP) [15] together with their resolution principles. Complete resolution is presented using the theoretical model developed by K.R. Apt [2, 3]. We then briefly describe the main lines of a local search process.

A CSP is a tuple (X, D, C) where $X = \{x_1, \cdots, x_n\}$ is a set of variables taking their values in their respective domains $D = \{D_1, \cdots, D_n\}$. A constraint $c \in C$ is a relation $c \subseteq D_1 \times \cdots \times D_n$ [1]. In order to simplify notations, D will also denote the Cartesian product of D_i and C the union of its constraints. A tuple $d \in D$ is a solution of a CSP (X, D, C) if and only if $\forall c \in C, d \in c$.

2.1   Solving a CSP with Complete Resolution Techniques

As mentioned in introduction, complete resolution methods are mainly based on a systematic exploration of the search space, which corresponds obviously to the set of possible tuples. To avoid the combinatorial grow up of this exploration, these methods use particular heuristics to prune the search space. The most popular of these techniques (i.e., constraint propagation) is based on local consistency properties. A local consistency (e.g., [9, 11]) is a property of the constraints which allows the search mechanisms to delete values from variables domains which cannot lead to solutions. We may mention node consistency and arc consistency [10] as famous examples of local consistencies. Complete search algorithms use constraint propagation techniques and splitting. Constraint propagation consists in examining a subset (usually a single constraint) C' of C, deleting some inconsistent values (from a local consistency point of view) of the domains of variables appearing in C' and to propagate this domain reduction to domains of variables appearing in $C \setminus C'$. When no more propagation is possible and the solutions are not reached, the CSP is split into sub-CSPs (generally, the domain of a variable is split into two sub-domains, leading to two sub-CSPs) on which propagation is applied again, and so on until the solutions are reached.

K.R. Apt proposed in [2, 3] a general theoretical framework for modeling such reduction operators. In this context, domain reduction corresponds to the

---

[1] Note that for sake of simplicity, we consider that each constraint is over all the variables $x_1, \ldots, x_n$. However, one can consider constraints over some of the x_i. Then, the notion of scheme [2, 3] can be used to denote sequences of variables.

computation of a fixpoint of a set of functions over a partially ordered set. These functions, called *reduction functions*, abstract the notion of constraint.

The computation of the least common fixpoint of a set of functions F is achieved by the following algorithm:

GI: Generic Iteration Algorithm

$d := \perp$;
$G := F$;
While $G \neq \emptyset$ do
$\quad$ choose $g \in G$;
$\quad G := G - \{g\}$;
$\quad G := G \cup update(G, g, d)$;
$\quad d := g(d)$;
endwhile

where G is the current set of functions still to be applied ($G \subseteq F$), d is a partially ordered set (the domains in case of CSP), and for all G, g, d the set of functions $update(G, g, d)$ from F is such that:

- $\{f \in F - G \mid f(d) = d \wedge f(g(d)) \neq g(d)\} \subseteq update(G, g, d)$.
- $g(d) = d$ implies that $update(G, g, d) = \emptyset$.
- $g(g(d)) \neq g(d)$ implies that $g \in update(G, g, d)$

Suppose that all functions in F are inflationary ($x \sqsubseteq f(x)$ for all x) and monotonic ($x \sqsubseteq y$ implies $f(x) \sqsubseteq f(y)$ for all x, y) and that $(D, \sqsubseteq)$ is finite. Then, every execution of the **GI** algorithm terminates and computes in d the least common fixpoint of the functions from F (see [2]).

Note that in the following we consider only finite partial orderings. Constraint propagation is now achieved by instantiating the **GI** algorithm:

- the $\sqsubseteq$ ordering is instantiated by $\supseteq$, the usual set inclusion,
- $d := \perp$ corresponds to $d := D_1 \times \ldots \times D_n$, the Cartesian product of the domains of the variables from the CSP,
- F is a set of monotonic and inflationary functions (called *domain reduction functions*) which abstract the constraints to reduce domains of variables. For example, one of the domain reduction functions to reduce Boolean variables using a $and(X, Y, Z)$ [2] constraint is defined by: if the domain of Z is $\{1\}$, then the domains of X and Y must be reduced to $\{1\}$.

The result is the smallest box (i.e., Cartesian product of domains) w.r.t. the given domain reduction functions that contains the solutions of the CSP.

At this point, in order to get the solutions of the CSP, one has to explore the reduced domains by enumeration or splitting techniques (and then, again, propagation, and so on). This usually implies an algorithmic process interleaving splitting and propagation phases. However, in the following, we will integrate splitting as a reduction function inside the **GI** algorithm, and we will extend the notion of CSP to sampled CSP on which an other type of reduction functions will be applied to mimic basic operations of local search algorithms.

---

[2] $and(X, Y, Z)$ represents the Boolean relation $X \wedge Y = Z$.

2.2 Solving CSP with Local Search

Given an optimization problem (which can be minimizing the number of violated constraints and thus trying to find a solution of the CSP), local search techniques [1] aim at exploring the search space, moving from a configuration to one of its neighbors. These moves are guided by a fitness function which evaluates the benefit of such a move in order to reach a local optimum. We will generalize the definition of local search in next sections.

For the resolution of a CSP (X, D, C), the search space can be usually defined as the set of possible tuples of $D = D_1 \times \cdots \times D_n$ and the neighborhood is a mapping $\mathcal{N} : D \to 2^D$. This neighborhood function defines indeed the possible moves from a configuration (a tuple) to one of its neighbors and therefore fully defines the exploration landscape. The fitness (or evaluation) function $eval$ is related to the notion of solution and can be defined as the number of constraints c such that $t \not\subseteq c$ (t being a tuple from D).

In this case, the problem to solve is indeed a minimization problem. Given a configuration $d \in D$, two basic strategies can be identified in order to continue the exploration of D:

- intensification: choose $d' \in \mathcal{N}(d)$ such that $eval(d') < eval(d)$.
- diversification: choose any other neighbor d'.

The intensification process only performs improving moves while diversification strategy allows the process to move to a worst neighbor w.r.t. the $eval$ function. Any local search algorithm is based on the management of these basic heuristics by introducing specific control features. Therefore, a local search algorithm can be considered as a sequence of moves on a structure ordered according to the evaluation function.

3 A Uniform Computational Framework

From these different CSP resolution approaches, our aim is to integrate the various involved computation processes in a uniform description framework. The purpose of this section is to instantiate the general computation scheme presented in Section 2.1.

Our idea is to extend the set of usual functions used in the generic iteration algorithm with splitting operators and local search strategies. Then, these search methods can be viewed as the computation of a fixpoint of a set of functions on an ordered set. Therefore, the first step of our work consists in defining the main structure.

3.1 Sampling the Search Space

As we have seen, domain reduction and splitting operate on domains of values while local search acts on a different structure, which usually corresponds to points of the search space. Here, we propose a more general and abstract definition based on the notion of sample.

Definition 1 (Sample). *Given a CSP (X, D, C), we define a sample function $\varepsilon : D \rightarrow 2^D$. By extension, $\varepsilon(D)$ denotes the set $\{\varepsilon(d) | d \in D\}$.*

Generally, $\varepsilon(d)$ is restricted to d and $\varepsilon(D) = D$, but it can also be a scatter of tuples around d, an approximation or a box covering d (e.g., for continuous domains). Moreover, it is reasonnable to impose that $\varepsilon(D)$ contains all the solutions. Indeed, the search space D is abstracted by $\varepsilon(D)$ to be used by LS.

In this context, a local search can be fully defined by a neighborhood function on $\varepsilon(D)$ and the set of visited samples for each local search path composed by a sequence of moves. Given a neighborhood function $\mathcal{N} : \varepsilon(D) \rightarrow 2^{\varepsilon(D)}$, we define the set of possible local search paths as $\mathcal{LS}_D =$

$$\bigcup_{i>0} \{p = (s_1, \cdots, s_i) \in \varepsilon(D)^i \mid \forall j, 1 \leq j < i - 1, s_{j+1} \in \mathcal{N}(s_j) \text{ and } s_1 \in \varepsilon(D)\}$$

since the fundamental property of local search relies on its exploration based on the neighborhood relation. From a practical point of view, a local search is limited to finite paths according to a stop criterion which can be a fixed maximum number of iterations or, in our context of CSP resolution, the fact that a solution is reached. For this concern, according to Section 2.2, we consider an evaluation function $eval : \varepsilon(D) \rightarrow I\!N$ such that $eval(s)$ represents the number of constraints unsatisfied by s and $eval(s)$ is equal to 0 iff s is a solution. We denote $s <_{eval} s'$ the fact that $eval(s) < eval(s')$.

Therefore, from a LS point of view, a result is either a search path leading to a solution or a search path of a maximum given size.

Definition 2. *We consider an order $\sqsubseteq_{ls}$ on $\mathcal{LS}_D$ defined by:*

$$(s'_1, \ldots, s'_m) \sqsubseteq_{ls} (s_1, \ldots, s_n) \text{ iff } eval(s_n) = 0 \text{ or } n \geq m.$$

Consider $p_1 = (a, b)$, $p_2 = (a, c)$ and $p_3 = (b)$ three elements of $\mathcal{LS}_D$ such that $eval(b) = 0$ (i.e., b is a solution). Then, they all correspond to possible results of a local search of size 2, and they are equivalent w.r.t. to Definition 2.

3.2   Computation Structure

We now instantiate the abstract framework of K.R. Apt described in Section 2.1.

Definition 3. *A sampled CSP (sCSP) is defined by a triple (D, C, p), a sample function ε, and a local search ordering $\sqsubseteq_{ls}$ where*

- $D = D_1, ..., D_n$
- $\forall c \in C, c \subseteq D_1 \times \ldots \times D_n$
- $p \in \mathcal{LS}_D$

Note that, in our definition, the local search path p should be included in the box defined by $\varepsilon(D)$. We denote $SCSP$ the set of $sCSP$ and we define now an ordering relation on the structure $(SCSP, \sqsubseteq)$.

Definition 4. *Given two sCSPs $\psi = (D, C, p)$ and $\psi' = (D', C, p')$,*

$$\psi \sqsubseteq \psi' \quad \text{iff} \quad D' \subseteq D \text{ or } (D' = D \text{ and } p \sqsubseteq_{ls} p').$$

This relation is extended on 2^{SCSP} as:

$$\{\phi_1, \ldots, \phi_k\} \sqsubseteq \{\psi_1, \ldots, \psi_l\} \quad \text{iff} \quad \forall \phi_i, (\exists \psi_j, \phi_i \sqsubseteq \psi_j \text{ and } \not\exists \psi_j, \psi_j \sqsubseteq \phi_i)$$

where $i \in [1..k], j \in [1..l]$.

Note that this ordering on sCSPs could be extended by also considering an order on constraints; this would enable constraint simplifications.

We denote ΣCSP the set 2^{SCSP} which constitutes the key set of our computation structure. We denote σCSP an element of ΣCSP. The least element $\bot$ is $\{(D, C, p)\}$, i.e., the initial σCSP to be solved.

3.3 Notion of Solution

Our framework is dedicated to CSP resolution and therefore we have to define precisely the notion of solution w.r.t. the previous computation structure. We should note that this notion is clear from each side of the resolution (i.e., complete and incomplete methods). From the complete resolution point of view, a solution of a CSP is a tuple which satisfies all the constraints. From the LS point of view, the notion of solution is related to the evaluation function *eval* which defines a solution as an element s of $\varepsilon(D)$ such that $eval(s) = 0$.

Given a sCSP $\psi = (D, C, p)$, these two points of view induce two sets of solutions $Sol_D(\psi) = \{d \in D | \forall c \in C, d \in c\}$ and $Sol_{\mathcal{LS}_D}(\psi) = \{(s_1, \cdots, s_n) \in \mathcal{LS}_D \mid eval(s_n) = 0\}$.

Definition 5. *Given a sCSP $\psi = (D, C, p)$, the set of solutions of ψ is defined by:*

$$Sol(\psi) = \{(d, C, p) | d \in Sol_D(\psi) \text{ or } p \in Sol_{\mathcal{LS}_D}(\psi)\}$$

This notion is extended to any σCSP Ψ as $Sol(\Psi) = \bigcup_{\psi \in \Psi} Sol(\psi)$.

3.4 Reduction Functions Definitions and Properties

We have now to define the notion of function on ΣCSP. Given an element $\Psi = \{\psi_1, \cdots, \psi_n\}$ of ΣCSP, we have to apply functions on Ψ which correspond to domain reduction, domain splitting, and local search. These functions may operate on various elements of Ψ, and for each ψ_i on some of its components. We should note that since we consider here finite initial CSPs, our structure is a finite partial ordering.

Definition 6 (Domain reduction function). *A domain reduction function is a function red on ΣCSP s.t. for all $\Psi = \{\psi_1, \ldots, \psi_n\} \in \Sigma CSP$, $red(\Psi) = \{\psi'_1, \ldots, \psi'_n\}$ and $\forall i \in [1 \cdots n]$:*

- either $\psi_i = \psi_i'$
- or $\psi_i = (D, C, p)$, $\psi_i' = (D', C, p')$ and $D \supseteq D'$ and $Sol_D(\psi_i) = Sol_D(\psi_i')$.

Note that this condition insures that $\Psi \sqsubseteq red(\Psi)$ and that the function is inflationary and monotonic on $(\Sigma CSP, \sqsubseteq)$. It allows one to reduce several domains of several $sCSPs$ of a σCSP at the same time. From a constraint programming point of view, no solution of the initial CSP is lost by a domain reduction function. This is also the case for domain splitting as defined below.

Definition 7 (Domain splitting). *A domain splitting function is a function sp on ΣCSP such that for all $\Psi = \{\psi_1, \ldots, \psi_n\} \in \Sigma CSP$:*

a. $sp(\Psi) = \{\psi_1', \ldots, \psi_m'\}$ *with $n \leq m$,*
b. $\forall i \in [1..n]$,
   - *either $\exists j \in [1..m]$ such that $\psi_i = \psi_j'$*
   - *or there exist $\psi_{j_1}', \ldots, \psi_{j_h}', j_1, \ldots, j_h \in [1..m]$ such that $Sol_D(\psi_i) = \bigcup_{k=1..h} Sol_D(\psi_{j_k}')$.*
c. *and, $\forall j \in [1..m]$,*
   - *either $\exists i \in [1..n]$ such that $\psi_i = \psi_j'$*
   - *or $\psi_j' = (D', C, p')$ and there exists $\psi_i = (D, C, p)$, $i \in [1..n]$ such that $D \supset D'$.*

Conditions a. and b. ensure that some sCSPs have been split into sub-sCSPs by splitting their domains (one or several variable domains) into smaller domains without discarding solutions (defined by the union of solutions of the ψ_i). Condition c. ensures that the search space does not grow: none of the domain of the sCSPs composing Ψ' is not included in one of the domain of some sCSP composing Ψ. Note that the domain of several variables of several sCSPs can be split at the same time.

Definition 8 (Local Search). *A local search function λ_N is a function*

$$\lambda_N \colon \Sigma CSP \to \Sigma CSP$$
$$\{\psi_1, \cdots, \psi_n\} \mapsto \{\psi_1', \cdots, \psi_n'\}$$

where

- *N is the maximum number of consecutive moves*
- *$\forall i \in [1..n]$*
   - *either $\psi_i = \psi_i'$*
   - *or $\psi_i = (D, C, p)$ and $\psi_i' = (D, C, p')$ with $p = (s_1, \cdots, s_k)$ and $p' = (s_1, \cdots, s_k, s_{k+1})$ such that $s_{k+1} \in \mathcal{N}(s_k) \cap D$ and $k + 1 \leq N$.*

N represents the maximum length of a local search path, i.e., the number of moves allowed in a usual local search process. A local search function can try to improve the sample of one or several sCSPs at once. Note that $\psi_i = \psi_i'$ may happen when:

1. $p \in Sol_{\mathcal{LS}_D}(\psi)$: the last sample s_n of the current local search path cannot be improved using λ_N,

2. $n = N$: the maximum allowed number of moves has been reached,
3. λ_N is the identity function on ψ_i, i.e., λ_N does not try to improve the local search path of the sCSP ψ_i. This might happen when no possible move can be performed (e.g., a descent algorithm has reached a local optimum or all neighbors are tabu in a tabu search algorithm [6]).

3.5 Solving σCSPs

The complete solving of a σCSP $\{(D_1, \ldots, D_n, C, p)\}$ now consists in instantiating the **GI** algorithm:

Computation Structure.

- the $\sqsubseteq$ ordering is instantiated by the ordering given in Definition 4,
- $d := \bot$ corresponds to $d := \{(D_1, \ldots, D_n, C, p)\}$, the Cartesian product of the variables domains and of the sample from the sCSP,
- F is a set of given monotonic and inflationary functions as defined in Section 3.4: domain reduction functions (extensions of usual domain reduction functions for CSPs), domain splitting functions (usual splitting mechanisms integrated as reduction functions), and local search functions (e.g., functions for descent, tabu search, ...).

Functions. We propose here an instantiation of the function schemes presented in the previous section.

From an operational point of view, reduction functions have to be applied on some selected $sCSP$s of a given σCSP. Therefore we have to consider functions driven by a selection operator. Given a selection function $select: A \to 2^B$ let us consider a function $f^{select}: A \to C$ such that $f^{select}(x) = g(y), y \in select(x)$ where $g: B \to C$. Therefore, f^{select} can be viewed as a non deterministic function. Formally, we may associate to any function f^{select} a family of deterministic functions $(f^i)_{i>0}$ such that $\forall x \in A, \forall y \in select(x), \exists k > 0, f^k(x) = g(y)$. If we consider finite sets A and B then this family is also finite.

This corresponds to the fact that all possible functions are needed for each σCSP that can result from the application of some functions on the initial σCSP to model the different possible executions of the resolution process [3].

We first define functions on $SCSP$ w.r.t. selection functions to select the domains on which the functions apply. Similarly and in order to extend operations on $SCSP$ to ΣCSP, we introduce a selection process which allows us to extract particular $sCSP$s of a given σCSP (see Figure 1).

Let us consider a domain selection function $Sel_D: SCSP \to 2^D$ and a $sCSP$ selection function $Sel_\psi: \Sigma SCSP \to \Sigma SCSP$.

---

[3] This is necessary in theory, however, in practice, only required functions are fed in the **GI** algorithm.

$\Psi \in \Sigma CSP$
$\Psi = \{\psi_1, \ldots, \psi_k, \ldots, \psi_n\}$

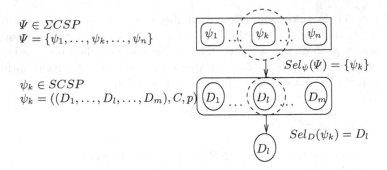

$Sel_\psi(\Psi) = \{\psi_k\}$

$\psi_k \in SCSP$
$\psi_k = ((D_1, \ldots, D_l, \ldots, D_m), C, p)$

$Sel_D(\psi_k) = D_l$

Fig. 1. Selection functions

Domain Reduction. We may first define a domain reduction operator on a single sCSP as:

$$red^{Sel_D} : SCSP \rightarrow SCSP$$
$$\psi = (D, C, p) \mapsto (D', C, p')$$

such that

1. $D = \{D_1, \cdots, D_n\}, D' = \{D'_1, \cdots, D'_n\}$ and $\forall 1 \leq i \leq n$
   - $D_i \in D \setminus Sel_D(\psi) \Rightarrow D'_i = D_i$
   - $D_i \in Sel_D(\psi) \Rightarrow D'_i \subseteq D_i$
2. $p' = p$ if $p \in \mathcal{LS}'_D$ otherwise p' is set to any sample chosen in $\varepsilon(D')$

Note that Condition 2. insures that the local search path associated to the sCSP stays in $\varepsilon(D')$ [4]. This function is extended to ΣCSP as:

$$red^{Sel_\psi, Sel_D} : \Sigma CSP \rightarrow \Sigma CSP$$
$$\Psi \mapsto (\Psi \setminus Sel_\psi(\Psi)) \bigcup\nolimits_{\psi \in Sel_\psi(\Psi)} red^{Sel_D}(\psi)$$

Splitting. We may first define a splitting operator on a single sCSP as:

$$sp_k^{Sel_D} : SCSP \rightarrow \Sigma CSP$$
$$\psi \mapsto \Psi'$$

with $\psi = (D_1, \ldots, D_h, \ldots, D_n, C, p)$ where $\{D_h\} = Sel_D(\psi)$ and
$\Psi' = \{(D_1, \ldots, D_{h_1}, \ldots, D_n, C, p_1), \cdots, (D_1, \ldots, D_{h_k} \ldots, D_n, C, p_k)\}$ such that

1. $D_h = \bigcup_{i=1}^{k} D_{h_i}$
2. for all $i \in [1..k]$, $p_i = p$ if $p \in \mathcal{LS}_{D_{h_i}}$ otherwise, p_i is set to any sample chosen in $\varepsilon(D_1, \ldots, D_{h_i}, \ldots, D_n)$.

---

[4] Note that we could keep $p' = (s_i)$ where s_i is the latest element of p which belongs to D', for instance, or a suitable sub-path of p. We have chosen to model here a restart from a randomly chosen sample after each reduction or splitting.

For the sake of readability we consider here the split of a single domain in the initial sCSP but it can obviously be extended to any selection function. The last condition is needed to satisfy the sCSP definition and corresponds to the fact that, informally, the samples associated to any sCSP belong to the box induced by their domains.

$$sp_k^{Sel_\psi, Sel_D} : \Sigma CSP \to \Sigma CSP$$
$$\Psi \mapsto (\Psi \setminus Sel_\psi(\Psi)) \bigcup\nolimits_{\psi \in Sel_\psi(\Psi)} sp_k^{Sel_D}(\psi)$$

Local Search. As mentioned above, local search is viewed as the definition of a partial ordering $\sqsubseteq_{ls}$ which is used for the definition of the ordering $\sqsubseteq$ on ΣCSP. The remaining components to be defined are now: 1) the strategy to obtain a local search path p' of length $n+1$ from a local search path p of length n, and 2) the stop criterion which is usually based on a fixed limited number of LS moves and, in this particular context of CSP resolution, the notion of reached solution. We first define a local search operator on $SCSP$ based on a function $strat: SCSP \to 2^{\varepsilon(D)}$ which defines the choice strategy of a given local search heuristics in order to move from a sample to one of its neighbors.

$$\lambda_N^{strat}: SCSP \to SCSP$$
$$\psi \mapsto \psi'$$

where

- N is the maximum number of moves
- $\psi = (C, D, p)$ and $\psi' = (C, D, p')$ with $p = (s_1, \cdots, s_n)$
  1. $p' = p$ if $p \in Sol_{\mathcal{LS}_D}$
  2. $p' = p$ if $n = N$
  3. $p' = (s_1, \cdots, s_n, s_{n+1})$ s.t. $s_{n+1} \in strat(\psi) \cap D$ otherwise

We provide here some examples of well known "move" heuristics.

- **Descent**: selects better neighbors
  $strat_d((D, C, (s_1, \cdots, s_n))) = \{s_{n+1} \in \varepsilon(D) \mid s_{n+1} <_{eval} s_n \wedge s_{n+1} \in \mathcal{N}(s_n)\}$
- **Strict Descent**: selects best improving neighbors
  $strat_{sd}((D, C, (s_1, \cdots, s_n))) = \{s_{n+1} \in \varepsilon(D) \mid s_{n+1} <_{eval} s_n \wedge s_{n+1} \in \mathcal{N}(s_n) \wedge \forall s' \in \mathcal{N}(s_n), s_{n+1} \leq_{eval} s'\}$
- **Random Walk**: selects all the neighbors
  $strat_{rw}((D, C, (s_1, \cdots, s_n))) = \{s_{n+1} \in \varepsilon(D) \mid s_{n+1} \in \mathcal{N}(s_n)\}$
- **Tabu of length l**: selects best neighbor not visited during the past l moves
  $strat_{tabu_l}((D, C, (s_1, \cdots, s_n))) = \{s_{n+1} \in \varepsilon(D) \mid \forall n - l \leq j \leq n, s_{n+1} \neq s_j \wedge s_{n+1} \in \mathcal{N}(s_n) \wedge \forall s' \in \mathcal{N}(s_n), s_{n+1} \leq_{eval} s'\}$

Note that, again, these functions satisfy the required properties (inflationary and monotonic) to be fed in the GI algorithm. Then this function is extended to ΣCSP as:

$$\lambda_N^{Sel_\psi, strat} : \Sigma CSP \to \Sigma CSP$$
$$\Psi \mapsto (\Psi \setminus Sel_\psi(\Psi)) \bigcup\nolimits_{\psi \in Sel_\psi(\Psi)} \lambda_N^{strat}(\psi)$$

Combination. The combination strategy is now totally managed by the "choose function" of the **GI** algorithm: different scheduling of functions lead to the same result (in term of least common fixpoint), but not with the same efficiency.

Note that in practice, we are not always interested in reaching the fixpoint of the **GI** algorithm, but we can also be interested in solutions such as: sCSPs which contain a solution for local search or a solution for constraint propagation. In this case, different runs of the **GI** algorithm with different strategies ("choose function") can lead to different solutions (e.g., in case of problems with several solutions, or several local minima).

Result of the GI Algorithm. We now compare the result of the GI algorithm w.r.t. the Definition 5 of solution of a σCSP.

Since we are in Apt's framework (concerning orderings and functions), given a σCSP Ψ and a set F of reduction functions (as defined above) the GI algorithm computes a common least fixpoint of the functions in F. Clearly, this fixpoint $glfp(\Psi)$ abstracts all the solutions of $Sol(\Psi)$:

- $\bigcup_{(d,C,p) \in Sol(\Psi)} d \supseteq \bigcup_{(d,C,p) \in glfp(\Psi)} d$
- for all $(D, C, p) \in Sol(\Psi)$ s.t. $p = (s_1, \ldots, s_n) \in Sol_{\mathcal{LS}_D}(\Psi)$ there exists a $(d, C, p') \in glfp(\Psi)$ s.t. $s_n \in \varepsilon(d)$.

The first item represents the fact that all domain reduction and splitting functions used in GI preserve solutions. The second item ensures that all solutions computed by LS functions are in the fixpoint of the GI algorithm.

In practice, one can stop the GI algorithm before the fixpoint is reached. For example, one can compute the fixpoint of the LS functions; in this case, only some applications of the CP functions can reduce the search space (and thus, the possible moves). This corresponds to the hybrid nature of the resolution process and the tradeoff between a complete and incomplete exploration of the space.

4   Experimentation

In this section, we present a prototype, developed in C++, which allows us to test hybridization on different CSP examples.

4.1   Functions and Strategies

We choose $\varepsilon(D_1, \cdots, D_n)$ as the Cartesian product $D_1 \times \cdots \times D_n$ ($\varepsilon(D) = D$). We consider the two selection functions $min(\Psi) = \{\psi\} \subseteq \Psi$ such that $\nexists \psi', \psi \sqsubseteq \psi'$ and $max(D) = \{D_i\}$ such that $\forall j \neq i, |D_i| \geq |D_j|$ (if there are several possible candidates choose the one with smallest index). A first set of domain reduction functions DR contains node and bound consistency operators (see [10]). The set SP contains the splitting operators $split_2^{min,max}$ and consist in cutting in two the largest domain of the minimal element of a σCSP. At last the set LS contains functions which corresponds to a tabu method: $\lambda_N^{min,strat_{tabu_l}}$.

The purpose of this section is not to test a high performance algorithm on large scale benchmarks but to prove the interest of our framework over various small problems.

According to the generic algorithm **GI**, note that one has to define a choose strategy at each iteration and to update the set of functions. Here we describe three different choose functions:

- $DR \cup SP$: in this case we consider the initial set of functions $F = DR \cup SP$ then the choose function is defined as: choose any $g \in G \cap DR$ or any $g \in G$ if $G \cap DR = \emptyset$ (G being the set of functions still to be applied in the **GI** algorithm). This simulates a complete backtracking algorithm.
- LS: here we consider $F = LS$. Note that in this case there is only one LS function for tabu search. We have also experimented a descent with random walk algorithm. In that case, reduction functions corresponding to descent and random walk strategies are applicable on each sCSP and one has to choose them alternatively with a certain probability.
- $DR \cup SP \cup LS$: we consider $F = DR \cup P \cup LS$. The choose function is: while $G \cap DR \neq \emptyset$ choose $g \in G \cap DR$; then choose any $g \in SP$; then while $G \cap LS \neq \emptyset$ choose $g \in G \cap LS$. In other terms, this strategy is: perform all possible domain reductions, then make a split, then a full local search; and iterate on this process.

Selected Problems. We propose various problems : **S+M=M**, a well-known crypto-arithmetic problem which consists in solving the equation $SEND + MORE = MONEY$ by assigning a different digit to each letter; **Marathon**, a problem of arrival in a race knowing particular information about the competitors (6 variables and 29 constraints); **Scheduling** problem (15 variables and 29 constraints); classical **Magic Square**, **Langford number** and **N-queens** benchmarks.

4.2   Experimental Results

The values given in the following table correspond to the truncated average of 50 independent runs. Concerning $DR \cup SP$, we count then the number of iterations of splitting operators which corresponds to the number of nodes in a classical backtracking algorithm. Concerning LS, we count the number of applied functions, which corresponds to the number of moves performed by the local search. We also mention the success rate. The computation time (t) is given in seconds. For $DR \cup SP \cup LS$, we limit the number of moves for each local search to $N = 100$, while for LS alone, a maximum of $500,000$ moves is allowed. Tabu list length l is set to 10.

We compare first the number of nodes with $DR \cup SP$ and $DR \cup SP \cup LS$ to get the first solution. Table 1 shows that $DR \cup SP \cup LS$ finds a solution with a smaller number of nodes compared to $DR \cup SP$ alone. In the combination, the relative efficiency of the LS part depends on the problem. For problems with one solution such as $S+M=M$, the benefit is less significant than for the other benchmarks (in particular N-queens).

Table 1. First solution ($DR \cup SP$ vs. $DR \cup SP \cup LS$ vs. LS)

Problem	$DR \cup SP$ (nodes | t)	$DR \cup SP \cup LS$ (nodes | moves | t)	LS (s. rate | moves | t)
$S+M=M$	(10 | 0.0)	(5.4 | 375.2 | 0.0)	(44% | 59294 | 5.6)
Marathon	(8 | 0.0)	(1 | 11.5 | 0.0)	(100% | 18 | 0.0)
Scheduling	(31 | 0.0)	(1 | 2.5 | 0.0)	(8% | 4726 | 59.1)
24-queens	(3329800 | 1631.2)	(1.2 | 62.8 | 0.6)	(100% | 201.7 | 2.1)
Magic-Square-4	(39 | 0.0)	(13.5 | 743 | 0.2)	(100% | 3423 | 2.0)
Langford 2 4	(4 | 0.0)	(1.6 | 95 | 0.0))	(100 % | 601 | 0.0)

Table 1 also shows the efficiency of the local consistency which guides the local search (see comparisons $DR \cup SP \cup LS$ vs. LS), in particular on $S+M=M$ and *Scheduling*. One should remark that the success rate of LS is also an important parameter which is really improved by the combination since in that case, hybrid solving always succeeds in finding one solution.

Computation time is, of course, strongly related to the implementation of the different operators. We may remark that this computation is improved by using $DR \cup SP \cup LS$ instead of LS alone. The comparison between $DR \cup SP$ and $DR \cup SP \cup LS$ is not really significant except on *N-queens* where the hybridization provides an important saving of time.

Finally, we have calculated the computing cost needed to get several solutions with $DR \cup SP \cup LS$ on a *Magic-Square-3* problem which has 8 solutions. The mechanisms progress together to get a set of distinct solutions by computing fewer nodes (about 25 % less for each solution) than a classical backtracking algorithm simulated by $DR \cup SP$. To get several distinct solutions is a really good asset compared to LS alone (which was not designed for computing different solutions) and could be very interesting for number of problems.

At last, similar experiments have been performed with a hill climbing algorithm and provided similar conclusions.

5   Perspectives and Conclusion

Most of hybrid approaches are ad-hoc algorithms based on a master-slave combination: they favor the development of systems whose efficiency is strongly related to a given class of CSPs.

In this paper, we have presented a global model which is more suitable for integrating different strategies of combination and for proving some properties of these combinations. We have shown that this work can serve as basis for the integration of LS and CP methods in order to highlight the connections between complete and incomplete techniques and their main properties.

In the future, we plan to extend our framework in order to handle optimization problems. From a LS point of view, this will change the *strat* functions used to create the reduction functions. From a CP point of view, algorithms such as Branch and Bound requires adding new constraints during resolution: this could be done using a new type of reduction function in our model.

An other future extension is to provide some "tools" to help designing finer strategies in the GI algorithm. To this end, we plan to extend works of [7] where strategies are built using some composition operators in the GI algorithm. Moreover, this will also open possibilities of concurrent and parallel application of reduction functions inside our model.

At last, we plan to complete our prototype implementation (Section 4) into a "fully" generic implementation of our framework in order to design and test new and finer efficient strategies of hybridization.

Ackowledgement. The authors are grateful to Willem Jan van Hoeve for the interesting remarks he made on a preliminary version of this paper and to the anonymous referees for their useful comments.

References

1. E. Aarts and J.K. Lenstra, editors. *Local Search in Combinatorial Optimization.* John Wiley and Sons, 1997.
2. K. Apt. From chaotic iteration to constraint propagation. In *24th International Colloquium on Automata, Languages and Programming (ICALP '97*, number 1256 in LNCS, pages 36–55. Springer, 1997. invited lecture.
3. K. Apt. The rough guide to constraint propagation. In *Proc. of the 5th International Conference on Principles and Practice of Constraint Programming (CP'99)*, volume 1713 of *LNCS*, pages 1–23, Springer, 1999. (Invited lecture).
4. K. Apt. *Principles of Constraint Programming.* Cambridge University Press, 2003.
5. F. Focacci, F. Laburthe, and A. Lodi. Local search and constraint programming. In *Handbook of Metaheuristics.* Kluwer, 2002.
6. F. Glover and M. Laguna. *Tabu Search.* Kluwer Academic Publishers, 1997.
7. L. Granvilliers and E. Monfroy. Implementing Constraint Propagation by Composition of Reductions. In C. Palamidessi, editor, *Proceedings of International Conference on Logic Programming*, LNCS 2916, pages 300–314. Springer, 2003.
8. N. Jussien and O. Lhomme. Local search with constraint propagation and conflict-based heuristics. *Artificial Intelligence*, 139(1):21–45, 2002.
9. A. Mackworth. *Encyclopedia on Artificial Intelligence*, chapter Constraint Satisfaction. John Wiley, 1987.
10. K. Mariott and P. Stuckey. *Programming with Constraints, An introduction.* MIT Press, 1998.
11. R. Mohr and T.C. Henderson. Arc and path consistency revisited. *Artificial Intelligence*, 28:225–233, 1986.
12. G. Pesant and M. Gendreau. A view of local search in constraint programming. In *Proc. of the Second International Conference on Principles and Practice of Constraint Programming*, number 1118 in LNCS, pages 353–366. Springer, 1996.
13. S. Prestwich. A hybrid search architecture applied to hard random 3-sat and low-autocorrelation binary sequences. In *Principle and Practice of Constraint Programming - CP 2000*, number 1894 in LNCS, pages 337–352. Springer, 2000.
14. P. Shaw. Using constraint programming and local search methods to solve vehicle routing problems. In *Principles and Practice of Constraint Programming - CP98*, number 1520 in LNCS, pages 417–431. Springer, 1998.
15. E. Tsang. *Foundations of Constraint Satisfaction.* Academic Press, London, 1993.

Arc-Consistency + Unit Propagation = Lookahead

Jia-Huai You and Guiwen Hou

Department of Computing Science
University of Alberta
Edmonton, Alberta, Canada

Abstract. *Arc-consistency* has been one of the most popular consistency techniques for space pruning in solving constraint satisfaction problems (CSPs), while *lookahead* appears to be its counterpart in answer set solvers. In this paper, we perform a theoretical comparison of their pruning powers, based on the translation of Niemelä from CSPs to answer set programs. Especially, we show two results. First, we show that lookahead is strictly stronger than arc-consistency. The extra pruning power comes from the ability to propagate *unique values* for variables, also called *unit propagation* in this paper, so that conflicts may be detected. This suggests that arc-consistency can be enhanced with unit propagation for CSPs. We then formalize this technique and show that, under the translation of Niemelä, it has exactly the same pruning power as lookahead.

1 Introduction

Among constraint programming frameworks, two have been given a lot of attention. One is the framework of constraint satisfaction problems (CSPs), and the other propositional satisfiability. Logic programming with the stable model semantics [6] can be viewed as a variant of the latter under a non-conventional semantics.

CSPs are typically solved by a systematic backtracking search algorithm, while at each choice point consistency of certain kind is maintained in order to prune the search space. A general notion of consistency is called k-consistency which requires that any partial solution for any $k - 1$ variables be consistently extended to a partial solution with any additional variable [4, 10]. The most popular degree of consistency is *arc-consistency*. A binary constraint is arc-consistent if and only if any assignment to any one of the variables in the constraint can be extended to a consistent assignment for the other variable. Many algorithms for maintaining arc-consistency for binary constraints have been developed and the optimal worst case complexity is known (cf. [2]).

Developed largely in parallel, satisfiability (SAT) solvers and later answer set solvers provide another framework for solving constraints, where a constraint problem is represented by clauses for the former and rules with default negation for the latter. Most complete solvers in this camp are based on the DP procedure (the Davis-Putnam-Logemann-Loveland algorithm) [1]. One of the main ideas for space pruning is that of *lookahead* - before a decision on a choice point is made, for each atom, if fixing the atom's truth value leads to a contradiction, the atom should then get the opposite truth value (cf. [3]). In this way, the atom gets a truth value propagated from already assigned atoms without going through a search process. In trying to derive a contradiction, fast constraint propagation algorithms are used. In SAT solvers the most popular technique is

B. Demoen and V. Lifschitz (Eds.): ICLP 2004, LNCS 3132, pp. 314–328, 2004.

unit propagation, and in answer set programming, a representative is Smodels' *expand* function [13].

Walsh [15] compares several encodings between CSPs and SAT. Generally speaking, unit propagation is weaker than arc-consistency. Gent [7], in extending an idea from Kasif [8], shows that the 'support encoding' of binary CSPs into SAT can have arc-consistency established by unit propagation. This is an interesting result. Essentially, for a variable x to take a value a, the support encoding encodes the set of values of the other variable that allows it. As the support for a value is encoded in SAT, unit propagation is sufficient for enforcing arc-consistency.

However, to our knowledge, lookahead as defined for SAT or answer set solvers has never been related to arc-consistency in the past. Question arises as how is the pruning power of lookahead compared to that of arc-consistency. If one is more powerful than the other, then why? Can the other be extended to make up the gap? Is such an extension new, or already present in the literature?

In this paper, we will answer these questions based on answer set programming, under some assumptions. The first assumption is that we only deal with binary constraints in this paper. We see no major technical hurdles in extending our results to n-ary constraints; nevertheless we will leave the details to the future version of this work. The second assumption is that we will fix the encoding from CSPs to answer set programs to be the one by Niemelä [12]. This encoding is probably the most straightforward translation from CSPs to answer set programs. Especially, no support information is explicitly encoded. Lastly, we shall choose a specific algorithm of lookahead for comparison at the detailed, technical level. We will thus fix the answer set programming system to be the system of Smodels [14]. However, we will rely only on normal logic programming in Smodels.

Under these assumptions, we show that lookahead prunes more search space than arc-consistency[1]. This result leads to the insight as what is missing in arc-consistency. This insight enables us to formalize the notion of arc-consistency with unique value propagation, or just *unit propagation*, a term borrowed from SAT, for CSPs. The extended algorithm turns out to have the same pruning power as lookahead. Arc-consistency with unit propagation appears to be new in the literature of CSPs; it differs from the notion of *arc-consistency look ahead* [2], which enforces full arc-consistency on all uninstantiated variables after each tentative assignment to the current variable is made.

The paper is organized as follows. The next section introduces CSPs. Section 3 introduces answer set programming and the lookahead algorithm as given in Smodels. In Section 4 we give Niemelä's translation and prove that lookahead is strictly stronger than arc-consistency. Then, in Section 5 we show the main result of this paper, namely arc-consistency plus unit propagation prunes exactly the same search space as does lookahead. In Section 6 we discuss some related work. Section 7 discusses some complexity results. We present an *optimal* worst case complexity result for lookahead. We then present a bound for computing the lookahead for the programs translated from CSPs by the method of Niemelä. Finally, Section 8 comments on the directions of future work.

---

[1] For the convenience of comparison, arc-consistency here technically refers to arc-consistency combined with node-consistency.

2   Constraint Satisfaction Problem

A constraint satisfaction problem (CSP) is a triple $\mathcal{A}(X, D, C)$ where $X = \{x_1, \ldots, x_k\}$ is a finite set of variables with respective domains $D = \{D_{x_1}, \ldots, D_{x_k}\}$ listing possible values for each variable, and $C = \{c_1, \ldots, c_m\}$ is a finite set of constraints. A *constraint* $c_i \in C$ is a relation defined on a subset S_i of X, S_i is called the *scope* of c_i. We may write $c_i(y_1, \ldots, y_n)$ to denote the scheme of the n-ary constraint c_i.

A *solution* to a CSP $\mathcal{A}(X, D, C)$ is an assignment where each variable is assigned a value from its domain such that all the constraints are satisfied. A constraint c_i is *satisfied* if and only if the assignment to variables in the scope of c_i yields a tuple in the relation c_i. We denote by $x \rightarrow a$ that variable x is assigned value $a \in D_x$.

Two CSPs are said to be *equivalent* if and only if they have the same set of solutions. A constraint c_i is partially instantiated if zero or more variables in its scope have been assigned a value from their perspective domains. A partial instantiation/assignment is *consistent* with constraint c_i if and only if the assignment yields a projection of a tuple in the relation of c_i. A partial assignment is consistent if and only if it is consistent with every constraint. A consistent partial assignment is also called a *partial solution*.

A CSP is typically solved by a backtrack algorithm that incrementally attempts to extend a partial solution to a complete solution. At each step, the current variable is assigned a value, if the partial assignment is consistent, we continue with the next variable; if not, we continue with the next value in the domain of the current variable; if all the values in the domain have been tried and fail to give a consistent assignment, we backtrack to the preceding variable and try alternative values in its domain. The search space can be pruned in a backtrack algorithm by employing domain reduction operations. The idea is to reduce the domains of the unassigned variables by maintaining certain type of consistency before committing to a choice. The reduction to an empty domain causes the algorithm to backtrack. During backtracking, domain reductions are undone to the point where an alternative instantiation of a variable is sought.

In this paper, we generally assume binary constraints if not said otherwise.

2.1   Consistency Techniques

The most interesting cases of k-consistency are *node-consistency* (when $k = 1$) and *arc-consistency* (when $k = 2$). Maintaining node-consistency is simple. Many algorithms for maintaining arc-consistency have been developed (cf. [2, 11]). In this section, we are interested mainly in what such an algorithm accomplishes than its efficiency. For this reason, we describe an abstract, nondeterministic procedure that combines node and arc consistency, and simply call it AC.

Algorithm AC

AC takes as input a CSP $\mathcal{A}(X, D, C)$, and performs the following domain reduction operations repeatedly until no domain can be further reduced.

1. For any $c \in C$, if there is exactly one uninstantiated variable x in its scope, remove d from D_x if d is inconsistent with the value of the instantiated variable in c.

2. For any $c \in C$ where both variables x and y in the scope of c are uninstantiated, remove any d from D_x for which there exists no value from D_y that, together with d, is consistent with c.

Example 1. Consider a CSP as described by the constraints $\{x < y, \ y < z, \ z \leq 3\}$, where $D_x = D_y = \{1,2,3\}$ and $D_z = \{2,3,4\}$. Enforcing node-consistency w.r.t. the last constraint reduces D_z to $D'_z = \{2,3\}$. Enforcing arc-consistency w.r.t. the first constraint reduces D_x to $D'_x = \{1,2\}$ Similarly, D_y is reduced to $D'_y = \{2,3\}$. Working on the constraint $y < z$ for variable y, D'_y is further reduced to $\{2\}$, which forces D'_x to become $\{1\}$ by the first constraint, and D'_z to become $\{3\}$ by the last constraint. By now, no further reduction is possible. ∎

In the sequel, given a CSP, we will denote by k the maximum domain size and e the number of constraints. It is known that for binary CSPs, the optimal worst case complexity is $O(ek^2)$. This is the worst case complexity of the algorithm, named AC-4, for checking and enforcing arc-consistency [2]. In the following, we also assume there are as many constraints as variables in $\mathcal{A}(X, D, C)$, so that we can simply refer to e for discussion of complexity.

3   Constraint Propagation in Smodels

In this section, we introduce constraint propagation in Smodels for normal logic programs, which consist of rules of the form

$$A \leftarrow B_1, ..., B_m, \text{not } C_1, ..., \text{not } C_n.$$

where A, B_i and C_i are function-free atoms, and not C_i is called a *default negation*. The head A may be omitted, in which case it serves as a constraint where the body must be false in any model. In systems like Smodels [14] and DLV [9] these programs are instantiated to ground instances for the computation of stable models. In the remainder of this paper, we only deal with ground programs.

The stable model semantics is defined over the ground instantiation of a given logic program in two stages [6]. The idea is that one guesses a set of atoms, and then tests whether the atoms in the set are precisely the consequences. In the first stage, given a program P and a set of atoms M, the *reduct* of P w.r.t. M is defined as:

$$P^M = \{a \leftarrow b_1, ..., b_m \mid a \leftarrow b_1, ..., b_m, \text{not } c_1, ..., \text{not } c_n \in P$$
$$\text{and } \forall i \in [1..n], c_i \notin M\}$$

Since P^M is a program without default negation, its deductive closure $\{\phi \mid P^M \vdash \phi, \phi$ is an atom in $L\}$, is the least model of P^M. Then, M is a *stable model* of P iff M is the least model of P^M.

Additional Notations: Atoms and default negations are both called *literals*. A set of literals is consistent if there is no atom ϕ such that ϕ and not ϕ are both in the set. $Atoms(\Phi)$ denotes the set of distinct atoms appearing in Φ where Φ is any syntactic entity. The expression $not(\text{not } \phi)$ is identified with ϕ. Given a set of literals B, $B^+ =$

$\{\xi \mid \xi$ is an atom in $B\}$ and $B^- = \{\xi \mid$ not $\xi \in B\}$. Let Q be a set of atoms. $not(Q) = \{\text{not } \phi \mid \phi \in Q\}$.

Constraint propagation in Smodels is carried out by the function $lookahead(P, A)$, where P is a program and A a set of literals representing a partial truth value assignment. Given A, $lookahead(P, A)$ picks up each unassigned atom q and assume a truth value; if it leads to a conflict, we know that q should get the opposite truth value in extending A. Truth values are propagated in lookahead by a function called $expand(P, A)$, which returns a superset of A, representing the process of propagating the values of the atoms in A to some additional atoms. These functions have been proved to be correct in the sense that any stable model M for program P that agrees with A (meaning $A^+ \subseteq M$ and $A^- \cap M = \emptyset$) must agree with the set returned by such a function [13].

The functions expand and lookahead are given in Figures 1 and 2, respectively.

> $Function\ expand(P, A)$
> $repeat$
> $A' := A$
> $A := Atleast(P, A)$
> $A := A \bigcup \{\text{not } \phi \mid \phi \in Atoms(P) \text{ and } \phi \notin Atmost(P, A)\}$
> $until\ A = A'$
> $return\ A.$

Fig. 1. Function $expand(P, A)$

> $Function\ lookahead(P, A)$
> $repeat$
> $A' := A$
> $A := lookahead\_once(P, A)$
> $until\ A = A'$
> $return\ A.$

> $Function\ lookahead\_once(P, A)$
> $B := Atoms(P) - Atoms(A)$
> $B := B \bigcup not\ (B)$
> $while\ B \neq \emptyset\ do$
> $take\ any\ literal\ \chi \in B$
> $A' := expand(P, A \bigcup \{\chi\})$
> $B := B - A'$
> $if\ conflict(P, A')\ then$
> $return\ expand(P, A \bigcup \{not\ (\chi)\})$
> $end\ while$
> $return\ A.$

Fig. 2. Function $lookahead(P, A)$

$Atleast(P, A)$ in the expand function returns a superset of A by repeatedly applying four propagation rules until no new literals can be deduced. Let r be a rule in program P of the form: $r = h \leftarrow a_1, ..., a_n, \text{not } b_1, ..., \text{not } b_m$. Define

$$min_r(A) = \{h \mid \{a_1, ..., a_n\} \subseteq A^+, \{b_1, ..., b_m\} \subseteq A^-\}$$
$$max_r(A) = \{h \mid \{a_1, ..., a_n\} \bigcap A^- = \emptyset, \{b_1, ..., b_m\} \bigcap A^+ = \emptyset\}$$

The four propagation rules in $Atleast(P, A)$ are:

1. If $r \in P$, then $A := A \bigcup min_r(A)$.
2. If there is an atom a such that for all $r \in P$, $a \notin max_r(A)$, then $A := A \bigcup \{not\ a\}$.
3. If an atom $a \in A$, there is only one $r \in P$ for which $a \in max_r(A)$, and there is a literal x such that $a \notin max_r(A \bigcup \{x\})$, then $A := A \bigcup \{not\ x\}$.
4. If $not\ a \in A$ and there is a literal x such that for some $r \in P$, $a \in min_r(A \bigcup \{x\})$, then $A := A \bigcup \{not\ x\}$.

The propagation rule 1 adds the head of a rule to A if the body is true in A. If there is no rule with a as the head whose body is not false w.r.t. A, then a cannot be derived by any (consistent) extension of A, and thus cannot be in any stable model agreeing with A. Rule 3 says that if $a \in A$, the only rule with a as the head must have its body true in A. Rule 4 forces the body of a rule to be false if the head is false in A.

The function $Atmost(P, A)$ is defined as the least fixpoint of a function $f(B)$ such that, given a rule $r = h \leftarrow a_1, ..., a_n, not\ b_1, ..., not\ b_m$ in P, $f(B)$ contains h if a_i's are in $B - A^-$, and none of the b_j's is in A^+. By including $not\ \xi$ if $\xi \notin Atmost(P, A)$, Atmost helps determine *unfounded atoms* in the same way as in computing the well-founded model [5].

Finally, in lookahead_once, the function $conflict(P, A)$ returns true if $A^+ \cap A^- \neq \emptyset$ and false otherwise.

Some lemmas are needed later in this paper. Lemma 1 below is proved in Simons' thesis [13]. Lemma 1 is used to prove Lemma 2 which has been known as a folklore in the past. Lemma 3 appears to be new, which will be used later to prove some complexity results. The proofs of these lemmas are omitted here.

Lemma 1. $expand(P, A)$ *is monotonic in the parameter* A.

Lemma 2. $lookahead(P, A)$ *returns the same set, independent of any order in which literals are chosen from* B *in the while loop of* $lookahead\_once(P, A)$.

Given a logic program P, it is convenient to construct a *dependency graph* for P: for each rule $a \leftarrow b_1, ..., b_m, not\ c_1, ..., not\ c_n$ in P, there is a positive edge from a to each b_i, $1 \leq i \leq m$, and a negative edge from a to each c_j, $1 \leq j \leq n$. P has a *positive loop* if in its dependency graph there is a path from an atom to itself which only contains positive edges.

Lemma 3. *If a program* P *has no positive loops, then* $expand(P, A)$ *can be computed in time linear in the size of* P.

4   AC Versus Lookahead

In this section we first present Niemelä's translation [12], and then show that lookahead is strictly stronger than AC.

4.1   Translation from CSPs to Logic Programs

Niemelä's translation is not limited only to binary constraints, so we will present this translation for n-ary constraints. Let $\mathcal{A}(X, D, C)$ be an n-ary CSP.

The translation of Niemelä [12] consists of three parts. The first part specifies the *uniqueness property* - a variable in CSP can only be assigned with one value. For each variable $x_i \in X$ and its domain $D_{x_i} = \{a_1, ..., a_l\}$, we use an atom, $x_i(a_j)$, to represent whether or not x_i gets the value a_j. Thus, for each $1 \leq j \leq l$, we add a rule

$$x_i(a_j) \leftarrow \text{not } x_i(a_1), ..., \text{not } x_i(a_{j-1}), \text{not } x_i(a_{j+1}), ..., \text{not } x_i(a_l). \quad (1)$$

In the second part, constraints are expressed. For each constraint scheme $c_i(x_1, ..., x_n)$ where $c_i \in C$, and each tuple $(a_1, ..., a_n) \in c_i$, we add

$$sat(c_i) \leftarrow x_1(a_1), ..., x_n(a_n). \quad (2)$$

Finally, we express that every constraint in $C = \{c_1, ..., c_m\}$ must be satisfied by

$$sat \leftarrow sat(c_1), ..., sat(c_m). \quad (3)$$

$$f \leftarrow \text{not } f, \text{not } sat. \quad (4)$$

where f is a new symbol.

The rules in 3 and 4 can be omitted if we ask a stable model generator to compute the stable models containing $sat(c_1), ..., sat(c_m)$. This is what we assume in the rest of this paper. We will let $sat(C) = \{sat(c_1), ..., sat(c_m)\}$.

Given a CSP $\mathcal{A}(X, D, C)$, we denote by $P_\mathcal{A}$ the logic program translated from it. The size of $P_\mathcal{A}$ is calculated as follows. For each variable the uniqueness property is expressed by at most k rules with at most k literals each. For binary constraints, the number of tuples in a constraint is at most k^2. As we have e constraints, we get

Proposition 1. *For any (binary) CSP $\mathcal{A}(X, D, C)$, $P_\mathcal{A}$ can be constructed in $O(ek^2)$ time. The size of $P_\mathcal{A}$ is also bounded by $O(ek^2)$.* ∎

One question one would like to ask is, under this translation, whether the propagation by the expand function is powerful enough to enforce arc-consistency. The answer is NO, as shown by the following example.

Example 2. Consider a CSP $\mathcal{A}(X, D, C)$ with one constraint $c(x, y) = \{(0, 0), (1, 1)\}$ where $D_x = \{0, 1, 2\}$ and $D_y = \{0, 1\}$. Under Niemelä's translation, we have only one rule with $x(2)$ as the head:

$$x(2) \leftarrow \text{not } x(0), \text{not } x(1).$$

and two rules with $sat(c)$ as the head:

$$sat(c) \leftarrow x(0), y(0).$$
$$sat(c) \leftarrow x(1), y(1).$$

While enforcing arc-consistency removes 2 from D_x, we do not deduce not $x(2)$ in the call $expand(P_\mathcal{A}, sat(C))$. However, if we perform lookahead, by picking up $x(2)$ in $lookahead\_once(P_\mathcal{A}, sat(C))$, $expand(P_\mathcal{A}, sat(C) \cup \{x(2)\})$ deduces not $sat(c)$, resulting in a conflict with $sat(C)$. ∎

4.2   Lookahead is Stronger than AC

Theorem 1. *Let $\mathcal{A}(X, D, C)$ be a CSP. Suppose after an application of AC, D is reduced to D' . If for any variable $x_j \in X$, a value d is removed from D_{x_j}, then* not $x_j(d) \in lookahead(P_\mathcal{A}, sat(C))$.

Proof. Let $d_1, ..., d_s$ be the sequence of domain values removed from the respective domains $D_{x_1}, ..., D_{x_s}$ by AC, in that order. We show that there is a sequence of applications of *lookahead_once*, each resulting in not $x_i(d_i)$ being added, in the same order. Then, by Lemma 2, because the set of literals returned by $lookahead(P_\mathcal{A}, sat(C)\})$ is independent of the order in which literals are picked, the existence of the latter sequence is sufficient for the theorem to hold.

Suppose d_1 is removed from D_{x_1} w.r.t. a constraint $c \in C$ whose scheme includes x_1 and y as variables, due to the fact there is no value of y that, together with d_1 for x_1, is consistent with c. We show that if we pick up atom $x_1(d_1)$ in *lookahead_once*$(P_\mathcal{A}, sat(C))$, and continue with the call $expand(P_\mathcal{A}, sat(C) \cup \{x_1(d_1)\})$, a conflict will be deduced.

By applying the propagation rule 3 in the function Atleast to the program rule in $P_\mathcal{A}$ with $x_1(d_1)$ as the head, for each $d' \in D_{x_1}$ such that $d' \neq d_1$, we have not $x_1(d') \in expand(P_\mathcal{A}, sat(C) \cup \{x_1(d_1)\})$. Thus, the bodies of the rules with $sat(c)$ as the head are all false except possibly those with $x_1(d_1)$ in the body. But since there is no $v \in D_y$ such that d_1 for x_1 and v for y would give a partial solution for c, there is simply no rule in $P_\mathcal{A}$ with $sat(c)$ as the head that contains $x_1(d_1)$ in the body. By the propagation rule 2 in the function Atleast, we deduce not $sat(c)$, resulting in a conflict with $sat(C)$.

Similar argument applies if d_1 is removed by maintaining node-consistency.

The proof for the rest of d_i's is by exactly the same argument under the setting: after d_1 is removed, the resulting CSP can be re-expressed as $\mathcal{A}'(X, D', C)$, which is equivalent to $\mathcal{A}(X, D, C)$ by the correctness of arc-consistency; and after obtaining not $x_j(d_1)$, the resulting program where $x_1(d_1)$ is false (thus any rule with $x_1(d_1)$ in the positive body is removed, so are the only rule with $x_1(d_1)$ as the head and all of the occurrences of not $x_1(d_1)$ in the body of any rule) is equivalent to the program $P_{\mathcal{A}'}$. ∎

Together with Theorem 1, the following example shows that lookahead is strictly stronger than AC.

Example 3. Consider a CSP[2] that consists of three variables x, y and z, both with the domain $\{0, 1\}$, and the following constraints:

$$c_1(x, y) = \{(0, 0), (1, 1)\}$$
$$c_2(y, z) = \{(0, 1), (1, 0), (1, 1)\}$$
$$c_3(z, x) = \{(0, 0), (1, 1)\}$$

It is clear that AC cannot reduce any domain. A backtracking algorithm that begins with the assignment $x \to 0$ would need backtrack. Now, suppose $x(0)$ is selected by lookahead_once. Then a conflict is arrived at so that not $x(0)$ is added. One can verify that the function lookahead alone is able to generate the unique solution to the CSP. ∎

---

[2] This example was contributed by Dr. Guan-Shieng Huang in a group discussion at the Institute of Information Science, Academy Sinica, Taipei.

5   AC with Unit Propagation

The insight revealed in the last section suggests that some space pruning power is missing in arc-consistency when compared with lookahead. In this section we identify what is missing.

Given a CSP $\mathcal{A}(C, X, D)$ and a partial solution Π, we define a function that extends Π as follows:

$unit\_propagate(\mathcal{A}, \Pi)$
$= \Pi \cup \{x \rightarrow a \mid c(y, x) \in C \text{ or } c(x, y) \in C, \text{ and } y \rightarrow b \in \Pi \text{ such that}$
$\qquad a \text{ is the only value in } D_x \text{ that is consistent with } b\}$

That is, in a binary constraint, if the unassigned variable has exactly one value in its domain that is consistent with the value of the instantiated variable, the unassigned variable must be given this value, providing Π.

A collection of pairs Π is said to be in *conflict* if and only if there are distinct values d and d' such that for some variable x, $x \rightarrow d, x \rightarrow d' \in \Pi$. The notion of conflict is needed because, as we will see shortly, the function unit_propagate may lead to such a conflict.

The function $unit\_propagate^*(\mathcal{A}, \Pi)$ below calls $unit\_propagate(\mathcal{A}, \Pi)$ repeatedly until nothing can be further propagated or a conflict is reached. That is,

$$Function\ unit\_propagate^*(\mathcal{A}, \Pi)$$
$$repeat$$
$$\Pi' := \Pi$$
$$\Pi := unit\_propagate(\mathcal{A}, \Pi')$$
$$if\ \Pi\ is\ in\ conflict\ then$$
$$return\ ``conflict"$$
$$until\ \Pi = \Pi'$$
$$return\ \Pi.$$

Example 4. Let $\mathcal{A}(X, D, C)$ be a CSP with $X = \{x, y\}$, $D_x = D_y = \{0, 1\}$, and C consisting

$$c_1(x, y) = \{(0, 1), (1, 0)\} \quad c_2(y, x) = \{(0, 0), (1, 1)\}$$

Given $\Pi = \{x \rightarrow 0\}$, $unit\_propagate^*(\mathcal{A}, \Pi)$ returns "conflict" because the set returned by $unit\_propagate(\mathcal{A}, \Pi \cup \{y \rightarrow 1\})$ is $\{x \rightarrow 0, y \rightarrow 1, x \rightarrow 1\}$.   ∎

Now we strengthen the process of enforcing arc-consistency by adding unit propagation, and name the function to be AC^+. Again, we describe it as an abstract, nondeterministic procedure.

Algorithm AC^+

AC^+ takes as input a CSP $\mathcal{A}(X, D, C)$, and performs the following domain reduction operations repeatedly until no domain can be further reduced.

1. For any $c \in C$, if there is exactly one uninstantiated variable x in its scope, remove any d from D_x if d is inconsistent with the value of the instantiated variable in c.

2. For any $c \in C$ where both variables x and y in the scope of c are uninstantiated, remove any d from D_x if

   (a) there is no value in D_y that, together with d, is consistent with c; or

   (b) $unit\_propagate^*(\mathcal{A}, \{x \rightarrow d\})$ returns "conflict".

AC^+ is obviously correct. The only addition is part (b), in which case the conflict is a sufficient ground for removing d. Note that when the domains of all affected variables have more than one consistent value, the process of unit propagation stops. So the overhead is proportional to the occurrences of unique values for variables during unit propagation.

Theorem 2. *Let $\mathcal{A}(C, X, D)$ be a CSP. Suppose after an application of AC^+, D is reduced to D'. Then, for any variable $x \in X$, a value d is removed from D_x iff $not\ x(d) \in lookahead(P_\mathcal{A}, sat(C))$.*

Proof. (Sketch) As was done in the proof of Theorem 1, it suffices to consider the first removal in the case of CSP, and the first call to the function $lookahead\_once$ in the other direction. Below, AC refers to the part of AC^+ without unit propagation.

($\Rightarrow$) In conjunction with the proof of Theorem 1, we will be considering the effect of unit propagation only. Suppose a_0 is removed from D_{y_0} in AC^+, because the call $unit\_propagate^*(\mathcal{A}, \{y_0 \rightarrow a_0\})$ returns "conflict". Suppose also that we pick up $y_0(a_0)$ in the function call $lookahead\_once(P_\mathcal{A}, sat(C))$. (Note that this is a valid assumption because the order of picking up literals is unimportant, cf. Lemma 2.) We need to show that the set returned by $expand(P_\mathcal{A}, sat(C) \cup \{y_0(a_0)\})$ is in conflict.

Suppose "conflict" returned by $unit\_propagate^*(\mathcal{A}, \{y_0 \rightarrow a_0\})$ is due to the sequence of unit propagations recorded as follows:

$$\{y_0 \rightarrow a_0, y_1 \rightarrow a_1, ..., y_n \rightarrow a_n, y_{n+1} \rightarrow a_{n+1}\} \tag{5}$$

where $y_0 = y_{n+1}$ and $a_0 \neq a_{n+1}$. We show, by a simple induction on n, that each $y_{i+1}(a_{i+1}), 0 \leq i \leq n+1$, is deduced by the function Atleast, and therefore a conflict is generated due to $y_0 = y_{n+1}$ and $a_0 \neq a_{n+1}$.

The base case is trivial as $y_0(a_0)$ is given in the call $expand(P_\mathcal{A}, sat(C) \cup \{y_0(a_0)\})$. Now, for any $i \geq 0$, assume $y_i(a_i)$ is deduced and show that $y_{i+1}(a_{i+1})$ is deduced. Since $y_i(a_i)$ is deduced, by the propagation rule 3 in Atleast, $not\ y_i(d')$ is deduced, for each $d' \in D_x$ such that $d' \neq a_i$. Thus, any rule encoding a constraint $c \in C$ involving variable y_i may only have a non-false body that contains $y_i(a_i)$. Let c's scope include y_i and y_{i+1}. Now a_{i+1} is the only value in $D_{y_{i+1}}$ that is consistent with a_i for y_i. It follows that there is exactly one rule with $sat(c)$ as the head, i.e.,

$$sat(c) \leftarrow y_i(a_i), y_{i+1}(a_{i+1}).$$

By the propagation rule 3 in Atleast, $y_{i+1}(a_{i+1})$ is deduced, generating a conflict.

($\Leftarrow$) Suppose $expand(P_\mathcal{A}, \{y_0(a_0)\} \cup sat(C))$ generates a conflict. We show that if AC does not remove a_0 from D_{y_0}, $unit\_propagate^*(\mathcal{A}, \{y_0 \rightarrow a_0\})$ in AC^+ must return "conflict".

Now assume AC does not remove a_0 from D_{y_0}. By the propagation rule 3, $y_0(a_0)$ causes not $y_0(d)$, for any $d \in D_{y_0}$ such that $d \neq a_0$, to be deduced. Since AC does not remove a_0 from D_{y_0}, for each constraint $c(y_0, y_1) \in C$ (similarly for any constraint $c'(y_1, y_0) \in C$) there are rules in P_A containing $y_0(a_0)$ in the body which are not made false by the addition of not $y_0(d)$ where $d \in D_{y_0}$ and $d \neq a_0$. That is,

$$sat(c) \leftarrow y_0(a_0), y_1(b_1).$$
$$\cdots\cdots$$
$$sat(c) \leftarrow y_0(a_0), y_1(b_k).$$

where $k \geq 1$. It is clear that further deduction can be made only if $k = 1$, so that the propagation rule 3 becomes applicable. Clearly, this corresponds to the propagation made by $unit\_propagate(A, \{y_0 \to a_0\})$. Let's denote b_1 by a_1. Then we witness the sequence as generated in Equation 5. As $expand(P_A, \{y_0(a_0)\} \cup sat(C))$ leads to a conflict, the corresponding sequence, as in Equation 5, must have $y_0 = y_{n+1}$ and $a_0 \neq a_{n+1}$. This leads to the generation of "conflict" by AC^+. ∎

6 Related Work

In the literature it is often felt that arc-consistency may be too expensive to be beneficial in real applications. Hence a restricted version, called *forward checking* (FC) where the values from the domains of uninstantiated variables (also called *future variables*) are filtered out if they are inconsistent with the current instantiation, is sometimes preferred.

Experiments show, however, that for problems with relatively tight constraints and relatively sparse constraint graphs, algorithms where future variables are checked against each other could substantially outperform FC [4]. This approach is called *arc-consistency look ahead*, where full arc-consistency on all uninstantiated variables are enforced following each tentative value assignment to the current variable. If a variable's domain becomes empty during this process, the current candidate value is rejected. An implementation of this approach is given in [2] (page 135, Fig. 5.10).

We use the following example to explain the difference between arc-consistency look ahead and arc-consistency with unit propagation.

Example 5. Consider a CSP with $X = \{x_1, x_2, x_3, x_4\}$, all the variables with domain $\{0, 1\}$, and the following constraints

$$c_1(x_1, x_2) = \{(0,0), (0,1), (1,1)\}$$
$$c_2(x_2, x_3) = \{(0,0), (0,1), (1,1), (1,0)\}$$
$$c_3(x_3, x_4) = \{(0,0), (1,1)\}$$
$$c_4(x_4, x_3) = \{(0,1), (1,0)\}$$

One can see that c_3 and c_4 together cannot yield a consistent assignment between x_3 and x_4. But arc-consistency cannot detect it. In fact, arc-consistency enforced on this CSP does not remove any domain value.

Now consider arc-consistency look ahead. Suppose the current variable is x_1. Let us tentatively assign x_1 with 0. Now, Since enforcing arc-consistency involves two variables, with a tentative assignment to the current variable, consistency check is among triplets, much stronger than arc-consistency alone. However, one can see that since the spot of conflict is unrelated to variable x_1, the inconsistency cannot be detected.

However, with AC^+, 0 is removed from D_{x_3}, so is 1, resulting in an empty domain, hence that this CSP has no solution can be answered without search. ∎

In the above example, one can also see that if we perform arc-consistency look ahead for *all* future variables, it then coincides with arc-consistency with unit propagation. The precise relationship between arc-consistency with unit propagation and arc-consistency look ahead is an interesting question to be answered in a further investigation.

7 Complexity Results

Despite the popularity of Smodels, the complexity of its key component, lookahead, has not been studied carefully. In this section we will see that its complexity is higher than what researchers assumed previously.

Theorem 3. *Let P be a program, n be the size of P and m the number of distinct atoms appearing in P. Then, the running time for lookahead is bounded by $O(nm^3)$.*

Proof. The expand function in lookahead is bounded by $O(nm)$ as both functions Atleast and Atmost can be computed in time linear in n, and there are at most m rounds of iterations. For lookahead, since after $2m$ rounds of iterations (each atom is tested for being true and false respectively), at least one conflict must be deduced for it to continue, there are at most $O(m^2)$ total rounds of iterations. Thus, a call to lookahead takes at most $O(nm^3)$ time. ∎

If we take program size as the only parameter, our bound translates to $O(n^4)$, which is higher than the folklore $O(n^3)$. Now, by constructing a program that takes lookahead at least $O(nm^3)$ time to run in the worst case, we show that this bound is optimal. That is, our worst case complexity cannot be lowered further.

We construct a program consisting of three parts, P_1, P_2, and P_3. The idea is that P_1 will make lookahead call lookahead_once (hence the expand function) $O(m^2)$ times in the worst case; in each call to expand, P_2 makes it call Atleast and Atmost $O(m)$ times; and P_3 makes each call to Atmost take $O(n)$ time to run.

Let us construct P_1. We start with $2s$ atoms, $a_1, .., a_s$ and $a'_1, .., a'_s$. P_1 contains the following rules:

$$\forall i \in [1..s-1], \qquad a_i \leftarrow \text{not } a_i, \, a_{i+1}.$$
$$\forall i \in [1..s], \qquad a_i \leftarrow \text{not } a'_i.$$
$$a'_i \leftarrow \text{not } a_i.$$
$$and \qquad a_s \leftarrow \text{not } a_s.$$

The idea in this example is simple. Let us consider only literals not a_i, $1 \le i \le s$. Suppose each time when lookahead_once is called, it picks up a literal in the order: not a_1, not a_2, ..., not a_s. In the first round, only when we get to not a_s are we able to deduce a conflict and hence conclude a_s. In the ith round we conclude a_{s-i+1}, and so on. Thus, the total number of calls is $s(s + 1)/2$, quadratic in s. That is, P_1 in the worst case makes lookahead call expand $O(s^2)$ times.

Now we construct P_2. Suppose there are additional $2s'$ atoms, $c_1, ..., c_{s'}$ and $b_1, ..., b_{s'}$. Then P_2 is:

$$\forall i \in [1..s], \qquad c_1 \leftarrow \text{not } a_i.$$
$$\forall i \in [1..s'], \qquad b_i \leftarrow \text{not } c_i.$$
$$b_i \leftarrow b_i.$$
$$\forall i \in [1..s' - 1], \quad c_{i+1} \leftarrow \text{not } b_i.$$

It is clear that each time when not a_i is picked up by lookahead once, it makes expand call Atleast and Atmost, alternately, each s' times. At the ith round, Atleast generates c_i and then not b_i is added, as b_i is not derivable by Atmost and becomes *unfounded*. Thus, P_2 makes expand call Atleast and Atmost $O(s')$ times.

The goal of P_3 is to make Atmost *thrashing* hence linear time must be taken each time when it is called. Suppose there are additional s'' atoms, $p_1, ..., p_{s''}$. Then we construct P_3 as:

$$\forall i \in [2..s'], \qquad p_1 \leftarrow \text{not } c_i.$$
$$\forall i \in [1..s'' - 1], \quad p_{i+1} \leftarrow p_i.$$

Recall that in the expand function Atmost is called after each call to Atleast, and P_2 makes this repetition s' times. According to the algorithm that implements Atmost ([13], page 39, procedure $atmost()$), in the first call to Atmost, all p_i are derived, because none of c_i, $2 \leq i \leq s'$, were deduced by the first call to Atleast. In the second round, as Atleast generated c_2, the computation of Atmost must be re-done. The procedure $atmost()$ first removes p_1 from the closure, due to the rule $p_1 \leftarrow \text{not } c_2$, and subsequently all of the p_i's; and it then puts p_1 back into the closure due to the rules $p_1 \leftarrow \text{not } c_i, i > 2$, and subsequently all p_i's. Clearly, the running time is proportional to s''. That is, each invocation of Atmost in this case takes $O(s'')$ time to run.

Note that in our construction, there is no restriction on the possible values for s, s', and s''. Thus, we may simply make $s = s' = s''$, and let $P = P_1 \cup P_2 \cup P_3$. Let m be the number of distinct atoms appearing in P and n the size of P. It is clear that s and s' are both linear in m and s'' is linear in n.

Putting all the arguments together, we conclude

Theorem 4. $O(nm^3)$ *is the optimal worst time complexity for lookahead as implemented in Smodels.* ∎

Note that this result is specifically for lookahead as implemented in Smodels. In particular, it does not rule out the possibility of developing more efficient algorithms for lookahead whose worst time complexities are lower. This is an interesting yet important question to be investigated in the future.

As the final result of this section, we give a bound for lookahead when it is used to solve CSPs based on Niemelä's translation.

Theorem 5. *Let $\mathcal{A}(X, D, C)$ be a (binary) CSP. Under the translation of Niemelä, the time taken by lookahead is bounded by $O(e^3 k^4)$.*

Proof. The size of the translated program is bounded by $O(ek^2)$. By Lemma 3, since the translated program has no positive loops, the bound on the expand function is also $O(ek^2)$. There are ek number of variables in the translated program. As lookahead_once is called $O(e^2k^2)$ times in the worst case, and each with one call to expand, we get the total time $O(e^3k^4)$. ∎

8   Future Directions

Despite their proximity, in the past constraint propagation in answer set programming has rarely been compared with consistency techniques in solving CSPs. In this paper, we establish a theoretical connection between arc-consistency used in CSPs and lookahead in answer set programming. In particular, we show that arc-consistency enhanced with unit propagation coincides with lookahead under Niemelä's translation from binary CSPs to logic programs. Since Niemelä's translation does not contain positive loops, the relationships studied here can be established similarly for lookahead as used in SAT.

The relations established in this paper only began the first step in this direction. Many more questions remain, among which *bounds consistency* as used in CSPs appears particularly interesting, not only because it is effective in reducing large numeric domains, but also because it appears to have no counterpart in answer set solvers. Traditionally, numeric constraints have been a weak spot in SAT-based approaches. We would like to see the arsenals of constraint propagation techniques in answer set programming also include a form of "bounds consistency", so that the search space due to large numeric domains may be reduced effectively.

Answer set solvers may also benefit from global constraints such as AllDifferent. One way to extend an answer set solver with such a special constraint is by writing an answer set program that implements it. Another way is to build special propagation rules into an answer set solver to support special language constructs for special constraints.

The relationships established in this paper are based on a particular translation from CSPs to answer set programs. The question remains open as whether the same conclusions hold for other translations. Since lookahead in Smodels is a general algorithm without fine tuning for binary constraints, the complexity given in Theorem 5 for performing arc-consistency with unit propagation is quite high. It is interesting to design a special, more efficient algorithm for arc-consistency with unit propagation. One such algorithm will be reported in a forthcoming paper by the authors.

On the other hand, we believe that the algorithm for lookahead as implemented in Smodels can be improved. Any trick in our argument for Theorem 4 points to such a possibility. For example, our argument depends on the implementation function $atmost()$ in Simons' thesis. Is there an algorithm for Atmost that can avoid the thrashing behavior? As another example, our argument also relies on a particular order in which literals are chosen by lookahead_once to make the worst case happen. Are there heuristics that are likely to avoid bad orders? Here, the purpose is to reduce the overhead of lookahead, hence these type of heuristics should be able to be computed very efficiently.

Acknowledgement

Early discussions on the topic by the first author with Ilkka Niemelä, Patrik Simons, and Tomi Janhunen helped set the stage for this investigation. The work is supported by the Natural Sciences and Engineering Research Council of Canada. The work by Jia-Huai You is also assisted by a grant under "Chunhui" plan from the Ministry of Education of China.

References

1. M. Davis, G. Logemann, and D. Loveland. A machine program for theorem proving. *Communications of the ACM*, 5(7):394–397, July 1962.
2. Rina Dechter. *Constraint Processing*. Morgan Kaufmann, 2003.
3. J.W. Freeman. *Improvements to propositional satisfiability search algorithms*. PhD thesis, Department of Computer and Information Science, University of Pennsylvania, 1995.
4. E.C. Freuder. Synthesizing constraint expressions. *CACM*, 21(11):958–966, 1978.
5. A. Van Gelder, K. Ross, and J. Schlipf. The well-founded semantics for general logic programs. *Journal of the ACM*, 38(3):620–650, 1991.
6. M. Gelfond and V. Lifschitz. The stable model semantics for logic programming. In *Proc. 5th ICLP*, pages 1070–1080. MIT Press, 1988.
7. Ian Gent. Arc consistency in SAT. In *Proc. ECAI 2003*, pages 121–125, 2002.
8. S. Kasif. On the parallel complexity of discrete relaxation in constraint satisfaction networks. *Artificial Intelligence*, pages 275–286, 1990.
9. N. Leone et al. DLV: a disjunctive datalog system, release 2000-10-15. At http:// www.dbai.tuwien.ac.at/proj/dlv/, 2000.
10. A. Mackworth. Consistency in networks of relations. *Artificial Intelligence*, 8(1):99–118, 1977.
11. K. Marriott and P. Stucky. *Programming with Constraints*. MIT Press, 1998.
12. I. Niemelä. Logic programs with stable model semantics as a constraint programming paradigm. *Annals of Math. and Artificial Intelligence*, 25(3-4):241–273, 1999.
13. P. Simons. *Extending and Implementing the Stable Model Semantics*. PhD thesis, Helsinki University of Technology, Helsinki, Finland, 2000.
14. P. Simons, I. Niemelä, and T. Soininen. Extending and implementing the stable model semantics. *Artificial Intelligence*, 138(1-2), 2002.
15. T. Walsh. CSP vs. SAT. In *Proc. Principles and Practice of Constraint Programming*, pages 441–456, 2000.

The *period* Constraint

Nicolas Beldiceanu* and Emmanuel Poder

LINA FRE CNRS 2729, École des Mines de Nantes,
4 rue Alfred Kastler, La Chantrerie, BP 20722, 44307 Nantes Cedex 3, France
{Nicolas.Beldiceanu,Emmanuel.Poder}@emn.fr

Abstract. The *period* constraint restricts the smallest period of a sequence of domain variables to be equal to a given domain variable. This paper first provides propositions for evaluating the feasible values of the smallest period of a sequence of domain variables. Then, it gives propositions for pruning the variables of the sequence in order to achieve one out of several possible smallest periods. The generalisation of the *period* constraint to the case where the equality between two domain variables is replaced by any condition is also considered.

1 Introduction

From a constraint perspective a first way to cope with some problems encountered in the area of combinatorial pattern matching [3] is to introduce variables that take their values within a set of strings; this set is then represented by a regular language. In this context, various constraints [6] can be implemented using finite automata. However, if for compatibility reasons with existing constraints, one wants to stick [9] to domain variables, then a way to proceed is to replace each fixed letter $s[i]$ of a sequence s by a domain variable[1]; the corresponding domain contains all the potential letters that $s[i]$ can take. Now, to each classical problem of computing a given sequence characteristic we associate a constraint, which enforces a given domain variable to be equal to the characteristic we consider on a sequence of domain variables. This process is illustrated on the following concrete example. As a characteristic, consider *the period* of a sequence of domain variables $V_0 \, V_1 \cdots V_{m-1}$ (i.e. the smallest natural number p such that $V_i = V_{i+p}$ for all $i \in \{0, 1, \ldots, m - p - 1\}$) and the corresponding constraint period($P, Sequence$), where:

- P is a domain variable,
- *Sequence* is a list $[V_0, V_1, \ldots, V_{m-1}]$ of m domain variables.

The *period* constraint holds iff P is the period of the sequence $V_0 \, V_1 \cdots V_{m-1}$. For instance, period($3, [1, 1, 4, 1, 1, 4, 1, 1]$) holds since 3 is the smallest period out of all periods $3, 6, 7$ and 8 of the sequence 1 1 4 1 1 4 1 1.

---

* This work was undertaken when the author was at SICS.

[1] A *domain variable* is a variable that ranges over a finite set of integers; $dom(V)$ denotes the set of possible values of variable V, while $min(V)$ and $max(V)$ denote respectively the minimum and the maximum value of V.

B. Demoen and V. Lifschitz (Eds.): ICLP 2004, LNCS 3132, pp. 329–342, 2004.
© Springer-Verlag Berlin Heidelberg 2004

The *period* constraint was generalised in [1, page 110] by considering an explicit binary constraint instead of the equality constraint used in its original definition. This binary constraint is provided as a third argument of the generalised *period* constraint. For instance, the constraint period$(2, [3, 1, 4, 6, 9, 7], <)$ holds since $3 < 4 < 9$, $1 < 6 < 7$ and since $3 < 1 < 4 < 6 < 9 < 7$ does not hold. As a motivating example for the *period* constraint and its generalisation, consider a cyclic scheduling problem of the following type: given a list of persons and a list of possible working periods (i.e. morning, afternoon, night, day off), the task is to determine a schedule over a period of one month, which provides for each person and each day the corresponding working period. In addition, each person has to work in a cyclic way, i.e. according to an unknown work pattern that is repeated with the assumption that days off do not break any cycle. To model this kind of periodicity we replace the equality constraint $X = Y$ by the constraint $(X = Y) \vee (X = 0) \vee (Y = 0)$ (assuming that 0 corresponds to a day off). The use of constraints for solving other types of cyclic scheduling problems is presented in [2] and [8].

No filtering algorithm was yet available, neither for the *period* constraint itself, nor for its generalisation. As usual within constraint programming, we only have partial information about the sequence we consider and its potential smallest periods. So our problem is not to have an efficient algorithm for computing the period of a given sequence [5], [7], but rather to perform the following tasks:

- On one side, we want to discard from the domain of P those values, which can't be the smallest period of any sequence that can be constructed from the domains of $V_0, V_1, \ldots, V_{m-1}$ by replacing each variable by one value of its domain,
- On the other side, we want to remove from the domains of $V_0, V_1, \ldots, V_{m-1}$ those values such that we can't generate any sequence for which the smallest period belongs to the domain of P.

As an illustrative example of the previous tasks, consider the constraint period$(P, [V_0, V_1, V_2, V_3, V_4, V_5, V_6, V_7])$, where the initial domains of the variables are as follows: $dom(P) = \{3, 4, 5, 8\}$, $dom(V_0) = \{2\}$, $dom(V_1) = \{2\}$, $dom(V_2) = \{2, 6, 9\}$, $dom(V_3) = \{2, 4\}$, $dom(V_4) = \{2, 8\}$, $dom(V_5) = \{2, 8\}$, $dom(V_6) = \{2, 6, 8, 9\}$, $dom(V_7) = \{2\}$. We first want to find out that 3 and 8 are not feasible smallest periods for all the potential sequences, which can be generated from the domains of $V_0, V_1, \ldots, V_7$. In fact, on one hand 3 is not a feasible smallest period since all variables $V_0, V_1, \ldots, V_7$ would have to be fixed to value 2 which would enforce a smallest period of 1^2. On the other hand, 8 is also not possible since 7 is a period, possibly not the smallest, of the sequence $V_0 \, V_1 \cdots V_7$. In order to achieve the only remaining smallest periods of 4 or 5, we restrict the domains of the variables V_5 and V_6. Hence, $dom(V_5) = \{2\}$ and $dom(V_6) = \{2, 6, 9\}$.

The paper is organised as follows. Section 2 sets up some basic required notions from the area of combinatorial pattern matching. Section 3 shows how to

---

^{2} Independently of the fact that value 1 is or is not in the domain of P.

handle the ground case of the *period* constraint, i.e. the case when all variables
are already fixed. Section 4 presents some propositions and their corresponding
implementation, which allow discarding infeasible periods within a sequence of
domain variables. Finally, Section 5 introduces propositions that combine the
apparently feasible values of the smallest period P with the potential values
of the variables of the sequence $V_0\ V_1 \cdots V_{m-1}$ in order to prune the domains
of $V_0, V_1, \ldots, V_{m-1}$. All propositions related to pruning consider the basic *period* constraint itself. Their adaptation for the generalised *period* constraint is
systematically investigated.

2 Background

This section follows the presentation of Crochemore et al. [4]. A *sequence* on
an alphabet A is a finite series of elements of A. In our context, A consists of
all those natural numbers, which occur in the initial domains of the variables
$V_0, V_1, \ldots, V_{m-1}$ of the *period* constraint. Within the rest of this paper, the expression "a sequence $V_0\ V_1 \cdots V_{m-1}$" should be interpreted as "all sequences,
which can be obtained from the domains of the variables $V_0, V_1, \ldots, V_{m-1}$ by replacing each variable by one value of its domain". The *empty sequence* is denoted
by ε. The *length* of a sequence s is the number of elements of its corresponding
series and is denoted by $|s|$. For $i \in \{0, 1, \ldots, |s| - 1\}$, $s[i]$ denotes the i-th letter
of s. Within a given sequence, the character $*$ denotes any letter of A. A nat-
ural number p such that $1 \le p \le |s|$ is a *period* of a non-empty sequence s if
$s[i] = s[i+p]$ for all $i \in \{0, 1, \ldots, |s| - p - 1\}$. The *period* of a non-empty sequence
s corresponds to its smallest period[3] and is denoted by $per(s)$. A sequence r is
a *factor* of a sequence s if there exists two sequences u and v such that $s = urv$;
when $u = \varepsilon$, r is a *prefix* of s; when $v = \varepsilon$, r is a *suffix* of s; when $r \neq s$, r
is called a *proper factor* of s. The factor $s[i]\ s[i+1] \cdots s[j]$ of s is denoted by
$s[i..j]$. A *border* of a non-empty sequence s is a proper factor of s, which is both
a prefix and a suffix of s. For a sequence s, $Bord(s)$ denotes the longest border
among all the borders of s. A standard relation between the longest border and
the period of a non-empty sequence s is $|s| - |Bord(s)| = per(s)$. As an example
consider again the sequence 1 1 4 1 1 4 1 1. It has four borders ε, 1, 1 1 and
1 1 4 1 1 and a smallest period of $8 - 5 = 3$. One way for computing the longest
border of a non-empty sequence s is to calculate the *border table* of s defined
as $bord[k] = |Bord(s[0..k])|$ for $k \in \{0, 1, \ldots, |s| - 1\}$. Crochemore et al. (see [4,
page 39]) give an $\Theta(|s|)$ algorithm for computing the border table that is based
on the following recurrence:

$$Bord(ua) = \begin{cases} Bord(u)a & \text{if } Bord(u)a \text{ is a prefix of } u, \\ Bord(Bord(u)a) & \text{else.} \end{cases} \tag{1}$$

---

[3] Within this paper keep in mind the difference between "a period" and "**the** period"
of a sequence s. A sequence s may have several periods, but **the** period designates
its minimum period.

3   Handling the Ground Case of the *period* Constraint

Given a generalised $period(P, [V_0, V_1, \ldots, V_{m-1}], ctr)$ constraint where $V_0, V_1, \ldots,$ V_{m-1} are fixed, we need to compute the period of $V_0 V_1 \cdots V_{m-1}$ and check whether it belongs or not to $dom(P)$. When ctr corresponds to the equality constraint we can directly reuse the algorithm that computes the border table mentioned at the end of the previous section and exploit the identity $per(V_0 V_1 \cdots V_{m-1}) = m - |Bord(V_0 V_1 \ldots V_{m-1})|$. But what should we do when ctr is not the equality constraint? To partially answer this question, we first extend the notion of border and then show how to adapt the recurrence used for computing the border under the hypothesis that ctr satisfies the transitivity property[4]. In that case, as for the equality constraint, we get a complexity of $O(m)$. Otherwise, if ctr does not satisfy the transitivity property we use the algorithm which checks each potential period; it has an overall complexity of $O(m^2)$. These two algorithms will also be used in the rest of this paper for evaluating the period of a completely fixed factor of a sequence.

Definition 1. *A border of a non-empty sequence s according to a binary constraint ctr corresponds to two proper factors u and v of s, such that:*

- *u and v have the same length which is called the* length *of the border,*
- *u is a prefix of s,*
- *v is a suffix of s,*
- *ctr(u[i], v[i]) holds for all $i \in \{0, 1, \ldots, |u| - 1\}$.*

Those two longest proper factors of s are respectively denoted by $Pbord(s, ctr)$ and $Sbord(s, ctr)$; $Lbord(s, ctr)$ designates their common length.

Proposition 1. *Let ctr be a binary constraint satisfying the transitivity property. Then:*

$$Lbord(ua, ctr) = \begin{cases} Lbord(u, ctr) + 1 & \text{if } ctr(u[Lbord(u, ctr) + 1], a) \text{ holds,} \\ Lbord(Pbord(u, ctr)a, ctr) & \text{else.} \end{cases}$$

(2)

Proof. Let $v = v_0 v_1 \cdots v_n = ua$ and $p = Lbord(u, ctr)$. Then, $\forall i \in \{0, 1, \ldots, p - 1\} : ctr(v_i, v_{n-p+i})$ holds.

1. CASE where $ctr(v_p, v_n)$ holds:

$$\wedge \begin{matrix} \forall i \in \{0, 1, \ldots, p-1\} : ctr(v_i, v_{n-p+i}) \text{ holds} \\ ctr(v_p, v_n) \text{ holds} \end{matrix} \left. \right\} \Rightarrow \begin{matrix} \forall i \in \{0, 1, \ldots, p\} : \\ ctr(v_i, v_{n-p+i}) \text{holds.} \end{matrix}$$

   Hence, $Lbord(v, ctr) = p+1$. So $Lbord(ua, ctr) = Lbord(u, ctr)+1$ is satisfied.
2. CASE where $ctr(v_p, v_n)$ does not hold:
   $Pbord(u, ctr)a = v_0 v_1 \cdots v_{p-1} a = v_0 v_1 \cdots v_{p-1} v_n$. Let $q = Lbord(Pbord(u, ctr)a, ctr)$. Then $\forall j \in \{0, 1, \ldots, q-2\} : ctr(v_j, v_{(p+1)-q+j})$ and $ctr(v_{q-1}, v_n)$

---

[4] $\forall X, Y, Z \ (ctr(X, Y) \wedge ctr(Y, Z)) \Rightarrow ctr(X, Z)$.

both hold. When $j \in \{0, 1, \ldots, q-2\}$, $(j+p-q) \in \{p-q, p-q+1, \ldots, p-2\}$ and for $i = p + 1 - q + j$, $ctr(v_i, v_{n-p+i})$ becomes $ctr(v_{p+1-q+j}, v_{n+1-q+j})$. Let a given $j \in \{0, 1, \ldots, q-2\}$. If ctr satisfies the transitivity property then

$$\wedge \left. \begin{array}{l} ctr(v_j, v_{p+1-q+j}) \text{ holds} \\ ctr(v_{p+1-q+j}, v_{n+1-q+j}) \text{ holds} \end{array} \right\} \Rightarrow ctr(v_j, v_{n+1-q+j}) \text{ holds}.$$

So, $\forall j \in \{0, 1, \ldots, q-2\} : ctr(v_j, v_{n+1-q+j})$ holds. Furthermore, $ctr(v_{q-1}, v_n)$ holds. Then, $Lbord(ua, ctr) \geq q$.

Finally, since the recurrence (2) considers the borders of u in decreasing lengths, it computes a border of maximum length. □

When ctr satisfies the transitivity property, the algorithm based on the previous recurrence can be adapted by changing the inequality test (see [4, page 39, line 4 of the algorithm]) by the test that the binary constraint ctr does not hold.

4 Searching for the Infeasible Smallest Periods

As a basic fact, we have that the period of a sequence of domain variables $V_0 \, V_1 \cdots V_{m-1}$ belongs to $\{1, 2, \ldots, m\}$. The aim of this section is to detect infeasible smallest periods for the sequence $V_0 \, V_1 \cdots V_{m-1}$. For this purpose, we first introduce four propositions, which remove from $dom(P)$ infeasible periods according to the fact that some variables do not take the same value. Finally, the last propositions of this section use the fact that, if p is a feasible period for a given sequence s, it follows that the smallest period of s can't exceed p.

Proposition 2. *Let r be a factor of a sequence s. Then, $per(s) \geq per(r)$.*

Proof. Straightforward from the definition of the period of a sequence. □

Example 1. Consider the sequence $s = * 5 * 0 \ 2 \ 1 \ 0 \ * * 3 \ 5 \ 3 \ 5 \ * \ * \ *$, where $*$ stands for a not yet fixed variable. Since the factors 5, 0 2 1 0 and 3 5 3 5 have a respective period of 1, 3 and 2, the period of s is greater than or equal to 3.

Proposition 2 is used for evaluating a lower bound of the period of a sequence of variables $V_0 V_1 \cdots V_{m-1}$ by computing the period of each factor of s that only consists of fixed variables of s and by stating that P is greater than or equal to those computed periods. This is achieved in $O(m)$ by scanning the variables $V_0, V_1, \ldots, V_{m-1}$ from left to right and by computing the border tables of each completely fixed factor of s.

Remark 1. Proposition 2 is still valid for any type of binary constraint.

Proposition 3. *Consider a sequence $s = V_0 V_1 \cdots V_{m-1}$ and two distinct positions i and j such that $0 \leq i < j \leq m - 1$ and $V_i \neq V_j$. Then, $(j - i)$ can't be a period of s.*

Proof. Straightforward from the definition of the period of a sequence.   □

Example 2. Consider the sequence $s = * \, 5 \, * \, * \, * \, * \, * \, 9 \, * \, * \, *$. Since the difference between the position of 9 and the position of 5 is equal to $7 - 1 = 6$, 6 can't be equal to the period of s.

Proposition 3 is used to check each variable, which was fixed since the last time the *period* constraint was woken according to the other fixed variables. When the *period* constraint is posted, we create a table $forbid[1..m]$ and initialise all its entries to 0. Its $(j - i)$-th entry will be set to 1 as soon as we find two fixed variables V_i and V_j such that $V_i \neq V_j$ $(i < j)$. For each new variable which was fixed this is achieved in $O(m)$.

Remark 2. As Proposition 2, Proposition 3 is still valid for any type of binary constraint, provided that we replace $V_i \neq V_j$ by the negation of the binary constraint *ctr*.

Proposition 4. *Consider a sequence $s = V_0 \, V_1 \cdots V_{m-1}$ and a natural number p such that $1 < p \leq m - 1$. If p is not a period of s then every number that exactly divides p, can't be a period of s.*

Proof. Let q be a divisor of p such that $p = \alpha \cdot q$ $(\alpha \in \mathbb{N}^*)$. We prove the contrapositive statement. Assume q is a period of s. It implies that for any $i \in \{0, 1, \ldots, m - p - 1\} : V_i = V_{i+q}, V_{i+q} = V_{i+2 \cdot q}, \ldots, V_{i+(\alpha-1) \cdot q} = V_{i+\alpha \cdot q}$. Therefore, by transitivity, $V_i = V_{i+\alpha \cdot q}$ i.e. $V_i = V_{i+p}$ and so p is a period of s.

     □

Example 3. Consider again Example 2. Since 6 was not a period of s, the numbers 3, 2 and 1 that exactly divide 6, can't be a period of s.

We reuse the table $forbid[1..m]$ introduced for the implementation of Proposition 3. Each time the $(j - i)$-th entry is set to 1, all the natural numbers that exactly divide $(j - i)$ are removed from P; the corresponding entries in the table $forbid[1..m]$ are also set to 1.

Remark 3. From the previous proof, Proposition 4 is still valid for a binary constraint which satisfies the transitivity property. We give an example showing that Proposition 4 can't be used when the binary constraint does not satisfy the transitivity property. For this purpose, consider the binary constraint defined by the condition $(X = Y) \vee (X = 0) \vee (Y = 0)$. According to this condition, 4 is not a period of the sequence 1 0 0 0 2 0 0 0 1 (since $V_0 = 1$ and $V_4 = 2$ are distinct and take both a value different from 0); however 2 and 1 are periods of the previous sequence.

We now introduce a proposition which removes infeasible periods even when variables of the sequence are not yet fixed.

Notation 1 *Consider a sequence* $s = V_0 \ V_1 \cdots V_{m-1}$ *and a natural number* p *such that* $1 \leq p \leq m - 1$*. Let*

$$I_i^p = \bigcap_{\substack{0 \leq k \leq m-1 \\ k \equiv i \pmod{p}}} dom(V_k)$$

be the intersection of the domains of the variables belonging to the i-*th* ($i \in \{0, 1, \ldots, p - 1\}$*) group of variables according to* p*. Note that if* $p > \lfloor \frac{m}{2} \rfloor$ *then* $I_i^p = dom(V_i)$ *for* $i \in \{m - p, m - p + 1, \ldots, p - 1\}$*.*

Proposition 5. *Consider a sequence* $s = V_0 \ V_1 \cdots V_{m-1}$ *and a natural number* p *such that* $1 \leq p \leq m - 1$*. Then, (a)* p *is not a period of* s *if and only if (b) there exists* $i \in \{0, 1, \ldots, p - 1\}$ *such that* $I_i^p = \emptyset$*.*

Proof.

- (a) $\Rightarrow$ (b): If p is not a period then, by definition of a period, for any sequence $v_0 v_1 \cdots v_{m-1}$ where $v_0 \in dom(V_0), v_1 \in dom(V_1), \ldots, v_{m-1} \in dom(V_{m-1})$ there exists $i \in \{0, 1, \ldots, m - p - 1\}$ such that $v_i \neq v_{i+p}$. Therefore $I_i^p = \emptyset$.
- (b) $\Rightarrow$ (a): We prove the contrapositive statement. Let assume that p is a period of s. Then, there exists $v_0 \in dom(V_0), v_1 \in dom(V_1), \ldots, v_{m-1} \in dom(V_{m-1})$ such that $s = v_0 v_1 \cdots v_{m-1}$ has a period p i.e. $v_i = v_{i+p}$ for $i \in \{0, 1, \ldots, m - p - 1\}$. Therefore, $I_i^p = \{v_i\}$ for $i \in \{0, 1, \ldots, p - 1\}$ is not empty.   □

Example 4. Consider the sequence $s = V_0 * * * V_4 * * * V_8 * *$ with the following domains for the variables: $dom(V_0) = \{1, 2\}$, $dom(V_4) = \{0, 2\}$ and $dom(V_8) = \{0, 1\}$. Since the intersection $dom(V_0) \cap dom(V_4) \cap dom(V_8)$ is empty, 4 can't be a period of s.

Proposition 5 requires in the worst-case $\frac{m \cdot (m-1)}{2}$ intersections between domains ($m - 1$ for $p = 1$, $m - 2$ for $p = 2$, ..., 1 for $p = m - 1$). After application of Proposition 5, only feasible periods, possibly not smallest feasible periods, remain in the domain of P.

Remark 4. Proposition 5 can be generalised, for a binary constraint $ctr(X, Y)$, if we provide a necessary and sufficient condition for checking whether a conjunction of binary constraints of the form

$$\bigwedge_{\substack{0 \leq k \leq m-1 \\ k \equiv i \pmod{p}}} ctr(V_k, V_{k+p})$$

($i \in \{0, 1, \ldots, p - 1\}$) has at least one solution. For instance, consider the binary constraint $(X = Y) \vee (X = 0) \vee (Y = 0)$ introduced in the motivating example related to the cyclic scheduling problem. In this context, a necessary and sufficient condition is that for all factor $s[\alpha \cdot \cdot \beta]$ of s such that:

- $(\alpha \equiv i \pmod{p}) \wedge ((\alpha - p < 0) \vee (0 \in dom(V_{\alpha-p})))$,
- $(\beta \equiv i \pmod{p}) \wedge ((\beta + p > m - 1) \vee (0 \in dom(V_{\beta+p})))$,
- $0 \notin dom(V_j)$ for any j such that $(\alpha \le j \le \beta) \wedge (j \equiv i \pmod{p})$,

the intersection

$$\bigcap_{\substack{\alpha \le k \le \beta \\ k \equiv i \pmod{p}}} dom(V_k)$$

is not empty.

We now come to propositions that handle the fact that P has to be the smallest period of sequence s.

Proposition 6. *Consider a sequence $s = V_0\, V_1 \cdots V_{m-1}$ and a natural number b such that $1 \le b \le \lfloor \frac{m}{2} \rfloor$. Let p denote the period of the sequence $s[0..b-1]s[m-b..m-1]$. The period of s is less than or equal to $\lceil \frac{b}{p} \rceil \cdot p + m - 2 \cdot b$.*

Proof. We search for a feasible period of s, no matter which values are assigned to the $m - 2 \cdot b$ variables of $s[b..m - b - 1]$. For this purpose, we first remove the previous variables from s and compute a feasible period p of the remaining sequence. Then, we deduce a feasible period of s as following:

- If $p \ge b$ ($\lceil \frac{b}{p} \rceil \cdot p = p$) then $\forall i \in \{0, 1, \ldots, b-1\}$ we have $i + p \ge m - b$ and $p + m - 2 \cdot b$ is a period of s,
- Else ($p < b$). We consider the smallest multiple $\lceil \frac{b}{p} \rceil \cdot p$ of p such that $\forall i \in \{0, 1, \ldots, b-1\} : i + \lceil \frac{b}{p} \rceil \cdot p \ge m - b$. Then, $\lceil \frac{b}{p} \rceil \cdot p + m - 2 \cdot b$ is a period of s. □

Example 5. Consider the sequence $s = 3\,1**8***2\,3\,1$. Since the period of the sequence 3 1 3 1 is 2, the period of s is less than or equal to $\lceil \frac{2}{2} \rceil \cdot 2 + 11 - 2 \cdot 2 = 9$, no matter what value is assigned to the not yet fixed variables.

Proposition 6 is used to adjust the upper bound of the period of the sequence $s = V_0\, V_1 \cdots V_{m-1}$ by considering the concatenation of the largest suffix and prefix of same length of fixed variables of s and by computing its smallest period. This has a worst-case complexity of $O(m)$.

Remark 5. When $p \ge b$ Proposition 6 is valid for any binary constraint. Otherwise ($p < b$), it is also still valid for a binary constraint that satisfies the transitivity property: the transitivity is required to ensure that the multiple $\lceil \frac{b}{p} \rceil \cdot p$ of period p is still a period.

Proposition 7. *Consider a sequence $s = V_0\, V_1 \cdots V_{m-1}$ and $s' = s[0..b - 1]s[m - b..m - 1]$ where b is the greatest integer in $\{1, 2, \ldots, \lfloor \frac{m}{2} \rfloor\}$ such that all variables of s' are fixed but exactly one single variable, for instance V. The period of s is less than or equal to*

$$p = \max_{v \in dom(V)} \left(\left\lceil \frac{b}{p_v} \right\rceil \cdot p_v + m - 2 \cdot b \right)$$

where p_v is the period of s' when $V = v$.

Proof. Proposition 7 is a generalisation of Proposition 6 in the sense that s' contains a non-fixed variable. For each potential value of the domain of the non-fixed variable we compute an upper bound of the period of s and keep the maximum of the upper bounds.   □

Example 6. Consider the sequence $s = 1\ V_1\ 2\ V_3\ V_4\ 2\ 1\ 1\ 2$ with the following domains for the variables: $dom(V_1) = \{1,2\}$ and $dom(V_3) = dom(V_4) = \{0,1,\ldots,9\}$. Then, $s' = 1\ V_1\ 2\ 1\ 1\ 2$, $p_1 = 3$, $p_2 = 4$ and the period of s is less than or equal to $max(3,4) + 9 - 2 \cdot 3 = 7$.

Proposition 7 is used to adjust the upper bound of the period of the sequence $s = V_0\ V_1 \cdots V_{m-1}$ by considering the concatenation of the leftmost and rightmost groups of variables (of same length) of s with one non-fixed variable in the concatenation.

Remark 6. When $min_{v \in dom(V)}(p_v) \geq b$ Proposition 7 is valid for any binary constraint. Otherwise, it is also still valid for a binary constraint, which satisfies the transitivity property.

Proposition 8. *Consider a sequence $s = V_0\ V_1 \cdots V_{m-1}$ and a natural number $p \in \{2,3,\ldots,m\}$. Assume that each I_k^p ($k \in \{0,1,\ldots,p-1\}$) is reduced to only one single value. If there exists a period $q < p$ of $I_0^p\ I_1^p \cdots I_{p-1}^p$ where q divides exactly p then p can't be the period of s.*

Proof. Since $I_0^p\ I_1^p \cdots I_{p-1}^p$ is completely fixed, there exists for sequence s only one solution of period p. Furthermore, if there exists a period $q < p$ of $I_0^p\ I_1^p \cdots I_{p-1}^p$ where q divides exactly p, then q is also a period of s. Therefore p can't be the smallest period of s.   □

Example 7. Consider the sequence $s = V_0\ V_1 \cdots V_{11}$ with the following domains for the variables: $dom(V_i) = \{0,1,\ldots,9\}$ for $i \in \{0,1,5,6,7,8,10,11\}$, $dom(V_2) = dom(V_4) = \{1\}$ and $dom(V_3) = dom(V_9) = \{0\}$. For $p = 4$, we have $I_0^4 = I_2^4 = \{1\}$, $I_1^4 = I_3^4 = \{0\}$ and the single solution $s = 1\ 0\ 1\ 0\ 1\ 0\ 1\ 0\ 1\ 0\ 1\ 0$. Since 2 is a period of $I_0^4\ I_1^4\ I_2^4\ I_3^4 = 1\ 0\ 1\ 0$ then 4 can't be the period of s.

Proposition 8 is used to check that an apparently feasible period p of a sequence $s = V_0\ V_1 \cdots V_{m-1}$ is not the period of s. For this purpose, we compute $I_0^p\ I_1^p \cdots I_{p-1}^p$ and, if this sequence is completely fixed, we calculate its smallest period q. If that period q is strictly less than p and divides exactly p, we remove p from $dom(P)$. Assuming that $I_0^p, I_1^p, \ldots, I_{p-1}^p$ were already computed (see Notation 1) the complexity for testing an apparently feasible period p is equal to the complexity of computing the period of $I_0^p\ I_1^p \cdots I_{p-1}^p$, i.e. is equal to $O(p)$.

Remark 7. Proposition 8 is still valid for a binary constraint which satisfies the equivalence property[5].

---

[5] *ctr* satisfies the *equivalence* property if *ctr* has the following three properties: Reflexivity ($\forall X\ ctr(X,X)$), symmetry ($\forall X,Y\ ctr(X,Y) \Rightarrow ctr(Y,X)$) and transitivity ($\forall X,Y,Z\ (ctr(X,Y) \wedge ctr(Y,Z)) \Rightarrow ctr(X,Z)$).

The following weaker form of Proposition 8 is first used for pruning the period of a sequence. This is because it has an overall complexity of $O(m)$ that is independent from the number of periods to check.

Proposition 9. *Consider a sequence s containing a factor a^k, where a stands for an element of the alphabet Λ and $k > 1$ for a strictly positive natural number. Then, the period of s can't be equal to $2, 3, \ldots, k$.*

Proof. Let any $p \in \{1, 2, \ldots, k\}$. s is containing a factor a^k implies that $I_i^p = \{a\}$ for $i \in \{0, 1, \ldots, p - 1\}$. Since $I_0^p \ I_1^p \cdots I_{p-1}^p$ has a period of $1 < p$ and since 1 divides exactly p, then Proposition 8 tells us that p can't be a period of s. $\quad\square$

Example 8. Consider the sequence $s = * \ 0 \ 0 \ 0 \ 0 \ * \ *$. Since s contains the factor 0^4, its period can't be equal to 2, 3 and 4.

Proposition 9 is used by computing the size of the largest factor for which all variables are fixed to the same value and by pruning P according to this number.

5   Pruning According to the Potential Periods

The aim of this section is to give rules for pruning the variables $V_0, V_1 \ldots, V_{m-1}$ so to enforce the period of $V_0 \ V_1 \ldots V_{m-1}$ to be one of the values of the domain of P. Most of these rules are based on the propositions presented in the previous section. We start with a proposition directly derived from the definition of the period of a sequence.

Proposition 10. *Consider a sequence $s = V_0 \ V_1 \cdots V_{m-1}$.*

1. *For all i such that $max(P) \leq i \leq m - 1$ we remove from $dom(V_i)$ all values that don't belong to*

$$\bigcup_{\substack{0 \leq l < i \\ (i - l) \in dom(P)}} dom(V_l).$$

2. *For all i such that $0 \leq i \leq m - 1 - max(P)$ we remove from $dom(V_i)$ all values that don't belong to*

$$\bigcup_{\substack{i < k \leq m - 1 \\ (k - i) \in dom(P)}} dom(V_k).$$

Proof. From the definition of the period of a sequence, if $i - max(P) \geq 0$ then V_i has to be equal to a variable V_l such that $(i - l) \in dom(P)$. Using constructive disjunction[6] [10] on the previous equalities leads to remove all values not in

$$\bigcup_{\substack{0 \leq l < i \\ (i - l) \in dom(P)}} dom(V_l).$$

The second part of Proposition 10 is proved in a similar way. $\quad\square$

---

[6] We remove those values that are discarded by all the equality constraints associated to the potential periods.

Example 9. Consider the sequence $s = V_0\ V_1\ V_2\ V_3\ V_4\ V_5$ with the following domains for the variables: $dom(V_0) = \{0, 1, 2, 8\}$, $dom(V_1) = \{0, 1\}$, $dom(V_2) = \{2, 8\}$, $dom(V_3) = \{0, 1\}$, $dom(V_4) = \{1, 2, 6\}$ and $dom(V_5) = \{0, 1\}$. Furthermore, assume that P has to take value 2 or value 4. Part 1 of Proposition 10 considers variables V_4 and V_5: For V_4, since $dom(V_0) \cup dom(V_2) = \{0, 1, 2, 8\}$ then $6 \in dom(V_4)$ has to be removed from $dom(V_4)$ in order to achieve a smallest period of 2 or 4. No pruning occurs for V_5. Similarly, from part 2 of Proposition 10, since $dom(V_2) \cup dom(V_4) = \{1, 2, 6, 8\}$ then $0 \in dom(V_0)$ has to be removed from $dom(V_0)$.

For a given value *val*, finding all variables from which it has to be removed according to Proposition 10 is similar to the problem of finding all occurrences of a sequence r which contains jokers within a sequence t which does not contains any joker. A joker is a special letter $ which does not belong to the alphabet A and which can be matched to any character of the alphabet A. The length of sequence t is m and its i-th position $t[i]$ is equal to 1 if $val \in dom(V_i)$ and 0 otherwise. The sequence r, we want to localise within t, is defined as follows:

- $r[0] = 1$ represents the value we want to prune,
- For $i \in dom(P)$: $r[i] = 0$ (0 represents the fact that we don't want to find value *val* at any position corresponding to a potential period of s),
- For $i \notin dom(P)$ and $i < max(P)$: $r[i] =\$$ ($ represents the fact that we don't care finding value *val* or not, for all those positions which do not correspond to potential periods of s).

Using a standard algorithm from [4, page 266] allows finding all occurrences of r within t in time $O(n \cdot p \cdot m)$ where $n \cdot p$ is the number of intervals of consecutive values of $dom(P)$.

Example 10. Consider again the previous example where $s = V_0\ V_1\ V_2\ V_3\ V_4\ V_5$ with the following domains for the variables: $dom(V_0) = \{0, 1, 2, 8\}$, $dom(V_1) = \{0, 1\}$, $dom(V_2) = \{2, 8\}$, $dom(V_3) = \{0, 1\}$, $dom(V_4) = \{1, 2, 6\}$ and $dom(V_5) = \{0, 1\}$. Assume that we want to localise those variables from which we can remove value 0. We first build the sequence $t = 1\ 1\ 0\ 1\ 0\ 1$ for which the i-th $(0 \le i < m)$ position contains 1 when $0 \in dom(V_i)$ and 0 otherwise. Since $dom(P) = \{2, 4\}$, we search the occurrences of the sequence $r = 1\ \$ \ 0\ \$ \ 0$ within t and find one single match when the first positions of both sequences coincide. Therefore, we can remove value 0 from $dom(V_0)$.

Remark 8. Proposition 10 is still valid for a binary constraint for which we can provide a complete filtering algorithm for a conjunction of binary constraints of the form $ctr(X, Y_1) \wedge ctr(X, Y_2) \wedge \cdots \wedge ctr(X, Y_n)$.

In Proposition 10 we consider, for a variable V_i, only its immediate neighbours according to all its potential periods. In order to remove more values one could restrict $dom(V_i)$ to:

$$\bigcup_{p \in dom(P)} dom(I^p_{i \bmod p}).$$

In that case, pruning all the domains of variables $V_0, V_1 \cdots, V_{m-1}$ requires $m \cdot size(P)$ unions and $\frac{m \cdot (m-1)}{2}$ intersections between domains, where $size(P)$ denotes the number of values of $dom(P)$. Note that it still does not allow to get a complete pruning since potential periods and not smallest potential periods are considered.

The next proposition is derived from Proposition 4 and Proposition 5.

Proposition 11. *Note q the least common multiple of the potential values of P and assume $q < m$. For each $i \in \{0, 1, \ldots, min(q, m - q) - 1\}$, the domains of the variables $V_i, V_{i+q}, \ldots, V_{i+\lfloor \frac{m-i-1}{q} \rfloor \cdot q}$ are restricted to I_i^q.*

Proof. Since q is a multiple of the period of s (no matter which values are assigned to the not yet fixed variables of s), the contraposition of Proposition 4 tells us that q is also a period of s. We prune according to that fact. □

Example 11. Consider the sequence $s = V_0 \; V_1 \; V_2 \; V_3 \; V_4 \; V_5 \; V_6 \; V_7 \; V_8 \; V_9$ with the following domains for the variables: $dom(V_0) = dom(V_1) = dom(V_2) = dom(V_3) = dom(V_4) = \{1, 2\}$ and $dom(V_5) = dom(V_6) = dom(V_7) = dom(V_8) = dom(V_9) = \{0, 2\}$. Furthermore, assume that $dom(P) = \{1, 2, 3\}$. Since 6 is the least common multiple of the previous values, the domains of the following pairs of variables (V_0, V_6), (V_1, V_7), (V_2, V_8) and (V_3, V_9) are respectively restricted to the intersections $dom(V_0) \cap dom(V_6) = \{2\}$, $dom(V_1) \cap dom(V_7) = \{2\}$, $dom(V_2) \cap dom(V_8) = \{2\}$ and $dom(V_3) \cap dom(V_9) = \{2\}$.

Remark 9. Proposition 11 is still valid for a binary constraint $ctr(X, Y)$ which satisfies the transitivity property and for which we can provide a complete filtering algorithm for a conjunction of binary constraints of the form

$$\bigwedge_{\substack{0 \leq k \leq m-1 \\ k \equiv i \pmod{q}}} ctr(V_k, V_{k+q}) \qquad (i \in \{0, 1, \ldots, q - 1\}).$$

The next proposition is directly derived from Proposition 9.

Proposition 12. *Consider a sequence $s = V_0 \; V_1 \cdots V_{m-1}$ containing a factor $a^{k_1} \; V_i \; a^{k_2}$, where a stands for an element of the alphabet A, k_1 and k_2 for two strictly positive natural numbers and V_i ($1 \leq i \leq m-2$) for a not yet fixed domain variable. If the domain of the period of s is included within $\{2, 3, \ldots, k_1 + k_2 + 1\}$ then V_i can't take value a.*

Proof. The reverse of Proposition 9 tells us that, if p_i is both in P and satisfies $p_i \leq k_1 + k_2 + 1$, then s can't contain the factor $s = a^{k_1 + k_2 + 1}$. Therefore V_i can't take value a. □

Example 12. Consider the sequence $s = 0 \; 0 \; V_2 \; 0 \; V_4 \; V_5$ and assume the period of s to be 2, 3 or 4. Since s contains the factor $s = 0^2 \; V_2 \; 0^1$, V_2 can't take 0 as value.

A simple scan through positions $0, 1, \ldots, m-1$ of sequence s allows localising those factors $a^{k_1} V_i a^{k_2}$ from which one can prune a not yet fixed variable V_i ($1 \leq i \leq m-2$).

Let us now introduce Proposition 13, which is derived from Proposition 6.

Proposition 13. *Consider a sequence $s = V_0 V_1 \cdots V_{m-1}$ and $s' = s[0..b-1]s[m-b..m-1]$ where b is the greatest integer in $\{1, 2, \ldots, \lfloor \frac{m}{2} \rfloor\}$ such that all variables of s' are fixed but exactly one single variable, for instance V. Let $v \in dom(V)$ and p the period of s' when V is fixed to v. If $\lceil \frac{b}{p} \rceil \cdot p + m - 2 \cdot b$ is strictly less than the minimum value of $dom(P)$ then V can't take value v.*

Proof. If the period of s' is p then Proposition 6 tells us that the period of s is less than or equal to $\lceil \frac{b}{p} \rceil \cdot p + m - 2 \cdot b$. Therefore, if $\lceil \frac{b}{p} \rceil \cdot p + m - 2 \cdot b$ is strictly less than the minimum value of $dom(P)$, s has a period not in $dom(P)$. So to avoid it, v has to be removed from $dom(V)$. □

Example 13. Consider the sequence $s = 1\,2\,3\,6*9\,1\,V_7\,3$ where V_7 corresponds to a not yet fixed domain variable. If the period of s is strictly greater than 6 (i.e. $min(dom(P)) > 6$) then V_7 should not be fixed to value 2. Otherwise s would have a border $b = 1\,2\,3$ and therefore a smallest period less than or equal to 6, which contradict the hypothesis.

Remark 10. Remark 5 also holds for Proposition 13.

We conclude this section with a remark concerning the implementation of the propositions introduced in this paper. We apply in priority Propositions 1, 2, 3, 4, 6, 9 and 12 where only fixed variables of the sequence s are considered. These propositions are used each time a new variable of s is fixed. Then, we apply Propositions 7 and 13 on the prefix and the suffix of s where only one single non-fixed variable is considered. Concerning Propositions 5, 8, 10 and 11, they might require an important number of intersections or unions of domains and it is still an open question how to use them in an efficient way.

6 Conclusion

We have revisited the classical notion of period of a sequence from a constraint point of view. We have extended this notion in order to handle any comparison condition between two characters. Finally, for each proposition Pr, we have systematically shown how to extend it (when possible) or how to characterise a required property on the comparison condition for using Pr.

From a broader perspective we hope that the paper will awake the interest for turning other classical problems from the area of combinatorial pattern matching, such as distance between sequences or local periods, to new constraints. In fact, it is often possible to turn to a constraint an algorithm which computes a result from an input. This is achieved by breaking the distinction between input and output parameters.

References

1. Beldiceanu, N.: Global Constraints as Graph Properties on Structured Network of Elementary Constraints of the Same Type. SICS Technical Report T2000/01, (2000).
2. Bockmayr, A., Pisaruk, N., Aggoun, A.: Network Flow Problems in Constraint Programming. 7th International Conference of Principles and Practice of Constraint Programming - CP 2001, Paphos, Cyprus, (November 26 - December 1, 2001), Proceedings. Lecture Notes in Computer Science, Vol. 2239, Springer-Verlag (2001) 196-210.
3. Crochemore, M. and Rytter, W.: Text Algorithms. Oxford University Press, New York (1994).
4. Crochemore, M., Hancart, C. and Lecroq, T.: Algorithmique du texte. Vuibert, Paris (2001), in French.
5. Czumaj, A. and Gasieniec, L.: On the Complexity of Determining the Period of a String. Combinatorial Pattern Matching, 11th Annual Symposium, CPM 2000, Montreal, Canada, (June 21-23, 2000), Proceedings. Lecture Notes in Computer Science, Vol. 1848, Springer-Verlag (2000) 412-422.
6. Golden, K. and Pang, W.: Constraint Reasoning over Strings. Principles and Practice of Constraint Programming - CP 2003, vol. 2833 of Lecture Notes in Computer Science, Springer-Verlag (2003) 377-391.
7. Hikita, T. and Goto, E.: An O(N) algorithm for finding periodicity of a sequence using hash coding. Information Processing Letters $6(2)$ (1977) 69-71.
8. Pesant, G.: A Filtering Algorithm for the Stretch Constraint. 7th International Conference of Principles and Practice of Constraint Programming - CP 2001, Paphos, Cyprus, (November 26 - December 1, 2001), Proceedings. Lecture Notes in Computer Science, Vol. 2239, Springer-Verlag (2001) 183-195.
9. Pesant, G.: A Regular Language Membership Constraint for Sequences of Variables. 2nd Interntional Workshop on Modelling and Reformulating Constraint Satisfaction Problems, Principles and Practice of Constraint Programming - CP 2003, Kinsale, Ireland, (September 29 - October 3, 2003), Proceedings, 110-119.
10. Van Hentenryck, P., Saraswat, V. and Deville, Y.: Design, Implementation and Evaluation of the Constraint Language cc(FD). In A. Podelski, ed., Constraints: Basics and Trends. Lecture Notes in Computer Science, Vol. 910, Springer-Verlag (1995).

Non-viability Deductions
in Arc-Consistency Computation

Camilo Rueda* and Frank D. Valencia**

[1] Dept. of Computer Science, Universidad Javeriana Cali
Cali, Colombia
crueda@puj.edu.co
[2] Dept. of Information Technology, Uppsala University
Uppsala, Sweden
frankv@it.uu.se

Abstract. Arc-Consistency (AC) techniques have been used extensively in the study of Constraint Satisfaction Problems (CSP). These techniques are used to simplify the CSP before or during the search for its solutions. Some of the most efficient algorithms for AC computation are AC6++ and AC-7. The novelty of these algorithms is that they satisfy the so-called *four desirable properties* for AC computation. The main purpose of these interesting properties is to reduce as far as possible the number of constraint checks during AC computation while keeping a reasonable space complexity. In this paper we prove that, despite providing a remarkable reduction in the number of constraint checks, the four desirable properties do not guarantee a minimal number of constraint checks. We therefore refute the minimality claim in the paper introducing these properties. Furthermore, we propose a *new desirable property* for AC computation and extend AC6++ and AC-7 to consider such a property. We show theoretically and experimentally that the new property provides a further substantial reduction in the number of constraint checks.

1 Introduction

Constraint satisfaction problems (CSP) occur widely in engineering, science and the arts. Applications are frequently reported in production planning, resource allocation [BLN01], music composition [AADR98], Verification [EM97], Security [BB01] Bioinformatics [GW94] and many others. In fact, a CSP is any problem that can be expressed as that of finding, from a finite set of possibilities, a collection of values satisfying some given particular properties. These properties are represented by relations called constraints.

In its general setting the constraint satisfaction problem has been proved to be NP-complete. Nevertheless, in many real world instance a solution can be found with reasonable time and space efficiency when appropriate techniques are applied. The most frequently used are so-called *consistency* techniques. The main idea in these techniques is to use constraints not only to test the validity of a solution but as a sort of devices

---

* The contribution of Camilo Rueda was supported by the **AVISPA** Project.
** The contribution of Frank D. Valencia was supported by the **PROFUNDIS** Project.

B. Demoen and V. Lifschitz (Eds.): ICLP 2004, LNCS 3132, pp. 343–355, 2004.
© Springer-Verlag Berlin Heidelberg 2004

for detecting inconsistencies and for pruning from the original set of possibilities some values that cannot appear in a solution. The reduced CSP taking into account only the remaining values is said to satisfy a given (weak) notion of consistency. One such notion is *arc consistency*. Consistency procedures are usually invoked repeatedly during search so it is very important to have efficient consistency algorithms. Even savings by a constant factor can have important overall performance consequences in some situations.

Finding better arc consistency algorithms has thus been an ongoing research topic for more than two decades. Building from algorithm AC-3 [Mac77], improvements such as AC-4 [MH86], AC-6 [Bes94], AC6++, AC-7 (see [BR99]) have been proposed. The standard way to compare arc consistency algorithms is by the number of constraint checks they perform. In [BR95] the so-called *four desirable properties* (FDP) for AC algorithms were defined and shown to provide a remarkable reduction in the number of constraint checks. Moreover, in [BR95] it is claimed that algorithms (such as AC6++ and AC-7) satisfying the FDP are optimal in the number of constraint checks.

Our contributions are the following: we show that even when complying with the FDP an AC algorithm can still perform unnecessary constraint checks (e.g., AC-6++ and AC-7). We thus refute the above optimality claim. We prove that there is a family of CSP's for which these unnecessary constraint checks can be rather significant. We also define a new property and show how AC algorithms satisfying it can avoid those redundant checks. This property is parameterized in a set of inference rules. We give two such rules and show their validity. We give a general AC algorithm taking into account the new property and show its correctness. We then use it to orthogonally extend AC-6++ and AC-7 into algorithms maintaining the new property and show how they improve over the originals in some benchmark and randomly generated problems.

Recently, [vD02] has proposed a particular constraint processing ordering heuristic that can lead to savings of constraint checks similar to ours. Our idea is independent of constraint ordering and so leaves more room to variations in constraint ordering heuristics. This is important theoretically because the optimality claim for FDP compliant algorithms is wrt to analysis that assume the same particular constraint ordering. It is important in practice because a particular ordering may encode useful knowledge about the problem domain. On the other hand, efficient implementations of our idea seem to require particular value orderings, so it may leave less room to value ordering heuristics.

2   CSP and AC: Concepts, Assumptions and Concerns

A *Constraint Satisfaction Problem* (CSP) consists of a given finite set of variables with their corresponding finite domain of values, and a given set of constraints over the variables. The constraints specify allowed value assignments for the corresponding variables. A CSP *solution* is a value assignment for the variables satisfying all the constraints. Since CSP's are NP-complete [GJ79], usually they are simplified by using pre-processing techniques, most notably Arc-Consistency (AC). This technique, also used *during* the search of CSP's solutions, involves the removal of some values that cannot be in any solution.

In AC we are only concerned with binary constraints, so we confine ourselves to CSP's where all the constraints are binary relations; i.e., *binary CSP's*.

We can define a (binary) CSP as a tuple $\langle V, D, C \rangle$ where $V = \{x_1, \ldots, x_n\}$ is a set of *variables*, $D = \{D_1, \ldots, D_n\}$ is a set of *domains* with each D_i specifying the domain of $x_i \in V$, and C is a set of *constraints* $C_{ij} \subseteq D_i \times D_j$. We define the predicate $C_{ij}(v, w)$ to be true iff $(v, w) \in C_{ij}$. Without loss of generality, for each pair (x_i, x_j) of variables in V, *we assume that there is at most one constraint* $C_{ij} \in C$. A tuple $(v_1, \ldots, v_n) \in D_1 \times \ldots \times D_n$ is a *solution* iff for each $C_{ij} \in C$, $C_{ij}(v_i, v_j)$.

Example 1. Let $V = \{x_1, x_2, x_3\}$, $D = \{D_1, D_2, D_3\}$ with $D_1 = D_3 = \{1, 2\}$ and $D_2 = \{0, 1, 2\}$. Define $C_{12} = \{(v, w) \in D_1 \times D_2 \mid v \leq w\}$ and $C_{23} = \{(v, w) \in D_2 \times D_3 \mid v \leq w\}$. Consider the CSP $\langle V, D, \{C_{12}, C_{23}\} \rangle$. The tuples $(1, 1, 1), (1, 1, 2), (1, 2, 2), (2, 2, 2)$ are solutions, but no tuple having 0 as its second component (i.e., of the form $(\_, 0, \_)$) can be a solution.   □

2.1 Bidirectionality

Let $\langle V, D, C \rangle$ be a CSP. Notice that if $C_{ij} \in C$, augmenting the CSP with a constraint C_{ji} which is the *converse* of C_{ij} (i.e., $C_{ji} = C_{ij}^{-1} = \{(w, v) \mid (v, w) \in C_{ij}\}$) does not restrict any further the CSP, i.e., the CSP's solutions remain the same. Intuitively, C_{ij} and its converse C_{ji} represent exactly the same constraint except that C_{ij} can be viewed as a constraint going from x_i to x_j while C_{ji} as going from x_j to x_i. The reader may care to augment the CSP's constraints in Example 1 with the converses C_{21} and C_{32} and verify that the resulting CSP's solutions are the same as the ones to the original CSP.

If a CSP has a converse C_{ji} for each of its constraints C_{ij} then it is said to satisfy the *bidirectionality* property. Without loss of generality, we shall confine our attention to *CSP's satisfying the bidirectionality property* as usually done for AC.

2.2 Arc-Consistency and Viability

As mentioned before, the idea behind AC computation is to eliminate from the domains of a given CSP some values that cannot be in any of its solutions. We say that such values are not *viable*.

Definition 1 (Support and Viability). *Let* $P = \langle V, D, C \rangle$ *be a CSP where* $D = \{D_1, \ldots, D_n\}$. *Let* $D_1' \subseteq D_1 \ldots D_n' \subseteq D_n$. *Suppose that* $C_{ij} \in C$, $v \in D_i'$ *and* $w \in D_j'$.

We say that w *is a* **support** *for* v *(wrt* C_{ij}*) iff* $C_{ij}(v, w)$. *Also, we say that* v *is* **viable** *wrt* D_j' *iff there exists a support for* v *in* D_j'. *Furthermore, we say that* v *is* **viable** *wrt* $D_1' \times \ldots \times D_n'$ *iff for all* $C_{ik} \in C$, v *is viable wrt* D_k'.

Example 2. Let P be the CSP $\langle V, D, C \rangle$ with V and D as in Example 1 and C as the set containing the constraints C_{12} and C_{23} in Example 1 plus its converses C_{21} and C_{32}.

Notice that 2 is a support in D_2 for $1, 2 \in D_1$. Also notice that $0 \in D_2$ is not viable wrt D_1, so it cannot be in any solution to P. We shall see that in AC computation, $0 \in D_2$ must be removed.   □

The AC algorithms use a graph whose nodes and arcs correspond to the variables and constraints, respectively, of the input CSP. Given a CSP $P = \langle V, D, C \rangle$, define G_P as the graph with nodes $Nodes(G_P) = \{i \mid x_i \in V\}$ and arcs $Arcs(G_P) = \{(i, j) \mid C_{ij} \in C\}$. Let us recall the definition of arc-consistency:

Definition 2 (AC Graphs). *Let* $P = \langle V, D, C \rangle$ *be a CSP where* $D = \{D_1, \ldots, D_n\}$ *and let* $D'_1 \subseteq D_1 \ldots D'_n \subseteq D_n$.

An arc (i, j) *in* G_P *is said to be* **arc-consistent** *wrt* D'_i *and* D'_j *iff every* $v \in D'_i$ *is viable wrt* D'_j. *Also* G_P *is said to be* **arc-consistent** *wrt* $D'_1 \times \ldots \times D'_n$ *iff every arc* (i, j) *in* G_P *is arc-consistent wrt* D'_i *and* D'_j.

Furthermore, we say that G_P *is* **maximal arc-consistent** *wrt* $\rho = D'_1 \times \ldots \times D'_n$ *iff* G_P *is arc-consistent wrt* ρ *and there are no* $D''_1 \supset D'_1, \ldots, D''_n \supset D'_n$ *such that* G_P *is arc-consistent wrt* $D''_1 \times \ldots \times D''_n$.

Example 3. Let $P = \langle V, D, C \rangle$ as in Example 2. Notice that G_P is not arc-consistent wrt $D_1 \times D_2 \times D_3$ but it is wrt $\emptyset \times \emptyset \times \emptyset$. Verify that G_P is maximal arc-consistent wrt $D_1 \times D'_2 \times D_3$ where $D'_2 = D_2 - \{0\}$.   □

Computing Arc-Consistency

Given a $P = \langle V, D, C \rangle$ where $D = \{D_1, \ldots, D_n\}$, the outcome of an AC algorithm on input P, is a $P' = \langle V, D', C \rangle$ with $D' = \{D'_1, \ldots, D'_n\}$, $D'_k \subseteq D_k$ ($1 \leq k \leq n$) such that G_P is maximal arc-consistent wrt $D'_1 \times \ldots \times D'_n$.

Usually, an AC algorithm takes each arc (i, j) of G_P and removes from D_i those values that are not viable wrt D_j (i.e., not having support in D_j). This may cause the viability of some values, previously supported by the removed ones from D_i, to be checked again by the algorithm.

Constraint Checks. The standard comparison measure for the various AC algorithms is the *number of constraint checks* performed (i.e., checking whether $C_{ij}(v, w)$ for some C_{ij} and $v \in D_i$, $w \in D_j$) [Bes94, BR95, BFR95]. It has been shown analytically and experimentally [BFR95] that if we assume a large cost per constraint check or *demonstrate* large enough savings in the number of constraint checks, the constraint checks count will dominate overhead concerns.

In the next section we shall see several properties aiming at reducing substantially the number of constraint checks from simple but useful observations.

Domain Ordering $\prec$. Henceforth, we presuppose a total underlying order $\prec$ on the CSP's domains as typically done for AC computation [Bes94, BR95, BFR95]. In practice, $\prec$ corresponds to the ordering on the data structure representing the domains. In our examples, we shall take $\prec$ to be the usual "less" relation $<$ on the natural numbers.

We can now recall the general notion of support lower-bound. Such a notion denotes a value before which no support for a given value can be found.

Definition 3 (Support Lower-Bound). *Let* $P = \langle V, D, C \rangle$ *be a CSP where* $D = \{D_1, \ldots, D_n\}$ *and let* $D'_1 \subseteq D_1 \ldots D'_n \subseteq D_n$. *For all* $C_{ij} \in C$, *the value* $w \in D'_j$ *is a* **support lower-bound** *in* D'_j *for* $v \in D'_i$ *iff for every* $w' \in D'_j$ *with* $w' \prec w$, $C_{ij}(v, w')$ *does not hold.*

Example 4. Let P be as in Example 2. Assume that the total ordering $\prec$ on the domains is $<$. Then $1 \in D_2$ is a support lower-bound in D_2 for $1, 2 \in D_1$.   □

(Notice that a support lower-bound for v is not necessarily a support of v.)

In the next sections, we shall see that simple and general notions, such as support lower-bound and bidirectionality (which are usually assumed in AC), can reduce substantially the number of constraints checks.

3 Four Desirable Properties of AC Computation

Modern AC algorithms satisfy the so-called *four desirable properties* of a AC computation given in [BR95, BFR95]. These are very simple and practical properties aiming at reducing the number of constraint checks while keeping a reasonable space complexity. In practice, algorithms satisfying these properties have shown to be very successful [BR95, BFR95].

In the following we assume that $D_1, \ldots, D_n$ represent the current CSP domains of during AC computation. The desirable properties require (of an AC algorithm) that:

1. $C_{ij}(v, w)$ should not be checked if there is w' still in D_j such that $C_{ij}(v, w')$ was already successfully checked.
2. $C_{ij}(v, w)$ should not be checked if there is w' still in D_j such that $C_{ji}(w', v)$ was already successfully checked.
3. $C_{ij}(v, w)$ should not be checked if:
   a. $C_{ij}(v, w)$ was already succesfully or unsuccessfully checked, or
   b. $C_{ji}(w, v)$ was already succesfully or unsuccessfully checked.
4. The space complexity should be $O(ed)$ where e, d are the cardinalities of the set of constraints and the largest domain, respectively, of the input CSP.

The properties can be justified as follows. An AC algorithm checks $C_{ij}(v, w)$ when establishing the viability of v wrt D_j (i.e., the algorithm needs to find a support for v in D_j if any, otherwise it should remove v from D_i). Now, the value v in (1) has already a support, i.e., it is viable, if such a w' still exists in D'_j ; so there is no need to check whether $C_{ij}(v, w)$. Property (2) can be explained similarly by using bidirectionality. Property 3.a states that there is no need of doing the same constraint check more than once, and 3.b states that, by bidirectionality, if we have checked $C_{ji}(w, v)$ then we already know the result of checking $C_{ij}(v, w)$. Property (4) states a restriction on the space that can be used (see [BR95] for further details).

The AC algorithm AC-3 does not satisfy Properties (1-3); AC-4 does not satisfy Properties 1,2,3.b, and 4; AC-6 does not satisfy Properties 2 and 3b (the ones using bidirectionality); AC-Inference does not comply with Property 4. The modern algorithms AC6++ and AC-7 preserve the four properties.

The AC6++ and AC-7 algorithms differ mainly in the order that values and arcs are considered during AC computation. The latter propagates the effects of removing a value as soon as possible (i.e., to reconsider the viability of the values supported by the removed one). In practice, this heuristic seems to save unnecessary constraint checks. Experimentally, AC-7 has shown to outperform AC6++.

In [BR95] it is also claimed that the four desirable properties guarantee a minimal number of constraint checks. This claim is in the context of CSP's where nothing is known about the particular semantics of the constraints and wrt the order in which values, variables and arcs are considered during AC computation. Hence, AC6++ performs a minimal number of constraint checks according to the order used by this algorithm, but still it may perform more constraint checks than AC-7 which uses a different order.

The above four properties are of important practical significance. Nevertheless, we believe that they are not enough to guarantee the minimal number of constraint checks, thus contradicting the claim mentioned above. In the next section, we shall show that even when complying with the four desirable properties, an AC algorithm can still perform a substantial number of unnecessary constraint checks.

4   New Desirable Property and and Non-viability Deductions

A drawback of the four desirable properties is that they allow checking $C_{ij}(v, w)$ even when the non-viability of v or w could have been deduced by using only the general notions of bidirectionality and support lower-bound, and information about previous constraint checks – i.e., without using any particular semantic properties of the constraints under consideration. In our view, the check of $C_{ij}(v, w)$ under the above conditions would be unnecessary.

Let us illustrate the above with the following example:

Example 5. Let P be the CSP defined in Example 4. Suppose that during AC computation an algorithm satisfying the four desirable properties checks, first of all, the viability of the values in D_1 and immediately after the viability of the values in D_3. Furthermore, suppose that the search for support in D_2 is done according to $\prec$.

After establishing the viability of all the values in D_1, the algorithm has checked that for every value $v \in D_1$, $C_{12}(v, 0)$ does not hold. Furthemore, after establishing the viability of the values in D_3, the algorithm has checked that for every value $w \in D_3$, $C_{32}(w, 0)$ holds.

Nevertheless, notice that for any $w \in D_3$ checking $C_{32}(w, 0)$ is really unnecessary, because after checking for the viability of the values in D_1 one can deduce that $0 \in D_2$ is not viable.

Here is a proof of the non-viability of $0 \in D_2$: Recall from Example 4 that $1 \in D_2$ is a support lower-bound in D_2 for $1, 2 \in D_1$. Now $0 \prec 1$, so after checking for the viability of $1, 2 \in D_1$, we can conclude from Definition 3 that $\neg C_{12}(1, 0)$ and $\neg C_{12}(2, 0)$. By bidirectionality $\neg C_{21}(0, 1)$ and $\neg C_{21}(0, 2)$. Hence we can *deduce*, from Definition 1, that $0 \in D_2$ is not viable.   □

4.1   Unnecessary Constraint Checks

One can verify that both AC6++ and AC-7 may indeed perform the unnecessary constraint checks mentioned in the above example. Also notice that the number of unnecessary constraint checks in the above example is $d = |D_3|$. However, as shown below, one can generalize Example 5 to a family of CSP's for which the numbers of unnecessary constraint checks is about ed^2, where e is the number of constraints and d is the size of the largest domain.

In the following theorem, by *unnecessary constraint check* we mean that the check can be avoided by using only bidirectionality, the notion of support lower-bound, and information about previous constraint checks.

Theorem 1. *There is family of CSP's for which the number of unnecessary constraint checks during AC computation, even when complying with the four desirable properties, can be $\Omega(ed^2)$, where e is the number of constraints and d the size of the largest domain.*

Proof (Outline). Let $P = \langle V, D, C \rangle$ where $D = \{D_1, \ldots, D_n\}$ with all the domains being of a same even size. Decree that for any $(i, j) \in Arcs(G_P)$, $i < j$, the first half of the values in D_j (according to the domain ordering $\prec$) are not viable wrt D_i.

Let us suppose that we have an AC algorithm satisfying the four desirable properties. Assume that the algorithm checks first of all the viability of the values in D_1 wrt D_n (i.e., it searches supports in D_n for the values in D_1), then D_2 wrt $D_n, \ldots, D_{n-1}$ wrt D_n, and then D_1 wrt D_{n-1}, D_2 wrt D_{n-1} and so on. Furthermore, suppose that the search for support is done according to $\prec$.

After establishing the viability of the values in D_1, it is possible to deduce, by using the notion of bidirectionality and support lower-bound (as in Example 5), that the values in the first half of D_n are not viable. Now, for each $k = 2, \ldots, n-1$, the four desirable properties *do not prevent* the algorithm from checking unnecessarily $C_{kn}(v, w)$ for every $v \in D_k$ and every w in the first half of D_n. The same happens for $k = 2, \ldots, n-2$ wrt D_{n-1}, and so on. It then follows that the algorithm can perform $\Omega(ed^2)$ unnecessary constraint checks.   □

4.2 New Desirable Property

In order to avoid unnecessary constraint checks of the kind above, we could suggest the following new desirable property: $C_{ij}(v, w)$ should not be checked if it can be deduced via bi-directionality and the notion of support-lower bound that v or w is not viable. We shall use "deduce" in a loose sense of the word: We mean that one can conclude, without performing further constraint checks, that v (or w) is not viable.

Nevertheless, there could be many other ways of deducing non-viability (e.g., special properties of constraints, domains, etc). Hence, we find it convenient to define the new desirable property wrt to fixed *non-viability deduction system* S; i.e, a set of *inference rules* that allows us to deduce the non-viability of some values. We assume that whether a given value can be deduced in S as non-viable can always be decided. The fifth desirable property wrt a fixed S can be stated as follows:

5. $C_{ij}(v, w)$ should not be checked if it can be deduced, in the underlying non-viability inference system S, that v or w are not viable.

Of course some deduction systems may be of little help. For example if S is the empty set of rules, in which case both AC-6++ and AC-7 would trivially satisfy the fifth property. Other example is a deduction system in which deciding the non-viability of a given value cannot be done with $O(ed)$ in space – see the fourth desirable property. Next we give more helpful but general deduction systems (inference rules).

Non-viability Deductions

In the following properties, we give two simple and general inference rules for non-viability deduction to avoid unnecessary constraint checks of the kind illustrated in Example 5 and stated in Theorem 1.

Property 1 (Support LOWEST-Bound). Let $P = \langle V, D, C \rangle$ be a CSP where $D = \{D_1, \ldots, D_n\}$ and let $D'_1 \subseteq D_1 \ldots D'_n \subseteq D_n$. Suppose that SLB_{ij} is the **least** value (wrt $\prec$) in a given set containing a support-lower bound in D'_j for each $v \in D'_i$. The following is a valid non-viability inference rule:

$$\text{If } w \in D'_j \text{ and } w \prec SLB_{ij} \text{ then } w \text{ is not viable wrt } D'_i.$$

Proof. By using the notions of support lower-bound (Definition 3) and bidirectionality. $\qquad\square$

The above property says that a value can be deduced as non-viable if it is less than every support-lower bound for (all the values of) a given domain. The property can be implemented by using an array SLB such that $SLB[i, j]$ keeps the least support-lower bound in D_j for the values in D_i. We shall discuss this issue in Section 5.1.

Property 2 (Support Upper-Bound Cardinality). Let $P = \langle V, D, C \rangle$ be a CSP where $D = \{D_1, \ldots, D_n\}$ and let $D'_1 \subseteq D_1 \ldots D'_n \subseteq D_n$. Suppose that $sub_{ij}(v)$ denotes an upper bound on the number of supports of $v \in D'_i$ in D'_j. The following is a valid non-viability inference rule:

$$\text{If } sub_{ij}(v) = 0 \text{ then } v \text{ is not viable wrt } D'_j.$$

Proof. Immediate $\qquad\square$

We can implement the above property by having counters of the form $sub_{ij}(v)$ initially set to $|D_j|$. Then counter $sub_{ij}(v)$ decreases each time a check of $C_{ij}(v, w)$ is found to be false, a support $w' \in D_j$ for v is eliminated, or some value supported by v is eliminated. Once $sub_{ij}(v) = 0$ we can proceed as if v did not exist in D_i. We shall discuss this in Section 5.1.

In the next sections we shall also illustrate experimentally that despite its simplicity, the above deduction rules indeed provide a substantial reduction in the number of constraint checks for CSP's where nothing is known about the particular semantics of the constraints.

5   AC Algorithms with Non-viability Deductions

In this section we first present a new generic AC algorithm, here called AC[$\mathcal{S}$], which is parametric in an underlying non-viability deduction system $\mathcal{S}$. The algorithm is based on AC-5 and it can be instantiated to produce other AC algorithms such as AC-4, AC-5, AC-3, AC6++ and AC-7.

The generic AC algorithm removes the values deduced as being non-viable immediately. This can be justified as follows: If propagating the consequences of removing a value as soon as possible is a good heuristic (as shown by AC-7 [BFR95]) then it is reasonable to perform removals as soon as possible. The non-viability deductions can also help to detect promptly values that must be removed.

In the following we assume that $P = \langle V, D, C \rangle$ represents the CSP on input of which AC[$\mathcal{S}$] is to perform AC. Furthermore, we assume that $D_1, \ldots, D_n$ represent the current CSP's domains during the AC computation.

Most AC algorithms use a waiting list Q containing elements that have been removed and for which we need to propagate the effects of their elimination. In AC[$\mathcal{S}$], Q contains elements of the form $\langle (i,j), w \rangle$, where (i,j) is an arc and w is value which has been removed from D_j, thus making us reconsider the viability of some values in D_i supported by w.

As AC-5, AC[$\mathcal{S}$] is parametric in the procedures ArcCons and LocalArcCons (Figure 1) whose implementation can give rise to various AC algorithms. The procedure ArcCons(i, j, Δ_i, Δ_j) computes the set of values $\Delta_i \subseteq D_i$ without support in D_j and the set of values $\Delta_j \subseteq D_j$ deduced, wrt $\mathcal{S}$, as being non-viable. The procedure LocalArcCons($i, j, w, \Delta_i, \Delta_j$) is similar except that it computes the set of values $\Delta_i \subseteq D_i$ without support in D_j which were previously supported by a value w removed from D_j.

procedure ArcCons(**in** i, j, **out** Δ_i, Δ_j)
Pre: $(i,j) \in Arcs(G_P)$
Post: $\Delta_i = \{v \in D_i \mid \forall w \in D_j : \neg C_{ij}(v, w)\}$
      $\Delta_j = \{w \in D_j \mid P \vdash_{\mathcal{S}} w \text{ is not viable }\}$

procedure LocalArcCons(**in** i, j, w, **out** Δ_i, Δ_j)
Pre: $(i,j) \in Arcs(G_P) \wedge w \notin D_j$
Post: $\Delta_i = \{v \in D_i \mid C_{ij}(v, w) \wedge \forall w' \in D_j : \neg C_{ij}(v, w')\}$
      $\Delta_j = \{w' \in D_j \mid P \vdash_{\mathcal{S}} w' \text{ is not viable }\}$

Fig. 1. The ArcCons and Local ArcCons Procedures. Notation $P \vdash_{\mathcal{S}} E$ means that E can be deduced in the inference system $\mathcal{S}$ from the current information about P.

The AC[$\mathcal{S}$] algorithm (see Figure 2) has two phases. In the first one, called initialization phase (Lines 1-7), AC[$\mathcal{S}$] enforces each arc (i,j) to be arc-consistent wrt to the current D_i and D_j. In the second one, called propagation phase (Lines 8-15), it propagates the effects of all the removed values. Notice that the removed values are put in Q and they stay in there until the effects of their elimination are propagated.

The following theorem states that the outcome of AC[$\mathcal{S}$] on a CSP $P = \langle V, D, C \rangle$ where $D = \{D_1, \ldots, D_n\}$, is a CSP $P' = \langle V, D', C \rangle$ with $D' = \{D'_1, \ldots, D'_n\}$, $D'_k \subseteq D_k$ ($1 \leq k \leq n$) such that G_P is maximal arc-consistent wrt $D'_1 \times \ldots \times D'_n$.

Theorem 2 (Correctness of AC[$\mathcal{S}$]). *The algorithm AC[$\mathcal{S}$], Figure 2, is correct wrt its precondition and postcondition.*

Proof (Outline). Suppose that the AC[$\mathcal{S}$] algorithm runs on input $P = \langle V, C, D \rangle$ with $D = \{D_1, \ldots, D_n\}$. Let $\rho_f = D_{1_f} \times \ldots \times D_{n_f}$ be such that G_P is maximal arc-consistent wrt ρ_f.

Let D_{i_0} be the initial D_i and D_{i_k} with $k > 0$ be the current D_i after the k-th elimination of a Δ_m (Lines 6-7 and 14-15) from some $D_{m_{k-1}}$. Let $\rho_k = D_{1_k} \times \ldots \times D_{n_k}$. It is sufficient to prove that AC[$\mathcal{S}$] terminates with a final ρ_k, $k \geq 0$, such that $\rho_k = \rho_f$.

From the specification of ArcCons and LocalArcCons, it is easy to verify that any value is removed from $D_{i_{k-1}}$ only if it is found non-viable wrt ρ_{k-1}; either it did not

Algorithm AC[$\mathcal{S}$] (**in-out** P)
Pre: P is a CSP $\langle V, D, C \rangle$ with $D = \{D_1, \ldots, D_n\}$
Post: G_{P_0} is maximal arc-consistent wrt $D_1 \times \ldots \times D_n$
1. $Q \leftarrow \emptyset$
2. **for each** $(i, j) \in Arcs(G_P)$ **do**
3.   ArcCons$(i, j, \Delta_i, \Delta_j)$
4. $Q \leftarrow Q \cup \{\langle (k, i), v \rangle \mid (k, i) \in Arcs(G_P) \wedge v \in \Delta_i\}$
5. $Q \leftarrow Q \cup \{\langle (k, j), w \rangle \mid (k, j) \in Arcs(G_P) \wedge w \in \Delta_j\}$
6. $D_i \leftarrow D_i - \Delta_i$
7. $D_j \leftarrow D_j - \Delta_j$
8. **while** $Q \neq \emptyset$ **do**
9.   **choose** $\langle (i, j), w \rangle \in Q$
10.   LocalArcCons$(i, j, w, \Delta_i, \Delta_j)$
11. $Q \leftarrow Q - \{\langle (i, j), w \rangle\}$
12. $Q \leftarrow Q \cup \{\langle (k, i), v \rangle \mid (k, i) \in Arcs(G_P) \wedge v \in \Delta_i\}$
13. $Q \leftarrow Q \cup \{\langle (k, j), w \rangle \mid (k, j) \in Arcs(G_P) \wedge w \in \Delta_j\}$
14. $D_i \leftarrow D_i - \Delta_i$
15. $D_j \leftarrow D_j - \Delta_j$

Fig. 2. The generic AC[$\mathcal{S}$] algorithm. Notation P_0 denotes the CSP P when input to the algorithm.

have a support or it was deduced in $\mathcal{S}$ as being non-viable. Now one can prove by induction on k that if $v \notin D_{i_k}$ then $v \notin D_{i_f}$. So, the first invariant of AC[$\mathcal{S}$] is the following:

$$\rho_f \subseteq \rho_k \subseteq \rho_{k-1} \subseteq \ldots \subseteq \rho_0. \tag{1}$$

Also, from the specification of ArcCons and LocalArcCons, one can verify that after the initialization phase (Lines 1-8) every value has a support in the current domains or in the waiting list Q. More precisely, let $Val(Q)$ be the set of domain values appearing in Q; during the propagation phase, the second invariant of AC[$\mathcal{S}$] is:

$$\forall (i, j) \in G_P, \forall v \in D_{i_k}, \exists w \in D_{j_k} \cup Val(Q) : C_{ij}(v, w). \tag{2}$$

The algorithm terminates when $Q = \emptyset$. Hence, from Definition 2 and the second invariant, G_P is arc-consistent wrt the ρ_k at termination time. Furthermore, from the first invariant we have $\rho_f \subseteq \rho_k$. It then follows that G_P is maximal arc-consistent wrt the ρ_k at termination time, as wanted.

It only remains to prove termination; i.e., that the propagation phase terminates (Lines 8-15). Observe that once an element $\langle (i, j), w \rangle$ is taken from Q it is never put back in Q. In each iteration in the propagation phase, an element is taken from Q. Furthermore, there can be no more than ed elements in Q, where $e = |C|$ and d is the size of the largest domain. Hence, ed is an upper-bound on the number of iterations of the propagation phase.   □

5.1   Implementation: AC6-3+ and AC-7+

We have implemented the non-viability inference rules given in Properties 1 and 2 for AC6++ and AC-7. We call AC6-3+ the algorithm that (orthogonally) extends AC6++

with the support *lowest*-bound inference rule (Property 1) and AC-7+ the one that extends (orthogonally) AC-7 with the support upper-bound cardinality rule (Property 2).

The algorithm AC6-3+ has a three-dimensional array slb used exactly as in AC6++. Each entry $slb[i, j, v]$ represents a support *lower*-bound for $v \in D_i$ in D_j – in fact the greatest one so far found by the algorithm; see [BR95] for more details. In addition, AC6-3+ has a two-dimensional array SLB. Each entry $SLB[i, j]$ keeps the *least* of all $slb[i, j, v]$ for all $v \in D_i$. Justified by Property 1, every value in $w \in D_j$ less than $SLB[i, j]$ is removed from D_j before checking any constraint of the form $C_{kj}(u, w)$ or $C_{kj}(w, u)$.

As for AC-7+, we use an additional three-dimensional array sub. Each array entry $sub[i, j, v]$ represents a lower-bound on the number of supports in D_j for $v \in D_i$. Initially, each $sub[i, j, v]$ is set to $|D_j|$. Then the algorithm decreases $sub[i, j, v]$ each time $C_{ij}(v, w)$ is found to be false, a support $w' \in D_j$ for v is eliminated, or some value supported by v is eliminated. Justified by Property 2, v is removed from D_i whenever $sub[i, j, v]$ becomes zero.

Both extended algorithms have the same worst-case complexities of their predecessors AC6++ and AC-7. More precisely, both AC6++ and AC-7+ have $O(ed^2)$ worst-case time complexity and $O(ed)$ worst-case space complexity, where e is the number of constraints and d the size of the largest domain [BR95, BFR95]. They also satisfy the four desirable properties as a result of being orthogonal extensions of AC6++ and AC-7. Furthermore, they satisfy the new desirable property wrt their underlying non-viability deduction rules, thus they can save some unnecessary constraint checks. In the next section, we shall show experimental evidence of these savings.

6 Experimental Results

Here we show some of our experimental results obtained from CSP's typically used to compare AC algorithms [Bes94, BR95, BFR95]. We compared AC6++ vs AC6-3++ and AC-7 vs AC-7+ in benchmark CSP's [Van89] as well as randomly generated CSP's [Bes94, BR95, BFR95]. Each comparison was performed wrt fifty instances of each problem.

For the ZEBRA problem [Van89] we obtained the following results in terms of constraint checks (ccs):

AC6++ : 717 ccs	AC-7 : 640 ccs
AC6-3+ : 639 ccs	AC-7+ : 594 ccs

As for the combinatorial problem suggested in [Van89], we obtained:

AC6++ : 977 ccs	AC-7 : 966 ccs
AC6-3+ : 783 ccs	AC-7+ : 826 ccs

For the randomly generated problems, following [Bes94, BR95, BFR95], we took the following as parameters of the generation: the number of variables, the size of the domains, the probability of having a constraint between any two variables, and the probability for any two values to be support of each other. In Figure 3 we show some results corresponding to the values of the parameters used in experiments of [BR95]. On

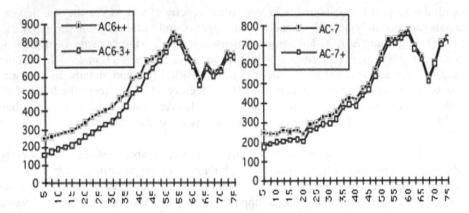

Fig. 3. AC6++ vs AC6-3+ (left) and AC-7 vs AC-7+ (right) on random generated problems with 20 variables, at most 5 values per domain, and 30% probability of having a constraint between two variables. The horizontal axis represents the probability percentage that two values support each other. The vertical axis represents the number of constraint checks.

average, we obtained that the reduction in the number of constraint checks by AC6-3+ and AC-7+ wrt AC6++ and AC-7 (respectively), was about 10%. We also observed that the numbers of values deduced as being non-viable was proportional to the reduction in the number of constraint checks. Moreover, even when the number of non-viability deductions was small, the number of constraint checks was significantly reduced.

7   Concluding Remarks

We have shown that, despite providing a remarkable reduction in the number of constraint checks, the four desirable properties of AC computation still allow a substantial number of unnecessary constraint checks – in the sense that the checks could have been avoided by deducing, only from general constraint properties and previous constraint-checks, the non-viability of some values. We also suggested a new desirable property which provides a further substantial reduction in the number of constraint checks. We modified some of the best known AC algorithms to satisfy the property and showed experimentally the benefits of the modified algorithms.

Since the reduction in the number of constraint checks by the new property depends on the non-viability of values, we believe it is practical for problems with strong structural properties (i.e., strong constrains, large domains, etc). As future work, we plan to identify and implement more inference rules to deduce non-viability efficiently.

Acknowledgements

Many thanks to Christian Bessière and Marc van Dongen for helpful comments on this work.

References

[AADR98] C. Agon, G. Assayag, O. Delerue, and C. Rueda. Objects, time and constraints in openmusic. In *ICMC98*, pages 1–12. ICMA, 1998.

[BB01]   G. Bella and S. Bistarelli. Soft constraints for security protocol analysis: Confidentiality. In *PADL01*, volume 1990 of *LNCS*, pages 108–122, 2001.

[Bes94]   C. Bessiére. Arc-consistency and arc-consistency again. *Artificial Intelligence*, 65(1):179–190, 1994.

[BFR95]   C. Bessière, E. C. Freuder, and J. C. Régin. Using inference to reduce arc consistency computation. In *ICAI-95*, pages 592–599, 1995.

[BLN01]   P. Baptiste, C. Le Pape, and W. Nuijten. *Constraint-Based Scheduling. Applying Constraint programming to Scheduling Problems*. Kluwer, 2001.

[BR95]   C. Bessière and J. C. Régin. Using Bidirectionality to Speed Up Arc-Consistency Processing. In *Constraint Processing, Selected Papers*, volume 923 of *LNCS*, pages 157–169. Springer-Verlag, 1995.

[BR99]   C. Bessiére and E. C. Freuder J. C. Régin. Using constraint metaknowledge to reduce arc consistency computation. *Artificial Intelligence*, 107(1):125–148, 1999.

[EM97]   J. Esparza and S. Melzer. Model checking LTL using constraint programming. In *18th International Conference on Application and Theory of Petri Nets*, volume 1248 of *LNCS*. Springer-Verlag, 1997.

[GJ79]   R. Garey and D.S. Johnson. *Computers and Intractability. A Guide to the Theory of NP-Completeness*. W. H. Freeman and Company, 1979.

[GW94]   C. Gaspin and E. Westhof. The determination of secondary structures of RNA as a constraint satisfaction problem. In *Advances in molecular bioinformatics*. IOS Press, 1994.

[Mac77]   A. K. Mackworth. Consistency in Networks of Relations. *Artificial Intelligence*, 8:99–118, 1977.

[MH86]   R. Mohr and T. C. Henderson. Arc and path consistency revisited. *Artificial Intelligence*, 28(2):225–233, 1986.

[Van89]   P. Van Hentenryck. *Constraint Satisfaction in Logic Programming*. MIT Press, Cambridge, MA, 1989.

[vD02]   Marc R. C. van Dongen. AC-3_d an efficient arc-consistency algorithm with a low space-complexity. In *CP02*, volume 2470 of *LNCS*, pages 755–760, 2002.

Compiling Prioritized Circumscription into Answer Set Programming

Toshiko Wakaki[1] and Katsumi Inoue[2]

[1] Shibaura Institute of Technology
307 Fukasaku, Minuma-ku, Saitama-City, Saitama 337–8570 Japan
twakaki@sic.shibaura-it.ac.jp
[2] National Institute of Informatics
2-1-2 Hitotsubashi, Chiyoda-ku, Tokyo 101–8430 Japan
ki@nii.ac.jp

Abstract. In computing circumscription by logic programming, circumscription is usually transformed into some target logic program whose answer sets (or stable models) yield the Herbrand models of circumscription. In this paper, we propose a new method of computing models of prioritized circumscription in answer set programming, which is correct and more efficient than previous approaches. The basic idea of our approach is to transform a given circumscription into a general extended disjunctive program whose answer sets (if exist) yield strictly preferred models to a given candidate model with respect to the preorder $\leq^{P^1 > \cdots > P^k ; Z}$. Hence its inconsistency enables us to determine models of prioritized circumscription. Based on our new method, a circumscriptive model generator has already been implemented. Its performance for some interesting examples of circumscription is also addressed.

1 Introduction

Circumscription [14, 15] was proposed to formalize the commonsense reasoning under incomplete knowledge. So far many studies have been proposed to explore the approach of the use of logic programming for the automation of circumscription. Such approaches were based on the relationship between the semantics of circumscription and the semantics of the target logic programs.

Gelfond and Lifschitz [8] was the first to propose a computational method for some restricted class of prioritized circumscription, which compiles circumscriptive theories into stratified logic programs. Though their method is computationally efficient, the applicable class is too limited. Afterwards, Sakama and Inoue proposed two methods. The first one [19] is for a class of parallel circumscription without function symbols, which compiles circumscription into a normal disjunctive program whose semantics is given by stable models, and the second one [20, 21] is for a class of parallel circumscription as well as prioritized circumscription without function symbols, which compiles circumscription into a prioritized logic program [20, 21] (or PLP, for short) whose semantics is given by preferred answer sets. However, only the semantic issues are given for the second one and the procedure to compute preferred answer sets of PLPs was left as their future works. Under such situations, Wakaki and Satoh [23] proposed a

B. Demoen and V. Lifschitz (Eds.): ICLP 2004, LNCS 3132, pp. 356–370, 2004.

method for a class of parallel circumscription as well as prioritized circumscription without function symbols, which compiles circumscription into an extended logic program whose semantics is given by answer sets. Their method enables to extend Sakama and Inoue's first method to become applicable for a class of prioritized circumscription without function symbols. However, the number of rules becomes large when the input size grows. Another problem in both Sakama and Inoue's first method [19] and Wakaki and Satoh's one [23] is that they have to compute the *characteristic clauses* [10] of the given axiom set in advance, which must be computed elsewhere by some consequence-finding procedure instead of answer set programming. Recently, Wakaki et al. [24] proposed a procedure of computing preferred answer sets of Sakama and Inoue's PLP in *answer set programming* (ASP, for short), one of whose purposes was to implement Sakama and Inoue's second method to compute circumscription mentioned above. Implementing the procedure [24], it is found that Sakama and Inoue's second method [21, Theorems 3.8 and 3.9] (or [20, Lemma 3.7 and Theorem 3.8]) is not correct for computing models of circumscription.

Thus, the motivation of this research is to develop a correct and efficient method to compute models of parallel and prioritized circumscription in ASP. To achieve the correctness, we will establish a new translation of prioritized circumscription into a logic program, which is inspired by a translation technique used in [24]. Roughly speaking, the basic idea of our approach is to translate a given circumscription into a general extended disjunctive program whose answer sets (if exist) yield strictly preferred models for a given candidate model with respect to the preorder $\leq^{P^1 > \cdots > P^k; Z}$. Hence if it is inconsistent, we can decide that the candidate model is a model of prioritized circumscription. We give the soundness and completeness theorems for our method of computing models of circumscription. To gain the efficiency, we will not rely on any preprocessing other than ASP. Thus, the advantage of our new method over the previous methods by [19, 23] is that we do not have to compute the characteristic clauses, whose time complexity is exponential in the propositional case. As far as the authors know, our evaluation results show that our approach is more efficient than any other previous implemented procedures such as the method using integer programming [16].

The rest of this paper is structured as follows. In Section 2, we provide preliminaries. In Section 3, we present our translated logic program, soundness and completeness theorems for our method, the procedure of computing models of circumscription, and the experimental results under the current implementation of our procedure. We finish this paper by comparing our approach with related work in Section 4.

2   Preliminaries

We briefly review the basic notions used throughout this paper.

2.1   Circumscription

Let $A(P, Z)$ be a sentence of a first order theory, P be a tuple of *minimized predicates* and Z be a tuple of *variable predicates*. Q denotes the rest of the predicates occurring in A, called the *fixed predicates*. Then *parallel circumscription of P for $A(P, Z)$ with Z varied* [14] is defined by a second order formula as follows:

$$Circum(A; P; Z) \stackrel{def}{=} A(P, Z) \land \neg \exists pz (A(p, z) \land p < P).$$

where p, z are tuples of variables which have the same arity to P, Z respectively. We write $Circum(A; P)$ when the last argument Z in $Circum(A; P; Z)$ is empty. If P is decomposed into disjoint parts $P^1, \cdots, P^k$, and the members of P^i are assigned a higher priority than the members of P^j for $i < j$, then *prioritized circumscription of $P^1 > \cdots > P^k$ for A with Z varied* is denoted by $Circum(A; P^1 > \cdots > P^k; Z)$, which is also defined by a second order formula. Due to the space limitation, its definition is omitted (see [14]). Prioritized circumscription for $k = 1$ coincides with parallel circumscription.

Definition 1 Let P, Z, Q be tuples of minimized predicates, variable predicates and fixed predicates respectively. For a structure M, let $|M|$ be its universe and $M[\![K]\!]$ the interpretations of all individual, function, and predicate constants K in the language. For any two structures M_1, M_2, we write $M_1 \leq^{P;Z} M_2$ if
> (i) $|M_1| = |M_2|$,
> (ii) $M_1[\![Q]\!] = M_2[\![Q]\!]$,
> (iii) $M_1[\![P]\!] \subseteq M_2[\![P]\!]$.

Definition 2 Let $P^1, \cdots, P^k$ be k disjoint parts of P in Definition 1. For any two structures M_1, M_2, we write $M_1 \leq^{P^1 > \cdots > P^k; Z} M_2$ if

(i) $|M_1| = |M_2|$,
(ii) $M_1[\![Q]\!] = M_2[\![Q]\!]$,
(iii) a. $M_1[\![P^1]\!] \subseteq M_2[\![P^1]\!]$,
   b. For every $i \leq k$, if for every $1 \leq j \leq i - 1$, $M_1[\![P^j]\!] = M_2[\![P^j]\!]$, then $M_1[\![P^i]\!] \subseteq M_2[\![P^i]\!]$.

The preorder $\leq^{P^1 > \cdots > P^k; Z}$ for $k = 1$ coincides with $\leq^{P;Z}$.
We write $M_1 <^{P^1 > \cdots > P^k; Z} M_2$ if $M_1 \leq^{P^1 > \cdots > P^k; Z} M_2$ and $M_2 \not\leq^{P^1 > \cdots > P^k; Z} M_1$. With respect to $\leq^{P^1 > \cdots > P^k; Z}$, we say that M_1 is *preferred* to M_1 if $M_1 \leq^{P^1 > \cdots > P^k; Z} M_2$, and M_1 is *strictly preferred* to M_1 if $M_1 <^{P^1 > \cdots > P^k; Z} M_2$. We say that M_1 and M_2 are *tie* if $M_1 \leq^{P^1 > \cdots > P^k; Z} M_2$ and $M_2 \leq^{P^1 > \cdots > P^k; Z} M_1$.

Definition 3 With respect to $\leq^{P^1 > \cdots > P^k; Z}$ a structure M is *minimal* in a class S of structures if $M \in S$ and there is no structure $M' \in S$ such that $M' <^{P^1 > \cdots > P^k; Z} M$.

Proposition 1 *A structure M is a model of $Circum(A; P; Z)$ iff M is minimal in the class of models of A with respect to $\leq^{P;Z}$ [14].*

Proposition 2 *A structure M is a model of $Circum(A; P^1 > \cdots > P^k; Z)$ iff M is minimal in the class of models of A with respect to $\leq^{P^1 > \cdots > P^k; Z}$ [14].*

2.2   General Extended Disjunctive Programs

A *general extended disjunctive program* (GEDP) [11] is a set of rules of the form:
$$L_1; \cdots; L_k; not L_{k+1}; \cdots; not L_l$$
$$\leftarrow L_{l+1}, \ldots, L_m, not L_{m+1}, \ldots, not L_n, \tag{1}$$
where each L_i ($n \geq m \geq l \geq k \geq 0$) is a classical literal, i.e. either an atom a or its negation $\neg a$ preceded by the classical negation sign $\neg$, and ";" represents a disjunction. The rule with $k = 0$ is called an *integrity constraint*. A rule with variables stands for the set of its ground instances.

The semantics of a GEDP is given by the *answer sets* [9, 11] as follows.

Definition 4   Let Lit_P be the set of all ground literals in the language of P. First, let P be a *not*-free GEDP (i.e., for each rule $k = l, m = n$). Then, $S \subseteq Lit_P$ is an *answer set* of P if S is a minimal set satisfying the conditions:

1. For each ground instance of a rule $L_1; \cdots; L_k \leftarrow L_{l+1}, \ldots, L_m$ in P, if $\{L_{l+1}, \ldots, L_m\} \subseteq S$, then $L_i \in S$ for some i ($1 \leq i \leq l$); In particular, for each integrity constraint $\leftarrow L_1, \ldots, L_m$ in P, $\{L_1, \ldots, L_m\} \not\subseteq S$ holds;
2. If S contains a pair of complementary literals, then $S = Lit_P$.

Second, let P be any GEDP and $S \subseteq Lit_P$. The *reduct* of P by S is a *not*-free GEDP P^S obtained as follows:
  A rule $L_1; \cdots; L_k \leftarrow L_{l+1}, \ldots, L_m$ is in P^S
iff there is a ground rule of the form (1) in P such that $\{L_{k+1}, \ldots, L_l\} \subseteq S$ and $\{L_{m+1}, \ldots, L_n\} \cap S = \emptyset$.

Then, S is an answer set of P if S is an answer set of P^S. An answer set is *consistent* if it is not Lit_P. The answer set Lit_P is said *contradictory*. A GEDP is *consistent* if it has a consistent answer set; otherwise, it is *inconsistent*.

3   Computing Models of Circumscription

In this section, we introduce a sound and complete procedure for computing models of parallel circumscription $Circum(A; P; Z)$ or prioritized circumscription $Circum(A; P^1 > \cdots > P^k; Z)$. We assume that A is a first order theory without function symbols and is given by a set of clauses of the form:
$$A_1 \vee \cdots \vee A_\ell \vee \neg B_1 \vee \cdots \vee \neg B_m, \tag{2}$$
where A_i ($1 \leq i \leq \ell$) and B_j ($1 \leq j \leq m$) are atoms. Also, we consider *Herbrand models* of A, which has the effect of introducing both the *domain closure assumption* (DCA) and the *unique name assumption* (UNA) into A [21]. We suppose that any clause in A with variables stands for the set of its ground instances expanded by individual constants occurring in DCA. Hereafter, let U be the *Herbrand Universe* of A, and H be the *Herbrand base* of A.

3.1   Translation for Generating Strictly Preferred Models

We translate a parallel or prioritized circumscription into ASP in two steps. In the first step, given a parallel or prioritized circumscription, the set A of clauses is translated into the following GEDP in a similar way to [20, 21], each of whose answer sets is a Herbrand model of A.

Definition 5   Given $Circum(A; P^1 > \cdots > P^k; Z)$ (or $Circum(A; P; Z)$ if $k = 1$), Π is the GEDP defined as follows:

(i) For any clause (2) in A, Π has the rule:
$$A_1; \cdots; A_\ell \leftarrow B_1, \ldots, B_m. \tag{3}$$
(ii) For any fixed or variable predicate μ in Σ, Π has the rule:
$$\mu(\mathbf{x}) \; ; \; not \; \mu(\mathbf{x}) \leftarrow . \tag{4}$$

Here $\mathbf{x}$ is the tuple of variables in each predicate.

Definition 6 Let P, Z, Q be the same sets in Definition 1. For any two structures M_1, M_2, we write $M_1 \leq^P M_2$ if
> (i) $M_1 \leq^{P;Z} M_2$,
> (ii) $M_1[\![Z]\!] = M_2[\![Z]\!]$.

Then with respect to a logic program Π, the following Theorem 1 holds.

Theorem 1. *Let Π be the GEDP as in Definition 5. Then, (i) M is an answer set of Π if and only if M is a minimal Herbrand model with respect to $\leq^P$ in the set of Herbrand models of A. (ii) In case of $Z = \emptyset$, M is an answer set of Π if and only if M is a model of $Circum(A; P)$.*

Proof: See Appendix.

Having the GEDP Π, the next step determines the models of the given parallel or prioritized circumscription based on the order $<^{P;Z}$ (or $<^{P^1>\cdots>P^k;Z}$) on the set of answer sets of Π. To this end, we constructs a logic program $T[\Pi; P; Z; M]$ (or $T[\Pi; P^1, \ldots, P^k; Z; M]$) from the given parallel or prioritized circumscription and any answer set M of Π. The proposed translation here is inspired by the idea in Wakaki *et al.*'s method [24] to compute preferred answer sets of PLPs [20, 21]. The construction of the logic program $T[\Pi; P^1, \ldots, P^k; Z; M]$ (or $T[\Pi; P; Z; M]$ for $k = 1$) is based on the techniques of *renaming atoms* and *meta-programming* as follows.

First, we encode the given answer set M of Π as well as some other answer set M' of Π within an answer set of $T[\Pi; P^1, \ldots, P^k; Z; M]$. This encoding enables us to check whether $M' <^{P^1>\cdots>P^k;Z} M$ holds or not. To this end, we use *renaming atoms* such that each atom $L \in H$ in M is renamed by the newly introduced atom L^*. Then, this technique symbolically enables us to embed the given answer set M as the set M^* of renamed atoms L^*, together with another answer set M' within an answer set of $T[\Pi; P^1, \ldots, P^k; Z; M]$.

Second, we use a *meta-programming* technique in order to decide

$$M' <^{P^1 > \cdots > P^k; Z} M$$

with respect to two answer sets M and M' of Π, where a comparison between an atom $a \in M$ and some atom $b \in M'$ is required. For such a comparison in our approach, it should be symbolically known that the newly introduced symbol L^* is the renamed atom for the corresponding atom $L \in H$. Therefore, not only we introduce a new constant L_t for each atom $L \in H$ as well as its renamed atom L^*, but also we provide predicate symbols m_1 and m_2 such that, with respect to any constant L_t corresponding to an atom $L \in H$ as well as its renamed atom L^*, $m_1(L_t)$ means $L \in M$ for the given answer set M, while $m_2(L_t)$ means $L \in M'$ for another answer set M'.

In the following, the set of renamed atoms L^*s is defined as H^*, and the set of newly introduced constants L_ts is defined as C.

Definition 7 H^* and C are defined as follows.

$$H^* \stackrel{def}{=} \{L^* \mid L \in H\}$$

$$C \stackrel{def}{=} \{L_t \mid L \in H\}$$

where H is finite, so are H^* and C.

3.1.1 Parallel Circumscription

We are ready to show the transformed logic program $T[\Pi; P; Z; M]$ for parallel circumscription as follows.

Definition 8 Let Π be the GEDP constructed from $Circum(A; P; Z)$ according to Definition 5, and M be an answer set of Π. Then $T[\Pi; P; Z; M]$ is the GEDP defined as:

$$T[\Pi; P; Z; M] \stackrel{def}{=} \Pi \cup \Gamma \cup \Xi.$$

Here, Γ is the set of *domain dependent* rules as follows:

1. $L^* \leftarrow,$ for each $L \in M$,
   where each $L^* \in H^*$ is the renamed atom corresponding to $L \in M$,

2. $m_1(L_t) \leftarrow L^*,$ $m_2(L_t) \leftarrow L,$
   for every $L \in H$, its renamed atom $L^* \in H^*$ and the ground term $L_t \in C$ expressing the atom L,

3. $minp(L_t) \leftarrow,$
   for ground term $L_t \in C$ representing the atom $p(\mathbf{t}) \in H$ whose predicate symbol p is in P, and

4. $fixed(L_t) \leftarrow,$
   for every term $L_t \in C$ representing the atom $q(\mathbf{t}) \in H$ whose predicate symbol q is in Q,

where $minp$ and $fixed$ are newly introduced predicate symbols, and $\mathbf{t}$ occurring in items 3 and 4 is a tuple of elements in U for each predicate. Ξ is the set of *domain independent* rules instantiated over constants in C as follows:

5. $\quad h_1 \leftarrow m_1(x),\ fixed(x),\ not\ m_2(x),$
    $\quad h_2 \leftarrow m_2(x),\ fixed(x),\ not\ m_1(x),$
    $\quad h \leftarrow not\ h_1, not\ h_2,$

6. $\quad c \leftarrow m_1(x),\ minp(x),\ not\ m_2(x),$
    $\quad d \leftarrow m_2(x),\ minp(x),\ not\ m_1(x),$

7. $\quad subsetp \leftarrow h,\ c,\ not\ d,$

8. $\quad \leftarrow not\ subsetp,$

where h_1, h_2, h, d, $subsetp$ are newly introduced propositional symbols. Rules of items 5, 6 and 7 check $M' <^{P;Z} M$ using the conditions (ii), (iii) in Definition 1 where M_1 and M_2 are regarded as some answer set M' and the given answer set M in this case, respectively. Rules of item 5 mean that h becomes true if $M'[\![Q]\!] = M[\![Q]\!]$. Rules of item 6 mean that c (or d) becomes true if there is some atom $a \in M \setminus M'$ (or $a \in M' \setminus M$) whose predicate symbol is in P. Thus, Item 7 means that, with respect to the given answer set M, $subsetp$ becomes true for any answer set M' such that $M' <^{P;Z} M$. Item 8 means that the inconsistency is derived if $subsetp$ is not true.

The following theorems hold for the translated logic program $T[\Pi; P; Z; M]$, whose proofs are omitted since they are special case (i.e. $k = 1$) for proofs of Theorem 4 and Theorem 5 given in Appendix.

Theorem 2. *Given $Circum(A; P; Z)$, let M be an answer set of Π.*
If $T[\Pi; P; Z; M]$ is consistent, then for any answer set E of $T[\Pi; P; Z; M]$, there is an answer set M' of Π such that $M' <^{P;Z} M$ where $M' = E \cap H$. Conversely, if there is an answer set M' of Π such that $M' <^{P;Z} M$, $T[\Pi; P; Z; M]$ is consistent and has an answer set E such that $E \cap H = M'$.

Corollary 1 *Given $Circum(A; P; Z)$, let M be an answer set of Π. Then, $T[\Pi; P; Z; M]$ is inconsistent if and only if there is no answer set M' of Π such that $M' <^{P;Z} M$.*
Proof: This is immediately proved as the contrapositive of Theorem 2.

Theorem 3. *(Soundness and Completeness Theorem)*
Given $Circum(A; P; Z)$, $T[\Pi; P; Z; M]$ is inconsistent for an answer set M of Π if and only if M is a model of $Circum(A; P; Z)$.

Example 1. Let us consider parallel circumscription $Circum(A; ab_1, ab_2; p)$ [1] where $P = \{ab_1, ab_2\}$, $Q = \{q, r\}$, $Z = \{p\}$. A is given by the set of clauses as follows:

$$\{\neg p(x) \lor ab1(x) \lor \neg r(x),\ p(x) \lor ab2(x) \lor \neg q(x),\ r(n),\ q(n)\}$$

[1] This is the well-known *Quaker and Republican's problem.*

where x is an individual variable and n is a constant. Then the GEDP Π is constructed from $Circum(A; ab_1, ab_2; p)$ as follows:

Π: $ab_1(x) \leftarrow p(x), r(x)$, $p(x) \; ; \; ab_2(x) \leftarrow q(x)$,
   $r(n) \leftarrow, \quad q(n) \leftarrow, \qquad p(x) \; ; \; not \; p(x) \leftarrow,$
   $q(x) \; ; \; not \; q(x) \leftarrow, \qquad r(x) \; ; \; not \; r(x) \leftarrow .$

Π has the following two answer sets M_1, M_2:

$$M_1 = \{r(n), q(n), ab_2(n)\}, \quad M_2 = \{r(n), q(n), p(n), ab_1(n)\}.$$

Corresponding to the Herbrand base $H = \{p(n), q(n), r(n), ab_1(n), ab_2(n)\}$, we prepare H^* and $\mathcal{C}$ as follows.

$$H^* = \{p^*(n), q^*(n), r^*(n), ab_1{}^*(n), ab_2{}^*(n)\}, \quad \mathcal{C} = \{pn, qn, rn, ab1n, ab2n\}.$$

Then for M_1, $T[\Pi; P; Z; M_1] = \Pi \cup \Gamma_1 \cup \Xi$ is constructed with the following Γ_1:

$\Gamma_1:$ $r^*(n) \leftarrow, \quad q^*(n) \leftarrow, \quad ab_2{}^*(n) \leftarrow, \quad m_1(pn) \leftarrow p^*(n),$
   $m_1(qn) \leftarrow q^*(n), \quad m_1(rn) \leftarrow r^*(n), \quad m_1(ab1n) \leftarrow ab_1{}^*(n),$
   $m_1(ab2n) \leftarrow ab_2{}^*(n), \quad m_2(pn) \leftarrow p(n), \quad m_2(qn) \leftarrow q(n),$
   $m_2(rn) \leftarrow r(n), \quad m_2(ab1n) \leftarrow ab_1(n), \quad m_2(ab2n) \leftarrow ab_2(n),$
   $minp(ab1n) \leftarrow, \quad minp(ab2n) \leftarrow, \quad fixed(qn) \leftarrow, \quad fixed(rn) \leftarrow .$

In this case, both $T[\Pi; P; Z; M_1]$ and $T[\Pi; P; Z; M_2]$ are inconsistent. Therefore, according to Theorem 3, we can conclude that both M_1 and M_2 are models of $Circum(A; ab_1, ab_2; p)$.

3.1.2 Prioritized Circumscription

The translated logic program $T[\Pi; P^1, \ldots, P^k; Z; M]$ for prioritized circumscription is shown as follows.

Definition 9 Suppose a tuple P of predicates is decomposed into k disjoint parts $P^1, \ldots, P^k$. Let Π be the GEDP constructed from $Circum(A; P^1 > \cdots > P^k; Z)$ according to Definition 5, and M be an answer set of Π.
   Then $T[\Pi; P^1, \ldots, P^k; Z; M]$ is the GEDP defined as:

$$T[\Pi; P^1, \ldots, P^k; Z; M] \overset{def}{=} \Pi \cup \Gamma \cup \Xi.$$

Here, Γ is the set of *domain dependent* rules, which has not only the same rules of items 1, 2, 4 from Γ given in Definition 8 but also rules of item 3 as follows:

3. $minp_i(L_t) \leftarrow,$
   for every term $L_t \in \mathcal{C}$ representing the atom $p(\mathbf{t}) \in H$ whose predicate p is in P^i $(1 \leq i \leq k)$

where each $minp_i$ $(1 \leq i \leq k)$ is a newly introduced predicate symbol. Ξ is the set of *domain independent* rules instantiated over constants in $\mathcal{C}$ as follows:

5. $h_1 \leftarrow m_1(x), \ fixed(x), \ not \ m_2(x),$
    $h_2 \leftarrow m_2(x), \ fixed(x), \ not \ m_1(x),$
    $h \leftarrow not \ h_1, not \ h_2,$

6. $c_i \leftarrow m_1(x), \ minp_i(x), \ not \ m_2(x),$
    $d_i \leftarrow m_2(x), \ minp_i(x), \ not \ m_1(x),$
    $eq_i \leftarrow not \ d_i, not \ c_i.$ $(1 \leq i \leq k)$

7. $smaller_1 \leftarrow h, \ c_1, not \ d_1,$
    $smaller_i \leftarrow h, eq_1, \ldots, eq_{i-1}, \ c_i, not \ d_i,$ $(2 \leq i \leq k)$
    $subsetp \leftarrow smaller_i,$ $(1 \leq i \leq k)$

8. $\leftarrow not \ subsetp,$

where h_1, h_2, h, d_i, c_i, eq_i, $smaller_i$ and $subsetp$ are propositional symbols. Rules of items 5, 6 and 7 check $M' <^{P^1 > \cdots > P^k; Z} M$ using the conditions (ii), (iii) in Definition 2. Rules of item 7 means that, with respect to the given answer set M, $subsetp$ becomes true for any answer set M' such that $M' <^{P^1 > \cdots > P^k; Z} M$. Thus due to item 8, the inconsistency is derived if $subsetp$ is not true.

With respect to the translated logic program $T[\Pi; P^1, \ldots, P^k; Z; M]$ for prioritized circumscription, the following theorems hold.

Theorem 4. *Given $Circum(A; P^1 > \cdots > P^k; Z)$, let M be an answer set of Π. If $T[\Pi; P^1, \ldots, P^k; Z; M]$ is consistent, then for any answer set E of $T[\Pi; P^1, \ldots, P^k; Z; M]$, there is an answer set M' of Π such that $M' <^{P^1 > \cdots > P^k; Z} M$ where $M' = E \cap H$. Conversely, if there is an answer set M' of Π such that $M' <^{P^1 > \cdots > P^k; Z} M$, $T[\Pi; P^1, \ldots, P^k; Z; M]$ is consistent and has an answer set E such that $E \cap H = M'$.*

Proof: See Appendix.

Corollary 2 *Given $Circum(A; P^1 > \cdots > P^k; Z)$, let M be an answer set of Π. Then, $T[\Pi; P^1, \ldots, P^k; Z; M]$ is inconsistent if and only if there is no answer set M' of Π such that $M' <^{P^1 > \cdots > P^k; Z} M$.*

Proof: This is immediately proved as the contrapositive of Theorem 4.

Theorem 5. *(Soundness and Completeness Theorem)*
Given $Circum(A; P^1 > \cdots > P^k; Z)$, $T[\Pi; P^1, \ldots, P^k; Z; M]$ is inconsistent for an answer set M of Π if and only if M is a model of $Circum(A; P^1 > \cdots > P^k; Z)$.

Proof: See Appendix.

Example 2. Consider prioritized circumscription $Circum(A; ab_1 > ab_2; p)$. A is the same as in Example 1, and let $P^1 = \{ab_1\}$, $P^2 = \{ab_2\}$. Then for the answer set M_1, $T[\Pi; P^1, P^2; Z; M_1] = \Pi \cup \Gamma_1' \cup \Xi$ is constructed with Γ_2 as follows:

$$\Gamma_2 = \{\Gamma_1 \setminus \{minp(ab_1n) \leftarrow, minp(ab_2n) \leftarrow\}\} \cup \{minp_1(ab_1n) \leftarrow, \ minp_2(ab_2n) \leftarrow\}$$

where M_1 and Γ_1 are given in Example 1. In this case, $T[\Pi; P^1, P^2; Z; M_1]$ is inconsistent, but $T[\Pi; P^1, P^2; Z; M_2]$ is consistent. Thus we can conclude that only M_1 is a model of $Circum(A; ab_1 > ab_2; p)$ by Theorem 5.

3.2 Procedure to Compute Circumscriptive Models

We show the sound and complete procedure *CircModelsGenerator* which generates all models of the given circumscription based on Theorem 3 and Theorem 5. In order to decide the minimal ones among the answer sets of Π, the procedure makes use of the inconsistency checking of the logic program $T[\Pi; P^1, \ldots, P^k; Z; M]$ whose answer sets (if exist) yield strictly preferred models to M with respect to $\leq^{P^1 > \cdots > P^k; Z}$. Surprisingly our procedure is very simple and elegant though its encoding has a *guess and check* structure as follows.

Procedure 1 *CircModelsGenerator(A; $P^1, \cdots, P^k; Z; \Delta$)*

Input: $Circum(A; P^1 > \cdots > P^k; Z)$ (or $Circum(A; P; Z)$ if $k = 1$)
Output: the set Δ of all models of $Circum(A; P^1 > \cdots > P^k; Z)$

1. Generate the GEDP Π from A, Z, Q according to Definition 5, and compute the set AS of all answer sets of Π. $\Delta := \emptyset$.
2. If AS is the empty set $\emptyset$, then $\Delta := AS$, return Δ.
3. For any answer set $S \in AS$, if $T[\Pi; P^1, \ldots, P^k; Z; S]$ is inconsistent, then $\Delta := \Delta \cup \{S\}$.
4. return Δ.

3.3 Implementation and Experimental Results

The procedure *CircModelsGenerator* presented in Section 3.2 has been implemented using the ASP solver *dlv* [6] and the C++ programming language. The current implementation is running under the Linux and Windows operating systems. Some of experimental results and performance under the Linux on a 2.5 GHz Pentium IV computer are shown as follows.

Example 3. In Examples 6 and 12 in [16], parallel circumscription $Circum(A; p, q; r)$ and prioritized circumscription $Circum(A; p, r > q)$ are respectively given, where A is the set of clauses as follows[2]:

$$\{ p(a) \vee q(a) \vee r(a), \ r(a) \supset r(b), \ p(b) \vee q(b), \ r(c) \vee p(c), \ p(c) \supset r(d)\}$$

Our implementation computes correctly 4 models w.r.t. $Circum(A; p, q; r)$ in 4 msec and 2 models w.r.t. $Circum(A; p, r > q)$ in 5 msec. These are average CPU times repeated 20 times to eliminate inaccuracies caused by the system clock.

Example 4. $Circum(A; e_1 > e_2 > e_3 > c; p, v, m)$ expresses the meeting scheduling problem in [22] where A is the set of clauses as follows:

$$\{ c(1) \vee c(2) \vee c(3), \ p(x) \supset c(x), \ v(x) \supset c(x), \ m(x) \supset c(x),$$
$$c(x) \wedge \neg e_1(x) \supset p(x), \ c(x) \wedge \neg e_2(x) \supset v(x), \ c(x) \wedge \neg e_3(x) \supset m(x),$$
$$\neg p(1), \ \neg v(3), \ \neg m(2)\}$$

---

[2] These are counter-examples to Theorem 3.8 and Theorem 3.9 in [21] (or Lemma 3.7 and Theorem 3.8 in [20]) respectively. In fact, 30 models are computed for $Circum(A; p, q; r)$ according to their Theorem 3.8 in [21] (or Lemma 3.7 in [20]).

It has the unique model $M_1 = \{\ c(2),\ e_3(2),\ p(2),\ v(2)\}$, which is computed correctly in 365 msec by our current implementation. On the other hand, prioritized circumscription: $Circum(A;\ e_1 > e_2,\ e_3 > c;\ p,\ v,\ m)$ has two models M_1 and $M_2 = \{\ c(3),\ e_2(3),\ p(3),\ m(3)\}$, which are also computed in 383 msec by the current implementation. These are also average CPU times repeated 10 times.

4   Related Work and Conclusion

We presented a new method of compiling parallel and prioritized circumscription without function symbols into answer set programming. In computing circumscription by logic programming, almost all previous methods [8, 20, 23, 21] translate a given circumscription into some semantically equivalent logic program. In our new approach, a given circumscription is translated into a logic program whose answer sets (if exist) yield strictly preferred models to a given candidate model. Hence its inconsistency enables us to determine models of prioritized circumscription. With respect to complexity, it is well known that model checking of circumscription is coNP-complete [3] and literal entailment from circumscription is Π_2^p-complete [5]. As for the proposed procedure, it calls an ASP solver polynomial order times. Our procedure has been implemented using ASP solver. Under the current implementation, models of circumscription are correctly computed. Our performance presented in Section 3.3 is faster than or comparable with that of figures ($30 \sim 420$ msec) shown in [16, p.75] which are taken to compute minimal models using integer programming. To the best of our knowledge, there are not enough benchmarks for the implemented systems to compute prioritized circumscription. Thus it may be concluded that our approach is more efficient than any other previous implemented methods of computing prioritized circumscription.

Our approach of computing circumscriptive models is inspired by [24]. It turns out that Janhunen and Oikarinen's approach for testing the equivalence of logic programs [13, 17] is based on a similar technique. Their approach and ours construct the translated logic programs for the respective purposes using technique of *renaming atoms*. More precisely speaking, answer sets of our translated logic program yield the *strictly preferred models* with respect to the preorder $\leq^{P^1 > ... > P^k; Z}$ used to check the minimality for each candidate Herbrand model, whereas answer sets of their translated logic program yield the *counter-examples* used to check the equivalence of two logic programs. Thus, our encoding technique may become one of general techniques or frameworks using ASP for problem solving whose complexity is in the second level of the polynomial hierarchy.

Using a different preference ordering, Brewka *et al.* [1, 2] proposed similar approaches to ours to compute preferred models of logic programs with ordered disjunction [1] and for answer set optimization [2]. Their both approaches use two programs, a generator and a tester which correspond to Π and $T[\Pi; P^1, \ldots, P^k; Z; M]$ respectively for our approach. However, their implementation is different from ours since their generator and the tester are run in an interleaved fashion which is similar technique used in Janhunen *et al.* [12].

Eiter *et al.* [7] explore the implementation of preference semantics for logic programs by means of *meta-programming* in ASP. Their approach enables to compute preferred answer sets for three different kinds of preferential ASPs including Delgrande *et al.*'s approach [4]. Their basic meta-interpreter P_I has the "guess and check" structure, which is similar to our procedure. Our approach also uses the technique of the meta-programming, but its idea and aim are different from those of Eiter *et al.*'s meta-programming.

Finally, in future work, we want to to improve the procedure presented in this paper to enhance the efficiency by pruning the search space based on the similar intelligent backtracking technique proposed by [12, 18].

Acknowledgments

We would like to thank the anonymous referees for their valuable comments.

References

1. Brewka, G., Niemelä, I. and Syrjänen, T.: Implementing Ordered Disjunction Using Answer Set Solvers for Normal Programs, *Proc. of 8th European Conf. on Logics in Artificial Intelligence (JELIA 2002)*, LNAI 2424, pages 444–455, Springer, 2002.
2. Brewka, G., Niemelä, I. and Truszczynski, M.: Answer set Optimization, *Proc. of 17th Int. Joint Conf. on Artificial Intelligence (IJCAI 2003)*, pages 867–872, 2003.
3. Cadoli, M.: The complexity of model checking for circumscriptive formulae, *Information Processing Letters 44*, pages 113–118, 1992.
4. Delgrande, J. P., Schaub, T. and Tompits, H.: A framework for compiling preferences in logic programs, *Theory and Practice of Logic Programming 3*(2), pages 129–187, 2003.
5. Eiter, T. and Gottlob, G.: Propositional circumscription and extended closed-world reasoning are Π_2^p-Complete. *Theoretical Computer Science 114* (2), pages 231–245, 1993.
6. Eiter, T., Leone, N., Mateis, C., Pfeifer, G. and Scarcello, F.: A deductive system for nonmonotonic reasoning, *Proc. of LPNMR 1997*, LNCS 1265, pages 364-375, Springer, 1997. URL http://www.dbai.tuwien.ac.at/proj/dlv/
7. Eiter, T., Faber, W., Leone, N. and Pfeifer G.: Computing preferred answer sets by meta-interpretation in answer set programming, *Theory and Practice of Logic Programming 3* (4-5), pages 463–498, 2003.
8. Gelfond, M. and Lifschitz, V.: Compiling circumscriptive theories into logic programs. *Proc. of AAAI 1988*, pages 455–459, 1988.
9. Gelfond, M. and Lifschitz, V.: Classical negation in logic programs and disjunctive databases. *New Generation Computing 9*, pages 365–385, 1991.
10. Inoue, K.: Linear resolution for consequence finding, *Artificial Intelligence 56*, pages 301–353, 1992.
11. Inoue, K. and Sakama, C.: On positive occurrences of negation as failure. *Proc. of KR 1994*, pages 293–304, 1994.
12. Janhunen, T., Niemelä, I. Simons, P. and You, J.: Unfolding Partiality and Disjunctions in Stable Model Semantics, *Proc. of KR 2000*, pages 411–422, 2000.
13. Janhunen, T. and Oikarinen, E.: Testing the equivalence of logic programs under stable models semantics, *Proc. of 8th European Conf. on Logics in Artificial Intelligence (JELIA 2002)*, LNAI 2424, pages 493–504, Springer, 2002.
14. Lifschitz, V.: Computing circumscription. *Proc. of IJCAI'85*, pages 121–127, 1985.

15. McCarthy, J.: Applications of circumscription to formalizing commonsense knowledge. *Artificial Intelligence 28*, pages 89–116, 1986.
16. Nerode, A., Ng, R. T. and Subrahmanian, V.S.: Computing circumscriptive databases, part I: theory and algorithms, *Information and Computation*, Vol. 116, pages 58 – 80, 1995
17. Oikarinen, E. and Janhunen, T.: Verifying the equivalence of logic programs in the disjunctive case, *Proc. of 7th Int. Conf. on Logic Programming and Nonmonotonic Reasoning (LPNMR 2004)*, LNAI 2923, pages 180–193, Springer, 2004.
18. Pfeifer, G.: Improving the Model Generation/Checking Interplay to Enhance the Evaluation of Disjunctive Programs, *Proc. of 7th International Conference on Logic Programming and Nonmonotonic Reasoning (LPNMR 2004)*, LNAI 2923, pages 220–233, Springer, 2004.
19. Sakama, C. and Inoue, K.: Embedding circumscriptive theories in general disjunctive programs, *Proc. of 3rd Int. Conference on Logic Programming and Nonmonotonic Reasoning (LPNMR 1995)*, LNAI 928, pages 344-357, Springer, 1995.
20. Sakama, C. and Inoue, K.: Representing priorities in logic programs. *Proc. of Joint Int. Conf. and Sympo. on Logic Programming (JICSLP'96)*, pages 82–96, 1996.
21. Sakama, C. and Inoue, K.: Prioritized logic programming and its application to commonsense reasoning, *Artificial Intelligence 123*, pages 185–222, 2000.
22. Satoh, K.: Formalizing soft constraints by interpretation ordering, *Proc. of 9th European Conference on Artificial Intelligence (ECAI 1990)*, pages 585–590, 1990.
23. Wakaki, T. and Satoh, K.: Compiling prioritized circumscription into extended logic programs. *Proc. of IJCAI'97*, pages 182–187, 1997.
24. Wakaki, T., Inoue, K., Sakama, C. and Nitta, K.: Computing preferred answer sets in answer set programming, *Proc. of 10th International Conference on Logic for Programming Artificial Intelligence and Reasoning (LPAR 2003)*, LNAI 2850, pages 259–273, Springer, 2003.

Appendix: Proofs of Theorems

Proof of Theorem 1

Proof: (i) Let $\mathcal{P}$, $\mathcal{Q}$, $\mathcal{Z}$ be disjoint subsets of the Herbrand base H of A such that $\mathcal{P}$, $\mathcal{Q}$, $\mathcal{Z}$ are sets of ground instances for minimized predicates, fixed predicates, and variable predicates respectively. It is obvious that any answer set M of Π is a Herbrand model of A since M satisfies the rules of the form (3) in Π. In addition, any answer set M such that $S \subseteq M$ for any set $S \in 2^{\mathcal{Q} \cup \mathcal{Z}}$ satisfies all rules of the form (4) in Π. Then,

    M is an answer set of Π

    iff M is an answer set of Π^M

    iff M is a minimal Herbrand model of $A \cup \{\mu(\mathbf{x}) \; ; \; not \; \mu(\mathbf{x}) \leftarrow\}^M$

    iff M is a minimal Herbrand model of $A \cup \{M \cap (\mathcal{Q} \cup \mathcal{Z})\}$

    iff M is minimal with respect to the set inclusion ($\subseteq$) in the set of Herbrand
        models of A each of whose extension of $\mathcal{Q} \cup \mathcal{Z}$ coincides with $M \cap (\mathcal{Q} \cup \mathcal{Z})$.

    iff M is minimal with respect to $\leq^P$ in the set of all Herbrand models of A.

(ii) It is obvious due to the result of (i).   □

Proof of Theorem 4 Let $\mathcal{P}^1, \ldots, \mathcal{P}^k$ be disjoint subsets of $\mathcal{P}$, each of which is a set of atoms with the predicate from P^i $(1 \leq i \leq k)$.

Proof: ($\Longrightarrow$) Since $T[\Pi; P^1, \ldots, P^k; Z; M] = \Pi \cup \Gamma \cup \Xi$ is consistent, it holds that *subsetp* $\in E$ for any answer set E of $T[\Pi; P^1, \ldots, P^k; Z; M]$, and E is also an answer set of $T[\Pi; P^1, \ldots, P^k; Z; M] \setminus \{\leftarrow not\ subsetp\}$. Then, since $\Gamma \cup \Xi \setminus \{\leftarrow not\ subsetp\}$ is a stratified logic program whose each rule has the ground head atom not occurring in H, E is an augmented answer set of Π which not only includes some answer set of Π but also has ground head atoms of the rules in $\Gamma \cup \Xi \setminus \{\leftarrow not\ subsetp\}$. Thus $M' = E \cap H$ should be an answer set of Π. According to item 1 in Definition 8, it is obvious that $M^* = E \cap H^*$ is a renamed answer set of a given answer set M such that each $L^* \in M^*$ is a renamed literal w.r.t $L \in M$. Then, according to item 2,

$$m_1(a_t) \in E \quad \text{iff} \quad a^* \in M^* \quad \text{(i.e. } a \in M)$$
$$m_2(b_t) \in E \quad \text{iff} \quad b \in M' = E \cap H$$

where $a_t \in \mathcal{C}, a^* \in H^*$ w.r.t $a \in H$ and $b_t \in \mathcal{C}$ w.r.t $b \in H$. Thus, according to rules in Definition 9, it follows that, for any answer set E of $T[\Pi; P^1, \ldots, P^k; Z; M]$,

  $subsetp \in E$

iff $smaller_i \in E$ for some i ($1 \le i \le k$)

iff $h \in E$, $eq_j \in E$, $c_i \in E$ and $d_i \notin E$ for $1 \le j \le i - 1$ and $1 \le \exists i \le k$

iff $h_1 \notin E$, $h_2 \notin E$, $eq_1 \in E, \ldots, eq_{i-1} \in E$ $c_i \in E$ and $d_i \notin E$

iff $\neg$ ($\exists a_t \in \mathcal{C}$ s.t. $m_1(a_t) \in E \wedge fixed(a_t) \in E \wedge m_2(a_t) \notin E$) $\wedge$
  $\neg$ ($\exists b_t \in \mathcal{C}$ s.t. $m_2(b_t) \in E \wedge fixed(b_t) \in E \wedge m_1(b_t) \notin E$)$\wedge$
  $\bigwedge_{j=1}^{i-1} \{\neg (\exists e_t^j \in \mathcal{C}$ s.t. $m_1(e_t^j) \in E \wedge minp_j(e_t^j) \in E \wedge m_2(e_t^j) \notin E)\wedge$
  $\neg(\exists g_t^j \in \mathcal{C}$ s.t. $m_2(g_t^j) \in E \wedge minp_j(g_t^j) \in E \wedge m_1(g_t^j) \notin E)\} \wedge$
  $\neg$ ($\exists u_t \in \mathcal{C}$ s.t. $m_2(u_t) \in E \wedge minp_i(u_t) \in E \wedge m_1(u_t) \notin E)\wedge$
  ($\exists v_t \in \mathcal{C}$ s.t. $m_1(v_t) \in E \wedge minp_i(v_t) \in E \wedge m_2(v_t) \notin E)$

iff $\neg$ ($\exists a \in \mathcal{Q}$ s.t. $a \in M \wedge a \notin M'$) $\wedge \neg$ ($\exists b \in \mathcal{Q}$ s.t. $b \in M' \wedge b \notin M$) $\wedge$
  $\bigwedge_{j=1}^{i-1} \{\neg$ ($\exists e^j \in \mathcal{P}^j$ s.t. $e^j \in M \setminus M'$) $\wedge \neg$ ($\exists g^j \in \mathcal{P}^j$ s.t. $g^j \in M' \setminus M)\}$
  $\wedge \neg$ ($\exists u \in \mathcal{P}^i$ s.t. $u \in M' \setminus M$) $\wedge$ ($\exists v \in \mathcal{P}^i$ s.t. $v \in M \setminus M'$)

iff $(M'[\![Q]\!] = M[\![Q]\!]) \wedge \bigwedge_{j=1}^{i-1}(M'[\![P^j]\!] = M[\![P^j]\!]) \wedge (M'[\![P^i]\!] \subset M[\![P^i]\!])$

iff $M' <^{P^1 > \cdots > P^k; Z} M$ where $M' = E \cap H$.

($\Longleftarrow$) Suppose that there is an answer set M' of Π such that $M' <^{P^1 > \cdots > P^k; Z} M$. Now, we define a set τ as follows:

$$\tau \overset{def}{=} T[\Pi; P^1, \ldots, P^k; Z; M] \setminus \{\leftarrow not\ subsetp\}$$

It is easily shown that, not only any answer set F of τ is an augmented answer set of Π such that $N = F \cap H$ for some answer set N of Π but also for any answer set N of Π, there is some answer set F of τ such that $F \cap H = N$. According to the assumption, M' is also an answer set of Π. Therefore, there should be some answer set F' of τ such that $F' \cap H = M'$. With respect to F', it is obvious that $M^* = F' \cap H^*$ is a renamed answer set of a given answer set M according to item 1 in Definition 8, and due to item 2,

$$m_1(a_t) \in F' \quad \text{iff} \quad a^* \in M^* \quad \text{(i.e. } a \in M)$$
$$m_2(b_t) \in F' \quad \text{iff} \quad b \in F' \cap H = M'$$

Since for such an answer set F' of τ, $M' <^{P^1 > \cdots > P^k; Z} M$ where $M' = F' \cap H$ is satisfied, it follows that, for $M' = F' \cap H$,

  $M' <^{P^1 > \cdots > P^k; Z} M$

iff $(M'\llbracket Q \rrbracket = M\llbracket Q \rrbracket) \wedge \bigwedge_{j=1}^{i-1}(M'\llbracket P^j \rrbracket = M\llbracket P^j \rrbracket) \wedge (M'\llbracket P^i \rrbracket \subset M\llbracket P^i \rrbracket)$ for $\exists i \leq k$

iff $h \in F'$, $eq_1 \in F', \ldots, eq_{i-1} \in F'$, $c_i \in F'$ and $d_i \notin F'$

iff $smaller_i \in F'$ for $1 \leq \exists i \leq k$

iff $subsetp \in F'$

Hence F' should be also an answer set of $T[\Pi; P^1, \ldots, P^k; Z; M]$ which satisfies $M' <^{P^1 > \cdots > P^k; Z} M$ for $M' = F' \cap H$. Therefore $T[\Pi; P^1, \ldots, P^k; Z; M]$ is consistent.   □

Proof of Theorem 5

Proof: Let $\mathcal{M}_A$ and $\mathcal{AS}$ be the sets of Herbrand models of A and Π respectively.
($\Longrightarrow$) Suppose that $T[\Pi; P^1, \ldots, P^k; Z; M]$ is inconsistent for a given answer set M of Π. Then according to Corollary 2, there is not any answer set M' of Π such that $M' <^{P^1 > \cdots > P^k; Z} M$. Hence, for any answer set $M' \in \mathcal{AS}$ such that $M'\llbracket Q \rrbracket = M\llbracket Q \rrbracket$, if M' is not tie w.r.t. M, it follows that,

$$M <^{P^1 > \cdots > P^k; Z} M', \tag{5}$$

where $\quad M\llbracket P^j \rrbracket = M'\llbracket P^j \rrbracket \quad (j = 1, \ldots, i-1)$ and
$\quad\quad M\llbracket P^i \rrbracket \subset M'\llbracket P^i \rrbracket$ for $\exists i \leq k$.

Since such $M' \in \mathcal{AS}$ is minimal in $\mathcal{M}_A$ with respect to $\leq^P$ due to Theorem 1, for any answer set $M'' \in \mathcal{M}_A \backslash \mathcal{AS}$ such that $M'\llbracket Q \rrbracket = M''\llbracket Q \rrbracket$ and $M'\llbracket Z \rrbracket = M''\llbracket Z \rrbracket$, it follows that,

$$M' <^P M'', \quad \text{where } M'\llbracket P \rrbracket \subset M''\llbracket P \rrbracket \text{ and } P = P^1 \cup \cdots \cup P^k. \tag{6}$$

Thus according to (5) and (6), with respect to M and such $M'' \in \mathcal{M}_A \backslash \mathcal{AS}$ via $M' \in \mathcal{AS}$ such that $M\llbracket Q \rrbracket = M'\llbracket Q \rrbracket = M''\llbracket Q \rrbracket$, the following holds transitively.

$$M <^{P^1 > \cdots > P^k; Z} M'', \tag{7}$$

where $\quad M\llbracket P^j \rrbracket = M''\llbracket P^j \rrbracket \quad (j = 1, \ldots, \ell-1)$ and
$\quad\quad M\llbracket P^\ell \rrbracket \subset M''\llbracket P^\ell \rrbracket$ for $1 \leq \exists \ell \leq i$.

Thus, due to (5) and (7), for any answer set $N \in \mathcal{M}_A$ which is not tie w.r.t. M and $N\llbracket Q \rrbracket = M\llbracket Q \rrbracket$,

$$M <^{P^1 > \cdots > P^k; Z} N \tag{8}$$

is derived. On the other hand, for $M' \in \mathcal{AS}(\subseteq \mathcal{M}_A)$ which is tie w.r.t. M,

$$M' \not<^{P^1 > \cdots > P^k; Z} M \tag{9}$$

due to Corollary 2. As a result, due to (8) and (9), there is no model $N \in \mathcal{M}_A$ such that $N <^{P^1 > \cdots > P^k; Z} M$. Therefore, M is minimal in $\mathcal{M}_A$ with respect to $\leq^{P^1 > \cdots > P^k; Z}$, which means that M is a model of $Circum(A; P^1 > \cdots > P^k; Z)$.

($\Longleftarrow$) The contrapositive is proved. That is, in the following, we prove that if $T[\Pi; P^1, \ldots, P^k; Z; M]$ is consistent for an answer set M of Π, then M is not a model of $Circum(A; P^1 > \cdots > P^k; Z)$.

Suppose that $T[\Pi; P^1, \ldots, P^k; Z; M]$ is consistent for an answer set M of Π. Then, according to Theorem 4, there exists some answer set M' of Π such that $M' <^{P^1 > \cdots > P^k; Z} M$. Since both M and M' are Herbrand models in $\mathcal{M}_A$, M is not minimal in $\mathcal{M}_A$ with respect to $\leq^{P^1 > \cdots > P^k; Z}$ due to Definition 3. Thus, M is not a model of $Circum(A; P^1 > \cdots > P^k; Z)$ due to Proposition 2.   □

Enhancing the Magic-Set Method
for Disjunctive Datalog Programs

Chiara Cumbo[1], Wolfgang Faber[2], Gianluigi Greco[1], and Nicola Leone[1]

[1] Dipartimento di Matematica, Università della Calabria, 87030 Rende, Italy
{cumbo,greco,leone}@mat.unical.it
[2] Institut für Informationssysteme, TU Wien, 1040 Wien, Austria
faber@kr.tuwien.ac.at

Abstract. We present a new technique for the optimization of (partially) bound queries over disjunctive datalog programs. The technique exploits the propagation of query bindings, and extends the Magic-Set optimization technique (originally defined for non-disjunctive programs) to the disjunctive case, substantially improving on previously defined approaches.

Magic-Set-transformed disjunctive programs frequently contain redundant rules. We tackle this problem and propose a method for preventing the generation of such superfluous rules during the Magic-Set transformation. In addition, we provide an efficient heuristic method for the identification of redundant rules, which can be applied in general, even if Magic-Sets are not used.

We implement all proposed methods in the DLV system – the state-of-the-art implementation of disjunctive datalog – and perform some experiments. The experimental results confirm the usefulness of Magic-Sets for disjunctive datalog, and they highlight the computational gain obtained by our method, which outperforms significantly the previously proposed Magic-Set method for disjunctive datalog programs.

1 Introduction

Disjunctive datalog (Datalog$^{\vee}$) programs are logic programs where disjunction may occur in the heads of rules [1, 2]. Disjunctive datalog is very expressive in a precise mathematical sense: it allows to express every property of finite ordered structures that is decidable in the complexity class Σ_2^P [2]. Therefore, under widely believed assumptions, Datalog$^{\vee}$ is strictly more expressive than *normal* (*disjunction-free*) datalog which can express only problems of lower complexity. Importantly, besides enlarging the class of applications which can be encoded in the language, disjunction often allows for representing problems of lower complexity in a simpler and more natural fashion (see [3]).

Recently, disjunctive datalog is employed in several projects, mainly due to the availability of some efficient inference engines, such as the DLV system [4] and the GnT system [5]. E.g., in [6] this formalism has been shown to be very well-suited for database repair, and the European Commission has funded a couple of IST projects focusing on the exploitation of disjunctive datalog in "hot" application areas like information integration and knowledge management[1].

---

[1] The exploitation of disjunctive datalog for information integration is the main focus of the INFOMIX project (IST-2001-33570); while an application of disjunctive datalog for knowledge management is studied in ICONS (IST-2001-32429).

B. Demoen and V. Lifschitz (Eds.): ICLP 2004, LNCS 3132, pp. 371–385, 2004.
© Springer-Verlag Berlin Heidelberg 2004

The increasing application of disjunctive datalog systems stimulates the research on algorithms and optimization techniques, which make these systems more efficient and more widely applicable. Within this framework, we investigate here a promising line of research consisting of the extension of deductive database techniques and, specifically, of binding propagation techniques exploited in the Magic-Set method [7–12], to nonmonotonic logic languages like disjunctive datalog.

Intuitively, the goal of the Magic-Set method (originally defined for non-disjunctive datalog queries only) is to use the constants appearing in the query to reduce the size of the instantiation by eliminating "a priori" a number of ground instances of the rules which cannot contribute to the derivation of the query goal.

The first extension of Magic-Set method to disjunctive programs is due to [13], where the author observes that binding propagation strategies have to be changed for disjunctive rules so that each time a head predicate receives some binding from the query, it eventually propagates this relevant information to all the other head predicates as well as to the body predicates (see Section 3.1). An algorithm implementing the above strategy has been also proposed in [13]. Roughly, it is a rewriting algorithm that bloats the program with some additional predicates (called *collecting* predicates), besides the standard "magic" ones (intrinsic in the Magic-Set method) in order to make the propagation strategy work – in the following we call this algorithm Auxiliary Predicates Method (APM).

In this paper we provide fresh and refined ideas (w.r.t. [13]) for extending the Magic-Set method to disjunctive datalog queries. In particular, we observe that the method in [13] has two major drawbacks. First, the introduction of the new (collecting) predicates enlarges the size of the grounding and consequently reduces the gain that could be potentially achieved by the optimization. Second, several redundant (which are subsumed by the rest of the program) rules are frequently generated by the application of this method. Since the number of rules in a program is a critical performance factor, these redundancies can deteriorate run-time behavior. In extreme cases this overhead alone can outweigh the benefits of the optimization – since the evaluation of a disjunctive datalog program requires exponential time in the size of its instantiation, a polynomial increase in the size of the program instantiation may give an exponential increase in the program evaluation time.

Here, we address both problems above. Specifically, the main contribution is the following:

▷ **We define a new Magic-Set method for disjunctive datalog.** The new method, called Disjunctive Magic-Set (DMS), overcomes some drawbacks of the previous magic-set methods for disjunctive datalog. We provide an algorithm for the proposed DMS method, which involves a generalization of sideways information passing to the disjunctive case. Importantly, we formally prove the correctness of the DMS method by showing that given a query Q over a program P, the brave and cautious answers of Q over P coincide, respectively, with the brave and cautious answers of Q over P', where P' is the rewriting of P under DMS.

▷ **We design effective techniques for avoiding redundant rules.** The head-to-head binding propagation needed for disjunctive programs (see [13] and Section 3.1), very often causes the generation of many redundant rules (both APM and DMS are affected by this problem). We experimentally observe that the presence of redundant rules slows down the computation significantly, and may even counterpoise the advantages of the magic sets optimization. Thus, we design two techniques for redundant-rules prevention and elimination, respectively. The former technique prevents some cases of generation of redundant rules, by storing some extra information on the binding-propagation flow. Since the problem of redundant-rule identification is untractable (like clause subsumption), to eliminate "a posteriori" redundant rules (which could not be avoided by the former technique), we design a new and efficient heuristic for identifying redundant rules. Note that this heuristic is not specific for the disjunctive Magic-Set method, and can be applied for any type of logic program, even in the presence of unstratified negation and constraints. The enhancement of DMS with both our redundancy prevention and elimination techniques, yields an improved method, called Optimized Disjunctive Magic-Set Method (ODMS).

▷ **We implement all the proposed methods and techniques.** In particular, we implement the DMS method and its enhancements for redundancy prevention and elimination (yielding ODMS), in the DLV system [4] – the state-of-the-art implementation of disjunctive datalog. Both DMS and ODMS are fully integrated in the DLV system, and their are completely transparent to the end user that can simply enable them by setting the corresponding option. The interested reader can retrieve from `http://www.dlvsystem.com/magic/` a downloadable executable of the DLV system in which an option for using DMS or ODMS is provided – the same url contains some hints for its usage.

▷ **We evaluate the efficiency of the implemented method:** We have performed extensive experiments using benchmarks reported in the literature, comparing the performance of the DLV system without optimization, with APM of [13], with DMS, and with ODMS. These experiments show that our methods, especially ODMS, yields speedups in many cases and only rarely produces mild overheads w.r.t. the native DLV system, greatly improving on APM of [13].

2 Preliminaries

2.1 Disjunctive Datalog Queries

A *disjunctive rule* r is of the form $a_1 \vee \cdots \vee a_n :- b_1, \cdots, b_k.$, where $a_1, \cdots, a_n$, $b_1, \cdots, b_k$ are atoms and $n \geq 1$, $k \geq 0$. The disjunction $a_1 \vee \cdots \vee a_n$ is the *head* of r, while the conjunction $b_1, \ldots, b_k$ is the *body* of r. Moreover, let $H(r) = \{a_1, \ldots, a_n\}$ and $B(r) = \{b_1, \ldots, b_k\}$. A non-disjunctive rule with an empty body (i.e. $n = 1$ and $k = 0$) is called a *fact*. If a predicate is defined only by facts, it is referred to as *EDB predicate*, otherwise as *IDB predicate*. Throughout this paper, we assume that rules are *safe*, that is, each variable of a rule r appears in a positive literal of the body of r. A *disjunctive datalog program* (short. Datalog$^\vee$ program) $\mathcal{P}$ is a finite set of rules; if $\mathcal{P}$ is disjunction-free, then it is a *datalog program* (Datalog program). A *query* Q is a non-empty conjunction $b_1, \cdots, b_k$ of atoms.

Given a program $\mathcal{P}$, we denote by $ground(\mathcal{P})$ the set of all the rules obtained by applying to each rule $r \in \mathcal{P}$ all possible substitutions from the variables in r to the set of all the constants in $\mathcal{P}$. The semantics of a program $\mathcal{P}$ is given by the set $\mathcal{MM}(\mathcal{P})$ of the subset-minimal models of $\mathcal{P}$. Note that on Datalog$^\vee$ the notion of *answer set* [1] coincides to the notion of minimal model.

Let $\mathcal{P}$ be a Datalog$^\vee$ program and let $\mathcal{F}$ be a set of facts. Then, we denote by $\mathcal{P}_\mathcal{F}$ the program $\mathcal{P}_\mathcal{F} = \mathcal{P} \cup \mathcal{F}$. Given a query $\mathcal{Q}$ and an interpretation M of $\mathcal{P}$, $\vartheta(\mathcal{Q}, M)$ denotes the set containing each substitution ϕ for the variables in $\mathcal{Q}$ such that $\phi(\mathcal{Q})$ is true in M. The answer to a query $\mathcal{Q}$ over $\mathcal{P}_\mathcal{F}$, under the *brave* semantics, denoted by $Ans_b(\mathcal{Q}, \mathcal{P}_\mathcal{F})$, is the set $\cup_M \vartheta(\mathcal{Q}, M)$, such that $M \in \mathcal{MM}(\mathcal{P} \cup \mathcal{F})$. The answer to a query $\mathcal{Q}$ over the facts in $\mathcal{F}$, under the *cautious* semantics, denoted by $Ans_c(\mathcal{Q}, \mathcal{P}_\mathcal{F})$, is the set $\cap_M \vartheta(\mathcal{Q}, M)$, such that $M \in \mathcal{MM}(\mathcal{P} \cup \mathcal{F}) \neq \emptyset$. If $\mathcal{MM}(\mathcal{P} \cup \mathcal{F}) = \emptyset$, then all substitutions over the universe for variables in $\mathcal{Q}$ are in the cautious answer. Finally, we say that programs $\mathcal{P}$ and $\mathcal{P}'$ are *bravely* (resp. *cautiously*) *equivalent* w.r.t. $\mathcal{Q}$, denoted by $\mathcal{P} \equiv_{\mathcal{Q},b} \mathcal{P}'$ (resp. $\mathcal{P} \equiv_{\mathcal{Q},c} \mathcal{P}'$), if for any set $\mathcal{F}$ of facts $Ans_b(\mathcal{Q}, \mathcal{P}_\mathcal{F}) = Ans_b(\mathcal{Q}, \mathcal{P}'_\mathcal{F})$ (resp. $Ans_c(\mathcal{Q}, \mathcal{P}_\mathcal{F}) = Ans_c(\mathcal{Q}, \mathcal{P}'_\mathcal{F})$).

2.2   Magic-Set for Non-disjunctive Datalog Queries

We will illustrate how the Magic-Set method simulates the top-down evaluation of a query by considering the program consisting of the rules $\mathrm{path}(X, Y) :- \mathrm{edge}(X, Y).$ and $\mathrm{path}(X, Y) :- \mathrm{edge}(X, Z), \mathrm{path}(Z, Y).$ together with query $\mathrm{path}(1, 5)?$.

Adornment Step: The key idea is to materialize, by suitable *adornments*, binding information for IDB predicates which would be propagated during a top-down computation. These are strings of the letters b and f, denoting bound or free for each argument of an IDB predicate. First, adornments are created for query predicates. The adorned version of the query above is $\mathrm{path}^{bb}(1, 5)$.

The query adornments are then used to propagate their information into the body of the rules defining it, simulating a top-down evaluation. Obviously various strategies can be pursued concerning the order of processing the body atoms and the propagation of bindings. These are referred to as Sideways Information Passing Strategies (*SIPS*), cf. [9]. Any SIPS must guarantee an iterative processing of all body atoms in r. Let q be an atom that has not yet been processed, and v be the set of already considered atoms, then a SIPS specifies a propagation $v \rightarrow_\chi q$, where χ is the set of the variables bound by v, passing their values to q.

In the first rule of the example ($\mathrm{path}(X, Y) :- \mathrm{edge}(X, Y).$) a binding is only passed to the EDB predicate edge (which will not be adorned), yielding the adorned rule $\mathrm{path}^{bb}(X, Y) :- \mathrm{edge}(X, Y)$. In the second rule, $\mathrm{path}^{bb}(X, Y)$ passes its binding information to $\mathrm{edge}(X, Z)$ by $\mathrm{path}^{bb}(X, Y) \rightarrow_{\{X\}} \mathrm{edge}(X, Z)$. $\mathrm{edge}(X, Z)$ itself is not adorned, but it gives a binding to Z. Then, we consider $\mathrm{path}(Z, Y)$, for which we obtain the propagation $\mathrm{path}^{bb}(X, Y), \mathrm{edge}(X, Z) \rightarrow_{\{Y, Z\}} \mathrm{path}(Z, Y)$. This causes the generation of the adorned atom $\mathrm{path}^{bb}(Z, Y)$, and the resulting adorned rule is $\mathrm{path}^{bb}(X, Y) :- \mathrm{edge}(X, Z), \mathrm{path}^{bb}(Z, Y)$.

In general, adorning a rule may generate new adorned predicates. This step is repeated until all adorned predicates have been processed, yielding the *adorned program*, in our example it consists of the rules $\mathrm{path}^{bb}(X, Y) :- \mathrm{edge}(X, Y).$ and $\mathrm{path}^{bb}(X, Y) :- \mathrm{edge}(X, Z), \mathrm{path}^{bb}(Z, Y)$.

Generation Step: The adorned program is used to generate *magic rules*, which simulate the top-down evaluation scheme. Let the *magic version* ***magic***(p^α) for an adorned atom p^α be defined as $\texttt{magic\_}p^\alpha$ in which all arguments labeled f in α are eliminated.

Then, for each adorned atom p in the body of an adorned rule r_a, a magic rule r_m is generated such that (i) the head of r_m consists of ***magic***(p), and (ii) the body of r_m consists of the magic version of the head atom of r_a, followed by all of the predicates of r_a which can propagate the binding on p. In our example we generate $\texttt{magic\_path}^{bb}(Z, Y) \texttt{:- magic\_path}^{bb}(X, Y), \texttt{edge}(X, Z).$

Modification Step: The adorned rules are modified by including magic atoms generated in Step 2 in the rule bodies. The resultant rules are called *modified rules*. For each adorned rule whose head is h, we extend the rule body by inserting ***magic***(h). In our example, $\texttt{path}^{bb}(X, Y) \texttt{:- magic\_path}^{bb}(X, Y),\ \texttt{edge}(X, Y).$ and $\texttt{path}^{bb}(X, Y) \texttt{:-} \texttt{magic\_path}^{bb}(X, Y),\ \texttt{edge}(X, Z),\ \texttt{path}^{bb}(Z, Y).$ are generated.

Processing of the Query: For each adorned atom g^α of the query, (1) the *magic seed* ***magic***(g^α). is asserted, and (2) a rule g :- g^α is produced. In our example we generate $\texttt{magic\_path}^{bb}(1, 5).$ and $\texttt{path}(X, Y) \texttt{:-} \texttt{path}^{bb}(X, Y).$

The complete rewritten program consists of the magic, modified, and query rules. Given a non-disjunctive datalog program $\mathcal{P}$, a query $\mathcal{Q}$, and the rewritten program $\mathcal{P}'$, it is well known (see e.g. [7]) that $\mathcal{P}$ and $\mathcal{P}'$ are equivalent w.r.t. $\mathcal{Q}$, i.e., $\mathcal{P} \equiv_{\mathcal{Q},b} \mathcal{P}'$ and $\mathcal{P} \equiv_{\mathcal{Q},c} \mathcal{P}'$ hold (since brave and cautious semantics coincide for non-disjunctive datalog programs).

3 Magic-Set Method for Disjunctive Datalog Programs

In this section we present the Disjunctive Magic-Set algorithm (short. DMS) for the optimization of disjunctive datalog programs, which has been implemented and integrated into the DLV system [4]. Before discussing the details of the algorithm, we informally present the main ideas that have been exploited for enabling the Magic-Set method to work on disjunctive programs.

3.1 Binding Propagation in Datalog$^\vee$ Programs: Some Key Issues

As first observed in [13], while in nondisjunctive programs bindings are propagated only head-to-body, any sound rewriting for disjunctive programs has to propagate bindings also head-to-head in order to preserve soundness. Roughly, suppose that a predicate p is relevant for the query, and a disjunctive rule r contains p(X) in the head. Then, besides propagating the binding from p(X) to the body of r (as in the nondisjunctive case), a sound rewriting has to propagate the binding also from p(X) to the other head atoms of r. Consider, for instance, a Datalog$^\vee$ program $\mathcal{P}$ containing rule $p(X) \lor q(Y) \texttt{:-} a(X, Y), r(X).$ and the query p(1)?. Even though the query propagates the binding for the predicate p, in order to correctly answer the query, we also need to evaluate the truth value of q(Y), which indirectly receives the binding through the body predicate a(X, Y). For instance, suppose that the program contains facts a(1, 2), and r(1); then atom q(2) is relevant for query p(1)? (i.e., it should belong to the magic set of the query), since the truth of q(2) would invalidate the derivation of p(1) from the above rule, because of the minimality of the semantics. It follows that, while propagating the binding, the head atoms of disjunctive rules must be all adorned as well.

However, the adornment of the head of one disjunctive rule r may give rise to multiple rules, having different adornments for the head predicates. This process can be somehow seen as "splitting" r in multiple rules. While this is not a problem in the nondisjunctive case, the semantics of a disjunctive program may be affected. Consider, for instance, the program $p(X, Y) \lor q(Y, X) :- a(X, Y)$. in which p and q are mutually exclusive (due to minimality), since they do not appear in any other rule head. Assuming the adornments p^{bf} and q^{bf} to be propagated, we might obtain rules whose heads have the form $p^{bf}(X, Y) \lor q^{fb}(Y, X)$ (derived while propagating p^{bf}) and $p^{fb}(X, Y) \lor q^{bf}(Y, X)$ (derived while propagating q^{bf}). These rules could support two atoms $p^{bf}(m, n)$ and $q^{bf}(n, m)$, while in the original program $p(m, n)$ and $p(n, m)$ could not hold simultaneously (due to semantic minimality), thus changing the original semantics.

The method proposed in [13] circumvents this problem by using some auxiliary predicates which collect all facts coming from the different adornments. For instance, in the above example, two rules of the form `collect_p(X, Y) :- p^{fb}(X, Y)`. and `collect_p(X, Y) :- p^{bf}(X, Y)`. are added for predicate p. The main drawback of this approach is that collecting predicates, while resolving the semantic problem, bloat the program with additional rules reducing the gain of the optimization.

A relevant advantage of our algorithm (confirmed also by an experimental analysis) is that we do not use collecting predicates; rather, we preserve the correct semantics by stripping off the adornments from non-magic predicates in modified rules. Other computational advantages come from our adornment technique, which is obtained by extending non-disjunctive SIPS to the disjunctive case.

3.2 DMS Algorithm

The salient feature of our algorithm is that we generate modified and magic rules on a rule-by-rule basis. To this end, we exploit a stack S of predicates for storing all the adorned predicates to be used for propagating the binding of the query: At each step, an element is removed from S, and each defining rule is processed at a time. Thus, adorned rules do not have to be stored.

The algorithm DMS (see Figure 1) implements the Magic-Set method for disjunctive programs. Its input is a disjunctive datalog program $\mathcal{P}$ and a query $\mathcal{Q}$. Note that the algorithm can be used for non-disjunctive rules as a special case. If the query contains some non-free IDB predicates, it outputs a (optimized) program $\mathrm{DMS}(\mathcal{Q}, \mathcal{P})$ consisting of a set of *modified* and *magic* rules, stored by means of the sets *modifiedRules*$(\mathcal{Q}, \mathcal{P})$ and *magicRules*$(\mathcal{Q}, \mathcal{P})$, respectively. The main steps of the algorithm DMS are illustrated by means of the following running example.

Example 1 (Strategic Companies [14]). We are given a collection C of companies producing some goods in a set G, such that each company $c_i \in C$ is controlled by a set of other companies $O_i \subseteq C$. A subset of the companies $C' \subset C$ is a *strategic set* set if it is a minimal set of companies producing all the goods in G, such that if $O_i \subseteq C'$ for

```
Input:   A Datalog∨ program P, and a query Q = g₁(t₁),...,gₙ(tₙ).
Output:  The optimized program DMS(Q, P).
var  S: stack of adorned predicates; modifiedRules(Q, P), magicRules(Q, P): set of rules;
begin
  1. if g₁(t₁),...,gₙ(tₙ) has some IDB predicate then
  2.    modifiedRules(Q, P):=∅; ⟨S, magicRules(Q, P)⟩:=BuildQuerySeeds(Q);
  3.    while S ≠ ∅ do
  4.        pᵅ:=S.pop();
  5.        for each rule r ∈ P: p(t) v p₁(t₁) v ... v pₙ(tₙ) :- q₁(s₁),...,qₘ(sₘ) do
  6.            rₐ:=Adorn(r,pᵅ,S);
  7.            magicRules(Q, P) := magicRules(Q, P) ⋃ Generate(rₐ);
  8.            modifiedRules(Q, P) := modifiedRules(Q, P) ⋃ {Modify(rₐ)};
  9.        end for
 10.    end while
 11.    DMS(Q, P):=magicRules(Q, P) ⋃ modifiedRules(Q, P);
 12.  return DMS(Q, P);
 13. end if
end.
```

Fig. 1. Disjunctive Magic-Set Method

some $i = 1, \ldots, m$ then $c_i \in C'$ must hold. This scenario can be modelled by means of the following program $\mathcal{P}_{sc}$.

$r_1 :$ sc(C_1) v sc(C_2) :- produced_ by(P, C_1, C_2).
$r_2 :$ sc(C) :- controlled_ by(C, C_1, C_2, C_3), sc(C_1), sc(C_2), sc(C_3).

Moreover, given a company $c \in C$, we consider a query $\mathcal{Q}_{sc} = $ sc(c) asking whether c belongs to some strategic set of C.   □

The computation starts in step 2 by initializing $modifiedRules(Q, P)$ to the empty set. Then, the function **BuildQuerySeeds** is used for storing in $magicRules(Q, P)$ the magic seeds, and pushing on the stack S the adorned predicates of Q. Note that we do not generate any query rules, because the transformed program will not contain adornments.

Example 2. Given the query $\mathcal{Q}_{sc} = $ sc(c) and the program $\mathcal{P}_{sc}$, **BuildQuerySeeds** creates magic_sc^b(c). and pushes sc^b onto the stack S.   □

The core of the technique (steps 4-9) is repeated until the stack S is empty, i.e., until there is no further adorned predicate to be propagated. Specifically, an adorned predicate p^α is removed from the stack S in step 4, and its binding is propagated in each (disjunctive) rule r in $\mathcal{P}$ of the form

$r :$ p(t) v p₁(t₁) v ... v pₙ(tₙ) :- q₁(s₁), ..., qₘ(sₘ).

with n ≥ 0, having an atom p(t) in the head (step 5).
Adorn. Step 6 performs the adornment of the rule. Different from the case of non-disjunctive programs, the binding of the predicate p^α needs to be also propagated to the atoms p₁(t₁),...,pₙ(tₙ) in the head. We achieve this by defining an extension of any non-disjunctive SIPS to the disjunctive case. The constraint for such a disjunctive SIPS is that head atoms (different from p(t)) cannot provide variable bindings, they can only *receive* bindings (similarly to negative literals in standard SIPS). So they should

be processed only once all their variables are bound or do not occur in yet unprocessed body atoms[2]. Moreover they cannot make any of their free-variables bound.

The function ***Adorn*** produces an adorned disjunctive rule from an adorned predicate and a suitable unadorned rule by employing the refined SIPS, pushing all newly adorned predicates onto S. Hence, in step 6 the rule r_a is of the form

$$r_a : \; p^{\alpha}(t) \; \vee \; p_1^{\alpha_1}(t_1) \; \ldots \; p_n^{\alpha_n}(t_n) :- q_1^{\beta_1}(s_1), \ldots, q_m^{\beta_m}(s_m).$$

Example 3. Consider again Example 1. When sc^b is removed from the stack, we first select rule r_1 and the head predicate $sc(C_1)$. Then, the adorned version is

$$r'_{1_a} : \; sc^b(C_1) \; \vee \; sc^b(C_2) :- \text{produced\_by}(P, C_1, C_2).$$

Next r_1 is processed again, this time with head predicate $sc(C_2)$, producing

$$r''_{1_a} : \; sc^b(C_2) \; \vee \; sc^b(C_1) :- \text{produced\_by}(P, C_1, C_2).$$

and finally, processing r_2 we obtain

$$r_{2_a} : \; sc^b(C) :- \text{controlled\_by}(C, C_1, C_2, C_3), \; sc^b(C_1), \; sc^b(C_2), \; sc^b(C_3).$$

$\square$

Generate. The algorithm uses the adorned rule r_a for generating and collecting the magic rules in step 7. Since r_a is a disjunctive rule, ***Generate*** first produces a non-disjunctive intermediate rule by moving head atoms into the body. Then, the standard technique for Datalog rules, as described in *Generation Step* in Section 2, is applied.

Example 4. In the program of Example 3, from the rule r'_{1_a} first its non-disjunctive intermediate rule

$$sc^b(C_1) :- sc^b(C_2), \text{produced\_by}(P, C_1, C_2).$$

is produced, from which the magic rule

$$\text{magic\_}sc^b(C_2) :- \text{magic\_}sc^b(C_1), \; \text{produced\_by}(P, C_1, C_2).$$

is generated. Similarly, from the rule r''_{1_a} we obtain

$$\text{magic\_}sc^b(C_1) :- \text{magic\_}sc^b(C_2), \; \text{produced\_by}(P, C_1, C_2).$$

and finally r_{2_a} gives rise to the following rules

$$\text{magic\_}sc^b(C_1) :- \text{magic\_}sc^b(C), \; \text{controlled\_by}(C, C_1, C_2, C_3).$$
$$\text{magic\_}sc^b(C_2) :- \text{magic\_}sc^b(C), \; \text{controlled\_by}(C, C_1, C_2, C_3).$$
$$\text{magic\_}sc^b(C_3) :- \text{magic\_}sc^b(C), \; \text{controlled\_by}(C, C_1, C_2, C_3).$$

$\square$

---

[2] Recall that the safety constraint guarantees that each variable of a head atom also appears in some positive body-atom.

Modify. In step *8* the modified rules are generated and collected. The only difference to the non-disjunctive case is that the adornments are stripped off the original atoms – see Section 3.1. Hence, the function *Modify* constructs a rule of the following form

$$p(t) \lor p_1(t_1) \lor \dots \lor p_n(t_n) \; :\text{-} \; \textbf{\textit{magic}}(p^\alpha(t)), \textbf{\textit{magic}}(p_1^{\alpha_1}(t_1)), \dots, \textbf{\textit{magic}}(p_n^{\alpha_n}(t_n)),$$
$$q_1(s_1), \dots, q_m(s_m).$$

Finally, after all the adorned predicates have been processed the algorithm outputs the program $\text{DMS}(\mathcal{Q}, \mathcal{P})$.

Example 5. In our running example, we derive the following set of modified rules:

$r'_{1_m} :\; \text{sc}(C_1) \; \text{v} \; \text{sc}(C_2) :\text{-}\, \text{magic\_sc}^b(C_1),\, \text{magic\_sc}^b(C_2),\, \text{produced\_by}(P, C_1, C_2).$
$r''_{1_m} :\; \text{sc}(C_2) \; \text{v} \; \text{sc}(C_1) :\text{-}\, \text{magic\_sc}^b(C_2),\, \text{magic\_sc}^b(C_1),\, \text{produced\_by}(P, C_1, C_2).$
$r_{2_m} :\; \text{sc}(C) :\text{-}\, \text{magic\_sc}^b(C),\, \text{controlled\_by}(C, C_1, C_2, C_3),\, \text{sc}(C_1),\, \text{sc}(C_2),\, \text{sc}(C_3).$

where r'_{1_m} (resp. r''_{1_m}, r_{2_m}) is derived by adding magic predicates and stripping off adornments for the rule r'_{1_a} (resp. r''_{1_a}, r_{2_a}). Thus, the optimized program $\text{DMS}(\mathcal{Q}_{sc}, \mathcal{P}_{cs})$ comprises the above modified rules as well as the magic rules in Example 4, and the magic seed $\text{magic\_sc}^b(c)$. □

3.3 Query Equivalence Results

We conclude the presentation of the DMS algorithm by formally proving its soundness. To this aim proofs in [13] cannot be reused, due to the many differences w.r.t. our approach. The result is shown by first establishing a relationship between the minimal models of the program $\text{DMS}(\mathcal{Q}, \mathcal{P})$ and of the program $rel(\mathcal{Q}, \mathcal{P})$ constructed as follows.

Given a set $\mathcal{S}$ of ground rules of $\mathcal{P}$, we denote by $\mathbf{R}(\mathcal{S})$ the set $\{r \in ground(\mathcal{P}) \mid \exists r' \in \mathcal{S}, \exists q \in B(r') \cup H(r') \text{ s.t. } q \in H(r)\}$. Then, $rel(\mathcal{Q}, \mathcal{P})$ is the least fixed point of the following succession $rel_0(\mathcal{Q}, \mathcal{P}) = \{r \in ground(\mathcal{P}) \mid \exists ground(q) \in Q \cap H(r)\}$, and $rel_{i+1}(\mathcal{Q}, \mathcal{P}) = \mathbf{R}(rel_i(\mathcal{Q}, \mathcal{P}))$, for each $i > 0$.

Notice that the correspondence between the models of $\text{DMS}(\mathcal{Q}, \mathcal{P})$ and of $rel(\mathcal{Q}, \mathcal{P})$ can be established by focusing on non-magic atoms only. Thus, we next exploit the following notation. Given a model M and a predicate symbol g, we denote by $M[g]$ the set of atoms in M whose predicate symbol is g. Then, $M[\mathcal{P}]$ denotes the set of atoms in M whose predicate symbol appears in the head of some rule of $\mathcal{P}$. Finally, given a set of interpretations S, let $S[g] = \{M[g] | M \in S\}$ and $S[\mathcal{P}] = \{M[\mathcal{P}] | M \in S\}$.

Lemma 1. *Given a Datalog$^\lor$ program $\mathcal{P}$, and a query $\mathcal{Q}$. Then, it holds that $\forall M' \in \mathcal{MM}(\text{DMS}(\mathcal{Q}, \mathcal{P}))$, and $\exists M \in \mathcal{MM}(rel(\mathcal{Q}, \mathcal{P}))$ s.t. $M = M'[rel(\mathcal{Q}, \mathcal{P})]$.*

Lemma 2. *Given a Datalog$^\lor$ program $\mathcal{P}$, and a query $\mathcal{Q}$. Then, it holds that $\forall M \in \mathcal{MM}(rel(\mathcal{Q}, \mathcal{P}))$, and $\exists M' \in \mathcal{MM}(\text{DMS}(\mathcal{Q}, \mathcal{P}))$ s.t. $M = M'[rel(\mathcal{Q}, \mathcal{P})]$.*

Armed with the above results, we can prove the following.

Theorem 1 (Soundness of the DMS Algorithm). *Let $\mathcal{P}$ be a Datalog$^\lor$ program, let $\mathcal{Q}$ be a query. Then, $\text{DMS}(\langle \mathcal{Q}, \mathcal{P} \rangle) \equiv_{\mathcal{Q}, b} \mathcal{P}$ and $\text{DMS}(\langle \mathcal{Q}, \mathcal{P} \rangle) \equiv_{\mathcal{Q}, c} \mathcal{P}$ hold.*

Proof (Sketch). Let $\overline{rel}(Q, P)$ denote the set $ground(P) - rel(Q, P)$. After lemmas 1 and 2, it suffices to prove that $rel(Q, P) \equiv_{Q,b} P$ and $rel(Q, P) \equiv_{Q,c} P$. In fact, we can show that $ground(P)$ is partitioned into two modules (see definitions and notations in [2]), i.e., $rel(Q, P) \rhd \overline{rel}(Q, P)$, that can be hierarchically evaluated. Thus, the models of P are such that $\mathcal{MM}(P) = \bigcup_M \mathcal{MM}(M \cup \overline{rel}(Q, P))$, for each $M \in \mathcal{MM}(rel(Q, P))$, where for the sake of simplicity the model M is also used for denoting the set of the corresponding ground facts in it.

The results follows by observing that for each predicate q in Q, $\mathcal{MM}(P)[q] = (\mathcal{MM}(P)[rel(Q, P)])[q]$. In fact, we can show that $\mathcal{MM}(P)[rel(Q, P)] = \mathcal{MM}(rel(Q, P))$. Then, it suffices to observe that for each predicate q in Q, the set of ground rules having q in the head is in $rel_0(Q, P) \subseteq rel(Q, P)$.   □

4 Redundant Rules: Prevention and Checking

Both the DMS method described above and APM of [13] have a common drawback: Numerous redundant rules may be generated, which can deteriorate the optimization. For instance, in Example 5 the first two modified rules coincide, and this might happen even if the two head predicates differ. We stress that our rewriting algorithm already drastically reduces the impact of such phenomena, as it does not introduce additional predicates and rules (apart from magic rules). Nevertheless, since this aspect is crucial for the optimization process, we next devise some strategies for further reducing the overhead.

Let P be a disjunctive datalog program, and let r_1 and r_2 be two rules of P. Then, r_1 is *subsumed* by r_2 (denoted by $r_1 \sqsubseteq r_2$) if there exists a substitution ϑ for $H(r_2) \cup B(r_2)$, such that $\vartheta(H(r_2)) \subseteq H(r_1)$ and $\vartheta(B(r_2)) \subseteq B(r_1)$. Finally, a rule r_1 is *redundant* if there exists a rule r_2 such that $r_1 \sqsubseteq r_2$. Unfortunately, deciding whether a rule is subsumed by another rule is a hard task:

Theorem 2. *Let P be a disjunctive datalog program, and let r_1 and r_2 be two rules of P. Then, the problem of deciding whether $r_1 \sqsubseteq r_2$ is NP-complete in the number of variables of r_1 (program complexity). Hardness holds even for $B(r_1) = B(r_2) = \emptyset$.*

The above result strongly motivates the design of methods for preventing the generation of redundant rules as well as of polynomial time heuristics for their identification. The latter aspect is also of interest outside the context of the Magic-Set method.

4.1 Prevention of Redundant Rules

There are two typical situations in which redundant rules may be generated: **(S1)** when adorning a disjunctive rule with two predicates having the same adornment and arguments, and **(S2)** when adorning a rule with an adorned predicate, which stems solely from a previous adornment of the same rule.

Example 6. **(S1)** Assume that the adorned predicates p^b and s^b are used for propagating the binding in the rule $p(X)$ v $s(X)$:- $a(X)$. Then, both of the modified rules will eventually result in $s(X)$ v $p(X)$:- $magic\_s^b(X)$, $magic\_p^b(X)$, $a(X)$.   □

The source of the redundancy lies in the fact that disjunctive rules may be adorned by two distinct predicates (s^b and p^b in the example) sharing the same bound variables.

Example 7. **(S2)** Consider the rule $s(X, Z) \lor p(X, Y) :- a(X), b(Y), c(Z)$. and the query $s(1, 2)$?. By adorning with s^{bb} we obtain the modified rule

$$r_1 : s(X, Z) \lor p(X, Y) :- \texttt{magic\_s}^{bb}(X, Z), \texttt{magic\_p}^{bf}(X), a(X), b(Y), c(Z).$$

and p^{bf} is pushed onto the stack, which gives rise to

$$r_2 : s(X, Z) \lor p(X, Y) :- \texttt{magic\_s}^{bf}(X), \texttt{magic\_p}^{bf}(X), a(X), b(Y), c(Z).$$

which is not syntactically subsumed by nor subsumes r_1.

Nonetheless, if p^{bf} is generated only by the above rule, then r_2 will add no significant information as for the relevance of s^{bf}, as it would propagate to s^{bf} the same binding it had received from predicate s itself. Conversely, if the predicate p^{bf} is eventually generated by some other rules, then it must also be considered for adorning the above rule, since it may provide additional new information.   □

Situation **S1** is easy to implement: In the function **Generate** we add a check whether the creation of the modified rule is necessary. Let $r : p_1(t_1) \lor \ldots \lor p_n(t_n) :- q_1(s_1), \ldots, q_m(s_m)$. be a disjunctive rule, and p_i^α be an adorned predicate that has already been used for generating the modified rule r_m. Then, any other adorned predicate $p_j^{\alpha'}$ such that (i) p_j has the same arguments of p_i and (ii) each argument of p_i has the same adornment in α and α', will generate for r a modified rule r'_m with $r'_m \sqsubseteq r_m$.

This check can be implemented by storing for each adorned predicate the set of rules it has already adorned, and it can be proven to be sound and complete.

Situation **S2** requires more effort. It implies that an adorned predicate should not always be applied to the whole program. To achieve this, we associate a *target* to each adorned predicate. The first time a predicate p^α is pushed on the stack, it is marked for being used for adorning all the rules but the one that has generated it; this target is termed *allButSource*. Then, if at a certain point p^α is generated again, then two situations may occur:

- if p^α has been marked *allButSource* and already used for adorning the program (hence has been removed from the stack), then the new predicate will be inserted in the stack by marking it for adorning only the rule which was the source of the first generation of p^α (that has not been adorned yet); such a target is called *onlySource*.
- if p^α has been not yet used, then it is simply marked for being used for adorning all the program, giving rise to target *all*.

In the implementation we associate to each adorned predicate also the rule that generated it. Then, we modify step *6* in Fig. 1 as follows. A rule r considered for being adorned with a predicate p^α is actually adorned if and only if (i) the target of p^α is *onlySource* and r has generated the adornment p^α, or (ii) the target of p^α is *allButSource* and r has not generated the adornment p^α, or (iii) the target of p^α is *all*.

Due to space limits, we omit the correctness proofs of the above solutions.

4.2   Identifying Redundant Rules

Even though the above strategies may significantly reduce the redundancy within the rewritten program, we also exploit a (post-processing) technique for identifying those redundant rules whose generation could not be prevented. Specifically, we implemented a heuristic for rule subsumption checking that has been integrated into the core of the DLV system, and that can be invoked to identify redundancy in any type of program. The heuristic is based on the following observation.

Proposition 1. *Let r_1 and r_2 be two disjunctive rules. Then, r_1 subsumes r_2 if and only if there exists an ordering of all the atoms in $H(r_1) \cup B(r_1)$ of the form $l_1, \ldots, l_m$ and a sequence of substitutions $\vartheta_1, \ldots, \vartheta_m$, such that for each $l_i \in B(r_1)$ (resp. $l_i \in H(r_1)$), there exists $l_i' \in B(r_2)$ (resp. $l_i' \in H(r_2)$) with $(\vartheta_1 \cup \ldots \cup \vartheta_{i-1})(l_i) = \{l_i'\}$.*

Roughly, we try to construct the sequence $l_1, \ldots, l_m$ of the above proposition and the associated substitutions $\vartheta_1, \ldots, \vartheta_m$ in an incremental way. At each step i, we choose an atom l_i in r_1 which has not yet been processed such that there exists a candidate l_i' in r_2 for being subsumed. Moreover, if many atoms in r_i satisfy the above condition, we greedily select the one which subsumes the maximum number of atoms, and among these we prefer those with the maximum number of distinct variables not yet matched.

5   Experimental Results

5.1   Compared Methods, Benchmark Problems and Data

In order to evaluate the impact of the proposed methods, we compare DMS and ODMS both with the traditional DLV evaluation without *Magic-Sets* and with the APM method proposed in [13]. For the comparison, we consider the following benchmark problems that have been already used to assess APM in [13] (see therein for more details):

- *Simple Path:* Given a directed graph G and two nodes a and b, does there exist a unique path connecting a to b in G? The graph is the same as the one reported in [13], and the instances are generated by varying the number of nodes.
- *Ancestor:* Given a genealogy graph storing information of relationship (father/ brother) among people and given two persons p_1 and p_2, is p_1 an ancestor of p_2? The structure of the "genealogy" graph is the same as the one presented in [13], and the instances are generated by varying the number of nodes, i.e., the number of persons, in the graph.
- *Strategic Companies:* The problem has been formalized in Example 1. The instances are generated according to the ideas presented in [13], by grouping the companies in suitable clusters. Let G be the cluster such that c is in G. Then, the instances are generated with $|G| = 250$, while the number of companies outside G is varied.

5.2   Results and Discussion

The experiments have been performed on Pentium III machines running GNU/Linux. The DLV prototype used was compiled with GCC 2.95. For every instance, we have allowed a maximum running time of 1800 seconds (half an hour) and a maximum memory usage of 256MB. On all problems, DMS outperforms APM, even without considering the time for the rewriting needed in [13], which is also not reported in the figures.

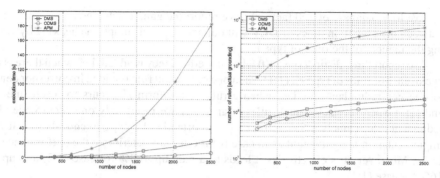

Fig. 2. *Simple Path:* Execution time *(Left)* and Number of rules instances *(Right)*

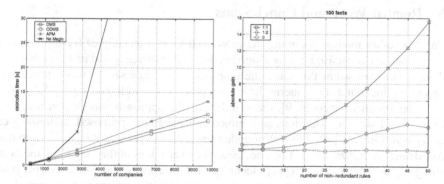

Fig. 3. Timing in *Strategic Companies (Left)* and Impact of subsumption checking *(Right)*

The results for *Simple Path* are reported in Figure 2. The diagram on the left shows that DMS scales much better than APM on this problem and that ODMS provides additional speed-up. The main reason can be understood by looking at the right diagram, in which the numbers of ground rules are reported: The overhead of the auxiliary rules for APM is evident, it generates about 25 times more rules than DMS. We did not include pure DLV (No Magic) in the diagrams, as it is dramatically slower; e.g. the instance with 255 nodes takes about 195 seconds. Finally, the experimental results for *Ancestor* are very similar to the ones for *Simple Path*.

On the left of Figure 3 we report the results for *Strategic Companies*. The advantages of the Magic-Set method (in both implementations) are evident. Anyhow, we can see that APM performs and scales worse than DMS, while ODMS provides even better performance *and* scaling.

Finally, on the right of Figure 3, we report a more detailed analysis on the impact of subsumption checking. In particular, we want to check whether the application of subsumption checking is computationally heavy (how much performance gets worse in a bad case where no redundant rule is identified). To this end, we test a program with two types of rules, specifically r_i : $p_i(X) \vee q_i(X) :\text{-} a(X), b(X).$ and r_i' : $p_i(X) \vee q_i(X) :\text{-} a(X).$, where a and b are *EDB* predicates, and where each rule of the form r_i is subsumed by a rule of the form r_i'.

We fix a database of 100 facts, and we report the gain, calculated as the difference between the execution times of DLV without and with subsumption checking by varying the number of the rules of type r_i.

We report three distinct runs: (0) when no redundancy is added, i.e., when there is no occurrence of rules of type r_i', (1:1) when one redundant rule is added in correspondence to one non-redundant one, i.e., when a rule of the form r_i' occurs for each rule r_i, and (1:2) when for each pair of rules r_i and r_{i+1} we insert only one occurrence of a redundant rule, namely either r_i' or r_{i+1}'. Importantly, the experiments show that the implementation is lightweight as in case (0) it does not deteriorate the performance of DLV. Moreover, it is effective as it leads to a gain up to 3% for case (1:2) and up to 16% for case (1:1).

6 Related Work and Conclusions

The Magic-Set method is among the most well-known techniques for the optimization of positive recursive Datalog programs due to its efficiency and its generality, even though other focused methods, e.g. the supplementary magic set and other special techniques for linear and chain queries have been proposed as well (see, e.g., [15, 7, 16]).

After seminal papers [8, 9], the viability of the approach was demonstrated e.g. in [17, 18]. Later on, extensions and refinements have been proposed, addressing e.g. query constraints in [10], the well-founded semantics in [11], or integration into cost-based query optimization in [12]. The research on variations of the Magic-Set method is still going on. For instance, in [19] a technique for the class of *soft-stratifiable* programs is given, and in [13] an elaborated technique for disjunctive programs is described.

In this paper, we have elaborated on the issues addressed in [13]. Our approach is similar in spirit to APM, but differs in several respects:

– DMS avoids the use of auxiliary predicates needed for APM, yielding a significant computational benefit.
– DMS is a flexible framework for enhancements and optimizations, as it proceeds in a localized fashion by analyzing one rule at time, while APM processes the whole program at time.
– ODMS extends DMS by employing effective methods for avoiding the generation of and for identifying still left-over redundant rules.
– ODMS has been integrated into the DLV system [4], profitably exploiting the DLV internal datastructures and the ability of controlling the grounding module.
– We could experimentally show that our ODMS implementation outperforms APM on benchmarks taken from the literature.

It has been noted (e.g. in [11]) that in the non-disjunctive case, memoing techniques lead to similar computations as evaluations after Magic-Set transformations. Also in the disjunctive case such techniques have been proposed, e.g. Hyper Tableaux [20], for which a similar relationship might hold. However, we leave this issue for future research, and follow [11] in noting that an advantage of Magic-Sets over such methods is that they can be more easily combined with other database optimization techniques.

Concerning future work, our objective is to extend the Magic-Set method to the case of disjunctive programs with constraints and unstratified negation, such that it can be fruitfully applied on arbitrary DLV programs. We believe that the framework developed in this paper is general enough to be extended to these more involved cases.

References

1. Gelfond, M., Lifschitz, V.: Classical Negation in Logic Programs and Disjunctive Databases. New Generation Computing **9** (1991) 365–385
2. Eiter, T., Gottlob, G., Mannila, H.: Disjunctive Datalog. ACM TODS **22** (1997) 364–418
3. Eiter, T., Faber, W., Leone, N., Pfeifer, G.: Declarative Problem-Solving Using the DLV System. In Minker, J., ed.: Logic-Based Artificial Intelligence. Kluwer (2000) 79–103
4. Leone, N., Pfeifer, G., Faber, W., Eiter, T., Gottlob, G., Perri, S., Scarcello, F.: The DLV System for Knowledge Representation and Reasoning (2004) To appear. Available via http://www.arxiv.org/ps/cs.AI/0211004.
5. Janhunen, T., Niemelä, I., Simons, P., You, J.H.: Partiality and Disjunctions in Stable Model Semantics. In: KR 2000, April 12-15, Morgan Kaufmann (2000) 411–419
6. Arieli, O., Denecker, M., Van Nuffelen, B., Bruynooghe, M.: Database repair by signed formulae. In: FoIKS 2004. LNCS 2942., Springer (2004) 14–30
7. Ullman, J.D.: Principles of Database and Knowledge Base Systems. Computer Science Press (1989)
8. Bancilhon, F., Maier, D., Sagiv, Y., Ullman, J.D.: Magic Sets and Other Strange Ways to Implement Logic Programs. In: PODS'86. (1986) 1–16
9. Beeri, C., Ramakrishnan, R.: On the power of magic. JLP **10** (1991) 255–259
10. Syuckey, P.J., Sudarshan, S.: Compiling query constraints. In: PODS'94, ACM Press (1994) 56–67
11. Kemp, D.B., Srivastava, D., Stuckey, P.J.: Bottom-up evaluation and query optimization of well-founded models. Theoretical Computer Science **146** (1995) 145–184
12. Seshadri, P., Hellerstein, J.M., Pirahesh, H., Leung, T.Y.C., Ramakrishnan, R., Srivastava, D., Stuckey, P.J., Sudarshan, S.: Cost-based optimization for magic: Algebra and implementation. In: SIGMOD Conference 1996, ACM Press (1996) 435–446
13. Greco, S.: Binding Propagation Techniques for the Optimization of Bound Disjunctive Queries. IEEE TKDE **15** (2003) 368–385
14. Cadoli, M., Eiter, T., Gottlob, G.: Default Logic as a Query Language. IEEE TKDE **9** (1997) 448–463
15. Greco, S., Saccà, D., Zaniolo, C.: The PushDown Method to Optimize Chain Logic Programs (Extended Abstract). In: ICALP'95. (1995) 523–534
16. Ramakrishnan, R., Sagiv, Y., Ullman, J.D., Vardi, M.Y.: Logical Query Optimization by Proof-Tree Transformation. JCSS **47** (1993) 222–248
17. Gupta, A., Mumick, I.S.: Magic-sets Transformation in Nonrecursive Systems. In: PODS'92. (1992) 354–367
18. Mumick, I.S., Finkelstein, S.J., Pirahesh, H., Ramakrishnan, R.: Magic is relevant. In: SIGMOD Conference 1990. (1990) 247–258
19. Behrend, A.: Soft stratification for magic set based query evaluation in deductive databases. In: PODS 2003, ACM Press (2003) 102–110
20. Baumgartner, P., Furbach, U., Niemelä, I.: Hyper Tableaux. In: JELIA'96. LNCS 1126, Springer (1996) 1–17

Rectilinear Steiner Tree Construction Using Answer Set Programming

Esra Erdem[1] and Martin D.F. Wong[2]

[1] Institut für Informationssysteme 184/3,
Technische Universität Wien, 1040 Wien, Austria
esra@kr.tuwien.ac.at
[2] Department of Electrical and Computer Engineering
University of Illinois at Urbana-Champaign, Urbana, IL 61801, USA
mdfwong@uiuc.edu

Abstract. We introduce a new method for Rectilinear Steiner Tree (RST) construction in a graph, using answer set programming. This method provides a formal representation of the problem as a logic program whose answer sets correspond to solutions. The answer sets for a logic program can be computed by special systems called answer set solvers. We describe the method for RST construction in the context of VLSI routing where multiple pins in a given placement of a chip are connected by an RST. Our method is different from the existing methods mainly in three ways. First, it always correctly determines whether a given RST routing problem is solvable, and it always produces a solution if one exists. Second, some enhancements of the basic problem, in which lengths of wires connecting the source pin to sink pins are restricted, can be easily represented by adding some rules. Our method guarantees to find a tree if one exists, even when the total wire length is not minimum. Third, routing problems with the presence of obstacles can be solved. With this approach, we have computed solutions to some RST routing problems using the answer set solver CMODELS.

1 Introduction

The Steiner tree problem is a combinatorial search problem that asks for a connected graph spanning a given set of points such that the total "length" of edges is minimum. In this paper, we consider a variation of Steiner trees whose edges are composed of horizontal or vertical line segments. Such a Steiner tree is called a Rectilinear Steiner Tree (RST) [1]. Here the length of an edge is the number of segments contained in that edge. This problem is NP-complete [2]. The computational problem we are interested in is to construct an RST connecting a set of given vertices in an undirected graph in the presence of obstacles. Consider, for instance, the tree shown in Figure 1 that connects all points labeled $p0, \dots, p30$ without passing through the obstacles, shown in black. Since the total number of segments covered by this tree is minimum, this tree is an RST.

B. Demoen and V. Lifschitz (Eds.): ICLP 2004, LNCS 3132, pp. 386–399, 2004.

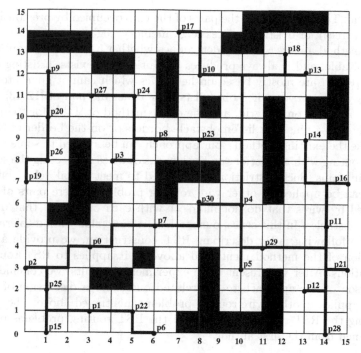

Fig. 1. An RST routing problem along with its solution.

We introduce a new method for RST construction using answer set programming (ASP) [3–5] – a declarative programming methodology that can be used to solve combinatorial search problems. The idea of ASP is to represent a given computational problem as a logic program whose answer sets (stable models) [6, 7] correspond to solutions to the given problem. Systems that compute answer sets for a logic program are called answer set solvers. For instance, SMODELS with its front-end LPARSE[1] is one of the answer set solvers that are currently available. System CMODELS[2] is another answer set solver, and it also uses LPARSE as its front-end. In the main part of this paper, we assume that the reader has some familiarity with the language of LPARSE [4].

We describe the RST construction problem as a logic program in the language of LPARSE, and use the answer set solver CMODELS to compute solutions. For instance, the solution presented in Figure 1 is computed using CMODELS.

In this paper, we consider RST construction in the context of VLSI routing. Automatic routing of wires has been the premier application of RSTs since Hanan's original paper [8]. (See [9] for the work on RST routing applications). The problem shown in Figure 1 can be viewed as a routing problem where multiple "pins", i.e., $p0, \ldots, p30$, are connected via an RST. This problem differs from other RST routing applications studied earlier in that there are obstacles

---

[1] http://www.tcs.hut.fi/Software/smodels/
[2] http://www.cs.utexas.edu/users/tag/cmodels/

on the grid. The obstacles are the parts of the chip occupied by previously routed nets (i.e., trees), or existing devices (e.g., memory, registers).

Our method always correctly determines whether a given RST routing problem is solvable, and it always produces a solution if it exists. Existing methods such as [10, 11] are mostly based on heuristics which cannot guarantee finding a routing solution even when one exists. The exact method of [12, 13] does not consider obstacles on the grid, and the exact method of [14] is for the problems with only 3 or 4 pins that lie on obstacle borders or on the border of the grid.

Unlike the existing methods, our approach can be applied to some variations of RST routing with restrictions on the lengths of wires connecting the source pin to the sink pins. Such restrictions are needed to meet signal delay constraints. It also can be applied to other wire routing problems where pairs of pins are connected by wires that do not intersect with each other and that do not go through obstacles. In this sense, our method is more elaboration tolerant [15].

In the following, after describing RST construction, we provide a detailed description of the method mentioned above as it applies to RST routing and its variations. After we present some experimental results, we conclude with a comparison of our approach to the related ones, and a discussion of how our method applies to other wire routing problems mentioned above. The programs describing the RST routing domain and the RST routing problems below can be obtained from the first author.

2   RST Construction

We describe RST construction as a graph problem. Recall that a *Steiner tree* for a set S of vertices in a graph (V, E) $(S \subseteq V)$ is a tree (V', E') that is a subgraph of (V, E) where $S \subseteq V'$ and the total length of edges in E' is minimum. A *Rectilinear Steiner Tree (RST)* for a set S of vertices in a graph (V, E) $(S \subseteq V)$ is a Steiner tree (V', E') for S in (V, E) such that the edges in E' are horizontal or vertical line segments. In this paper, the length of an edge is the number of segments contained in that edge. The problem of computing an RST is NP-complete [2].

In the computational problem we are solving, the input graph (V, E) is a grid. Given a set S of points on this grid, our goal is to find a tree in the grid that connects all the points in S such that the total number n of unit segments covered by the tree is minimum, or to determine that there does not exist such a tree. Note that since the edges E of the given graph are vertical or horizontal, the edges of the tree in this graph are also vertical or horizontal. Therefore, the trees we compute are RSTs.

To make sure that all points in S are connected via a tree on the grid, we use the following proposition:

Proposition 1 *For any finite graph (V, E), and any set $V' \subseteq V$, the following conditions are equivalent: (a) there exists a subgraph of (V, E) with the set V' of vertices that is a tree; (b) there exists a vertex $v \in V'$ such that every vertex in V' is reachable from v in V'.*

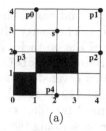 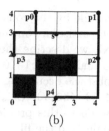

(a)   (b)

Fig. 2. (a) An RST routing problem with the source pin s and 5 sink pins $p0, \ldots, p4$. A solution to this problem is presented in (b).

```
const maxX = 4. const maxY = 4.

source(2,3).
sink(0,1,4). sink(1,4,4). sink(2,4,2). sink(3,0,2). sink(4,2,0).

obstacle(1,3,1). obstacle(0,1,0).
```

Fig. 3. Input file for the problem from Figure 2(a).

Proposition 1 allows us to specify one of the given points as the "source" point, and ensure that, for every other point ("sink" point), there is a path connecting it to the source point in the grid. When n is minimum, the union of paths connecting sink points to the source point forms an RST.

In some variations of RST construction, we put restrictions on the lengths of paths between the source point and sink points. For instance, we can ensure that the length of each path connecting a source point to a sink point is at most l. In another variation, we can put restrictions on the lengths of specific paths.

When we put restrictions on the lengths of paths, we may not find an RST. However, a smallest graph connecting the sink points and the source point that satisfies the given length restrictions is a tree:

Proposition 2 *Let $G = (V, E)$ be a finite graph, and s be a vertex in V. Let V' be a subset of V, and $H = (V, E')$ be a connected subgraph of G. If the total length of edges in E' is minimum subject to the condition, for every vertex $x \in V'$, the length of a path connecting x to s in H is less than some given number l_x, then H is a tree.*

3   Input and Output of CMODELS

In our approach, the solutions of the RST routing problems are characterized by the truth values of the atoms covered(S,X,Y) ("If S=h then the horizontal segment connecting the points (X,Y) and (X+1,Y) is covered by the graph; if S=v then the vertical segment connecting the points (X,Y) and (X,Y+1) is covered by the graph").

Consider, for instance, the problem shown in Figure 2(a). This problem is described to CMODELS by the file presented in Figure 3. The size of the grid is represented in that file by the constants maxX and maxY. These numeric values are defined in each particular routing problem. The source pin and the sink pins are specified. Next, we describe the shape of the obstacles in this example by obstacle(1,3,1) and obstacle(0,1,0). Here, obstacle(X1,X2,Y) expresses that there is an obstacle occupying the points covered by the rectangle defined by the points (X1,Y), (X2,Y), (X1,Y+1), and (X2,Y+1).

To find a solution to this problem we need the file rst.lp, describing the RST routing domain, and the file point.lp, describing the grid points that are not covered by obstacles. Parts of file rst.lp are discussed in the next section. Given the files rst.lp and point.lp with the file presented in Figure 3, and an upper bound n=12 on the total wire length, CMODELS finds the following tree:

```
Answer set:
covered(h,0,3) covered(h,1,3) covered(h,2,0) covered(h,2,3)
covered(h,3,0) covered(h,3,3) covered(v,0,2) covered(v,1,3)
covered(v,4,0) covered(v,4,1) covered(v,4,2) covered(v,4,3)
```

shown in Figure 2(b). CMODELS also determines that there is no tree whose total length is less than 12. It follows that the tree above is a solution.

4   The RST Routing Domain

As described in Section 2, we construct RSTs from paths connecting sink points to the source point. Every path is characterized by the truth values of the atoms in(S,N,X,Y) ("If S=h then the horizontal segment connecting the points (X,Y) and (X+1,Y) occurs in Path N – a path connecting sink pin N to the source pin; if S=v then the vertical segment connecting the points (X,Y) and (X,Y+1) occurs in Path N").

In the file rst.lp, first sets of atoms of the form in(S,N,X,Y) are "generated" by the choice rule

```
{in(S,N,X,Y)} :- segment(S), path(N), point(X,Y).
```

where point(X,Y) defines, in the file point.lp, the grid points that are not blocked by obstacles. Then these sets are "tested" with some constraints expressing the following:

  (i)   the set describes a subgraph of the grid,
 (ii)   the subgraph contains paths connecting the sink points to the source point, and
(iii)   the size of the subgraph is minimum.

Due to Proposition 1, condition (ii) expresses that the subgraph contains a tree connecting the sink points and the source point. With condition (iii), this subgraph forms a solution to the RST routing problem.

First, for (i), we eliminate the sets that contain vertical segments connecting a point (X,Y) on the grid that is not blocked by an obstacle to the point (X,Y+1) that is blocked by an obstacle (or is above the upper edge of the grid):

```
:- in(v,N,X,Y), path(N), point(X,Y), not point(X,Y+1).
```

A similar constraint is added for horizontal segments.

Next, for (ii), we eliminate the sets that do not contain paths connecting the sink points to the source point by adding the following constraints.

To express that the end points of a path should be in that path, we define the atom at(N,X,Y) ("the point (X,Y) is in Path N"). We express that the end points of Path N, specified in a problem description file, should be in Path N by the constraint:

```
:- not at(N,X,Y), ends(N,X,Y).
```

We need to make sure that the end points of Path N cannot be connected to two or more points in the path, whereas each of the other points of Path N should be connected to exactly two points in the path. For that, we define the atom at(N,X,Y,D) ("the unit segment that begins at the point (X,Y) and goes in the direction D occurs in Path N"). We make sure that the end points of Path N cannot be connected to two or more points by the constraint

```
:- 2{at(N,X,Y,D):direction(D)},
   path(N), ends(N,X,Y).
```

Each of the other points of Path N cannot be connected to exactly one point

```
:- 1{at(N,X,Y,D):direction(D)}1,
   path(N), point(X,Y), not ends(N,X,Y).
```

and cannot be connected to more than three points.

```
:- 3{at(N,X,Y,D):direction(D)},
   path(N), point(X,Y), not ends(N,X,Y).
```

That is, each of these points should be connected to exactly two points.

Finally, for (iii), we eliminate the sets where the total wire length is larger than n by adding the constraint

```
:- n+1 {covered(S,X,Y):segment(S):point(X,Y)}.
```

where covered(S,X,Y) is defined as

```
covered(S,X,Y) :- in(S,N,X,Y), segment(S), path(N), point(X,Y).
```

If the total wire length n is minimum then the graph generated by the program above is an RST. For instance, with the routing domain described above, CMODELS finds the tree presented in Figure 1 with n=76. For n=75, CMODELS determines that there is no answer set for the program; therefore, the tree presented in Figure 1 is an RST.

5   Restricting the Lengths of Wires

An RST routing problem may involve constraints on the lengths of some wires connecting the sink pins to the source pin, to meet some signal delay constraints.

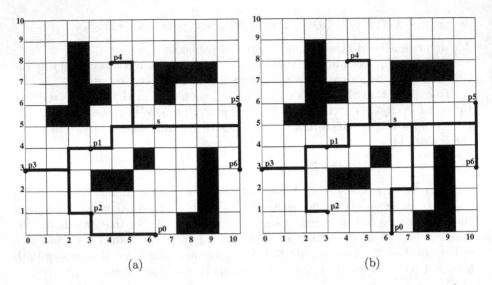

Fig. 4. (a) An RST routing problem with 7 sink pins, along with a solution where the total wire length is minimum, and the length of each wire is at most 13. (b) A near-solution to the RST routing problem in (a) where the length of Path 0 is required to be at most 8.

We can express that any wire cannot be longer than a specific value, say l, by adding to the problem description the constraint

```
:- l+2 {at(N,X,Y):point(X,Y)}, path(N).
```

In other words, no path connecting the source pin to a sink pin covers l+1 unit segments on the grid. Consider, for instance, the problem shown in Figure 4(a), along with a solution. In this solution, the total wire length is minimum (n=26), and each wire length can be at most 13 (l=13). There is no solution for this problem with n=26 and l=12.

We can put restrictions on the length of a specific wire as well. For instance, for the problem described in Figure 4(a), we can express that the wire corresponding to Path 0 cannot be longer than 8 by adding to the problem description the constraint

```
:- 8+2 {at(0,X,Y):point(X,Y)}.
```

After this change, a tree can be found by CMODELS as shown in Figure 4(b). Here, the total wire length is 28, and each wire length is at most 13; there is no solution with the total wire length being less than 28.

When we put restrictions on the lengths of wires, we may not find an RST. For instance, when we restrict the length of Path 0 above, a connected graph with minimum total wire length n=26 does not exist. However, due to Proposition 2, we know that a smallest graph connecting the sink pins to the source pin that satisfies the given length restrictions is a tree. For instance, the graph

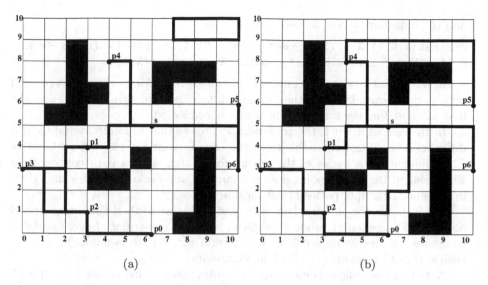

(a)   (b)

Fig. 5. (a) A cyclic graph and (b) a tree connecting the sink pins $p0, ..., p6$ to the source pin s.

in Figure 4(b) satisfies the restriction on the length of Path 0, and there is no such graph that has a smaller total length (n<28).

6 Constructing Trees

If the upper bound n for the total number of the segments covered by the paths is not tight enough then the graph generated by the program described in Section 4 may not be a tree, i.e., there may be cycles as in Figure 5(a). Since a path connecting a sink point to the source point does not contain any cycles, these cycles are of the two forms: either they do not contain any of the sink points and the source point, or they are formed by different paths. In Figure 5(a), we can see both kinds of cycles.

To make sure that the graph generated by the program described in Section 4 is a tree, due to the definition of a tree, we need to make sure that every point covered by the graph is reachable from the source point via exactly one path. For that, we add to the program describing the RST routing domain the constraint

```
:- at(N,X,Y), at(N1,X,Y), not reachable(N,N1,X,Y),
   point(X,Y), path(N;N1), N<=N1.
```

Here `reachable(N,N1,X,Y)` expresses that every point `(X,Y)` covered by Paths N and N1 is reachable from the source point via the segments covered by both paths, and it has a straightforward recursive definition. The base case is defined by the rule

```
reachable(N,N1,X,Y) :- source(X,Y), path(N;N1), N <= N1.
```

and the inductive step is defined by rules like

```
reachable(N,N1,X+1,Y) :- reachable(N,N1,X,Y), path(N;N1), N <= N1,
  in(h,N,X,Y), in(h,N1,X,Y), point(X,Y), point(X+1,Y).
```

In the case of N = N1, the constraint above expresses that every point covered by a path is reachable from the source point. This eliminates the cycles of the first form, and makes sure that the graph is connected.

In the case of N ≠ N1, the constraint expresses that a point covered by two different paths is not reachable from the source point via two different paths. This eliminates the cycles of the second form, and, since a path connecting a sink point to the source point does not contain any cycles, it makes sure that, in a connected graph, paths do not form any cycles.

For instance, for the problem presented in Figure 5(a), if the upper bound on the total wire length is set to 40 then, with the constraint above, CMODELS computes the tree in Figure 5(b). If the total wire length is minimum (n=26) then CMODELS computes the RST in Figure 4(a).

Note that the program describing the routing domain in Section 4 is a "tight" program, and it becomes "nontight" with the definition of reachability above [16].

7   Experimental Results

In the computational problem we are solving, the input consists of a program describing the locations of the pins and the obstacles on a grid (Section 3), the program describing the RST routing domain (Section 4), and an upper bound n on the total wire length. Given this input, CMODELS computes a graph that connects the pins without going through the obstacles where the total wire length is at most n, or determines that such a graph does not exist. Our goal is to compute an RST (Section 2), if it exists. For that, first we make sure that the given upper bound is not too small so that CMODELS can compute a solution, and then we call CMODELS on the given input programs with decreasing values of the upper bound until we reach the minimum total wire length. (Alternatively, binary search can be used.) We reach the minimum total wire length n, when CMODELS computes a solution for the upper bound n, and determines that a solution does not exist for the upper bound $n - 1$.

To make the computation more efficient, we introduce two "circles" with a given radius around the endpoints of a path we are looking for, and require that the path be contained in the union of these circles. This modification sometimes improves the computation time of CMODELS significantly. For instance, for the problem shown in Figure 1, introducing circles of radius=8 around the endpoints improves the computation time of a solution (n=76) by a factor of 10. However, adding circles around endpoints can prevent CMODELS from finding a solution to a solvable problem if the value of radius is too small. For instance, for the problem above, if we reduce radius by 1 then we cannot find a solution. For this reason, when we reach an upper bound, for which there is no solution with circles, we continue the process of computing an RST without introducing any circles.

Problems	# of sink pins	n	CPU time
A	15	58	14
		57*	67
B	20	68	17
		67*	128
C	25	74	21
		73*	450
D	30	76	23
		75*	164

Fig. 6. Computation times for problems $A, \ldots, D$ on a 15×15 grid when the total wire length (n) is minimum.

Another way to make the computation of an RST more efficient is to prohibit "adjacencies" of unit segments. (Two unit segments are *adjacent* if they form the opposite sides of a unit square.) This is possible due to the following proposition.

Proposition 3 *Let (V, E) be a rectilinear tree where each edge is a unit segment. Then there exists a rectilinear tree (V, E') without any adjacencies of unit segments such that $|E'| = |E|$.*

With no adjacencies, for instance, the computation time of a solution (n=76, radius=8) for the problem in Figure 1 can be improved by a factor of 7.

Given the programs describing a specific routing problem and describing the RST routing domain, with n and radius specified, CMODELS transforms the programs into a propositional theory [17], and calls a SAT solver to compute the models of this theory, which are identical to the answer sets for the given programs[3]. In our experiments, we use CMODELS (Version 2.01) and LPARSE (Version 1.0.13), with the SAT solver ZCHAFF (Version Z2003.11.04)[4]. All CPU times presented below are in seconds for a PC with a 733 MHz Intel Pentium III processor and 256MB RAM, running SuSE Linux (Version 8.1).

We consider 4 problems $A, \ldots, D$ on a grid of size 15×15 with 15, 20, 25, 30 sink pins respectively. Note that the RST problems in VLSI routing typically have small number of sink pins (e.g., less than 10), so our test problems are of reasonable size for that application. Figure 6 shows the computation times for these problems, when radius=8. This value of radius is small enough to find a solution to each problem with the minimum total wire length. The character * denotes that the problem does not have a solution. For instance, problem A does not have a solution where the total wire length is 57; CMODELS finds this out in 67 seconds, without introducing any circles.

When we relax the restriction on the total wire length to compute a tree (as in Section 6), the computation times sometimes decrease. For instance, for problem B, a solution with the minimum total wire length (n=68) is computed in 17 seconds. If we allow the total wire length to be at most 85, a tree of size 79 is computed in 7 seconds.

---

[3] For nontight programs, CMODELS operates with a "generate and test" approach [18].
[4] http://www.ee.princeton.edu/~chaff/zchaff.php

Problems	# of sink pins	n	l	CPU time
A	15	58	16	17
			15*	16
B	20	68	19	40
			18*	59
C	25	74	17	32
			16*	40
D	30	76	21	69
			20*	82

Fig. 7. Computation times for problems $A, \ldots, D$ on a 15×15 grid when the total wire length (n) is minimum, and each wire length is at most l.

Figure 7 shows the computation times for problems $A, \ldots, D$ when the length of each wire connecting a sink pin to the source pin is bounded by l. The results are for radius=8. Compared to the results in Figure 6, we can see that restricting the length of each wire by l sometimes increases the computation time. For instance, for problem D, computing a solution with n=76 takes 23 seconds whereas a solution with n=76 and l=21 takes 69 seconds.

Another answer set solver that we can use to solve the routing problems with our formalizations above is SMODELS. However, solutions to the problems above can be computed faster using CMODELS. For instance, a problem with 7 pins on a 10×10 grid can be solved by CMODELS in less than a second whereas a solution can not be found in less than a minute with SMODELS (Version 2.27).

One way to extend our approach to problems with larger grid size is to consider a small set of points on the grid that would be sufficient to construct a tree. These points can be identified by the following hierarchical process in a multi-level manner. At the first level, we consider the given $n \times n$ grid as an $(n/m) \times (n/m)$ small grid. Each point of this small grid represents a $m \times m$ subgrid of the given grid. We construct an RST on this small grid using CMODELS, and obtain the points of the given grid covered by this RST. We repeat this process by decreasing m at each level until we obtain a small set of points on the grid that would be sufficient to construct a tree. Note that a tree computed by this process is not guaranteed to have the minimum total length. We have implemented the algorithm above as a PERL program, and experimented with two problems E and F on a 100×100 grid with 5 and 10 pins respectively. For each problem, first we have obtained a subgraph of the grid that is sufficient to find a tree that connects the given pins, by considering the given grid first as a 10×10 grid, then as a 20×20 grid, then as a 25×25 grid, and finally as a 50×50 grid. This process takes 20 seconds for problem E and 36 seconds for problem F. After that, we have computed some trees connecting the given pins over these subgraphs. Figure 8 shows these computation times when radius=30. For instance, we can compute a tree of size 157 in 75 seconds for problem F.

8   Discussion

We have introduced a formal method for RST construction, in the context of VLSI routing, using answer set programming. This method provides a concise formal representation of the problem as a logic program whose answer sets correspond to solutions. The answer sets for the given formalism are computed using the answer set solver CMODELS.

Our method always correctly determines whether a given RST routing problem, possibly with the presence of obstacles, is solvable, and finds a solution if one exists. The two other exact methods for RST routing are presented in [14] and [12, 13]. In [14], the authors consider RST problems with 3 or 4 pins. They identify the possible topologies, and then describe exact algorithms for each topology. Our method is more general in that any number of pins can be connected by an RST without having to identify all possible topologies. In [12, 13], the authors do not consider obstacles. The idea for RST construction is first to generate some full Steiner trees (Steiner trees where the source and the sink points are the leaves of the tree) for subsets of the given pins, and then to construct a Steiner tree from a subset of these full Steiner trees. Our method is more general in that RST construction in the presence of obstacles can be handled.

Other existing methods for RST construction such as [10, 11] are based on heuristics which cannot guarantee finding a routing solution even when one exists.

Another difference of our method from the ones mentioned above is that it allows us to solve variations of RST routing where some restrictions are put on the lengths of paths connecting the sink points to the source pin. For instance, we can ensure that the length of each path connecting a source pin to a sink pin is at most l. In another variation, we can put restrictions on the lengths of specific paths. In such cases, our method guarantees that we find a tree even when the total wire length is not minimum.

In some routing problems, the goal is to connect pairs of pins with wires, and the solutions consist of paths that are required not to intersect with each other, and that do not intersect with obstacles. For instance, a routing problem, along with its solution computed by CMODELS, is displayed in Figure 9. Such problems can be solved with our formalization (Section 2), by adding to the problem description the constraint

```
:- at(N,X,Y), at(N1,X,Y), N<N1, path(N), path(N1), point(X,Y).
```

expressing that no two paths intersect[5]. As in the case of RST routing problem, variations of these routing problems, in which lengths of wires and distances between them come into play, can easily be represented by slight modifications.

---

[5] For routing problems, where pairs of pins are connected, some other ASP representations are presented in [19–21], and one is due to Tommi Syrjänen (personal communication, July 31, 2000). With the formalization above, such routing problems can be solved more efficiently. For instance, a problem with 20 pairs of pins on a grid of 15×15 can be solved in 21 seconds with our program, using about 80MB of memory. With the encoding of [20], the computation time is 57 seconds and the used memory is about 300MB. A solution for this problem cannot be found in less than a minute with the other formalizations. In our formalization, paths are defined in terms of segments, and the grid does not have to be rectangular. This allows us to solve RST routing problems avoiding cycles and with a hierarchical approach.

Problems	# of pins	n	CPU time
E	5	111	16
		115	9
		119	6
F	10	157	75
		163	64
		170	32

Fig. 8. Computation times for problems E and F on a 100×100 grid when the total wire length is at most n, using hierarchical routing.

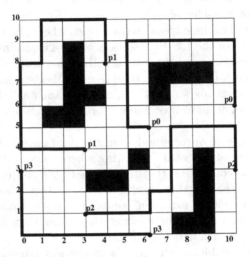

Fig. 9. A routing problem where pairs of pins are connected.

For instance, we can solve bus routing problems where all wires connecting pairs of pins should be of the same length so that the signal delays through all wires are equal. In another enhancement, we can prohibit the adjacency of wires, to avoid signal interferences. In this sense, this representation method is elaboration tolerant.

Acknowledgments

We have had useful discussions with Vladimir Lifschitz on the formalizations of the problems. Derek Corneil has helped us with Proposition 2. Ilkka Niemelä has suggested to us introducing "circles" around the end points of paths. Sinan T. Erdoğan has implemented a program to visualize the solutions computed by CMODELS. Selim T. Erdoğan and Vladimir Lifschitz have provided helpful comments on earlier drafts. Much of this work was done while the first author was at the University of Toronto, and this was made possible by Hector Levesque and Ray Reiter. The work of the first author was partially supported by FWF under project P16536-N04. The work of the second author was partially supported by NSF under grants CCR-0244236 and CCR-0306244.

References

1. Hanan, M.: On Steiner's problem with rectilinear distance. SIAM Journal on Applied Mathematics **14** (1966) 255–265
2. Garey, M.R., Johnson, D.S.: The rectilinear Steiner tree problem is NP complete. SIAM Journal of Applied Mathematics **32** (1977) 826–834
3. Marek, V., Truszczyński, M.: Stable models and an alternative logic programming paradigm. In: The Logic Programming Paradigm: a 25-Year Perspective. (1999) 375–398
4. Simons, P., Niemelä, I., Soininen, T.: Extending and implementing the stable model semantics. Artificial Intelligence **138** (2002) 181–234
5. Lifschitz, V.: Answer set programming and plan generation. Artificial Intelligence **138** (2002) 39–54
6. Gelfond, M., Lifschitz, V.: The stable model semantics for logic programming. In: Logic Programming: Proc. of the Fifth Int'l Conference and Symposium. (1988) 1070–1080
7. Gelfond, M., Lifschitz, V.: Classical negation in logic programs and disjunctive databases. New Generation Computing **9** (1991) 365–385
8. Hanan, M.: Net wiring for large scale integrated circuits. Tech. report, IBM (1965)
9. Lengauer, T.: Combinatorial Algorithms for Integrated Circuit Design. (1990)
10. Nielsen, B.K., Winter, P., Zachariasen, M.: An exact algorithm for the uniformly-oriented steiner tree problem. In: Proc. of ESA-10 (2002) 760–771
11. Zhou, H.: Efficient steiner tree construction based on spanning graphs. In: ACM Int'l Symposium on Physical Design. (2003)
12. Warme, D.M.: A new exact algorithm for rectilinear steiner trees. In the Int'l Symposium on Mathematical Programming (1997)
13. Zachariasen, M.: Rectilinear full steiner tree generation. Networks **33** (1999) 125–143
14. Ganley, J.L., Cohoon, J.P.: Routing a multi-terminal critical net: Steiner tree construction in the presence of obstacles. In: Proc. of the Int'l Symposium on Circuits and Systems. (1994) 113–116
15. McCarthy, J.: Elaboration tolerance. In progress (1999)
16. Erdem, E., Lifschitz, V.: Tight logic programs. Theory and Practice of Logic Programming **3** (2003) 499–518
17. Lloyd, J.: Foundations of Logic Programming. (1984)
18. Lierler, Y., Maratea, M.: Cmodels-2: SAT-based answer sets solver enhanced to non-tight programs. In: Proc. of LPNMR-7. (2004) 346–350
19. Erdem, E., Lifschitz, V., Wong, M.: Wire routing and satisfiability planning. In: Proc. of the First Int'l Conference on Computational Logic. (2000) 822–836
20. Erdem, E.: Theory and Applications of Answer Set Programming. PhD thesis, University of Texas at Austin (2002), Department of Computer Sciences.
21. East, D., Truszczyński, M.: More on wire routing with ASP. In: Working Notes of the AAAI Spring Symposium on Answer Set Programming. (2001)

Adding Domain Dependent Knowledge into Answer Set Programs for Planning

Xiumei Jia, Jia-Huai You, and Li Yan Yuan

Department of Computing Science
University of Alberta
Edmonton, Alberta, Canada

Abstract. We investigate the methodology of utilizing domain dependent knowledge in solving the planning problem in answer set programming. We provide a classification of domain dependent knowledge, and for each class, a coding scheme. In this way, domain dependent knowledge can be encoded into an existing program. Experiments are conducted to illustrate the effect of adding domain dependent knowledge for benchmark planning problems, which show that adding domain dependent knowledge in many cases substantially improves the search efficiency.

1 Introduction

The planning problem is to find a sequence of actions that leads from the initial state to the goal state. The problem is computationally difficult. It is PSPACE-complete to determine if a given planning instance has any solution [6]. By fixing the length of plans, the complexity reduces to NP-completeness.

As a recent addition to the paradigm of declarative programming, answer set programming (ASP) under the stable model semantics [9], has been used to solve the planning problems [4, 14, 15, 18, 21], where a planning problem is represented by a program specifying the constraints and rules that must be satisfied by any plan, and each answer set corresponds to a solution to the given planning problem.

Although the methodology for solving the planning problem in ASP is generally well-understood, the methodology for extracting and encoding domain dependent knowledge is not. The work in [20] showed how procedural knowledge expressed by temporal formulas can be encoded into answer set planning. In general, however, the questions remain for anyone who chooses to use ASP to solve a planning problem: what types of domain dependent knowledge one should look for, how each type may be encoded into an existing program, and what kind of pitfalls to avoid. The work reported here is intended to serve as an important step in finding answers to these questions. There is a growing belief that domain dependent knowledge could be the key to future performance gains [15, 23].

To utilize domain dependent knowledge, one needs to extract knowledge from the planning domain. A classification of the knowledge can serve as a guidance as how domain dependent knowledge may be extracted. We are aware of no previous work in the literature that classifies domain dependent knowledge for planning, especially in the

B. Demoen and V. Lifschitz (Eds.): ICLP 2004, LNCS 3132, pp. 400–415, 2004.
© Springer-Verlag Berlin Heidelberg 2004

context of ASP. In this report we first classify domain dependent knowledge into five categories. In addition, a coding scheme in ASP is provided for each class. The idea is that domain dependent knowledge is encoded into an existing solution either by adding new constraints or by strengthening the conditions of some action rules.

Domain dependent knowledge has been incorporated into a number of systems, e.g., CPlan [22], TLPlan [1], and TALplan [5]. Our approach differs from these works. First, domain dependent knowledge is not encoded into the underlying search algorithm, as was done in CPlan. That is, the information we use does not make references to the underlying planning algorithm. Second, in contrast with TLPlan and TALplan, we do not build a new language for the encoding of domain dependent knowledge. In our case, the knowledge is encoded as constraints into the original program in the same language.

The next section reviews answer set programming for planning. Section 3 classifies domain dependent knowledge. We then begin to present and discuss experimental results on five benchmark planning problems, each with some unique characteristics. In Section 4, one can find the experiment setup and a description of the benchmarks. Section 5 presents and summarizes experimental results, with Section 6 commenting on the related work and future directions. The programs and test data used in our experiments can be found at http://www.cs.ualberta.ca/~you/thesis-xiumei/Program.htm.

2   Answer Set Programming for Planning

In this paper, ASP refers to logic programming under the stable model semantics. A logic program consists of rules of the form $A \leftarrow B_1, ..., B_m, \text{not } C_1, ..., \text{not } C_n.$, where A, B_i and C_i are function-free atoms. Such a rule is called a *basic rule*. The head A may be omitted, in which case it serves as a constraint where the body must be false in any stable model. In systems like Smodels and DLV these programs are instantiated to ground instances for the computation of stable models. The definition of stable model is given in [9].

ASP has been extended with new constructs [17], in particular

choice rule : $\{h_1, \ldots, h_m\} \leftarrow body.$
cardinality constraint : $L\{a_1, ..., a_n, \text{not } b_1, ..., \text{not } b_m\}U$

In a choice rule, if the body is satisfied then any subset of the head may be included in a stable model. In a cardinality constraint, L and U are integers giving the lower and upper bounds of the constraint, respectively. It is satisfied by a model if the cardinality of the subset of the literals satisfied by the model is between the integers L and U, inclusively. A cardinality constraint can be used just like a literal anywhere in a rule.

To solve a planning problem in ASP, we need to represent: (a) *fluents* and *actions*; (b) *initial* and *goal* states; and (c) an *action system*. The fluents and actions are represented by predicates in logic programs. For actions and state-related fluents, we add a state parameter T to explicitly represent in which state the fluents and actions are about. To represent an action system for planning, four groups of rules are needed.

- *Action choice*: which actions should be chosen;
- *Affected objects*: what objects are affected by an action;
- *Effects*: if affected, what are the effects on the affected objects; and
- *Frame axioms*: if not affected by any action at a state, the fluents that hold at the current state remain to hold in the next state.

An action system can be realized in ASP by the following encoding. In the first two rule schemes below, action choice is represented by a choice rule, along with a constraint preventing an action and its conflicting actions from happening at the same state (such as moving a block to two distinct locations at the same state). In the next two rules, affected object is identified and change of property specified. Finally, a frame axiom formulates that a property of an object holds at the current state will continue to hold at the next state if the object is not affected by any action at the current state.

$$\{action(Obj_1, ..., Obj_n, T)\} \leftarrow preconditions.$$
$$\leftarrow action(Obj_1, ..., Obj_n, T), conflictingAction(Obj_1, ..., Obj_m, T).$$
$$affected(Obj, T) \leftarrow action(T).$$
$$property_2(Obj, T + 1) \leftarrow action(T), property_1(Obj, T).$$
$$property(Obj, T + 1) \leftarrow \text{not } affected(Obj, T), property(Obj, T).$$

3   Classification of Domain Dependent Knowledge

In this section, a classification of the nature of domain dependent knowledge is proposed. If the domain dependent knowledge does not rule out any optimal plan (measured by the number of actions in this paper) for the underlying planning domain, we call the knowledge *optimality* knowledge (adapted from [12]). All the domain dependent knowledge discussed here is optimality knowledge.

We often refer to the *gripper problem* [16] for illustration. The goal of this problem is to transport all the balls from one room to the other by a robot. To accomplish this, the robot is allowed to *move* from one room to the other, and use its two grippers to *pick up* and *put down* balls. Each gripper can hold one ball at a time. Here, parallel actions are allowed: two grippers could pick up or put down balls at the same state[1].

3.1   End State Knowledge

The end state knowledge (ESK) is the domain information about the initial state and goal state. It extracts static information about these states.

With the knowledge about the initial or goal properties of an object, taking an action on this object may be redundant. For example, in the gripper problem, if a ball is already in the goal room, then *pickup* will be a redundant action for this ball. However if the ball is on a gripper and the robot is not in the ball's goal room, *putdown* is a wasted action. ESK can be formulated by the following rule:

$$\text{if } \chi \text{ then } not \ Action \tag{1}$$

where χ represents initial or goal properties of an object which holds at the current state, *Action* represents the action that affects χ. This ensures that an action not to occur at a state under the condition of χ at this state.

---

[1] Encoding that allows parallel actions is generally simpler, since there is not need to restrict that only one action at a time is allowed.

To encode ESK into the original program, we simply put not χ into *Action*'s preconditions. The only rules that are affected by ESK are action rules. Thus, we have the coding scheme for ESK:

$$HeadAction(Obj, .., T) \leftarrow preconditions, \text{not } \chi. \tag{2}$$

where $HeadAction(Obj, .., T)$ denotes the head of the corresponding action rule in the original program.

3.2 State Relationship Knowledge

During the construction of a plan, the relationships among the properties of two or more states are good sources of domain knowledge. We identify two subclasses here.

Relationship about state properties. A relationship among the properties that concern multiple states is established by a sequence of actions. Such a relationship should not exist if the action sequences that construct it introduce redundant actions to plans.

For example, for the gripper domain, the effect, "return a ball back to its original room", can be expressed by a relation among three properties: $\{at(A, R, T_0),$ not $at(A, R, T_0 + 1), at(A, R, T_1)\}$ where $T_1 > T_0 + 1$, and $at(A, R, T)$ means A is in room R at state T. This relationship can be formed, among others, by the following sequence of actions: gripper G picks up ball A at T, moves to another room at $T + 1$, moves back to the original room at $T + 2$, and puts ball down at $T + 3$. Destroying such a relationship will prune all the action sets that construct the relationship. This type of knowledge can be formulated as well as encoded by a a constraint, $\leftarrow \chi_1, ..., \chi_n$, where $\chi_1, ..., \chi_n$ together construct the "bad" relationship.

Relationship among state conditions and actions. Another subclass of SRK concerns the relationships among state conditions and actions. The SRK of this subclass is the same as ESK described earlier except it may not be related to end states. We will therefore refer to Rules 1 and 2 for its formulation and encoding. E.g., one piece of SRK in the blocks world, in the form of Rule 1, is

$$\textbf{if not } goodTower(Y, T) \textbf{ then not } move(X, Y, T)$$

which says that if block Y is not on a *good tower* at T, do not move X onto Y. A good tower is one in which the blocks are already at their goal positions. According to the encoding for ESK (cf. Rule 2), we can define a predicate $goodTower(X, T)$ and add it as a condition into the action rules that move a block onto another block.

3.3 Procedural Knowledge

Procedural knowledge (PK) extracts sequential information from the sequence of actions in final plans. This type of knowledge is powerful because it provides a shortcut for deriving new actions directly from "existing" ones. It can also provide extra constraints among actions to guarantee the right sequence in the final plans.

We identify four subtypes of PK that frequently appear in planning domains. First, we single out procedural knowledge with *unknown objects* (that occur in action predicates). E.g., boarding a bus at one location should precede unboarding it at another location. The latter location may be unknown from the planning domain. On the other hand, the object *bus* is known to refer to the same bus.

For PK where the objects are all known, we distinguish the knowledge with *known state distances* from the one with *unknown state distances*. In addition, any procedural knowledge can be *total* or *partial*. While the latter specifies a strict order among n actions, total knowledge in addition requires that when any $n - 1$ actions occur at their specified positions in a sequence, the remaining nth action must also occur in the sequence at its specified position.

In general, we need to consider orderings among not only single actions but sets of actions. We now give the details.

Total procedural knowledge with known state distances. Let $action_i(T_i)$ be an action that occurs at state T_i. The notation, $c : action_i(T_i) \prec_k action_j(T_j)$, expresses that under the condition c, once either action occurs in a plan, the other must also occur in the same plan; and in the plan $action_j$ must occur k states later than $action_i$, where k is a numerical expression.

Notation: $n(action_1(T) \mid \cdots \mid action_i(T))m$ denotes that, of all the i actions, l actions in the list may occur at state T where $n \leq l \leq m$.

Total procedural knowledge with known state distances can be formulated by

$$c : \chi_1(T_1) \prec_{k_{1,2}} \chi_2(T_2) \prec_{k_{2,3}} \cdots, \prec_{k_{n-1,n}} \chi_n(T_n) \qquad (3)$$

where $\chi_i(T_i)$ is of the form $action_i(T_i)$ or $n(action_1(T) \mid \cdots \mid action_m(T))m$. This rule says that under the condition represented by c, once any $n - 1$ elements in the list occur in a plan in the specified order, the nth element must occur in the same plan and all the elements must occur in the specified order with said state distances.

To encode the above rule in ASP, for each element $\chi_i(T_i)$, we construct the following logic program rule:

$$\chi_i'(T_i) \leftarrow \chi_1'(T_1), ..., \chi_{i-1}'(T_{i-1}), \chi_{i+1}'(T_{i+1}), ..., \chi_n'(T_n),$$

$$c, T_2 - T_1 = k_{1,2}, ..., T_n - T_{n-1} = k_{n-1,n}. \qquad (4)$$

where if $\chi_i(T_i)$ is of the form $action_i(T_i)$, $\chi_i' = \chi_i$; if χ_i is of the form $n(action_{j_1}(T) \mid \cdots \mid action_{j_q}(T))m$, $\chi_i' = n\{action_{j_1}(T), \cdots, action_{j_q}(T)\}m$.

Partial procedural knowledge with known state distances. Partial procedural knowledge with known state distances can be formulated by

$$c : \chi_1(T_1) \sqsubset_{k_{1,2}} \chi_2(T_2) \sqsubset_{k_{2,3}}, ..., \sqsubset_{k_{n-1,n}} \chi_n(T_n) \qquad (5)$$

where $\chi_j(T_j)$ is of the form $action_i(T_i)$ or $n(action_1(T) \mid \cdots \mid action_l(T))m$. $k_{i,i+1}$ is a number representing the state distance of T_i and T_{i+1}. This rule says, under the condition represented by c, (1) if all the actions in the sequence occur in a plan, their state distances must be those specified in the rule; and (2) if, for all j, $1 \leq j \leq i$, all actions represented by $\chi_j(T_j)$ occur at state T_j in a plan in the sequence specified by the rule, then action(s) $\chi_{i+1}(T_{i+1})$ must occur in the same plan $k_{i,i+1}$ states later.

Partial PK provides a single directed dependency relation between sets of actions. The action(s) at the right side of $\sqsubset$ depend on all of the action(s) at the left side, but the converse need not be true. This relation is useful for pruning search space in planning. Once the left side action(s) occurs in a plan, the right side action(s) can be directly added into the same plan. As an example, the following partial PK in the gripper problem

$$(goalRoom(R_2), at(robot, R_1, T_1)) : pickup(G, A, T_1) \sqsubset_1 move(robot, R_1, R_2, T_2)$$

says that if the robot picks up ball A at state T_1, it must move to the ball's goal room at the next state. However, it is not always true that if the robot moves to the goal room it must pick up A at the previous state, since this room is the destination of many balls.

Partial PK can be encoded as: for each $\chi_i(T_i)$ where $2 \leq i \leq n$, construct the rule

$$\chi_i'(T_i) \leftarrow c, \chi_1'(T_1), ..., \chi_{i-1}'(T_{i-1}), T_2 - T_1 = k_{1,2}, ..., T_i - T_{i-1} = k_{i-1,i}. \quad (6)$$

where $\chi_i'(T_i) = \chi_i(T_i)$ if $\chi_i(T_i)$ is of the form $action_i(T_i)$, and if $\chi_i(T_i)$ is of the form $n(action_1(T)| \cdots |action_l(T))m$ then $\chi_i'(T_i) = n\{action_1(T), \cdots , action_l(T)\}m$.

Procedural knowledge with unknown state distances. This can be expressed by Rule 5 or Rule 3 without subscripts under the symbol for ordering. Suppose, if $action_1$ and $action_2$ occur in a plan then $action_1$ should occur before $action_2$. Since the distance is unknown, given $action_1$ there could be many candidate states for $action_2$. Although one can use a choice rule with the set of actions in all candidate states as the head, the number of candidate states will multiply when we specify a sequence of such actions. Encoding by constraints is a good choice in this case, especially for two (sets of) actions $\chi_i(T_i)$ and $\chi_j(T_j)$, where $\chi_i(T_i)$ should precede $\chi_j(T_j)$ under the condition c:

$$\leftarrow \chi_i(T_i), \chi_j(T_j), c, T_i > T_j.$$

where $\chi_i(T_i) = \chi_i(T_i)$ if it is of the form $action_i(T_i)$, if $\chi_i(T_i)$ is of the form $n(action_1(T)| \cdots |action_l(T))m$, $\chi_i'(T_i) = n\{action_1(T), \cdots , action_l(T)\}m$.

Procedural knowledge with unknown objects. From the coding point of view, the problem of capturing unknown objects in action predicates is identical to the one of capturing unknown state distances. Thus, the discussion for PK with unknown state distances applies.

3.4 Symmetry Knowledge

Symmetry knowledge (SK) is the knowledge of checking and breaking symmetries. To capture symmetry knowledge, we must discover symmetric objects and break them.

Definition 1. [22]
Two plans M_1 and M_2 are isomorphic if M_1 can be obtained from M_2 by exchanging an object e with another object e' in M_2. Objects e and e' are called symmetric objects.

Symmetry discovery. In ASP for planning, two objects obj_1 and obj_2 in a planning domain are symmetric at the current state T if they have the following properties:

1. The properties of obj_1 and obj_2 that are required to hold at the goal state must be the same, and must not hold at the current state.

2. They are from the same domain (that is, of the same type).
3. Their properties which hold at the current state T are the same.
4. The same action cannot be performed on obj_1 and obj_2 at the same state, but the different orders (of the action working on them) will derive isomorphic plans[2].

In the gripper problem for example, there are two classes of objects: grippers (left and right) and balls. Both of these two types of objects are possible symmetric objects. The balls A and B are symmetric objects when:

1. The properties which are required to hold at the goal state are the same: staying in the goal room. At the current state, they are both in the initial room.
2. They are of the same type (both are balls).
3. Their properties at the current state are the same: they are located in the same room, the initial room, not being held by any grippers.
4. Action $pickup(Gripper, Ball, T)$ cannot perform on two balls at the same time since one gripper can hold only one ball at a time. However, the plan where the gripper first picks up ball A is isomorphic to the plan where the same gripper first picks up ball B.

To detect symmetry, a new predicate is constructed for each type of symmetric object. In the rule scheme below, the body consists of the properties 1-3 for obj_1 and obj_2. The property number 4 cannot be encoded using predicate or inference rules. It depends on the judgment of the user.

$$symmetric(objType, A, B, T) \leftarrow state(T), objType(A), objType(B),$$

$$goal\_properties(A), goal\_properties(B),$$

$$current\_properties(A, T), current\_properties(B, T). \qquad (7)$$

The properties of A and B which hold at the current state T must not be the same as their properties that are required to hold at the goal state.

Take the object type $ball$ in the gripper domain as an example. We construct the following rule to detect symmetric objects:

$$symmetric(ball, A, B, T) \leftarrow ball(A), ball(B), state(T), initRoom(R_1), R_1 \neq R_2,$$
$$goalAt(A, R_2), goalAt(B, R_2), at(A, R_1, T), at(B, R_1, T).$$

where $ball(A)$ and $ball(B)$ correspond to property number 2. Since there are only two rooms, R_2 which is not the initial room must be the goal room. $initRoom(R)$, $at(A, R, T)$ and $at(B, R, T)$ are properties that hold at the current state T for A and B. $goalAt(A, R_2)$ and $goalAt(B, R_2)$ are properties that must hold at the goal state. Since ball A and B are in the initial room, their properties that must hold at the goal state do not hold at the current state.

Symmetry breaking. There are several ways to break symmetries. Symmetry breaking during search [10] is a recent development which adds constraints during search, to ensure that any assignment symmetric to the one already considered will not be explored. This approach requires a modification of the underlying planning algorithm.

---

[2] This property is essential, since if obj_1 and obj_2 can be "performed" by the same action at the same state, we do not need to differentiate them.

Another way to break symmetry is to add constraints to a program in order to force symmetric solutions into one [8, 19]. This is the approach adopted in our work. First, symmetric objects form an ordered list. Then, we ensure that the relevant action rules are applied only to the least element among all symmetric objects.

New predicates are constructed to assign each symmetric object an order. Suppose $a_1, a_2, \ldots, a_n$ is a list with elements from domain $objType$. Such a list can be represented using the predicates: $head(objType, a_1)$, $list(objType, a_2, a_1)$, ..., $list(objType, a_n, a_{n-1})$, where $head(objType, a_1)$ represents that the list contains the objects of type $objType$ and the head of the list is a_1, $list(objType, a_2, a_1)$ tells that in the list a_2 follows a_1, and so on. Under this representation, every object in the list can be given a number as its order, as done by the following rules:

$$order(objType, A, 1) \leftarrow head(objType, A). \tag{8}$$

$$order(objType, B, N + 1) \leftarrow list(objType, B, A), order(objType, A, N). \tag{9}$$

Rule 8 initializes the order of the head element in the list as 1, and Rule 9 gives an incremental number to the element in the list and the last element gets the largest number. These rules guarantee that each object in the list gets a distinct number.

To get the object with the least number in a list, the following rules can be used:

$$greater(objType, A, B, T) \leftarrow symmetric(objType, A, B, T), N_b > N_a,$$
$$order(objType, A, N_a), order(objType, B, N_b). \tag{10}$$

$$nonLess(objType, 1, A, T) \leftarrow symmetric(objType, A, B, T),$$
$$greater(objType, A, B, T), A \neq B. \tag{11}$$

$$least(objType, 1, A, T) \leftarrow \text{not } nonLess(objType, 1, A, T),$$
$$symmetric(objType, A, B, T). \tag{12}$$

To break symmetries, the least symmetric object should be chosen. For this, an extra condition can be added to the body of an action rule on symmetric objects as

$$HeadAction(Obj, SymObj, ..., T) \leftarrow body, least(objType, 1, SymObj, T). \tag{13}$$

where $SymObject$ denotes a symmetric object, $HeadAction(Object, SymObject, ..., T)$ and $body$ denote the head and the body literals, respectively, of the original rule.

If parallel actions are allowed on the same set of symmetric objects, or we allow more than one least element (sometime it is desirable not to break all symmetries; see Subsections 5.4 and 5.6), we need to construct additional rules to identify the least N objects.

3.5   Distance Knowledge

If the lower bound needed to change properties of an object (or all objects of a type) which hold at the current state to properties which hold at the goal state is less than the available steps, then the current partial plan cannot lead to a plan within the given number of steps.

In the following, Rule 14 expresses the computation of lower bound; to stop the search once the lower bound is greater than the available steps, we construct Rule 15 where *steps* is the maximum length for plan.

$$lowerBound(Obj, N, T) \leftarrow current\_conditions(Obj, T), goal\_conditions(Obj),$$
$$other\_facts, N = formulaToComputeLowerBound. \quad (14)$$
$$\leftarrow lowerBound(Obj, N, T), N > (steps - T). \quad (15)$$

4　Experiments Setup and Benchmarks

We have implemented a range of test domains to determine how simple it is to specify domain dependent knowledge using our encodings, and how effective the domain dependent knowledge is for pruning the search space in planning. In our empirical tests we run Smodels 2.26 on a Pentium IV 1.5GHz machine with 1GB RAM.

We tested our encodings with five planning domains. The logistics domains [3], the blocks world domains [11] and the gripper domains are from the CPlan testbed. The elevator planning domains are from the AIPS planning competition in 2000 [2] while the ferry domains are from TLPlan distribution [1]. In our encoding of these problems parallel actions are allowed.

Experiments are conducted as follows: for each type of domain dependent knowledge, and for each of the five benchmarks, we run instances without any domain dependent knowledge, and then the same instances with the encoding of the knowledge added. In this way, we could see the effect of each type of domain knowledge. We sometimes had to design specific instances where a particular type of knowledge is not strong in order to see the impact of the overhead.

The gripper problem has been described in Section 2. The blocks world problem is well-known. The remaining three benchmark problems are described here.

Logistics World: There are two types of vehicles, trucks and airplanes. Trucks can be used to transport packages within a city, and airplanes to transport packages between airports. The problem in this domain starts with a collection of packages at various locations in various cities, and the goal is to redistribute these packages to their destinations.

Ferry World: With actions of boarding and unboarding, the ferry can transport, one car at a time, all the cars to their destinations. The sources and destinations of cars may be different.

Elevator Domain: There is an elevator which will transport passengers from their initial floors to their goal floors. There are three types of objects: the elevator called $lift$, a number of passengers, and several floors. The elevator can move up and down to any floor. When it stops at a floor, any passenger in the elevator can be unboarded, and any passenger waiting at the floor can be boarded on to the elevator. The goal of the problem is to transport all the passengers to their destination floors.

Table 1. Experiments for the gripper problem with/without domain knowledge (have solution)

#ball	steps	Time (seconds)								
		without	ESK	SRK	PK01	PK02	PK03	PK01+02	SK	DK
4	7	0.78	0.13	0.12	0.53	0.18	0.09	0.19	0.06	0.13
5	11	136.07	11.02	5.76	46.33	65.40	23.87	12.55	0.88	199.53
6	11	2611.74	11.89	21.23	440.77	148.34	177.41	23.74	9.53	549.63
7	15	> 2 days	2947	788.41	47132	38435	11550	7245	298.39	>2 days

5 Experimental Results

In the tables that follow[3], the column labeled "steps" is the length of the plan, the group column labeled "time (seconds)" shows the the search time to find the first plan, or the answer *no* when the instance has no solution. Each column under it either shows the search time *without* any domain dependent knowledge (under the column labeled "without"), or the search time *with* a particular kind of domain dependent knowledge.

Any test run will be stopped after 2 days of running, in which case the corresponding entry is filled with "> 2 days".

5.1 Experiments with End State Knowledge

In each table, the experimental results with ESK are shown in the column under the label ESK. End state knowledge can be extracted from all transportational problems. Once an object gets to its goal location, it should not be moved after that. Also, its goal location is not related to the goal locations of other objects. ESK for the blocks world problem is not strong, since the positions of the blocks are interrelated. A block reaches its own goal position does not mean it will stay at that position. It depends on whether all the blocks under it are at their goal positions.

The performance gain for ESK is impressive. The more difficult an instance is, the better ESK works. E.g., in Table 1, when there are 5 balls, the encoding with ESK is 12 times faster than the one without it. When the number of balls is 6, the encoding with ESK is 200 times faster.

5.2 Experiments with State Relationship Knowledge

These results appear under the table column labeled SRK. For transportational problems, that a moved object is moved back involves the location property at three states. This knowledge is used in the experiments of all domains except the block world, for which two other experiments are conducted. The column SRK01 in Table 7 employs the SRK: *do not move a block from table to table*, while SRK02 uses the knowledge: *do not move block X to block Y if Y is not on a good tower*. In the latter case, we defined a new predicate $goodTower(X, T)$[4].

State relationship knowledge is a reliable source for pruning the search space.

---

[3] For lack of space, we organized the experimental results for one benchmark into one table. The reader needs to check out a column from each table when reading the text.

[4] That this particular domain knowledge for the blocks world is very effective for space pruning is previously known.

5.3   Experiments with Procedural Knowledge

The blocks world problem has very little sequential patterns in final plans.

For the gripper domain, we experimented with several types of procedural knowledge. PK0n below are the column labels in the tables.

1. PK01. A gripper must pick up a ball before putting it down. This is partial PK with known state distance.
2. PK02. If a gripper picks up a ball at T, it must put it down at $T + 2$, and vice versa. This is total PK with known state distance.
3. PK03. If robot is in room R then its movement from R to another room occurs after a pickup or putdown action, and vice versa. This is total PK knowledge with unknown state distance.

We note that between PK01 and PK02, either is strictly stronger than the other. Neither rule prunes all the wasted actions that the other could. Applying these two rules together therefore works better. The results are given under the column labeled PK01+02.

The procedural knowledge used for other domains are:

- PK05 (logistics): Truck loads a package, and then at some later state unloads it.
- PK06 (elevator): Do not stop at a floor if the lift does not board or unboard any passengers at the next state.
- PK07 (ferry): Unloading a car must occur two states later than boarding the same car at a different location.
- PK08 (ferry): If ferry boards a car at state T, then the ferry should move to its destination.

We obtained performance gains for almost all the test cases that stopped within 2 days.

5.4   Experiments with Symmetry Knowledge

Not every planning domain has symmetry. In the blocks world, since parallel actions are allowed, there is no symmetry left. Changing the order of action move will totally change the plan. Also, any two blocks that have the same properties must be at the *table* and be clear. Then, these two blocks can be moved at the same state. They are not symmetric objects.

We conducted experiments for the gripper problem, the logistics problem, and the ferry problem, based on the encoding proposed in Section 3. It turns out that symmetry knowledge for the gripper problem is very effective, due to the fact that the presence of symmetry is very strong and easy to identify - all the balls that have not been moved are all symmetric.

The use of symmetry knowledge is generally less effective for the logistics problem, because the presence of symmetry is not substantial. Our analysis shows that only when at a state T, two trucks (or two airplane) have not loaded any packages, and they are at the same location, can these two trucks be symmetric objects. This case rarely happens. In the instances tested for the logistics domain, p01, p02 and p04 have little symmetry, and as such the overhead makes the performance worse, while p05 and p07 have some

Table 2. Experiments for the gripper problem with/without domain knowledge (no solution)

#ball	steps	Time (seconds)							
		without	ESK	SRK	PK01	PK02	PK01+02	SK	DK
4	6	0.28	0.06	0.07	0.21	0.10	0.08	0.05	0.01
5	10	372.99	6.07	9.08	96.29	60.32	18.45	2.73	0.09
6	10	937.72	10.96	15.63	178.41	132.45	34.91	3.86	0.09
7	14	> 2 days	1350.55	2990.46	>2 days	>2 days	>2 days	558.52	0.16

symmetries, in one of which the performance gain is minimum while in the other a hard instance is solved efficiently.

For the ferry problem, the effect of SK heavily depends on the problem instance. If, at the initial state, many cars are at the same location and they have the same goal location, then these cars are symmetric objects for action *board*. Otherwise, the symmetry is not strong. In Tables 5 and 6, f03 and f03n are designed without symmetries.

5.5   Experiments with Distance Knowledge

The effect of utilizing distance knowledge depends on two factors. First, the longer the lower bound is, the earlier can the pruning occur and therefore is more effective. The second concerns the amount of overhead in computing the lower bound at each state.

For the gripper domain, the lower bound can be computed by a formula for any state, it's the number of steps to transfer all the balls that are not at their goal room to their goal room. If a test case has no solution, it involves no search, and stops right away (see Table 2).

For the ferry domain, due to parallel actions, there is no easy formula for the computation of the minimum steps to move *all* the cars to their destinations. We may choose the biggest lower bound among all lower bounds for individual cars. In this case, before the lower bound becomes effective, the properties of all the objects in the domain have to be checked in order to compute it. The effort required to do this is not much less than that required to backtrack without checking the lower bound, which is why distance knowledge in the ferry domain tends to make search performance worse. Also, in the ferry domain, the distance knowledge only works at the last five states (corresponding to the case where the car and the ferry are at different locations and the ferry is not empty). This is why in most of our test instances, the performance becomes worse. This discussion also applies to the elevator problem.

For the logistics domain, although the distance knowledge works the same way as in the ferry domain, the lower bound for some packages can be nine, which is comparable to the length of the final plans. The distance knowledge can therefore work at very early states which is why distance knowledge works better in the logistics domain than in the ferry domain. This discussion also applied to the blocks world domain.

5.6   Summary of Experimental Results

Our experiments show that each class of domain dependent knowledge can prune some search space, but the extent depends on the planning domain and the type of knowledge.

Table 3. The elevator problem with/without domain knowledge (have solution)

instance	#passenger	#floor	steps	Time (seconds)				
				without	ESK	SRK	PK06	DK
E02	3	5	10	2.14	0.13	1.75	0.75	2.52
E03	4	7	12	70.01	2.50	50.43	11.48	95.21
E04	5	9	14	853.86	13.40	608.79	115.33	7151.46
E05	6	11	14	3676.65	112.91	890.52	247.11	>2 days

Table 4. The logistics world with/without domain knowledge (have solution)

instance	#package	steps	Time (seconds)					
			without	ESK	SRK	PK05	SK	DK
p01	6	9	2.16	1.29	1.27	2.06	4.83	2.33
p02	5	7	1.88	2.39	1.24	1.63	12.73	3.08
p04	7	9	3.16	1.31	2.29	2.90	8.00	1.98
p05	4	11	70.28	56.07	51.71	60.86	58.31	66.31
p07	10	9	> 2 days	43.11	41.26	>2 days	320.43	119.61

Table 5. The ferry problem with/without domain knowledge (have solution)

instance	#car	#location	steps	Time (seconds)						
				without	ESK	SRK	PK07	PK08	SK	DK
f01	4	4	11	1.04	0.15	0.84	2.22	0.32	0.63	1.55
f02	5	4	12	3.09	0.56	2.15	1.80	3.25	1.41	2.63
f03	5	6	12	7.29	1.93	12.68	3.71	2.94	10.49	10.26
f04	5	4	15	124.44	3.08	40.15	1.70	2.66	45.10	165.96
f05	4	4	16	150.61	112.50	61.04	16.68	4.67	8.58	436.96

Table 6. The ferry problem with/without domain knowledge (no solution)

instance	#car	#location	steps	Time (seconds)						
				without	ESK	SRK	PK07	PK08	SK	DK
f01n	4	4	10	0.48	0.10	0.31	0.38	0.47	0.28	0.54
f02n	5	4	11	2.72	0.36	2.15	0.99	1.37	0.92	2.93
f03n	5	6	11	12.78	1.51	4.14	2.93	3.31	4.52	9.76
f04n	5	4	14	45.86	4.86	30.93	3.88	21.38	8.12	55.60
f05n	4	4	15	122.94	36.72	22.35	11.12	13.68	7.43	136.15

End state knowledge, state relationship knowledge and procedural knowledge can prune bad actions for almost all the planning domains and the improvement can be up to 3 orders of magnitude.

Symmetry knowledge can improve search efficiency, but the overhead is a concern. When symmetry is strong in a planning domain, its use improves search efficiency significantly. Otherwise, the encoding of the knowledge may increase the search space. Therefore, breaking all the symmetries in the problem may not always be an optimal strategy; sometimes we may leave some symmetries in the program.

Table 7. The blocks world problem with/without domain knowledge (have solution)

instance	#blocks	steps	Time (seconds)				
			without	ESK	SRK01	SRK02	DK
bw.16	16	8	3.20	2.21	3.08	1.09	8.33
bw.17	17	9	2424.42	2202.83	7.78	1.75	17.73
bw.18	18	10	3146.80	2728.86	53.79	2.58	102.39
bw.20	20	10	22.70	10.49	13.14	1.56	102.23
bw.21	21	11	> 2 days	>2 days	24.56	2.10	112.47
bw.25	25	15	> 2 days	>2 day	>2 days	17.80	>2 days

Distance knowledge can improve search efficiency, but not for every domain. If the lower bound for all the objects in the domain can be computed, it can be used as a checker to stop an invalid partial plan at an early stage. If only the lower bound for each object in the domain can be computed, the improvement depends on the coverage of the distance knowledge. If the distance knowledge only works on the last few states, then the overhead may outweigh the benefit. If the distance knowledge works at almost all the states, the improvement can be significant, especially for hard instances.

Combining different classes of domain dependent knowledge can prune more search space. For example, we can add end state knowledge and symmetry knowledge to a logic program representing a planning problem. Since these two classes of knowledge prune different sets of redundant actions, the encoded knowledge can compensate each other. Take the gripper problem as an example. The end state knowledge can prune redundant actions for the balls that are already in the goal room. If the balls are in the goal room, then no actions need to be undertaking for these balls. On the other hand, symmetry knowledge prunes bad actions on the balls that are not in the goal room. Therefore, combining these two classes of knowledge can prune more search space.

The use of some knowledge may make other knowledge useless. For example, in the same gripper problem. If we apply procedural knowledge to specify that the sequence "a gripper first picks up a ball, then moves it to the goal room, puts it down, and moves back to the beginning room" is in final plans. At the same time, we also apply end state knowledge saying that when a ball a and a gripper g are in the beginning room at any state T, action $putdown(g, a, T)$ should not be taken, and if the ball is in the goal room, action $pickup(g, a, T)$ should not be taken. Then, the state relationship knowledge " do not move a ball back to a room" becomes useless after applying the above two classes of knowledge.

6 Related Work and Future Direction

Procedural knowledge has been used in GOLOG, a logic programming language based on a situation calculus theory of actions [13, 7]. The range of procedural knowledge described in this report is far wider than that used in GOLOG. We can capture not only sequential information for specific actions, but also the sequence of sets of actions, even the sequence of the whole plan can be specified.

In [20] constraints on sequence of actions are expressed by temporal formulas whose interpretation is realized by an answer set program. Our work emphasizes the patterns of procedural knowledge that appear frequently in planning domains. Since we do not rely on an interpreter written as part of the planning program, the overhead in our method seems to be generally smaller.

Distance knowledge is first used in CPlan [22], where lower and upper bounds on how many steps needed for a variable to change from one value to another are computed when applying distance knowledge. In CPlan, these bounds are computed only at the initial state. Since, in our encodings, the length is given, the upper bound becomes irrelevant. The lower bound is however extended to any state except the goal state.

A pending investigation is to identify the classes of new atoms in the coding of domain dependent knowledge that are *non-split*, in the sense that their values can be determined solely by the atoms in the original planning solution. As such, these atoms need not participate in the search, and as a result, the overhead can be reduced.

Based on the formalization and standard encoding of each class of domain knowledge, an important area for future research is to design a system for automatically generating and translating domain specific knowledge to be added to the encoding of planning domains in answer set programming.

Acknowledgement

The work by Jia-Huai You was partially supported by the *Chunhui plan* under the Ministry of Education of China.

References

1. F. Bacchus and F. Kabanza. Using temporal logics to express search control knowledge for planning. *Artificial Intelligence*, 116(1,2):123–191, 2000.
2. F. Bacchus, H. Kautz, D.E. Smith, D. Long, H. Geffner, and J. Koehler. AIPS-00 Planning Competition. In *http://www.cs.toronto.edu/aips2000/*, 2000.
3. A. L. Blum and M. L. Furst. Fast planning through planning graph analysis. In *Proc. IJCAI-95*, pages 1636–1642, 1995.
4. Y. Dimopoulos, B. Nebel, and J. Keohler. Encoding planning problems in non-monotonic programs. In *Proc. European Conf. on Planning*, pages 169–181. Springer-Verlag, 1997.
5. P. Doherty and J. Kvarnstom. TALplanner: An empirical investigation of a temporal logic-based forward chaining planner. *TIME'99*, pages 47–54, 1999.
6. K. Erol, D. Nau, and V. S. Subrahmanian. Complexity, decidability and undecidability results for domain-independent planning. *Artificial Intelligence*, 76(1-2):75–88, 1995.
7. A. Finzi, F. Pirri, and R. Reiter. Open world planning in the situation calculus. In *Proc. AAAI-2000*, pages 754–760, 2000.
8. A. Frisch, I. Miguel, and T. Walsh. CGRASS: A system for transforming constraint satisfaction problems. In *Proc. Joint Workshop of the ERCIM/CologNet area on Constraint Solving and Constraint Logic Programming*, pages 15–30, 2002.
9. M. Gelfond and V. Lifschitz. The stable model semantics for logic programming. In *Proc. 5th ICLP*, pages 1070–1080. MIT Press, 1988.
10. I. P. Gent and B. M. Smith. Symmetry breaking during search in constraint programming. Research Report 99.02, School of Computer Studies, University of Leeds, 1999.
11. N. Gupta and D. Nau. On the complexity of blocks-world planning. *Artificial Intelligence*, 56:223–254, 1992.

12. H. Kautz and B. Selman. Planning as satisfiability. In *Proc. 10th European Conference on Artificial Intelligence*, pages 359–363, 1992.
13. H. J. Levesque, R. Reiter, and etc. GOLOG: A logic programming language for dynamic domains. *Journal of Logic Programming*, pages 59–83, 1997.
14. V. Lifschitz. Action languages, answer sets and planning. In K.R. Apt et al., editor, *The Logic Programming Paradigm: A 25-Year Perspective*, pages 357–371. Springer, 1999.
15. V. Lifschitz. Answer set programming and plan generation. *Artificial Intelligence*, 138:39–54, 2002.
16. I. Miguel. Symmetry-breaking in planning: schematic constraints. In *Proc. CP'01 Workshop on Symmetry in Constraints (SymCon '01)*, pages 17–24, 2001.
17. I. Niemelä and P. Simons. Extending the Smodels system with cardinality and weight constraints. In *Jack Minker, editor, Logic-Based Artificial Intelligence, pages 491-521, Kluwer Academic Publishers*, pages 491–521, 2000.
18. I. Niemelä. Logic programs with stable model semantics as a constraint programming paradigm. *Annals of Math. and Artificial Intelligence*, 25(3-4):241–273, 1999.
19. B. Smith. Reducing symmetry in a combinatorial design problem, Research Report 2001.01. Technical report, University of Leeds, 2001.
20. T. C. Son, C. Baral, and S. McIlraith. Planning with different forms of domain-dependent control knowledge - an answer set programming approach. In *Proc. 6th LPNMR*, pages 226–239, 2001.
21. V.S. Subrahmanian and C. Zaniolo. Relating stable models and ai planning domain. In *Proc. ICLP-95*, 1995.
22. P. Van Beek and X. Chen. Cplan: a constraint programming approach to planning. In *Proc. AAAI-99*, 1999.
23. D. Wilkins and M. desJardins. A call for knowledge-based planning. *AI Magazine*, 22(1), 2001.

Multi-agent Coordination as Distributed Logic Programming

David Robertson

Informatics, University of Edinburgh

Abstract. A novel style of multi-agent system specification and deployment is described, in which familiar methods from computational logic are re-interpreted to a new context. One view of multi-agent system design is that coordination is achieved via an interaction model in which participating agents assume roles constrained by the social norms of their shared task; the state of the interaction reflecting the ways these constraints are mutually satisfied within some system for synchronisation that is open and distributed. We show how to harness a process calculus; constraint solving; unfolding and meta-variables for this purpose and discuss the advantages of these methods over traditional approaches.

1   Introduction

We are interested in the specification and deployment of multi-agent systems, which we define as systems of distributed components in which components can usefully be viewed as autonomous problem solvers that must collaborate in order to perform complex tasks. There are numerous difficulties in constructing such systems, beyond the normal difficulties associated with building individual agents. These specific issues include the following:

- Maintaining the conformity of interaction necessary to perform a shared task reliably without sacrificing the autonomy of each agent. One solution to this problem is to define a model of the interaction with which agents interact (via some appropriate controller) in order to perform a given task. Control and state information essential to the task resides in that model, minimising the impact on individual agents.
- Ensuring that when necessary an agent can determine its current role and obligations in the interaction, and not requiring that any agent monitor the interaction when that is unnecessary.
- Allowing constraints on variables established locally by agents to be shared by other agents if appropriate and for those others to be able to adapt these constraints.

Although it may seem surprising that standard methods from computational logic can be applied simply and directly to these sorts of issues, we shall explain how this can be done – in the process establishing a new niche for such methods. To emphasise the parallels between issue and method we write each section title in the form $I = M$, where I is an issue for multi-agent system design and M is the corresponding logic programming method. The methods taken together provide a basic formal approach to

B. Demoen and V. Lifschitz (Eds.): ICLP 2004, LNCS 3132, pp. 416–430, 2004.

designing and (in appropriate circumstances) deploying multi-agent systems. Section 2 describes key aspects of earlier research by others that relate to our approach.

In Section 9 we shall demonstrate how these methods work together on a short but (by current standards) complex scenario. The scenario, which concerns ordering and configuration of a computer, is as follows:

> An internet-based agent acting on behalf of a customer wants to buy a computer but doesn't know how to interact with other agents to achieve this so it contacts a service broker. The broker supplies the customer agent with the necessary interaction information. The customer agent then has a dialogue with the given computer vendor in which the various configuration options and pricing constraints are reconciled before a purchase finally is made.

To deal with this scenario we shall introduce the basic components of a Lightweight Coordination Calculus (LCC). In Section 3 we introduce the basic calculus. We then, in Section 4, show how this permits multi-agent social norms to be controlled by mutual constraints on variables determining their message passing behaviour. Sections 5 and 6 show how traditional transformation methods may be applied to execute LCC specifications in distributed environments. Section 7 describes how finite domain constraint solving can be used to make protocols less brittle. Section 8 shows how LCC protocols are suited to brokering of interactions between agents – a key issue for open systems like the Web.

2 Background

Although we use the popular term "agent" in our research, an interest in coordination of processes in open, distributed environments extends more broadly across computer science. Much of the topical interest has come from burgeoning technological efforts – in particular the semantic web and multi-agent systems. There has, however, been long term interest in the logic programming community.

In [1] LCC is described from the perspective of those wishing to coordinate semantic web services, where the point of contact for LCC is the process specification component of (rapidly evolving) service specification languages. Seen from this perspective, the closest existing research is from those using temporal logics to specify different aspects of required service behaviours: for individual services (*e.g.* [2]); shared models for coordinating services (*e.g.* [3]) or the process of composing services (*e.g.* [4, 5]). In [6] LCC is presented as a compact way to describe electronic institutions of the sort recently made popular in the agent community through use of finite state machine models of coordination [7, 8].

In logic programming there is a history of interest in parallel computation and consequently an involvement in coordinating the distributed computations in multi-agent systems. One form of involvement is to invent a form of logic programming language that gives an overall architecture for coordination. The Go! language [9], for example, provides a multi-threaded environment in which agents may be coordinated via a shared memory store of beliefs, desires and intentions. In contrast to such languages, LCC requires nothing more than a traditional Prolog system to achieve its form of coordination

– the primary interest being in using specifications written in LCC to coordinate processes that may individually be in different environments. Perhaps closer to LCC is the work being done on modelling multi-agent coordination using logic programs, for example in [10] where the Event Calculus is used to specify and analyse social constraints between agents (the motivation for this being similar to that of [4]). A translator has been written from LCC to a version of the Event Calculus, although most of our current research on verification of LCC protocols operates more directly from the LCC notation [11].

3   Interaction Model = Process Calculus

LCC borrows the notion of role from agent systems that enforce social norms but reinterprets this in a process calculus. Process calculi have been used before to specify social norms (see for example [7]) but LCC is, to our knowledge, the first to be used directly in computation for multi-agent systems. Social norms in LCC are expressed as the message passing behaviours associated with roles. The most basic behaviors are to send or receive messages, where sending a message may be conditional on satisfying a constraint and receiving a message may imply constraints on the agent accepting it. The choice of constraint language depends on the constraint solvers used and we shall discuss this more fully in subsequent sections. More complex behaviours are specified using the connectives *then*, *or* and *par* for sequence, choice and parallelisation respectively. A set of such behavioural clauses specifies the message passing behaviour expected of a social norm. We refer to this as the interaction framework. Its syntax is as shown in Figure 1.

$$Framework := \{Clause, \ldots\}$$
$$Clause := Agent :: Dn$$
$$Agent := a(Type, Id)$$
$$Dn := Agent \mid Message \mid Dn \; then \; Dn \mid Dn \; or \; Dn \mid Dn \; par \; Dn \mid null \leftarrow C$$
$$Message := M \Rightarrow Agent \mid M \Rightarrow Agent \leftarrow C \mid M \Leftarrow Agent \mid C \leftarrow M \Leftarrow Agent$$
$$C := Term \mid C \wedge C \mid C \vee C$$
$$Type := Term$$
$$M := Term$$

Where *null* denotes an event which does not involve message passing; *Term* is a structured term in Prolog syntax and *Id* is either a variable or a unique identifier for the agent.

Fig. 1. Syntax of LCC dialogue framework

LCC is not the first specification language to describe social norms, although it is believed to be the first such logic programming language. Conversation policy languages (*e.g.* [12]) are similar to LCC in the sense that they apply constraints to the behaviours permitted by agents, thus giving a safe envelope of operation for agents. In Section 7 we shall consider this issue in more detail. LCC is also temporal, since it imposes partial orderings on message passing between agents, so in this respect it resembles efforts in the semantic web service arena to represent individual service behaviours (*e.g.* [2]); shared models for coordinating services (*e.g.* [3]) or the process of composing services (*e.g.* [4,5]). A third view of LCC is as a way of describing state change during multi-agent interaction. In this aspect it resembles systems like Islander [7,8] that represent social norms as finite state systems in which agents "move" between states according to given constraints. In Section 5 we describe a different view of state change but, first, we consider briefly the interplay in LCC between social norms and constraints.

4   Social Norms = Mutual Constraints

The LCC language ensures coherence of interaction between agents by imposing constraints relating to the messages they send and receive in their chosen roles. The clauses of a protocol are arranged so that, although the constraints on each role are independent of others, the ensemble of clauses operates to give the desired overall behaviour. For instance, the LCC protocol:

$$a(r1, A_1) :: offer(X) \Rightarrow a(r2, A_2) \leftarrow p(X) \ then \ accept(X) \Leftarrow a(r2, A_2)$$
$$a(r2, A_2) :: offer(X) \Leftarrow a(r1, A_1) \ then \ accept(X) \Rightarrow a(r1, A_1) \leftarrow q(X)$$
$$\tag{1}$$

places two constraints on the variable X: the first ($p(X)$)is a condition on the agent in role $r1$ sending the message $offer(X)$ and the second ($q(X)$) is a condition on the agent in role $r2$ sending message $accept(X)$ in reply. By (separately) satisfying $p(X)$ and $q(X)$ the agents mutually constrain the variable X.

How does each agent satisfy constraints? LCC allows two options:

– Internally according to whatever knowledge and reasoning strategies it possesses. This is the normal assumption in most multi-agent systems, yet it is not always ideal. In particular we sometimes would like to use knowledge specifically for a social interaction but not require an agent to internalise it (*e.g.* if that knowledge might be inconsistent with an agent's own beliefs). In such cases LCC offers a second option:
– Externally using a set of Horn clauses defining common knowledge assumed for the purposes of the interaction. Like the LCC protocols themselves, this common knowledge is passed between agents along with messages during interaction (see Section 6) so it is ephemeral - lasting only as long as the interaction.

In Section 7 we consider constraint satisfaction in more detail but first we describe the basic mechanism provided in LCC for changing the state of the interaction during message passing.

5   Interaction State Change = Unfolding

In multi-agent systems with predictable behaviours we must be able to reason about state change. In Section 6 we shall discuss the distinction between state that is private to individual agents and state associated with their interaction. Before this we describe how the state of the interaction from the perspective of an individual agent's role may change. The mechanism for performing this basic operation is a form of unfolding familiar from logic program transformation.

Unfolding of a Horn clause with respect to a set of Horn clauses is done by selecting a unit goal in the body of that clause and matching it to the head of a copy of an appropriate clause in the set. The body of that matched clause then replaces the unit goal in the original clause. State change in LCC uses a similar method.

Recall that the behaviour of an agent in a given role is determined by the appropriate LCC clause. Figure 2 gives a set of rewrite rules that are applied to give an unfolding of a LCC clause C_i in terms of protocol $\mathcal{P}$ in response to the set of received messages, M_i, producing: a new LCC clause C_n; an output message set O_n and remaining unprocessed messages M_n (a subset of M_i). These are produced by applying the protocol rewrite rules above exhaustively to produce the sequence from i to n:

$$\langle C_i \xrightarrow{M_i, M_{i+1}, \mathcal{P}, O_i} C_{i+1}, \; \ldots \; C_{n-1} \xrightarrow{M_{n-1}, M_n, \mathcal{P}, O_n} C_n \rangle$$

We refer to the rewritten clause, C_n, as an expansion of the original clause, C_i and write $expanded(C_i, M_i, \mathcal{P}, C_n, O_n)$ when this expansion is performed. In the next section we describe how this basic expansion method is used for multi-agent coordination.

6   Coordination = Distributed Clauses

To coordinate an interaction between multiple agents, each agent must know its constraints on when to send and receive messages. We want this to have as low an impact as possible on the engineering of agents so the mechanism for achieving this should be modular, acting as an intermediary between the agent and the medium used to transmit messages. The module we supply has the following elements:

- A message encoder/decoder for receiving and transmitting messages from whatever message passing media are being used to transport messages between agents. For example, if the JADE platform is being used for inter-agent communication then the encoder/decoder must be able to read JADE messages (which use the FIPA-ACL performative language) and translate these into LCC protocol expressions; similarly for other platforms.
- A protocol expander that decides how to expand a protocol received via a message. This was described in Section 5.
- A constraint solver capable of deciding whether constraints passed to it by the protocol expander are satisfiable. This was introduced in Section 4 and is extended in Section 7.

Given the above, expression 2 defines how an agent can react to a received message M addressed to its identifier, X, in the role R and carrying protocol, $\mathcal{P}$. S is the store of LCC clauses already known to the agent, from which an appropriate clause C_i may be drawn if it has already been involved in this role or, if not, C_i may be drawn from $\mathcal{P}$. After expansion to C_n the clause is replaced in S to give new clause store S_n. The

The following ten rules define a single expansion of a clause. Full expansion of a clause is achieved through exhaustive application of these rules. Rewrite 1 (below) expands a protocol clause with head A and body B by expanding B to give a new body, E. The other nine rewrites concern the operators in the clause body. A choice operator is expanded by expanding either side, provided the other is not already closed (rewrites 2 and 3). A sequence operator is expanded by expanding the first term of the sequence or, if that is closed, expanding the next term (rewrites 4 and 5). A parallel operator expands on both sides (rewrite 6). A message matching an element of the current set of received messages, M_i, expands to a closed message if the constraint, C, attached to that message is satisfied (rewrite 7). A message sent out expands similarly (rewrite 8). A null event can be closed if the constraint associated with it can be satisfied (rewrite 9). An agent role can be expanded by finding a clause in the protocol with a head matching that role and body B – the role being expanded with that body (rewrite 10).

$$A :: B \xrightarrow{M_i,M_o,\mathcal{P},O} A :: E \qquad\qquad if\ B \xrightarrow{M_i,M_o,\mathcal{P},O} E$$

$$A_1\ or\ A_2 \xrightarrow{M_i,M_o,\mathcal{P},O} E \qquad\qquad if\ \neg closed(A_2)\ \wedge$$
$$A_1 \xrightarrow{M_i,M_o,\mathcal{P},O} E$$

$$A_1\ or\ A_2 \xrightarrow{M_i,M_o,\mathcal{P},O} E \qquad\qquad if\ \neg closed(A_1)\ \wedge$$
$$A_2 \xrightarrow{M_i,M_o,\mathcal{P},O} E$$

$$A_1\ then\ A_2 \xrightarrow{M_i,M_o,\mathcal{P},O} E\ then\ A_2 \qquad if\ A_1 \xrightarrow{M_i,M_o,\mathcal{P},O} E$$
$$A_1\ then\ A_2 \xrightarrow{M_i,M_o,\mathcal{P},O} A_1\ then\ E \qquad if\ closed(A_1)\ \wedge$$
$$A_2 \xrightarrow{M_i,M_o,\mathcal{P},O} E$$

$$A_1\ par\ A_2 \xrightarrow{M_i,M_o,\mathcal{P},O_1\cup O_2} E_1\ par\ E_2 \qquad if\ A_1 \xrightarrow{M_i,M_n,\mathcal{P},O_1} E_1\ \wedge$$
$$A_2 \xrightarrow{M_n,M_o,\mathcal{P},O_2} E_2$$

$$C \leftarrow M \Leftarrow A \xrightarrow{M_i,M_i-\{M \Leftarrow A\},\mathcal{P},\emptyset} c(M \Leftarrow A)\ if\ (M \Leftarrow A) \in M_i\ \wedge$$
$$satisfy(C)$$

$$M \Rightarrow A \leftarrow C \xrightarrow{M_i,M_o,\mathcal{P},\{M \Rightarrow A\}} c(M \Rightarrow A) \qquad if\ satisfied(C)$$
$$null \leftarrow C \xrightarrow{M_i,M_o,\mathcal{P},\emptyset} c(null) \qquad\qquad if\ satisfied(C)$$
$$a(R,I) \leftarrow C \xrightarrow{M_i,M_o,\mathcal{P},\emptyset} a(R,I) :: B \qquad if\ clause(\mathcal{P}, a(R,I) :: B)\ \wedge$$
$$satisfied(C)$$

A protocol term is decided to be closed, meaning that it has been covered by the preceding interaction, as follows:

$$closed(c(X))$$
$$closed(A\ or\ B) \leftarrow closed(A) \vee closed(B)$$
$$closed(A\ then\ B) \leftarrow closed(A) \wedge closed(B)$$
$$closed(A\ par\ B) \leftarrow closed(A) \wedge closed(B)$$
$$closed(X :: D) \leftarrow closed(D)$$

$satisfied(C)$ is true if C can be solved from the agent's current state of knowledge.
$satisfy(C)$ is true if the agent's state of knowledge can be made such that C is satisfied.
$clause(\mathcal{P}, X)$ is true if clause X appears in the dialogue framework of protocol $\mathcal{P}$, as defined in Figure 1.

Fig. 2. Rewrite rules for expansion of a protocol clause

resulting set of output messages, O_n can then be sent to appropriate agents via whatever message encoder is provided.

$$react(M, X, R, \mathcal{P}, \mathcal{S}, O_n, \mathcal{S}_n) \leftarrow clause\_for\_role(\mathcal{P}, a(R, X), \mathcal{S}, C_i) \wedge \quad (2)$$
$$expanded(C_i, \{M\}, \mathcal{P}, C_n, O_n) \wedge$$
$$replace(C_i, C_n, \mathcal{S}, \mathcal{S}_n)$$

$$clause\_for\_role(\mathcal{P}, a(R, X), \mathcal{S}, a(R, X) :: D) \leftarrow$$
$$a(R, X) :: D \in \mathcal{S} \vee \quad (3)$$
$$(\neg(a(R, X) :: D \in \mathcal{S}) \wedge a(R, X) :: D \in \mathcal{P})$$

The reactive definition above is one of a range of ways that LCC protocols may be used in coordinating distributed interactions. To date we have built two other forms of deployment mechanism:

- A Java-based mechanism, implemented by Walton, in which a thread is created for each role and these threads then control the message passing. Although this paper views LCC from a logic programming perspective, this illustrates that one does not necessarily require a Prolog interpreter to compute with it.
- A Prolog-based mechanism in which clause store, $\mathcal{S}$, is not resident on each agent but carried with the protocol as messages are sent. This has the advantage that it requires no clause storage on agents but it works only for interactions that are linear, in the sense that at any given time only one agent has the protocol. In Section 7 we return to this form of interaction when dealing with finite domain restrictions on variables in protocols.

LCC is intended to be as neutral to the choice of mechanism for communicating between agents so it is natural (and desirable) that several such mechanisms exist for it. It is not neutral, however, to the choice of constraint solver. In the next section we discuss in more detail the interplay between constraints and protocol.

7   Interaction Scope = Constraint Space

In previous sections we have not discussed in detail the way in which constraints stipulated in protocols are satisfied. The hooks given for this in Figure 2 (via the predicates $satisfy(C)$ and $satisfied(C)$) tacitly assume a solver that would find a satisfiable instance of constraint C. It is, however, well known that satisfying instances of constraints too early can result in the wrong instance being selected. The price paid for this in standard logic programs is the computational cost of backtracking. In multi-agent interactions we do not have this option because messages sent to other agents remain sent and we cannot assume that agents having received messages are able to backtrack, since they may not be implemented in a language that supports backtracking. Hence if we rely entirely on satisfying instances of constraints our protocols are liable to be brittle.

One remedy for brittleness is to have a more sophisticated view of mutual constraints between agents (recall Section 4) in which we maintain a constraint space that bounds the scope of the interaction. With a finite domain constraint solver, for instance, this constraint space can be described by the range constraints on all the variables in the protocol clauses expanded by participating agents. Applying this to our initial example of mutual constraints in expression 1, if the range of values permitted for X by $p(X)$ is $\{1, 2, 3\}$ while the range of values permitted for X by $q(X)$ is $\{2, 3, 4\}$ then were we to demand instances for variables in all constraints then the agent in role $r1$ might (arbitrarily) choose $p(1)$ and consequently send $offer(1)$ to the agent in role $r2$. Unfortunately, $r2$ would then need to satisfy $q(1)$ in order to reply with an acceptance and it cannot. The brittle protocol then, in the absence of a means of backtracking, can only fail. Were we instead to use a finite domain solver we would obtain the range $\{1, 2, 3\}$ for $p(X)$ and, since $q(X)$ is constraining the same variable at the time it is called, this would be reduced to $\{2, 3\}$ - a range that would be attached to the variable returned in the $accept(X)$ message. By maintaining a constraint space we make our protocols less brittle.

To maintain a constraint space during interaction between agents we must send, along with each message, a description of that space. For a finite domain solver this description might be in the form of variable ranges for each variable in the expanded protocol clauses. These ranges must then be applied on each expansion step, thus maintaining the ranges as constraints change. The simplest way of doing this, given that a protocol may be distributed across any number of agents, is to restrict our interactions to those which are linear (in the sense given at the end of Section 6) and send along with the protocol the clause store, S (this time defining the state of the interaction between all participants) and a set, V, containing the current restriction for each variable in the clauses of S. Individual agents then react to messages in a similar way to definition 2, except in this case the $react$ definition follows a sequence of messages, M_i to M_n, between (possibly different) agents, X_i in role R_i to X_j in role R_j, with each instance of $react$ changing both the clause store S and its variable restrictions, V.

$$\langle react(M_i, X_i, R_i, \mathcal{P}, \mathcal{S}_i, \mathcal{V}_i, M_{i+1}, \mathcal{S}_{i+1}, \mathcal{V}_{i+1}), \ \dots \qquad (4)$$
$$react(M_{n-1}, X_j, R_j, \mathcal{P}, \mathcal{S}_{n-1}, \mathcal{V}_{n-1}, M_n, \mathcal{S}_n, \mathcal{V}_n)\rangle$$

In Section 9 we give a detailed example of this sort of mechanism in operation, where the variable restrictions are finite domain restrictions and the constraint solver is a finite domain solver. Before reaching this example we cover the final concept we consider essential for open agent systems: the ability to broker interactions.

8 Brokering = Meta-variables

A broker is a kind of Web service that, upon being asked by a client to suggest a collaboration appropriate for some task, will send that client a description of the dialogue with which the client can initiate that collaboration. Brokering is required in open agent systems, where agents newly entering an environment may not know the forms of social norm expected and may not even know which agents are available. A basic, generic definition of brokering is represented succinctly using expressions 5 and 6 below.

A broker, B, can receive a request for a protocol for a task, T, and will send the protocol $\mathcal{P}$ if it has it.

$a(broker, B) ::$
$\quad ask(send\_protocol(T)) \;\Leftarrow\; a(client(B), A) \;\;then$
$\quad inform(protocol(T, \mathcal{P})) \;\Rightarrow\; a(client(B), A) \;\leftarrow\; protocol\_for\_task(A, T, \mathcal{P})$

$$\text{(5)}$$

A client, A, for broker, B, can send a request for a protocol for a task, T; then receives the protocol segment $\mathcal{P}$; then continues its protocol by following $\mathcal{P}$.

$a(client(B), A) ::$
$\quad ask(send\_protocol(T)) \;\Rightarrow\; a(broker, B) \;\leftarrow\; have\_task(T) \;\;then$
$\quad inform(protocol(T, \mathcal{P})) \;\Leftarrow\; a(broker, B) \;\;then$
$\quad \mathcal{P}$

$$\text{(6)}$$

The generality of this definition of brokering comes from the last step in clause 6 which allows a protocol sent via a message to be inserted into the protocol followed by the recipient of that message. This is similar to the construction of executable goals in logic programming languages, but moved to a distributed dialogue setting.

Notice also that this form of brokering appears to be compatible with forms of brokering and matchmaking developed elsewhere (for example [13]). The point at which matchmaking occurs in the protocol above is when the $protocol\_for\_task(A, T, \mathcal{P})$ constraint is solved in clause 5, producing a protocol, $\mathcal{P}$, for collaboration to solve task T. Different matchmaking algorithms solve this constraint with differing levels of sophistication:

- "Yellow pages" brokers normally allow only propositional tasks and would return as $\mathcal{P}$ a protocol only of the form:

$$ask(Q) \;\Rightarrow\; a(R, S) \;\;then\;\; inform(A) \;\Leftarrow\; a(R, S)$$

  where Q is a query appropriate for the task, T; A is the identifier of the agent who may answer that query while in role R; and A is the answer obtained in response.

- Brokers returning linear sequences of agent interactions (*e.g.* [14]) generalise yellow pages brokering by offering more than one query-response interaction in performing a task, so $\mathcal{P}$ can in this case be of the form:

$$ask(Q_1) \;\Rightarrow\; a(R_1, S_1) \;\;then\;\; inform(A_1) \;\Leftarrow\; a(R_1, S_1) \;\;then\;\; \dots$$
$$\dots \;\;then\;\; ask(Q_n) \;\Rightarrow\; a(R_n, S_n) \;\;then\;\; inform(A_n) \;\Leftarrow\; a(R_n, S_n)$$

  where n is the number of agents needed to perform the task. More sophisticated brokers of this type can generate conditional messages in $\mathcal{P}$ to deal with constraints such as ontology translation between terms in messages.

- Brokers exist for assembling more complex structures for $\mathcal{P}$. Those of which we are aware assume that process specifications for each individual service are available (expressed in a language such as DAML-S) and use a planning system to compose these service components into a plan for service invocation. Examples of such systems include the planning component of the RETSINA system [13] and the SHOP2 system applied to DAML-S [15]. Protocols in our LCC language could be viewed as a form of plan that might be constructed using methods analogous to those of the RETSINA and SHOP2 experiments. It is not yet clear, however, whether these plan-based composition methods can be applied directly to composition of LCC protocols.

A customer, C, can send a request to vendor, V, to buy an item, X, that the customer needs and believes the vendor sells. Then the customer takes the role of negotiator with the vendor.

$$a(customer, C) ::$$
$$ask(buy(X)) \Rightarrow a(vendor, V) \leftarrow need(X) \wedge sells(X, V)\ then \qquad (7)$$
$$a(neg\_customer(X, V, [\,]), C)$$

A negotiating customer with a set, S, of negotiated attributes of the desired item, X, either receives an offer of a new attribute, A, and accepts that (continuing in the negotiating role with A added to S) or it receives a request to commit to the current set of negotiated attributes and replies with the constraints, C_a, it wishes to impose on those attributes; then receives confirmation from the vendor of the final values, F, for the attributes once the customer's constraints have been applied at the vendor's side.

$$a(neg\_customer(X, V, S), C) ::$$
$$\left(\begin{array}{l} offer(A) \Leftarrow a(neg\_vendor(X, C, \_), V)\ then \\ accept(A) \Rightarrow a(neg\_vendor(X, C, \_), V) \leftarrow acceptable(A)\ then \\ a(neg\_customer(X, V, [att(A)|S]), C) \end{array} \right)$$
$$or$$
$$\left(\begin{array}{l} ask(commit) \Leftarrow a(neg\_vendor(X, C, \_), V)\ then \\ tell(commit(S, C_a)) \Rightarrow a(neg\_vendor(X, C, \_), V) \leftarrow choose(S, C_a)\ then \\ tell(sold(F)) \Leftarrow a(neg\_vendor(X, C, \_), V) \end{array} \right)$$
$$\qquad (8)$$

A vendor, V, receives a request from a customer, C, to buy an item, X; then takes the role of negotiator with the customer over the attribute set, S, that applies to that item.

$$a(vendor, V) ::$$
$$ask(buy(X)) \Leftarrow a(customer, C)\ then \qquad (9)$$
$$a(neg\_vendor(X, C, S), V) \leftarrow attributes(X, S)$$

A negotiating vendor with a set, S, of negotiable attributes of the desired item, X, either takes the first element, A, of S and offers it to the customer for acceptance (continuing then in its negotiating role with the remaining attributes, T) or if S is empty it asks the customer to commit to the attributes they have discussed and receives the customer's constraints, C_a, on the final values of those attributes then, if these are satisfiable, it informs the customer of the final attribute values, F, for the sold item.

$$a(neg\_vendor(X, C, S), V) ::$$
$$\left(\begin{array}{l} offer(A) \Rightarrow a(neg\_customer(X, V, \_), C) \leftarrow S = [A|T] \wedge available(A)\ then \\ accept(A) \Leftarrow a(neg\_customer(X, V, \_), C)\ then \\ a(neg\_vendor(X, C, T), V) \end{array} \right)$$
$$or$$
$$\left(\begin{array}{l} ask(commit) \Rightarrow a(neg\_customer(X, V, \_), C) \leftarrow S = [\,]\ then \\ tell(commit(F, C_a)) \Leftarrow a(neg\_customer(X, V, \_), C)\ then \\ tell(sold(F)) \Rightarrow a(neg\_customer(X, V, \_), C) \leftarrow C_a \end{array} \right)$$
$$\qquad (10)$$

Fig. 3. Protocol for our example

9   Example Combining Sections 3 to 8

We now combine the elements introduced earlier to demonstrate how they apply to the scenario given at the end of Section 1. Figure 3 describes the protocol for interaction between vendor and supplier.

The agents involved in the protocol of Figure 3 must be capable of satisfying the constraints it imposes. Some of the axioms used in constraint solving might be standard for all agents, in which case they are shared among all agents (and propagated with the protocol). The definition necessary to choose constraints on attributes is an example of this sort of standardisation, since all agents would be assumed to have precisely the same interpretation of $choose/2$, which constructs a conjunctive constraint on attribute values from a set of attribute names. Expression 11 gives a definition, which assumes that a predicate $choice/2$ that determines each constraint is satisfiable by the agent asked to choose.

$$choose([att(Att)|T], C \wedge R) \leftarrow choice(Att, C) \wedge choose(T, R)$$
$$choose([], true) \tag{11}$$

As an example of knowledge private to an agent, we now define for the customer the ranges of acceptable values for attributes of the personal computer under discussion. For instance, the customer would accept disk space of 40 or above. We also define how the specific values for attributes are chosen by the customer from the ranges agreed via earlier dialogue with the vendor: the maximum from the range being taken for every attribute except for price which is minimised.

$$
\begin{aligned}
&need(pc) \\
&sells(pc, s1) \\
&acceptable(disk\_space(D)) \leftarrow D\ in\ 40..sup \\
&acceptable(monitor\_size(M)) \leftarrow M\ in\ 15..sup \\
&acceptable(price(\_, \_, P)) \leftarrow P\ in\ 800..2000 \\
&choice(disk\_space(D), true) \\
&choice(monitor\_size(M), true) \\
&choice(price(\_, \_, P), minimise(P))
\end{aligned}
\tag{12}
$$

The vendor agent's local constraints are defined in a similar way to that of the customer. We define the available ranges for the attributes needed to configure a PC and relate these to its price via a simple equation (the aim being to demonstrate the principle of relating constraints rather than to have a realistic pricing policy).

$$
\begin{aligned}
&attributes(pc, [disk\_space(D), monitor\_size(M), price(D, M, P)]) \\
&available(disk\_space(D)) \leftarrow D\ in\ 40..80 \\
&available(monitor\_size(M)) \leftarrow M\ in\ 15..18 \\
&available(price(D, M, P)) \leftarrow 1000 + ((M - 15) * 100) + ((D - 40) * 10)\ \#=\ P \\
&minimise(V) \leftarrow fd\_min(V, Vm) \wedge V\ in\ Vm..Vm
\end{aligned}
\tag{13}
$$

The sequence of message passing that follows from the protocol of Figure 3 and the constraints of expressions 11, 12 and 13 is shown below. The dialogue iterates between a customer, $b1$, and a vendor, $s1$. Each illocution shows: the type of the agent sending the message; the message itself; the type of agent to which the message is sent; and the variable restrictions applying to the message (the term $r(V, C)$ relating a finite domain constraint C to a variable V). The first illocution is the customer making initial contact with the vendor. Illocutions two to seven then are offers of ranges for attributes ($disk\_space$, $monitor\_size$ and $price$) each of which are accepted by the customer. At illocution eight the vendor, which has worked through all its relevant attributes, asks for commitment from the customer. In reply, the customer asks the vendor to minimise its price (the variable C in illocution nine). Finally, the vendor offers a sale at a price of 1000 (it having decided simply to take the minimum of the current range restriction on C). The variables for $disk\_space$ and $monitor\_size$ (B and A respectively) are left without commitment, although the vendor could have committed to these if it so desired.

Sender : $a(customer, b1)$
Message : $ask(buy(pc))$
Recipient : $a(vendor, s1)$
Restrictions : $[]$

Sender : $a(neg\_vendor(pc, b1, [disk\_space(A), monitor\_size(B), price(A, B, \_)]), s1)$
Message : $offer(disk\_space(A))$
Recipient : $a(neg\_customer(pc, s1, \_), b1)$
Restrictions : $[r(A, [[40|80]])]$

Sender : $a(neg\_customer(pc, s1, []), b1)$
Message : $accept(disk\_space(A))$
Recipient : $a(neg\_vendor(pc, b1, \_), s1)$
Restrictions : $[r(A, [[40|80]])]$

Sender : $a(neg\_vendor(pc, b1, [monitor\_size(A), price(B, A, \_)]), s1)$
Message : $offer(monitor\_size(A))$
Recipient : $a(neg\_customer(pc, s1, \_), b1)$
Restrictions : $[r(B, [[40|80]]), r(A, [[15|18]])]$

Sender : $a(neg\_customer(pc, s1, [att(disk\_space(A))]), b1)$
Message : $accept(monitor\_size(B))$
Recipient : $a(neg\_vendor(pc, b1, \_), s1)$
Restrictions : $[r(B, [[15|18]]), r(A, [[40|80]])]$

Sender : $a(neg\_vendor(pc, b1, [price(A, B, C)]), s1)$
Message : $offer(price(A, B, C))$
Recipient : $a(neg\_customer(pc, s1, \_), b1)$
Restrictions : $[r(C, [[1000|1700]]), r(B, [[15|18]]), r(A, [[40|80]])]$

Sender : $a(neg\_customer(pc, s1, [att(monitor\_size(A)), att(disk\_space(B))]), b1)$
Message : $accept(price(B, A, C))$
Recipient : $a(neg\_vendor(pc, b1, \_), s1)$
Restrictions : $[r(C, [[1000|1700]]), r(B, [[40|80]]), r(A, [[15|18]])]$

Sender : $a(neg\_vendor(pc, b1, []), s1)$
Message : $ask(commit)$
Recipient : $a(neg\_customer(pc, s1, \_), b1)$
Restrictions : $[]$

Sender : $a(neg\_customer(pc, s1, [att(price(A, B, C)), att(monitor\_size(B)), att(disk\_space(A))]), b1)$
Message : $tell(commit([att(price(A, B, C)), att(monitor\_size(B)), att(disk\_space(A))], minimise(C)))$
Recipient : $a(neg\_vendor(pc, b1, \_), s1)$
Restrictions : $[r(C, [[1000|1700]]), r(B, [[15|18]]), r(A, [[40|80]])]$

Sender : $a(neg\_vendor(pc, b1, []), s1)$
Message : $tell(sold([att(price(A, B, 1000)), att(monitor\_size(B)), att(disk\_space(A))]))$
Recipient : $a(neg\_customer(pc, s1, \_), b1)$
Restrictions : $[r(B, [[15|18]]), r(A, [[40|80]])]$

Recall that the means of each agent maintaining an appropriate role in the interaction is by expanding the clause it selects for its initial role (see Section5). The term below is the fully expanded clause used by agent $b1$ in the role of a customer. By following through the nesting in this clause, the reader may reconstruct the expansions of the initial customer clause (clause 7 in Figure 3) performed using the transformations of Figure 2 and observe that this allows the message sequence for the customer described above.

$$
\begin{aligned}
&a(customer, b1) :: \\
&\quad c(ask(buy(pc))) \Rightarrow a(vendor, s1)) \text{ then} \\
&\quad (a(neg\_customer(pc, s1, []), b1) :: \\
&\qquad c(offer(disk\_space(A))) \Leftarrow a(neg\_vendor(pc, b1, \begin{bmatrix} disk\_space(A), \\ monitor\_size(B), \\ price(A, B, 1000) \end{bmatrix}), s1)) \text{ then} \\
&\qquad c(accept(disk\_space(A))) \Rightarrow a(neg\_vendor(pc, b1, \begin{bmatrix} disk\_space(A), \\ monitor\_size(B), \\ price(A, B, 1000) \end{bmatrix}), s1)) \text{ then} \\
&\qquad (a(neg\_customer(pc, s1, [att(disk\_space(A))]), b1) :: \\
&\qquad\quad c(offer(monitor\_size(B))) \Leftarrow a(neg\_vendor(pc, b1, \begin{bmatrix} monitor\_size(B), \\ price(A, B, 1000) \end{bmatrix}), s1)) \text{ then} \\
&\qquad\quad c(accept(monitor\_size(B))) \Rightarrow a(neg\_vendor(pc, b1, \begin{bmatrix} monitor\_size(B), \\ price(A, B, 1000) \end{bmatrix}), s1)) \text{ then} \\
&\qquad\quad (a(neg\_customer(pc, s1, \begin{bmatrix} att(monitor\_size(B)), \\ att(disk\_space(A)) \end{bmatrix}), b1) :: \\
&\qquad\qquad c(offer(price(A, B, 1000)) \Leftarrow a(neg\_vendor(pc, b1, [price(A, B, 1000)]), s1)) \text{ then} \\
&\qquad\qquad c(accept(price(A, B, 1000)) \Rightarrow a(neg\_vendor(pc, b1, [price(A, B, 1000)]), s1)) \text{ then} \\
&\qquad\qquad (a(neg\_customer(pc, s1, \begin{bmatrix} att(price(A, B, 1000)), \\ att(monitor\_size(B)), \\ att(disk\_space(A)) \end{bmatrix}), b1) :: \\
&\qquad\qquad\quad c(ask(commit) \Leftarrow a(neg\_vendor(pc, b1, []), s1)) \text{ then} \\
&\qquad\qquad\quad c(tell(commit(\begin{bmatrix} att(price(A, B, 1000)), \\ att(monitor\_size(B)), \\ att(disk\_space(A)) \end{bmatrix}, minimise(1000))) \Rightarrow \\
&\qquad\qquad\qquad a(neg\_vendor(pc, b1, []), s1)) \text{ then} \\
&\qquad\qquad\quad c(tell(sold(\begin{bmatrix} att(price(A, B, 1000)), \\ att(monitor\_size(B)), \\ att(disk\_space(A)) \end{bmatrix})) \Leftarrow a(neg\_vendor(pc, b1, []), s1))))))
\end{aligned}
$$

Although this example is compact it demonstrates capabilities beyond standard semantic web service specification languages (such as OWL-S), which do not allow recursion over data structures and therefore could not represent a recursive negotiation like the one in this example. It also allows the protocol of Figure 3 to be brokered to any agent asking for it (that brokering interaction also being represented using clauses 5 and 6 of Section 8) – a capability not possessed by other forms of computation for agent social norms. Finally, it demonstrates a simple way of managing finite domain constraints across multi-agent interactions.

10 Conclusions

A criticism of the LCC approach from the mainstream semantic web or agent communities might be that it too closely resembles logic programming. It is true that the language described in this paper uses data structures familiar to logic programmers but those that are highly specific to Prolog (*e.g.* the list expressions used) are not essential to LCC and could be replaced by others according to taste. The essence of LCC is its mixture of process calculus and Horn clauses. Both of these aspects do appear in the mainstream (though sometimes heavily disguised), for example in the process component of OWL-S specifications or in the rule-based reasoners being constructed to supplement Description Logic reasoners for semantic web services. The advantage of being closer to logic programming than is fashionable in the mainstream is that we are able to make our specifications executable through simple, well known methods that (because they are well established) we know can be taught to engineers of more traditional systems. Many comparable specification languages in the semantic web services domain do not possess this advantage.

The emphasis of this paper is on the way in which we adapt traditional methods to this new application. The agents research group at Edinburgh is developing LCC in ways we shall describe in other papers:

- Walton ([11]) has produced a translator from a variant of the language to Promela, allowing him to model check protocols using the SPIN model checker.
- McGinnis ([16, 17]) is exploring how to make interactions more adaptable by allowing transformations to the protocol by participating agents, leading to notions of "safe" adaptations.
- Barker is applying LCC to the problem of experiment coordination on e-science grids, requiring him to reconcile the data-flow paradigm assumed by many grid service architectures with the messaging processes of LCC.
- Guo ([18]) is studying how to translate to LCC from traditional business process modelling languages.
- Hassan ([19]) is developing more sophisticated forms of constraint management beyond those described in the current paper.

Ultimately, our aim is to produce a single form of specification that supports specification, analysis and modelling for complex, coordinated, multi-agent systems.

References

1. Robertson, D.: A lightweight method for coordination of agent oriented web services. In: Proceedings of AAAI Spring Symposium on Semantic Web Services, California, USA (2004)
2. Decker, K., Pannu, A., Sycara, K., Williamson, M.: Designing behaviors for information agents. In: Proceedings of the First International Conference on Autonomous Agents. (1997)
3. Giampapa, J., Sycara, K.: Team-oriented agent coordination in the retsina multi-agent system. Technical Report CMU-RI-TR-02-34, Robotics Institute, Carnegie Mellon University (2002)

4. McIlraith, S., Son, T.: Adapting golog for composition of semantic web services. In: Proceedings of the Eighth International Conference on Knowledge Representation and Reasoning. (2002) 482–493
5. Sheshagiri, M., desJardins, M., Finin, T.: A planner for composing services described in daml-s. In: International Conference on Automated Planning and Scheduling. (2003)
6. Robertson, D.: A lightweight coordination calculus for agent social norms. In: AAMAS Workshop on Declarative Agent Languages and Technologies, New York, USA (2004)
7. Esteva, M., Padget, J., Sierra, C.: Formalizing a language for institutions and norms. In: Intelligent Agents VIII, Lecture Notes in Artificial Intelligence. Volume 2333. Springer-Verlag (2002) 348–366
8. Esteva, M., de la Cruz, D., Sierra, C.: Islander: an electronic institutions editor. In: Proceedings of the 1st International Joint Conference on Autonomous Agents and MultiAgent Systems. (2002) 1045–1052
9. Clark, K.L., McCabe, F.G.: Go! for multi-threaded deliberative agents. In Leite, J.A., Omicini, A., Sterling, L., Torroni, P., eds.: Declarative Agent Languages and Technologies, First International Workshop, DALT 2003. Melbourne, Victoria, July 15th, 2003. Workshop Notes. (2003) 17–32
10. Artikis, A., Pitt, J., Sergot, M.: Animated specifications of computational societies. In Castelfranchi, C., Lewis Johnson, W., eds.: Proceedings of the 1st International Joint Conference on Autonomous Agents and MultiAgent Systems, Bologna, Italy, Association for Computing Machinery (2002) 1053–1061
11. Walton, C.: Model checking multi-agent web services. In: Proceedings of AAAI Spring Symposium on Semantic Web Services, California, USA (2004)
12. Kagal, L., Finin, T., Joshi, A.: A policy language for pervasive systems. In: Fourth IEEE International Workshop on Policies for Distributed Systems and Networks. (2003)
13. Paolucci, M., Sycara, K., Kawamura, T.: Delivering semantic web services. Technical Report CMU-RI-TR-02-32, Robotics Institute, Carnegie Mellon University (2003)
14. Robertson, D., Correa da Silva, F., Agusti, J., Vasconcelos, W.: A lightweight capability communication mechanism. In: Proceedings of the 13th International Conference on Industrial and Engineering Applications of Artificial Intelligence and Expert Systems, New Orleans, Louisiana (2000)
15. Wu, D., Parsia, B., Sirin, E., Hendler, J., Nau, D.: Automating daml-s web services composition using shop2. In: Proceedings of 2nd International Semantic Web Conference. Volume 2870 of Lecture Notes in Computer Science., Springer-Verlag (2003) 195–210
16. McGinnis, J., Robertson, D., Walton, C.: Using distributed protocols as an implementation of dialogue games. In: Proceedings of the First European workshop on Multi-Agent Systems. (2003)
17. McGinnis, J., Robertson, D.: Dynamic and distributed interaction protocols. In: Proceedings of the Fourth Symposium on Adaptive Agents and Multi-Agent Systems. (2004)
18. Li, G., Chen-Burger, J., Robertson, D.: Mapping a business process model to a semantic web services model. In: Proceedings of the IEEE International Conference on Web Services, San Diego (2004)
19. Hassan, F., Robertson, D.: Constraint relaxation to reduce brittleness of distributed agent ppotocols. In: Proceedings of the ECAI Workshop on Coordination in Emergent Agent Societies, Valencia, Spain (2004)

Logic Programs with Annotated Disjunctions

Joost Vennekens, Sofie Verbaeten*, and Maurice Bruynooghe

Department of Computer Science, K.U.Leuven
Celestijnenlaan 200A
B-3001 Leuven, Belgium
{joost.vennekens,sofie.verbaeten,maurice.bruynooghe}@cs.kuleuven.ac.be

Abstract. Current literature offers a number of different approaches to what could generally be called "probabilistic logic programming". These are usually based on Horn clauses. Here, we introduce a new formalism, Logic Programs with Annotated Disjunctions, based on disjunctive logic programs. In this formalism, each of the disjuncts in the head of a clause is annotated with a probability. Viewing such a set of probabilistic disjunctive clauses as a probabilistic disjunction of normal logic programs allows us to derive a possible world semantics, more precisely, a probability distribution on the set of all Herbrand interpretations. We demonstrate the strength of this formalism by some examples and compare it to related work.

1 Introduction

The study of the rules which govern human thought has, apart from traditional logics, also given rise to logics of probability [10]. As was the case with first order logic and logic programming, attempts have been made to derive more "practical" formalisms from these probabilistic logics. Research in this field of "probabilistic logic programming" has mostly focused on ways in which probabilistic elements can be added to Horn clause programs. We, however, introduce in this work a formalism which is based on disjunctive logic programming [15].

This is a natural choice, as disjunctions themselves – and therefore disjunctive logic programs – already represent a kind of uncertainty. Indeed, they can, to give just one example, be used to model indeterminate effects of actions. Consider for instance the following disjunctive clause:

$$heads(Coin) \lor tails(Coin) \leftarrow toss(Coin).$$

This clause offers quite an intuitive representation of the fact that tossing a coin will result in either heads or tails. Of course, this is not all we know. Indeed, if a coin is not biased, we know that it has equal probability of landing on heads or tails. In the formalism of *Logic Programs with Annotated Disjunctions* or *LPADs*,

---

* Sofie Verbaeten is a Postdoctoral Fellow of the Fund for Scientific Research - Flanders (Belgium) (F.W.O. - Vlaanderen).

B. Demoen and V. Lifschitz (Eds.): ICLP 2004, LNCS 3132, pp. 431–445, 2004.

this can be expressed by annotating the disjuncts in the head of such a clause with a probability, i.e.

$$(heads(Coin) : 0.5) \vee (tails(Coin) : 0.5) \leftarrow toss(Coin), \neg biased(Coin).$$

Such a clause expresses the fact that for each coin c, precisely one of the following clauses will hold: $heads(c) \leftarrow toss(c), \neg biased(c)$, i.e. the unbiased coin c will land on heads when tossed, or $tails(c) \leftarrow toss(c), \neg biased(c)$, i.e. the unbiased coin c will land on tails when tossed. Both these clauses have a probability of 0.5.

Such annotated disjunctive clauses can be combined to model more complicated situations. Consider for instance the following LPAD:

$$(heads(Coin) : 0.5) \vee (tails(Coin) : 0.5) \leftarrow toss(Coin), \neg biased(Coin).$$
$$(heads(Coin) : 0.6) \vee (tails(Coin) : 0.4) \leftarrow toss(Coin), biased(Coin).$$
$$(fair(coin) : 0.9) \vee (biased(coin) : 0.1).$$
$$(toss(coin) : 1).$$

Similarly to the first clause, the second clause of the program expresses that a biased coin lands on heads with probability 0.6 and on tails with probability 0.4. The third clause says that a certain coin, *coin*, has a probability of 0.9 of being fair and a probability of 0.1 of being biased; the fourth clause says that *coin* is certainly (with probability 1) tossed.

As mentioned previously, each ground instantiation of an annotated disjunctive clause represents a probabilistic choice between several non-disjunctive clauses. Similarly, each ground instantiation of an LPAD represents a probabilistic choice between several non-disjunctive logic programs, which are called *instances* of the LPAD. This intuition can be used to define a probability distribution on the set of Herbrand interpretations of an LPAD: the probability of a certain interpretation I is the probability of all instances for which I is a model. As in [11], this probability distribution defines the semantics of a program.

These notions will be formalized in Section 2, where we describe the syntax and semantics of LPADs. We illustrate our formalism further by presenting some examples in Section 3: it is shown how a Hidden Markov Model and Bayesian network can be represented by an LPAD, and how LPADs can represent actions with uncertain effects in a situation calculus setting. In Section 4 we give an overview of, and compare our work with, existing formalisms for probabilistic logic programming. It is shown that, while the semantics of LPADs is similar to that of some existing approaches, they do offer significant advantages by providing a natural way of representing relational probabilistic knowledge and as such constitute a useful contribution to the field of probabilistic logic programming. We conclude and discuss future work in Section 5. An extended version of this paper is given in [26].

2   Logic Programs with Annotated Disjunctions

A Logic Program with Annotated Disjunctions consists of a set of rules of the following form:

$$(h_1 : \alpha_1) \vee \cdots \vee (h_n : \alpha_n) \leftarrow b_1, \ldots, b_m. \tag{1}$$

Here, the h_i and b_i are, respectively, atoms and literals of some language and the α_i are real numbers in the interval $[0, 1]$, such that $\sum_{i=1}^{n} \alpha_i = 1$. For a rule r of this form, the set $\{(h_i : \alpha_i) \mid 1 \leq i \leq n\}$ will be denoted as $head(r)$, while $body(r) = \{b_i \mid 1 \leq i \leq m\}$. If $head(r)$ contains only one element $(a : 1)$, we will simply write this element as a.

We will denote the set of all ground LPADs as $\mathcal{P_G}$.

The semantics of an LPAD is defined using its grounding. For the remainder of this section, we therefore restrict our attention to ground LPADs. Furthermore, in providing a formal semantics for such a program $P \in \mathcal{P_G}$, we will, in keeping with logic programming tradition [14], also restrict our attention to its Herbrand base $H_B(P)$ and consequently to the set of all its Herbrand interpretations $\mathcal{I}_P = 2^{H_B(P)}$. In keeping with [11], the semantics of an LPAD will be defined by a probability distribution on $\mathcal{I}_P$:

Definition 1. *Let P be in $\mathcal{P_G}$. An admissible probability distribution π on $\mathcal{I}_P$ is a mapping from $\mathcal{I}_P$ to real numbers in $[0, 1]$, such that $\sum_{I \in \mathcal{I}_P} \pi(I) = 1$.*

We would now like to select one of these admissible probability distributions as our intended semantics. To illustrate this process, we consider the grounding of the example presented in the introduction:

$$(heads(coin) : 0.5) \vee (tails(coin) : 0.5) \leftarrow toss(coin), \neg biased(coin).$$
$$(heads(coin) : 0.6) \vee (tails(coin) : 0.4) \leftarrow toss(coin), biased(coin).$$
$$(fair(coin) : 0.9) \vee (biased(coin) : 0.1).$$
$$toss(coin).$$

As already mentioned in the introduction, each of these ground clauses represents a probabilistic choice between a number of non-disjunctive clauses. By choosing one of the possibilities for each clause, we get a non-disjunctive logic program, for instance:

$$heads(coin) \leftarrow toss(coin), \neg biased(coin).$$
$$heads(coin) \leftarrow toss(coin), biased(coin).$$
$$fair(coin).$$
$$toss(coin).$$

Such a program is called an *instance* of the LPAD. Note that this LPAD has $2 \cdot 2 \cdot 2 = 8$ different instances. Such an instance can be assigned a probability by assuming independence between the different choices. This is a reasonable assumption to make, because – as in classical logic programming – it should be possible to read each clause independently from the others; dependence should be modeled within one clause. Indeed, in our example it makes perfect sense to assume that the probability of a non-biased coin landing on heads is independent of the probability of a biased coin landing on heads and of the probability of a certain coin being fair. As such, the probability of the above instance of the example is $0.5 \cdot 0.6 \cdot 0.9 \cdot 1 = 0.27$.

We now formalize the above ideas. The notion of a selection function formalizes the idea of choosing, for each ground instantiation of a rule in an LPAD, one of the atoms in its head.

Definition 2. *Let P be a program in $\mathcal{P}_{\mathcal{G}}$. A selection σ is a function which selects one pair $(h : \alpha)$ from each rule of P, i.e. $\sigma : P \to (H_B(P) \times [0,1])$ such that for each r in P, $\sigma(r) \in head(r)$. For each rule r, we denote the atom h selected from this rule by $\sigma_{atom}(r)$ and the selected probability α by $\sigma_{prob}(r)$. Furthermore, we denote the set of all selections σ by $\mathcal{S}_P$.*

Each selection σ defines an instance of the LPAD.

Definition 3. *Let P be a program in $\mathcal{P}_{\mathcal{G}}$ and σ a selection in $\mathcal{S}_P$. The instance P_σ chosen by σ is obtained by keeping only the atom selected for r in the head of each rule $r \in P$, i.e. $P_\sigma = \{ ``\sigma_{atom}(r) \leftarrow body(r)" \mid r \in P \}$.*

The process of defining the semantics of an LPAD through its instances, is similar to how so-called *split programs* are used in [21] to define the *possible model semantics* for (non-probabilistic) disjunctive logic programs. The main difference is that a split program is allowed to contain more than one non-disjunctive clause for each original disjunctive clause, as the possible model semantics aims to capture both the exclusive and inclusive interpretations of disjunction. In contrast, a probabilistic rule in an LPAD expresses the fact that exactly one atom in the head holds (with a certain probability) as a consequence of the body of the rule being true. Of course, in such a semantics, the inclusive interpretation of disjunctions can be simulated by adding additional atoms to explicitly represent the conjunction of two or more of the original disjuncts. It is worth noting that the semantics of the preferential reasoning formalism *Logic Programs with Ordered Disjunctions* [5], is also defined using a similar notion of instances[1].

Next, we assign a probability to each selection σ in $\mathcal{S}_P$, which induces a probability on the corresponding program P_σ. As motivated above, we assume independence between the selections made for each rule.

Definition 4. *Let P be a program in $\mathcal{P}_{\mathcal{G}}$. The probability of a selection σ in $\mathcal{S}_P$ is the product of the probabilities of the individual choices made by that selection, i.e.*

$$C_\sigma = \prod_{r \in P} \sigma_{prob}(r).$$

The instances of an LPAD are normal logic programs. The meaning of such programs is given by their models under a certain formal semantics. For example, all common semantics for logic programs agree that the meaning of the above instance of the coin-program, is given by the Herbrand interpretation

---

[1] We would like to thank an anonymous reviewer of a previous draft for pointing this out to us.

$\{toss(coin), fair(coin), heads(coin)\}$. The instances of an LPAD therefore define a probability distribution on the set of interpretations of the program. More precisely, the probability of a certain interpretation I is the probability of all instances for which I is a model.

Returning to the example, there is one other instance of this LPAD which has $\{toss(coin), fair(coin), heads(coin)\}$ as its model, namely

$$heads(coin) \leftarrow toss(coin), \neg biased(coin).$$
$$tails(coin) \leftarrow toss(coin), biased(coin).$$
$$fair(coin).$$
$$toss(coin).$$

The probability of this instance is $0.5 \cdot 0.4 \cdot 0.9 \cdot 1 = 0.18$. Therefore the probability of the interpretation $\{toss(coin), fair(coin), heads(coin)\}$ is $0.5 \cdot 0.4 \cdot 0.9 \cdot 1 + 0.5 \cdot 0.6 \cdot 0.9 \cdot 1 = 0.5 \cdot (0.4 + 0.6) \cdot 0.9 \cdot 1 = 0.45$.

Of course, there are a number of ways in which the semantics of a non-disjunctive logic program can be defined. In our framework, uncertainty is modeled by annotated disjunctions. Therefore, a non-disjunctive program should contain *no* uncertainty, i.e. it should have a single two-valued model. Indeed, this is the only way in which an LPAD can be seen as specifying a *unique* probability distribution, without assuming that the "user" meant to say something he did not actually write. Consider for instance the program: $\{a \leftarrow \neg b.\ b \leftarrow \neg a.\}$. Any reasonable probability distribution specified by this program, would have to assign a probability α to the interpretation $\{a\}$ and $1 - \alpha$ to $\{b\}$. However, if such a probability distribution were intended, one would simply have written: $(a : \alpha) \vee (b : 1 - \alpha)$.

Therefore, we will take the meaning of an instance P_σ of an LPAD to be given by its well founded model $WFM(P_\sigma)$ [24] and require that all these well founded models are two-valued. If, for instance, the LPAD is acyclic (meaning that all its instances are acyclic [1]), this will always be the case.

Definition 5. *An LPAD P is called* sound *iff for each selection σ in $\mathcal{S}_P$, the well founded model of the program P_σ chosen by σ is two-valued.*

The probabilities on the elements σ of $\mathcal{S}_P$ are then naturally extended to probabilities on interpretations. The following distribution π_P^* gives the semantics of an LPAD P.

Definition 6. *Let P be a sound LPAD in $\mathcal{P}_{\mathcal{G}}$. For each of its interpretations I in $\mathcal{I}_P$, the probability $\pi_P^*(I)$ assigned by P to I is the sum of the probabilities of all selections which lead to I, i.e. with $S(I)$ being the set of all selections σ for which $WFM(P_\sigma) = I$:*

$$\pi_P^*(I) = \sum_{\sigma \in S(I)} C_\sigma.$$

It is easy to show that – for a sound LPAD – this distribution π_P^* is indeed an admissible probability distribution [26].

Proposition 1. *Let P be a sound LPAD in $\mathcal{P}_\mathcal{G}$. Then π_P^* is an admissible probability distribution.*

There is a strong connection between the interpretations $I \in \mathcal{I}_P$ for which $\pi_P^*(I) > 0$ and traditional semantics for disjunctive logic programs. First of all, each such interpretation I with $\pi_P^*(I) > 0$ is also a *possible model* [21] of the LPAD (when ignoring the probabilities, of course). Secondly, each *stable model* [8] of the LPAD is such an interpretation. Moreover, in most cases, the stable model semantics coincides precisely with this set of interpretations. Only for programs where the same atom appears in the head of different clauses, as for instance $\{(a : 0.5) \vee (b : 0.5). \quad a.\}$, can there be a difference. Indeed, this example has a unique stable model $\{a\}$, but in our probabilistic framework $\pi_P^*(\{a, b\}) = 0.5$. From a modeling perspective, this difference makes sense, because in an LPAD a clause like the first one represents a kind of "experiment", of which the disjuncts in its heads are possible outcomes. As such, there is no reason why a being true should preclude b as a possible outcome of the experiment denoted by the first clause.

Of course, we are not only interested in the probabilities of interpretations, but also in the probability of a formula ϕ under the semantics π_P^*. This is defined as the sum of the probabilities of the interpretations in which the formula is true:

Definition 7. *Let P be a sound LPAD in $\mathcal{P}_\mathcal{G}$. Slightly abusing notation, for each formula ϕ, the probability $\pi_P^*(\phi)$ of ϕ according to P is the sum of the probabilities of all interpretations in which ϕ holds, i.e.*

$$\pi_P^*(\phi) = \sum_{I \in \mathcal{I}_P^\phi} \pi_P^*(I).$$

with $\mathcal{I}_P^\phi = \{I \in \mathcal{I}_P \mid I \models \phi\}$.

Calculating such probabilities is the basic inference task of probabilistic logic programs. Usually, the formulas are restricted to being *queries*, i.e. existentially quantified conjunctions. While inference algorithms are not the focus of this work, we will nevertheless briefly explain how this inference task is related to inference for logic programs.

The probability of a formula is defined as the sum of the probabilities of all interpretations in which it is true. The probability of such an interpretation is, in turn, defined in terms of the probabilities of the normal logic programs which can be constructed from the LPAD. Hence, finding a proof for the query, gives us already "part" of the probability of the query. To compute the entire probability of the query, it suffices to find all proofs and to appropriately combine the probabilities associated with the heads of the clauses appearing in these proofs.

In Section 4 on related work, we will discuss a formalism called the Independent Choice Logic [20]. For this formalism, an inference algorithm has been developed, which operates according to the principles outlined in the previous paragraph. Furthermore, a source-to-source transformation from acyclic LPADs to ICL exists, which allows this algorithm to also be applied to acyclic LPADs. Moreover, as this transformation is polynomial in the size of the input program, this shows that acyclic LPADs are in the same complexity class as ICL.

In [26], we show that the semantics presented in this section is consistent with that proposed in Halpern's fundamental article [11], in which a general way of formalizing a certain type of probabilistic knowledge through a possible world semantics was introduced.

3 Examples

We present four examples and refer to [26] for more examples.

A Hidden Markov Model. The Hidden Markov Model in Figure 1 can be modeled by the following LPAD.

$$(state(s0, s(T)) : 0.7) \vee (state(s1, s(T)) : 0.3) \leftarrow state(s0, T).$$
$$(state(s1, s(T)) : 0.8) \vee (state(s2, s(T)) : 0.2) \leftarrow state(s1, T).$$
$$state(s2, s(T)) \leftarrow state(s2, T).$$
$$(out(a, T) : 0.2) \vee (out(b, T) : 0.8) \leftarrow state(s0, T).$$
$$(out(b, T) : 0.9) \vee (out(c, T) : 0.1) \leftarrow state(s1, T).$$
$$(out(b, T) : 0.3) \vee (out(c, T) : 0.7) \leftarrow state(s2, T).$$
$$state(s0, 0).$$

This program corresponds nicely to the way in which one would tend to explain the semantics of this HMM in natural language. For instance, the first clause could be read as: "if the HMM is in state s_0, then it can either go to state s_1 or stay in state s_0."

It is worth noting that this

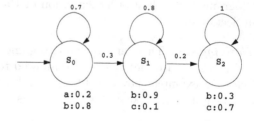

Fig. 1. A Hidden Markov Model.

LPAD has an infinite grounding. As such, each particular instance of this LPAD has a probability of zero. However, our semantics remains well-defined and still assigns an appropriate non-zero probability to each finite string, through an infinite sum of such zero probabilities. Moreover, the aforementioned transformation from LPADs to ICL is also able to deal with such programs, since it does not instantiate any variables. As the inference-algorithm of ICL does not need to compute the grounding of a program, but rather searches for "proofs" of a query in an SLD-like manner, this allows these probabilities to be effectively computed as well.

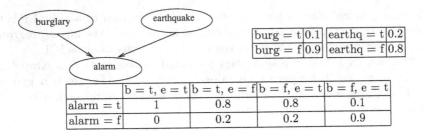

	b = t, e = t	b = t, e = f	b = f, e = t	b = f, e = t
alarm = t	1	0.8	0.8	0.1
alarm = f	0	0.2	0.2	0.9

Fig. 2. A Bayesian network.

A Bayesian network. The Bayesian network in Figure 2 can also be represented in our formalism. This is done by explicitly enumerating the possible values for each node. In this way, every Bayesian network can be represented as an LPAD.

$$(burg(X,t) : 0.1) \vee (burg(X,f) : 0.9).$$
$$(earthq(X,t) : 0.2) \vee (earthq(X,f) : 0.8).$$
$$alarm(X,t) \leftarrow burg(X,t), earthq(X,t).$$
$$(alarm(X,t) : 0.8) \vee (alarm(X,f) : 0.2) \leftarrow burg(X,t), earthq(X,f).$$
$$(alarm(X,t) : 0.8) \vee (alarm(X,f) : 0.2) \leftarrow burg(X,f), earthq(X,t).$$
$$(alarm(X,t) : 0.1) \vee (alarm(X,f) : 0.9) \leftarrow burg(X,f), earthq(X,f).$$

Actually, this LPAD represents several "versions" of the original Bayesian network, namely one for each instantiation of X. As such, this representation is similar to the *knowledge based model construction*-formalism of Bayesian Logic Programs [12], a first-order extension of Bayesian networks, which is discussed in Section 4.

Throwing dice. There are some board games which require a player to roll a six (using a standard die) before he is allowed to actually start the game itself. The following example shows an LPAD which defines a probability distribution on how long it could take a player to do this.

$$(on(D,1,s(T)) : 1/6) \vee (on(D,2,s(T)) : 1/6) \vee \cdots \vee (on(D,6,s(T)) : 1/6)$$
$$\leftarrow time(T), die(D), \neg on(D,6,T).$$
$$start\_game(s(T)) \leftarrow time(T), on(D,6,T).$$
$$time(s(T)) \leftarrow time(T).$$
$$time(0). \qquad die(die).$$

The first rule of this LPAD is the most important one. It states that if the player has not succeeded in getting a six on his current attempt, he will have to try again. Note that, because of the use of negation-as-failure in the body of this clause, the atoms $on(D,1,s(T)), \ldots, on(D,5,s(T))$ are only needed to serve as alternatives for $on(D,6,s(T))$. As such, in the context of this example, this clause could equivalently be written as for instance:

$$(on(D, 6, s(T)) : 1/6) \lor (not\_six : 5/6) \leftarrow time(T), die(D), \neg on(D, 6, T).$$

Moreover, instead of the atom *not_six*, any atom not appearing in the rest of the program could be used. We therefore simply abbreviate such clauses by

$$(on(D, 6, s(T)) : 1/6) \leftarrow time(T), die(D), \neg on(D, 6, T).$$

Situation calculus. LPADs can also be used to model indeterminate actions. To demonstrate this, we will consider a variant of the turkey shooting problem. If we try to shoot a healthy turkey, there are three possible outcomes: we can miss (with probability 0.2), we can hit but merely wound it (with probability 0.5) or we can immediately succeed in killing it (with probability 0.3). Trying to shoot a wounded turkey can have two possible effects: we can miss, in which case the turkey simply remains wounded (with probability 0.3 – wounded turkeys are of course less mobile than their healthy counterparts), or we can hit and kill it (with probability 0.7). If the turkey is already wounded and we wish to save our bullets, we can also simply wait to see whether it will succumb to its wounds (with probability 0.4). However, this also gives the turkey a chance to rest and as such it could recover from its injuries (with probability 0.1).

The following LPAD models this problem, using the situation calculus.

$$(holds(healthy, do(shoot, S)) : 0.2) \lor holds(wounded, do(shoot, S)) : 0.5)$$
$$\lor \, holds(dead, do(shoot, S)) : 0.3) \leftarrow holds(healthy, S).$$
$$(holds(wounded, do(shoot, S)) : 0.3) \lor (holds(dead, do(shoot, S)) : 0.7)$$
$$\leftarrow holds(wounded, S).$$
$$(holds(healthy, do(wait, S)) : 0.1) \lor (holds(wounded, do(wait, S)) : 0.5)$$
$$\lor \, holds(dead, do(wait, S)) : 0.4) \leftarrow holds(wounded, S).$$
$$holds(dead, do(A, S)) \leftarrow holds(dead, S), action(A).$$
$$holds(Prop, do(wait, S)) \leftarrow holds(Prop, S), \neg holds(wounded, S).$$
$$holds(healthy, s0). \quad action(wait). \quad action(shoot).$$

The probability distribution defined by this LPAD specifies, for instance, that the probability $\pi^*(holds(dead, do(wait, do(shoot, s0))))$ of the turkey being dead after shooting and waiting, is $0.3 + 0.5 \cdot 0.4 = 0.5$. Once again, this probability can also be effectively computed by applying the transformation from LPADs to ICL.

4   Related Work

There is a large body of work concerning probabilistic logic programming. Due to space limitations, we refer to [25] and [26] for more details, references, and comparisons with LPADs.

An important class of probabilistic logic programming formalisms are those following the *Knowledge Based Model Construction* or KBMC approach. Such formalisms allow the representation of an entire "class" of propositional models, from which, for a specific query, an appropriate model can then be constructed "at run-time". This approach was initiated by Breese et al [4] and Bacchus [2]. Examples are: *Context-Sensitive Probabilistic Knowledge Bases* of Ngo and Haddawy [19], *Probabilistic Relational Models* of Getoor et al [9], and *Bayesian Logic Programs* of Kersting and De Raedt [12].

A formal comparison between LPADs and Bayesian Logic Programs (BLPs) is given in [26]. A BLP can be seen as representing a (possibly infinite) set of Bayesian networks. Each ground atom represents a random variable, which can take on a value from a domain associated with its predicate. An implication in a clause of a BLP is not a logical implication, but rather an expression concerning probabilistic dependencies. This makes the reading of a BLP – at least for those acquainted with logic programming – less natural. Another difference is that, although it is possible to simulate classical negation in BLPs, they do not incorporate non-monotonic negation. In some cases, this can lead to longer and less intuitive programs.

The most natural way of modelling the coin-example of the introduction, is by the following BLP:

$$side(Coin) \leftarrow toss(Coin), biased(Coin).$$

$$biased(coin).$$

$$toss(coin).$$

With each of these clauses, a conditional probability table or CPT has to be associated, which defines the conditional probability of each value for a random variable associated with a ground instantiation of the atom in the head of the clause, given the values of the random variables associated with the corresponding ground instantiations of the atoms in the body. In the case of the example, these are as follows. The atoms $toss(Coin)$ and $biased(Coin)$ are abbreviated to, respectively, $t(C)$ and $b(C)$.

side(C)	t(C) = t, b(C) = t	t(C) = t, b(C) = f	t(C) = f, b(C) = t	t(C) = f, b(C) = f
heads	0.6	0.5	0	0
tails	0.4	0.5	0	0
NA	0	0	1	1

biased(coin)	
t	0.6
f	0.4

toss(coin)	
t	1
f	0

Note that, in order to simulate the fact that we are only interested in the position of coins *after* they have been tossed, the domains of the random variables corresponding to ground instantiations of $side(C)$ had to be extended with the "don't care"-value NA (not applicable).

In [26] it is formally shown that the semantics of a BLP can be expressed by an LPAD, which explicitizes the implicit argument of each atom, i.e. its "value", and enumerates all the elements in the domain. This process is similar to that which was used in Section 3 to model a Bayesian network by an LPAD. Conversely, it is shown that quite a large subset of all LPADs can be represented as BLP. This is done by making each atom a boolean random variable, i.e. one with domain $\{true, false\}$, simulating the logical semantics of clauses by appropriate conditional probabilities and introducing for each clause a new random variable to explicitly represent the choice between the disjuncts in its head. This process, however, often leads to BLPs which are not very natural. For instance, the LPAD-clause

$$(heads(Coin) : 0.5) \vee (tails(Coin) : 0.5) \leftarrow toss(Coin), \neg biased(Coin).$$

would be transformed to the set of clauses

$$heads(Coin) \leftarrow toss(Coin), not\_biased(Coin), ch(Coin).$$
$$tails(Coin) \leftarrow toss(Coin), not\_biased(Coin), ch(Coin).$$
$$ch(Coin).$$

with the following CPTs:

$heads(C)$	$t(C) = t, nb(C) = t, ch(C) = 1$	$\cdots$
t	1	0
f	0	1

$tails(C)$	$t(C) = t, nb(C) = t, ch(C) = 2$	$\cdots$
t	1	0
f	0	1

$ch(C)$	
1	0.5
2	0.5

Another class of formalisms, besides that of KBMC, are those which grew out of an attempt to extend logic programming with probability. Among these formalisms, *Programming in Statistical Modeling* (PRISM) [23] and the *Independent Choice Logic* (ICL) [20] deviate the least from classical logic programming. ICL is a probabilistic extension of abductive logic programming. An ICL program consists of both a logical and a probabilistic part. The logical part is an acyclic, normal logic program. The probabilistic part consists of a set of clauses of the form (in LPAD syntax): $(a_1 : \alpha_1) \vee \cdots \vee (a_n : \alpha_n)$. The atoms a_i in such clauses are called abducibles. Each abducible may only appear once in the probabilistic part of an ICL program; in the logical part of the program, abducibles may only appear in the bodies of clauses.

Syntactically, each ICL program is clearly an LPAD. In [26] it was shown that this embedding of ICL into LPADs preserves the original semantics of ICL (as formulated in [20]). Conversely, each acyclic LPAD can be transformed into one in this restricted syntax [26]. This is done by creating new, artificial atoms, which explicitly represent the process of choosing a disjunct from the head of a clause, as is illustrated by the following ICL-version of the coin-example of the introduction:

$$heads(Coin) \leftarrow toss(Coin), \neg biased(Coin), fair\_heads(Coin).$$
$$tails(Coin) \leftarrow toss(Coin), \neg biased(Coin), fair\_tails(Coin).$$
$$heads(Coin) \leftarrow toss(Coin), biased(Coin), biased\_heads(Coin).$$
$$tails(Coin) \leftarrow toss(Coin), biased(Coin), biased\_tails(Coin).$$
$$(fair\_heads(Coin) : 0.5) \lor (fair\_tails(Coin) : 0.5).$$
$$(biased\_heads(Coin) : 0.6) \lor (biased\_tails(Coin) : 0.4).$$
$$(fair(coin) : 0.9) \lor (biased(coin) : 0.1).$$
$$toss(coin).$$

On the first author's web site[2] a Prolog program can be found which performs this transformation. As such, even though LPADs do not (yet) have an implemented inference algorithm of their own, it is already possible to solve queries to acyclic LPADs by using the ICL algorithm.

It should be noted that, although these two formalisms are similar in terms of theoretical expressive power, they are nevertheless quite different in their practical modeling properties. Indeed, ICL (and of course the corresponding subset of LPADs) is ideally suited for problem domains such as diagnosis or theory revision, in which it is most natural to express uncertainty on the *causes* of certain effects. The greater expressiveness of LPADs (in the sense that LPADs allow more natural representations of certain types of knowledge), on the other hand, makes these also suited for problems such as modeling indeterminate actions, in which it is most natural to express uncertainty on the *effects* of certain causes. Of course, this is not surprising, as a similar relationship exists between the non-probabilistic formalisms on which ICL and LPADs are based: [22] proves that abductive logic programming and disjunctive logic programming are essentially equivalent; however, history has shown that both these formalisms are valid ways of representing knowledge, with each having problem domains for which it is better suited than the other.

LPADs are not the only probabilistic formalism based on disjunctive logic programming. In *Many-Valued Disjunctive Logic Programs* of Lukasiewicz [16] probabilities are associated with disjunctive clauses as a whole. In this way, uncertainty of the implication itself – and *not*, as is the case with LPADs, of the disjuncts in the head – is expressed. In our work, the goal is not to represent uncertainty about the truth of a disjunctive clause. In fact, given an LPAD and a model of it, all the corresponding non-probabilistic disjunctive rules are true in the interpretations which have non-zero probability. Instead, LPADs are to be used in situations where one has uncertainty about the consequence (head) of a given conjunction of atoms (body).

All the works mentioned above use point probabilities. There are however also a number of formalisms using probability intervals: *Probabilistic Logic Programs* of Ng and Subrahmanian [18], their extension to *Hybrid Probabilistic Programs* of Dekhtyar and Subrahmanian [7] and *Probabilistic Deductive Databases* of Lakshmanan and Sadri [13]. Contrary to our approach, programs in these

---

formalisms do not define a *single* probability distribution, but rather a *set* of possible probability distributions, which – in a sense – allows one to express a kind of "meta-uncertainty", i.e. uncertainty about which distribution is the "right" one. Moreover, the techniques used by these formalisms tend to have more in common with constraint logic programming than "normal" logic programming.

We also want to mention the *Stochastic Logic Programs* of Muggleton and Cussens [6, 17]. In this formalism probabilities are attached to the selection of clauses in the Prolog inference algorithm, which basically results in a first-order version of stochastic context free grammars. Because of this formalism's strong ties to Prolog, it appears to be quite different from LPADs and indeed all of the other formalisms mentioned here.

More recently, Baral et al. developed *P-log* [3]. While the principles underlying this formalism and its semantics seem quite related to ours, there are quite some differences in the execution of these ideas; more specifically, P-log is not an extension of logic programming, but rather a new language which "compiles to" answer set programs. As such, the precise relation between LPADs and P-log is currently not clear.

5   Conclusion and Future Work

In Section 2, Logic Programs with Annotated Disjunctions were introduced. In our opinion, this formalism offers a natural and consistent way of describing complex probabilistic knowledge in terms of a number of (independent) simple choices, an idea which is prevalent in for instance [20]. Furthermore, it does not ignore the crucial concept of conditional probability, which underlies the entire "Bayesian movement", and does not deviate from the well established and well known non-probabilistic semantics of first-order logic and logic programming. Indeed, as shown in Section 2, for an LPAD P, the set of interpretations I for which $\pi_P^*(I) > 0$, is a subset of the possible models of P and a (small) superset of its stable models.

While the comparison with related work such as ICL (Section 4) showed that the ideas underlying this formalism and its semantics are not radically new, we feel it offers enough additional advantages in providing a natural representation of relational probabilistic knowledge, to constitute a useful contribution to the field of probabilistic logic programming. In future work, we hope to demonstrate this further, by presenting larger, real-world applications of LPADs. We also plan further research concerning a proof procedure and complexity analysis for LPADs.

Finally, there are a number of possible extensions to the LPAD formalism which should be investigated. For example, it might prove useful to allow the use of variables in the probabilistic annotations and incorporate aggregates, in order to allow a more concise representation of certain basic probability distributions. In such a way, one would be able to express, for instance, that if one chooses a person at random from a room in which there are m men and f women, the probability of having chosen a man is $\frac{m}{m+f}$:

$$(male(C) : \frac{M}{P}) \vee (female(C) : \frac{F}{P}) \leftarrow chosen(C),$$
$$M = count(X, male(X)), F = count(X, female(X)), P = M + F.$$

Because of the logical nature of LPADs and their instance-based semantics, it should be fairly straightforward to add such extensions to the language in a natural way. In other formalisms, such as BLP or ICL, this appears to be more difficult.

References

1. K.R. Apt and M. Bezem. Acyclic programs. *New Generation Computing*, 9:335–363, 1991.
2. F. Bacchus. Using first-order probability logic for the construction of bayesian networks. In *Proceedings of the Sixth Conference on Uncertainty in Artificial Intelligence*, pages 219–226, 1993.
3. C. Baral, M. Gelfond, and N. Rushton. Probabilistic reasoning with answer sets. In *Proc. Logic Programming and Non Monotonic Reasoning, LPNMR'04*, pages 21–33. Springer-Verlag, 2004.
4. J.S. Breese, R.P. Goldman, and M.P. Wellman. Introduction to the special section on knowledge-based construction of probabilistic and decision models. *IEEE Transactions on Systems, Man, and Cybernetics*, 24(11):1577–1579, 1994.
5. G. Brewka. Logic programming with ordered disjunction. In *Proceedings of the 18th National Conference on Artificial Intelligence, AAAI-2002. Morgan Kaufmann, 2002.*, pages 100–105, 2002.
6. J. Cussens. Stochastic logic programs: Sampling, inference and applications. In *Proceedings of the Sixteenth Annual Conference on Uncertainty in Artificial Intelligence*, pages 115–122. MK, 2000.
7. A. Dekhtyar and V.S. Subrahmanian. Hybrid probabilistic programs. *Journal of Logic Programming*, 43(3):187–250, 2000.
8. M. Gelfond and V. Lifschitz. Classical negation in logic programs and disjunctive databases. *New generation computing*, 9:365–385, 1991.
9. L. Getoor, N. Friedman, D. Koller, and A. Pfeffer. Learning Probabilistic Relational Models. In S. Dzeroski and N. Lavrac, editors, *Relational Data Mining*, pages 7–34. Springer-Verlag, 2001. to appear.
10. J. Y. Halpern. *Reasoning about uncertainty*. MIT press, 2003.
11. J.Y. Halpern. An analysis of first-order logics of probability. *Artificial Intelligence*, 46:311–350, 1989.
12. K. Kersting and L. De Raedt. Bayesian logic programs. In J. Cussens and A. Frisch, editors, *Work-in-Progress Reports of the Tenth International Conference on Inductive Logic Programming (ILP-2000)*, 2000.
13. L.V.S. Lakshmanan and F. Sadri. Probabilistic deductive databases. In M. Bruynooghe, editor, *Proceedings of the International Symposium on Logic Programming*, pages 254–268. MIT Press, 1994.
14. J.W. Lloyd. *Foundations of Logic Programming*. Springer-Verlag, 2nd edition, 1987.
15. J. Lobo, J. Minker, and A. Rajasekar. *Foundations of Disjunctive Logic Programming*. MIT Press, 1992.

16. T. Lukasiewicz. Fixpoint characterizations for many-valued disjunctive logic programs. In *Proceedings of the 6th International Conference on Logic Programming and Nonmonotonic Reasoning (LPNMR'01)*, volume 2173 of *Lecture Notes in Artificial Intelligence*, pages 336–350. Springer-Verlag, 2001.

17. S. Muggleton. Learning stochastic logic programs. *Electronic Transactions in Artificial Intelligence*, 5(041), 2000.

18. R.T. Ng and V.S. Subrahmanian. Probabilistic logic programming. *Information and Computation*, 101(2):150–201, 1992.

19. L. Ngo and P. Haddawy. Answering queries from context-sensitive probabilistic knowledge bases. *Theoretical Computer Science*, 171(1–2):147–177, 1997.

20. D. Poole. The Independent Choice Logic for modelling multiple agents under uncertainty. *Artificial Intelligence*, 94(1-2):7–56, 1997.

21. C. Sakama. Possible model semantics for disjunctive databases II (extended abstract). In *Logic Programming and Non-monotonic Reasoning*, pages 107–114, 1990.

22. C. Sakama and K. Inoue. On the equivalence between disjunctive and abductive logic programs. In *International Conference on Logic Programming*, pages 489–503, 1994.

23. T. Sato and Y. Kameya. PRISM: A language for symbolic-statistical modeling. *Proceedings of IJCAI 97*, pages 1330–1335, 1997.

24. A. Van Gelder, K.A. Ross, and J.S. Schlipf. The Well-Founded Semantics for General Logic Programs. *Journal of the ACM*, 38(3):620–650, 1991.

25. J. Vennekens and S. Verbaeten. A general view on probabilistic logic programming. In *Proceedings of the 15th Belgian-Dutch Conference on Artificial Intelligence*, pages 299–306, 2003. http://www.cs.kuleuven.ac.be/~joost/bnaic.ps.

26. J. Vennekens and S. Verbaeten. Logic programs with annotated disjunctions. Technical Report CW386, K.U. Leuven, 2003.
http://www.cs.kuleuven.ac.be/~joost/techrep.ps.

Abstract Interpretation-Based Mobile Code Certification*

Elvira Albert[1], Germán Puebla[2], and Manuel Hermenegildo[2,3]

[1] SIP, Complutense University of Madrid
elvira@sip.ucm.es
[2] Fac. de Informática, Technical U. of Madrid
{german,herme}@fi.upm.es
[3] Depts. of Comp. Sci. and El. and Comp. Eng., U. of New Mexico
herme@unm.edu

Current approaches to mobile code safety – inspired by the technique of *Proof-Carrying Code* (PCC) [4] – associate safety information (in the form of a *certificate*) to programs. The certificate (or *proof*) is created by the code supplier at compile time, and packaged along with the untrusted code. The consumer who receives the code+certificate package can then run a *checker* which, by a straightforward inspection of the code and the certificate, is able to verify the validity of the certificate and thus compliance with the safety policy. The main practical difficulty of PCC techniques is in generating safety certificates which at the same time: i) allow expressing interesting safety properties, ii) can be generated automatically and, iii) are easy and efficient to check.

We propose an automatic approach to PCC which makes use of *abstract interpretation* [2] techniques for dealing with the above issues. While our approach is general, we develop it for concreteness in the context of (Constraint) Logic Programming, (C)LP, because this paradigm offers a good number of advantages, especially the maturity and sophistication of the analysis tools available. *Assertions* are used to define the safety policy. Such assertions are syntactic objects which allow expressing "abstract" – i.e. symbolic – properties over different *abstract domains*. The first step in our method then involves automatically inferring a set of *safety assertions* (corresponding to the analysis results), using abstract interpretation, and taking as a starting input the program, the predefined assertions available for library predicates, and any (optional) assertions provided by the user for user-defined predicates. The safety policy consists in guaranteeing that the safety assertions hold for the given program in the context of the desired abstract domain. This is automatically provided by the inference process and its correctness ensured by the proved correctness of the process.

The *certification* process – i.e., the generation of a safety certificate by the code supplier which is as small as possible – is in turn based on the idea that only a particular *subset* of the analysis results computed by abstract interpretation-

---

* This work was funded in part by projects ASAP (EU IST FET Programme Project Number IST-2001-38059) and CUBICO (MCYT TIC 2002-0055). Part of this work was performed during a research stay of Elvira Albert and Germán Puebla at UNM supported by respective grants from the Secretaría de Estado de Educación y Universidades. Manuel Hermenegildo is also supported by the Prince of Asturias Chair in Information Science and Technology at UNM.

B. Demoen and V. Lifschitz (Eds.): ICLP 2004, LNCS 3132, pp. 446–447, 2004.

based fixpoint algorithms needs to be used to play the role of certificate for attesting program safety. In our implementation, the high-level assertion language of [5] is used and the certificate is automatically generated from the results computed by the *goal dependent* fixpoint abstract interpretation-based analyzer of [3]. These analysis results are represented by means of two data structures in the output: the *answer table* and the *arc dependency table*. We show that a particular subset of the analysis results – namely the answer table – is sufficient for mobile code certification. A verification condition generator computes from the assertions and the answer table a *verification condition* in order to attest compliance of the program with respect to the safety policy. Intuitively, the verification condition is a conjunction of boolean expressions whose validity ensures the consistency of a set of assertions. The automatic *validator* attempts to check its validity. When the verification condition is indeed checked, then the answer table is considered a valid certificate.

In order to retain the safety guarantees, the consumer, after receiving the program together with the certificate from the supplier, can trust neither the code nor the certificate. Thus, in the *validation* process, the consumer not only checks the validity of the answer table received but it also (re-)generates a trustworthy verification condition, as it is done by the supplier. The crucial observation in our approach is that the *validation* process performed by the code consumer is similar to the above certification process but replacing the fixpoint analyzer by an *analysis checker* which *does not need to compute a fixpoint*. It simply *checks* the analysis, using an algorithm which is a very simplified *one-pass* analyzer. Intuitively, since the certification process already provides the fixpoint result as certificate, an additional analysis pass over it cannot change the result. Thus, as long as the answer table is valid, a single cycle over the code validates the certificate.

We believe that our proposal can bring the expressiveness and automation which is inherent to abstract interpretation-based techniques to the area of mobile code safety. In particular, the expressiveness of existing abstract domains will be useful to define a wider range of safety properties. Furthermore, in the case of (C)LP the approach inherits the inference power and automation of the abstract interpretation engines developed for this paradigm. A complete description of the method (and related techniques) can be found in [1].

References

1. E. Albert, G. Puebla, and M. Hermenegildo. An Abstract Interpretation-based Approach to Mobile Code Safety. TR CLIP8/2003.0, T. U. of Madrid, Nov. 2003.
2. P. Cousot and R. Cousot. Abstract Interpretation: a Unified Lattice Model for Static Analysis of Programs by Construction or Approximation of Fixpoints. POPL'77, pages 238–252, 1977.
3. M. Hermenegildo, G. Puebla, K. Marriott, and P. Stuckey. Incremental Analysis of Constraint Logic Programs. *ACM TOPLAS*, 22(2):187–223, March 2000.
4. G. Necula. Proof-Carrying Code. *POPL'97*, pages 106–119. ACM Press, 1997.
5. G. Puebla, F. Bueno, and M. Hermenegildo. An Assertion Language for CLP. In *Analysis and Visualization Tools for Constraint Programming*, pages 23–61. Springer LNCS 1870, 2000.

Labeled Logic Programs

Steve Barker

Dept. Computer Science, King's College, London, UK

Abstract. In this communication, we describe work-in-progress on "webized" logic programs, and the use of these programs for policy formulation and exchange in the context of conducting e-commerce.

A number of practical and theoretical issues remain to be addressed in the context of conducting e-commerce. When agents engage in business transactions via the Web, the notions of policy specification and implementation are fundamentally important. For instance, when one business b_1 considers trading with another business b_2, b_1 will request information from b_2 on things like b_2's pricing policies, discounting policies, refund policies, and lead times. Moreover, the policy information that b_2 releases to b_1 may depend on b_2's perception of b_1 as a possible trading partner e.g., whether b_2 believes (either from direct experience or by experiences reported by a trusted third-party) that b_1 is likely to be a potential "bad debtor" or a "prompt payer". The information that b_2 releases to b_1 is controlled by using a usage policy specification.

Logic programs have a number of attractive features that make them suitable for policy representation. For example, logic programs permit the high-level, declarative specification of requirements by using a language for which well known formal semantics are defined, and for which efficient operational methods have been developed. Nevertheless, extended forms of logic programs are desirable to better meet the requirements of e-commerce applications. To address this need, we introduce labeled normal clause programs.

A *labeled normal clause* is a formula of the following form where C is an atom, v_i is an empty set or a singleton that is the URI for a non-local source (e.g., an ontology) that includes the definition of an atom in the set $\{A_1, A_2, \ldots, A_m, B_1, B_2, \ldots, B_n\}$, and *not* is negation-as-failure:

$$C \leftarrow v_1 : A_1, v_2 : A_2, \ldots, v_m : A_m,$$
$$not\ v_{m+1} : B_1, not\ v_{m+2} : B_2, \ldots,$$
$$not\ v_{m+n} : B_n.$$

A *labeled logic program* is a finite set of labeled normal clauses. For most (all?) policy specifications in practice, labeled logic programs will be locally stratified and function-free.

In addition to labeled logic programs, we introduce a markup language for enabling policy information to be exchanged between agents that engage in e-trading. Our markup language extends *RuleML* [2] to enable a variety of different

B. Demoen and V. Lifschitz (Eds.): ICLP 2004, LNCS 3132, pp. 448–449, 2004.

forms of policy information to be exchanged. We refer to this language as ERML (viz., extended RuleML).

The most important feature of ERML is that it permits comparison operators in the set $\Phi = \{<, \leq, =, \neq, \geq, >\}$ and the arithmetic operators in the set $\Gamma = \{+, -, \div, \times, mod, abs\}$ to be expressed by using markup. Our motivations for using Γ and Φ, over a finite domain of natural numbers, is that much information that is expressed in policies either requires to be represented and manipulated in numeric form or may be equivalently represented and manipulated in numeric form. Arithmetic is a universally accepted *inter lingua*, and all computational systems will implement the simple form of arithmetic that we propose for policy specifications. Moreover, by imposing some not too restrictive conditions on the use of comparison operators and arithmetic operators (e.g., the restriction to *ground arithmetic expressions* [1]), the soundness and completeness of the operational semantics of rule engines that process policy information can be ensured.

Because arithmetic may be soundly implemented in the hardware or software used by rule engines, we claim that our approach remains within the realms of "pure-belief" systems [3]. Given the importance of arithmetic and comparison operators in practical policy formulation, we argue that these notions ought to be given first-class status in a markup language for policy representation. Moreover, we argue that *procedural attachments* [3], which have been proposed for implementing the operators in $\Gamma \cup \Phi$, should only be used for application-specific requirements, rather than for defining things like comparison operators and arithmetic operations, which are needed for expressing policy requirements *in general*.

In implementations of our approach, a compiler is used to transform a labeled logic program into a language for implementation (e.g., XSB PROLOG or SQL). The URIs in a labeled logic program may be mapped to import statements or file manipulation functions in the implementation language. Another compiler can perform bidirectional translations of PROLOG and SQL to/from ERML.

To demonstrate a practical application of our approach, we show how a usage control model may be formulated to protect a range of Web resources from unauthorized access requests.

References

1. K. Apt, From Logic Programming to Prolog, Prentice Hall, 1997.
2. H. Boley, S. Tabet, and G. Wagner, Design Rationale of RuleML: A Markup Language for Semantic Web Rules, SWWS 2001, 381–401, 2001.
3. B. Grosof, Representing E-commerce Rules via Situated Courteous Logic Programs, Electronic Commerce Research and Applications, 3(1), 2–20, 2004.

Xcerpt and XChange –
Logic Programming Languages for Querying
and Evolution on the Web*

François Bry, Paula-Lavinia Pătrânjan, and Sebastian Schaffert

Institute for Informatics, University of Munich
http://www.pms.ifi.lmu.de/

Motivation. The *Semantic Web* is an endeavor aiming at enriching the existing Web with meta-data and data (and meta-data) processing so as to allow computer systems to actually *reason* with the data instead of merely *rendering* it. To this aim, it is necessary to be able to *query* and *update* data and meta-data. Existing Semantic Web query languages (like DQL[1]) are special purpose, they are not capable of processing generic Web data. On the other hand, the language *Xcerpt* [1] [2] presented in the poster is a general purpose language that can query any kind of XML data and at the same time, being based on logic programming, provides advanced reasoning capabilities. Likewise, the maintenance and evolution of data on the (Semantic) Web is necessary: the Web is a "living organism" whose dynamic character requires languages for specifying its evolution. This requirement regards not only updating data from Web resources, but also the propagation of changes on the Web. These issues have not received much attention so far, existing update languages (e.g. XML-RL Update Language [3]) and reactive languages [4] for the Web offer the possibility to execute simple update operations and, moreover, important features needed for propagation of updates on the Web are still missing. The language *XChange* also presented in the poster builds upon the query language Xcerpt and provides advanced, Web-specific capabilities, such as propagation of changes on the Web (*change*) and event-based communications between Web sites (*exchange*).

Xcerpt: Querying Data on the Web. Xcerpt is a declarative, rule-based query language for Web data based on logic programming. An Xcerpt program contains at least one *goal* and some (maybe zero) *rules*. Rules and goals consist of query and construction patterns, called *terms* in analogy to other logic programming languages. Terms represent tree-like (or graph-like) structures.

Data terms are used to represent XML documents and the data items of a semistructured database.

Query terms are patterns matched against Web resources represented by data terms. They are similar to the latter, but augmented by *variables*, possibly with

* This research has been funded by the European Commission and by the Swiss Federal Office for Education and Science within the 6th Framework Programme project REWERSE number 506779 (cf. http://rewerse.net).
[1] DAML Query Language, http://www.daml.org/dql.

variable restrictions (the possible bindings are restricted to certain subterms), by *partial term specifications* (omitting subterms irrelevant to the query), and by additional query constructs like *subterm negation, optional subterm specification,* and *descendant.*

Construct terms serve to reassemble variables so as to construct new data terms. Again, they are similar to the latter, but augmented by *variables* (acting as place holders for data selected in a query) and the *grouping construct* all (which serves to collect all instances that result from different variable bindings).

Construct-Query Rules (short: rules) relate a construct term to a query consisting of AND and/or OR connected query terms. Xcerpt rules might be *chained* like active or deductive database rules to form complex query programs.

XChange: Evolution of Data on the Web

Exchanging Events on the Web. The language XChange aims at establishing reactivity, expressed by *reaction rules*, as communication paradigm on the Web. With XChange, communication between Web sites is peer-to-peer, i.e. all parties have the same capabilities and can initiate communication, and synchronisation can be expressed, so as to face the fact that communication on the Web might be unreliable and cannot be controlled by a central instance. The processing of events is specified in XChange by means of event-raising rules, event-driven update rules, and event-driven transaction rules. *Event-raising rules* specify events that are to be constructed and raised as reaction to incoming (internal or external) events.

Propagating Changes on the Web. XChange provides the capability to specify relations between complex updates and execute the updates conformly. To deal with network communication problems, an explicit specification of synchronisation operations on updates is needed, a (kind of) control which logic programming languages lack. *Update rules* are rules specifying (possibly complex) updates. The head of an update rule contains patterns for the data to be modified augmented with update operations (i.e. insertion, deletion, replacement), called *update terms*, and the desired synchronisation operations. Since it is sometimes necessary to execute *complex updates* in an *all-or-nothing manner*, the concept of *transactions* is supported by the language XChange.

References

1. Bry, F., Schaffert, S.: Towards a Declarative Query and Transformation Language for XML and Semistructured Data: Simulation Unification. In: Proc. Int. Conf. on Logic Programming (ICLP). LNCS 2401, Springer-Verlag (2002)
2. Bry, F., Schaffert, S.: An Entailment for Reasoning on the Web. In: Proc. of Rules and Rule Markup Languages for the Web (RuleML03), Springer-Verlag (2003)
3. Liu, M., Lu, L., Wang, G.: A Declarative XML-RL Update Language. In: Proc. Int. Conf. on Conceptual Modeling (ER 2003). LNCS 2813, Springer-Verlag (2003)
4. Papamarkos, G., Poulovassilis, A., Wood, P.T.: Event-condition-action rule languages for the semantic web. In: Workshop on Semantic Web and Databases, Berlin (2003)

Protein Folding Simulation in CCP

Alessandro Dal Palù[1], Agostino Dovier[1], and Federico Fogolari[2]

[1] Dip. di Matematica e Informatica, Univ. di Udine
Via delle Scienze 206, 33100 Udine, Italy
{dalpalu,dovier}@dimi.uniud.it
[2] Dip. Scientifico-Tecnologico, Univ. di Verona
Strada Le Grazie 15, 37134 Verona, Italy
fogolari@sci.univr.it

Background. A protein is a list of linked units called aminoacids. There are 20 different kinds of aminoacids and the typical length of a protein is 100–500 units. The Protein Structure Prediction Problem (PSP) is the problem of predicting the 3D native conformation of a protein, when its aminoacid sequence is known. The process for reaching this state is called the *protein folding*. This work deals with *ab-initio* prediction, based on *Anfinsen thermodynamic hypothesis* [1] which states that the conformation adopted by a protein (also known as the *native* conformation) is the one with minimum free energy. We can identify two main problems: the first is to choose a representation of the protein and an energy function, which must be at minimum for native-like conformations. The second is, given the representation and the energy function, to find the 3D conformation that minimizes the function. Due to intrinsic computational limits, no general solution to the latter problem is currently available. In particular, simulation-based techniques that take into account all atoms constituting the aminoacids (and the solvent) and simulate the folding process approximating atom interactions, run extremely slow due to the huge number of calculations.

Results. In this work we adopt a simplified representation of a protein where each aminoacid is represented by a center of interaction. This simplification, while loosing some details, has the advantage of being computationally tractable and of having smoother potential landscapes. A recently developed empirical contact energy function [3], already used in constraint-based approach to the problem [4], is modified and augmented by local terms which describe bond lengths, bend angles, and torsion angles. The energy term related to bond lengths is designed to keep the distance of two consecutive aminoacids in the chain fixed. The bend angle and the torsion angle potentials are a statistical mean of the behaviour of the aminoacids, extracted from analysis performed on the Protein Data Bank [2].

With this energy function the problem is approached by a high-level simulation method which makes use of concurrent constraint programming. Basically, each aminoacid of the protein is viewed as an independent process that moves in the space and communicates with other aminoacids. Each process waits for a communication of the modification of other processes' position; after receiving a message, it stores the information in a list and performs a move. The new position is computed using a Montecarlo simulation, based on the spatial information

B. Demoen and V. Lifschitz (Eds.): ICLP 2004, LNCS 3132, pp. 452–453, 2004.

available to the aminoacid, which may not be the current dislocation of the protein, due to asynchrony in the communication. Once the move is performed, the aminoacid communicates its new position to all the others. The code has been implemented in Mozart [5], where it is natural to model concurrent programs in a simple notation mixing classes, constraints, and logic variables. During the computation each process keeps track of the whole history of the folding. There are various parameters to be correctly set to properly model the system; with the currently computed values we are able to properly obtain helices (see figure on the right). There are also difficulties that arise due to concurrency; among them there is the asyncronization between the communication and the moves of the aminoacids, which lead to modification of the energy landscape.

Conclusions. We have presented a preliminary concurrent constraint implementation of protein folding simulation. The results are promising. As far as we know, all current parallel approaches to the Protein Folding are simply a division of the computational load between the processors, while here we are starting to model the problem in a real concurrent setting. We wish to concentrate our efforts in this direction, developing more sophisticated communication strategies and especially some cooperative approach, in which the cooperation strategy adapts to the current configuration. The target is to derive a model that is able to represent the dynamical evolution of the system and that exploits these features to perform faster searches for the minimum energy point in the space of conformations. However, the actual energy function is too simple to capture all the complex interactions between the aminoacids; for this reason we would like to introduce the representation of the so-called *side chain* of an aminoacids and to use some already tested potentials. Moreover, we are planning to integrate this software with other tools, both from the constraint minimization side and from the molecular dynamics side.

References

1. C. B. Anfinsen. Principles that govern the folding of protein chains. *Science*, 181:223–230, 1973.
2. H. M. Berman et al. The Protein Data Bank. *Nucleic Acids Research*, 28:235–242, 2000. http://www.rcsb.org/pdb/.
3. M. Berrera, H. Molinari, and F. Fogolari. Amino acid empirical contact energy definitions for fold recognition in the space of contact maps. *BMC Bioinformatics*, 4(8), 2003.
4. A. Dal Palù, A. Dovier, and F. Fogolari. Protein folding in $CLP(\mathcal{FD})$ with empirical contact energies. In *Recent Advances in Constraints*, vol. 3010 of *Lecture Notes in Artificial Intelligence*, pp. 250–265, 2004.
5. Univ. des Saarlandes, Sweedish Inst. of Computer Science, and Univ. Catholique de Louvain. The Mozart Programming System. www.mozart-oz.org.

Applying CLP to Predict Extra-Functional Properties of Component-Based Models

Olivier Defour, Jean-Marc Jézéquel, and Noël Plouzeau

INRIA-Rennes, Campus universitaire de Beaulieu,
Avenue du général Leclerc 35042 Rennes Cedex, France
{olivier.defour,jean-marc.jezequel,noel.plouzeau}@irisa.fr

Abstract. A component is the basic re-usable unit of composition to build composite systems by connecting to others through their provided and required ports. Checking the functional compliance between provided and required ports is necessary to build functional systems. At the same time, one of the most important issues today in Component-Based Software Engineering (CBSE) is the prediction of the composite structure Quality of Service (QoS) at design time, using the extrafunctional properties of its components. This paper focuses on this specific CBSE issue, and the use of Constraint Logic Programming (CLP) in this context. For each component providing and requiring services, we propose to specify the QoS properties as required and provided operations, called dimensions, on the component ports. In this model, a QoS property can depend on other QoS attributes, and be constrained by OCL pre- and post-conditions. From this model, the QoS aspect of a component is translated into a QoS system of non-linear constraints over the reals: the dimensions and their pre/post-conditions as variables controlled by non-linear constraints. These constraints are either inequalities that bound the admissible QoS values, or non-linear functions that bind QoS properties between them. Using the CLP, we are able to determine if a QoS system can be satisfied, and to predict what quality level is required by the assembly from its environment, as a set of admissible intervals. The CLP is a general framework that can be implemented with a realistic effort, to reason about the component-based models QoS properties at design time, that is one of the most important issues in CBSE.

1 Introduction

The Component-Based Software Engineering (CBSE) community considers any software system as an assembly of components, and promotes methods, technologies and tools in this sense. Software components enable practical reuse: building new solutions by combining bought and home made components improves quality and supports rapid development [4].

Specifications languages for component-based models are yet available, such as UML2.0. However, these models focus only on the functional aspects: the required and provided services, and the connections between components. The

B. Demoen and V. Lifschitz (Eds.): ICLP 2004, LNCS 3132, pp. 454–455, 2004.
© Springer-Verlag Berlin Heidelberg 2004

extra-functional aspect, also called Quality of Service (QoS), is another important part of component-based specifications. This aspect has specific issues, such as:

- monitoring of the QoS properties;
- reasoning about the QoS of an assembly [3].

This paper presents the interest of constraint logic programming over the real (CLP(R)) applied to this last issue.

2   Reasoning on the QoS of an Assembly

A QoS property, also called a dimension [2], is a valuable quantity. Its type is a totally ordered set, such as integer, real, or low; medium; high. Moreover, dependency relationships exist between the dimensions of provided and required service. In order to take into account these properties, we propose to model dimensions as operations, and QoS contracts (set of dimensions) as interfaces [1]. The required or provided levels of quality can be expressed using OCL pre/post conditions.

This metamodel extends usual UML2.0 metaclasses only, and so it is easy to implement into case tool. A model transformation translates the QoS aspect of a QoS-aware component-based model into CLP(R) code where: (1) the components are first order predicates which their arguments are dimensions, constrained in the body by the pre/post conditions, (2) the connections and compositions are conjunctions of component predicates.

3   Conclusion

The CLP(R) is a general framework to handle and reason about the QoS of component-based models. It checks the (QoS) validity of an assembly, and computes an approximated levels of quality. In future works, the model transformation will take into account behavior models, and QoS mutant operators will be developed to (QoS) test a component.

References

1. Defour O., Jézéquel J.M., Plouzeau N. Extra-functional contracts support in components Component Based Software Engineering (CBSE7), Edinburgh, May 2004.
2. Frolund S. and Koistinen J. QoS specification in distributed object systems *Distributed Systems Engineering, vol. 5, July 1998, The British Computer Society*
3. Stafford J. and Scott H. The Software Engineering Institute's Second Workshop on Predictable Assembly: Landscape of compositional predictability SEI Report CMU/SEI-2003- TN-029, 2003.
4. Szyperski C. Component software, beyond object oriented programming *2nd ed., Addison-Wesley, 2002*

Main Results of the OADymPPaC Project

Pierre Deransart

INRIA-Rocquencourt, BP 105, 78153 Le Chesnay Cedex, France
Pierre.Deransart@inria.fr

Abstract. The 3 years OADymPPaC project ended may 2004.

The expected impacts of the project were of three kinds: new results in constraint program development and debugging, and visualization of dynamic phenomena; improvement of the industrial and academic platforms: constraint solvers and their tools for constraint program development and modules of visualization, enhancement of several platforms (GNU-Prolog, PaLM, Choco, CHIP); contribution to the teaching of the programming with constraints.

All results (reports and systems) may be found at the project URL:
http://contraintes.inria.fr/OADymPPaC

The French RNTL[1] 3 years OADymPPaC (Tools for Dynamic Analysis and Debugging of Constraint Programs) project ended May 2004.

The project consortium included four academic partners: INRIA (G. Arnaud, P. Deransart (coordinator), L. Langevine, F. Fages, J.-D. Fekete), Ecole des Mines de Nantes (N. Jussien, M. Gonhiem), INSA/IRISA Rennes (M. Ducassé, E. Jahier), the University of Orléans (G. Ferrand, W. Lesaint, A. Tessier), and two industrial partners: COSYTEC (A. Aggoun, R. Martin) and ILOG (T. Baudel).

Most results are in reports, and research or industrial prototypes: **new resolution tracers** for control of the search space and constraint propagation: [1, 2] for GNU-Prolog, tracers developed for PaLM [3], and CHIP V5 of COSYTEC [4]; enhanced constraint programming platforms [5]; **new constraints debugging tools** [6, 7], and **new visualization paradigms** [8–10].

But the main result issued by the project is the definition of a new *generic trace format* based on an abstract semantics of finite domain solvers [11–13]. This generic trace enables debugging tools to be defined almost independently from finite domain solvers, and conversely, tracers to be built independently from these tools.

The trace syntax is represented using an XML DTD, called "gentra4cp.dtd" and described in [14]. A compliant trace is encoded in an XML format according to this DTD and follows the described semantics.

---

[1] "Réseau National de recherche et d'innovation en Technologies Logicielles ", a French Government Research Program launched in 1999.

B. Demoen and V. Lifschitz (Eds.): ICLP 2004, LNCS 3132, pp. 456–457, 2004.

References

1. Langevine, L.: Codeine, a Propagation Tracer for GNU-Prolog (2004)
   http://contraintes.inria.fr/~langevin/codeine.
2. Langevine, L., Deransart, P., Ducassé, M.: A propagation tracer for GNU-Prolog:
   from formal definition to efficient implementation. In Palamidessi, C., ed.: Proc. of
   19th International Conference on Logic Programming (ICLP 2003). Volume 2916.,
   Springer Verlag (2003) 269–283
3. Jussien, N., Barichard, V.: The PaLM system: explanation-based constraint programming. In: Proceedings of TRICS: Techniques foR Implementing Constraint
   programming Systems, a post-conference workshop of CP 2000, Singapore (2000)
   118–133 Available at
   http://www.emn.fr/jussien/publications/jussien-WCP00.pdf.
4. COSYTEC: CHIP++ V5.6, alpha version. http://www.cosytec.com (2004)
5. Debruyne, R., Ferrand, G., Jussien, N., Lesaint, W., Ouis, S., Tessier, A.: Correctness of constraint retraction algorithms. In: FLAIRS'03: Sixteenth International
   Florida Artificial Intelligence Research Society Conference, St. Augustine, Florida,
   USA, AAAI press (2003) 172–176
6. Fages, F.: CLPGUI: a generic graphical user interface for constraint logic programming over finite domains. In Tessier, A., ed.: Proceedings of the 12th Workshop
   on Logic Programming Environments (WLPE'02), Copenhagen (2002) Available
   as CoRR:cs.SE/0207048.
7. Ducassé, M., Langevine, L.: Automated analysis of CLP(FD) program execution
   traces. In Stuckey, P., ed.: Proceedings of the International Conference on Logic
   Programming, Lecture Notes in Computer Science, Springer-Verlag (2002) Poster.
   Extended version available at http://www.irisa.fr/lande/ducasse/.
8. Baudel, T., et al: ILOG VISUAL CP reference manual (2003) Manufactured and
   freely distributed by ILOG,
   http://www2.ilog.com/preview/Discovery/gentra4cp/.
9. Gonhiem, M., Jussien, N., Fekete, J.D.: Visualizing explanations to exhibit
   dynamic structure in constraint problem satisfaction. In O'Sullivan, B., ed.:
   Proceedings of the third International Workshop on User Interaction in Constraint Satisfaction (UICS'03), Cork University (Ireland) (2003) Available at
   http://www.cs.ucc.ie/~osullb/UICS-03/.
10. G. Arnaud: PAVOT Reference Manual (2004)
    http://contraintes.inria.fr/~arnaud/pavot/.
11. Deransart, P., Ducassé, M., Langevine, L.: A generic trace model for finite domain
    solvers. In O'Sullivan, B., ed.: Proceedings of the second International Workshop
    on User Interaction in Constraint Satisfaction (UICS'02), Cornell University (USA)
    (2002) Available at
    http://www.cs.ucc.ie/~osullb/UICS-02/papers/deransart_et_al-uics02.ps.
12. Ferrand, G., Lesaint, W., Tessier, A.: Theoretical foundations of value withdrawal
    explanations for domain reduction. Electronic Notes in Theoretical Computer Sci-
    ence **76** (2002) http://www.elsevier.com/gej-ng/31/29/23/126/23/26/76008.pdf.
13. Langevine, L., Deransart, P., Ducassé, M.: A generic trace schema for the porta-
    bility of CP(FD) debugging tools. In Apt, K., Fages, F., Rossi, F., Szeredi, P.,
    Vancza, J., eds.: Recent Advances in Constraints, 2003. Number 3010 in LNAI.
    Springer Verlag (2004)
14. Deransart, P., al.: Generic Trace Format for Constraint Programming, version
    2.1. Technical report, INRIA, EMN, University of Orléans, Cosytec, ILOG (2004)
    http://contraintes.inria.fr/OADymPPaC/Public/Trace.

FDBG, the CLP$\mathcal{FD}$ Debugger Library of SICStus Prolog[*]

Dávid Hanák, Tamás Szeredi, and Péter Szeredi

Budapest University of Technology and Economics
{dhanak,tszeredi}@inf.bme.hu, szeredi@cs.bme.hu

1 Introduction

Debugging tools serve an important role in software development. This also holds for constraint programming and CLP($\mathcal{FD}$) in particular, where it is often necessary to observe how the domains of various variables behave, how different constraints linked by shared variables affect each other, etc. There are numerous projects for implementing debuggers for CLP($\mathcal{FD}$) systems. Some have committed themselves to interactive tools, others have chosen assertion based methods, and a large number of publications deal with trace generation and analysis.

We have decided to develop a trace based debugger for the CLP($\mathcal{FD}$) library of SICStus Prolog, a library which neatly embeds the theory of finite domain constraints into Prolog. The SICStus environment has an advanced and extensible debugger for the base language, but until recently it has lacked direct support to observe the run of constraint programs. The goal of FDBG (which is short for Finite domain DeBuGger) is to fill in this gap.

FDBG was written almost entirely in Prolog, as user space code, no native routines were used directly. The library (along with its source code) is part of the SICStus Prolog distribution versions 3.9 and upwards, and is documented in detail in the SICStus User's Manual.

2 Debugger Services

FDBG consists of two loosely coupled parts. The core is responsible for making the run of a CLP($\mathcal{FD}$) program observable by translating it into a sequence of *events*. The outer layer consists of a collection of configurable and extensible *visualizers* and utility predicates which process and display the events according to the needs of the user. The two are linked together through a simple interface.

CLP(FD) Events. By observing the process of CLP($\mathcal{FD}$) problem solving we can conclude that events can belong to two classes. The events of the first class called *constraint events* occur when a constraint does some propagation on the domains of its variables. Events belonging to the second class are *labeling events*, representing decisions made during the exploration of the search space. Events of

---

[*] The subject is presented in full detail at the WLPE'04 workshop.

B. Demoen and V. Lifschitz (Eds.): ICLP 2004, LNCS 3132, pp. 458–459, 2004.

these two classes appear interleaved in a trace log, as labeling triggers additional propagation, after which labeling is resumed, etc.

Every event intercepted by the FDBG core is described with a Prolog term and then dispatched to the appropriate visualizers. Most visualizers, such as the default ones provided by FDBG, display the event in the trace log. Consequently, a log usually contains a block of lines for each event. However, in general a visualizer can do any kind of processing or analysis.

Basic Services. To make FDBG produce a verbose text log of the trace events using its built-in visualizers, a CLP($\mathcal{FD}$) program needs no modification. All the user needs to do is to turn on the debugger before invoking the main program.

For constraint events, the default log entry consists of the name and actual arguments of the constraint, and the list of variables narrowed in that particular step, showing their domains *before* and *after* the propagation took place. Variables are identified by their names, which are assigned either implicitly by the debugger core, or explicitly by the user. A sample of such a trace with explicitly assigned names can be seen on Fig 1.

For labeling events, an entry contains the name of the variable being labeled, and describes the way its domain is divided. This can either be the selection of a single value or narrowing to a subset of its domain. Alternative choices branching off the same choicepoint can be recognized as such by a unique identifier included in the log.

Advanced Features. A useful service of FDBG is the *naming of variables* and terms in general. An advantage of naming is that built-in visualizers will use the specified name to refer to variables wherever they appear in the log. The user can also easily identify these variables anywhere from the program by using the *annotation* service, which replaces variables with descriptive Prolog terms.

If the user is unsatisfied with the output of the default visualizers or finds it hard to understand, he has the opportunity to customize them, or to write his own visualizers. FDBG provides an easy way to switch between the built-in and custom visualizers, and they may also be used simultaneously. An example custom log can be seen on Fig. 2.

Writing visualizers also provides a simple means to filter trace events, or to silently wait for the occurrence of an event and start the Prolog debugger at that point.

The figures below show two snippets from two traces of the 4-queen problem. The first one was printed by the built-in visualizer, while the second one, showing the entire checkerboard, was created by a custom visualizer.

```
                                    no_threat(4,<queen_3>,1)
                                       [ . X . . ]
      no_threat(4,<queen_3>,1)         [ . . . X ]
         queen_3: {1}\/{3} -> {1}      [ X . - . ]
         Constraint exited.            [ X . X X ]
```

Fig. 1. Basic log entry   **Fig. 2.** Custom log entry

Development of Semantic Debuggers
Based on Refinement Calculus

Rohit N. Kundaji and R.K. Shyamasundar

School of Technology and Computer Science, Tata Institute of Fundamental Research,
Homi Bhabha Road, Mumbai 400005, India
{rohit,shyam}@tcs.tifr.res.in

Introduction

Translation validation based on *refinement mappings* has been effectively used for validating compiled programs [1, 2]. Debugging programs is a very important stage in the software development cycle. An important issue for the debugger-user communication aspect is that of *transparency* which is the illusion wherein the user gets an impression that he is debugging his source. A debugger is said to exhibit *transparent behaviour* if it returns exactly the same response for all requests as it would if the target program were not optimized. A debugger that behaves differently for an optimized program exhibits *non-transparent behaviour*. Various approaches have been envisaged in [3] for debugging optimized programs. In this paper, we show how we can use the methodology of translation validation of optimized programs to design and develop semantic transparent debuggers that permits modifications of variables only if consistent. Our approach uses the proof rule for validating optimized programs described in [4]. Further, we have been able to automate the process of validation and build prototype debuggers in Prolog.

The notion of refinement forms the basis for defining correct translation of an abstract code to a concrete code. With $\mathcal{V}_A$: set of variables, $\mathcal{O}_A$: set of observable variables , Θ_A: initial condition, $\mathcal{T}_A$: finite set of transitions, let $S_A =< \mathcal{V}_A, \mathcal{O}_A, \Theta_A, \mathcal{T}_A >$ be an abstract system and similarly $S_C =< \mathcal{V}_C, \mathcal{O}_C, \Theta_C, \mathcal{T}_C >$ be the concrete system. A concrete system is said to implement a given abstract system specification, iff it is a refinement of the abstract system. We say that S_C is a refinement (correct translation) of S_A if for every finite S_C-computation $\sigma^C : s_0^C, ..., s_m^C$, there exists a finite maximal S_A-computation $\sigma^A : s_0^A, ..., s_k^A$, such that $s_m^C[x] = s_k^A[X]$ for every $X \in \mathcal{O}_A$, $x \in \mathcal{O}_C$. The rule for establishing refinement described in [4] is summarized below:

(a) Establish a control abstraction $\mathcal{K} : CP_C \rightarrow 2^{CP_A}$ mapping each value of the concrete control variable π_C into one or more corresponding values of the abstract control variable π_A; note that it should map the initial and terminal locations of the source and the target respectively.

(b) For each node p in the source, form two invariants (with auxiliary variables), ϕ_{Ap}, containing only source variables and ϕ_{Cp} containing only target variables.

(c) Establish a data abstraction mapping $\alpha : (pr_1 \rightarrow v_1 = E_1) \wedge ... \wedge (pr_n \rightarrow v_n = E_n)$ that associates with some source state variables $v_i \in \mathcal{V}_A - \pi_A$, an expres-

B. Demoen and V. Lifschitz (Eds.): ICLP 2004, LNCS 3132, pp. 460–461, 2004.

sion E_i over the concrete state variables, conditional on the concrete boolean expression pr_i.

(d) For each pair of nodes i, j such that there is a simple path from i to j in the control path of $\mathcal{S}_C$, form the verification condition (π refers to control points):

$$C_{ij} : \bigwedge_{p \in \mathcal{K}(i)} \bigvee_{q \in \mathcal{K}(j)} (\pi_A = p) \wedge \alpha \wedge \phi_{Cp} \wedge \phi_{Ap} \wedge \mathcal{A}_{Ai} \wedge \mathcal{A}_{Ci} \wedge \rho_{ij}^C \to$$

$$\exists (\mathcal{V}'_A \cup AVS'_{Aj} \cup AVS'_{Cj}) : \alpha' \wedge \phi'_{Cq} \wedge \phi'_{Aq} \wedge \mathcal{A}'_{Aj} \wedge \mathcal{A}'_{Cj} \wedge \rho_{pq}^A$$

(e) Establish the validity of all the generated verification conditions.

Symbolic Debugging of Optimized Code

Our idea of generating a semantic debugger lies in abstracting the above proof rules for the given debugging features in terms of Prolog clauses. For instance, consider the design of a very simple debugger that requires us to (i) view the values of all *Observable Variables* in source code at any given point of execution and (ii) modify values of source variables at any location in the middle of execution and continue execution taking into account the modified values of variables. If one uses optimized transformations, it is not easy to guarantee the above features easily. From the point of translation validation, we need only one cut point for every basic block. However, from the symbolic debugging point of view, ideally, we need every source level statement location to be included in the cut point set. In our approach, we have revised some possible solutions, when the ideal scenario doesn't hold. Further, our methodology has the capability of allowing us to include every source location in the cut point set. Our implementation uses the functionality of such a system and maps the state of target system to the source system. It also allows users to modify the values of source variables and maps the modified state back to the concrete system from where execution can be continued.

Some of the advantages of our method are: (i) it is not restricted to any specific source and target languages, (ii) only uses information generated during translation validation phase and does not involve complex algorithms or calculations on the part of the debugger leading to high dependability, (iii) allows modification of source variables during execution and continue execution without recompilation, (iv) allows us to frame complex assertions in temporal logic and verify the validity of the assertions, and (v) we can examine the states at which these assertions are violated.

References

1. A. K. Bhattacharjee, S. D. Dhodapkar, K. Karunakar, B. Rajan, R. K. Shyamasundar (2000), *System for Object Code Validation*, LNCS, 1926, pp. 152-169.
2. A. Pnueli, M. Siegel, and O. Shtrichman, (1998), *Translation Validation for Synchronous Languages*, LNCS 1443, pp. 235-246.
3. C.M. Tice, (1999), Non Transparent Debugging of Optimized Code, *Ph.D. Thesis*, Univ. of California, at Berkeley.
4. R. Kundaji, and R.K. Shyamasundar (2003), *Refinement Calculus: A basis for translation, validation, debugging and certification*, AMiLP-3, Verona, pp. 195-205.

A Tracer Driver to Enable Debugging, Monitoring and Visualization of CLP Executions from a Single Tracer*

Ludovic Langevine[1] and Mireille Ducassé[2]

[1] INRIA Rocquencourt
ludovic.langevine@inria.fr
[2] IRISA/INSA de Rennes
mireille.ducasse@irisa.fr

Tracers provide users with useful information about program executions. A tracer can be used for many purposes. Embedded in an interactive console, it enables users to investigate program executions. It can also be the front-end of visualization tools, or it can be used by an automatic process to monitor execution behaviors. For each purpose, the requested information is similar but slightly different. It is therefore important to be able to interact with the tracer in order to tune the sent information.

We propose a so-called "tracer driver". From a single tracer, it provides a powerful front-end for multiple dynamic analysis tools while limiting the overhead of the trace generation. The tracer driver can be used both synchronously and asynchronously. The relevant execution information is specified by flexible event patterns. A large variety of trace data can be given either systematically or "on demand". The proposed tracer driver has been designed and experimented in the context of constraint logic programming, within Codeine, a tracer for GNU-Prolog [1], and connected to a set of graphical tools.

Tracer Driver. A CLP execution trace is a sequence of elementary events. The tracer is a module of the traced execution that is called at each execution event. Each event is filtered by the *tracer driver*. The tracer driver decides whether the event is relevant or not for the current analyses. In order to do so, the tracer driver manages a base of *event patterns* that specify the relevant events and what trace data has to be generated for each event. The tracer driver is connected to an analyzer which processes the trace and produces abstractions of it (e.g. graphical views, statistics or bug reports). The tracer driver adapts the actual trace to the needs of the analyzer at a given moment.

An event pattern can be asynchronous: at each matching event, some data is traced and the execution goes on. An event pattern can also be synchronous: at each matching event, some data is traced and the execution is frozen, waiting for analyzer requests. Then, the analyzer can investigate more deeply the current state of the execution: the **current** primitive of the tracer driver allows to retrieve some pieces of data. The analyzer can also modify the base of patterns:

---

* This work has been partially supported by the French RNTL project OADymPPaC, http://contraintes.inria.fr/OADymPPaC/ and by Région Île-de-France.

B. Demoen and V. Lifschitz (Eds.): ICLP 2004, LNCS 3132, pp. 462–463, 2004.

```
visu_prop:  when port = reduce and isNamed(var) and (not cstrType='assign')
            and delta notcontains [maxInt]
            do current(cstr=C and var=V), call spy_propag(C,V)
symbolic:   when port in [reduce,suspend]
            and (cstrType = 'fd_element_var' or cstrType = 'fd_exactly')
            do_synchro call symbolic_monitor
```

Fig. 1. Examples of patterns for visualization and monitoring

reset the event-pattern base; **add** a pattern to the base or **remove** it. The **go** primitive ends the synchronous session and resumes the execution.

Event Patterns. An event pattern specifies a class of interesting events that should be traced. It specifies also what pieces of trace data have to be traced for each instance of this event-class and whether the pattern is synchronous or not. The specification of the event class is made thanks to unary and binary predicates on the event attributes. Event class are expressed by combination of such elementary conditions, using conjunction, disjunction and negation. During the execution, each pattern is compiled into a finite automaton. On each event, the pattern is checked against the current event using this automaton.

Fig. 1 presents two patterns activated in parallel. The first pattern is visualization oriented. It requests the trace of all the domain reductions made by constraints that do not come from the labeling procedure and that do not remove the maximal integer value. It stores the reducing constraint and the reduced variable. Those data can be used to compute some statistics and to visualize the impact of each constraint on its variables. This pattern is asynchronous: the requested data are sufficient for the visualization and the patterns do not have to be modified. The second pattern is monitoring-oriented: it freezes the execution at each domain reduction made by a symbolic constraint. This pattern allows the monitoring of the filtering algorithms used for these two constraints.

Emulation of Traditional Analyses. The classical dynamic analysis schemata can be emulated in our framework. Primitive tracing (simple output of the trace in a given channel) is done by specifying the relevant trace data at the execution beginning with asynchronous patterns. Standard tracing (output of the trace in an interactive console) is done by specifying synchronous event patterns. debugging primitives are implemented by modifying patterns on the fly.

Conclusion. We have presented a framework to easily adapt a tracer to the needs of an analyzer. This adaptation is done thanks to a *tracer driver* that enables both synchronous and asynchronous communication. An incremental base of event patterns specifies what data has to be traced. The classical analysis schemata can be implemented in this framework.

References

1. Langevine, L., Ducassé, M., Deransart, P.: A propagation tracer for gnu-prolog: from formal definition to efficient implementation. In Palamidessi, C., ed.: Proc. of ICLP'03. LNCS, Mumbai, India (2003)

Grid Service Selection with PPDL*

Massimo Marchi[1], Alessandra Mileo[1], and Alessandro Provetti[2]

[1] DSI-DICO, Univ. degli Studi di Milano. Milan, I-20135 Italy
marchi@dsi.unimi.it, mileo@dico.unimi.it
[2] Dip. di Fisica, Univ. degli Studi di Messina. Messina, I-98166 Italy
ale@unime.it

Abstract. The application of the novel PPDL (Policy Description Language with Preferences) specification language to Grid-Service Selection is presented. We describe an architecture based on interposing the policy enforcement engine between the calling application and the client stubs. This way, our solution is fully declararive and remains transparent to the client application.

This poster article reports on our experimental application of PPDL to the standard Grid Service architecture. PPDL, which is formally described below, is a declarative language that extends the Policy Description Language PDL [2] by permitting the specification of preferences on how to enforce integrity constraints. The declarative semantics of PPDL policies is given by translation into Brewka's Logic Programs with Ordered Disjunctions (LPOD) [3]. Translated LPOD programs will then be fed to the *Psmodels* solver [4], which has shown a reasonable efficency.

Grid Services Architecture. Web Services is a distributed technology using a set of well-defined protocol derived from XML and URI that achieves a large interoperability between different client/server implementations. In our experiments, we use GT3 Grid Services, an extension of Web Services (WS) coded in Java. Typically, each communication between client and server is made through a coupled object, called *stub*. When a client application needs a service, it queries the UDDI Registry to retrieve a list of Web Services that fit its request. The query response passed to the client application can be i) *the first* in the list of results, ii) *randomly* chosen or iii) *user-chosen* through some *static* meta-information stored in the UDDI.

In contrast, our approach allows user-defined policies that are evaluated *dynamically* and *client-side*. The policy module shown in Figure 1 catches all starting invocations from client, stores all available servers returned by the UDDI, applies the connection policy by translating it into a LPOD program, invokes *Psmodels* and, according to the result, *routes* the call.

* Thanks to E. Bertino, S. Costantini, J. Lobo and M. Ornaghi. Work supported by the Information Society Technologies programme of the European Commission, Future and Emerging Technologies under the IST-2001-37004 WASP project.

B. Demoen and V. Lifschitz (Eds.): ICLP 2004, LNCS 3132, pp. 464–466, 2004.

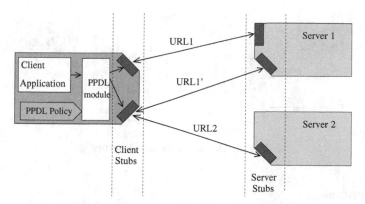

Fig. 1. PPDL module on WS client.

Policies Specification and Enforcement. Some of these authors have developed PPDL [5] as an extension of PDL [2]. Even though PPDL has rather simple constructs and is prima-facie less expressive than the traditional Knowledge Representation languages, it allows capturing the essence of routing control while keeping the so-called *business logic* outside the client applications; (P)PDL policies can be changed at any time transparently from the applications, which do not need rewriting.

A PPDL policy is defined as a set of ECA-style rules P_i and a set of consistency-maintenance rules M_i:

P_i : $e_1, \ldots e_m$ **causes** a **if** C
M_i : **never** $a_1 \times \ldots \times a_n$ **if** C'

where C, C' are Boolean conditions, $e_1, \ldots e_m$ are *events* (requests), a is an *action* to be executed and $a_1 \ldots a_n$ are actions that, intuitively, cannot execute *simultaneously*. Notice that PPDL rules are evaluated and applied in parallel and in a discrete-time framework. If applying the policy yields a set of actions that violates one of the M_i (for monitor) rules, then the PPDL interpreter will *cancel* some of the actions. The decision on which action to drop has been addressed in our work [5,6] and it corresponds to applying the ordered disjunction operator ($\times$) of LPODs [3] into the M_i rules. Both the declarative and operational semantics of PPDL policies are given by translation into LPODs.

To sum it up, Fig. 2 shows how PPDL policies are employed in our architecture.

An Example Specification. Suppose we want to i) send calls to the *add(x,y)* function to a server providing it (to be found on a look-up table) but ii) *prefer* sending calls to host *zulu* over host *mag* whenever x is greater than 100. Assuming that we have a look-up table mapping each WS *interface* into a PPDL constant, e.g. *iMath*, the PPDL rules are as follows:

request(iMath.M(L)) **causes** send(URL, iMath.M(L)) **if** table (URL, iMath).
never send(*mag*, iMath.M(L)) $\times$ send(*zulu*, iMath.M(L)) **if** M=add, L[0]> 100.

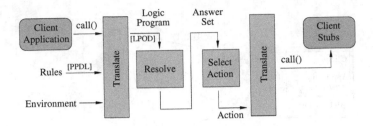

Fig. 2. Our software architecture

References

1. Marchi M., Mileo A. and Provetti A., 2004. *Specification and execution of policies for Grid Service Selection.* Poster at ICWS2004 conference. IEEE press.
2. Chomicki J., Lobo J. and Naqvi S., 2003. *Conflict Resolution using Logic Programming.* IEEE Transactions on Knowledge and Data Engineering 15:2.
3. Brewka, G., 2002. *Logic Programming with Ordered Disjunction.* Proc. of AAAI-02.
4. PSMODELS: *http://www.tcs.hut.fi/Software/smodels/priority/*
5. Bertino E., Mileo A. and Provetti A., 2003. *Policy Monitoring with User-Preferences in PDL.* Proc. of NRAC 2003 Workshop. Available from *http://mag.dsi.unimi.it/*
6. Bertino, E., Mileo, A. and Provetti, A., 2003. User Preferences VS Minimality in PPDL. Proc. of *AGP03,* Available from *http://mag.dsi.unimi.it/*

Concurrent Constraint Programming
and Tree–Based Acoustic Modelling*

Moritz Neugebauer

Department of Computer Science, University College Dublin, Dublin 4, Ireland
moritz.neugebauer@ucd.ie

The design of acoustic models is key to a reliable connection between acoustic waveform and linguistic message in terms of individual speech units. We present an original application of concurrent constraint programming in this important area of spoken language processing. The application presented here employs concurrent constraint programming – represented by Mozart/Oz [1] – to overcome the problem of sparse training data in order to provide context-dependent acoustic models for automatic speech recognition.

State–of–the–art automatic speech recognition relies on standard pattern recognition algorithms, i.e. Hidden–Markov models (HMMs), to estimate representative yet robust acoustic models from a limited amount of speech data. In tree-based acoustic modelling, phonetic decision trees are employed to predict models for phonetic contexts which are not contained in the training data [2]. To this end, phoneme contexts are classified using phonetic categories of speech sounds. The assumption behind this is that context phonemes which belong to the same class have similar acoustic effects on the phoneme in question. This results in clustered phonetic contexts and a reduced number of acoustic models. Thus, tree-based acoustic modelling represents one approach to maintaining the balance between model complexity and available training data when building a HMM-based speech recogniser.

We employ concurrent constraint programming in Mozart/Oz to implement this crucial component of statistical training for large vocabulary speech recognition. The principal idea which led us to apply this paradigm to speech recognition based on decision trees was to perform deterministic inferences among the trained models first, in order to avoid superfluous case distinctions. This method is known as *propagate and distribute* where propagation performs simple inferences and distribution performs case distinctions. The procedure presented here is comprised of four steps as described below.

Characteristic acoustic parameters of a specific speech unit are trained in terms of context-dependent phonemes (allophones) which take into consideration the left and right phoneme context, respectively. Then, a phonetic specification system such as the International Phonetic Alphabet which divides the set of phonemes into several phonetic classes is formalised. This step benefits

---

* This material is based upon works supported by the Science Foundation Ireland under Grant No. 02/IN1/ I100. The opinions, findings and conclusions or recommendations expressed in this material are those of the authors and do not necessarily reflect the views of Science Foundation Ireland.

B. Demoen and V. Lifschitz (Eds.): ICLP 2004, LNCS 3132, pp. 467–468, 2004.

from a specific property of the Mozart language as it provides open and closed feature structures. Since Mozart does not offer types or sorts as a built-in data type, a type inheritance system has been implemented on top of the (previously untyped) feature structures.

Given this phonetic knowledge base, binary decision trees are generated in a fully unified way. This means that decision tree-based clustering of individual Markov states can operate on a fully typed feature system thereby ensuring consistent and efficient knowledge representation.

Finally, the size of the acoustic models is reduced by tying of shared states among individual Markov models. Each tree is built using a top-down sequential optimisation procedure. Initially, all of the states to be clustered are placed in the root node of the tree. The information gain of the training data is calculated on the assumption that all of the states in that node are tied. This node is then split into two by finding the phonetic class which partitions the states in the parent node such that the information gain is maximised.

The statistical framework of decision trees in acoustic modelling provides two major advantages over the previous rule–based or bottom–up approaches. First, the classification and prediction power of the decision tree allows model units or contexts to be synthesised, which do not occur in the training data. Second, the node splitting procedure of decision tree-based state tying is a model selection process. Both aspects are being modelled in the tree constraint domain. The three final steps which make use of concurrent constraint programming techniques provide a way of maintaining a balance between model complexity and the number of parameters in order to render a robust model parameter estimation using feature constraints and decision trees.

Our study indicates that optimal decision tree building procedures can be made both computationally feasible and that they can significantly improve robustness and quality of acoustic models. The proposed concurrent constraint-based approach was tested and compared with related work. Our results indicate that acoustic modelling using tree constraints in Mozart/Oz leads to promising results with regard to model quality and recognition performance while building on concurrent optimisation strategies performed on detailed phonetic knowledge [3].

References

1. Smolka, G.: The Oz programming model. In van Leeuwen, J., ed.: Computer Science Today. Volume 1000 of Lecture Notes in Computer Science., Springer Verlag (1995) 324–343
2. Young, S.J., Odell, J.J., Woodland, P.C.: Tree-based state tying for high accuracy acoustic modelling. In: Proceedings of the ARPA Human Language Technology Workshop, Plainsboro, NJ (1994) 307–312
3. Neugebauer, M.: Constraint Programming and Subphonetic Acoustic Modelling. PhD thesis, Department of Computer Science, University College Dublin (in preparation)

MProlog: An Extension of Prolog
for Modal Logic Programming

Linh Anh Nguyen

Institute of Informatics, University of Warsaw
ul. Banacha 2, 02-097 Warsaw, Poland
nguyen@mimuw.edu.pl

Abstract. We introduce our implemented modal logic programming system MProlog. This system is written in Prolog as a module for Prolog. Codes, libraries, and most features of Prolog can be used in MProlog programs. The system contains a number of built-in SLD-resolution calculi for modal logics, including calculi for useful multimodal logics of belief.

Modal logics can be used to reason about knowledge, belief, actions, etc. A number of authors have proposed modal extensions for logic programming; see [7] for a survey and [6, 1, 3, 4] for later works. There are two approaches for modal logic programming: the direct approach and the translational approach. The first approach directly uses modalities, while the second one translates modal logic programs to classical logic programs.

Despite that the theory of modal logic programming has been studied in a considerable number of works, it has not received much attention in practice. But if we want to use modal logics for practical applications, then modal logic programming deserves for further investigations, especially in practical issues.

In [3, 4], we proposed a general framework for developing semantics of modal logic programs and gave sound and complete SLD-resolution calculi for a number of modal logics, including calculi for useful multimodal logics of belief. Our framework uses a direct approach for handling modalities and does not require any special restriction on occurrences of modal operators (the used language is as expressive as the general modal Horn fragment). Starting from the purely logical formalism of [3, 4], we have built a real system called MProlog [5] for modal logic programming. The implemented system adds extra features to the logical formalism in order to increase usefulness of the language. It is written in Prolog as a module for Prolog and can run in SICStus Prolog and SWI-Prolog. Codes, libraries, and most features of Prolog can be used in MProlog programs in a pure way. This gives MProlog capabilities for real applications. MProlog has been designed to obtain high effectiveness and flexibility. For effectiveness, classical fragments are interpreted by Prolog itself and a number of options can be used for MProlog to restrict the search space. For flexibility, there are three kinds of predicates (classical, modal, and dum[1]) and we can use and mix different calculi in an MProlog program.

---

[1] i.e. classical predicates which are defined using modal formulae

B. Demoen and V. Lifschitz (Eds.): ICLP 2004, LNCS 3132, pp. 469–470, 2004.

MProlog has a very different theoretical foundation than the implemented Molog system [2]. In MProlog, a labeling technique is used for existential modal operators instead of skolemization. We also provide and use new technicalities like normal forms of modalities or pre-orders between modal operators. MProlog also eliminates drawbacks of Molog (e.g., MProlog gives computed answers).

Our system contains a number of built-in SLD-resolution calculi for modal logics, including calculi for multimodal logics intended for reasoning about multi-degree belief, for use in distributed systems of belief, or for reasoning about epistemic states of agents in multi-agent systems. SLD-resolution calculi for MProlog are specified using our framework given in [3, 4] and written in Prolog. They contain rules (used as meta-clauses) for handling properties of the base modal logic, definitions of auxiliary predicates, and definitions for a number of required predicates (e.g., to specify the normal form of modalities).

In MProlog, modalities are represented as lists, e.g., $\Box_i \Diamond_j\, q(x)$ is represented as $[bel(I), pos(J)] : q(X)$, and $\Box_x god\_exists \leftarrow christian(x)$ is represented as $[bel(X)]$: god_exists :- $christian(X)$. Notations of modal operators depend on how the base SLD-resolution calculus is defined. As another example, for MProlog-$\Box$ [4], which disallows existential modal operators in program clauses and goals, we represent $\Box_{i_1} \ldots \Box_{i_k}$ as $[I1, \ldots, Ik]$.

Syntactically, an MProlog program is a Prolog program. Each modal clause in an MProlog program is of one of the following forms:

$$Context : (Head :- Body). \quad \text{or} \quad Head :- Body.$$

where *Context* is a list representing a modality, *Head* is of the form E or $M : E$, E is a classical atom, and M is a list containing one modal operator.

In summary, our MProlog system is a tool for experimenting with applications of modal logic programming to AI. It is also a tool for developing and experimenting with new SLD-resolution calculi for modal logic programming.

References

1. M. Baldoni, L. Giordano, and A. Martelli. A framework for a modal logic programming. In *Joint Int. Conf. and Symp. on Logic Prog.*, p.52–66. MIT Press, 1996.
2. L. Fariñas del Cerro. Molog: A system that extends Prolog with modal logic. *New Generation Computing*, 4:35–50, 1986.
3. L.A. Nguyen. A fixpoint semantics and an SLD-resolution calculus for modal logic programs. *Fundamenta Informaticae*, 55(1):63–100, 2003.
4. L.A. Nguyen. Multimodal logic programming and its applications to modal deductive databases. *manuscript (served as a technical report), available on Internet at http://www.mimuw.edu.pl/~nguyen/papers.html*, 2003.
5. L.A. Nguyen. Source files, calculi, and examples of MProlog. *Available on Internet at http://www.mimuw.edu.pl/~nguyen/mprolog*, 2004.
6. A. Nonnengart. How to use modalities and sorts in Prolog. In C. MacNish, D. Pearce, and L.M. Pereira, editors, *Proceedings of JELIA'94*, LNCS 838, pages 365–378. Springer, 1994.
7. M.A. Orgun and W. Ma. An overview of temporal and modal logic programming. In D.M. Gabbay and H.J. Ohlbach, editors, *Proc. First Int. Conf. on Temporal Logic*, LNAI 827, pages 445–479. Springer-Verlag, 1994.

Probabilistic Choice Operators as Global Constraints: Application to Statistical Software Testing

Matthieu Petit and Arnaud Gotlieb

IRISA-INRIA, Campus de Beaulieu, 35042 Rennes cedex, France
{Matthieu.Petit,Arnaud.Gotlieb}@irisa.fr

Probabilistic Concurrent Constraint Programming (PCCP) [3] is an extension of Concurrent Constraint Programming (CCP) [5] where probabilistic choice operators are introduced to represent the randomness or uncertain behaviour of processes. A probabilistic choice between two processes can be though of as flipping a coin : head the first process is triggered, tail it is the second. Based on this theoretical framework, it seems possible to extend the classical CCP over finite domains framework [4] with probabilistic choice operators.

Our aim is to define probabilistic choice operators as global constraints of the CCP over finite domains paradigm [4] and to apply this framework to deal with a specific Software Testing problem [1]. Global constraints are a good way for giving global semantics to complex constraints. Furthermore, such operators appear to the user like single constraints and so can be awaked and treated efficiently by the constraint propagation algorithm. A part of our work is to establish the relationships between probabilistic choice operators, global constraints and the PCCP semantic framework.

Gupta et al. pioneered the inclusion of probabilistic choice operators in CCP to address several applications areas, such as stochastic processes [3].

Example 1 (extracted from [3])
choose X from $\{0,1\}$ with distribution $\{\frac{1}{2},\frac{1}{2}\}$ in $[tell\ (X = Z)]$
$\|$ choose Y from $\{0,1\}$ with distribution $\{\frac{1}{2},\frac{1}{2}\}$
in $[if\ Z = 1\ then\ tell\ (Y = 1)]$.

After the example running, Z is constrained to 0 with a probability $\frac{1}{2}$ (event $X = 0$), to 1 with a probability $\frac{1}{4}$ (event $X = 1 \wedge Y = 1$) and the process fails with a probability $\frac{1}{4}$ (event $X = 1 \wedge Y = 0$).

Our current implementation includes new global constraints of SICStus Prolog's library clp(FD) like the `choose_unif` global constraint.

Example 2 (Example 1 running)
```
?-choose_unif(X,0..1,[X#=Z]),choose_unif(Y,0..1,[ask(Z#=1,Y#=1)]).
```
Here is an output sequence of several launches (we get the distribution $p(Z = 0) = \frac{1}{2}$, $p(Z = 1) = \frac{1}{4}$ and $p(\text{fail}) = \frac{1}{4}$, as expected).

X=1, Y=1, Z=1	X=0, Y=0, Z=0	no	X=1, Y=1, Z=1	X=0, Y=1, Z=0	no	X=0, Y=1, Z=0	X=0, Y=0, Z=0	...

B. Demoen and V. Lifschitz (Eds.): ICLP 2004, LNCS 3132, pp. 471–472, 2004.
© Springer-Verlag Berlin Heidelberg 2004

In [2], we proposed to transform the problem of the automatic test data generation into a Constraint Logic Programming over finite domains problem. Our work aims at extending this framework to address a new problem : the statistical structural testing application [6]. In this testing method, we use a probabilistic test data selection, i.e. the use of a random test data generator to cover a selected testing criterion (such as the all-paths criterion). It requires constructing a non-uniform generator over the input domain of the program, which aims at giving the highest probability to activate each criterion element, including the most difficult to reach. This allows a good coverage of test criteria and reduces the cost of the test oracle construction.

Example 3 *Test criterion : covering all-paths.*

```
if X = 0 then C1 else C2 ; if Y = 0 then C3 else C4
```

Statistical structural testing aims at constructing a random test data generator where the events $(X = 0 \wedge Y = 0)$, $(X = 0 \wedge Y \neq 0)$, $(X \neq 0 \wedge Y = 0)$ *and* $(X \neq 0 \wedge Y \neq 0)$ *have the same probability* $(\frac{1}{4})$. *Here is a first model of this problem in PCCP:*

choose U *from* $\{0,1\}$ *with distribution* $\{\frac{1}{2}, \frac{1}{2}\}$
  in $[$*if* $U = 0$ *then* $[$*tell* $(X = 0) \parallel C1] \parallel$ *if* $U = 1$ *then* $[$*tell* $(X \neq 0) \parallel C2]]$
$\parallel$ *choose* V *from* $\{0,1\}$ *with distribution* $\{\frac{1}{2}, \frac{1}{2}\}$
  in $[$*if* $V = 0$ *then* $[$*tell* $(Y = 0) \parallel C3] \parallel$ *if* $V = 1$ *then* $[$*tell* $(Y \neq 0) \parallel C4]]$.

To conclude, we believe that implementing probabilistic choice operators as global constraints is interesting. In the one hand, this gives the possibility of using a powerful probabilistic choice operator in the CCP over finite domains framework. In the other hand, it seems to be adequate to address the problem of random test data generator for statistical structural testing. The implementation as an extension of the clp(FD) library of SICStus Prolog is in progress.

References

1. Richard A. DeMillo and A. Jefferson Offutt. Constraint-based automatic test data generation. *IEEE Trans. Softw. Eng.*, 17(9):900–910, 1991.
2. A. Gotlieb, B. Botella, and M. Rueher. A clp framework for computing structural test data. In *Computational Logic (CL)*, pages 399–413, LNAI 1891, 2000.
3. V. Gupta, R. Jagadeesan, and P. Panangaden. Stochastic processes as concurrent constraint programs. In *Symposium on POPL*, pages 189–202, 1999.
4. P. Van Hentenryck, V. A. Saraswat, and Y. Deville. Design, implementation, and evaluation of the constraint langage cc(FD). *Journal of Logic Programming*, 1998.
5. V. A. Saraswat, M. Rinard, and P. Panangaden. Semantic foundations of concurrent constraint programming. In *Symposium on POPL*, pages 333–352, 1991.
6. P. Thévenod-Fosse and H. Waeselynck. An Investigation of Statistical Software Testing. *Journal of Software Testing, Verification and Reliability*, 1991.

Constraint-Based Synchronization and Verification of Distributed Java Programs

Rafael Ramirez and Juanjo Martinez

Pompeu Fabra University
Ocata 1, 08003 Barcelona, Spain
Tel: +34 935422165, Fax: +34 935422202
rramirez@iua.upf.es, juanjo.martinez@upf.edu

Introduction. Constraint-based synchronization pioneered by (concurrent) logic and concurrent constraint programming is a powerful mechanism for elegantly synchronizing concurrent and distributed computations. It supports a declarative model of concurrency that avoids explicitly suspending and resuming computations. This extended abstract briefly outlines (1) a new model for high-level concurrent and distributed programming based on constraint entailment, (2) its implementation (for both uniprocessors and distributed systems) as an extension to the Java programming language, and (3) how model-based verification methods can be directly applied to programs in the resulting language.

The model. The basic idea is to use a constraint logic program to represent the (usually infinite) set of constraints of interest. The constraints themselves are of the form $X < Y$, read as "X precedes Y" or "the execution time of X is less than the execution time of Y", where X and Y are events, and $<$ is a partial order. The constraint logic program (CLP) is defined as follows[1]. Constants range over events classes $E, F, \ldots$ and there is a distinguished (postfixed) functor $+$. Thus the terms of interest, apart from variables, are $e, e+, e++, \ldots, f, f+, f++, \ldots$. The idea is that e represents the first event in the class E, $e+$ the next event, etc. Thus, for any event X, $X+$ is implicitly preceded by X, i.e. $X < X+$. We denote by $e(+N)$ the N-th event in the class E. Programs facts or *predicate constraints* are of the form $p(t_1, \ldots, t_n)$ where p is a user defined predicate symbol and t_i $(1 \leq i \leq n)$ are ground terms. Program rules or *predicate definitions* are of the form $p(X_1, \ldots, X_n) \leftarrow B$ where the X_i are distinct variables and B is a rule body restricted to contain variables in $\{X_1, \ldots, X_n\}$. A program is a finite collection of rules and is used to define a family of partial orders over events. Intuitively, this family is obtained by unfolding the rules with facts indefinitely[2], and collecting the (ground) *precedence constraints* of the form $e < f$. Multiple rules for a given predicate symbol give rise to different partial orders. We abbreviate the set of clauses: $H \leftarrow Cs_1, \ldots, H \leftarrow Cs_n$ by the *disjunction constraint* $H \leftarrow Cs_1; \ldots; Cs_n$ (disjunction is specified by the usual disjunction operator ';').

The interpreter. The constraint logic program as defined above has a procedural interpretation that allows a correct specification to be executed in the sense

---

[1] For a complete description, see [3].

[2] In general, *reactive* concurrent programs on which we are focusing, do not terminate.

B. Demoen and V. Lifschitz (Eds.): ICLP 2004, LNCS 3132, pp. 473–474, 2004.

that processes run only as permitted by the constraints represented by the program. This procedural interpretation is based on an incremental execution of the program and a *lazy* generation of the corresponding partial orders. Constraints are generated by the CLP only when needed to reason about the execution times of current events. A detailed description of the interpreter can be found in [3]).

Processes coordination. Processes interact with each other by performing simple operations on a shared constraint store. In the distributed case, the constraint store is a shared, network-accessible repository for constraints and objects. Processes can perform operations to *check* if the execution of a particular event is entailed by the constraints in the store, to *write* new objects into the store, or to *read* objects in the store. Synchronization is achieved only by using the *check* operation. The rest of the operations are non-blocking. The behavior of the operations described above distinguishes our approach from other coordination models, especially blackboard architectures [1].

Program verification. We have applied the SMV model checking system [2] to verify properties of our programs. We have implemented a prototype which automatically translates an extended finite-state Java program into a model M in SMV's description language. Thus, it suffices to code the property we want to verify using the specification language of SMV resulting in a CTL (computation tree logic) formula p, and run SMV with inputs M and p.

Implementation. Prototype Java implementations for both uniprocessors and distributed systems have been written. Both implementations are articulated in two main components: The *parser* parses the text file containing the constraints, builds the data structures required by the interpreter, and checks for some possible semantic and syntactic errors in the text file, e.g. infinite loops in predicate definitions, correct number and type of predicate arguments, etc. The *interpreter* is an object which decides whether or not Java threads suspend upon reaching a *check* operation during execution. When a thread reaches a check operation m, a request is sent to the interpreter to determine whether the current event e associated with m is *disabled*, i.e. it appears on the right of a precedence constraint $X < e$, or *enabled*, i.e. otherwise, w.r.t. the *system constraints*. If e is found to be disabled, the thread is blocked until e becomes enabled, otherwise the thread proceeds execution at the instruction immediately after m. *Fairness* is implicitly guaranteed by our implementation. Although fairness is provided as the default, users, however, may intervene by specifying priority events.

Acknowledgments. This work has been partially funded by the Spanish TIC project ProMusic (TIC2003-07776-C02-01).

References

1. Carriero, N. and Gelernter, D. 1991. *How to write parallel programs: A first course.* MIT Press.
2. McMillan, K.L. 1993. *Symbolic Model Checking.* Kluwer Academic Publishers.
3. Ramirez, R., Santosa, A.E., Yap, R. 2000. *Concurrent programming made easy,* IEEE International Conference on Engineering of Complex Computer Systems, IEEE Press.

JmmSolve: A Generative Java Memory Model Implemented in Prolog and CHR

Tom Schrijvers[*]

Dept. of Computer Science, K.U.Leuven, Belgium

Abstract. The memory model of a programming language specifies the interaction between multiple threads and main memory. Basically, the model says for every value obtained by a read operation in a program by what write operation it has been produced. In a multi-threaded unsynchronized program this need not be a deterministic linking from reads to writes. For a multi-platform language such as Java, a memory model is essential to guarantee portability of programs.

However, several undesirable properties of the current Java Memory Model (JMM) have been revealed: it is not an easy model to understand by programmers, gives rise to some unwanted behavior and is hard to implement on current hardware architectures. Because of this, Java Specification Request 133 [2] has called for a new JMM that fixes the current problems.

The Concurrent Constraint-based Memory Machines (CCMMs) proposal by Vijay Saraswat [3] is a framework to express and study different declarative memory models. CCMMs are different from other proposals in that it does not express a memory model in terms of imperative operational semantics, but in terms of constraints. This should facilitate reasoning about the model and its properties, e.g. the *no thin-air reads* property is structurally proved in [3].

Because of the declarative constraint-based nature of CCMMs we have chosen constraint logic programming (CLP) as the technology for this generative implementation. In particular, JmmSolve has been implemented in the latest version of SWI-Prolog [4], with its new support for constraint programming: attributed variables and a Constraint Handling Rules (CHR) [1] system.

CCMMs associate an event program with a source program. The event program is an abstraction that only keeps the relevant information for the memory model. Every statement in a source program corresponds with several events, i.e. read/write/lock/unlock/... operations on a source variable in a particular thread. Together with these events equality constraints are imposed over values read and written, e.g. for an assignment of an expression to a variable the value written to the variable should be equal to the expression.

CCMMs models main memory as a constraint store that processes the events with their constraints. Events are processed in batches called action sets. Every thread can contribute any number of events with corre-

* Research Assistant of the Fund for Scientific Research - Flanders (Belgium)(F.W.O. - Vlaanderen)

B. Demoen and V. Lifschitz (Eds.): ICLP 2004, LNCS 3132, pp. 475–476, 2004.

sponding constraints to an action set. Such an action set is added as a whole by the store. The addition takes care of the following:

- Events in the action set are ordered with respect to events already present in the store.
- Events in the action set are ordered with respect to other events in the action set, but in a different thread.
- Read operations are linked to write operations.

The above three steps depend on the particular rules of the underlying ordering model. For example, the Sequential Consistency model only allows interleaved sequentialization of instructions, while the Happens Before model is more relaxed and imposes less ordering.

CCMMs has set itself, in addition to the requirements of JSR-133, the requirement to be generative. This means that given a program it should be possible to generate all valid executions, in particular all valid linkings of reads to writes. It is the goal of JMMSOLVE to prove this point by providing exactly such a generative implementation of CCMMs.

The current working of JMMSOLVE is as follows. A source program (in a simplified syntax) is read in and converted to an event program with constraints. The event program is partitioned into one action set for the initialization and one for all the threads. Both action sets are added to an empty store together with the necessary ordering constraints according to the memory model. Finally all valid linkings from reads to writes are generated for each action set.

The compiler from source to event programs is rather straightforward, using DCGs. On the other hand, the generative part of JMMSOLVE, uses a mix of ordinary Prolog and CHR constraints. CHR constraints are used in particular:

- For the ordering constraint and the related event visibility. The semantics are captured in several CHR rules and can be modified according to the underlying instantiation of the CCMMs framework.
- For a simple arithmetic and finite domain constraint solver. These are currently only prototype implementations with minimal functionality. They can later be replaced with fully featured constraint solvers.

The current implementation of JMMSOLVE is available for download at `http://www.cs.kuleuven.ac.be/~toms/jmmsolve/` and contains rules for the Happens Before model.

References

1. T. Frühwirth. Constraint Handling Rules. In A. Podelski, editor, *Constraint Programming: Basics and Trends*, number 910 in Lecture Notes in Computer Science, pages 90–107. Springer Verlag, March 1995.
2. W. Pugh. Proposal for java memory model and thread specification revision. JSR-133, http://www.jcp.org/en/jsr/detail?id=133.
3. V. Saraswat. Concurrent Constraint-based Memory Machines: A framework for Java Memory Models (Preliminary Report). Technical report, IBM, March 2004.
4. J. Wielemaker. SWI-Prolog's Home. http://www.swi-prolog.org/.

Agent Oriented Logic Programming Constructs in Jinni 2004

Paul Tarau

Department of Computer Science and Engineering
University of North Texas
tarau@cs.unt.edu
http://www.cs.unt.edu/~tarau

Jinni 2004 [1] (available from http://www.binnetcorp.com/Jinni) expresses various agent programming constructs in terms of an Object Oriented Logic Programming layer implemented on top of a Java-based Prolog compiler. The architecture provides a high degree of compositionality through the use of a small set of orthogonal programming language constructs.

Objects: provide proven program composition and code reuse mechanisms and allow extension of libraries of behaviors and knowledge processing components.

Logic: Logic programming provides well understood, resolution-based inference mechanisms. Beyond clause selection in the resolution process and generalized parameter passing, unification provides flexible search in message queues and databases.

Inference Engines: execution of multiple independent goals are provided for implementing complex reactive patterns in agent programs.

Coordination: agent coordination is separated from the details of agent communication and the agent's computational mechanisms (engines). Jinni 2004 provides coordination through blackboards - databases with intelligent, constraint-based search - instead of conventional message passing.

Remote Action: Jinni supports a simple client-server style remote call mechanism as a building block for various forms of remote action.

Object Oriented Prolog with Cyclical Multiple Inheritance: Inheritance can be seen as a special purpose inference mechanism. Traditional inheritance has been confined to trees (simple inheritance) or lattices (multiple inheritance). This contrasts with the dominant information sharing model - the Web - which has an arbitrary directed graph structure (handled quite well despite its size and growth). While limiting the scope of inheritance in procedural languages makes sense, given the presence of side effects, an arbitrary directed graph model is worth trying out in the context of declarative languages endowed with a formally simpler and cleaner semantics. With this in mind, *cyclical multiple inheritance* looks like a natural choice for designing an object oriented structuring mechanism around a logic programming language. The multiple cyclical depth first inheritance mechanism is implemented by keeping the path consisting of the list of visited *includes*, when (at compile time) predicates not defined locally, are brought from files or URLs. In the presence of multiple *includes*, a depth-first

B. Demoen and V. Lifschitz (Eds.): ICLP 2004, LNCS 3132, pp. 477–478, 2004.
© Springer-Verlag Berlin Heidelberg 2004

order for finding definitions ensures that a dominant main inheritance tree prevails in case of ambiguity. This cyclical inheritance mechanism allows reuse of Prolog code located virtually everywhere on the Web from a *local* perspective.

Inference Engines, Answer Generation and Control: Independently of its multi-threading mechanism, Jinni 2004 provides "first class" inference engines - separate instances of its dynamically growing/shrinking runtime system (consisting of a heap, stack and trail) which can be controlled through a simple *iterator*-style API that allows users (and their agents) to start, explore and stop a Prolog goal's answer computations.

Thread Coordination with Blackboard Constraints and Remote Execution: Jinni threads can be launched locally or remotely. Blackboards are global (one per Jinni process) databases which provide thread coordination. Jinni extends Linda coordination by using *constraint* solving for the selection of matching terms, instead of plain unification. Blackboard operations can be combined with remote predicate calls to allow interaction between threads distributed in different Jinni processes.

Agent Programming with Agent Classes and Inference Engines: Agent classes are built on top of Jinni's Object Oriented Prolog system. An Agent Class provides a *goal set* and a *specialized inference engine* working as query interpreter on a separate thread. In a client-server setting this can be seen as a generalized service processor. An agent instance feeds the query interpreter while listening as a server on a port. It also creates a thread for each goal in the goal set. Agent instances have unique global identities provided by a broker agent and communicate through remote or local blackboards. Each agent instance runs its own set of goal threads. To implement a minimalist agent consisting of client, server and goal threads, with a self-centered behavior loop in which the goal component requests through the agent's client component to ask the agent's server component to print out a stream of messages. The agent class is simply a combination of client and server classes together with one or more (background) goal threads. As Jinni agents are not based on a monolithic *sense-plan-act-sense* agent loop, it is possible to easily interleave planning and with reactive loops using blackboard constraints for synchronization. Multi-agent architectures are supported through a combination of P2P-connected broker agents which provide unique global IDs to registered agents and TCP-IP tunneling allowing agents to function as virtual servers behind firewalls.

An increasing number of past and ongoing projects are using our agent architecture for applications ranging from virtual personalities and 3D graph visualization to online trading agents and internet-based teaching tools. We plan to extend our agent class libraries to cover a larger diversity of agent programming patterns in a number of different application domains.

References

1. Paul Tarau. The Jinni 2004 Prolog Compiler: a High Performance Java and .NET based Prolog for Object and Agent Oriented Internet Programming. Technical report, BinNet Corp., 2004.
   URL: http://www.binnetcorp.com/download/jinnidemo/JinniUserGuide.html.

Author Index

Lecture Notes in Computer Science

For information about Vols. 1–3070

please contact your bookseller or Springer

Vol. 3125: D. Kozen (Ed.), Mathematics of Program Construction. X, 401 pages. 2004.

Vol. 3124: J.N. de Souza, P. Dini, P. Lorenz (Eds.), Telecommunications and Networking - ICT 2004. XXVI, 1390 pages. 2004.

Vol. 3123: A. Belz, R. Evans, P. Piwek (Eds.), Natural Language Generation. X, 219 pages. 2004. (Subseries LNAI).

Vol. 3122: K. Jansen, S. Khanna, J.D.P. Rolim, D. Ron (Eds.), Approximation, Randomization, and Combinatorial Optimization. IX, 428 pages. 2004.

Vol. 3121: S. Nikoletseas, J.D.P. Rolim (Eds.), Algorithmic Aspects of Wireless Sensor Networks. X, 201 pages. 2004.

Vol. 3120: J. Shawe-Taylor, Y. Singer (Eds.), Learning Theory. X, 648 pages. 2004. (Subseries LNAI).

Vol. 3118: K. Miesenberger, J. Klaus, W. Zagler, D. Burger (Eds.), Computer Helping People with Special Needs. XXIII, 1191 pages. 2004.

Vol. 3116: C. Rattray, S. Maharaj, C. Shankland (Eds.), Algebraic Methodology and Software Technology. XI, 569 pages. 2004.

Vol. 3114: R. Alur, D.A. Peled (Eds.), Computer Aided Verification. XII, 536 pages. 2004.

Vol. 3113: J. Karhumäki, H. Maurer, G. Paun, G. Rozenberg (Eds.), Theory Is Forever. X, 283 pages. 2004.

Vol. 3112: H. Williams, L. MacKinnon (Eds.), Key Technologies for Data Management. XII, 265 pages. 2004.

Vol. 3111: T. Hagerup, J. Katajainen (Eds.), Algorithm Theory - SWAT 2004. XI, 506 pages. 2004.

Vol. 3110: A. Juels (Ed.), Financial Cryptography. XI, 281 pages. 2004.

Vol. 3109: S.C. Sahinalp, S. Muthukrishnan, U. Dogrusoz (Eds.), Combinatorial Pattern Matching. XII, 486 pages. 2004.

Vol. 3108: H. Wang, J. Pieprzyk, V. Varadharajan (Eds.), Information Security and Privacy. XII, 494 pages. 2004.

Vol. 3107: J. Bosch, C. Krueger (Eds.), Software Reuse: Methods, Techniques and Tools. XI, 339 pages. 2004.

Vol. 3106: K.-Y. Chwa, J.I. Munro (Eds.), Computing and Combinatorics. XIII, 474 pages. 2004.

Vol. 3105: S. Göbel, U. Spierling, A. Hoffmann, I. Iurgel, O. Schneider, J. Dechau, A. Feix (Eds.), Technologies for Interactive Digital Storytelling and Entertainment. XVI, 304 pages. 2004.

Vol. 3104: R. Kralovic, O. Sykora (Eds.), Structural Information and Communication Complexity. X, 303 pages. 2004.

Vol. 3103: K. Deb, e. al. (Eds.), Genetic and Evolutionary Computation – GECCO 2004. XLIX, 1439 pages. 2004.

Vol. 3102: K. Deb, e. al. (Eds.), Genetic and Evolutionary Computation – GECCO 2004. L, 1445 pages. 2004.

Vol. 3101: M. Masoodian, S. Jones, B. Rogers (Eds.), Computer Human Interaction. XIV, 694 pages. 2004.

Vol. 3100: J.F. Peters, A. Skowron, J.W. Grzymała-Busse, B. Kostek, R.W. Świniarski, M.S. Szczuka (Eds.), Transactions on Rough Sets I. X, 405 pages. 2004.

Vol. 3099: J. Cortadella, W. Reisig (Eds.), Applications and Theory of Petri Nets 2004. XI, 505 pages. 2004.

Vol. 3098: J. Desel, W. Reisig, G. Rozenberg (Eds.), Lectures on Concurrency and Petri Nets. VIII, 849 pages. 2004.

Vol. 3097: D. Basin, M. Rusinowitch (Eds.), Automated Reasoning. XII, 493 pages. 2004. (Subseries LNAI).

Vol. 3096: G. Melnik, H. Holz (Eds.), Advances in Learning Software Organizations. X, 173 pages. 2004.

Vol. 3095: C. Bussler, D. Fensel, M.E. Orlowska, J. Yang (Eds.), Web Services, E-Business, and the Semantic Web. X, 147 pages. 2004.

Vol. 3094: A. Nürnberger, M. Detyniecki (Eds.), Adaptive Multimedia Retrieval. VIII, 229 pages. 2004.

Vol. 3093: S. Katsikas, S. Gritzalis, J. Lopez (Eds.), Public Key Infrastructure. XIII, 380 pages. 2004.

Vol. 3092: J. Eckstein, H. Baumeister (Eds.), Extreme Programming and Agile Processes in Software Engineering. XVI, 358 pages. 2004.

Vol. 3091: V. van Oostrom (Ed.), Rewriting Techniques and Applications. X, 313 pages. 2004.

Vol. 3089: M. Jakobsson, M. Yung, J. Zhou (Eds.), Applied Cryptography and Network Security. XIV, 510 pages. 2004.

Vol. 3087: D. Maltoni, A.K. Jain (Eds.), Biometric Authentication. XIII, 343 pages. 2004.

Vol. 3086: M. Odersky (Ed.), ECOOP 2004 – Object-Oriented Programming. XIII, 611 pages. 2004.

Vol. 3085: S. Berardi, M. Coppo, F. Damiani (Eds.), Types for Proofs and Programs. X, 409 pages. 2004.

Vol. 3084: A. Persson, J. Stirna (Eds.), Advanced Information Systems Engineering. XIV, 596 pages. 2004.

Vol. 3083: W. Emmerich, A.L. Wolf (Eds.), Component Deployment. X, 249 pages. 2004.

Vol. 3080: J. Desel, B. Pernici, M. Weske (Eds.), Business Process Management. X, 307 pages. 2004.

Vol. 3079: Z. Mammeri, P. Lorenz (Eds.), High Speed Networks and Multimedia Communications. XVIII, 1103 pages. 2004.

Vol. 3078: S. Cotin, D.N. Metaxas (Eds.), Medical Simulation. XVI, 296 pages. 2004.

Vol. 3077: F. Roli, J. Kittler, T. Windeatt (Eds.), Multiple Classifier Systems. XII, 386 pages. 2004.

Vol. 3076: D. Buell (Ed.), Algorithmic Number Theory. XI, 451 pages. 2004.

Vol. 3075: W. Lenski (Ed.), Logic versus Approximation. IX, 205 pages. 2004.

Vol. 3074: B. Kuijpers, P. Revesz (Eds.), Constraint Databases and Applications. XII, 181 pages. 2004.

Vol. 3073: H. Chen, R. Moore, D.D. Zeng, J. Leavitt (Eds.), Intelligence and Security Informatics. XV, 536 pages. 2004.

Vol. 3072: D. Zhang, A.K. Jain (Eds.), Biometric Authentication. XVII, 800 pages. 2004.

Vol. 3071: A. Omicini, P. Petta, J. Pitt (Eds.), Engineering Societies in the Agents World. XIII, 409 pages. 2004. (Subseries LNAI).